To Be Continued
An Annotated Guide to Sequels

To Be Continued
An Annotated Guide to Sequels
Second Edition

by
Merle L. Jacob
and
Hope Apple

Oryx Press
2000

© 2000 by The Oryx Press
4041 North Central at Indian School Road
Phoenix, Arizona 85012-3397

Library of Congress Cataloging-in-Publication Data

Jacob, Merle.
    To be continued : an annotated guide to sequels / Merle Jacob and Hope Apple.—
2nd ed.
        p. cm.
    Includes bibliographical references and index.
    ISBN 1-57356-155-X (alk. paper)
        1. Sequels (Literature)—Bibliography. 2. Prose literature—Bibliography. I. Apple,
Hope. II. Title.

Z6514.S4 J33   2000
[PN3448.S47]
016.80883—dc21   00-042782
                                                         CIP

We would like to dedicate this book to six people who have been influential in our lives: our parents, Alex and Sally Jacob and Paul and Hope Cousley, and our friends and mentors, Mary Radmacher and Dorothy Rasmussen.

CONTENTS

PREFACE

The best books are those that keep us up reading into the night or lure us to read when we should be doing something else. As we approach the end of one of these books, however, we are curious, but a bit frustrated. Even though we are happy to know the fates of the characters who fascinate us, we do not want the book to end because we have enjoyed it so much. Luckily there are some books that satisfy both our need to know the outcome and our desire to know more. They are called sequels.

Since the early 1800s authors such as James Fenimore Cooper, Honore de Balzac, and Alexandre Dumas have made their readers happy by writing memorable stories and then continuing to follow those wonderful plots and characters through sequels. It is for readers who love fiction in sequels that this book was compiled.

Since the first edition came out five years ago, numerous librarians have told us how useful this book has been in helping them find sequels for their patrons and how much patrons have enjoyed using it themselves. The publishing trend of the last five years has also seen many more authors writing sequels, whether they are new authors writing new series, or established authors writing sequels to novels they published much earlier.

In the years since *To Be Continued* was published, we have continued to collect authors and titles that we considered sequels to add to our second edition. Our methodology for searching for these books begins with our reading of *Library Journal, Booklist, Publishers Weekly, Kirkus Reviews, the New York Times Book Review, Locus,* and *Romantic Times* for reviews of new fiction. We also check reference books for more authors and series titles. Sources such as *Fiction Catalog, Book Review Digest,* and *Twentieth Century Authors,* along with

other readers advisory tools such as *Books in Print Plus* and Ingram's *i* Page have also been used. We searched publishers catalogs, especially for Christian fiction, which is often not reviewed. Citation information was verified against *OCLC*. When there were questions, bibliographies such as the *Dictionary of Literary Biography* and individual author bibliographies were checked. Whenever possible we looked at the individual books or, if they weren't available, at book reviews. A list of some of the sources that we found useful follows this preface.

To establish some parameters for the work, we looked for a meaningful definition of a sequel, but were unable to find one in the dictionaries of literary terms. *The American Heritage Dictionary of the English Language* defines a sequel as "a literary work complete in itself but continuing the narrative of an earlier work." For the purpose of this bibliography, we define sequels as novels that tell a continuing story or are united by a regional, social, or philosophical theme. Often authors do not use the term sequel to define their works, but may use terms such as series, trilogy, or saga. Despite the variations in terms, we consider novels to be sequels if they fit our definition.

In compiling this bibliographic guide, we have concentrated on novels in English, for adult audiences, which are available in American libraries. We have also included some sequels that are partly or completely composed of short stories, such as the P.G. Wodehouse Jeeves stories. Other than genuine collaborations, we have excluded sequels that are the product of more than one author, such as the Star Trek and Dr. Who books. Also excluded are sequels that have only been published in one-volume editions in America. We excluded mysteries because we believe that most mystery series lack a sense of continuity or passage of time and, like the Star Trek books, are only connected by their main character or characters. Their plots rarely continue from book to book. More important, mysteries, as a genre, are already covered in several excellent reference works, such as Allan J. Hubin's *Crime Fiction II: 1749–1990 A Comprehensive Bibliography* (Garland Publishing, 1994) and *St. James Guide to Crime Mystery Writers,* 4th edition (St. James Press, 1996).

For this edition, we have added 660 new or updated sequels. We have added many Christian fiction, romance, and science fiction sequels because there has been an explosion in the number of series written in these genres. As careful as we were in looking for updates, we are sure that we have missed some updates, because these books are often not reviewed.

Entries

Each bibliographical entry contains the following information:

Author   Names are entered as they appear in library catalogs. If a pseudonym is used, the author's actual name is also given. Cross references are entered under variations of the author's name. The bibliographical difficulties presented by pseudonyms, changed names, and transliterated authors' names will always be with us, but we have tried for as much accuracy as possible by using authoritative sources such as OCLC, the Twentieth Century Authors series, and *Dictionary of Literary Biography.*

Series Title   The series title, if there is one, follows the entry number. If there is no series title, the space is left blank.

Title   Titles are listed in the chronological order of fictional events. In some cases the author or a critical source has indicated a preferred reading order. For some series with complex overlapping plot lines, the titles are listed in order of publication.

Publisher   The first American publisher is listed. A few titles published only in Eng-

land are included for the sake of completeness.

Publication date   The first American publication date is listed, followed by the original publication date if it is two years or more before the American publication.

Annotation   Time, place, and the characters and narrative threads that tie the novels together are described. Books for which no time period is indicated are in time settings contemporary with their publication dates.

Genre   A work of genre fiction tends to follow an established pattern of writing style, tone, plot, character, and setting. Because library patrons often find genre designations helpful in selecting fiction, we have placed many series in one or more of the following broadly defined genre categories. Many novels, however, fit in no genre classification.

> *Adventure.*   Novels filled with a rapid sequence of action-filled events.
>
> *Animal Story.*   Novels whose central characters are animals who frequently exhibit human characteristics.
>
> *Christian Fiction.*   Novels that contain no explicit sex, violence, or obscene language and whose characters rely on their Christian faith to help them overcome obstacles.
>
> *Coming of Age.*   Novels that show the growth and development of young people as they overcome obstacles and mature.
>
> *Crime Novel.*   Novels that depict criminals and people from the dark side of society involved in illegal activities and violence.
>
> *Espionage.*   Novels in which spies or intelligence-gathering organizations uncover secret information for their governments or agencies.
>
> *Family Saga.*   Novels featuring a large-scale narrative extending over time and following one or two families or groups of people through at least two generations.

Fantasy. Novels that describe an imagined world where magic or other forces that cannot be explained by science or the laws of nature are in effect.

Gentle Read. Novels that have no explicit sex or violence and stress the goodness of people.

Historical Fiction. Novels that take place in a time period at least one generation earlier than the date they were written.

Historical Romance. Novels that are centered on a love story that takes place in the past.

Horror. Novels that feature vampires, supernatural beings, ghosts, and/or the occult and produce a sense of fear in the reader.

Humor. Novels that feature funny characters or events or spoof real people or events.

Naval Adventure. Novels following the action-filled events surrounding men in the navy, usually during wartime.

Romance. Novels centered on a love story between a man and woman who must overcome obstacles before they can find happiness.

Science Fiction. Novels that speculate about future events, particularly those involving scientific discoveries or life forms from other worlds.

Sports. Stories that follow the exploits of athletes as they face the rigors of competition.

Technothriller. Novels featuring action-filled events that revolve around the use of military equipment, weapons, or technology as a major element of the story.

War. Novels set during wartime in which combatants or civilians that are caught up in the war play central roles.

Western. Novels about life in the American West that feature charac-

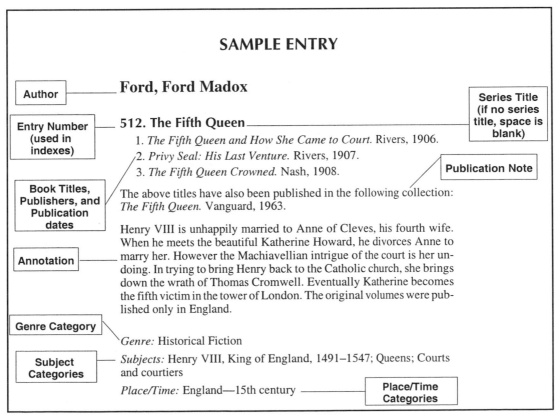

SAMPLE ENTRY

Author ──── **Ford, Ford Madox**

Series Title (if no series title, space is blank)

Entry Number (used in indexes) ── **512. The Fifth Queen**

1. *The Fifth Queen and How She Came to Court.* Rivers, 1906.
2. *Privy Seal: His Last Venture.* Rivers, 1907.
3. *The Fifth Queen Crowned.* Nash, 1908.

Publication Note

Book Titles, Publishers, and Publication dates

The above titles have also been published in the following collection: *The Fifth Queen.* Vanguard, 1963.

Annotation ── Henry VIII is unhappily married to Anne of Cleves, his fourth wife. When he meets the beautiful Katherine Howard, he divorces Anne to marry her. However the Machiavellian intrigue of the court is her undoing. In trying to bring Henry back to the Catholic church, she brings down the wrath of Thomas Cromwell. Eventually Katherine becomes the fifth victim in the tower of London. The original volumes were published only in England.

Genre Category ──── *Genre:* Historical Fiction

Subject Categories ──── *Subjects:* Henry VIII, King of England, 1491–1547; Queens; Courts and courtiers

Place/Time: England—15th century ──── Place/Time Categories

ters such as cowboys, Indians, mountain men, settlers, and ranchers.

Subjects   Each entry includes a list of subject categories covered in the series, such as aristocracy, business, Christian life. Also included are **Literary Forms** such as allegories, autobiographical stories, diaries, etc., which do not fit in the genre categories. Subjects and literary forms are in order by relevance to the series.

Subject terms were selected from *Sears List of Subject Headings, 15th Edition.* NY: H. W. Wilson, 1994. In the event that *Sears* did not contain a needed subject heading, the Library of Congress subject headings were used. On the rare occasion when neither of these sources produced an appropriate term, the authors created a new subject term. Subject headings were limited to no more than six.

Place/Time   Each entry includes a list of time and place categories covered in the series, such as Austria—1945–1980, Chicago (Ill.)—1900–1945. Place/Time terms are in order by relevance to the series.

Terms were selected from *Sears List of Subject Headings, 15th Edition* and from the Library of Congress subject headings, using the same guidelines as were used in selecting the subject terms. Generally, one to three time/place terms were assigned per series. However, for some series, especially those in the fantasy and science fiction genres, time/place terms were not applicable, and therefore not assigned.

Indexes

Following the main entry section are four indexes:

- Title
- Genre
- Subjects and Literary Forms
- Time and Place

These indexes will give readers further access to sequels.

We hope that this bibliography will help librarians and their patrons to identify specific sequel titles and also to search more generally for a favorite genre or subject that has been published in sequel form.

We have attempted to make our bibliography as comprehensive as possible but do not claim that it is definitive and welcome suggestions, additions, or corrections.

We would like to express our appreciation for the resources of the Chicago Public Library and Skokie Public Library, which made the creation of a bibliography of this magnitude possible.

Merle Jacob
Director of Library Collection Development
Chicago Public Library

Hope Apple
Freelance researcher, writer,
and former reference librarian

Useful Sources

Adamson, Lynda G. *American Historical Fiction: An Annotated Guide to Novels for Adults and Young Adults.* Phoenix, AZ: The Oryx Press, 1999.

————. *World Historical Fiction: An Annotated Guide to Novels for Adults and Young Adults.* Phoenix, AZ: The Oryx Press, 1999.

Anatomy of Wonder: A Critical Guide to Science Fiction. NY: R. R. Bowker, 1995.

Books in Print Plus. NY: R. R. Bowker, 2000.

Book Review Digest. NY: H. W. Wilson Co., 1905–to date.

Contemporary Authors. Detroit: Gale Research, volumes 1–185.

Contemporary Authors New Revision Series. Detroit: Gale Research, volumes 1–89.

Contemporary Novelists. 6th edition. Detroit: St. James Press, 1996.

Dictionary of Literary Biography. Detroit: Gale Research, volumes 1–219.

Fantasy Literature: A Reader's Guide. NY: Garland Publishing, 1990.

Fiction Catalog. 11th edition. NY: H. W. Wilson Co., 1986.

Fiction Catalog. 12th edition. NY: H. W. Wilson Co., 1991.

Fiction Catalog. 13th edition. NY: H. W. Wilson Co., 1996.

Gerhardstein, Virginia Brokaw. *Dickinson's American Historical Fiction*. Metuchen, NJ: Scarecrow Press, 1986.

Herald, Diana. *Fluent in Fantasy*. Englewood, CO: Libraries Unlimited, 1999.

———. *Genreflecting: A Guide to Reading Interests in Genre Fiction*. 5th edition. Englewood, CO: Libraries Unlimited, 2000.

Husband, Janet, and Husband, Jonathan. *Sequels; An Annotated Guide to Novels in Series*. 3rd edition. Chicago: American Library Association, 1997.

Olderr, Steven. *Olderr's Fiction Index 1988–1990*. Chicago: St. James Press, 1989, 1990, 1991.

———. Young Adult Fiction Index 1988–1990. Chicago: St. James Press, 1989, 1990, 1991.

Pearl, Nancy. *Now Read This. A Guide to Mainstream Fiction 1978–1998*. Englewood, CO. Libraries Unlimited, 1999.

Pringle, David. *The Ultimate Guide to Science Fiction*. MA: Scolar Press, 1995.

Ramsdell, Kristin. *Romance Fiction: A Guide to the Genre*. Englewood, CO: Libraries Unlimited, 1999.

The Reader's Adviser. 14th edition. NY: R. R. Bowker, 1994.

Royce, William Hobart. *Balzac As He Should Be Read: The Comedie Humaine Arranged in Logical Order of Reading According to Time of Action*. NY: A. Giraldi, 1946.

Simkin, John. *The Whole Story: 3000 Years of Series & Sequels*. NJ: D. W. Thorpe, 1999.

St. James Guide to Horror, Ghost & Gothic Writers. Detroit: St. James Press, 1998.

St. James Guide to Fantasy Writers. Detroit: St. James Press, 1996.

St. James Guide to Science Fiction Writers. 4th edition. Detroit: St. James Press, 1996.

Twentieth Century Romance and Historical Writers. 3rd edition. Detroit: St. James Press, 1994.

Twentieth Century Western Writers. 2nd edition. Detroit: St. James Press, 1991.

What Do I Read Next? A Reader's Guide to Current Genre Fiction. Detroit: Gale Research, 1990–.

MAIN ENTRY SECTION

Adams, Douglas

1. Dirk Gently

1. *Dirk Gently's Holistic Detective Agency.* Simon & Schuster, 1987.
2. *The Long Dark Tea-Time of the Soul.* Simon & Schuster, 1988.

Unlike most scientific detectives, Dirk Gently deduces with his psychic abilities and his belief in the interconnectedness of things. Never lacking for big issues and enormous opposing forces, Dirk first saves humanity from extinction, then confronts beings, who are in fact Norse gods, involved in an explosion at Heathrow Airport.

Genre: Fantasy; Humor; Science Fiction
Subjects: Detectives; Holism

2. The Hitchhiker Series

1. *The Hitchhiker's Guide to the Galaxy.* Crown, 1980.
2. *The Restaurant at the End of the Universe.* Crown, 1982.
3. *Life, the Universe, and Everything.* Crown, 1982.
4. *So Long, and Thanks for All the Fish.* Harmony, 1984.

The above titles have also been published in the following collections: *The Hitchhiker's Quartet.* Harmony, 1986. *The More Than Complete Hitchhiker's Guide: Complete and Unabridged.* Crown, 1989.

5. *Mostly Harmless.* Harmony, 1992.

The Hitchhiker's Guide to the Galaxy is a travel book being revised by incognito alien Ford Prefect, who is on a visit to Earth just as the planet is about to be destroyed to make way for an intergalactic expressway. Ford manages to save his very British friend Arthur Dent and the two set off as stowaways through a universe ruled by the addled two-headed galactic president Zaphad Beeblebox. After many exciting adventures with Ford, Zaphad, and Zaphad's girlfriend Trillium, Arthur returns to an intact but changed Earth and finds love with a young woman who may be a bit deranged but may also have discovered the secret of happiness.

Genre: Fantasy; Humor; Science Fiction
Subjects: Earth, destruction of; Interplanetary voyages

Adams, Richard

3.

1. *Watership Down.* Macmillan, 1972.
2. *Tales from Watership Down.* Knopf, 1996.

In search of a new location for a warren, three rabbits (Hazel, Bigwig, and Fiver) encounter danger and adventure, learning about themselves and the world in the process. The sequel continues the stories of the rabbit warren interspersed with tales of the mythical rabbit hero El-ahrairah.

Genre: Fantasy
Subjects: Rabbits; Mythical animals; Allegories

4. The Beklan Empire

1. *Shardik.* Simon & Schuster, 1975.
2. *Maia.* Knopf, 1985.

The Beklan Empire, a mythical tropical realm with a barbaric, sensual culture, connects these two tales, one of Shardik, a great bear who is thought to be divine, and the other of Maia, a young girl who is sold as a concubine but uses her position among the rich and powerful to improve her society.

Genre: Fantasy
Subjects: Bears; Concubinage; Society, primitive

Aksyonov, Vassily

5.

1. *Generations of Winter.* Random House, 1994.
2. *The Winter's Hero.* Random House, 1996.

From 1925 to 1953, the Gradov family is swept up in the purges, wars, and privations of the Stalinist era. Patriarch Boris, the physician, becomes a general and a deputy in the Supreme Soviet and survives the turmoil of the period until he is called to treat the dying Stalin. His daughter Nina is a poet who is forced out of Moscow. Sons Kirill and Nikita support the regime until they are accused of being anti-Stalinist and are exiled to Siberia. During World War II, Nikita is called back into service. Grandchildren Yolka and Boris must try to survive the final years of Stalin's madness. The vast panorama of Soviet history is revealed in these sprawling novels that incorporate real and imagined characters, Russian legends, folklore, and history.

Genre: Family Saga; Historical Fiction
Subjects: Family life; World War II 1939–1945; Soviet Union; Stalin, Joseph 1879–1953

Place/Time: Soviet Union—1917–1945; Soviet Union—1945–1980; Soviet Union—1980–1991

Alcott, Louisa May

6.
1. *Little Women or Meg, Jo, Beth, and Amy.* Roberts, 1868.
2. *Little Men or Life at Plumfield with Jo's Boys.* Roberts, 1871.
3. *Jo's Boys or How They Turned Out.* Roberts, 1886.

These beloved classics tell the story of the March girls, Meg, Jo, Beth, and Amy, from childhood through middle age in New England. Each sister is very different: Beth is the homebody; Jo is the tomboy; Meg is the practical one; and Amy, the youngest, is interested only in herself. Their father is fighting in the Civil War, and the girls help their mother, Marmee, make ends meet. When they grow up, Meg marries and has several children; Amy marries Laurie, the grandson of their neighbor, Mr. Laurence; Jo, who never wanted to marry, finally marries a middle-aged German professor who encourages her to write. Jo and Professor Bhaer set up a school for boys. When their two boys grow up, they help expand the school to a college for men and women.

Genre: Gentle Read
Subjects: Family life; Mothers and daughters; Mothers and sons; Sisters
Place/Time: New England—19th century

Aldiss, Brian W.

7. Helliconia Trilogy
1. *Helliconia Spring.* Atheneum, 1982.
2. *Helliconia Summer.* Atheneum, 1983.
3. *Helliconia Winter.* Atheneum, 1985.

The inhabitants of Alvernus, Earth's observation station in outer space, watch events unfold on Helliconia, a planet whose seasons are centuries long. As the planet passes into spring, a young man emerges from the dark mysteries of a religious cult to found the city of Oldorando. In the summer, Billy Xiao Pin comes to Helliconia from Alvernus risking infection with the virus that is death to outsiders. Winter brings an invasion of the Phagors, vicious beasts who throughout the history of the planet have made war on man.

Genre: Science Fiction
Subjects: Life on other planets; Seasons; Space stations; Viruses

Aldrich, Bess Streeter

8.
1. *A Lantern in Her Hand.* Appleton, 1928.
2. *A White Bird Flying.* Appleton, 1931.

As a bride in the mid-1800s, Abbie Deal goes by covered wagon to Nebraska. She lives out her long life on the prairies where her descendant, Laura, later struggles to find her own identity.

Genre: Historical Fiction
Subjects: Women; Frontier and pioneer life; Prairie life
Place/Time: Nebraska—19th century

Aldridge, James

9. Rupert Royce
1. *A Captive in the Land.* Doubleday, 1962.
2. *The Statesman's Game.* Doubleday, 1966.

The Cold War serves as the background for the adventures of an eccentric Englishman who becomes involved in East-West relations when he rescues a Russian who has survived a plane crash in the Arctic. He subsequently takes advantage of his family's position of power and wealth in the shipping industry to deal with the Russians and eventually turns his attention to Communist China.

Subjects: Cold war; Capitalists and financiers; Rescues; Communism; Shipping
Place/Time: Arctic regions—1945–1980; England—1945–1980; Soviet Union—1945–1980; Soviet Union—1980–1991; China—1945–1980

Aleichem, Sholem. *See Sholem Aleichem*

Alexander, Sidney

10.
1. *Michelangelo, the Florentine.* Random House, 1957.
2. *The Hand of Michelangelo.* M. Casalini, 1965.
3. *Nicodemus: The Roman Years.* Ohio University Press, 1984.

The Italian Renaissance is vividly evoked in this series of historical novels about the life of Michelangelo. The books follow the young man as he learns his art then creates masterpieces for the popes in Rome.

Genre: Historical Fiction
Subjects: Michelangelo Buonarroti, 1475–1564; Renaissance; Artists; Sculptors; Popes; Cathedrals
Place/Time: Florence (Italy)—15th century; Rome (Italy)—16th century; Italy—15th century; Italy—16th century

Alexie, Sherman

11.
1. *The Lone Ranger and Tonto Fist Fight in Heaven.* Atlantic Monthly Press, 1993.
2. *Reservation Blues.* Atlantic, 1995.

On the Spokane Indian Reservation Victor views his community and his people mired in alcohol, violence, and despair. He sees young men dreaming of escape, old people ignored, and everyone hears their ancestors laughing in the trees. Victor sees beyond the grimness to the humor and the culture of his people. When a stranger arrives at the reservation with a magical guitar, Victor and his friends use the guitar to form an all-Indian rock and roll band. As the groups plays in small clubs and then goes on tour they attract groupies. The more they succeed, the more they lose their native American culture and their souls.

Subjects: Native Americans; Music
Place/Time: Washington (state) 1980–

Allen, Henry Wilson. *See Fisher, Clay*

Allen, Hervey

12. The Disinherited Series
1. *The Forest and the Fort.* Farrar & Rinehart, 1943.
2. *Bedford Village.* Farrar, 1944.
3. *Toward the Morning.* Rinehart, 1948.

The above titles have also been published in the following collection: *City in the Dawn.* Rinehart, 1950.

Salathiel Albine, raised by American Indians, is returned to colonial settlers in the Pennsylvania forests during the French and Indian Wars. His life during these times is shaped by the tensions among the American Indians, the British, and the colonists.

Genre: Historical Fiction
Subjects: United States—French and Indian War, 1755–1763; Frontier and pioneer life; Native Americans; Boys; Native Americans—captivities
Place/Time: Pennsylvania—19th century

Allen, James Lane

13. Kentucky Series
1. *A Kentucky Cardinal: A Story.* Harper, 1895.
2. *Aftermath: Part Second of "A Kentucky Cardinal."* Harper, 1896.

The above titles have also been published in the following collection: *A Kentucky Cardinal and Aftermath.* Macmillan, 1924.

Adam Moss, a young 19th-century Southerner, prefers his almost mystical relationship with plants and animals to human society until he meets his neighbor, the lovely Georgianna. Their love survives her unfortunate attempt to put it to the test, but her death following the birth of their child plunges Adam back into his previous existence as a hermit whose greatest joy is the woods and meadows.

Subjects: Hermits; Nature; Love; Husbands and wives
Place/Time: Kentucky—19th century

Allen, Roger McBride

14. Hunted Earth
1. *The Ring of Charon.* Tor, 1990.
2. *The Shattered Sphere.* Tor, 1994.

In the process of conducting a scientific demonstration involving the Ring of Charon around Pluto's moon, astrophysicist Larry Chao seems to have destroyed Earth. In actuality, the gravity wave beam released by Chao has activated a signal that sets in motion a plan of the alien Charonians to kidnap Earth. In Earth's solar system, the remaining humans discover their missing planet's fate and start a rescue effort, while in a distant stellar system Earth is in the midst of a conflict between the Charonians and another alien race.

Genre: Science Fiction
Subjects: Kidnapping; Extraterrestrial beings; Rescues; Interplanetary wars

Allis, Marguerite

15. Ashbel Field Series
1. *Now We Are Free.* Putnam, 1952.
2. *To Keep Us Free.* Putnam, 1953.
3. *Brave Pursuit.* Putnam, 1954.
4. *The Rising Storm.* Putnam, 1955.
5. *Free Soil.* Putnam, 1958.

Ashbel Field returns to Connecticut after the Revolutionary War and moves his family to the new western frontier in Ohio. Five generations of his family fight to tame the frontier, to win a woman's right to education, and to bring about the abolition of slavery. Lafayette Field moves from Ohio to Kansas and fights to have it admitted to the Union as a free state.

Genre: Family Saga; Historical Fiction
Subjects: Frontier and pioneer life; Abolitionists; Slavery
Place/Time: Ohio—19th century; Kansas—19th century

Alten, Steve

16.
1. *Meg.* Doubleday, 1997.
2. *The Trench.* Penguin, 1999.

Carcharodon megalodon is an ancient ancestor of the shark, which has survived in a deep ocean abyss. When Jonas Taylor, a paleontologist, is helping a friend test the waters in the ocean trench, their instruments are destroyed. They watch in horror as one of the creatures devours another and the surviving meg is pregnant. Taylor kills it and raises the offspring in captivity, but it escapes and leads everyone on a nonstop race until Taylor and the creature fight to the death.

Genre: Horror; Adventure
Subjects: Adventure; Animals
Place/Time: Pacific Ocean—1980–

Alvarez, Julia

17.
1. *How the Garcia Girls Lost Their Accents.*
   Algonquin Books, 1991.
2. *Yo!* Algonquin Books, 1997.

Through interconnected vignettes, the lives of the four Garcia sisters are powerfully retold. The sisters are brought to America as young girls so the family can escape the political horrors in the Domincan Republic. Adapting to life in America is difficult and often confusing especially when the girls are hurt by prejudice against Spanish-speaking students. Daughter Yolanda, or Yo, becomes a writer who uses her family's history as the basis for her books. Yo's story is told by the many people who know her and each reveals a different side of her.

Subjects: Sisters; Family life; Immigrants; Hispanic Americans
Place/Time: Dominican Republic—1945–1980; New York (N. Y.)—1945–1980; New York (N. Y.)—1980–

Anand, Valerie

18. Bridges over Time
1. *The Proud Villeins.* St. Martin's, 1992.
2. *The Ruthless Yeoman.* St. Martin's, 1993.
3. *Women of Ashdon.* St. Martin's, 1993.
4. *The Faithful Lovers.* St. Martin's, 1994.
5. *The Cherished Wives.* St. Martin's, 1995.

From 1036 to 1800, the free-spirited women of the Whitmead family rebel inwardly and outwardly against their selfish, chauvinistic husbands, lovers, and fathers. In 1036 French knight Sir Ivon de Clairpont crosses the channel to try to conquer the English throne, but is defeated and sold into slavery by William the Conqueror. His descendants fight to become freemen and to better their lives. A marriage of convenience brings the Ashdon estate into the family, and it is the Whitmead women who save it through the turmoil of family fights and English history.

Genre: Family Saga; Historical Fiction
Subjects: William I, King of England, 1028–1087; Middle Ages; Feudalism; Husbands and Wives; England—history, 1714–1837
Place/Time: England—multicentury span

Anderson, Kevin J. *See* Herbert, Brian

Anderson, Poul

19.
1. *Operation Chaos.* Doubleday, 1971.
2. *Operation Luna.* Tor, 1999.

Since magic has returned to the world in the 20th century, beings who were once thought to be the stuff of legends now serve practical purposes. Steve Matucheck, who, in addition to being an engineer, is also a werewolf, and his wife Virginia, an expert witch, first face the world's most powerful demon as they battle against Black Magic. Next the couple wages war on evil spirits who are sabotaging the United States space program in an effort to keep humanity on Earth.

Genre: Fantasy; Science Fiction
Subjects: Werewolves; Witchcraft; Magic; Good and evil; Space flight

20.
1. *Harvest of Stars.* Tor, 1993.
2. *The Stars Are Also Fire.* Tor, 1994.
3. *Harvest the Fire.* Tor, 1995.
4. *The Fleet of Stars.* Tor, 1997.

Starting in the near future and extending many generations beyond are these stories of the domination of human life by technology, corporate power, and a cult devoted to repressively rational concepts. The brilliant leader of Fireball Industries, Anson Guthrie, achieves near immortality by downloading himself into a computer and opposing the philosophical-religious movement of Avantism. However, he finds his strongest opponent is another computer clone of himself. Meanwhile yet another version of Guthrie explores the stars. Anson's descendant Dagny and her own descendants create a lunar colony that later becomes a breeding ground for revolutionaries who oppose the increasing technological control of society. Guthrie returns to Earth to investigate the findings of a solar lens in deep space.

Genre: Science Fiction
Subjects: Technology and civilization; Computers; Business; Cults; Space colonies

21. Alternate World Sequence
1. *Three Hearts and Three Lions.* Doubleday, 1961.
2. *Midsummer Tempest.* Doubleday, 1974.

A unique mixture of modern-day characters, actual historical figures, and magical beings come together in these romantic tales of adventure. In the first tale, a Dane injured in World War II is transported centuries back in time to engage in heroic deeds in Carolingian Europe. In the second work, Shakespearean characters come to life to help an English prince support Charles I and assist fairy spirits in their struggle against the forces of the Industrial Revolution.

Genre: Fantasy
Subjects: Time travel; Fairies; Shakespeare, William, 1564–1616—characters; Charles I, King of England, 1600–1649
Place/Time: Europe—9th century; England—17th century; England—18th century

22. Technic History Series
1. *War of the Wing-Men.* (Alternate title: *The Man Who Counts.*) Ace, 1958.
2. *Trader to the Stars.* Doubleday, 1964.
3. *The Trouble Twisters.* Doubleday, 1966.
4. *Satan's World.* Doubleday, 1969.

5. *Mirkheim.* Berkley, 1977.
6. *The Earth Book of Stormgate.* Berkley, 1978.
7. *Ensign Flandry.* Chilton, 1966.
8. *A Circus of Hells.* New American Library, 1970.
9. *The Rebel Worlds.* New American Library, 1969.
10. *Mayday Orbit.* Ace, 1961.
11. *Earthman, Go Home!* Ace, 1960.

The above two titles have also been published in the following collection: *Flandry of Terra.* Chilton, 1965.

12. *We Claim These Stars.* Ace, 1959.
13. *A Knight of Ghosts and Shadows.* Doubleday, 1974.
14. *The Game of Empire.* Baen, 1985.
15. *Let the Spacemen Beware!* (Alternate title: *The Night Face.*) Ace, 1963.

In the 23rd century, a mercantile union of traders and adventurers travels through the galaxies transferring goods and cultural elements between planets. The earlier stories are dominated by spice and liquor entrepreneur Nicholas Van Rijn whose flamboyant personality and deeds match the expansionist mood of the times. In contrast, a darker character, agent Dominic Flandry, becomes the protagonist in later works set beyond the high point of the Terran Empire, when the federation decays and questions of right and wrong become more difficult to judge.

Genre: Science Fiction
Subjects: Interplanetary voyages; Merchants; Spies

Anderson, Roberta. *See Michaels, Fern*

Andrews, Raymond

23.
1. *Appalachee Red.* Dial Press, 1978.
2. *Rosiebelle Lee Wildcat Tennessee.* Dial Press, 1980.
3. *Baby Sweets.* Dial Press, 1983.

This raucous and compassionate tale depicts the people of Appalachee, a small town in Muskhogean County, Georgia, from 1917 to 1959. Red is the bastard son of the town's most influential white man and his African American maid. Red must learn to live in a town that is rapidly changing from social, industrial, and political pressure.

Genre: Historical Fiction
Subjects: Southern states; Race relations; African Americans; Cultural conflict; Prejudices
Place/Time: Georgia—1900–1945; Georgia—1945–1980

Andrews, V. C. (Victoria C.)

24.
1. *Tarnished Gold.* Pocket Books, 1996.

2. *Ruby.* Pocket Books, 1994.
3. *Pearl in the Mist.* Pocket Books, 1995.
4. *All That Glitters.* Pocket Books, 1995.
5. *Hidden Jewel.* Pocket Books, 1995.

Gabriel Landry leads a happy life in her Louisiana bayou until she is raped by rich cannery owner Octavius Tate. To spare her family, Gabriel agrees to have the baby and give it up to the Tates. Paul Tate grows up not knowing his real heritage. He falls in love with Ruby, a Cajun girl who also has a dark secret in her past. As the two try to find love, they must discover the shocking truth of their heritage, which could destroy them.

Genre: Horror
Subjects: Family life; Child abuse
Place/Time: Louisiana—1980–

25. Casteel Family
1. *Web of Dreams.* Pocket Books, 1990.
2. *Heaven.* Pocket Books, 1985.
3. *Dark Angel.* Pocket Books, 1986.
4. *Fallen Hearts.* Pocket Books, 1988.
5. *Gates of Paradise.* Pocket Books, 1989.

Heaven Leigh Casteel is the brightest child in a poor West Virginia hillbilly family. When her stepmother runs away, her father sells the children to different families. The children spend their lives searching for each other and for the love they lost and trying to undo their traumatic past.

Subjects: Child abuse; Family life; Brothers and sisters
Place/Time: Boston (Mass.)—1980–; Massachusetts—1980–

26. Cutler Family
1. *Dawn.* Pocket Books, 1990.
2. *Secrets of the Morning.* Pocket Books, 1991.
3. *Twilight's Child.* Pocket Books, 1992.
4. *Midnight Whispers.* Pocket Books, 1992.

Dawn Longchamp tries to recover from the abuse she received from her mother's family. That child abuse haunts her during her own marriage, then shatters her daughter Christie, though Dawn has tried to shield her from the family secrets.

Subjects: Child abuse; Family life; Mothers and daughters
Place/Time: New York (N. Y.)—1980–

27. Dollanganger Family
1. *Garden of Shadows.* Pocket Books, 1987.
2. *Flowers in the Attic.* Pocket Books, 1979.
3. *Petals on the Wind.* Pocket Books, 1980.
4. *If There Be Thorns.* Pocket Books, 1981.
5. *Seeds of Yesterday.* Pocket Books, 1984.

The evil that begins with the marriage of Malcolm and Olivia Foxworth in *Garden of Shadows* sets the stage for the horrors that afflict their four innocent children, who are locked away in an attic. Even after they escape from the attic, the family horror cannot be hidden, and the children and their children must confront their past throughout their tortured lives.

Genre: Horror
Subjects: Child abuse; Family life; Children; Emotionally disturbed children
Place/Time: Virginia—1980–

Andric, Ivo

28.
1. *The Bridge on the Drina.* Macmillan, 1959, 1945.
2. *Bosnian Chronicle.* Knopf, 1963, 1945.
3. *The Woman from Sarajevo.* Knopf, 1965, 1945.

The tortured history of Bosnia from the 17th century to the early 20th century is shown through the people who have lived through the occupation and wars that have shaped the country. Through much of the history, the Turks control the area. Later the town of Travnik is the scene for clashes between Napoleon's forces and the Turks. Then Bosnia becomes the scene for the assassination that triggers World War I.

Genre: Historical Fiction
Subjects: War; Bosnia—history
Place/Time: Bosnia—multicentury span

Angoff, Charles

29.
1. *Journey to the Dawn.* Beechhurst Press, 1951.
2. *In the Morning Light.* Beechhurst Press, 1952.
3. *The Sun at Noon.* Beechhurst Press, 1955.
4. *Between Day and Night.* Yoseloff, 1959.
5. *The Bitter Spring.* Yoseloff, 1961.
6. *Summer Storm.* Yoseloff, 1963.
7. *Memory of Autumn.* Yoseloff, 1968.
8. *Winter Twilight.* Yoseloff, 1970.
9. *Seasons of Mists.* Yoseloff, 1971.
10. *Mid-Century.* A. S. Barnes, 1973.
11. *Toward the Horizon.* A. S. Barnes, 1978.

The Jewish Polonsky family leaves czarist Russia in 1900 and migrates to Boston. Events affecting their lives, family relationships, and new home, and the formation of the state of Israel are followed through the various family members.

Genre: Family Saga; Historical Fiction
Subjects: Jews; Family life; Israel
Place/Time: Boston (Mass.)—1900–1945; Israel—1945–1980; Massachusetts—1900–1945

Ansay, A. Manette

30.
1. *Vinegar Hill.* Viking, 1994.

2. *Read This and Tell Me What It Says.* Massachusetts Press, 1995.

The people of Holly's Field, Wisconsin, have to face poverty, sickness, aging, and abuse. Jimmy and Ellen Grier and their two young children move back to Jimmy's parents' farm. There Ellen finds her in-laws to be a bitter abusive couple who make her life unbearable until she gets up the courage to leave. In the town, a young girl becomes a compulsive thief when she is pressured by her family's hopes for her academic success. Another wife sees her husband desert her, but he keeps calling to remind her to put the dog out. All of the characters in this harsh town develop a strength and a resourcefulness that help them deal with their troubled lives.

Subjects: Country life; Small town life; Family life
Place/Time: Wisconsin—1980–

Anthony, Evelyn. *Pseud.* of Evelyn Bridget Patricia Stephens Ward-Thomas

31.
1. *Rebel Princess.* Crowell, 1953.
2. *Royal Intrigue.* Crowell, 1954.
3. *Far Fly the Eagles.* Crowell, 1955.

Fourteen-year-old Catherine comes to Russia to marry the half-witted Grand Duke Peter. Having survived her marriage to Peter, she becomes Catherine the Great, Empress of Russia, and embarks on a turbulent and passionate 20-year reign. Her line ends tragically with the short reign of her epileptic son Peter.

Genre: Historical Fiction
Subjects: Catherine I, Empress of Russia, 1684–1727; Courts and courtiers; Queens
Place/Time: Russia—18th century

32.
1. *The Defector.* Coward, McCann & Geoghegan, 1981.
2. *Avenue of the Dead.* Coward, McCann & Geoghegan, 1982.
3. *Albatross.* Putnam, 1983.
4. *The Company of Saints.* Putnam, 1984.

British intelligence agent Davina Graham unravels Russian KGB plots against the Western alliance, but her overriding aim is to find the KGB agent who murdered her husband years earlier. Amid the rivalries and feuds of the various intelligence agencies, Davina finds treachery at every turn.

Genre: Espionage
Subjects: Secret service; International intrigue; Spies; Murder and murderers
Place/Time: Soviet Union—1945–1980; Soviet Union—1980–1991; England—1945–1980

Anthony, Mark

33. The Last Rune

1. *Beyond the Pale.* Bantam, 1999.
2. *The Keep of Fire.* Bantam, 1999.

Contact with a mystical rune transports bartender Travis Wilder and emergency room physician Grace Becket from Colorado to the magical, but sinister, land of Eldh where Grace learns witchcraft and becomes a healer. After returning to Earth, Travis discovers that he is being followed by dark creatures who want to learn of his Eldh experience. When a plague that causes its victims to burst into flame afflicts both Earth and Eldh, Travis travels back to Eldh in the hope that he and Grace can find a cure for the strange disease.

Genre: Fantasy
Subjects: Imaginary kingdoms; Magic; Diseases; Good and evil; Fire

Anthony, Piers (*Pseud. of* Piers Anthony Dillingham Jacob) *and* Margoff, Robert E.

34. Kelvin Knight

1. *Dragon's Gold.* Tor, 1987.
2. *Serpent's Silver.* Tor, 1988.
3. *Chimaera's Copper.* Tor, 1990.
4. *Orc's Opal.* Tor, 1990.
5. *Mouvar's Magic.* Tor, 1992.

In a fantasy world where the shape of one's ears is all important, young Kelvin struggles with good and evil while trying to fulfill the wizard Mouvar's prophecy of the triumph of a united kingdom. Along the way, Kelvin marries and produces telepathic children, one a dragon, who becomes the target of the wicked witch Zady.

Genre: Fantasy
Subjects: Imaginary kingdoms; Good and evil; Telepathy; Prophecies

Anthony, Piers. *Pseud. of* Piers Anthony Dillingham Jacob

35. Apprentice Adept

1. *Split Infinity.* Ballantine, 1980.
2. *Blue Adept.* Ballantine, 1981.
3. *Juxtaposition.* Ballantine, 1982.
4. *Out of Phaze.* Putnam, 1987.
5. *Robot Adept.* Putnam, 1988.
6. *Unicorn Point.* Putnam, 1989.
7. *Phaze Doubt.* Putnam, 1990.

In this combination of fantasy and science fiction, characters pass between two interlocking worlds, encountering danger, adventure, romance, and—frequently—their alternate selves. Proton is a scientific world full of computers, robots, and pollution. Dragons, elves, and unicorns inhabit Phaze, an illogical world of magic.

Genre: Fantasy; Science Fiction
Subjects: Technology and civilization; Magic

36. Aton

1. *Chthon.* Ballantine, 1967.
2. *Phthor.* Berkley, 1975.

Interspersed with a series of flashbacks into his earlier life is the story of Aton Five, who is forced to work a garnet mine in a cruel alien society on the far edge of the galaxy. The tale continues with the experiences of Aton's son, who lives in the caverns with little human contact other than his parents until he meets an intriguing young woman who calls herself Ex.

Genre: Science Fiction
Subjects: Life on other planets; Cruelty; Mines and mining; Caves

37. Battle Circle

1. *Sos the Rope.* Pyramid, 1968.
2. *Var the Stick.* Bantam, 1973.
3. *Neq the Sword.* Corgi, 1975.

In the century following a nuclear holocaust, the survivors are reduced to living so barbarically that each man's favorite weapon becomes part of his name. Having gained control of the nomadic tribes of the time, Sos and Var conflict with an industrial group that controls the supply of arms. Ultimately Neq emerges and attempts to rebuild this strange, primitive but technological society.

Genre: Science Fiction
Subjects: Arms and armor; Nuclear warfare; Nomads

38. Cal, Veg, and Aquilon

1. *Omnivore.* Ballantine, 1968.
2. *Orn.* Avon, 1971.
3. *Ox.* Avon, 1976.

The intellectual Cal, the lovely, artistic Aquilon, and the powerful vegetarian Veg return from exploring the planet Nacre, bringing with them the Mantas, tropical fungi that endanger life on Earth. Next the three travel to a prehistoric planet, which they name Paleo, where they try to save the great bird Orn from the extinction that civilization will bring. In their last adventure, they are assisted by the Mantas, who accompany them in their struggle to escape from a web that has trapped them in time and space.

Genre: Science Fiction
Subjects: Explorers; Life on other planets; Ecology; Rare animals

39. Geodyssey

1. *Isle of Woman.* St. Martin's, 1993.
2. *Shame of Man.* Tor, 1994.
3. *Hope of Earth.* Tor, 1997.
4. *Muse of Art.* Tom Doherty Assoc., 1999.

The story of humanity is retold through a series of tales that show the history of two families who are continually reborn. From prehistoric days through America in the 21st century, Ember and Blaze love each other but are always kept apart. Their various stories show the ecological impact of humans on history. In the second book, Anthony again follows two families through several thousand years and many different cultures as he explores Earth's multicultural history. The tales continue through ancient Athens, leap to the gang culture of the 1990s, and explore the environmental challenges of the near future.

Genre: Fantasy
Subjects: Reincarnation; Love; Ecology

40. Mode
1. *Virtual Mode.* Putnam, 1991.
2. *Fractal Mode.* Putnam, 1992.
3. *Chaos Mode.* Putnam, 1994.

Colene, a neglected, suicidal teenager, rescues Darius, an attractive, but possibly unbalanced young man who tells her of another wonderful reality to which he wants to take her. Discouraged by her disbelief, he vanishes but regrets his decision. Through a series of adventures they are reunited and fall into the magical world of Oria with Sequiro, the telepathic horse, and Provos, the woman who remembers only the future. Finally, Colene's unique experiences equip her with some skills that allow her to deal with her difficult family on a visit to Earth.

Genre: Fantasy
Subjects: Teenagers; Love

41. Xanth
1. *A Spell for Chameleon.* Ballantine, 1977.
2. *The Source of Magic.* Ballantine, 1979.
3. *Castle Roogna.* Ballantine, 1979.
4. *Centaur Aisle.* Ballantine, 1982.
5. *Ogre, Ogre.* Ballantine, 1982.
6. *Night Mare.* Ballantine, 1983.
7. *Dragon on a Pedestal.* Ballantine, 1983.
8. *Crewel Lye: A Caustic Yarn.* Ballantine, 1985.
9. *Golem in the Gears.* Ballantine, 1986.
10. *Vale of the Vole.* Avon, 1987.
11. *Heaven Cent.* Avon, 1988.
12. *Man from Mundania.* Avon, 1989.
13. *Isle of View.* Morrow, 1990.
14. *Question Quest.* Avon, 1991.
15. *The Color of Her Panties.* Avon, 1992.
16. *Demons Don't Dream.* Tor, 1993.
17. *Harpy Thyme.* Tor, 1994.
18. *Geis of the Gargoyle.* Tor, 1994.
19. *Roc and a Hard Place.* Tor, 1995.
20. *Yon Ill Wind.* Tor, 1996.
21. *Faun and Games.* Tor, 1997.
22. *Zombie Lover.* Tor, 1998.
23. *Xone of Contention.* Tor, 1999.

Xanth is a land of magic, wit, puns, and fun, but some things are taken very literally. Shoes grow on shoe trees, for example. Demons and dragons mingle with characters with names such as D. Mentia and Chlorine. Sometimes events and characters in Xanth collide with those in the boring world of Mundania (our world).

Genre: Fantasy
Subjects: Magic; Language and languages

Appel, Allen

42.
1. *Time After Time.* Carroll & Graf, 1985.
2. *Twice Upon a Time.* Carroll & Graf, 1987.
3. *Till the End of Time.* Doubleday, 1990.

Historian Alex Balfour has the ability to travel between the present and past, but only to the time and place he is studying. However, he has no control over when he will time travel or how long he will stay. As Alex ventures to the Russian Revolution, the Pacific during World War II, and the American Indian Wars of the 1860s, he meets such famous people as Rasputin, John F. Kennedy, and General Custer. He also gets involved in cliff hanging situations that could trap him in the past.

Genre: Fantasy
Subjects: Time travel; Soviet Union—revolution, 1917–1921; World War II, 1939–1945—naval operations; Native Americans—wars
Place/Time: Soviet Union—1917–1945; Pacific Ocean—1900–1945; United States—19th century

Archer, Jeffrey

43.
1. *Kane and Abel.* Simon & Schuster, 1980.
2. *The Prodigal Daughter.* Simon & Schuster, 1982.

Born on the same day in 1906, William Kane, son of a wealthy family, and Abel Rosnovski, illegitimate son of a Polish baron, use their ambition and intelligence to achieve wealth, prestige, and power in Boston but in very different ways. Their 60-year rise to the top also causes a terrible feud between them. Abel's daughter and Kane's son meet and marry, causing a break with both families. Through her drive and hard work, Abel's daughter sets up a business, enters politics, and reunites the families.

Genre: Family Saga
Subjects: Wealth; Millionaires; Businessmen; Businesswomen; Self-made men
Place/Time: Boston (Mass.)—1900–1945; Boston (Mass.)—1945–1980; Massachusetts—1900–1945; Massachusetts—1945–1980

Arenas, Reinaldo

44.
1. *Singing from the Well.* Viking, 1987, 1967.
2. *Palace of the White Skunks.* Viking, 1990, 1975.
3. *Farewell to the Sea.* Viking, 1985, 1982.
4. *The Assault.* Viking, 1994.

This nightmarish view of Cuba before and after the revolution is written by one of Cuba's greatest authors. Through the grotesque fantasies and dreams of a young boy and a disillusioned revolutionary, Arenas explores the reality of Cuba during Batista and under Castro. He shows the despair of the Cuban people when their hopes are destroyed.

Subjects: Communism; Cuba—revolution, 1958–1959; Batista y Zaldivar, Fulgencio, 1901–1973; Castro, Fidel, 1926–
Place/Time: Cuba—1900–1945; Cuba—1945–1980

Argo, Ellen. *Pseud. of* Ellen Argo Johnson

45.
1. *Jewel of the Seas.* Putnam, 1977.
2. *Crystal Star.* Putnam, 1979.
3. *Yankee Girl.* Putnam, 1980.

In the early 1800s, Julia Logan learns to manage the men on board a Cape Cod sailing ship and to handle the storms of the South Atlantic on a voyage home from Hong Kong with her husband.

Genre: Historical Fiction
Subjects: Sailing vessels; Shipmasters; Women; Marriage
Place/Time: Cape Cod (Mass.)—19th century; Atlantic Ocean—19th century; Massachusetts—19th century

Arlen, Leslie. *Pseud. of* Christopher Nicole. *See also* Nicole, Christopher

46. The Borodins
1. *Love and Honor.* Jove, 1980.
2. *War and Passion.* Jove, 1981.
3. *Fate and Dreams.* Jove, 1981.
4. *Hope and Glory.* Jove, 1982.
5. *Rage and Desire.* Jove, 1982.
6. *Fortune and Fury.* Jove, 1984.

The Borodins are an aristocratic Russian family in the early 1900s. General Borodin is the unbending head of the family. His son Peter and daughters Ilona and Tatiana are passionate and headstrong. They fight the forces rising in Russia that threaten their birthright and become involved with American George Hayman during the Russian Revolution. Their children continue to be part of the Soviet Union through the Cold War.

Genre: Family Saga; Historical Romance
Subjects: Aristocracy; Family life; Brothers and sisters; Parents and children
Place/Time: Russia—1900–1917; Soviet Union—1917–1945; Soviet Union—1945–1980; Soviet Union—1980–1991

Armstrong, Campbell

47.
1. *Jig.* Morrow, 1987.
2. *Mazurka.* Harper, 1990.
3. *Mambo.* Harper, 1990.
4. *Jigsaw.* Little, Brown, 1995.

Frank Pagan is a member of Scotland Yard's antiterrorist group. He goes after IRA terrorists, master German terrorist Gunther Ruhr and elusive, beautiful terrorist Carlotta. Pagan's adventures take him from Britain to Ireland, the United States to Cuba, and France to Italy as he attempts to foil violent plots against the West.

Genre: Adventure; Espionage
Subjects: Spies; International intrigue; Secret service; Terrorism
Place/Time: England—1980–; Ireland—1980–; United States—1980–; Cuba—1980–

Arnold, Bruce

48.
1. *A Singer at the Wedding.* H. Hamilton, 1978.
2. *Song of the Nightingale.* H. Hamilton, 1980.
3. *The Muted Swan.* H. Hamilton, 1981.
4. *Running to Paradise.* H. Hamilton, 1983.

The emotional life of a British schoolboy in the 1950s is explored in this tetralogy. His violent father and vile stepmother give him much to ponder as he moves through his twenties and thirties.

Genre: Coming of Age
Subjects: Boys; Teenagers; Family life; Child abuse
Place/Time: England—1945–1980

Arundel, Honor

49.
1. *The Terrible Temptation.* Thomas Nelson, 1971.
2. *The Blanket Word.* Thomas Nelson, 1973.

Jan Meredith goes to college dreaming of an independent life. When she falls in love with Timothy, she refuses to get involved as she does not want to be tied down with a family and responsibility. Only after her mother's death does she realize love means many things.

Genre: Gentle Read; Romance
Subjects: College life
Place/Time: 1945–1980

Asaro, Catherine

50. Saga of the Skolian Empire
1. *Primary Inversion.* Tor, 1995.
2. *Catch the Lightning.* Tor, 1996.
3. *The Last Hawk.* Tor, 1997.
4. *The Radiant Seas.* St. Martin's, 1998.

In the far future, the Skolian Empire is one of the powers in a three-sided interstellar conflict. Space pilots in these war stories of the future deal with psionic powers and romance as their exploits take them through time and into alternate realities.

Genre: Science Fiction
Subjects: Interplanetary wars; Time travel; Extrasensory perception

Asch, Sholem

51.
1. *The Nazarene.* Putnam, 1939.
2. *The Apostle.* Putnam, 1943.
3. *Mary.* Putnam, 1949.
4. *Moses.* Putnam, 1951.
5. *The Prophet.* Putnam, 1955.

Yiddish author Asch's purpose in creating this biblical series, which explores Old Testament and early Christian history, was to reconcile the Christian and Jewish viewpoints. *The Nazarene* is narrated in part by modern characters who feel they are reincarnated men of biblical times and in part by Judas Iscariot. The final volume, *The Prophet*, goes back to the Old Testament figure, the second Isaiah, in Babylon of fifth century B.C.

Genre: Historical Fiction
Subjects: Biblical stories; Judaism; Christianity
Place/Time: Palestine—to 70 A. D.; Babylon—to 70 A. D.

Asimov, Isaac

52. Future History
1. *I, Robot.* Gnome Press, 1950.
2. *The Caves of Steel.* Doubleday, 1954.
3. *The Naked Sun.* Doubleday, 1957.

The above two titles have also been published in the following collection: *The Robot Novels.* Doubleday, 1971.

4. *The Rest of the Robots.* Doubleday, 1964.

Most of the robot short stories have also been published in the following collection: *The Complete Robot.* Doubleday, 1982.

5. *Robots of Dawn.* Doubleday, 1983.
6. *Robots and Empire.* Doubleday, 1985.
7. *The Currents of Space.* Doubleday, 1952.
8. *The Stars, Like Dust.* Doubleday, 1951.
9. *Pebble in the Sky.* Doubleday, 1950.

The above three titles have also been published in the following collection: *Triangle.* Doubleday, 1961.

10. *Prelude to Foundation.* Doubleday, 1988.
11. *Forward the Foundation.* Doubleday, 1993.
12. *Foundation.* Gnome Press, 1951.
13. *Foundation and Empire.* Gnome Press, 1952.
14. *Second Foundation.* Gnome Press, 1953.

The above three titles have also been published in the following collection: *Foundation Trilogy.* Doubleday, 1963.

15. *Foundation's Edge.* Doubleday, 1982.
16. *Foundation and Earth.* Doubleday, 1986.
17. *Foundation's Fear.* HarperCollins, 1997. (Written by Gregory Benford).
18. *Foundation and Chaos.* HarperCollins, 1998. (Written by Greg Bear).
19. *Foundation's Triumph.* HarperCollins, 1999. (Written by David Brin)

Toward the end of his career, Asimov assembled his novels and short stories in the above chronological order. Asimov's works fall roughly into three subgroups. The Robot Books (1–6) feature Asimov's positive attitude toward the relationship between robots and man. The stories begin with the reminiscences of Susan Calvin, a specialist instrumental in the early development of the robots, and continue as detective fiction, with interplanetary sleuth Elijah Baley assisted by a very human robot, Daneel Olivaw. The next works (7–9) follow the history of the expansion and resulting conflicts of the Trantorian Empire in its early stages, when mankind has spread out over the galaxy to escape from Earth, damaged and made partly uninhabitable by nuclear warfare. The initial Foundation Trilogy (12–14) chronicles the fate of two foundations established by psycho-historian Hari Seldon to minimize the effect of the collapse of the Trantorian Empire, whose complexity has created an impossibly delicate balance of forces.

The First Foundation engages in conflict with a powerful mutant known as the Mule, then with the more theoretical Second Foundation. Ultimately a young official of the First Foundation seeks a fusion of the good elements of the opposing forces and sets out to search for secrets that may be buried in the lost planet Earth.

Prelude to Foundation and *Forward the Foundation* (10–11), the latter published after the author's death, form a bridge between the Trantorian Empire and Foundation books by describing the early career of Hari Seldon. With the authorization of the Asimov estate, three distinguished writers of science fiction, Gregory Benford, Greg Bear, and David Brin, have continued the Foundation Saga with stories that fill in gaps in the Hari Seldon narrative and follow him into the latter years of his career.

Genre: Science Fiction
Subjects: Robots; Space colonies; Nuclear warfare; Detectives; Mutation (biology)

Assis, Machado de. *See* Machado de Assis

Asturias, Miguel Angel

53. Banana Republic Trilogy
1. *Strong Wind.* Delacorte Press, 1968.
2. *The Green Pope.* Delacorte Press, 1971.

3. *The Eyes of the Interred.* Delacorte Press, 1973.

Asturias won the 1967 Nobel Prize for this trilogy and his other works. A Central American republic is dominated and exploited by a powerful fruit company. The local people attempt to free themselves from the brutality and tyranny of the Tropical Banana Company and eventually bring its downfall.

Subjects: Business—unscrupulous methods; Revolutions and revolutionists; Peasant life
Place/Time: Central America—1945–1980

Attanasio, A. A.

54.
1. *The Dragon and the Unicorn.* HarperPrism, 1996.
2. *The Eagle and the Sword.* HarperPrism, 1997.
3. *The Wolf and the Crown.* HarperPrism, 1998.

Celtic and Norse myths blend in this retelling of the Arthurian legend. A cosmological conflict results from forces unleashed at the creation of the universe. Earth is the powerful Dragon with the Unicorn as a mystical controlling force. A demon who emerges from this clash of primal energy sources is born in human form and becomes the magician Merlin. Merlin recognizes the destructive elements in Arthur's nature, creates a magic sword to curb his willingness to kill, and guides him through his early years as King.

Genre: Fantasy
Subjects: Arthur, King; Merlin (legendary character); Demonology

Auel, Jean M.

55. Earth's Children
1. *The Clan of the Cave Bear.* Crown, 1980.
2. *The Valley of Horses.* Crown, 1982.
3. *The Mammoth Hunters.* Crown, 1985.
4. *Plains of Passage.* Crown, 1990.
5. *Shelters of Stone,* Crown, 2002

Young Cro-Magnon orphan Ayla is adopted into the Neanderthal clan of the cave bear. Her different traits and appearance create conflict, ultimately leading to her expulsion from the clan. She then wanders the vast expanse of Eastern Europe searching for her people.

Genre: Adventure; Historical Fiction
Subjects: Stone Age; Man, prehistoric; Women, prehistoric; Tribes; Clans; Adventure
Place/Time: Europe—prehistoric times

Austen-Leigh, Joan

56.
1. *A Visit to Highbury.* St. Martin's, 1996.
2. *Later Days at Highbury.* St. Martin's, 1996.

In the Sussex village of Highbury in the early 19th century, Mrs. Goddard, the mistress of the local school for girls, and her sister, Mrs. Pinkney, work quietly to help the younger women of the village find true love and marriage. Told through an exchange of letters between the two sisters, the romances of the young singles are retold while the changing times in the village are recounted. The author is the great-great-grandniece of Jane Austen and she uses the setting of Austen's *Emma* for her romances, but these books are not sequels to *Emma.*

Genre: Historical Romance
Subjects: Love; Letters (stories in letter form)
Place/Time: England—19th century

Bacchelli, Riccardo

57.
1. *The Mill on the Po.* Pantheon, 1950, 1938.
2. *Nothing New Under the Sun.* Pantheon, 1955, 1941.

The Scacerni family are millers in Italy's Po Valley at the start of the Napoleonic Wars. They and their descendants live through the tumultuous events from the unification of Italy to the end of World War I.

Genre: Family Saga; Historical Fiction
Subjects: War; Country life
Place/Time: Italy—19th century

Bacher, June Masters

58. Journey to Love
1. *Journey to Love.* Harvest House, 1985.
2. *Dreams Beyond Tomorrow.* Harvest House, 1985.
3. *Seasons of Love.* Harvest House, 1986.
4. *My Heart's Desire.* Harvest House, 1986.
5. *The Heart Remembers.* Harvest House, 1990.
6. *From This Time Forth.* Harvest House, 1991.

To escape her father's drunken rages, Rachel joins a wagon train going west. She marries Colby in name only, then struggles with storms, Indians, Colby's dreams, and her own faith before deciding what she really feels. She follows Colby to Superstition Mountain, where she works with other women of the community to thwart the evil men who would destroy their town. Only their faith saves them and makes them strong.

Genre: Christian Fiction; Historical Romance
Subjects: Frontier and pioneer life; Wagon trains; Christian life; Faith
Place/Time: Western states—19th century

59. Love Is a Gentle Stranger Series
1. *Love Is a Gentle Stranger.* Harvest House, 1983.
2. *Love's Silent Song.* Harvest House, 1983.
3. *Diary of a Loving Heart.* Harvest House, 1984.

4. *Love Leads Home.* Harvest House, 1984.
5. *Love Follows the Heart.* Harvest House, 1990.
6. *Love's Enduring Hope.* Harvest House, 1990.

When she is jilted, Chris Beth Kelly goes west to Oregon to teach school on the frontier. There she finds love with a minister and fights Indians, droughts, and plagues of grasshoppers. Her faith and commitment sustain her through her trials, but her children and friends must face their own problems as they struggle for a deeper understanding that only faith can give them.

Genre: Christian Fiction; Historical Romance
Subjects: Frontier and pioneer life; Family life; Christian life; Faith
Place/Time: Oregon—19th century

60. Love's Soft Whisper

1. *Love's Soft Whisper.* Harvest House, 1987.
2. *Love's Beautiful Dream.* Harvest House, 1987.
3. *When Hearts Awaken.* Harvest House, 1988.
4. *Another Spring.* Harvest House, 1988.
5. *When Morning Comes Again.* Harvest House, 1988.
6. *Gently Love Beckons.* Harvest House, 1989.

In the 1850s, Courtney is sent west as a companion to her cousin in the Columbia Territory of Oregon. There she meets Clint and falls in love, but their path is not smooth as they lose their first child and must fight storms that destroy their crops. Family rivalries challenge their bond, but their deepening love for each other and their strong faith see them through these tests until they realize their dreams.

Genre: Christian Fiction; Historical Romance
Subjects: Frontier and pioneer life; Family life; Christian life; Faith
Place/Time: Oregon—19th century

Baird, Wilhelmina

61.
1. *Crashcourse.* Ace, 1993.
2. *Clipjoint.* Ace, 1994.

In this future world movies are all too real. The audience, fitted with implants that allow them to feel the actors' emotions, love it—but what about the actors who must experience the action as if it's reality? Cassandra, her boyfriend Moke, and sidekick Dosh sign a contract to appear in a film knowing it's a risky life, but unaware that they'll be working with a mass murderess. Their adventures in cyber-cinema continue as a co-star who was thought dead mysteriously reappears.

Genre: Science Fiction
Subjects: Motion pictures; Actors and actresses; Violence; Bionics

Baker, Kage

62. The Company
1. *In the Garden of Iden.* Harcourt Brace, 1997.
2. *Sky Coyote.* Harcourt Brace, 1999.
3. *Mendoza in Hollywood.* Harcourt, 2000.

By conducting questionable experiments, a group of businessmen and scientists develop a process that creates immortal cyborgs who can travel through time and influence events that are not part of recorded history. Operative Mendoza travels from the 24th century to the reign of Bloody Mary in England to retrieve a species of holly that could cure cancer in the future, but which will become extinct without her intervention. Joseph has lived in many times and many places, but his current assignment is to transport a village of pre-Columbian Chumash American Indians to the future to rescue them from the white men who will soon exploit the west coast of the New World. Mendoza reappears in California of the 1860s where the American Civil War rumbles in the distance and a handsome British spy reminds her of a love who was lost to her centuries ago.

Genre: Science Fiction
Subjects: Time travel; Bionics; Immortality; Medicine; Native Americans; History; Love
Place/Time: England—16th century; North America—16th century; California—19th century

Baldwin, Faith

63.
1. *American Family.* Farrar & Rinehart, 1935.
2. *The Puritan Strain.* Farrar & Rinehart, 1935.

Turn-of-the-century New York and China are the backgrounds for this chronicle of the family of American missionary Tobias Condit. The saga continues with the conflicts of Tobias's daughter Elizabeth, who leaves a comfortable existence with her husband and son in America to follow a fascinating adventurer back to China.

Genre: Family Saga
Subjects: Missionaries
Place/Time: New York (N. Y.)—1900–1945; China—1900–1945

Ball, Margaret. *See* McCaffrey, Anne

Balmer, Edwin *and* Wylie, Philip

64.
1. *When Worlds Collide.* Stokes, 1933.
2. *After Worlds Collide.* Stokes, 1934.
The above titles have also been published in the following collection: *When Worlds Collide.* Lippincott, 1950.

When a group of scientists discovers that Earth is on a collision course with other planets, a spaceship is constructed to carry a small group of survivors to a new life on a distant planet.

Genre: Science Fiction
Subjects: Earth, destruction of; Interplanetary voyages

Balzac, Honore de

65. The Human Comedy

1. *The Chouans.* Nimmo, 1889.
2. *An Historical Mystery.* Roberts, 1891. (Alternate titles: *A Dark Affair* and *The Gondreville Mystery.*)
3. *Louis Lambert.* Roberts, 1889.
4. *The Philosopher's Stone.* J. Winchester, 1844. (Alternate titles: *The Quest of the Absolute* and *The Alkahest.*)
5. *The Celibates and Other Stories.* Gebbie, 1898.
6. *Daddy Goriot, or Unrequited Affection.* Ward & Lock, 1860. (Alternate titles: *Pere Goriot* and *Father Goriot.*)
7. *Eugenia Grandet.* J. Winchester, 1843.
8. *History of the Grandeur and Downfall of Cesar Birotteau.* Saunders, Otley, 1860. (Alternate title: *Cesar Birotteau.*)
9. *Lost Illusions.* Roberts, 1892.
10. *The Lily of the Valley.* Roberts, 1891.
11. *Splendors and Miseries of Courtesans.* G. Barrie, 1895.
12. *Gobseck and Other Stories.* Roberts, 1896.
13. *The Country Doctor.* Roberts, 1887.
14. *Luck and Leather: A Parisian Romance.* Brainard, 1843. (Alternate titles: *The Wild Ass's Skin* and *The Magic Skin.*)
15. *Ursula.* Roberts, 1891.
16. *Beatrix.* Roberts, 1895.
17. *The Village Rector.* Roberts, 1893.
18. *Cousin Bette.* Roberts, 1888.
19. *Cousin Pons.* Simpkin, Marshall, 1880.
20. *The Lesser Bourgeoisie.* Roberts, 1896. (Alternate titles: *The Petty Bourgeois* and *The Middle Classes.*)

Although Balzac dipped into other times and locations for the settings of some volumes of his enormous series The Human Comedy, his literary reputation rests primarily on his role as observer and chronicler of his own France of the first half of the 19th century. The personalities and social classes of his characters were more important to Balzac than plot. Consisting of 99 separate works, some not translated into English, The Human Comedy has a complex publishing history. Balzac wrote and published some of the works before the concept of the series was completely formed, then revised these titles to fit into the series. His concept of the series included eight general groups: Scenes of Private, Provincial, Parisian, Military, Political, and Country Life, and Philosophical and Analytical Studies, but these groups are not particularly helpful to the reader approaching the series.

The list above is based on the reading order and selection of seminal works from *Balzac As He Should Be Read: The Comedie Humaine Arranged in Logical Order of Reading According to Time of Action* (A. Giraldi, 1946) by Balzac scholar and bibliographer William Hobart Royce. Royce suggests that readers completely unfamiliar with Balzac should test their interest by reading *Daddy Goriot* (6). Royce's bibliography contains a complete catalog of The Human Comedy listed in both Balzac's categories and a reading order suggested by the chronology of events in the works.

Subjects: Social classes; Middle classes; Social problems; Country life; Family life; Politics—France
Place/Time: France—19th century

Banis, Victor

66.

1. *This Splendid Earth.* St. Martin's, 1978.
2. *The Earth and All It Holds.* St. Martin's, 1980.

The de Brussac family, who backs the losing side in postrevolutionary France in the 1840s, flees to California where they establish a successful vineyard. Years later their grandchildren must struggle to maintain their inheritance.

Genre: Family Saga; Historical Fiction
Subjects: Wine and wine making; Farm life
Place/Time: California—19th century

Banks, Iain

67.

1. *Consider Phlebas.* St. Martin's, 1988.
2. *Use of Weapons.* Bantam, 1992.

The Idirans believe they are in a holy war against the Communistic Culture and its Sentient Minds. Out of principle, the Culture opposes the fiercely religious Idirans. In the middle are mercenaries like Horza and the planets and people who are destroyed by these two empires intent on destroying each other.

Genre: Science Fiction
Subjects: Imaginary wars and battles; Mercenary soldiers

Banks, Lynne Reid. *See Reid Banks, Lynne*

Bantock, Nick

68.

1. *Griffin and Sabine: An Extraordinary Correspondence Written and Illustrated by Nick Bantock.* Chronicle, 1991.

2. *Sabine's Notebook: In Which the Extraordinary Correspondence of Griffin and Sabine Continues.* Chronicle, 1992.
3. *The Golden Mean: In Which the Extraordinary Correspondence of Griffin and Sabine Continues.* Chronicle, 1993.

A lonely British card designer, Griffin Moss, receives a letter from South Pacific islander Sabine Strohem. The two strike up a mystical correspondence as they delve into each other's souls through their hand-illustrated and written letters and postcards.

Subjects: Psychological novels; Friendship; Letters (stories in letter form)
Place/Time: London (England)—1980–; England—1980–

Banville, John

69.
1. *Book of Evidence.* Scribner, 1989.
2. *Ghosts.* Knopf, 1993.
3. *Athena.* Knopf, 1995.

Freddie Montgomery abandons his family in Spain and returns to Ireland to raise money. When he discovers that his mother has sold his late father's paintings to a dealer, Freddie tries to steal them back. In the process, he murders a maid and is sent to jail. Paroled 10 years later, he becomes a ghostwriter to a retired art historian who fraudulently authenticates paintings with Freddie's help. Using the name Morrow, Freddie is drawn into an art scam by a sinister underworld character.

Subjects: Authors; Art critics
Place/Time: Ireland—1980–

Barke, James

70. Immortal Memory
1. *The Wind That Shakes the Barley.* Macmillan, 1947.
2. *The Song in the Green Thorn Tree.* Macmillan 1948.
3. *The Wonder of All the Gay World.* Macmillan, 1950.
4. *The Crest of the Broken Wave.* Macmillan, 1953.
5. *The Well of the Silent Harp.* Macmillan, 1954.
6. *Bonnie Jean.* Collins, 1959. (This title has been published only in England.)

Mixing fictional characters with real people, Barke retells the life of Scottish poet Robert Burns. During the volatile late 1700s, Burns becomes the major poetic voice of his country. He falls in love with Jean Armour and uses his poems to celebrate love, patriotism, and rustic life.

Genre: Historical Fiction

Subjects: Burns, Robert, 1759–1796; Poets; Country life; Love
Place/Time: Scotland—19th century

Barker, Clive

71.
1. *The Great and Secret Show: The First Book of the Art.* Harper, 1989.
2. *Everville: The Second Book of the Art.* Harper, 1994.

Randolph Jaffe works in the Dead Letter Room in Omaha, Nebraska, and comes upon a network of mysterious revelations that provide him with great power. He leads the forces of darkness, and Richard Fletcher, a philanthropic scientist, leads the forces of light as they battle over the Quiddity. Later these two characters are drawn back in time to the dream realm of Quiddity where they fight malignant forces.

Genre: Horror
Subjects: Good and evil; Time travel
Place/Time: Omaha (Neb.)—1980–

Barker, Pat

72.
1. *Regeneration.* Dutton, 1992.
2. *The Eye in the Door.* Dutton, 1994.
3. *The Ghost Road.* Dutton, 1995.

In 1917, British officer and poet Siegfried Sassoon is sent to a hospital after he writes a piece condemning the war. Dr. William Rivers, the psychiatrist at the hospital, tries to treat him but finds Sassoon is very sane. Rivers begins to doubt his own role in curing his patients and then sending them back to be slaughtered. All of the men at the hospital lead double lives. Lieutenant Billy Prior is a working-class soldier who must betray the people who sheltered him. Charles Manning must hide his homosexuality, while Sassoon must reconcile his pacifist beliefs with his life as a soldier. The horrors of World War I are hauntingly portrayed in these poetic antiwar novels. The final novel in the trilogy won the Booker Prize.

Genre: Historical Fiction; War
Subjects: World War I, 1914–1918; Army, British; War
Place/Time: England—1900–1945

Barnes, Steven. *See* Niven, Larry

Barrie, J. M. (James Matthew)

73.
1. *Sentimental Tommy.* Scribner, 1896.
2. *Tommy and Grizel.* Scribner, 1898.

Tommy has an over-active imagination. As he grows up in Scotland, he cannot resist playing the hero whenever his mood calls for it. He uses his imagination to leave the slums and become a writer. However, he cannot succeed as a faithful lover or husband and finally accidentally dies by hanging.

Subjects: Marriage problems; Country life; Authors
Place/Time: Scotland—19th century

Barstow, Stan

74.
1. *A Kind of Loving.* Doubleday, 1961.
2. *Watchers on the Shore.* Doubleday, 1966.

Twenty-one-year-old Vic Brown's hasty marriage to his pregnant girlfriend Ingrid brings him nothing but heartache and boredom. Reaching out from the confines of this loveless union, Vic tries to find himself, in this stark and realistic look at a modern marriage in England.

Subjects: Marriage problems; Husbands and wives
Place/Time: England—1945–1980

Barthelme, Frederick

75.
1. *The Brothers.* Viking, 1993.
2. *Painted Desert.* Viking, 1995.

As he approaches his 44th birthday, Del Tribute faces a mid-life crisis. He is newly divorced, relocates to Biloxi, Mississippi, and is having an affair with his sister-in-law. When Del's brother Bud returns, Bud tries to repair his marriage. Del hooks up with a 27-year-old true-crime buff, Jenn, who decides the two of them need to see the world, visiting the sites of recent murders as they travel. Only after meeting numerous fanatics and a psychopath, do Jenn and Del begin to rethink their lives. These sardonic novels poke fun at the absurdities of modern sex, marriage, and relationships.

Subjects: Husbands and wives; Love affairs; Marriage problems
Place/Time: Mississippi—1980–

Bass, Milton R.

76.
1. *Jory.* Putnam, 1969.
2. *Mistr Jory.* Putnam, 1976.

In 1870, Jory is a 15-year-old gunman in the Old West. He kills a man who kicks his father, then flees to Texas. There the mild-mannered boy saves the life of a cattle baron and becomes the foreman of his spread. He fights cattle thieves, Indians, and gunmen.

Genre: Adventure; Historical Fiction; Western
Subjects: Frontier and pioneer life; Cattle drives; Cowboys
Place/Time: Texas—19th century

Bateman, Colin

77.
1. *Divorcing Jack.* Arcade, 1995.
2. *Of Wee Sweetie Mice and Men.* Arcade, 1997.

Dan Starkey is a Belfast columnist who can't keep out of trouble. When he has an affair, his lover is murdered, and Starkey becomes the principal suspect. He discovers that his lover's father is involved in Irish politics. As he hunts for a tape that reveals the man's past, he is pursued by the police and the IRA. Later Starkey goes to New York to cover the heavyweight fight between Mike Tyson and Irish hopeful Bobby McMaster. When McMaster's remarks about African Americans ignite protests, Starkey is again sucked into the turmoil and the violence.

Genre: Adventure
Subjects: Adventure; Violence; Love affairs
Place/Time: Ireland—1980–; New York (N. Y.)—1980–

Bates, H. E. (Herbert Ernest)

78. The Pop Larkin Chronicles
1. *The Darling Buds of May.* Little, Brown, 1958.
2. *A Breath of French Air.* Little, Brown, 1959.
3. *Hark, Hark, the Lark!* Little, Brown, 1960.
4. *Oh! To Be in England.* Farrar, Straus, 1963.
5. *A Little of What You Fancy.* Penguin, 1991, 1970.

Pop Larkin, the world's most affluent and amiable junk dealer, his wife, and six children are a happy-go-lucky lot on their farm in rural England. They work when they please and have unconventional adventures that are humorous and delightful.

Genre: Gentle Read; Humor
Subjects: Family life; Country life
Place/Time: England—1945–1980

Bayer, Valerie Townsend

79. Marlborough Gardens Quartet
1. *City of Childhood.* St. Martin's, 1992.
2. *The Metaphysics of Sex.* St. Martin's, 1992.
3. *Forbidden Objects.* St. Martin's, 1995.

In the 1920s, two women, American Harriet Van Buren and Londoner Rachel Lowe, reconstruct the life and house of Emma Forster, a forgotten Victorian novelist, through her letters, memoirs, excerpts from a novel, and family papers. She played, brawled, and grew up with 12 cousins at Marlborough Gardens in the 1830s. As a gawky girl, Emma fell in love with her Italian cousin Johan Lustig. As Emma and her cousins grow up, they must face the consequences of their own weaknesses and vices, and the turbulent revolutions in Europe in the 1840s and 1850s. The issues of women's subservience, anti-Semitism in Germany, and Victorian attitudes toward homosexuals are seen in Emma's letters.

Subjects: Authors; Children; Love; Cousins
Place/Time: England—19th century

Beach, Edward L.

80.
1.   *Run Silent, Run Deep.* Holt, 1955.
2.   *Dust on the Sea.* Holt, 1972.
3.   *Cold Is the Sea.* Holt, 1978.

Beach, a retired submarine commander who fought in World War II, has fashioned a realistic series based on his adventures. His commander, Rich Richardson, leads his men through the dangerous waters of the Pacific as they destroy Japanese ships and attack wolf packs in the China seas. During the Cold War, Richardson commands a nuclear submarine that must try to avoid a nearby Russian sub. These novels convey what it is like to work on a submarine during wartime.

Genre: Naval Adventure; War
Subjects: War; Cold war; World War II, 1939–1945—naval operations; Submarines; Navy, United States—officers
Place/Time: Pacific Ocean—1900–1945; Pacific Ocean—1945–1980

Beagle, Peter S.

81.
1.   *The Last Unicorn.* Viking, 1968.
2.   *The Unicorn Sonata.* Turner, 1996.

In her quest for her own kind, the unicorn, finding herself alone in the world, enlists the aid of the intrinsically good humans against the wicked, who may have made the unicorns disappear. Written over twenty years later, the sequel follows a young girl from her home in modern day Los Angeles to the magic realm of Shei'rah, the home of the unicorns, where she and her grandmother help to cure the mystical creatures of blindness.

Genre: Fantasy
Subjects: Unicorns; Mythical animals; Imaginary kingdoms; Good and evil

Bear, Greg. *See also* Asimov, Isaac (*Foundation and Chaos*)

82.
1.   *Legacy.* Tor, 1995.
2.   *Eon.* Bluejay Books, 1985.
3.   *Eternity.* Warner, 1988.

Thistledown, an asteroid turned starship, mysteriously appears from another reality and becomes the entrance to the Way, a corridor that gives humans the ability to travel through both time and space. An invasion by the alien Jarts forces Thistledown to separate from the Way leaving the tunnel a contained universe in space.

Genre: Science Fiction
Subjects: Time travel; Spaceships, Extraterrestrial beings

83.
1.   *Queen of Angels.* Warner, 1990.
2.   *Slant.* Tor, 1997.

In this near future world compulsory psychotherapy and artificial mood enhancers are a way of life. At the same time unemployment and addiction to near pornographic virtual reality afflict a large part of the population. In this environment, Los Angeles Police Inspector Mary Choy investigates a brutal mass murder committed by a celebrated poet. In the sequel a Seattle police officer tries to determine who or what is producing a state of national madness by tampering with artificial mood enhancers. Meanwhile two sentient computers battle for control of the country.

Genre: Science Fiction; Crime Novel
Subjects: Computers; Technology and civilization; Police; Crime and criminals
Place/Time: Los Angeles (Calif.)—1980–; Seattle (Wash.)—1980–

84.
1.   *The Forge of God.* St. Martin's, 1987.
2.   *Anvil of Stars.* Warner, 1992.

Arthur Gordon, former science advisor to the president, and Edward Shaw, professor of geology, are drawn into a strange alien invasion when a moon of Jupiter disappears and a volcanic mountain suddenly appears in Australia. When the aliens invade the Earth then destroy it, a band of survivors go to Mars, but they seek vengeance against the destroyers with the aid of another pan-galactic alien culture.

Genre: Science Fiction
Subjects: Extraterrestrial beings; Space colonies; Earth, destruction of

Beckett, Samuel

85.
1.   *Molloy.* Grove, 1955.
2.   *Malone Dies.* Grove, 1956.
3.   *The Unnamable.* Grove, 1958.
The above titles have also published in the following collection: *Molloy, Malone Dies, and the Unnamable: Three Novels.* Grove, 1959.

Through the narratives of three characters, Moran, the serious, conventional detective who seeks the incorrigible delinquent Molloy, the dying storyteller Malone, and a strange creature who speaks incoherently of the three, Beckett probes the uses of language and the tension between a self-centered existence and a life of involvement and commitment.

Subjects: Juvenile delinquency; Detectives; Selfishness; Philosophical novels

Beckford, William

86. Vathek
1. *Vathek: An Arabian Tale.* Lawrence & Bullen, 1893.
2. *The Episodes of Vathek.* Swift, 1912.

Originally written in French by an English author, the tale of Vathek, an Arabian caliph whose fascination with evil and the life of the senses leads him and his beloved to their destruction, has an ambiguous tone, at times moralistic, at others satirical or sensual. *The Episodes of Vathek* relates the tales of other sinners whom Vathek encounters in a sort of purgatory before he meets his fiery fate.

Genre: Fantasy
Subjects: Arabs; Good and evil; Hedonism

Becnel, Rexanne

87.
1. *The Bride of Rosecliffe.* St. Martin's, 1998.
2. *The Knight of Rosecliffe.* St. Martin's, 1999.
3. *The Mistress of Rosecliffe.* St. Martin's, 2000.

In 12th-century Wales, Rand FitzHugh is sent by the English King Henry to subdue the rebellious Welsh people. Josselyn of Carrey Du is the daughter of a Welsh lord, who is prepared to marry a man she hates if it will unite the Welsh against the English. When Rand captures Josselyn, neither imagines that love will bridge their distrust. Rand's younger brother Jasper FitzHugh is given Rhonwen, a Welsh loyalist, as a captive after she tries to kill him. Rhonwen, like Josselyn, learns the power of love that overcomes their hatred. A rogue Welsh knight goes to Rosecliffe Castle to reclaim his birthright, but he falls in love with his enemies' daughter.

Genre: Historical Romance
Subjects: Knights and knighthood; Lovers
Place/Time: Wales—12th century

Bedford, Sybille

88.
1. *A Favourite of the Gods.* Simon & Schuster, 1963.
2. *Compass Error.* Knopf, 1969.

Three wealthy aristocratic women—Anna, an American, her Italian-reared daughter Constanza, and her English-reared granddaughter Flavia—are at home in all the worldly cultural centers of Europe of the 1920s and 1930s, but are in conflict with each other.

Subjects: Mothers and daughters; Wealth; Aristocracy; Society novels
Place/Time: Europe—1900–1945

Beebe, Elswyth Thane. *See Thane, Elswyth*

Bellamann, Henry

89.
1. *Kings Row.* Simon & Schuster, 1940.
2. *Parris Mitchell of Kings Row.* Simon & Schuster, 1948.

Parris Mitchell goes to medical school before World War I, then sets up practice in the middle western town of Kings Row. When he becomes successful, his old friend Fulmer Green tries to stop his influence. While he is fighting Green, he must also battle his own feelings for another woman while remaining devoted to his fragile wife Elise.

Genre: Historical Fiction
Subjects: Medicine; Physicians; Small town life
Place/Time: Midwestern states—1900–1945

Bellamy, Edward

90.
1. *Looking Backward.* Ticknor, 1888.
2. *Equality.* Appleton, 1897.

Julian West awakens in 2000 A. D., unaged after 113 years of hypnotic sleep. He finds that he is in a utopian society where all work and share alike. He falls in love with his fiancee's great-granddaughter, who guides him through this new commonwealth. Bellamy comments on the greed and ruthlessness of society through his ideal utopia.

Subjects: Time travel; Love; Utopias

Belle, Pamela

91.
1. *Wintercombe.* St. Martin's, 1988.
2. *Herald of Joy.* St. Martin's, 1990.
3. *A Falling Star.* St. Martin's, 1990.
4. *Treason's Gift.* St. Martin's, 1993.

The romantic saga of three generations of the St. Barbe family sweeps from the start of the English Civil War in 1641 through the ascension of William of Orange. Silence, the first Lady St. Barbe, is left in charge of her husband's estate Wintercombe while he is fighting for the Puritans. When the estate is taken over by Royalists, Silence falls in love with Captain Nick Hellier. That love haunts her and her family as each generation must take sides in this religious battle, fight to maintain the estate, and reconcile the star-crossed lovers.

Genre: Family Saga; Historical Romance
Subjects: War
Place/Time: England—17th century

Bender, Carrie

92. Miriam's Journal
1. *A Fruitful Vine.* Herald Press, 1993.
2. *A Winding Path.* Herald Press, 1994.
3. *A Joyous Heart.* Herald Press, 1994.
4. *A Treasured Friendship.* Herald Press, 1996.
5. *A Golden Sunbeam.* Herald Press, 1996.

After caring for her aged parents until their death, Miriam finds that at 40 she is a single woman in an Amish community. Miriam would like to have a husband and children. Ultimately she marries Nate, an Amish farmer, who has four children. While their marriage is strong, Miriam has to deal with illness, strained friendships, and death. She finds that her faith in God is tested but becomes stronger. Told in diary format, these books reveal many fascinating details of Amish life.

Genre: Christian Fiction
Subjects: Christian life; Faith; Amish; Diaries (stories in diary form); Farm life
Place/Time: Pennsylvania—1980–

93. Whispering Brook Series
1. *Whispering Brook Farm.* Herald Press, 1995.
2. *Summerville Days.* Herald Press, 1996.
3. *Chestnut Ridge Acres.* Herald Press, 1997.

In the Pennsylvania Amish community, Nancy Petersheim and her family live on Whispering Brook Farm. Nancy and her brothers and sisters spend their days playing, working, and helping neighbors. Pigeon catching, buggy racing, farm chores, and nature walks round out their days in this peaceful community.

Genre: Christian Fiction
Subjects: Christian life; Faith; Amish; Farm life; Family life
Place/Time: Pennsylvania—1980–

Benford, Gregory. *See also* Clarke, Arthur C. (*Beyond the Fall of Night*) and Asimov, Isaac (*Foundation's Fear*)

94. Great Sky River
1. *Great Sky River.* Bantam, 1987.
2. *Tides of Light.* Bantam, 1989.
3. *Furious Gulf.* Bantam, 1994.

In the distant future, the domination of machines and artificial intelligence has reduced humanity to a low level of existence. A small group of refugees flees across the galaxy, encountering devastated planets and the cosmic designs of powerful cyborgs.

Genre: Science Fiction
Subjects: Bionics; Technology and civilization; Interplanetary voyages

95. In the Ocean of Night
1. *Deeper Than the Darkness.* Ace, 1970. (This title was revised as *The Stars in Shroud.* Berkley, 1978.)
2. *In the Ocean of Night.* Dial Press, 1977.
3. *Across the Sea of Suns.* Simon & Schuster, 1984.
4. *Sailing Bright Eternity.* Bantam, 1995.

While investigating a spacecraft imbedded in an asteroid, astronaut Nigel Walmsley discovers that aliens have visited Earth and tampered with the human mind. Although the incident nearly ends his career and essentially isolates him, Walmsley survives and 50 years later is part of a space mission to the star Ra, the source of a mysterious English language radio broadcast. Finally the astronaut joins with members of the Bishop family who are inexorably drawn toward the culmination of a conflict between mechanical and organic life forms.

Genre: Science Fiction
Subjects: Extraterrestrial beings; Interplanetary voyages

Bennett, Arnold

96.
1. *Clayhanger.* Dutton, 1910.
2. *Hilda Lessways.* Dutton, 1911.
3. *These Twain.* Doran, 1916.

Edwin Clayhanger wants to be an architect, but his father Darius objects. Throughout his life, Edwin constantly fights with his father and struggles to find his way. The same story is then retold through the eyes of his wife Hilda. Finally the strains of their marriage are examined through both their eyes.

Subjects: Marriage problems; Husbands and wives; Fathers and sons
Place/Time: England—1900–1945

Benson, Ann

97.
1. *The Plague Tales.* Delacorte, 1997.
2. *The Burning Road.* Delacorte, 1999.

Two societies, seven centuries apart, face the onslaught of devastating plagues, and two physicians try to deal with the outbreaks. In 14th-century England, Jewish physician Alejandro Canches tries to keep the royal court alive as the bubonic plague sweeps across Europe. Alejandro faces prejudice and mistrust until he finally flies to France and aids the peasants as they revolt. In 2007 England, Janie Crowe tries to deal with a world where antibiotics are no longer effective against disease, and the "outbreak" is killing the world. How each of these physicians and their societies face the medical horrors is told alternately, but the two become intertwined when Janie unleashes the microbes from the 14th-century plague on an unprepared London.

Genre: Historical Fiction; Science Fiction
Subjects: Medicine; Physicians; Jews; Middle ages; Viruses
Place/Time: England—14th century; England—1980–

Benson, E. F. (Edward Frederic)

98.
1. *Queen Lucia.* Doran, 1920.
2. *Lucia in London.* Doubleday Doran, 1928.
3. *Miss Mapp.* Doran, 1923.
4. *The Male Impersonator.* Doran, 1929.

The above titles have also been published in the following collection: *All About Lucia.* Doubleday, 1936.

5. *Mapp and Lucia.* Doubleday Doran, 1931.
6. *The Worshipful Lucia.* Doubleday Doran, 1935.
7. *Trouble for Lucia.* Doubleday Doran, 1939.

All of the above titles have also been published in the following collection: *Make Way for Lucia.* Crowell, 1977.

In prewar, small town England, the snobbish Lucia rules the town and is in and out of interesting situations. With her wonderful "enemy" Miss Mapp, she has adventures that satirize British upper-class life.

Genre: Humor
Subjects: Small town life; Social classes; Satire
Place/Time: England—1900–1945

Benzoni, Juliette

99.
1. *Lure of the Falcon.* Putnam, 1978.
2. *The Devil's Necklace.* Putnam, 1980.

Young Gilles Goelo leaves his native Breton to fight with Lafayette in the American Revolution. He returns with a title and an estate, and he fights to rescue his true love, Judith, from the hands of her evil relatives.

Genre: Historical Romance
Subjects: United States—revolution, 1775–1783
Place/Time: France—18th century; United States—18th century

100. Marianne Series
1. *Marianne.* Putnam, 1970.
2. *Marianne and the Masked Prince.* Putnam, 1971.
3. *Marianne and the Privateer.* Putnam, 1972.
4. *Marianne and the Rebels.* Putnam, 1974.
5. *Marianne and the Lords of the East.* Putnam, 1975.
6. *Marianne and the Crown of Fire.* Putnam, 1976.

Abandoned on her wedding night by her gambler husband, the beautiful Marianne flees to Paris where she becomes Napoleon's lover and a secret agent for him. Her adventures take her across Europe, to America, to the Ottoman Empire, and finally to Russia during Napoleon's invasion. She tries to save her emperor, her husband, and herself.

Genre: Historical Romance
Subjects: Spies; Adventure; Napoleon I, Emperor of the French, 1769–1821
Place/Time: Paris (France)—19th century; Europe—19th century; United States—19th century; France—19th century

Berent, Mark

101.
1. *Rolling Thunder.* Putnam, 1989.
2. *Steel Tiger.* Putnam, 1990.
3. *Phantom Leader.* Putnam, 1991.
4. *Eagle Station.* Putnam, 1992.
5. *Storm Flight.* Putnam, 1993.

Air Force pilots and commandos fight the North Vietnamese in this war series by an Air Force pilot. From Da Nang in 1965 to the Tet Offensive in 1968, Berent follows his men into battles in Laos, along the Ho Chi Min Trail, and even into Hanoi's infamous prison. Realistic action and flight scenes highlight this series, whose volumes follow the action of the Vietnam War year by year.

Genre: War
Subjects: Vietnamese War, 1961–1975; Air pilots; Soldiers—American; War
Place/Time: Vietnam—1945–1980

Berger, John

102. Into Their Labours
1. *Pig Earth.* Pantheon, 1979.
2. *Once in Europa.* Pantheon, 1987.
3. *Lilac and Flag.* Pantheon, 1990.

In a series of interconnected short stories, Berger shows the effect of modernization on the peasants of Alpine France. The various village peasants go about their daily lives as they try to deal with love, loss, solitude, and survival. As the forces of contemporary society change the rural landscape, the young people move to the city and try to find a place for themselves, but have little success.

Subjects: Country life; Peasants; Urbanization
Place/Time: France—1945–1980

Berger, Thomas

103.
1. *Little Big Man.* Delacorte Press, 1963.
2. *The Return of Little Big Man.* Little, Brown, 1999.

At the age of 112, Jack Crabb, a white man adopted by the Cheyenne, relates his version of Western history. He grew up with the Cheyenne, became a gunfighter, worked as a buffalo hunter, and was the only white survivor of Custer's Last Stand. All of the famous men of the West crossed his path—Wild Bill Hickock at the Deadwood Saloon, Wyatt Earp at the O.K. Corral, Sitting Bull at the reservation, and Buffalo Bill at his Wild West Show. Is Jack a naive innocent or the greatest of liars? No matter which, his riotous adventures reveal a very different Wild West.

Genre: Historical Fiction
Subjects: Satire; Western states; Native Americans; Cheyenne; Custer, George Armstrong, 1839–1876.
Place/Time: Western states—19th century

104.
1. *Crazy in Berlin.* Scribner, 1958.
2. *Reinhart in Love.* Scribner, 1962.
3. *Vital Parts.* R. W. Baron, 1970.
4. *Reinhart's Women.* Delacorte Press, 1981.

Carl Reinhart is an American GI stationed in Berlin at the end of World War II. As a German American, he feels guilty about the treatment of Jews in Nazi Germany. When he returns to Ohio, he eventually marries and has a family. However, nothing in his life goes the way it should, and the comic situations he gets himself involved with are both hilarious and eccentric.

Genre: Humor
Subjects: Soldiers—American; World War II, 1939–1945; Guilt; Holocaust, Jewish, 1933–1945; War
Place/Time: Berlin (Germany)—1900–1945; Ohio—1945–1980; Germany—1900–1945

Bergman, Ingmar

105.
1. *Best Intentions.* Arcade, 1993.
2. *Sunday's Children.* Arcade, 1994.

The famed film director tells the fictional story of the early years of his parents' marriage in Sweden. In 1909, Henrik Bergman, an impoverished divinity student, refuses to visit his dying grandmother because she has disowned his father. Henrik courts and marries Anna, but finds he has married a woman who stands up to him. Henrik's children fight their tyrannical father as aunts, uncles, servants, and friends drift in and out of the family's life.

Genre: Historical Fiction
Subjects: Autobiographical stories; Family life; Marriage problems
Place/Time: Sweden—1900–1945

Besher, Alexander

106.
1. *Rim: A Novel of Virtual Reality.* HarperCollins, 1994.
2. *Mir: A Novel of Virtual Reality.* Simon & Schuster, 1996.
3. *Chi: A Novel of Virtual Reality.* Simon & Schuster, 1999.

In the 21st century, humanity has learned to communicate with plants and animals, but is threatened by an insidious computer virus called Mir and by the possibility of being trapped in the virtual reality of cyberspace. Professor Frank Gobi is horrified to discover that his son Trevor has been trapped by a computer game manufactured by the large corporation that has just hired him. Years later Trevor becomes a hunter of the Mir virus, which has infected his girlfriend and is capable of destroying the entire World Wide Net of cyberspace.

Genre: Science Fiction
Subjects: Computers; Technology and civilization; Fathers and sons

Bienek, Horst

107. Gleiwitz Suite Series
1. *The First Polka.* Fjord Press, 1984.
2. *September Light.* Atheneum, 1987.
3. *Time Without Bells.* Atheneum, 1988.
4. *Earth and Fire.* Atheneum, 1988.

Noted German author Bienek chronicles life in the town of Gleiwitz, Upper Silesia, from the opening days of World War II in 1939 to the start of the Russian invasion in 1945. The inhabitants of this town on the border between Germany and Poland are used to being invaded by outsiders, and they try to ignore the turbulent events engulfing their town. Bienek focuses on the Piontek family as they grow up, marry, and die among raging conflicts.

Genre: Historical Fiction
Subjects: World War II, 1939–1945; Cities and towns; Family life
Place/Time: Germany—1900–1945

Biggins, John

108.
1. *A Sailor of Austria.* St. Martin's, 1994.
2. *The Emperor's Coloured Coat.* St. Martin's, 1995.

At 101, Ottokar Prohaska, the narrator, describes his adventures as a young man in the Royal Austro-Hungarian Navy from 1909 to 1918. He travels across Europe and Asia where he meets the Kaiser, lords, lovely ladies, and pirates. When World War I starts, he becomes a U-boat captain and travels to the shores of Italy, Germany, and Africa. He also recounts day to day life on the submarine and the battles that he and his men fight.

Genre: Naval Adventure
Subjects: Naval battles; Navy, Austro-Hungarian Empire; War; World War I, 1914–1918
Place/Time: Europe—1900–1945; Mediterranean region—1900–1945

Biggle, Lloyd, Jr.

109. Cultural Survey
1. *The Still, Small Voice of Trumpets.* Doubleday, 1968.
2. *The World Menders.* Doubleday, 1971.

In a galaxy inhabited by a variety of sentient life forms, the Interplanetary Relations Bureau works to liberate planets from authoritarian governments by promoting revolution from within. Adversaries include a tyrannical monarch and a god emperor with a powerful ruling class that has created a society ripe for a slave revolt.

Genre: Science Fiction
Subjects: Totalitarianism; Revolutions and revolutionists

110. Jan Darzek
1. *All the Colors of Darkness.* Doubleday, 1963.
2. *Watchers of the Dark.* Doubleday, 1966.
3. *This Darkening Universe.* Doubleday, 1975.
4. *Silence Is Deadly.* Doubleday, 1977.
5. *The Whirligig of Time.* Doubleday, 1979.

Though Earth is considered an uncivilized planet because its inhabitants lie, earthling Jan Darzek is put at the pinnacle of a galactic system that is kept in order by an enormous, wise computer called Supreme. With his venerable assistant Miss Schlupe, Darzek travels throughout the galaxy trying to outwit the evil Udef.

Genre: Science Fiction
Subjects: Computers; Truthfulness and falsehood; Espionage; Interplanetary voyages

Bigsby, Christopher

111.
1. *Hester.* Viking, 1994.
2. *Pearl.* Weidenfeld & Nicolson, 1996.

This retelling of Nathaniel Hawthorne's *The Scarlet Letter* is centered on the original characters and plot, but goes back in time before Hester's doomed love affair and follows the fate of her daughter Pearl. As a young woman, Hester marries the town eccentric, Roger Chillingsworth, and then flees from him when his behavior becomes macabre. On the boat to America, she meets Arthur Dimmesdale and falls in love with him. The second work tells of Pearl's journey to England to seek her origins. Like her mother, she falls in love with a preacher and discovers the difficulty of controlling her own destiny.

Genre: Historical Fiction
Subjects: Love affairs; Women; Mothers and daughters
Place/Time: New England—17th century; England—17th century

Binchy, Dan

112.
1. *The Neon Madonna.* St. Martin's, 1992.

2. *The Last Resort.* St. Martin's, 1993.

Father Jerry O'Sullivan leaves his Vatican post to be a parish priest in Brulagh, Ireland, but this little rural town is not the quiet haven it seems. The crafty Father Jerry is soon involved in the hilarious misadventures of the locals who get mixed up with politicians, IRA goons, moonshiners, and Yankee developers.

Genre: Humor
Subjects: Catholic faith; Catholic priests; Country life
Place/Time: Ireland—1980–

Bischoff, David F.

113.
1. *Star Fall.* Berkley, 1980.
2. *Star Spring.* Berkley, 1982.

Todd Spigot survives a body switch with a former assassin. He becomes the target of the victims' vengeful relatives, then is seen by a cyborg millionaire as a threat to his evil cosmic agenda.

Genre: Science Fiction
Subjects: Revenge; Bionics

Bischoff, David F. *and* Monteleone, Thomas F.

114. Dragonstar
1. *Day of the Dragonstar.* Berkley, 1983.
2. *Night of the Dragonstar.* Berkley, 1985.
3. *Dragonstar Destiny.* Berkley, 1989.

The human population of the Heinlein exploratory space mission is attacked by prehistoric animals that are part of the enormous spacecraft terrarium. Further human contact with the dinosaurs proves that the animals are intelligent and potentially subject to exploitation.

Genre: Science Fiction
Subjects: Outer space, exploration of; Prehistoric animals

Bishop, Michael

115. Urban Nucleus
1. *A Little Knowledge.* Berkley, 1977.
2. *Catacomb Years.* Berkley, 1979.
3. *Under Heaven's Bridge.* (Written with Ian Watson) Ace, 1982.

In the 21st century, the government of the United States has collapsed and been replaced by the Urban Federation of City States. Like other urban areas, the city of Atlanta is now under a dome with a society dominated by the influence of Ortho-Urban Christianity. Into this already unstable environment come aliens from 61 Cygni, who may be reincarnated humans and who rearrange the power structure as a result of their religious conversion.

Genre: Science Fiction
Subjects: Imaginary cities; Cults; Extraterrestrial beings

Bisson, Terry. *See* Miller, Walter M.

Bjarnhof, Karl

116.
1. *The Stars Grow Pale.* Knopf, 1958.
2. *The Good Light.* Knopf, 1959.

This is the haunting story of a Danish boy in the early 1900s coming to terms with his progressive blindness. He must acknowledge that he can no longer see, but will not stop loving life. At 14, he enters the Institute for the Blind in Copenhagen only able to see light. While there he discovers love, literature, art, and music, and he must finally admit he is blind.

Genre: Coming of Age
Subjects: Teenagers; Blindness
Place/Time: Denmark—1900–1945

Bjorkman, Edwin August

117.
1. *The Soul of a Child.* Knopf, 1922.
2. *Gates of Life.* Knopf, 1923.

Living in Sweden in the late 19th century with his parents and grandmother, Keith Wellander experiences life as a series of passages through walls of restraint and finally emigrates to America in his early twenties. These autobiographical works are exceptionally frank and honest reflections of the thoughts and feelings of a young boy.

Genre: Coming of Age
Subjects: Teenagers; Autobiographical stories
Place/Time: Sweden—1900–1945; United States—1900–1945

Bjorn, Thyra Ferre

118.
1. *Papa's Wife.* Rinehart, 1955.
2. *Papa's Daughter.* Rinehart, 1958.
3. *Mama's Way.* Rinehart, 1959.
4. *Dear Papa.* Holt, Rinehart & Winston, 1963.

In the early 1900s, Swedish housemaid Maria marries her pastor, and they move to New England. There they raise eight children in these heartwarming and humorous stories about family life.

Genre: Gentle Read; Historical Fiction; Humor
Subjects: Family life; Clergy
Place/Time: New England—1900–1945

Blackwell, Lawana

119. Gresham Chronicles
1. *The Widow of Larkspur Inn.* Bethany House, 1998.
2. *The Courtship of the Vicar's Daughter.* Bethany House, 1998.
3. *The Dowry of Miss Lydia Clark.* Bethany House, 1999.

When Julia Hollis is widowed, she takes her children to the only place they have left, Larkspur Inn in the late 1860s English village of Gresham. There she becomes the proprietor of a lodging house and falls in love with the curate, Andrew Phelps, a widower with two daughters. As they prepare for their marriage, Andrew's daughter Elizabeth becomes engaged to a young curate, but when an old flame comes to the village, Elizabeth begins to doubt her love. After Julia and Andrew are married, their three children go to Octavia Bartley School of Advanced Learning where Lydia Clark teaches them. When it is rumored that Lydia has a large dowry, Harold Sanders comes to court the plain schoolteacher. However, Lydia finds true love when she agrees to help a bashful archeologist. In the little village of Gresham, romance seems to affect both young and old.

Genre: Christian Fiction
Subjects: Love; Small town life; Faith; Family life
Place/Time: England—19th century

120. Victorian Serenade
1. *Like a River Glorious.* Tyndale House, 1995.
2. *Measures of Grace.* Tyndale House, 1996.
3. *Jewels for a Crown.* Tyndale House, 1996.
4. *Song of a Soul.* Tyndale House, 1997.

In Victorian England, Corrine Hammond makes her living by conning wealthy men out of their money. Her maid, Rachel, feels trapped in this life, and as a faithful Christian she needs a miracle to escape. The miracle happens when Corrine accepts Christ and gives up her evil ways. Corrine goes home to the family she abandoned, but is followed by a man she conned who wants to ruin her. Only Corrine's faith saves her. She passes on her faith to her daughter Jenny who is training with Florence Nightingale. When Jenny is assigned to a London hospital instead of one in Canada, Jenny must bend to God's will. Another daughter Deborah is given the opportunity to study opera with a famous singer, but Deborah is not prepared for the perils of life on the stage.

Genre: Christian Fiction
Subjects: Faith; Women; Crime and criminals; Nurses and nursing; Singers
Place/Time: England—19th century

Blair, Clifford

121.
1. *The Guns of Sacred Heart.* Walker, 1991.
2. *Storm over the Lightning.* Walker, 1993.

In the middle of a raging snowstorm, cowboy Tom Langston takes refuge in a mountain cabin with wounded Marshall Breck Stever and his prisoner Ned Tayback. Later schoolteacher Sharon Easton stumbles in. The four seek safety in a mission where Tayback's outlaws attack them. Tom and Sharon encounter more fights as they try to protect their small spread in the Oklahoma territory from greedy Eastern bad guys.

Genre: Western
Subjects: Cowboys; Outlaws
Place/Time: Oklahoma—19th century

Blakely, Mike

122.
1. *Shortgrass Song.* Forge, 1994.
2. *Too Long at the Dance.* Forge, 1996.

Shortly before the Civil War, the Holcomb family moves to Colorado's open range to set up a cattle farm. Mother Ella dies a few years later, and it is Buster, a freed black man, who helps hold the family together when father Ab joins the Union Army. After the War, Ab and his three sons, Matthew, Peter, and Caleb, build a huge ranch until homesteaders cut up the open range. After Matthew and Pete die, Caleb is attracted to Pete's widow Amelia, but he tries to resist the attraction. Caleb finds himself settling feuds, fighting in the Johnson County War, and battling a Native American uprising. Caleb uses his music and his humor to help him through his adventures.

Genre: Western
Subjects: Ranch life; Cowboys; Fathers and sons
Place/Time: Colorado—19th century

Blasco Ibanez, Vicente

123. Valencia Series
1. *The Three Roses.* Dutton, 1932. (Alternate title: *Rice and a Carriage.*)
2. *The Mayflower.* Dutton, 1921.
3. *The Cabin.* Knopf, 1924.
4. *The Torrent.* Dutton, 1921. (Alternate title: *Among the Oranges.*)
5. *Sonnica the Courtesan.* Duffield, 1912.
6. *Reeds and Mud.* Dutton, 1928.

The Valencia region of Spain, the author's birthplace, is the connecting thread in these stories. The leading characters range from a wealthy family in a state of decline to farmers and fishermen. Hannibal's attack on the Valencian castle of Sagunto in 219 B.C. is the basis for *Sonnica the Courtesan*, the only novel of this series not set in the 19th century.

Genre: Historical Fiction
Subjects: Spain—country life
Place/Time: Spain—3rd century B. C.; Spain—19th century

Bledsoe, Jerry

124.
1. *The Angel Doll: A Christmas Story.* Down Home Press, 1996.
2. *A Gift of Angels.* Down Home Press, 1999.

In the 1950s, the 10-year-old narrator and his best friend Whitey Black share a paper route in Thomasville, North Carolina. Whitey's little sister Sandy has survived polio, but she has a wasted leg and poor health. What Sandy loves is having Whitey read her favorite book, *The Littlest Angel,* to her. When Sandy asks for an angel doll for Christmas, Whitey and the narrator work to find a doll for her. Years later, the narrator looks for his old friend and finds Whitey's daughter Sandy, named after Whitey's sister. Sandy tells of Whitey's death in Vietnam trying to save a little Vietnamese girl from sniper fire. The narrator honors his friend by giving Whitey's granddaughter a very special Christmas gift.

Genre: Gentle Read
Subjects: Friendship; Boys; Christmas
Place/Time: North Carolina—1945–1980

Blish, James

125. Cities in Flight
1. *They Shall Have Stars.* Faber, 1956. (This title was revised as *Year 2018!* Avon, 1957.)
2. *A Life for the Stars.* Putnam, 1962.
3. *Earthman, Come Home.* Putnam, 1955.
4. *The Triumph of Time.* Avon, 1957.
The above titles have also been published in the following collection: *Cities in Flight.* Revised edition: Avon, 1970.

In the early 21st century, the United States is in danger of becoming a dictatorship, but in scientific circles a longevity drug and antigravity devices are being developed that centuries later produce a galaxy of wandering cities. These "Okies" spin off into space following decisions made by City Fathers, who are actually computers. The immortal Mayor Amalfi of the New York Okie emerges as a hero who flees an alien-earth conflict into the Magellanic Clouds only to perish in an apocalyptic end of time and birth of a new universe.

Genre: Science Fiction
Subjects: Imaginary cities; Longevity; Totalitarianism; End of the world

Bly, Stephen

126. Old California Series
1. *Red Dove of Monterey.* Crossway Books, 1998.
2. *The Last Swan in Sacramento.* Crossway Books, 1999.
3. *Proud Quail of the San Joaquin.* Crossway Books, 2000.

In California during the 1850s, Alena loses her father and is adopted by a leading Monterey family. Alena, however, becomes dissatisfied with her life until she meets Wilson Merced and marries him. Their daughter Martina must fight to save her family and their business when her husband goes to find gold. In Monterey when the local schoolteacher Christina Swan is fired, she goes to manage a ranch and runs into trouble with neighbor Kern Yager. They discover love through their faith.

Genre: Christian Fiction
Subjects: Faith; Love; Ranch life
Place/Time: California—19th century

Bodett, Tom

127.
1. *The End of the Road.* Morrow, 1989.
2. *The Big Garage on Clearshot: Growing Up, Growing Old, and Going Fishing at the End of the Road.* Morrow, 1990.

These interconnected sketches about the residents of End of the Road, Alaska, are similar in tone to Garrison Keillor's pieces about Lake Wobegon. In this mythical Alaska, Angus Wilson, Emmitt Frank, Tamara Dupree, and other residents live out their homespun and humorous lives.

Genre: Humor
Subjects: Small town life; Eccentrics and eccentricities

Boggs, Johnny D.

128.
1. *Hannah and the Horseman.* Thomas Bouregy, 1997.
2. *The Courtship of Hannah and the Horseman.* Thomas Bouregy, 1997.
3. *Riding with Hannah and the Horseman.* Thomas Bouregy, 1998.
4. *Hannah and the Horseman at the Gallows Tree.* Thomas Bouregy, 1998.
5. *Hannah and the Horseman on the Western Trail.* Thomas Bouregy, 1999.

Comely Hannah Scott was raised in an orphanage and now runs a ranch where she takes in orphans from West Texas in the 1880s. She's also in love with Pete Belissari, a Greek cowboy who catches wild mustangs for a living. As Hannah prepares for her wedding to Pete, she is kidnapped during a bank robbery and taken to the outlaw's hideout. Pete and Sheriff Buddy Pecos lead an assault on the hideout to save Hannah. Later Hannah, Pete, and Pecos set up a stagecoach line but have to fight gamblers and trail thugs to keep their stagecoach. The two then travel to Shafter, Texas, to find two orphans, but Pete is ambushed and Hannah charged with murder. It takes all of Hannah's wits to save herself and Pete, and afterward, they are forced to join a cattle drive to save their drought stricken ranch.

Again they must fight the elements and scoundrels to save their love and their ranch.

Genre: Western; Historical Romance
Subjects: Lovers; Cowboys; Ranch life; Women
Place/Time: Texas—19th century

Boissard, Janine

129.
1. *A Matter of Feeling.* Little, Brown, 1979.
2. *Christmas Lessons.* Little, Brown, 1984.
3. *A Time to Choose.* Little, Brown, 1985.
4. *Cecile.* Little, Brown, 1988.

Dr. and Mrs. Moreau and their four daughters are a warm and loving French family who live outside Paris. The children range in age from 12 to 21. Pauline, the third daughter, tells her story as she falls in love with an older man and the story of her sister Claire, who becomes pregnant. Shy young Cecile grows up and has her first love affair as her married sisters help her. The family struggles to preserve their integrity and their values.

Genre: Coming of Age
Subjects: Teenagers; Sisters; Love; Family life
Place/Time: Paris (France)—1945–1980; France—1945–1980

Bojer, Johan

130.
1. *The Great Hunger.* Moffat, Yard, 1919.
2. *The New Temple.* Century, 1928.

Peer Holm is a Norwegian immigrant who comes to the Midwest in the 1850s to farm. Peer's soul hungers for the divine on Earth, and he attains his goal—not through effort, success, or love, but through disaster, suffering, and sacrifice.

Genre: Historical Fiction
Subjects: Immigrants; Farm life; Faith
Place/Time: Midwestern states—19th century

Bonanno, Margaret

131.
1. *The Others.* St. Martin's, 1990.
2. *Otherwhere.* St. Martin's, 1991.
3. *Otherwise.* St. Martin's, 1993.

The "Others," who compose a pacifistic, scientifically advanced, and caring culture help raise the "People," who compose an ignorant, violent, and creative culture. However, the People eventually wipe out almost all of the Others using technology acquired from them and then unleash the same technology on each other. Lingri, an Other who has helped bring about the Other\People contact and who survives the devastation with her half-People son, narrates how the contact came about and then how the Others search for a safe haven.

Genre: Science Fiction
Subjects: Imaginary wars and battles; Technology and civilization; Cultural conflict

Bonner, Cindy

132.
1. *Lily.* Algonquin, 1992.
2. *Looking after Lily.* Algonquin, 1994.
3. *The Passion of Dellie O'Barr.* Algonquin, 1996.
4. *Right from Wrong.* Algonquin, 1999.

In McDade, Texas, Lily and Dellie De Lony are two young girls from a good church-going family. Lily is the passionate and adventuresome older sister who falls in love with Marion Beatty, the youngest son of the outlaw Beatty brothers. On Christmas Eve 1883, a vigilante group strikes out against the outlaws and only a few survive. Marion is sent to jail, and he asks his brother, Haywood, to look after pregnant Lily. Haywood plans to set Lily up, then leave her, but he does not expect to come to love Lily. Dellie, Lily's prim and proper younger sister, marries a rich husband, but finds she does not love him. Her affair with tenant farmer Andy Ashland involves her with the Populist movement and the early suffragists. In 1914, Sunny De Lony loves her cousin Gil, but their mothers keep them apart for several years. Gil goes off to war and Sunny marries someone else, but their love ultimately drives them from the town.

Genre: Historical Fiction; Western; Historical Romance
Subjects: Love; Outlaws; Women; Populist Movement
Place/Time: Texas—19th century

Borchardt, Alice

133.
1. *The Night of the Wolf.* Ballantine, 1999.
2. *The Silver Wolf.* Ballantine, 1998.

Set 800 years apart in the Roman Empire, these tales tell of two shape shifters who must deal with their dual natures. The young werewolf Maeniel, who lives in the Britain of the Roman occupation, realizes that he is indeed a shape shifter when his attraction to a human woman triggers his first transformation into werewolf form. He journeys to Rome where, centuries later, he encounters Regeane, a young noblewoman and distant relative of Charlemagne, who is also a werewolf. Regeane faces political intrigue surrounding her arranged marriage to a barbarian chieftain and the danger of being burned as a witch if her true nature is discovered.

Genre: Horror; Historical Fiction
Subjects: Werewolves; Aristocracy
Place/Time: Rome (Italy)—multicentury span

134.
1. *Devoted.* Dutton, 1995.

2. *Beguiled.* Dutton, 1996.

In the ninth century, Owen, the bishop of Chatalon, helps save the life of Elin of the Forest People from the Vikings who have invaded France. Owen and Elin fall in love. Later, when Owen is captured by the Vikings, Elin and her Forest People help rescue him. After Owen and Elin marry, they try to protect their town and build up their troops. Owen then sets out for his father's kingdom to get more help while Elin is left to defend the town. Gutsy battle scenes and graphic sex enliven the historical scenes.

Genre: Historical Romance
Subjects: Vikings; Husbands and wives
Place/Time: France—10th century

Borntrager, Mary Christner

135. Ellie's People
1. *Ellie.* Herald Press, 1988.
2. *Rebecca.* Herald Press, 1989.
3. *Rachel.* Herald Press, 1990.
4. *Daniel.* Herald Press, 1991.
5. *Reuben.* Herald Press, 1992.
6. *Andy.* Herald Press, 1993.
7. *Polly.* Herald Press, 1995.
8. *Sarah.* Herald Press, 1996.
9. *Mandy.* Herald Press, 1996.
10. *Annie.* Herald Press, 1997.

The tight-knit world of the Amish is lovingly shown through the eyes of Ellie, a young girl growing up in the community. The lives of her children, grandchildren, and brothers are depicted in each of the novels. The pressures of the outside world and the struggles to keep a strict faith are portrayed, as is the supportive community that helps members find their true faith.

Genre: Christian Fiction
Subjects: Teenagers; Christian life; Faith; Amish
Place/Time: Pennsylvania—1900–1945

Borrow, George

136.
1. *Lavengro: The Scholar, Gypsy, Priest.* Harper, 1851.
2. *Romany Rye.* Harper, 1857.

George, a young man interested in philosophy, wanders about Europe with a family of gypsies. As he lives with the gypsies, he reveals their ways as the vagabonds of Europe.

Subjects: Gypsies; Voyages and travels; Rogues and vagabonds
Place/Time: Europe—19th century

Bosse, Malcolm

137.
1. *The Warlord.* Simon & Schuster, 1983.
2. *Fire in Heaven.* Simon & Schuster, 1985.

General Tang is a warlord in northern China in 1927. He watches as his country is slowly torn apart by Chiang Kai-Shek in the south and Mao Tse-Tung in the north. As he tries to make alliances, he meets Vera Rogacheva, a czarist emigree, and Philip Embree, an American. Their lives and loves are intertwined with China's wars and the rise of Mao and the Communists.

Genre: Historical Fiction
Subjects: Communism; Politics—China; War; Mao Tse-Tung, 1893–1976; Chiang Kai-Shek, 1887–1975
Place/Time: China—1900–1945

Bova, Ben

138.
1. *Mars.* Bantam, 1992.
2. *Return to Mars.* Avon, 1999.

Navajo-Anglo geologist Jamie Waterman is a member of the first international expedition to the planet Mars and finally takes charge of the group when rivalries and factions threaten its survival. The discovery of a lichen-like life form gives impetus to a second mission of which Jamie is the commander. Jamie becomes fascinated by a mysterious cliff structure in a remote location, which he feels may be an indication of complex life on Mars at one time, but incidents of possible sabotage and the exploitive greed of one member of the mission distract him.

Genre: Science Fiction
Subjects: Mars (planet), exploration of; Outer space, exploration of; Native Americans; Scientists

139.
1. *Moonrise.* Avon, 1996.
2. *Moonwar.* Avon, 1998.

Astronaut Paul Stavenger and his wife Joanna dream of a domed city on the moon, which will be both a center for research and for utilization of the moon's vast resources. Their dream is close to becoming a reality, but when the lunar colony is threatened by various economic and political forces on Earth, a military conflict seems inevitable.

Genre: Science Fiction
Subjects: Astronauts; Moon; Space colonies; Husbands and wives

140.
1. *Privateers.* Tor, 1985.
2. *Empire Builders.* Tor, 1993.

The United States has abandoned space travel and exploration at this point in the future. American multimillionaire Dan Randolph first tries his own legitimate private program to combat what has become a Russian domination of space, but when his property is confiscated, he retaliates by becoming a privateer. In the sequel, Randolph joins a Lunar underground movement.

Genre: Science Fiction
Subjects: Privateering; Outer space, exploration of

141. Orion
1. *Orion.* Simon and Schuster, 1984.
2. *Vengeance of Orion.* Tor, 1988.
3. *Orion in the Dying Time.* Tor, 1990.
4. *Orion and the Conqueror.* Tor, 1994.
5. *Orion among the Stars.* Tor, 1995.

In the 20th-century he was John O'Ryan, but following his transformation into the superhuman warrior Orion by the mysterious Creators, he has traveled through time and space fulfilling a destined role of preserving the space-time continuum on which the future of the universe depends. Along the way Orion falls in love with the goddess Anya and does battle with his own Creators.

Genre: Science Fiction
Subjects: Time travel; Imaginary wars and battles; Gods and goddesses

142. Voyagers
1. *Voyagers.* Doubleday, 1981.
2. *The Alien Within.* Tor, 1986.
3. *Star Brothers.* Tor, 1990.

Astronaut/physicist Keith Stoner accepts almost certain death when he chooses to remain aboard an alien spaceship. However, he not only survives, but returns to Earth with his powers enhanced by alien technology and a type of accumulated knowledge that could help mankind avoid the tragedies and dangers that destroyed other civilizations.

Genre: Science Fiction
Subjects: Extraterrestrial beings; Bionics; Astronauts

Bowen, Peter

143.
1. *Yellowstone Kelly: Gentleman and Scout.* Jameson, 1987.
2. *Kelly Blue.* Crown, 1991.
3. *Imperial Kelly.* Crown, 1992.

In this burlesque rewrite of American history, Yellowstone Kelly starts his career as a scout for Colonel Nelson Miles in his war against the Nez Perce. He then hooks up with Buffalo Bill Cody and goes on a hunting expedition with a British duke. Later, at Cody's deathbed, he recalls his battles in the Civil War, his fights with the Mormons, and his life with the Sioux Indians. He then tries to avoid Theodore Roosevelt, but is dragged into the Spanish American War.

Genre: Historical Fiction
Subjects: Adventure; Native Americans; War; Frontier and pioneer life; Cody, William Frederick (Buffalo Bill), 1846–1917
Place/Time: Western states—19th century

Boyd, Donna

144.
1. *The Passion.* Avon, 1998.

2. *The Promise.* Avon, 1999.

In *The Passion,* Alexander Devoncroix is a 120-year-old leader of a werewolf pack who was at one time in love with a human woman, Tessa, despite the fact that she tried to kill him. Through her relationship with him, his beloved learns that werewolves secretly wield great power in the world and have been responsible for many important historical events. In *The Promise,* the scene shifts to a remote location in Alaska where a young widow rescues Alexander's werewolf son Nicholas from the wreckage of a plane crash.

Genre: Horror
Subjects: Werewolves; Love; Fathers and sons
Place/Time: United States—19th century; United States—1980–

Boyd, Jack

145. Cedar Gap Archives
1. *Life as It's Lived.* Texas Tech University Press, 1989.
2. *Boy Howdy!* Texas Tech University Press, 1990.
3. *If It Ain't Broke.* Texas Tech University Press, 1991.

Humorous small town tales from Boyd's column in the Abilene Texas Reporter News tell the stories of the 256 residents of Cedar Gap, Texas. The stories are all related and revolve around the regulars who come to the Palace Cafe to discuss everybody in the community in a down-home way.

Genre: Humor
Subjects: Small town life
Place/Time: Texas—1980–

Boyd, James

146.
1. *Drums.* Scribner, 1925.
2. *Marching On.* Scribner, 1927.

The Frasers come from Scotland in the years before the American Revolution and settle in North Carolina. When the war starts, they serve with John Paul Jones, then General Dan Morgan. Descendant James Fraser serves in the Civil War and falls in love with a wealthy planter's daughter.

Genre: Historical Fiction; War
Subjects: United States—revolution, 1775–1783; United States—Civil War, 1861–1865; War; Jones, John Paul, 1747–1792
Place/Time: North Carolina—18th century; North Carolina—19th century

Boyd, Martin

147. The Langtons
1. *The Cardboard Crown.* Dutton, 1952.
2. *A Difficult Young Man.* Reynal, 1955.

3. *Outbreak of Love.* Reynal, 1957.
4. *Much in Evidence.* Reynal, 1957.

Guy Langton narrates episodes in the history of his individualistic Anglo-Australian family beginning in the Victorian period and ending at the outbreak of World War I. He starts with his grandmother's diary, which reveals the tension between her longings for Europe and ties to Australia. The escapades of his flamboyant, irresponsible brother Dominic and the troubled marriage and sophisticated social circle of his Aunt Diana continue the family history.

Genre: Family Saga
Subjects: Family life
Place/Time: Australia—19th century; Australia—1900–1945

Boyd, Thomas Alexander

148.
1. *Through the Wheat.* Scribner, 1923.
2. *In Time of Peace.* Minton, 1935.

In this American version of *All Quiet on the Western Front,* William Hicks, a Marine, goes through World War I never distinguishing himself, but never flinching. In the final days of the war he becomes numb to the incessant attacks and brutality. After the war he marries and then has to fight the poverty of the Depression and Hoover's indifference to the plight of the average man.

Genre: War
Subjects: World War I, 1914–1918; Marine Corps, United States; Business depression, 1929
Place/Time: Europe—1900–1945; Midwestern states—1900–1945

Boylan, Clare

149.
1. *11 Edward Street.* Doubleday, 1992.
2. *Holly Pictures.* Summit, 1983.

From the poverty of a Dublin tenement in 1896 to a sheltered middle-class home in 1925, three generations of women deal with life. Elinore Devlin tries to raise her 10 children after her husband dies. Her daughter Daisy marries Cecil Cantwell and has to deal with his womanizing. Their daughters Nan and Mary lead a more sheltered life, but soon have to deal with hardship when their father's business is wiped out.

Genre: Family Saga; Historical Fiction
Subjects: Women; Family life; Poverty
Place/Time: Dublin (Ireland)—1900–1945; Ireland—1900–1945

Boylan, James Finney

150.
1. *The Planets.* Poseidon, 1991.
2. *The Constellations.* Random, 1994.

In Centralia, Pennsylvania, a town where an underground mine fire from the 1960s continues to burn, is the home of a strange and quirky group of residents. A former English teacher lives in an abandoned school while a policeman dresses up in a magician's costume. Phoebe Harrison and her friends go to a tattoo parlor, and all the characters come together at a school dance for a riotous ending. The slapstick antics of all the characters point out how little control people have over their lives.

Genre: Humor
Subjects: Small town life
Place/Time: Pennsylvania—1980–

Boyne, Walter J.

151.
1. *Trophy for Eagles.* Crown, 1989.
2. *Eagles at War.* Crown, 1991.
3. *Air Force Eagles.* Crown, 1992.

The growth of the airplane industry and the U.S. Air Force is told through the life of Frank Bandfield, flying ace and engineer. As he tries to build better planes and win flying races from the 1920s to the 1950s, he has to battle his nemesis Bruno Hofner and other villains who try to block the development of better planes. The books abound with technical information on flying and the development of jets and the B-47 bomber.

Genre: Adventure; Historical Fiction
Subjects: Airplanes; Air pilots; Air Force, United States; Adventure; War
Place/Time: United States—1900–1945; United States—1945–1980

Bradford, Barbara Taylor

152.
1. *A Woman of Substance.* Doubleday, 1979.
2. *Hold the Dream.* Doubleday, 1985.
3. *To Be the Best.* Doubleday, 1988.

Beautiful, willful Emma Harte rises from an impoverished youth to build a successful business empire, but she has to sacrifice love for success. As she grows older, she grooms her granddaughter Paula Amory O'Neill to succeed her as head of the powerful dynasty. Paula also finds that she must make personal sacrifices to keep the empire together.

Genre: Family Saga; Romance
Subjects: Businesswomen; Self-made women; Wealth; Women
Place/Time: England—1900–1945; Europe—1945–1980

Bradley, Marion Zimmer

153.
1. *Ghostlight.* Tor, 1995.
2. *Witchlight.* Tor, 1996.

3. *Gravelight.* Tor, 1997.
4. *Heartlight.* Tor, 1998.

The character of parapsychologist Truth Jourdemayne connects the first three of these modern day explorations of the occult. First Truth returns to a mysterious estate where her mother died and her father disappeared during a dark ritual years ago. In the following tale, Truth helps Winter Musgrave, a young woman who has lost her memory and senses that she is being pursued by a sinister invisible power. Next, Truth's research into the occult with the Bidney Institute takes her to a mountain town where there have been recurring paranormal phenomena as the result of the opening of a mysterious gate to another realm. The focus of the series shifts to Bidney Institute director Colin McLaren, who fought the black magic of the Nazis during World War II and was a friend of Truth's father before he disappeared in the 1960s.

Genre: Fantasy
Subjects: Supernatural phenomena; Witchcraft
Place/Time: United States—1900–1945; United States—1945–1980; United States—1980–

154.
1. *Black Trillium.* (Written with Julian May and Andre Norton) Doubleday, 1990.
2. *Blood Trillium.* (Written by Julian May) Bantam, 1992.
3. *Golden Trillium.* (Written by Andre Norton) Bantam, 1993.
4. *Sky Trillium.* (Written by Julian May) Del Rey, 1997.
5. *Lady of the Trillium.* Bantam, 1995.

Triplet daughters born to the queen of magical Ruwenda work out a prophecy made at their birth that they will save their kingdom from destruction. As they mature, they must deal with evil sorcerers, an aggressive neighboring king, and their own very different natures. Throughout their trials, they are guided and united by their talisman, the three-petaled black trillium, which blooms across the land united by the princesses. Two hundred years after the deaths of two of the sisters, the surviving sister Harramis, who rules as guardian and archimage, seeks a successor.

Genre: Fantasy
Subjects: Imaginary kingdoms; Triplets; Sisters; Charms; Prophecies

155.
1. *The Forest House.* Viking, 1994.
2. *Lady of Avalon.* Viking, 1997.
3. *The Mists of Avalon.* Knopf, 1982.

Written earlier in time, but occupying a place later in fictional chronology than the other two works, *The Mists of Avalon* relates the Arthurian legend from the perspective of the women in Arthur's life: the enticing Morgan le Fey, who is portrayed as the preserver of the ancient beliefs of magical Avalon in which the Mother Goddess is supreme, and Guenevere, whose love for Lancelot pulls her away from her duty to King Arthur and the new religion. *The Forest House* begins a tale of the forbidden love of a Druid girl for a young Roman officer who is part of the occupation of Britain. The birth of their son sets off a series of magical events which culminate in the birth of Arthur.

Genre: Fantasy
Subjects: Arthur, King; Morgan le Fey (legendary character); Guenevere, Queen (legendary character a.k.a. Guinevere); England—Anglo-Saxon period, 449–1066

156. Darkover
1. *Darkover Landfall.* DAW Books, 1972.
2. *Stormqueen.* DAW Books, 1978.
3. *Rediscovery: A Novel of Darkover.* DAW Books, 1993. (Written with Mercedes Lackey.)
4. *Hawkmistress!* DAW Books, 1982.
5. *Two to Conquer.* DAW Books, 1980.
6. *The Heirs of Hammerfell.* DAW Books, 1989.
7. *The Shattered Chain.* DAW Books, 1976.
8. *Spell Sword.* DAW Books, 1974.
9. *The Forbidden Tower.* DAW Books, 1977.
10. *Thendara House.* DAW Books, 1983.
11. *City of Sorcery.* DAW Books, 1984.
12. *Star of Danger.* Ace, 1965.
13. *The Winds of Darkover.* Ace, 1970.
14. *The Bloody Sun.* Ace, 1964.
15. *The Heritage of Hastur.* DAW Books, 1975.
16. *The Sword of Aldones, The Planet Savers.* Ace, 1962.
17. *Sharra's Exile.* DAW Books, 1981.
18. *The World Wreckers.* Ace, 1971.
19. *Exile's Song.* DAW Books, 1996.
20. *The Shadow Matrix.* DAW Books, 1997.
21. *Traitor's Sun.* DAW Books, 1999.

The following Darkover anthologies were written by Marion Zimmer Bradley in collaboration with other authors:

1. *The Keeper's Price.* DAW Books, 1980.
2. *The Sword of Chaos.* DAW Books, 1982.
3. *Free Amazons of Darkover.* DAW Books, 1985.
4. *The Other Side of the Mirror.* DAW Books, 1987.
5. *Red Sun of Darkover.* DAW Books, 1987.
6. *Four Moons of Darkover.* DAW Books, 1988.
7. *Domains of Darkover.* DAW Books, 1990.
8. *Leroni of Darkover.* DAW Books, 1991.
9. *Towers of Darkover.* DAW Books, 1993.
10. *Snows of Darkover.* DAW Books, 1994.

Two worlds, Darkover and Earth, meet in these works that leap back and forth in time to trace the intermingling of cultures, starting with the crash of a colonizing Terran spaceship on the planet Darkover. The telepathic, self-sufficient Darkovans may disdain the Terran reliance on community, bureaucracy, and technology, but throughout the Darkover tales, Terrans and Darkovans marry, reproduce, form friendships, pool their talents, and eventually discover their common heritage. *Note:* The novels listed above are in approximate order of events described, but may be read in any order. The short stories fill in the gaps in Darkovan history.

Genre: Fantasy; Science Fiction
Subjects: Space colonies; Telepathy; Technology and civilization

Bradley, Marion Zimmer *and* Lisle, Holly

157. Glenraven
1. *Glenraven.* Baen Books, 1996.
2. *In the Rift.* Baen Books, 1998.

A unique guidebook extolling the charms of Glenraven, an alpine country north of Italy, mysteriously appears in the lives of three women who want to get away from sorrow and danger. Sophie's child has recently died. Her friend JayJay is going through the breakup of her third marriage. Kate's life has been threatened. All are drawn into the magical land of Glenraven where adventures in the battle between good and evil, such as they have never imagined in the real world, await them.

Genre: Fantasy
Subjects: Imaginary kingdoms; Imaginary wars and battles; Good and evil

Brady, James

158.
1. *Further Lane.* St. Martin's, 1997.
2. *Gin Lane.* St. Martin's, 1998.
3. *The House That Ate the Hamptons.* St. Martin's, 1998.

News correspondent Beecher Stow returns to his family home in the East Hamptons. There he romps through the celebrity homes and the upper crust mansions of Hampton society. He meets gorgeous socialite Alix Dunraven as he writes a story on local guru Hannah Cutting. When Hannah turns up dead, Alix searches for her tell-all autobiography while Beecher tries to find out who murdered Hannah. Later Beecher and Alix visit the wealthier homes of South Hampton society. They attend the wedding of social climbers and get involved with an obnoxious morning deejay who has moved into the neighborhood. As the two move among the Middle Eastern potentates, Hollywood impresarios, social climbers, and upper crust society, they reveal the underside of life among the rich and famous.

Subjects: Society Novels; Wealth
Place/Time: New York (N. Y.)—1980–

Brady, Joan

159.
1. *God on a Harley.* Pocket Books, 1995.
2. *Heaven in High Gear.* Pocket Books, 1997.

Does God wear a leather jacket and drive a Harley? Disgruntled nurse Christine Moore discovers he does when a handsome, black-leather-jacketed Harley rider named Joe turns her life around. Christine is single, unhappy, and man hating. Joe changes her life by giving her six commandments that help her find herself and true love. Joe then helps Heather, a 29-year-old stripper, leave her cynical life and find a richer spiritual existence. As Heather talks to Joe she sees life in new way and Joe drives off on his Harley.

Genre: Christian Fiction
Subjects: Faith; Religion
Place/Time: United States—1980–

Bragg, Melvyn

160.
1. *The Hired Man.* Knopf, 1969.
2. *A Place in England.* Secker & Warburg, 1970.

John Tallentire is a farm laborer in rural England in 1898. When he marries and has a family, social and economic changes in England force him off the farm and into the towns. There he struggles to make a new life for his family. His son Joseph wants to be his own man, and after enduring hardships and World War I, finally opens a pub.

Genre: Historical Fiction
Subjects: Marriage problems; Fathers and sons; Cities and towns
Place/Time: England—1900–1945

Braine, John

161.
1. *Room at the Top.* Houghton Mifflin, 1957.
2. *Life at the Top.* Houghton Mifflin, 1962.

Climbing the corporate and social ladder in postwar Britain, Joe Lampton will do anything to attain wealth and social status. He finds, however, that he has traded personal freedom for elegant slavery.

Subjects: Ambition; Business; Social classes
Place/Time: England—1945–1980

Bramble, Forbes

162.
1. *Regent Square.* Coward, McCann & Geoghegan, 1977.
2. *The Iron Roads.* St. Martin's, 1981.

From the coronation of King George IV in 1820 through the Crimean War, Thomas Kelleway and his sons become lawyers and fight to establish themselves both in the courts and in society. Son John follows his father, but son Henry fights with his father. Henry becomes involved with a greedy businessman, George Hudson, who is building railroads in England. When Henry discovers the crimes Hudson has committed, he goes into politics to destroy Hudson.

Genre: Historical Fiction
Subjects: Fathers and sons; Law and lawyers; Social classes; Railroads
Place/Time: England—19th century

Briffault, Robert

163.
1. *Europa: The Days of Ignorance.* Scribner, 1935.
2. *Europa in Limbo.* Scribner, 1937.

Julian Bern wanders through Europe before and during World War I and cynically comments on life at that time. His travels and his friends lead him to all levels of society as Julian realistically and powerfully documents the disintegration he sees.

Genre: War
Subjects: World War I, 1914–1918; Travel; Degeneration; Social classes
Place/Time: Europe—1900–1945

Brin, David. *See also* Asimov, Isaac (*Foundation's Triumph*)

164. The New Uplift Trilogy
1. *Brightness Reef.* Bantam, 1995.
2. *Infinity's Shore.* Bantam, 1996.
3. *Heaven's Reach.* Bantam, 1998.

The planet Jijo has been abandoned to restore its ecological balance, but a group of sapient beings defies the quarantine of the Five Galaxies by settling on the planet and is joined in their secret civilization by humans from Earth. Seeming to fulfill a dark prophecy in the planet's religion, the starship Streaker arrives, unintentionally exposing Jijo to the machinations of the cruel Jophur, whose main goals are exploitation of the inhabitants and genocide.

Genre: Science Fiction
Subjects: Life on other planets; Space colonies

165. Uplift
1. *Sundiver.* Bantam, 1980.
2. *Startide Rising.* Bantam, 1983.
3. *The Uplift War.* Phantasia Press, 1987.
The above two titles have also been published in the following collection: *Earthclan.* Doubleday, 1987.

Uplift is a process of Earth's distant future that allows dolphins and chimpanzees to communicate with humans. It creates a relationship that figures in an intergalactic conflict between Terrans and alien beings.

Colonial planets, secrets of the history of the galaxy, and the potential for uplift in other species are the bones of contention in these hard science fiction adventures.

Genre: Science Fiction
Subjects: Interplanetary wars; Animal communication; Extraterrestrial beings

Brinig, Myron

166.
1. *Singermann.* Farrar & Rinehart, 1929.
2. *This Man My Brother.* Farrar & Rinehart, 1932.

Moses Singermann emigrates from Romania to America and establishes a business and a home for his family in the rough and tumble frontier town of Silver Bow, Montana. Twenty years later, the youngest son, Michael, returns from his home in the East to serve as a sympathetic observer of the ebb and flow of the family's fortunes.

Genre: Historical Fiction
Subjects: Small town life; Family life
Place/Time: Montana—1900–1945

Briskin, Jacqueline

167.
1. *Paloverde.* McGraw-Hill, 1978.
2. *Rich Friends.* Delacorte, 1976.

California from the rise of the railroads in 1880 to the turbulent 1960s is the setting for this family saga that covers the fortunes of four intertwining generations. Bud and 3Vee Van Vliet are the heirs to the Los Angeles ranch of Paloverde, and both love Amelia. While Bud marries Amelia, 3Vee fathers her daughter, Tess. Each succeeding generation finds that their loves are tragically crossed and that money cannot buy love.

Genre: Family Saga; Historical Romance
Subjects: Wealth
Place/Time: California—19th century; California— 1900–1945; California—1945–1980

Bristow, Gwen

168. The Plantation Trilogy
1. *Deep Summer.* Crowell, 1937.
2. *The Handsome Road.* Crowell, 1938.
3. *This Side of Glory.* Crowell, 1940.
   The above titles have also been published in the following collection: *Plantation Trilogy.* Crowell, 1962.

Judith Sheramy migrates to Louisiana in the 1800s and meets Philip Larne, the son of a wealthy South Carolina family. The two marry and struggle to keep their plantation through the Civil War. After the war, the lives of the wealthy Larnes and the poor Upjohns are followed to the period of the First World War.

Genre: Family Saga; Historical Fiction
Subjects: Plantation life; Wealth; Social classes
Place/Time: Louisiana—19th century; Louisiana— 1900–1945

Brooks, Terry

169.
1. *Running with the Demon.* Del Rey, 1997.
2. *A Knight of the Word.* Del Rey, 1998.
3. *Angel Fire East.* Del Rey, 1999.

John Ross, who has been anointed a Knight of the Word, comes to Hopewell, Illinois, to enlist the help of Nest Freemark in the battle against the demons of the Void who could devour humanity. John, an unassuming man in his thirties and Nest, a young girl from a working class background, seem unlikely warriors in the battle against evil, but Nest discovers her magical powers and is protected by a powerful ghost wolf. At one point, John retires from the conflict to run a shelter for the homeless, but is drawn back into the fray.

Genre: Fantasy
Subjects: Good and evil; Demonology; Imaginary wars and battles; Magic
Place/Time: Illinois—1980–

170. The Heritage of Shannara
1. *The Scions of Shannara.* Ballantine, 1990.
2. *The Druid of Shannara.* Ballantine, 1991.
3. *The Elf Queen of Shannara.* Ballantine, 1992.
4. *The Talismans of Shannara.* Ballantine, 1993.

Hundreds of years after the quests of Shea and his family, the Sword of Shannara has been lost, magic is forbidden, and the mysterious Shadowen threaten the realm. Guided by the shade of a Druid, descendants of Shea set off to search for the missing sword and for the elves, who have disappeared from the land.

Genre: Fantasy
Subjects: Imaginary kingdoms; Arms and armor; Magic

171. The Magic Kingdom of Landover
1. *Magic Kingdom for Sale—Sold!* Ballantine, 1986.
2. *The Black Unicorn.* Ballantine, 1987.
3. *Wizard at Large.* Ballantine, 1988.
4. *The Tangle Box.* Ballantine, 1994.
5. *Witches Brew.* Ballantine, 1995.

Landover may not be the perfect magical realm, but it looks good to unhappy Chicago lawyer Ben Holiday. Holiday becomes its king and finds himself dealing with dragons, rebellious barons, a hostile neighboring ruler, an incompetent wizard, and the helpful, but inconsistent fairy Willow. Some problems arise even in alternate realities: specifically taxes and con men.

Genre: Fantasy; Humor
Subjects: Law and lawyers; Imaginary kingdoms; Kings and rulers

172. Shannara
1. *First King of Shannara*. Del Rey, 1996.
2. *The Sword of Shannara*. Random House, 1977.
3. *The Elfstones of Shannara*. Ballantine, 1982.
4. *The Wishsong of Shannara*. Ballantine, 1985.

Bremen, the last Druid, allies himself with the King of the Elves, Jerle Shannara, to do battle with the Warlock Lord. Five hundred years later Shea Ohmsford discovers that he is the only man on earth who can save humanity. Armed with a cryptic Druid clue, Shea sets off on a search for the miraculous Sword of Shannara, which will enable him to do battle with the evil warlock. His descendants continue the quest for magic that will defeat the Powers of Darkness.

Genre: Fantasy
Subjects: Imaginary kingdoms; Good and evil; Magic

Brosnan, John
173. Sky Lords
1. *The Sky Lords*. St. Martin's, 1991.
2. *War of the Sky Lords*. St. Martin's, 1992.
3. *The Fall of the Skylords*. Gollancz, 1991.

As Earth's civilization is collapsing from gene wars, giant warships battle for supremacy above the Earth. The inhabitants of the feminist utopia of Minerva try to fight back. When Jan, one of the warriors of Minerva, is captured by a spaceship commander, she uses her position to fight to free her homeland.

Genre: Science Fiction
Subjects: Interplanetary wars; Feminism; Genetics

Brouwer, S. W.
174. Ghost Rider Series
1. *Morning Star*. Victor/Scripture, 1994.
2. *Moon Basket*. Victor, 1994.

Former bounty hunter, Samuel Keaton, meets a mysterious Sioux woman named Morning Star, who must reach her tribal home in the Black Hills. She masquerades as a man as she travels with Keaton, and she comes to love this man who defends her and other native Americans from corrupt white men. They battle their way to Laramie on the eve of the Battle of the Little Big Horn. Later Keaton becomes a marshall and must deal with a bank robbery and a double murder.

Genre: Christian Fiction; Western
Subjects: Native Americans; Western stories; Adventure; Faith
Place/Time: South Dakota—19th century

Brown, Sam
175.
1. *The Big Lonely*. Walker, 1992.
2. *The Long Drift*. Walker, 1995.

Casey Wills is a young cowboy on the huge XIT spread. As he mends fences, he is approached by Tatum Stagg who wants Casey to turn a blind eye to Stagg's cattle theft. Casey refuses and brings on the resulting action. Casey drifts from job to job until years later he decides to buy a ranch and settle down. He falls in love with a married woman and goes in search of her husband. He spends all his money on the search and ends up on another cattle drive. These offbeat westerns concentrate on the day-to-day life of the ordinary hard working people who made the West.

Genre: Western
Subjects: Cowboys; Ranch life
Place/Time: Western states—19th century

Bruchac, Joseph
176.
1. *Dawn Land*. Fulcrum, 1993.
2. *Long River*. Fulcrum, 1995.
3. *The Waters Between*. University Press, 1998.

At the end of the last ice age, Young Hunter, an Abenaki brave in what is now New England, must fight the Ancient Ones, evil giants who live off human flesh. After defeating the Ancient Ones, Young Hunter is warned of other dangers to his people through his dreams. Walking Hill (a woolly mammoth) and then a sea serpent in the lake the Only People use for food challenge Young Hunter, who must find the way to defeat them.

Genre: Historical Fiction
Subjects: Native Americans; Humans, prehistoric; Stone Age; Tribes
Place/Time: New England—prehistoric times

Bruckner, Christine
177.
1. *Gilly Flower Kid*. Fromm International Pub., 1982, 1975.
2. *Flight of Cranes*. Fromm International Pub., 1982, 1977.

Maximiliane von Quindt, a Prussian heiress, grows from a passive young wife to an iron-willed survivor during the three tumultuous decades spanning Germany's defeat after World War I to the arrival of Soviet troops into Prussia in 1944. She flees the Russians, works in the fields to feed herself and her children, and adapts to the changes in postwar Germany.

Genre: War
Subjects: World War I, 1914–1918; World War II, 1939–1945; Women
Place/Time: Germany—1900–1945; Germany—1945–1980

Brust, Steven

178.
1. *The Phoenix Guards.* Tor, 1992.
2. *Five Hundred Years After.* Tor, 1994.

Since Dragaerans live for centuries, these works, set 500 years apart in the early history of the decadent Dragaeran Empire, follow the same characters—court guard captain and narrator Khaavren, the empire's Dragonlord, and other aristocrats—through schemes, intrigues, and power plays of epic proportions. *The Viscount of Adrilankha*, which has not yet been published, will continue the series.

Genre: Fantasy
Subjects: Imaginary kingdoms; Degeneration; Longevity

179. Vlad Taltos
1. *Yendi.* Ace, 1984.
2. *Jhereg.* Ace, 1983.
3. *Teckla.* Ace, 1986.
4. *Taltos.* Ace, 1988.
5. *Phoenix.* Ace, 1990.
6. *Athyra.* Ace, 1993.
7. *Dragon.* Tor, 1998.

Because humans are discriminated against in Dragaeran society, it takes only a small push to send Vlad Taltos down the dangerous road to becoming an assassin. He is assisted by a telepathic flying reptile and the black arts he learned from his grandfather. Vlad becomes an idol to an unsophisticated country boy who watches the assassin engage in battle with the local sorcerer. Vlad's adventures continue as he enters into a conflict between royal houses over an ancient greatsword.

Genre: Fantasy
Subjects: Assassination; Witchcraft; Discrimination; Mythical animals

Buck, Pearl S.

180.
1. *The Good Earth.* Random House, 1931.
2. *Sons.* John Day, 1923.
3. *A House Divided.* Reynal & Hitchcock, 1935.

In prerevolutionary China, Wang Lung, a peasant, rises from poverty to wealth through hard work and the help of his wife O-lan. Their sons divide the land, and the youngest, Wang the Tiger, becomes a petty warlord. Yuan, Wang's son, studies in America and, when he returns to China in 1912, resolves to help China modernize by teaching agriculture.

Genre: Family Saga; Historical Fiction
Subjects: Peasants; Farm life
Place/Time: China—19th century

Budd, Lillian

181.
1. *April Snow.* Lippincott, 1951.
2. *Land of Strangers.* Lippincott, 1953.
3. *April Harvest.* Duell, 1959.

In Sweden in the late 1800s, the Christiansson family fight on their farm to stay above poverty. Their son, Carl works his way to Chicago, marries, and raises a family. His daughter Sigrid struggles in the year before World War I to get an education and support herself.

Genre: Historical Fiction
Subjects: Farm life; Family life; Poverty; Education
Place/Time: Sweden—19th century; Chicago (Ill.)—1900–1945; Illinois—1900–1945

Bujold, Lois McMaster

182. Vorkosigan
1. *Shards of Honor.* Baen, 1986.
2. *Barrayar.* Baen, 1991.
The above titles are published together in *Cordelia's Honor.* Baen, 1996.

3. *The Warrior's Apprentice.* Baen, 1986.
4. *The Vor Game.* Easton Press, 1990.
5. *Young Miles.* Baen, 1997.
6. *Cetaganda.* Baen, 1995.
7. *Borders of Infinity.* Baen, 1989.
8. *Brothers in Arms.* Baen, 1989.
9. *Mirror Dance.* Baen, 1994.
10. *Memory.* Baen, 1996.
11. *Komarr.* Baen, 1998.
12. *A Civil Campaign: A Comedy of Biology and Manners.* Simon & Schuster, 1999.

Although he is born a descendant of the powerful warrior class of Barrayar, Miles Vorkosigan is weak, physically disabled, and manic-depressive. In addition, he must live with the knowledge that, according to Barrayan custom, his mother's pregnancy should have been terminated once it became obvious that he would be born disabled. However, even though lacking physical strength, Miles proves himself to be a military genius and leader. In the midst of battle, he must suddenly cope with the appearance of his clone, Mark, who was created for dark purposes.

Genre: Science Fiction
Subjects: Life on other planets; Interplanetary wars; Physical handicaps; Good and evil

Bull, Bartle

183.
1. *The White Rhino Hotel.* Viking, 1992.
2. *A Cafe on the Nile.* Carroll & Graf, 1998.

At the end of World War I, a group of British settlers struggle to survive in Kenya. Safari leader Anton Rider and his wife Gwen lead the colonists and natives as they fall in love and fight off the villains including dwarf Olivio Fonseca Alavedo. Twenty years later, all of these people meet in Cairo before World War II. The dwarf Olivio owns the Cataract Cafe where Ryder shows up. He is to lead some Americans on safari in Ethiopia just as Colonel Grimaldi of the Italian air force is preparing for an attack on Ethiopia. The group must again fight the villains and scoundrels and save themselves as they flee the war.

Genre: Historical Fiction; Adventure
Subjects: Adventure; Country life; Farm life; War
Place/Time: Kenya—1900–1945; Cairo (Egypt)—1900–1945

Bulwer Lytton, Edward, Baron. *See* Lytton, Edward Bulwer, Baron

Bunch, Chris. *See* Cole, Allan

Bunn, T. Davis. *See also* Oke, Janette

184. The Priceless Collection
1. *Florian's Gate.* Bethany House, 1992.
2. *The Amber Room.* Bethany House, 1992.
3. *Winter Palace.* Bethany House, 1993.

The postcommunist world is seen through the eyes of London antique dealer Jeffrey Sinclair, who secretly meets with impoverished Eastern block people to purchase their antiques—the last remaining items of value that many have.

Genre: Christian Fiction
Subjects: Antiques; Poverty; Refugees; Christian life
Place/Time: London (England)—1980–; England—1980–

185. Rendezvous with Destiny
1. *Rhineland Inheritance.* Bethany House, 1993.
2. *Gibraltar Passage.* Bethany House, 1994.
3. *Sahara Crosswind.* Bethany House, 1994.
4. *Berlin Encounter.* Bethany House, 1995.
5. *Istanbul Express.* Bethany House, 1995.

In the aftermath of World War II, Captain Jake Barnes of the United States Army is transferred to the base near Baden-Baden in Germany. There he patrols the border and works with NATO intelligence to fight the rising power of Stalin. Later, French Captain Pierre Servais works with his friend Jake and discovers that his twin brother, whom he thought was killed in the Resistance, may be alive. As the Iron Curtain descends across the European continent, the two men use their wits and their strong faith in God to help them fight the tyranny around them.

Genre: Adventure; Christian Fiction; Espionage
Subjects: World War II, 1939–1945; Twins; Orphans; Christian life; International intrigue; Spies; Communism
Place/Time: Germany—1945–1980

Burgess, Anthony. *Pseud. of* John Anthony Burgess Wilson

186.
1. *Enderby.* Norton, 1968, 1963.
2. *Enderby Outside.* Heinemann, 1968.
3. *The Clockwork Testament or Enderby's End.* Knopf, 1975.
4. *Enderby's Dark Lady, Or No End to Enderby.* McGraw-Hill, 1984.

The above titles have also been published in the following collection: *The Complete Enderby.* Carroll & Graf, 1996.

The hilarious problems of minor English poet F. X. Enderby are retold as Burgess pokes fun at society in the late 1960s and early 1970s. Enderby is a middle-aged poet who can only practice his art in his bathroom. He is drawn out of his house to accept an award, but that leads him to lose his poetic gift and seek psychiatric help. Only when he starts to write again does he regain his sanity. Burgess is concerned with the practice of poetry and the place of the poet in 20th-century culture. *Enderby Outside* has only been published in England.

Genre: Humor
Subjects: Authors; Poets; Satire
Place/Time: London (England)—1945–1980; England—1945–1980

Burke, Fielding. *Pseud. of* Olive Tilford Dargan

187.
1. *Call Home the Heart.* Longmans, Green, 1932.
2. *A Stone Came Rolling.* Longmans, Green, 1932.

The burdens of poverty and a large family drive Ishma Waycaster from her North Carolina mountain life with a lovable, but unambitious, husband. Life with her lover in a mill town convinces her to return to her husband and try to better the lives of those she knows best.

Subjects: Poverty; Mountain life; Love affairs; Family life
Place/Time: North Carolina—1900–1945

Burns, Olive Ann

188.
1. *Cold Sassy Tree.* Ticknor & Fields, 1984.
2. *Leaving Cold Sassy: The Unfinished Sequel to Cold Sassy Tree.* Ticknor & Fields, 1992.

"I done ast her an' she's done said yes," Rucker Blakeslee tells his startled family of his plans to marry thirty-something Miss Love Simpson. Since Rucker is several times a grandfather and only three weeks a widower, most of his family and the residents of early 1900s Cold Sassy, Georgia, are properly shocked.

However, favorite grandson Will Tweedy provides a sympathetic narration of this May-December marriage and courtship—in that order. The sequel, left unfinished at the author's death, follows Will Tweedy into early manhood through the World War I period.

Subjects: Grandfathers; Marriage; Small town life; Love
Place/Time: Georgia—1900–1945

Burroughs, William S.

189.
1. *The Ticket That Exploded.* Grove, 1967, 1962.
2. *Nova Express.* Grove, 1966.
3. *Naked Lunch.* Grove, 1962, 1959.
4. *The Soft Machine.* Grove, 1966. (A revised and enlarged edition of this title was published by Calder, Boyars in 1968.)

Black comedy and science fiction mix in these stories of the attempts of the intergalactic Nova Police to thwart the activities of the Nova Mob on Earth without pushing them to the ultimate point of blowing up the planet. The primary goal of the Nova Mob, parasitic creatures who exploit the fears and addictive tendencies of humanity, is to control the mass media.

Genre: Humor; Science Fiction
Subjects: Gangsters; Police; Mass media

Butler, Octavia E.

190.
1. *Parable of the Sower.* Four Walls Eight Windows, 1993.
2. *Parable of the Talents.* Seven Stories Press, 1998.

In 2025, Lauren Olamina, a young black woman, leaves the walled community, which has afforded her some protection from a society fraught with environmental pollution and violence, to walk along the coast of California in search of a better life. In this dark depiction of the near future, Lauren's ability to empathize with other's pain is considered to be an affliction by those around her. A set of philosophical tenets she has been developing since she was twelve years old lead her to found Acorn, a new community in northern California. Her beliefs put her at odds with an extremist Christian element and result in a rift with her daughter and husband. The narrative leaps fifty years into the future to the perspective of Lauren's daughter in her own adult life.

Genre: Science Fiction
Subjects: Social problems; Violence; Religion; Mothers and daughters

191. Patternists
1. *Wild Seed.* Doubleday, 1980.
2. *Mind of My Mind.* Doubleday, 1977.
3. *Survivor.* Doubleday, 1978.
4. *Patternmaster.* Doubleday, 1976.
5. *Clay's Ark.* St. Martin's, 1984.

Beginning in 17th-century Africa and America, then continuing in the present and on into the near and distant future is this saga of a community of telepaths created by Doro, a vampiric creature who forms an antagonistic union with a powerful female shape shifter. In the present, the Patternists evolve into a cohesive group dealing with the sometimes negative power of their heightened mental abilities. In the near future, a group of missionaries flees to another planet to escape the psionic power of the Patternists. Ultimately, a benevolent leader rises to power in the telepathic community.

Genre: Fantasy; Science Fiction
Subjects: Telepathy; Eugenics
Place/Time: Africa—multicentury span; United States—multicentury span

192. Xenogenesis Trilogy
1. *Dawn.* Warner, 1987.
2. *Adulthood Rites.* Warner, 1988.
3. *Imago.* Warner, 1989.

The Oankali, aliens who rescue a segment of humanity from the aftermath of a nuclear holocaust, demand a price: to breed with the survivors to create a new race that will be vastly superior and also satisfy their need for genetic renewal. The survivor Lilith plays an important role in the Oankali's plan as a leader and mother to their hybrid offspring: first a son who appears human, but is torn by his dual nature, then a totally unique being whose powers threaten life itself.

Genre: Science Fiction
Subjects: Extraterrestrial beings; Eugenics; Nuclear warfare; Mothers

Butler, Samuel

193.
1. *Erewhon, or Over the Range.* Dutton, 1907, 1872.
2. *Erewhon Revisited, Twenty Years Later Both by the Original Discoverer of the Country and by His Son.* Dutton, 1910, 1901.

The nameless hero travels through the mountains of New Zealand and discovers a strange utopia where everything is topsy-turvy. He falls in love with Yram and sees the odd customs of Erewhon. People are put in jail for colds, and those who lie must learn to be straight. Twenty years later he returns with his son and sees the new religion that has taken over the country. Butler uses Erewhon to satirize contemporary English society and its views on science, crime, and religion.

Genre: Humor
Subjects: Utopias; Love; Satire
Place/Time: New Zealand—1900–1945

Butterworth, W. E. *See* Griffin, W. E. B.

Butts, Mary

194. The Taverner Novels
1. *Armed with Madness.* A. C. Boni, 1928.
2. *Death of Felicity Taverner.* Wishart & Co., 1932.

In the years after World War I, a group of friends living in the Cornish countryside become involved with a small jade cup that leads to Scylla Taverner being wounded by an insane friend. Later the friends investigate the death of Scylla's cousin Felicity while they try to keep Felicity's husband from destroying their woods.

Subjects: Friendship; Insanity; Death
Place/Time: England—1900–1945

Byatt, A. S.

195.
1. *The Virgin in the Garden.* Knopf, 1979.
2. *Still Life.* Scribners, 1985.
3. *Babel Tower.* Random House, 1996.

During Elizabeth II's coronation year in 1953, the three children of Bill Potter, a teacher at a progressive school in Yorkshire, England, become involved in relationships. Stephanie falls in love with a clergyman from a working-class background and marries him, which alienates her atheistic father. Frederica wins a role as Bess in the coronation festival's play and uses the play and the people she meets to have an affair. Their reclusive brother Marcus, who is taken in by his sister Stephanie, becomes the center of a tragedy while living with her. Frederica goes from affair to affair, lives in Provence, France, and enters Cambridge. These complex novels of ideas explore the nature and limits of communication in relationships and in art.

Subjects: Family life; Brothers and sisters
Place/Time: England—1945–1980; Provence (France)—1945–1980; France—1945–1980

Byrne, Beverly

196.
1. *A Lasting Fire.* Bantam, 1991.
2. *The Flames of Vengeance.* Bantam, 1991.
3. *The Firebirds.* Bantam, 1992.

From the 1400s to the 1980s, the Mendoza family is driven to maintain their wealth and their powerful bank, though their Jewish heritage must remain hidden or they will lose everything. Through the generations, powerful women, such as Sophie Valon and Lila Curan, wed the Mendoza men, then fight to control the Cordoba bank. The story moves from Spain to London, then to New York as the Mendoza clan seeks love and power.

Genre: Family Saga; Historical Romance
Subjects: Wealth; Bankers; Jews
Place/Time: Spain—multicentury span; London (England)—multicentury span; New York (N. Y.)—multicentury span; England—multicentury span

Cabell, James Branch

197. Biography of the Life of Manuel of Poictesme
1. *Beyond Life.* McBride, 1919.
2. *Figures of Earth.* McBride, 1921.
3. *The Silver Stallion.* McBride, 1926.
4. *Music from Behind the Moon.* Day, 1926.
5. *The Way of Ecben.* McBride, 1929.
6. *The White Robe.* McBride, 1928.
The above three titles have also been published in the following collection: *The Witch Woman.* Farrar, Straus, 1948.

7. *The Soul of Melicent.* (Alternate title: *Domnei.*) Stokes, 1913.
8. *Chivalry.* Harper, 1909. (Revised edition, McBride, 1928.)
9. *Jurgen.* McBride, 1919.
10. *The Line of Love.* Harper, 1905. (Revised edition, McBride, 1921.)
11. *The High Place.* McBride, 1923.
12. *Gallantry.* Harper, 1907. (Revised edition, McBride. 1928.)
13. *Something About Eve.* McBride, 1927.
14. *The Certain Hour.* McBride, 1916.
15. *The Cords of Vanity.* Doubleday, 1909. (Revised edition, McBride, 1920.)
16. *From the Hidden Way.* McBride, 1916. (Revised edition, McBride, 1924.)
17. *The Jewel Merchants.* McBride, 1921.
18. *The Rivet in Grandfather's Neck.* McBride, 1915.
19. *The Eagle's Shadow.* Doubleday, 1904. (Revised edition, McBride, 1923.)
20. *The Cream of the Jest.* McBride, 1917.
21. *Straws and Prayer-Books.* McBride, 1924.

In the medieval land of Poictesme, Manuel sets out to reclaim his position as ruler of the land and to find the ideal woman. His quest ends when he chooses to die rather than sacrifice his daughter Melicent. Tales mixing folklore, fantasy, and philosophical symbolism follow his descendants through 22 generations to 20th-century Virginia. Since this group of books was not originally planned as a series, several of the works were revised later to fit into the sequence.

Genre: Fantasy
Subjects: Imaginary kingdoms; Fathers and daughters

Cadell, Elizabeth

198.
1. *The Lark Shall Sing.* Morrow, 1955.

2. *The Blue Sky of Spring.* Hodder & Stoughton, 1956.
3. *Six Impossible Things.* Morrow, 1961.

When the six Wayne children are orphaned, they are sent to live with different families. Their home, Wood Mount, in the English countryside is rented out, but when the oldest child Lucille grows up, she decides to sell the home. The other siblings protest and have a reunion so they can try to keep their home. *The Blue of Spring* has only been published in England.

Genre: Gentle Read
Subjects: Brothers and sisters; Orphans; Houses
Place/Time: England—1945–1980

Caidin, Martin

199. The Six Million Dollar Man
1. *Cyborg.* Arbor House, 1972.
2. *Operation Nuke.* Arbor House, 1973.
3. *High Crystal.* Arbor House, 1974.
4. *Cyborg IV.* Arbor House, 1975.

Test pilot Steve Austin is given a choice following a crash: to remain a paraplegic or to go into government service as a fighting machine given superhuman powers by technology. With his body restored and enhanced, Austin steals experimental planes, uncovers secret submarine bases, enters a terrorist organization incognito, and discovers a powerful Indian crystal. This series was the basis for the television series *The Six Million Dollar Man.*

Genre: Science Fiction
Subjects: Bionics; International intrigue

Calder, Richard

200.
1. *Dead Girls.* St. Martin's, 1995.
2. *Dead Boys.* St. Martin's, 1996.
3. *Dead Things.* St. Martin's, 1997.

In the late twenty-first century, a nanotechnological virus has created lilims: adolescent girls who are robot-like aggressive sexual creatures. Ignatz Zwakh loses his love to the virus but manages to create a daughter from her reproductive organs. The virus soon spreads to the male population and appears to have far reaching consequences that may affect the structure of time itself.

Genre: Science Fiction
Subjects: Viruses; Degeneration; Teenagers; Sex

Caldwell, Janet Taylor. *See* Caldwell, Taylor

Caldwell, Taylor

201.
1. *Dynasty of Death.* Scribner, 1938.

2. *Eagles Gather.* Scribner, 1940.
3. *The Final Hour.* Scribner, 1944.

The saga of two French-American families—the Barbours and the Bouchards—is chronicled from 1837 to 1940. Ernest Barbour settles in Pennsylvania and sets up an armaments factory. He builds it into a powerful industry through underhanded dealings while he marries his children to the prominent Bouchard family. Their descendants become refined American aristocrats, but they use their money and power to thwart democracy until the Nazis make them realize what they will lose.

Genre: Family Saga; Historical Fiction
Subjects: Society novels; Wealth; Munitions; Corruption (in politics); Business—unscrupulous methods
Place/Time: Pennsylvania—19th century; Pennsylvania—1900–1945

Cameron, Elizabeth Jane. *See* Duncan, Jane

Camon, Ferdinando

202.
1. *The Fifth Estate.* Marlboro, 1987, 1970.
2. *Life Everlasting.* Marlboro, 1987, 1972.

In these lyrical, stream of consciousness novels, Camon pays tribute to the pre–World War II life of the rural Italian peasants. He tells their stories, legends, and struggles through a myriad of persons, both real and imaginary.

Subjects: Peasant life; Legends and folk tales; Stream of consciousness
Place/Time: Italy—1900–1945

Canham, Marsha

203.
1. *The Pride of Lions.* Paperjacks, 1988.
2. *The Blood of Roses.* Paperjacks, 1989.

Beautiful Catherine Ashbrooke is forced by her father to marry the winner of a duel, Alexander Cameron. She must fight to win his love and to keep him safe when she discovers he is a Scottish spy during the Jacobite uprising of 1745.

Genre: Historical Romance
Subjects: Spies; Jacobites
Place/Time: Scotland—18th century

Canning, Victor

204.
1. *The Runaways.* Morrow, 1972.
2. *Flight of the Grey Goose.* Morrow, 1973.
3. *The Painted Tent.* Morrow, 1974.

Fifteen-year-old Smiler has run away from an English reform school. On the same night that he escapes, a cheetah escapes from Longleat, an animal refuge. When the cheetah dies, Smiler raises her cubs and returns them to Longleat. Still on the run, he goes to Scotland where he helps a wounded grey goose. He finally settles on a farm where a peregrine falcon becomes his companion.

Genre: Coming of Age
Subjects: Animals; Runaways; Teenagers
Place/Time: England—1945–1980; Scotland—1945–1980

Card, Orson Scott

205. Ender Wiggin
1. *Ender's Game.* Tor, 1985.
2. *Speaker for the Dead.* Tor, 1986.
3. *Xenocide.* Tor, 1991.
4. *Children of the Mind.* Tor, 1996.
5. *Ender's Shadow.* Tor, 1999.

Spanning thousands of years in the distant future are the stories of Andrew Wiggin, nicknamed Ender, trained to exterminate an alien race that is subsequently found to be misunderstood rather than hostile. Ender travels through the galaxy with a mission of preserving sentient species, such as the Pequeninas or Piggies and the descendants of the Hive Queen. As Ender ages, the children he created using his own mental powers and the very human artificial intelligence, Jane, continue his quest. The adventures of Bean, a child of the streets who is a product of genetic experimentation, become part of Ender's life when Bean's talents bring him to the Battle School of the Future.

Genre: Science Fiction
Subjects: Genocide; Extraterrestrial beings; Interplanetary wars

206. Homecoming
1. *Memory of Earth.* Tor, 1992.
2. *The Call of Earth.* Tor, 1993.
3. *The Ships of Earth.* Tor, 1994.
4. *Earthfall.* Tor, 1995.
5. *Earthborn.* Tor, 1995.

Colonists of the planet Harmony have long been governed peacefully by a computer they call Oversoul, but now Oversoul must encourage some responsible citizens to help it return to Earth for repairs. In the meantime, conflict breaks out on Harmony. Although Oversoul is failing, it attempts to guide the colonists through the desert to the ancient starships that can return to Earth. Conflict breaks out among the colonists before, during, and after their return to Earth, which they find populated by sentient beings evolved from bats and rats.

Genre: Science Fiction
Subjects: Space colonies; Computers

207. Tales of Alvin Maker
1. *Seventh Son.* Tor, 1987.
2. *Red Prophet.* Tor, 1988.
3. *Prentice Alvin.* Tor, 1989.
4. *Alvin Journeyman.* Tor, 1995.
5. *Heartfire.* Tor, 1998.

The seventh son of a seventh son, Alvin grows up in a frontier America full of the magic and spells of both red and white people, and also inhabited by runaway slaves and historical figures such as William Henry Harrison. Alvin shows promise of being a mysterious messiah, but as he grows, his existence is threatened by the dark power of the insidious Unmaker, who drives him from his home and into a set of circumstances that force him to stand trial for his life. Alvin continues to battle the forces of darkness as he opposes witch trials in New England while his wife works to abolish slavery in the South.

Genre: Fantasy
Subjects: Magic; Mysticism; Good and evil
Place/Time: United States—18th century; United States—19th century

Carlson, Melody

208. Whispering Pine
1. *A Place to Come Home To.* Harvest House, 1999.
2. *Everything I Long For.* Harvest House, 2000.

Maggie Carpenter and her son Spencer move to Pine Mountain, Oregon, where she becomes the editor of the town newspaper. She works to help the town rebuild after a major highway is rerouted. When Spencer discovers a runaway girl named Leah in the forest, Maggie helps her find her biological father, but their search upsets the town.

Genre: Christian Fiction
Subjects: Faith; Small town life; Family life
Place/Time: Oregon—1980–

Carr, Caleb

209.
1. *The Alienist.* Random, 1994.
2. *The Angel of Darkness.* Random, 1997.

In 1896, New York Police Commissioner Theodore Roosevelt brings in Dr. Laszlo Kreizler, a psychologist or alienist, and *Times* reporter John Moore to help him solve the gruesome murders of young boys who were prostitutes. Kreizler compiles a profile of the serial killer while Moore tours the city's underworld, trying to find the killer before he strikes again. Later the three search for a woman who has kidnapped an infant. When Clarence Darrow defends the woman, it is Kreizler who must prove she is a serial killer.

Genre: Crime Novel; Historical Fiction
Subjects: Serial murders; Psychologists; Roosevelt, Theodore, 1858–1919
Place/Time: New York (N. Y.)—19th century

Carr, Philippa. *Pseud. of* Eleanor Hibbert. *See also* Plaidy, Jean

210. Daughters of England
1. *The Miracle at St. Bruno's.* Putnam, 1972.
2. *The Lion Triumphant.* Putnam, 1974.
3. *The Witch from the Sea.* Putnam, 1975.
4. *Saraband for Two Sisters.* Putnam, 1976.
5. *Lament for a Lost Lover.* Putnam, 1977.
6. *The Love-Child.* Putnam, 1978.
7. *The Song of the Siren.* Putnam, 1980.
8. *Will You Love Me in September.* Putnam, 1981.
9. *The Adultress.* Putnam, 1982.
10. *Knave of Hearts.* Putnam, 1983.
11. *Voices in a Haunted Room.* Putnam, 1984.
12. *The Return of the Gypsy.* Putnam, 1985.
13. *Midsummer's Eve.* Putnam, 1986.
14. *The Pool of St. Branok.* Putnam, 1987.
15. *The Changeling.* Putnam, 1989.
16. *Black Swan.* Putnam, 1990.
17. *A Time for Silence.* Putnam, 1991.
18. *The Gossamer Cord.* Putnam, 1992.
19. *We'll Meet Again.* Putnam, 1993.

The multigenerational saga of the Cornish Farland family follows its women from Tudor times to the end of World War II. Each book is set against a background of historical controversy, often involving the religious wars of the 16th and 17th centuries and involves two women of the family who must fight sinister forces. Although the family continues through the novels, each story is separate and the books can be read independently.

Genre: Family Saga; Historical Fiction; Historical Romance
Subjects: Women
Place/Time: England—multicentury span

Carroll, James

211.
1. *Mortal Friends.* Little, 1978.
2. *The City Below.* Houghton Mifflin, 1994.

The city of Boston and its Irish residents are the focus of these novels, which trace two families from the 1920s to the 1980s. Coleman Brady joins the IRA in the 1920s, but when he is betrayed, he flees to Boston. There he becomes a politician and joins Mayor James Curley in helping mob leader Gennaro Anselmo. When his son Collin discovers the truth about his father, a tragedy occurs. The Doyle brothers come of age in the Boston of the 1960s and form new political alliances. Nick joins the mob while Terry becomes part of the John F. Kennedy Camelot. Each struggles to bend Boston to his will.

Genre: Historical Fiction
Subjects: Irish—United States; Irish Republican Army; Politics—Massachusetts; Fathers and sons; Brothers

Place/Time: Ireland—1900–1945; Boston (Mass.)—1900–1945; Boston (Mass.)—1945–1980; Massachusetts—1900–1945; Massachusetts—1945–1980

Carroll, Lewis. *Pseud. of* Charles Dodgson

212.
1. *Alice's Adventures in Wonderland.* Macmillan, 1865.
2. *Through the Looking-Glass, and What Alice Found There.* Macmillan, 1872.

While written to entertain children, both novels are filled with Carroll's jokes, games, puzzles, tricks, parodies, and chess moves. He tells the tale of a young girl who falls down a rabbit hole and has wondrous adventures in a magical Wonderland, a dreamlike place inhabited by the Mad Hatter, the Cheshire Cat, the Mock Turtle, and other fantastic characters.

Genre: Fantasy
Subjects: Girls; Imaginary kingdoms

Carver, Jeffrey A.

213. The Chaos Chronicles
1. *Neptune Crossing.* Tor, 1994.
2. *Strange Attractors.* Tor, 1995.
3. *The Infinite Sea.* Tor, 1996.

Stuck in an unfulfilling job on one of the planets of Neptune, John Bandicut is suddenly chosen by the alien Quarx to rescue Earth from a collision with an object still far away across the solar system. John must steal a spaceship and allow one of the Quarx to live in his mind. His mission takes him out among the stars and into the depths of an ocean planet where a mysterious force called the Maw of the Abyss threatens the undersea dwellers.

Genre: Science Fiction
Subjects: Extraterrestrial beings; Rescues; Life on other planets; Interplanetary voyages

Cary, Joyce

214.
1. *Herself Surprised.* Harper, 1948.
2. *To Be a Pilgrim.* Harper, 1949.
3. *The Horse's Mouth.* Harper, 1950.

Three people in turn-of-the-century London pursue happiness and each other in highly individual ways. Easygoing sensualist Sara Monday, aristocratic lawyer Wilcher, and artist-rebel Gully Jimson each narrate one book as they interact with each other with comedy and sorrow.

Subjects: Bohemianism; Law and lawyers; Artists
Place/Time: London (England)—1900–1945; England—1900–1945

215.
1. *Prisoner of Grace.* Harper, 1952.
2. *Except the Lord.* Harper, 1953.
3. *Not Honour More.* Harper, 1955.

The world of Chester Nimmo, liberal politician, is depicted by himself, his wife Nina, and Captain Jim Latter, Nina's first love, second husband, and the third point of a 30-year-old triangle. The story begins in the first quarter of the 1900s and ends with England's general strike as the three relate the same story from different points of view.

Genre: Historical Fiction
Subjects: Politics—England; Love affairs
Place/Time: England—1900–1945

Castle, Jayne. *Pseud. of* Jayne Ann Krentz

216.
1. *Amaryllis.* Pocket Star, 1996.
2. *Zinnia.* Pocket Star, 1997.
3. *Orchid.* Pocket Star, 1998.

On the world of St. Helens, a planet colonized by earthlings, but cut off from contact with Earth, nearly the entire population has some psychic ability. To help with problem solving and even criminal investigation, experts called prisms are employed to help their clients focus this talent. Amaryllis assists in a corporate security investigation. Prism Zinnia helps a casino owner find a missing journal and a murderer. A businessman hires Orchid to utilize his ability to prevent a corporate takeover. Since the prism must work quite closely with her client, romance is a likely by-product of the relationship.

Genre: Science Fiction; Romance
Subjects: Extrasensory perception; Space colonies; Life on other planets; Love

Cavanaugh, Jack

217. American Family Portrait Series
1. *The Puritans.* Chariot Victor, 1994.
2. *The Colonists.* Chariot Victor, 1995.
3. *The Patriots.* Chariot Victor, 1996.
4. *The Adversaries.* Chariot Victor, 1996.
5. *The Pioneers.* Chariot Victor, 1996.
6. *The Allies.* Chariot Victor, 1997.
7. *The Victors.* Chariot Victor, 1998.
8. *The Peacemakers.* Chariot Victor, 1999.

From the Puritan Revolution in England to the War in Vietnam, each generation of the Morgan family faces the challenges of a changing America with strong Christian faith. Young Drew Morgan starts the family when he flees England and comes to America with the Puritans. His descendants fight on both sides of the American Revolution and the Civil War, and only faith holds the family together. Sons of later generations move West, fight in World War I and II, and face the

challenges of the 1960s and Vietnam. Each generation uses their devotion to face the problems of the times.

Genre: Christian Fiction; Family Saga
Subjects: Family life; Faith; War
Place/Time: United States—19th century; United States—1900–1945; United States—1945–1980

Cecil, Henry. *Pseud. of* Henry Cecil Leon

218.
1. *Brothers-in-Law.* Harper, 1955.
2. *Friends at Court.* Harper, 1957.
3. *Sober as a Judge.* Harper, 1958.

At 21, Roger Thursby becomes a law student in London, but his life is never usual. Somehow he is always involved with impossible witnesses and even more difficult family members. Eventually he becomes a High Court Judge with heavy responsibilities, but his friends get him involved in funny adventures.

Genre: Humor
Subjects: Law and lawyers; Trials
Place/Time: London (England)—1945–1980; England—1945–1980

Celine, Louis-Ferdinand. *Pseud. of* Louis-Ferdinand Destouches

219.
1. *North.* Delacorte, 1960.
2. *Castle to Castle.* Delacorte, 1968, 1957.
3. *Rigadoon.* Delacorte, 1974, 1969.

Destouches, alias Celine, though considered a major 20th-century writer, lived the later part of his life in France under a cloud, accused of collaborating with the Nazis. This semi-autobiographical trilogy is his response—the fragmentary, surrealistic account of his horrible and outrageously funny wartime experiences shared by his actress wife, their dog, and a theatrical friend.

Genre: War
Subjects: Autobiographical stories; World War II, 1939–1945; Surrealism; War
Place/Time: France—1900–1945

Cendrars, Blaise

220.
1. *Dan Yack.* Michael Kesend, 1987, 1929.
2. *Confessions of Dan Yack.* Peter Owen, 1990, 1929.

After an affair goes bad, English millionaire Dan Yack indulges his wanderlust and travels to Antarctica with his guests—a poet, a musician, and a sculptor. When they die, Yack eats and waits to be rescued. After further surreal adventures, he meets the daughter of an old mistress and marries her, but no matter what he does to please her, she still dies. Yack's strange journeys are a metaphor of the world's instability written in a literary cubist style.

Subjects: Millionaires; Survival (after airplane crashes, accidents, shipwrecks, etc.); Travel; Surrealism
Place/Time: Antarctic regions—1900–1945; England—1900–1945

Chadwick, Elizabeth

221.
1. *The Wild Hunt.* St. Martin's, 1991.
2. *The Running Vixen.* St. Martin's, 1992.
3. *The Leopard Unleashed.* St. Martin's, 1993.

Medieval Wales from 1098 to 1200 is the setting for this historical romance featuring three generations of star-crossed lovers. Judith of Ravenstow is married to Guyon, Lord of Ledworth, when she is 15. Guy must not only woo his bride, but fight feudal lords for King Henry I. Their daughter, Heulwen, and her love, Adam de Lacey, will help Henry's daughter Matilda, while their grandson, Renard, will continue fighting Norman and Welsh lords and love another spunky Welsh lass.

Genre: Family Saga; Historical Romance
Subjects: Courts and courtiers; Middle Ages; Feudalism
Place/Time: Wales—11th century; Wales—12th century

Chaikin, Linda

222. The Buccaneers Series
1. *Port Royal.* Moody Press, 1996.
2. *The Pirate and His Lady.* Moody Press, 1997.

In 18th-century Jamaica, Emerald Harwick works at a Christian school and plans to run away and marry the man she loves, indentured servant Baret. She has to keep her plans from her brutal father who has his own plans for Emerald. As Emerald and Baret try to escape the island, they are drawn into a pirate war over buried treasure. As the battle rages, Emerald has to fight for the man she loves.

Genre: Christian Fiction; Historical Romance
Subjects: Christian life; Faith; Pirates; Lovers
Place/Time: Jamaica—18th century

223. The Great Northwest
1. *The Empire Builders.* Bethany House, 1994.
2. *Winds of Allegiance.* Bethany House, 1996.

In the 1830s and 40s, settlers from America, England, and Russia settle in the Pacific Northwest and fight to conquer the land. Lumbermen, farmers, and adventurers try to claim the wealth of the territory, but come into conflict with each other. As the groups struggle, the fate of the land lies with independent people who stand by their integrity and hope.

Genre: Christian Fiction
Subjects: Faith; Frontier and pioneer life
Place/Time: Oregon—19th century

224. Heart of India
1. *Silk.* Bethany House, 1993.
2. *Under the Eastern Stars.* Bethany House, 1993.
3. *Kingscote.* Bethany House, 1993.

In the late 1700s under the surface of exotic India lay strong undercurrents of racial, religious, and political unrest. Coral Kendall, heiress to a silk plantation, confronts its values when she adopts an orphaned boy at the bottom of the rigid Hindu caste system. He is later abducted by Indian soldiers, and she struggles to find him. Coral then begins a school for the children of untouchables and thereby brings down the wrath of Sir Hugo Roxbury. Coral also must decide which of her two suitors she loves—adventurous Major Buckley or handsome Dr. Ethan Boswell.

Genre: Christian Fiction; Historical Fiction; Historical Romance
Subjects: Cultural conflict; Faith; Christian life
Place/Time: India—18th century

225. The Royal Pavilions
1. *Swords and Scimitars.* Bethany House, 1996.
2. *Golden Palaces.* Bethany House, 1996.
3. *Behind the Veil.* Bethany House, 1998.

During the Crusades, Norman knight Tancred Redwan rescues Helena, a beautiful Greek heiress, from western barbarians, but Helena faces more perils from the powerful Lysander family. The Lysanders betrayed her mother and now have given Helena to a Moslem prince. While in the palace of Prince Kalid in Moslem-controlled Antioch, Helena finds portions of the New Testament written by the apostle Paul. Helena discovers her faith and her love for Tancred as he rescues her, and they fight to flee the city.

Genre: Christian Fiction; Historical Romance
Subjects: Crusades; Knights and Knighthood; Faith; Middle Ages; Muslims; Love
Place/Time: Middle East—12th century

226. Trade Winds Series
1. *Captive Heart.* Harvest House, 1998.
2. *Silver Dreams.* Harvest House, 1998.
3. *Island Bride.* Harvest House, 1999.

In the late 1600s, the European nobility who live in Jamaica must battle buccaneers, pirates, and the Spanish. Lady Amber Buckington falls in love with French buccaneer Captain Marc Dubrett while Lady Devora Ashby is pledged to a Spanish don but loves another. English Captain Bruce Hawkins fights the Spanish to free Protestant prisoners and Inca Indians. All find that faith in God helps protect them from evil and brings them love.

Genre: Christian Fiction
Subjects: Faith; Pirates; Adventure
Place/Time: Caribbean region—17th century

Chalker, Jack

227. Changewinds
1. *When the Changewinds Blow.* Ace, 1987.
2. *Riders of the Winds.* Ace, 1988.
3. *War of the Maelstrom.* Ace, 1988.

From their existence as rather ordinary teenage girls, Sam and Charley are magically whisked off to Akalar, a world where the Changewinds, powerful gales controlled by rival sorcerers, might change a human into a beast. Sam and Charley get caught up in the magical battle between Klittichorn and Boolean and learn a good deal about themselves and each other.

Genre: Fantasy
Subjects: Teenagers; Winds; Imaginary wars and battles

228. The Dancing Gods
1. *The River of the Dancing Gods.* Ballantine, 1984.
2. *Demons of the Dancing Gods.* Ballantine, 1984.
3. *Vengeance of the Dancing Gods.* Ballantine, 1985.
4. *Songs of the Dancing Gods.* Ballantine, 1990.
5. *Horrors of the Dancing Gods.* Ballantine, 1995.

In the real world, Jack and Marge are destined to live only a few more minutes, but Ruddygore the sorcerer ferries them across the Sea of Dreams to Husaquahr, a magical land bordered by the River of the Dancing Gods. Once there, Jack becomes a warrior hero, and Marge discovers her magical powers, but they must engage in an ongoing battle against the evil of the charismatic Dark Baron and his minions.

Genre: Fantasy
Subjects: Rescues; Imaginary kingdoms; Imaginary wars and battles; Good and evil

229. The Quintara Marathon
1. *The Demons at Rainbow Bridge.* Ace, 1989.
2. *The Ninety Trillion Fausts.* Ace, 1991.
3. *The Run to Chaos Keep.* Ace, 1991.

In a galaxy ruled by three empires—The Exchange, the Mizlaplan, and the Mycohl—demons are discovered existing in a state of suspended animation. Once freed, the demons try to dominate the galaxy, but the threat unites the three empires against them.

Genre: Science Fiction
Subjects: Demonology; Interplanetary wars

230. Well World
1. *Midnight at the Well of Souls.* Ballantine, 1977.
2. *Exiles at the Well of Souls.* Ballantine, 1978.
3. *Quest for the Well of Souls.* Ballantine, 1978.
4. *The Return of Nathan Brazil.* Ballantine, 1979.
5. *Twilight at the Well of Souls.* Ballantine, 1980.
6. *Echoes of the Well of Souls.* Ballantine, 1993.
7. *Shadow of the Well of Souls.* Ballantine, 1994.
8. *Gods of the Well of Souls.* Ballantine, 1994.

Well World, a composite of interlocking realities created by ancient aliens, contains an all-powerful computer that controls events in the universe. The immortal Nathan Brazil and Mavra Chang have had a series of adventures in Well World and have returned to Earth. The last three works of the series form a trilogy that chronicles the experiences of the two after they are summoned back to Well World by what appears to be a meteor. Strange occurrences and mutations on Earth and difficulties that the two have in reaching Well World are symptoms of the insidious influence of the mysterious creature Kraang on the evolution of the universe.

Genre: Science Fiction
Subjects: Extraterrestrial beings; Computers; Immortality; Universe

231. Wonderland Gambit
1. *The Cybernetic Walrus.* Ballantine, 1995.
2. *The March Hare Network.* Ballantine, 1996.
3. *The Hot Wired Dodo.* Ballantine, 1997.

Cory Maddox's patent on a revolutionary computer system seems about to make him a wealthy man, but a corporate takeover ends his dream. A computer project involving virtual reality seems to be an attractive employment prospect, even though the originator Matthew Brand disappeared under mysterious circumstances. Gradually Cory realizes that what he is working on is not virtual reality, but the nature of reality itself. He begins to recall a previous life and is locked into a series of computer generated reincarnations from which only the missing Matthew Brand can supply an escape.

Genre: Science Fiction
Subjects: Computers; Reincarnation; Technology and civilization

Chamberlin, Ann

232.
1. *Sofia.* Forge, 1996.
2. *The Sultan's Daughter.* Forge, 1997.
3. *The Reign of Favored Women.* Forge, 1998.

Sofia Baffo, the beautiful daughter of the governor of Corfu, is in a convent in Venice when she is sent home to marry. On the voyage home, her ship is captured by Turks, and Sofia and sailor Giorgio Veniero are captured. In Constantinople, Sofia is sold into the Sultan's harem, while Giorgio is castrated and sold to the Sultan as a eunuch. In the harem Sofia uses her wiles to become the lover of Sultan Murad and the mother of his only son. Giorgio protects the Sultan's sister Esmikhan as she tries to bear a child. Infidelity, intrigue, and passion complicate all their lives as they struggle for power and love.

Genre: Historical Fiction
Subjects: Courts and courtiers; Women; Sex; Turks
Place/Time: Turkey—16th century

Charnas, Suzy McKee

233.
1. *Walk to the End of the World.* Ballantine, 1974.
2. *Motherlines.* Berkley, 1979.
3. *The Furies.* St. Martin's, 1994.
4. *The Conqueror's Child.* Tom Doherty Assoc., 1999.

Alldera escapes Holdfast, a male-dominated enclave where women are treated as slaves and are held responsible for a devastating nuclear holocaust that has left society at a barbaric level. She makes her home on the open plain outside of Holdfast with a society of amazons, who mate with horses and, although primitive in many ways, give her a sense of self-respect. However, she and her women companions decide to return to Holdfast and free their sisters from slavery. The focus of the tales changes to Alldera's daughter Sorrel, who was left in a community of women while her mother waged war on Holdfast. On her journey to be reunited with her mother, Sorrel brings with her an orphaned boy whom she has adopted, but whose fate will be unknown in a society where men are newly conquered slaves.

Genre: Science Fiction
Subjects: Nuclear warfare; Amazons; Sex discrimination

Chase, Loretta

234.
1. *Lord of the Scoundrels.* Avon, 1995.
2. *The Last Hellion.* Avon, 1998.

The "Mallory Hellions" Vere and Dain are both tall, dark, and handsome lords who are also egotistical. They meet their match in the arms of sensuous and headstrong ladies. The give and take of Regency era romance is wittily portrayed through four strong characters who learn that love is not predictable.

Genre: Historical Romance
Subjects: Romance; Courtship
Place/Time: England—18th century

Chase-Riboud, Barbara

235.
1. *Sally Hemings.* Viking, 1979.
2. *The President's Daughter.* Crown, 1994.

Did Thomas Jefferson have an affair with his mulatto slave Sally Hemings? Through flashbacks, Sally tells her story to a young census taker. She recounts her life with Jefferson at Monticello and in Paris. She loves him and bears him seven children, but is disillusioned when he refuses to free her from slavery. Their daughter Harriet leaves Monticello when she turns 21. With her white skin, red hair, and green eyes, she passes as white in New York, London, and Paris, but always feels she is living a lie.

Genre: Historical Fiction
Subjects: African Americans; Slavery; Love affairs; Mothers and daughters; Jefferson, Thomas, 1743–1826
Place/Time: Virginia—18th century; Virginia—19th century

Cheever, John

236.
1. *The Wapshot Chronicle.* Harper & Row, 1957.
2. *The Wapshot Scandal.* Harper & Row, 1964.

In this satirical chronicle spanning the 17th to the 20th century, the fortunes of the Wapshot family of St. Botolphs in New England decline, rise, and decline as Captain Leander Wapshot tries to keep his ferry boat. His sons will inherit their aunt's money if they marry and produce heirs, but they are frequently in hot water no matter what they try.

Subjects: Satire; Family life
Place/Time: New England—multicentury span

Cherry, Carolyn Janice. *See* Cherryh, C. J.

Cherryh, C. J. *Pseud. of* Carolyn Janice Cherry

237.
1. *Rider at the Gate.* Warner, 1995.
2. *Cloud's Rider.* Warner, 1996.

A group of stranded space colonists struggle to survive on a planet that, although rich in natural resources, is inhabited by telepathic wildlife who are capable of invading the human mind. Madness is the result of these telepathic invasions. The colonists' sole protection in this threatening land is the bond between certain humans and Nighthorses, powerful creatures who choose their human companions, but may themselves be influenced by violence and go rogue. Always lurking in the background is a still more powerful mysterious force than the known dangers, which the colonists have already faced.

Genre: Science Fiction
Subjects: Life on other planets; Animals; Horses; Telepathy

238.
1. *Foreigner: A Novel of First Contact.* DAW Books, 1994.
2. *Invader.* DAW Books, 1995.
3. *Inheritor.* DAW Books, 1996.

Marooned on the planet of the alien atevi, a group of colonists establishes an uneasy relationship with the aboriginal population by living on an island and relying on the atevi's interest in human technology and the diplomatic skills of their own ambassador to protect them from the atevi power structure in which assassination is registered and accepted as a logical solution to political disagreements. The return of the colonists' spaceship, which had mysteriously disappeared, and a split into factions of the human colony threaten the delicate balance that had been preserved by the human representative Bren Cameron. *Note:* The saga of the marooned colonists continues in a projected trilogy beginning with *Precursor*.

Genre: Science Fiction
Subjects: Space colonies; Extraterrestrial beings; Assassination

239.
1. *Precursor.* Penguin, 1999.

Taking up the narrative three years after the events of the *Foreigner* series, this projected trilogy begins with the return of the spaceship Phoenix to the colonists marooned on the planet of the atevi. Bren Cameron handles negotiations between the humans and atevi which are made more difficult by an alien invasion. *Note:* This series follows the Foreigner series.

Genre: Science Fiction
Subjects: Space colonies; Extraterrestrial beings; Spaceships

240.
1. *Fortress in the Eye of Time.* HarperPrism, 1995.
2. *Fortress of Eagles.* HarperPrism, 1998.
3. *Fortress of Owls.* HarperPrism, 1999.

The young man Tristen is a magical being brought to life by the wizard Mauryl to right ancient wrongs in the kingdom. Learning about living in the world as he travels, he journeys to the court of the young King Cefwyn and becomes involved in court intrigue. Tristen meets resistance when he becomes Duke of Amefel and must use his magic sword to defend the interests of his young king.

Genre: Fantasy
Subjects: Imaginary kingdoms; Good and evil; Magic; Courts and courtiers

241. The Book of Morgraine
1. *Gate of Ivrel.* DAW Books, 1976.
2. *Well of Shiuan.* DAW Books, 1978.
3. *Fires of Azeroth.* DAW Books, 1979.
   The above titles have also been published in the following collection: *The Book of Morgraine.* Doubleday, 1979.
4. *Exile's Gate.* DAW Books, 1988.

A series of time travel gates built by the alien qual have disrupted human life. The powerful Morgraine sets out to restore order by closing the gates and, with her magical sword, battling over the master gate.

Genre: Fantasy; Science Fiction
Subjects: Imaginary wars and battles; Time travel; Arms and armor

242. Chanur
1. *The Pride of Chanur.* DAW Books, 1982.
2. *Chanur's Venture.* Phantasia Press, 1984.
3. *The Kif Strikes Back.* Phantasia Press, 1985.
4. *Chanur's Homecoming.* DAW Books, 1986.
5. *Chanur's Legacy: A Novel of Compact Space.* DAW Books, 1992.

The Chanurs, a family of catlike sentient beings called hani, travel through space in a series of adventures that include rescuing a human from the evil, blood-thirsty kif and dealing with the Compact, an uneasy galactic trade alliance that brings together a variety of species that think and act quite differently.

Genre: Science Fiction
Subjects: Mythical animals; Interplanetary voyages; Good and evil

243. Ealdwood
1. *The Dreamstone.* DAW Books, 1983.
2. *The Tree of Swords and Jewels.* DAW Books, 1983.

Ealdwood, a magical woodland world, exists side by side with the violent world of men. The borders are seldom crossed, but Arafel the Sidhe, the Lady of Trees, ventures across and discovers Ciaran Cuilean, an elfish descendant living among men. Searching for his magical weapons and his own kind, Ciaran then crosses back into Ealdwood.

Genre: Fantasy
Subjects: Imaginary kingdoms; Forests and forestry; Magic

244. The Faded Sun
1. *The Faded Sun: Kesrith.* DAW Books, 1978.
2. *The Faded Sun: Shon'Jir.* DAW Books, 1979.
3. *The Faded Sun: Kutath.* DAW Books, 1980.

When the mri, mercenary subjects of the powerful female ruler Melein, are all but destroyed on the planet Kesrith, she sets out with her brother Niun and the human warrior Sten Duncan to find the original mri planet Kutath. Meilein establishes herself as ruler of the nomadic remnant of her people. Duncan, who has undergone a difficult transition to mri life, serves as link to the planet's other cultures.

Genre: Science Fiction
Subjects: Life on other planets; Women; Brothers and sisters; Nomads

245. Rusalka
1. *Rusalka.* Ballantine, 1989.
2. *Chernevog.* Ballantine, 1990.
3. *Yvgenie.* Ballantine, 1991.

In an ancient Russian forest, Eveshka is restored to life from her state as a destructive haunting spirit called a rusalka. She marries her mortal love Pyetr, but soon discovers that she, her husband, and their daughter must still contend with the dark powers of Chernevog, the wizard who killed her and turned her into a ghost.

Genre: Fantasy
Subjects: Ghost stories; Love; Witchcraft

Chesney, Marion

246. The Daughters of Mannerling
1. *The Banishment.* St. Martin's, 1995.
2. *The Intrigue.* St. Martin's, 1995.
3. *The Deception.* St. Martin's, 1996.
4. *The Folly.* St. Martin's, 1996.
5. *The Romance.* St. Martin's, 1997.
6. *The Homecoming.* St. Martin's, 1997.

On the splendid estate of Mannerling, Sir William Beverley, his wife, and their six beautiful daughters live the luxurious life of money, servants, and lavish balls until Sir William gambles it all away. Forced to move into a small house, the daughters have to learn to cook, sew, and take care of themselves. Each vows to win back her home by marrying the new lord of Mannerling, but love intervenes as each daughter tries to reclaim the estate. Each daughter marries for love until the youngest finally snags both the lord and love.

Genre: Historical Romance
Subjects: Sisters; Marriage; Romance
Place/Time: England—18th century

247. House for the Seasons
1. *The Miser of Mayfair.* St. Martin's, 1986.
2. *Plain Jane.* St. Martin's, 1986.
3. *The Wicked Godmother.* St. Martin's, 1987.
4. *Rake's Progress.* St. Martin's, 1987.
5. *The Adventuress.* St. Martin's, 1987.
6. *Rainbird's Revenge.* St. Martin's, 1988.

In Regency England, the house at 67 Clarges Street in London's fashionable Mayfair is rented out each season by various ladies who hope to find a husband. The servants, led by Mr. Rainbird, the butler, keep the house going and quietly work to help the ladies marry their loves. At the same time, the servants work to save their wages so they can buy their own inn and be independent. This is one of the few Regency Romances in which the servants play as important a role as the lovers.

Genre: Historical Romance
Subjects: Houses; Servants
Place/Time: England—19th century

248. The Poor Relations Series
1. *Lady Fortescue Steps Out.* St. Martin's, 1992.
2. *Miss Tonks Turns to Crime.* St. Martin's, 1993.
3. *Sir Philip's Folly.* St. Martin's, 1993.
4. *Mrs. Budley Falls from Grace.* St. Martin's, 1993.
5. *Colonel Sandhurst to the Rescue.* St. Martin's, 1994.
6. *Back in Society.* St. Martin's, 1994.

In Regency England, the Poor Relations is a London hotel very popular with the nobility because it is run by nobility who are down on their luck. Lady Fortescue, widowed and poor, opens her home as a hotel in order to live. She invites other poor aristocrats to join her. Each of the zany characters has humorous adventures as they try to keep the hotel going, and each finds romance along the way.

Genre: Historical Romance
Subjects: Hotels, taverns, etc.
Place/Time: England—19th century

249. School for Manners
1. *Refining Felicity.* St. Martin's, 1988.
2. *Perfecting Fiona.* St. Martin's, 1989.
3. *Enlightening Delilah.* St. Martin's, 1989.
4. *Finessing Clarissa.* St. Martin's, 1989.
5. *Animating Maria.* St. Martin's, 1990.
6. *Marrying Harriet.* St. Martin's, 1990.

The Tribble sisters, Effy and Amy, are society spinsters who have fallen on hard times. To make ends meet they groom young English ladies in the social graces so they can win acceptance in society and make good marriages. From Felicity to Harriet, each girl has her own delightful problem that the ever-diligent sisters must solve. Although sometimes the problem is not the girl but her parents, all ends well—even for the Tribbles.

Genre: Historical Romance
Subjects: Sisters; Society novels; Marriage brokers
Place/Time: England—19th century

250. Six Sisters
1. *Minerva.* St. Martin's, 1983.
2. *The Taming of Annabelle.* St. Martin's, 1983.
3. *Deidre and Desire.* St. Martin's, 1984.
4. *Daphne.* St. Martin's, 1984.
5. *Diana the Huntress.* St. Martin's, 1985.
6. *Frederica in Fashion.* St. Martin's, 1985.

In this Regency Romance series, the Reverend Armitage, in need of funds to finance his passion for the hunt, plans to marry his six beautiful and lively daughters to wealthy lords. How each sister snares her man and outdoes her sisters is lighthearted fun.

Genre: Historical Romance
Subjects: Sisters; Marriage
Place/Time: England—19th century

251. Traveling Matchmaker Series
1. *Emily Goes to Exeter.* St. Martin's, 1990.
2. *Belinda Goes to Bath.* St. Martin's, 1991.
3. *Penelope Goes to Portsmouth.* St. Martin's, 1991.
4. *Beatrice Goes to Brighton.* St. Martin's, 1991.
5. *Deborah Goes to Dover.* St. Martin's, 1992.
6. *Yvonne Goes to New York.* St. Martin's, 1992.

In 1800, when her late employer leaves her a legacy, Hannah Pym ends her career as a housekeeper for a life of travel and adventure on England's stagecoaches. With each trip, the adventurous Hannah meets numerous damsels in distress. Of course, there are innumerable problems to overcome, but the intrepid Miss Pym brings everyone to a happy ending—including herself.

Genre: Historical Romance
Subjects: Marriage brokers; Travel
Place/Time: England—19th century

Chiaverini, Jennifer

252.
1. *The Quilter's Apprentice.* Simon & Schuster, 1999.
2. *Round Robin.* Simon & Schuster, 2000.

When Sarah McClure and her husband move to Waterford, Pennsylvania, Sarah looks for a job and finally takes one helping elderly Sylvia Compson prepare her estate for sale. As Sarah helps her, Sylvia teaches her how to quilt. Over the quilting lessons, Sarah learns about Sylvia's family and is forced to face her own relationship with her mother. Sarah and Sylvia then decide to set up a quilting school from Sylvia's estate. The quilters work on a round robin quilt for Sylvia, and, as they work, they reveal their lives and problems with mothers, husbands, and children.

Subjects: Women; Quilts; Old age
Place/Time: Pennsylvania—1980–

Churchill, Winston

253.
1. *Richard Carvel.* Macmillan, 1899.
2. *The Crisis.* Macmillan, 1901.

Richard Carvel grows up in Maryland before the American Revolution. He fights with John Paul Jones during the battle between the "Bonhomme Richard" and "Serapis." His descendant, Virginia, is involved with the abolitionists, southern gentlemen, Confederate spies, and finally, a Union officer she loves and marries.

Genre: Historical Fiction; War
Subjects: United States—revolution, 1775–1783; Naval battles; Jones, John Paul, 1747–1792
Place/Time: Maryland—18th century; Maryland—19th century

Chute, Carolyn

254.
1. *The Beans of Egypt, Maine.* Ticknor & Fields, 1985.
2. *Letourneau's Used Auto Parts.* Ticknor & Fields, 1988.
3. *Merry Men.* Harcourt Brace, 1994.

The Beans of Egypt, Maine, are a dirt poor family who live in squalor in the backwoods. Earlene Pomerleau marries into the family and finds herself overcome by their poverty. Only a bit more enterprising are members of another clan, the Letourneaus, who work in the junkyard, but still lead lives just as dead-end as the Beans. The poor characters bring to life contemporary rural Maine.

Subjects: Poverty; Country life; New England
Place/Time: Maine—1980–

Claremont, Chris *and* Lucas, George

255.
1. *Shadow Moon.* Bantam, 1995.
2. *Shadow Dawn.* Bantam, 1997.
3. *Shadow Star.* Bantam, 1999.

This series begins with the adventures of the central character of the film *Willow.* The sorcerer Willow Ufgood is the godfather of Princess Elora, whose rule is threatened by evil forces. As the Shadow power grows, Elora accidentally unleashes an elemental force while learning magic. Soon Elora must face the fact that the leader of the sinister attackers, the Deceiver, may be her own dark twin.

Genre: Fantasy
Subjects: Imaginary kingdoms; Good and evil; Princesses; Imaginary wars and battles; Twins

Clarke, Arthur C. *See also* Preuss, Paul *and* Lee, Gentry

256.
1. *2001: A Space Odyssey.* New American Library, 1968.
2. *2010: Odyssey Two.* Ballantine, 1982.
3. *2061: Odyssey Three.* Ballantine, 1988.
4. *3001: The Final Odyssey.* Ballantine, 1997.

In collaboration with Stanley Kubrick, Clarke developed the screenplay for the landmark film *2001: A Space Odyssey* from his short story "The Sentinel" and actually wrote the full- length novel following the film. Space exploration takes on a mystical significance in this science fiction classic and its sequels. On a mission to Saturn, astronaut David Bowman almost becomes a victim of HAL, the spaceship computer, who seems to have developed an evil, vindictive personality. Bowman is propelled into deep space, encounters mysterious monoliths, and is reborn in a different form. In the sequels, space scientist Heywood Floyt sets off with an expedition to determine the fate of David Bowman and his spaceship *Discovery.* He encounters the transformed Bowman, the computer HAL, and the powerful monoliths. In the final work, Frank Poole, Bowman's fellow astronaut on the original mission who was presumed dead, is discovered alive drifting in space. Frank attempts to contact Bowman's mystical new consciousness.

Genre: Science Fiction

Subjects: Outer space, exploration of; Astronauts;
Computers

257. Mad Mind

1. *Against the Fall of Night.* Gnome, 1953. This
   title was revised as *The City and the Stars.*
   Harcourt Brace, 1956.)
2. *Beyond the Fall of Night.* (Written with
   Gregory Benford.)

The above titles were also published by Putnam
as a collection in a 1990.

In the far distant future, man has achieved immortality
but abandoned space travel after a galactic civilization
created and imprisoned a threatening force know as the
Mad Mind. Alvin, the only child in the last city on
Earth, breaks free of his beautiful, but confining culture to venture into space and encounter the Mad Mind.

Genre: Science Fiction
Subjects: Boys; Imaginary cities; Good and evil;
Space flight

258. Rama

1. *Rendezvous with Rama.* Harcourt Brace,
   1973.
2. *Rama II.* (Written with Gentry Lee) Bantam,
   1989.
3. *The Garden of Rama.* (Written with Gentry
   Lee) Bantam, 1991.
4. *Rama Revealed.* (Written with Gentry Lee)
   Bantam, 1994.

Since the Ramans do everything in threes, the huge,
technologically advanced and apparently empty
spaceship that comes toward Earth in the 22nd century
seems likely to return, and it does years later. With
three cosmonauts trapped aboard, the ship withstands
Earth's nuclear attack; reaches a Raman station; and
returns again with room for more human passengers
and, as a consequence, more trouble. On board the
spaceship, a dictatorial society that threatens the life of
Nicole, the former governor, develops. With the help
of her husband and a band of robots she escapes into
the strange environments of Rama, which are outside
the area inhabited by the colonists. *Note:* Coauthor
Gentry Lee has written a related series that takes place
in the Rama universe.

Genre: Science Fiction
Subjects: Spaceships; Space colonies; Extraterrestrial beings; Totalitarianism

Clavell, James

259.

1. *Shogun.* Atheneum, 1975.
2. *Tai-Pan: A Novel of Hong Kong.* Atheneum,
   1966.
3. *Gai-Jin.* Delacorte, 1993.
4. *Noble House.* Delacorte, 1981.
5. *Whirlwind.* Morrow, 1986.

This monumental saga—over 5,000 pages in five novels—depicts the clash of Asian and English culture

from the opening of Japan in 1600 to the fall of the
Shah of Iran in 1979. Clavell did not write the novels in
chronological order; instead he jumped back and forth
in time as he tells the story of the founding of Noble
House, the leading Hong Kong trading house, and its
Tai-Pan, Supreme leader, Dirk Struan, and his descendants. Grandson Mark enters Japan in 1862 and fights
Yoshi Toranaga, a descendant of Toranaga, the feudal
lord in *Shogun.* Both Struan and Toranaga's descendants meet again in *Whirlwind,* when they fight for oil
and gas concessions in Iran. Ruthless rivalries for position, power, money, and love propel all the leaders of
Noble House.

Genre: Family Saga; Historical Fiction
Subjects: Cultural conflict; Businessmen; Wealth;
Adventure; Business—unscrupulous methods
Place/Time: Hong Kong—multicentury span; Ja-
pan—multicentury span; Iran—multicentury span

Clayton, Jo

260. Drums of Chaos

1. *Drum Warning.* Tor, 1997.
2. *Drum Calls.* Tor, 1998.

Two worlds, Iomard and Glandair, have a powerful
connecting force called the Pneuma, which intensifies
as they come close together, producing an event called
the Settling or Corruption. According to tradition, as
the Settling approaches, a young hero will appear who
can control and channel the force that could destroy
both worlds. Cymel, a young woman who possesses
magical gifts, becomes the protector of Lyanz, who
may be the hero, but is opposed by powerful mages
who want to use the Pneuma for their own purposes.

Genre: Fantasy
Subjects: Heroes; Good and evil; Magic

Clemens, James

261. The Banned and the Banished

1. *Wit'ch Fire.* Ballantine, 1999.
2. *Wit'ch Storm.* Ballantine, 1999.

Elena lives a peaceful rural existence unaware that she
is the reincarnation of a powerful sorceress whose
skills will be essential to defeat the evil spirit called the
Dark One who is trying to seize power. Just as Elena is
beginning to sense her abilities the Dark One and his
followers try to capture her. Having eluded his
clutches, Elena and her companions set out to recover
the Blood Diary, a book endowed with potent magic
that could be the key to vanquishing the Dark One.

Genre: Fantasy
Subjects: Good and evil; Imaginary wars and battles;
Reincarnation; Magic

Clement, Hal

262. Mesklin

1. *Mission of Gravity*. Doubleday, 1954.
2. *Star Light*. Ballantine, 1971.

Since Mesklin is a planet with many times the gravitational pull of Earth, its own caterpillar-like inhabitants must retrieve an Earth space probe that lands there. The Mesklinite leader Barlennan emerges as a hero who goes on a mission of assistance to humans on the strange, enormous, heavy gravity planet Dhrawn.

Genre: Science Fiction
Subjects: Life on other planets; Space probes; Gravitation

263. Needle

1. *Needle*. Doubleday, 1950. (Alternate title: *From Outer Space*. Avon, 1957)
2. *Through the Eye of the Needle*. Ballantine, 1978.

The Hunter, an alien creature capable of assuming a variety of forms but most commonly existing as a parasite or symbiont, comes to Earth in search of a criminal. To carry out his plans, he enters the body of a young boy with whom he becomes good friends. When the symbiotic relationship begins to weaken the young man, the Hunter must seek help from his own race.

Genre: Science Fiction
Subjects: Boys; Extraterrestrial beings; Parasites

Cloete, Stuart

264.

1. *The Turning Wheels*. Houghton Mifflin, 1937.
2. *Watch for the Dawn*. Houghton Mifflin, 1939.
3. *The Hill of Doves*. Houghton Mifflin, 1941.
4. *The Mask*. Houghton Mifflin, 1957.

The Vander Berg family flees English South Africa and goes with the Boers on the Great Trek into the Transvaal. The novels graphically describe the Boer settlements and their inhabitants' hardships and loves from 1815 to 1880.

Genre: Historical Fiction
Subjects: Afrikaners; Farm life; Frontier and pioneer life
Place/Time: South Africa—19th century

Closs, Hannah

265.

1. *High Are the Mountains*. Vanguard Press, 1959.
2. *Deep Are the Valleys*. Vanguard Press, 1960.
3. *The Silent Tarn*. Vanguard Press, 1963.

The setting is 13th-century France, a feudal world torn by social, political, and religious upheavals. The people are divided between the Albigensian heretics and the Church of Rome. Rogerwolf of Foux is the son of Count Ramon. He is determined to avenge the deaths of his friends at the Siege of Carcassonne.

Genre: Historical Fiction
Subjects: Feudalism; Catholic faith; Persecution; Heretics, Christian
Place/Time: France—13th century

Cobb, James H.

266.

1. *Choosers of the Slain*. Putnam, 1996.
2. *Sea Strike*. Putnam, 1997.
3. *Sea Fighter*. Putnam, 2000.

In the year 2006, Commander Amanda Garrett must use her high-tech stealth destroyer U. S. S. *Cunningham* to stop Argentina from seizing mineral-rich Antarctica. Using the ship's state-of-the-art weaponry and its radar invisibility, Garrett defends her ship and her crew against a barrage of attacks. In her second outing, Garrett must take her ship to Chinese waters to stop nuclear weapons from getting into the wrong hands during the civil war in China. Again she must use her special weaponry to save the day. Later when she is put in charge of a U. N. Task force to stop an African civil war, Garrett's weapons are her only hope to stop the fighting.

Genre: Naval Adventure; War; Technothriller
Subjects: Navy, United States; Navy, United States—officers; Imaginary wars and battles
Place/Time: Pacific Ocean—2000–; China—2000–; Antarctica regions—2000–

Coccioli, Carlo

267.

1. *Heaven and Earth*. Prentice-Hall, 1952.
2. *The White Stone*. Simon & Schuster, 1960.

The story of a parish priest whose faith is threatened by his near death in World War II is told in part by a writer who searches for him in Italy and Mexico and finds him living in the woods searching for spiritual renewal.

Subjects: Faith; Catholic priests; World War II, 1939–1945
Place/Time: Italy—1900–1945; Mexico—1945–1980

Cochran, Molly *and* Murphy, Warren

268.

1. *The Forever King*. Tor, 1992.
2. *The Broken Sword*. Tor, 1997

King Arthur is reborn into the modern world. As these tales open, he is a 10-year-old boy guarded by a former

FBI agent who was Sir Galahad in a previous life. Merlin, the magician, appears to oppose two villains who want to control the power of the Holy Grail. When Arthur's magic sword Excalibur is broken, the knights of the Round Table come through a time warp to do battle. The narrative leaps back and forth between scenes set in modern day England and the United States and the legendary realm of Camelot.

Genre: Fantasy
Subjects: Arthur, King; Boys; Merlin (legendary character); Reincarnation; Time travel
Place/Time: England—1980–; United States—1980–

Coe, David B.

269. The LonTobyn Chronicles
1. *Children of Amarid.* Tor, 1997.
2. *The Outlanders.* Tor, 1998.

Ruled and guarded by kindly mages, the land of LonTobyn has been at peace for centuries, but a group of killers and thieves who appear to be mages are terrorizing the land and turning the population against their protectors. The young mage Jaryd and his uncle Baden undertake the task of defeating the evil spirit of a deceased mage, which seems to be the source of violence in the land. The adventures of the LonTobyn mages continue as Owl-Mage Orris journeys to the neighboring Lon-Ser, a land where technology has replaced magic, to get at the source of the troubles afflicting his land just as a band of raiders led by a powerful female assassin is planning an attack.

Genre: Fantasy
Subjects: Imaginary wars and battles; Magic; Good and evil

Coghlan, Peggie. *See* Stirling, Jessica

Colby, Merle Estes

270.
1. *All Ye People.* Viking, 1931.
2. *New Road.* Viking, 1933.

Young John Bray leaves his home in Vermont in 1810 to settle in Ohio, the West of his day. After his death, his widow marries aristocratic Martin Ward when Martin comes to Ohio. There they work to build their farm and the town. The social and economic life of early America is described in detail in these realistic novels.

Genre: Historical Fiction
Subjects: Farm life; Family life; Frontier and pioneer life
Place/Time: Ohio—19th century

Coldsmith, Don

271.
1. *Tallgrass: A Novel of the Great Plains.* Bantam, 1997.
2. *South Wind.* Bantam, 1998.

From 1541 to the middle of the 19th century, the lands west of the Mississippi are opened by white men who come into conflict with the native American tribes who live on the Great Plains. From the Spanish conquistadors to the French fur trappers, to the Lewis and Clark expedition, each wave of white men results in heightened tensions and conflict while also producing a series of unions between whites and Native Americans. In 1846 Jed Sterling, a Princeton-educated trapper who had been living with the Pawnee brings his African American wife to Kansas during the Bloody Kansas violence. For the next 30 years, he and other newcomers to Kansas are involved in opening up this frontier.

Genre: Historical Fiction
Subjects: Western states; Native Americans; Pawnee Tribe; Interracial marriage
Place/Time: Western states—multicentury span; Western states—19th century

272. The Spanish Bit Saga
1. *Runestone.* Bantam, 1995.
2. *Trail of the Spanish Bit.* Doubleday, 1980.
3. *The Elk-Dog Heritage.* Doubleday, 1982.
4. *Follow the Wind.* Doubleday, 1983.
5. *Buffalo Medicine.* Doubleday, 1981.
6. *Man of the Shadows.* Doubleday, 1983.
7. *Daughter of the Eagle.* Doubleday, 1984.
8. *Moon of Thunder.* Doubleday, 1985.
9. *The Sacred Hills.* Doubleday, 1985.
10. *Pale Star.* Doubleday, 1986.
11. *River of Swans.* Doubleday, 1986.
12. *Return to the River.* Doubleday, 1987.
13. *The Medicine Knife.* Doubleday, 1988.
14. *The Flower in the Mountains.* Doubleday, 1988.
15. *Trail from Taos.* Doubleday, 1989.
16. *Song of the Rock.* Doubleday, 1989.
17. *Fort De Chastaigne.* Doubleday, 1990.
18. *Quest for the White Bull.* Doubleday, 1990.
19. *Return of the Spanish.* Doubleday, 1991.
20. *Bride of the Morning Star.* Doubleday, 1991.
21. *Walks in the Sun.* Bantam, 1992.
22. *Thunderstick.* Doubleday, 1993.
23. *Track of the Bear.* Bantam, 1995.
24. *Child of the Dead.* Doubleday, 1995.
25. *Bearer of the Pipe.* Doubleday, 1995.
26. *Medicine Hat.* University of Oklahoma, 1997.

This saga of the Plains Indians begins in a prequel that presents Norse explorers surviving an Indian attack and gradually coming to understand the civilization of the Plains Indians of the 11th century. The story then picks up in the late 1600s and depicts the Native Americans as they were before contact with the white man.

When Spanish explorers, then French soldiers and American settlers enter the Mississippi region, the Indians' lives and culture are changed. The series centers on the Elk-Dog people and their foes, the Pawnees, from the late 1600s to the early 1800s. The stories cover several generations of families, and characters reappear in different books.

Genre: Family Saga; Historical Fiction
Subjects: Native Americans; Cultural conflict
Place/Time: Midwestern states—16th century; Midwestern states—17th century

Cole, Allan

273. The Timura Trilogy
1. *Wizard of the Winds.* Ballantine, 1997.
2. *Wolves of the Gods.* Ballantine, 1998.
3. *The Gods Awakened.* Ballantine, 1999.

Once they were friends and allies: the powerful sorcerer Safar Timura and the exiled orphan Prince Iraj Protarus. But after Safar helps Iraj ascend to the throne of Esmir, he is angered by the tyrannical ways of his former friend and brings about his downfall. Tired and sickened by court intrigue, Safar secludes himself, but must leave his mountain home when an evil force threatens the land and the spirit of the deceased Iraj appears as a wolflike shape-shifter.

Genre: Fantasy
Subjects: Magic; Kings and rulers; Good and evil; Imaginary kingdoms

Cole, Allan *and* Bunch, Chris

274.
1. *The Far Kingdoms.* Ballantine, 1994.
2. *The Warrior's Tale.* Ballantine, 1994.
3. *Kingdoms of the Night.* Ballantine, 1995.
4. *The Warrior Returns: An Epic Fantasy of the Anteros.* Ballantine, 1996.

In the first book, as a quest to prove his strength of character, Amalric sets out to find the legendary magical Far Kingdoms of the realm. Adding to the difficulty of the journey is the requirement that he and his companion Janos take with them a treacherous member of the magicians' guild. Worse still, Janos falls under the influence of black magic when they reach the Far Kingdoms. In the following book, Amalric's sister, Rali, the commander of the elite all-women's military force, must deal with danger and an insidious dark force during a sea voyage. As the series continues, an aging Amalric and Janos's granddaughter Janela journey into the Kingdoms of the Night where they encounter demons who threaten their world.

Genre: Fantasy
Subjects: Magic; Imaginary kingdoms; Voyages and travels; Brothers and sisters

Colegate, Isabel

275. Orlando King Series
1. *Orlando King.* Bodley Head, 1964.
2. *Orlando at the Brazen Threshold.* Bodley Head, 1971.
3. *Agatha.* Bodley Head, 1973.

The above titles have also been published in the following collection: *The Orlando Trilogy.* Viking Penguin, 1984.

In a modern Oedipus trilogy, Orlando, a successful young Englishman, is unwittingly responsible for the death of his friend and mentor. Orlando discovers the friend was his father only after he marries the man's attractive young widow. Blinded in the World War II bombing of London, Orlando is later reunited with his daughter Agatha. Finally Agatha chooses to help her brother, Paul, who has been convicted of treason, with grave consequences to herself.

Subjects: Mythology; Fathers and sons; Fathers and daughters; Brothers and sisters; Blindness; World War II, 1939–1945
Place/Time: England—1900–1945; England—1945–1980

Coleman, Lonnie

276.
1. *Beulah Land.* Doubleday, 1973.
2. *Look Away, Beulah Land.* Doubleday, 1977.
3. *The Legacy of Beulah Land.* Doubleday, 1980.

The passionate and stormy fortunes of the Kendrick family of Georgia are chronicled through the births, marriages, and deaths of its numerous members. From 1800 to 1861 they establish their plantation, Beulah Land, then defend it from Yankee soldiers during the Civil War. After the war, the Kendricks and their neighbors, the Davis family, struggle to bring their lives back to normal and establish a new society. Virtue and love triumph in the end.

Genre: Historical Romance
Subjects: Family life; Plantation life; United States—Civil War, 1861–1865
Place/Time: Georgia—19th century

Colette (Sidonie-Gabrielle)

277.
1. *Claudine at School.* A. C. Boni, 1930, 1900.
2. *Claudine in Paris.* Victor Gollancz, 1931, 1901.
3. *The Indulgent Husband.* Farrar & Rinehart, 1935, 1902. (Later retitled: *Claudine Married.*)

The above titles have also been published in the following collection: *The Complete Claudine.* Farrar, Straus & Giroux, 1976.

4. *Claudine and Annie.* Berkley, 1962, 1903.

Through these semi-autobiographical novels, Colette recounts the tales of Claudine, a mischievous French school girl, as she leaves her country home for Paris where she comes of age and marries. These short stories are written with a precocious sarcasm and candor.

Genre: Coming of Age
Subjects: Autobiographical stories; Girls; Marriage; Teenagers
Place/Time: Paris (France)—19th century; France—19th century

Collins, Jackie

278.
1. *Chances.* Warner, 1981.
2. *Lucky.* Simon & Schuster, 1985.
3. *Lady Boss.* Simon & Schuster, 1990.
4. *Vendetta: Lucky's Revenge.* Harper Collins, 1997.
5. *Dangerous Kiss.* Simon & Schuster, 1999.

This family saga follows the fortunes of Gino Santangelo, ex-hoodlum, Las Vegas casino owner, and sexual powerhouse, and his daughter, Lucky, who follows in his footsteps. When Gino has to leave the country because the IRS is after him, Lucky takes over his empire and fights competitors and lovers. After Gino and Lucky are reunited, she tries to take over a film studio for her third husband and is embroiled in Hollywood scandals and competition. Sex, money, sex, crime, sex, love affairs, and more sex are the hallmarks of this steamy rags to riches saga.

Genre: Family Saga
Subjects: Businesswomen; Gangsters; Gambling; Motion pictures
Place/Time: Las Vegas (Nev.)—1945–1980; Las Vegas (Nev.)—1980–; Nevada—1945–1980; Nevada—1980–

Colver, Alice Mary Ross

279.
1. *The Measure of the Years.* Dodd, 1954.
2. *There Is a Season.* Dodd, 1957.

The history of Stockbridge, Massachusetts, from 1739 to 1785 is intertwined with the Martin family. The father retires from the sea to a farm in Stockbridge. There he and his wife raise six children and live through Indian wars, the American Revolution, and a variety of family tragedies.

Genre: Historical Fiction
Subjects: Family life; Farm life; United States—revolution, 1775–1783
Place/Time: Massachusetts—18th century

Combs, Harry

280.
1. *Brules.* Lyford, 1992.

2. *The Scout.* Delacorte, 1995.

In 1916, Cat Brules is a reclusive Colorado mountain man who has seen the West he knew and loved disappear. He relates his adventures to a young engineering student. In 1867, Cat flees Kansas with a young prostitute after killing a man in a fight. Cat and Michelle, the prostitute, are captured by Comanches, and Michelle is killed. Cat stalks the Comanches as he takes his revenge. When his hatred wanes, he marries a Native American woman and becomes involved in the Indian wars of the 1870s and 1880s. As he ages, Cat slowly retreats to the mountains to live out his life.

Genre: Western
Subjects: Adventure; Western states; Mountain life; Native Americans
Place/Time: Western states—19th century; Colorado—19th century

Condon, Richard

281.
1. *Prizzi's Family.* Putnam, 1986.
2. *Prizzi's Honor.* Coward, McCann & Geoghegan, 1982.
3. *Prizzi's Glory.* Dutton, 1988.
4. *Prizzi's Money.* Crown, 1994.

Charley Partanna is the likable hit man for Don Corrado and the mob in New York City in the 1960s. He must keep the good guys from getting the Mafia and keep himself out of the hands of Maerose, Don Corrado's daughter. This black comedy satirizes the American dream as the mob becomes the average American family. Charley must protect Don Corrado from a vengeful politician, himself from a wife who is a hit woman, the mob as it franchises its enterprises, and finally Maerose as she takes over Charley and the mob. However, the Prizzi's are duped by Julia Ashbury when they get involved in a kidnapping plot.

Genre: Crime Novel
Subjects: Mafia; Husbands and wives; Kidnapping; Assassination; Satire
Place/Time: New York (N. Y.)—1945–1980

Coney, Michael G.

282. The Song of Earth
1. *The Celestial Steam Locomotive.* Houghton Mifflin, 1983.
2. *Gods of the Greataway.* Houghton Mifflin, 1984.
3. *Fang, the Gnome.* New American Library, 1988.
4. *King of the Scepter'd Isle.* New American Library, 1989.

Alternate time streams called happentraks, gnomes, and Arthurian characters figure in these tales of the legendary past and the distant future when a powerful godlike ruler, Starquin, controls Earth and the computer, Rainbow, keeps a segment of humanity immobilized in beautiful dreams.

Genre: Fantasy
Subjects: Time travel; Legends and folk tales; Kings and rulers; Computers; Dreams

Conley, Robert

283. The Real People
1. *The Way of the Priests.* Doubleday, 1992.
2. *The Dark Way.* Doubleday, 1993.
3. *The White Path.* Doubleday, 1993.
4. *The Way South.* Doubleday, 1994
5. *The Long Way Home.* Doubleday, 1994.

From legends and history, Conley tells the story of the Cherokee people before they were changed by the white man. In the 16th century, the Cherokees are dominated by their priests, who control every aspect of Indian life, but fail to see the dissatisfied masses. However when the Europeans come, the Cherokee society is changed, and the priests lose their hold over the people.

Genre: Historical Fiction
Subjects: Native Americans; Cherokee Indians
Place/Time: Georgia—16th century

Connell, Evan S.

284.
1. *Mrs. Bridge.* Viking, 1959.
2. *Mr. Bridge.* Knopf, 1969.

These novels recount the courtship and marriage of India and Walter Bridge of Kansas City from the 1920s through the 1940s. She is soft and befuddled while he is rigid and industrious. They raise three children and lead the typical upper-middle-class life of a Midwestern couple. The fascinating aspect of the novels is seeing the same events from India's point of view and then her husband's.

Subjects: Marriage; Husbands and wives; Family life; Middle classes
Place/Time: Kansas City (Mo.)—1900–1945; Missouri—1900–1945

Connery, Tom

285. Markham of the Marines
1. *Shred of Honour: A Markham of the Marines Novel.* Regnery, 1999.
2. *Honour Redeemed.* Regnery, 2000.
3. *Honour Be Damned.* Regnery, 2000.

In 1793, Lt. George Markham of the Royal Marines is suddenly thrust into command of a frigate's marine detachment when the ship's captain is killed. Markham is the illegitimate son of an English general and an Irish-Catholic mother. Because of his Irish background and a mysterious court martial years earlier, his men do not trust him. He must take his troops to Toulon and defend the town against the French troops of Napleon and French spies who want to see Markham dead. After escaping Toulon, he and his Marines go to Corsica to find Corsican leader General Paoli. Markham must fight the French, dally with the ladies, and escape death if he is to redeem his honor.

Genre: War; Naval Adventure
Subjects: War; Napoleonic Wars, 1800–1814; Royal Marines; Adventure
Place/Time: Atlantic Ocean—19th century; France—19th century; Corsica—19th century

Conrad, Joseph

286.
1. *The Rescue.* Doubleday, 1920.
2. *An Outcast of the Islands.* Appleton, 1896.
3. *Almayer's Folly: A Story of an Eastern River.* Macmillan, 1895.

European trader Tom Lingard wants to dominate the native kingdom in Malaya. He dreams of having great wealth and power, but the men who work for Lingard are weak and corrupt. Willem and Almayer lose their lives when their corruption brings down native wrath. Ultimately Lingard's megalomania causes his own death.

Genre: Adventure
Subjects: Traders; Ambition; Business; Adventure; Imperialism
Place/Time: Malaya—19th century

Conran, Shirley

287.
1. *Lace.* Simon & Schuster, 1982.
2. *Lace II.* Pocket Books, 1985.

International film star Lili searches for her mother through the decades and across continents. The homeless waif and four girlfriends go through men, marriages, and careers as they go from poverty to the jet set. Even after Lili finds her mother, she must uncover the secret her mother kept from her and foil the powerful men who want her. Sex, money, power, and torn lace underwear are the keys to Lili's success.

Genre: Romance
Subjects: Actors and actresses; Wealth; Friendship; Mothers and daughters
Place/Time: Europe—1945–1980; Europe—1980–

Cook, David

288.
1. *Walter.* Overlook, 1985.
2. *Winter Doves.* Overlook, 1985.

Walter is retarded. His mother is frustrated with him while his father is indifferent. His co-workers ridicule him, but Walter is a caring, loving person who learns to cope with injustice. Only later when he has been put in an institution does he feel that he has finally found a place for himself.

Subjects: Mental handicaps—children; Family life; Mental illness, care and treatment of
Place/Time: London (England)—1900–1945; London (England)—1945–1980; England—1900–1945; England—1945–1980

Cook, Glen

289. The Black Company
1. *The Black Company.* Tor, 1984.
2. *Shadows Linger.* Tor, 1984.
3. *The White Rose.* Tor, 1985.
4. *The Silver Spike.* Tor, 1989.
5. *Shadow Games.* Tor, 1989.
6. *Dreams of Steel.* Tor, 1990.
7. *Bleak Seasons.* Tom Doherty Assoc., 1996.
8. *She Is the Darkness.* Tor, 1997.
9. *Water Sleeps.* Tom Doherty Assoc., 1999.

A group of mercenaries working for an evil sorceress realize they are fighting on the wrong side, and eventually decide to work against their former employer. Their adventures continue as they battle the wicked Shadow-Masters and work against the power of an ancient artifact. The mercenaries are divided when part of the company is trapped in suspended animation under a glittering glassy plain.

Genre: Fantasy
Subjects: Mercenary soldiers; Good and evil; Magic; Imaginary wars and battles

290. The Garrett Files
1. *Sweet Silver Blues.* Signet, 1987.
2. *Bitter Gold Hearts.* Signet, 1988.
3. *Cold Copper Tears.* Signet, 1988.
4. *Old Tin Sorrows.* Signet, 1989.
5. *Dread Brass Shadows.* Roc, 1990.
6. *Red Iron Nights.* Roc, 1991.
7. *Deadly Quicksilver Lies.* Roc, 1994.
8. *Petty Pewter Gods.* Roc, 1995.
9. *Faded Steel Heat.* Roc, 1999.

Sword and sorcery themes mix with elements of the hard-boiled detective novel in these tales of P. I. Garrett whose turf, a town called TunFaire, is inhabited by elves, ogres, ghosts, and vampires. With the assistance of his girlfriend Tinnie and the half elf Morly Dotes, Garrett investigates cases, such as one that puts him in the middle of two pantheons of gods.

Genre: Fantasy; Crime Novel; Humor
Subjects: Detectives; Crime and criminals

Cook, Hugh

291. Chronicles of the Age of Darkness
1. *The Wizards and the Warriors.* C. Smythe, 1986.
2. *The Wordsmiths and the Warguild.* C. Smythe, 1987.
3. *The Women and the Warlords.* C. Smythe, 1989.
4. *The Walrus and the Warwolf.* Smythe/Dufour, 1989.
5. *The Wicked and the Witless.* Corgi, 1989.
6. *The Wishstone and the Wonder Workers.* Corgi, 1992.
7. *The Wizir and the Witch.* Corgi, 1992.
8. *The Werewolf and the Wormlord.* Corgi, 1991.
9. *The Worshippers and the Way.* Corgi, 1992.

In this sword and sorcery fantasy, warriors and wizards fight to save their world from the Swarms—a power that can turn living things to stone and rocks to life. Each book tells the story of different groups in the kingdom that are sent on a variety of quests. This fantasy series has a comic tone and a contemporary perspective. Books 4, 5, 6, 7, and 9 have only been published in England, and Book 8 has not yet been published.

Genre: Fantasy
Subjects: Imaginary wars and battles; Imaginary kingdoms; Witchcraft

Cooke, John Esten

292. Effingham
1. *The Virginia Comedians.* Appleton, 1854.
2. *Henry St. John, Gentleman.* Harpers, 1859.

Historical figures George Washington, Patrick Henry, and the great grandson of Pocahontas figure in these historical romances, which contrast two elements in colonial Virginia society: the aristocratic Effinghams and the hardworking, outgoing Waters family.

Genre: Historical Romance
Subjects: Washington, George, 1732–1799; Henry, Patrick, 1736–1799; Social classes
Place/Time: Virginia—18th century

293. Southern Army Campaign Series
1. *Surry of Eagle's Nest.* Bunce & Huntington, 1866.
2. *Hilt to Hilt.* G. W. Carleton, 1869.
3. *Mohun.* F. J. Huntington, 1869.

These memoirs of a fictitious staff officer who first served under Stonewall Jackson, then with Lee's regiments, paint a sympathetic, authentic picture of the Confederate Army at the close of the Civil War.

Genre: Historical Fiction
Subjects: United States—Civil War, 1861–1865; Jackson, Thomas Jonathan (Stonewall), 1824–1863; Army, Confederate States of America; Battles; War
Place/Time: Southern states—19th century

Cookson, Catherine

294.
1. *The Mallen Streak.* Dutton, 1973.

2. *The Mallen Girl.* Dutton, 1973.
3. *The Mallen Lot.* Dutton, 1974.

In the late 1800s in England, Thomas Mallen loses his estate to creditors and moves to a small cottage with his two wards and their governess. He takes up with his illegitimate son, Donald, and the two wreak havoc on everyone they meet. His daughter, Barbara, continues her father's unsavory ways as she tries to kill her rival for the man she loves. Eventually she destroys the lives of those around her and leaves her son and his girlfriend to finally find love.

Genre: Historical Romance
Subjects: Family life
Place/Time: England—19th century

295.
1. *Tilly.* Morrow, 1980.
2. *Tilly Wed.* Morrow, 1981.
3. *Tilly Alone.* Morrow, 1982.

After enduring a harsh childhood as well as accusations of witchcraft, Tilly becomes the mistress of Mark Sopwith, the lord of the manor. When he dies, she goes to Texas with his son, Matthew, where they establish a ranch and fight Indians. When Matthew dies, Tilly returns to Victorian England with her son and stepdaughter. At Sopwith Manor, she finds old friends and an old lover who help her face old conflicts and new challenges.

Genre: Historical Romance
Subjects: Frontier and pioneer life; Family life
Place/Time: Texas—19th century; England—19th century

296. Bill Bailey
1. *Bill Bailey.* Heinemann, 1986.
2. *Bill Bailey's Lot.* Bantam, 1987.
3. *Bill Bailey's Daughter.* Bantam, 1988.
The above titles have also been published in the following collection: *The Bailey Chronicles.* Summit, 1989.

In the rural north of England, diamond-in-the-rough contractor Bill Bailey moves into lovely young widow Fiona's home as a boarder. He soon becomes emotionally and legally attached to her and her children despite her mother's disapproval.

Genre: Romance
Subjects: Contractors; Widows; Love; Marriage
Place/Time: England—1980–

297. Mary Ann Shaughnessy
1. *A Grand Man.* Morrow, 1975, 1954.
2. *The Lord and Mary Ann.* Morrow, 1975.
3. *The Devil and Mary Ann.* Morrow, 1976, 1958.
4. *Love and Mary Ann.* Morrow, 1976, 1961.
5. *Life and Mary Ann.* Morrow, 1977, 1962.
6. *Marriage and Mary Ann.* Morrow, 1978, 1964.
7. *Mary Ann's Angels.* Morrow, 1978, 1965.
8. *Mary Ann and Bill.* Morrow, 1979, 1967.

Mary Ann Shaughnessy, the unconventional daughter of Irish working class parents in the north of England, first copes with her father's drinking problem, then with a benefactor's attempts to turn her into a elegant lady. After rejecting more polished suitors, she marries car mechanic, Corny Boyle, and produces twins who lead her on a merry chase.

Genre: Gentle Read
Subjects: Girls; Marriage; Love; Labor and laboring classes; Twins
Place/Time: England—1945–1980

Coonts, Stephen
298.
1. *Flight of the Intruder.* Naval Institute Press, 1986.
2. *The Intruders.* Pocket Books, 1994.
3. *Final Flight.* Doubleday, 1988.
4. *The Minotaur.* Doubleday, 1989.
5. *Under Siege.* Pocket Books, 1990.
6. *The Red Horseman.* Pocket Books, 1993.

Jack Grafton is an A-6 Intruder pilot during the Vietnamese War. He loves to fly and has the gung-ho will to win. However, the killing and dying that he sees forces him to decide whether to stay in the navy or to leave. Ultimately he can't give up the thrill of flying and commands a group of pilots on an aircraft carrier in the Mediterranean where he fights Arab terrorists. He helps develop new tactical aircraft, attacks drug dealers, and uncovers CIA plots. Grafton rises in the ranks to become a rear admiral and continues his nonstop adventures as he battles the enemies of America.

Genre: Adventure; Technothriller; War
Subjects: Adventure; Air pilots; Cold war; International intrigue; War
Place/Time: Vietnam—1945–1980; Mediterranean region—1945–1980; Mediterranean region—1980–; Washington (D. C.)—1945–1980; Washington (D. C.)—1980–

Cooper, James Fenimore
299. Leatherstocking Tales
1. *The Deerslayer.* Lea & Blanchard, 1841.
2. *The Last of the Mohicans.* Scribner, 1826.
3. *The Pathfinder.* Dodd, 1840.
4. *The Pioneers.* Dodd, 1822.
5. *The Prairie.* Dodd, 1827.

In upper New York state in the 1740s, Natty Bumpo, who has been raised by the Delaware chief Chingachgook, helps defend settlers against traitorous Indians and the French during the French and Indian War. As he grows older, he opposes society's destruction of the land and the animals and goes west. Natty is ever noble and fearless, the ideal American man of courage and action, and more than a little cornpone. The books are listed according to the chronology of events.

Genre: Historical Fiction; War
Subjects: Frontier and pioneer life; Native Americans; United States—French and Indian War, 1755–1763; Scouts and scouting
Place/Time: New York (state)—18th century

Cooper, Louise

300. Chaos Gate
1. *The Deceiver.* Bantam, 1991.
2. *The Pretender.* Bantam, 1991.
3. *The Avenger.* Bantam, 1992.

The tales of Order and Chaos continue through the narrative of the attempts of Ygorla, a young woman who is half human, half demon, to disrupt the balance between the Lords of Order and Chaos. Ygorla disables one of the Lords of Chaos by stealing his soul-stone and sets herself up as a cruel empress who practices black magic.

Genre: Fantasy
Subjects: Good and evil; Imaginary wars and battles

301. Indigo
1. *Nemesis.* Tor, 1989.
2. *Inferno.* Tor, 1989.
3. *Infanta.* Tor, 1990.
4. *Nocturne.* Tor, 1990.
5. *Troika.* Tor, 1991.
6. *Avatar.* Tor, 1992.
7. *Revenant.* Tor, 1993
8. *Aisling.* Tor, 1994.

Taking her new name from the color of a piece of glass from a broken family heirloom, a remorseful Princess Anghara renounces her royal position after youthful curiosity spurs her to defy her parents by entering the Tower of Regrets, thereby unleashing seven demons on the land. Accompanied by a telepathic wolf, Indigo follows the advice of the goddess Earth Mother to expiate her sins by traveling the world, searching down and destroying the evil beings.

Genre: Fantasy; Coming of Age
Subjects: Princesses; Good and evil; Atonement

302. Star Shadow
1. *Star Ascendant.* Tor, 1995.
2. *Eclipse.* HarperCollins, 1994.
3. *Moonset.* HarperCollins, 1995.

Written after the Time Master and Chaos Gate series, but earlier in fictional chronology, these works begin the continuing theme of the struggle between the forces of Order and Chaos. The control of the Lords of Chaos on the fate of humanity is weakening and is further undermined by the evil power of the First Magus of Order Vordegh and by the machinations of Iselia Darrow, a young disciple of Order, who is captured by the Chaos Riders on her wedding night.

Genre: Fantasy
Subjects: Imaginary wars and battles; Good and evil

303. Time Master Trilogy
1. *The Initiate.* Tor, 1985.
2. *The Outcast.* Tor, 1986.
3. *The Master.* Tor, 1987.

The forces of Order have seized control of the world and banished the gods of Chaos, who are seen as demons. Born in human form, Tarod is unaware that he is in truth an incarnation of one of the supreme beings of Chaos. He falls in love with a human woman, but once his true nature becomes known, he must travel through time to escape death as the rulers of Chaos battle for what they feel is their rightful place in the world.

Genre: Fantasy; Coming of Age
Subjects: Time travel; Imaginary wars and battles; Love

Cooper, William

304.
1. *Scenes from Provincial Life.* Cape, 1950.
2. *Scenes from Metropolitan Life.* Macmillan, 1961. (This book was never published in the United States.)
3. *Scenes from Married Life.* Dutton, 1984, 1961.

Books 1 and 3 have also been published in the following collection: *Scenes from Life.* Scribner, 1961.

4. *Scenes from Later Life.* Dutton, 1984.

Joe Lunn is a young British schoolteacher who feels that he is just beginning to live, while his country is on the brink of war in 1938. The narration follows Joe as he marries, contemplates a career change, and finally reaches retirement in the 1970s.

Subjects: Teachers; Marriage; World War II, 1939–1945
Place/Time: England—1900–1945; England—1945–1980

Copeland, Lori

305. Brides of the West
1. *Faith.* Tyndale, 1998.
2. *June.* Tyndale, 1999.
3. *Hope.* Tyndale, 1999.

In 1872, when their pastor father dies suddenly, the Kallahan sisters are left penniless. Each answers an ad for a Christian bride and goes west. Faith travels to Texas to wed a rancher, Nicholas Shepherd, but he keeps postponing the wedding. Faith meets a widower with a blind son and begins to teach him Braille. Soon Nicholas wonders if he has lost Faith to another man. June Kallahan goes to Seattle, but her future husband is ill and soon dies. June stays and works with an evangelist who has set up a local orphanage, but finds he is using the money for the orphans to build a church. As June falls in love with Pastor Sentell, they work to show the evangelist the error of his ways. Hope

Kallahan on her way west is kidnapped by a gang of payroll thieves, and federal agent Dan Sullivan must come to her rescue. Hope, however, works to convert both the criminals and Dan who believes God has thrown her into his life

Genre: Christian Fiction; Historical Fiction
Subjects: Faith; Lovers
Place/Time: Western states—19th century

Coppel, Alfred

306. The Goldenwing Cycle
1. *Glory.* Tor, 1993.
2. *Glory's War.* Tor, 1995.
3. *Glory's People.* Tor, 1996.

Three thousand years in the future, humanity has spread among the stars keeping many of the institutions and prejudices from Earth intact. The only connections between these worlds are enormous spaceships called Goldenwings staffed with technologically sophisticated crews who seem threatening to the insular planet populations. As the sentient spaceship Gloria Coeli and its crew sails through the galaxy, they encounter the institution of apartheid transplanted from South Africa, a Japanese space colony where a faster-than-light star drive is being developed, and a threatening force from deep space called the Terror, which feeds on human emotion.

Genre: Science Fiction
Subjects: Spaceships; Space colonies; Interplanetary voyages; Life on other planets; Cultural conflict

Cornwall, David. *See* Le Carre, John

Cornwell, Bernard

307.
1. *Sharpe's Triumph.* HarperCollins, 1999.
2. *Sharpe's Rifles.* Viking, 1988.
3. *Sharpe's Eagle.* Viking, 1981.
4. *Sharpe's Gold.* Viking, 1981.
5. *Sharpe's Battle.* Viking, 1995.
6. *Sharpe's Company.* Viking, 1982.
7. *Sharpe's Sword.* Viking, 1983.
8. *Sharpe's Enemy.* Viking, 1984.
9. *Sharpe's Honor.* Viking, 1985.
10. *Sharpe's Regiment.* Viking, 1986.
11. *Sharpe's Siege.* Viking, 1987.
12. *Sharpe's Revenge.* Viking, 1989.
13. *Sharpe's Waterloo.* Viking, 1990.
14. *Sharpe's Devil.* Viking, 1992.

In 1803, Richard Sharpe is a sergeant in India who becomes the unofficial aid to General Sir Arthur Wellesley, the future Duke of Wellington, during the fight against the Indian Mahratta Confederation. During the Peninsular War against Napolean in Spain in 1809, Sharpe becomes a lieutenant with the British 95th Rifles, and has to fight the French, difficult conditions, and snobbish British officers who resent the

lower-class upstart. Facing numerous suicidal missions, Sharpe uses heroics and derring-do to save himself and his men. The details of army life and war are realistically portrayed.

Genre: Adventure; Historical Fiction; War
Subjects: War; Adventure; Army, British—officers; Soldiers—British; Peninsular War, 1807–1814
Place/Time: Spain—19th century; India—19th century

308.
1. *Rebel.* HarperCollins, 1993.
2. *Copperhead.* HarperCollins, 1994.
3. *Battleflag.* HarperCollins, 1995.

Nate Starbuck is the discredited son of an abolitionist preacher. When he flees Boston after helping a femme fatale, he ends up in Richmond as the Civil War opens. Because he is a Northerner, he is distrusted, but finally joins Washington Faulconer, who is raising his own army to fight for the South. After fighting in the First Battle of Bull Run, he must cross enemy lines during battle to disprove espionage charges against him. He becomes a Confederate captain, but finds the incompetence of his friend General Faulconer threatens his troops. Only General Stonewall Jackson can help him, and then Starbuck fights with Jackson at the Second Battle of Manassas.

Genre: Adventure; War
Subjects: Adventure; Soldiers; United States—Civil War, 1861–1865; Jackson, Thomas Jonathan (Stonewall), 1824-1863
Place/Time: Boston (Mass.)—19th century; Richmond (Va.)—19th century; Massachusetts—19th century; Virginia—19th century

309.
1. *The Winter King.* St. Martin's, 1996.
2. *Enemy of God.* St. Martin's, 1997.
3. *Excalibur.* St. Martin's, 1998.

These tales of a very human King Arthur are narrated by his friend Derfel Cadarn, a former slave brought up by the wizard Merlin, who loves Ceinwyn, the princess Arthur rejects when he uses force to take Guinevere as his queen. Arthur's efforts to unite the warlords of the land behind him and the conflict between the followers of the old religion of the Britons and the disciples of Christianity form the backdrop for these stories that combine historical details and magical elements.

Genre: Fantasy; Historical Fiction
Subjects: Arthur, King; Guenevere, Queen (legendary character a.k.a. Guinevere); Merlin (legendary character); Religion; Magic

Cosic, Dobrica

310.
1. *Into the Battle.* Harcourt Brace, 1983, 1977.
2. *A Time of Death.* Harcourt Brace, 1978.
3. *Reach to Eternity.* Harcourt Brace Jovanovich, 1980.

4. *South to Destiny.* Harcourt Brace Jovanovich, 1981.

Abandoned by the Allies during World War I, Serbia waged a desperate battle for survival against the Austro-Hungarian Empire. Cosic portrays the face of war from the king down to the peasants.

Genre: Historical Fiction; War
Subjects: World War I, 1914–1918; War
Place/Time: Serbia—1900–1945

Cost, March. *Pseud. of* Peggy Morrison

311.
1. *The Hour Awaits.* Lippincott, 1952.
2. *Invitation from Minerva.* Lippincott, 1954.

Austrian Princess Victoria makes her way through London society of the early 1900s and has an intriguing relationship with an English professor. In *Invitation from Minerva*, Viccy is entertaining in her Tyrolean castle when an avalanche turns a dinner party into a dangerous situation that reveals a great deal about her distinguished guests.

Genre: Historical Romance
Subjects: Aristocracy; Society novels
Place/Time: London (England)—1900–1945; Austria—1900–1945; England—1900–1945

Cotton, Ralph W.

312.
1. *While Angels Dance: The Life and Times of Jeston Nash.* St. Martin's, 1994.
2. *Powder River.* St. Martin's, 1995.
3. *Cost of a Killing.* Pocket Books, 1996.
4. *Killer of Men.* Pocket Books, 1997.
5. *Trick of the Trade.* Pocket Books, 1997.

During the Civil War, young Jeston Nash kills another boy in self-defense and is forced to flee to Missouri. There he joins his cousins, Frank and Jesse James, as they ride with Quantrill's Raiders. After the war, he stays with the James gang as they rob and plunder their way across the state. Jesse and his friends steal a herd of horses and drive them to the Dakota Territory where they hope to sell them to the army. When they get there, they are immediately involved in Red Cloud's War. After meeting with Captain William Fetterman who believes his small troop can stop the Sioux, Nash joins Red Cloud until the Sioux massacre Fetterman and his men. Jeston wanders the West dodging outlaws and riding with General Custer. His adventures keep him in the midst of all the action.

Genre: Western
Subjects: Adventure; Western States; Native Americans; Horse trading; War
Place/Time: Western states—19th century; Missouri—19th century

Coulson, Juanita

313. Children of the Stars
1. *Tomorrow's Heritage.* Ballantine, 1981.
2. *Outward Bound.* Ballantine, 1982.
3. *Legacy of Earth.* Ballantine, 1989.
4. *The Past of Forever.* Ballantine, 1990.

In the 21st century, the Saunders, members of a powerful industrial family led by a strong-willed matriarch, battle over their differing attitudes toward space exploration and contact with aliens.

Genre: Family Saga; Science Fiction
Subjects: Mothers; Family life; Business; Outer space, exploration of

Coulter, Catherine

314.
1. *The Sherbrooke Bride.* Jove, 1992.
2. *Mad Jack.* Jove, 1999.
3. *The Courtship.* Jove, 2000.

In Regency England, Douglas Sherbrooke, Earl of Northcliffe, is sent to France on a secret mission just as he is to get married. He sends his cousin Tony to act as his proxy, but Tony falls in love with Melissande Chambers and the two run off and marry. Melissande's sister Alexandre becomes the proxy bride and works to get Douglas's love. At the estate of Grayson St. Cyres, his aunts and their valet Mad Jack descend on the household. However, Jack is really Winifrede Bascombe, a runaway girl hiding from her abusive stepfather. Jack steals one of St. Cyres's horses, and he goes after her and discovers her disguise. The two fall in love and finally marry. At the Sherbrooke estate, Spencer Hetherington meets tall Helen Mayberry, a friend of Grayson St. Cyres. Spencer is fascinated by her and is drawn into her plot to find Aladdin's lamp from an ancient scroll. On their search for the lamp, they fall in love.

Genre: Historical Romance
Subjects: Love; Lovers; Courtship
Place/Time: England—19th century

315.
1. *The Wyndham Legacy.* Putnam, 1993.
2. *The Nightingale Legacy.* Putnam, 1994.
3. *The Valentine Legacy.* Putnam, 1995.

Feisty women dominate the Wyndham family in Regency England. Josephina Cochrain is the illegitimate daughter of the Earl of Chase. Before his death, the earl marries Josephina's mother and leaves his estate to his daughter. However, obnoxious cousin Marcus Wyndham inherits the title, then marries Josephina who must win his love. Headstrong Caroline Derwent-Jones disobeys her guardian and finds herself in the arms of Lord Chilton, a lonely bachelor. Outspoken Jessie Warfield flees to America after a scandal ruins her reputation. James Wyndham comes after her, and all the characters from the previous books bring this sparkling romantic trilogy to a close.

Genre: Historical Romance
Subjects: Aristocracy; Love; Marriage; Illegitimacy; Courtship
Place/Time: England—19th century

316.
1. *Lord of Hawkfell Island.* Jove, 1993.
2. *Lord of Raven's Peak.* Jove, 1994.
3. *Lord of Falcon Ridge.* Jove, 1995.

Rorik Haraldsson, a Viking lord in England of 915 A.D., seeks to avenge the murder of his family by Einer Thorsson, by attacking Einer's castle and capturing his half-sister Mirana. Mirana, however, is not a hapless maid, but an independent woman who teaches the Viking women to fight for themselves and wins Rorik's love. Rorik's younger brother Merrik buys two slaves in Kiev and discovers one is a beautiful young girl who is a kidnapped noblewoman. She helps Merrik find a murderer and her kidnapper while winning his love. Cleve, emissary of Duke Rolo, goes to Ireland to seek the hand of Chessa, Princess of Ireland, for the Duke's son, but Chessa has to escape her suitors to find true love. Characters from the first two books help Chessa and Cleve.

Genre: Historical Romance
Subjects: Vikings; Brothers
Place/Time: England—10th century

317. Bride Trilogy
1. *The Sherbrooke Bride.* Jove, 1992.
2. *The Hellion Bride.* Jove, 1992.
3. *The Heiress Bride.* Putnam, 1992.

The Sherbrooke family faces numerous romantic entanglements in Regency England. Douglas Sherbrooke, Earl of Northclife, is duped into a marriage with an unwanted bride, Alexandra. The earl's brother, Ryder, goes to Jamaica to defend the Sherbrooke plantation and ends up marrying Sophie to save her from jail. The earl's sister, Joan, elopes to Scotland with her love, then finds hidden secrets in her new groom's castle. All the couples come together for the traditional happy ending.

Genre: Historical Romance
Subjects: Husbands and wives; Marriage
Place/Time: England—19th century; Jamaica—19th century; Scotland—19th century

Cournos, John

318. John Gombarov Series
1. *The Mask.* Doran, 1919.
2. *The Wall.* Dutton, 1921.
3. *Babel.* Boni & Liveright, 1922.

This autobiographical trilogy traces the life of a young Russian Jew who immigrates to America, becomes part of an intellectual circle in Philadelphia, then continues to try to find an outlet for his creativity in Europe on the brink of World War I.

Subjects: Autobiographical stories; Jews; Immigrants; Creation (literary, artistic, etc.)
Place/Time: Philadelphia (Pa.)—1900–1945; Europe—1900–1945; Pennsylvania—1900–1945

Courter, Gay

319.
1. *The Midwife.* Houghton, Mifflin, 1981.
2. *The Midwife's Advice.* Dutton, 1992.

Hannah Blair trains to be a midwife at Moscow's Imperial College in czarist Russia. Through her career, she becomes involved with noblewomen and the poor as she delivers their babies and listens to their troubles. She and her husband, Lazar, flee the Russian pogroms against Jews and go to New York. In New York, Hannah becomes a pioneering sex therapist fighting for women's rights and the legalization of birth control.

Genre: Historical Fiction
Subjects: Midwives; Social classes; Jews, persecution of; Birth control
Place/Time: Moscow (Russia)—1900–1917; New York (N. Y.)—1900–1945

Cowell, Stephanie

320.
1. *Nicholas Cooke.* Norton, 1993.
2. *The Physician of London.* Norton, 1995.

As a young boy, Nicholas Cooke sees his father hung as a thief and his mother turn to prostitution. His rage at his fate keeps him from going to Cambridge to study. After stabbing his brutal master, Nick flees to London where he meets Christopher Marlowe and becomes an actor with John Heminges's troop. Although he becomes a good actor, his restless nature leads him to join the army in Ireland. After the war, Nick returns to London where he marries Heminges's daughter and continues acting. Even though he is successful, he longs to become a priest. When his marriage fails, Nick finally goes to Cambridge to study for the priesthood and medicine. As a physician in London, he is lonely until he meets Thomas Wentworth and his daughter Cecily. His friendship with the Wentworths involves Nick with King Charles and his fight with Parliament, the scientific discoveries of William Harvey, and the religious battles of the early 1600s.

Genre: Historical Fiction
Subjects: Actors and actresses; Physicians; Catholic priests; Charles I, King of England, 1600–1649
Place/Time: England—17th century

Cowper, Richard. *Pseud. of* Colin Middleton Murry

321. White Bird of Kinship Trilogy
1. *The Road to Corlay.* Pocket Books, 1979.
2. *A Dream of Kinship.* Pocket Books, 1982.

3. *A Tapestry of Time.* Gollancz, 1982.

In this version of the future, Britain has become a group of very small islands inhabited by a society similar to that of the Middle Ages. A cult forms around the boy Tom who has the power to bring out the best in men through his music and the image of the White Bird. Centuries later, a religion with Tom as its central mystical figure is becoming dogmatic and rigid until another Tom with similar powers emerges.

Genre: Science Fiction
Subjects: Cults; Mysticism; Birds; Music

Coyle, Harold

322.
1. *Look Away.* Simon & Schuster, 1995.
2. *Until the End.* Simon and Schuster, 1996.

Wealthy Irish immigrant Edward Bannon is forced to send his sons away when they accidentally kill the woman they both love. Eldest son James goes to the Virginia Military Institute while son Kevin joins the New Jersey Militia in 1859. When the Civil War breaks out, the brothers are on opposite sides. From the Battle of Bull Run to Gettysburg, to the Wilderness Campaign to Appomattox, the brothers see the daily death, horror, and suffering of the War. As the war drags on, they become embittered and brutal and increasingly estranged from each other. The realistic descriptions of the battles and hospitals vividly portray this horrific war.

Genre: Historical Fiction; War
Subjects: War; Army, Confederate States of America; Army, United States; Brothers; Irish—United States; United States—Civil War, 1861–1865
Place/Time: United States—19th century; Southern states—19th century

Coyle, Neva

323. Summerwind Series
1. *A Door of Hope.* Bethany House, 1995.
2. *Inside the Private Hedge.* Bethany House, 1996.
3. *Close to a Father's Heart.* Bethany House. 1996.

When they graduate from high school in 1957, three young women must face the reality of growing up and leaving their fun days behind. Karissa Hill is popular and a member of the Summerwind High pep squad. When she secretly marries her high school sweetheart, she has to watch her friends go on to college and jobs while she stays home and deals with a tragic accident. Rita McCarron, on the other hand, wants to stay at home and help her family with their orange growing business. As her father's health fails, Rita must fight to hold the farm together. When Amy Weaver's mother dies suddenly, she must sort through the family papers where she discovers a secret her mother had kept hid-

den. Each young woman must look deep within herself to find faith and a path for the future.

Genre: Christian Fiction
Subjects: Faith; Christian life; Women
Place/Time: United States—1945–1980

Cradock, Fanny

324. Lorme Series
1. *The Lormes of Castle Rising.* Saturday Review Press, 1976.
2. *Shadows over Castle Rising.* Dutton, 1977.
3. *War Comes to Castle Rising.* Dutton, 1978.
4. *Wind of Change at Castle Rising.* Dutton, 1979.
5. *Uneasy Peace at Castle Rising.* W. H. Allen, 1979.
6. *Thunder over Castle Rising.* W. H. Allen, 1980.
7. *Gathering Clouds at Castle Rising.* W. H. Allen, 1981.
8. *Fateful Years at Castle Rising.* W. H. Allen, 1982.
9. *The Defence of Castle Rising.* W. H. Allen, 1984.

The Lormes have lived in Castle Rising for over 800 years. Now in Edwardian England, the family is at the peak of its power. Lord and Lady Aymthorp oversee an extended family of 40 that includes a bishop, a suffragette, numerous servants, and assorted scoundrels. From the 1890s through the 1920s, the family and its servants have love affairs, fight World War I, and survive tragedies in this lavish family saga. Books 5 to 9 have only been published in England and continue the family story.

Genre: Historical Fiction
Subjects: Family life; Aristocracy; Houses; Love affairs
Place/Time: England—1900–1945

Crawford, Dianna *and* Laity, Sally

325. Freedom's Holy Light
1. *The Gathering Dawn.* Tyndale House, 1994.
2. *The Kindled Flame.* Tyndale House, 1994.
3. *The Tempering Blaze.* Tyndale House, 1995.
4. *Fires of Freedom.* Tyndale House, 1996.
5. *Embers of Hope.* Tyndale House, 1996.
6. *The Torch of Triumph.* Tyndale House, 1997.

In 1770, the Harringtons, Haynes, and Thomas, come to America to find political and religious freedom. Susannah Harrington soon becomes involved in plots against the British while her brother Ted is in the British army. When Ted deserts the army, he is helped by his love, Jean Haynes, and her brother. As the Revolution breaks out, the families fight for General Washington and their newfound freedom.

Genre: Christian Fiction

Subjects: United States—revolution, 1775–1783;
Brothers and sisters; Faith
Place/Time: United States—18th century

Crawley, Aileen

326.
1. *The Bride of Suleiman.* St. Martin's, 1981.
2. *The Shadow of God.* St. Martin's, 1983.

In the 1500s, Khurrem, the Russian slave girl, becomes the bride of the Ottoman sultan Suleiman the Magnificent (1494–1566). Their love must survive the intrigues of the court and the war campaigns to keep the empire together.

Genre: Historical Romance
Subjects: Courts and courtiers; Suleiman I, Sultan of the Turks, 1495–1566
Place/Time: Turkey—16th century

Crichton, Michael

327.
1. *Jurassic Park.* Knopf, 1990.
2. *The Lost World.* Knopf, 1995.

On a fog-shrouded island off the coast of Costa Rica, a biotechnology financier has built an unusual theme park—a park inhabited by dinosaurs. These dinosaurs have been cloned from ancient DNA and are supposedly unable to breed, but chaos theoretician Ian Malcolm predicts that the animals' behavior is unstable. When a rival genetics firm tries to steal the dinosaur embryos, chaos erupts as the technology fails and the dinosaurs attack. Two children and a paleontologist are able to save the people in the park. While it seems that the dinosaurs have been destroyed, they are breeding in the Costa Rican jungle, and Malcolm and other scientists must return there to try to destroy the final remnants of dinosaurs.

Genre: Adventure
Subjects: Adventure; Escapes; Dinosaurs
Place/Time: Costa Rica—1980–

Crispin, A. C. *See also* Nolan, William F. (Witch World series—*Gryphon's Eyrie* and *Songsmith*)

328. Starbridge
1. *Starbridge.* Ace, 1989.
2. *Silent Dances.* Ace, 1990. (Written with Kathleen O'Malley).
3. *Shadow World.* Ace, 1991. (Written with Jannean Elliott).
4. *Serpent's Gift.* Ace, 1992. (Written with Deborah A. Marshall).
5. *Silent Songs.* Ace, 1994. (Written with Kathleen O'Malley).
6. *Ancestor's World.* Ace, 1996. (Written with King T. Jackson).

7. *Voices of Chaos.* Ace, 1998. (Written with Ru Emerson).

Starting with a story of first contact with the alien Simiu this series imagines a universe inhabited by several intelligent species united—although not always peacefully—by the Cooperative League of Systems. The Starbridge Academy becomes a training ground for representatives who go out among the stars to encourage understanding and unity among the races who vary widely not only in anatomy and psychology, but also in ethical and philosophical beliefs.

Genre: Science Fiction
Subjects: Life on other planets; Extraterrestrial beings; Outer space, exploration of

Criswell, Millie

329. Flowers of the West
1. *Wild Heather.* Warner, 1995.
2. *Sweet Laurel.* Warner, 1996.
3. *Prim Rose.* Warner, 1996.

Heather Martin wants to work on a newspaper, but in 1830 San Francisco, women don't work on newspapers. When she takes a job as a nanny for Brandon Montgomery, the owner of the city's largest newspaper, she finds she dislikes the man until passion brings the two together. Heather's sister Laurel seeks love in Denver where she tries to become a singer. Even though she can't sing, gambler Chance Rafferty hires her for his saloon. It isn't long before they too become attracted. Youngest sister Rose Elizabeth fights to save the family farm from an English duke and ends up falling in love with him.

Genre: Historical Romance
Subjects: Lovers; Marriage
Place/Time: San Francisco (Calif.)—19th century; Denver (Col.)—19th century

Cronin, A. J. (Archibald Joseph)

330.
1. *The Green Years.* Little, Brown, 1946.
2. *Shannon's Way.* Little, Brown, 1948.

When Robert Shannon is orphaned, he goes to Scotland to live with his mother's people. Of these, only his great-grandfather understands little boys. As Robert grows up, he enters medical school and dedicates his life to medical research.

Subjects: Orphans; Grandfathers; Boys; Physicians
Place/Time: Scotland—1900–1945

331.
1. *A Song of Sixpence.* Little, Brown, 1964.
2. *A Pocketful of Rye.* Little, Brown, 1969.

At the turn of the century, Laurence Carroll is a Catholic in an English Protestant town. When his father dies, his life is a struggle, but he is helped by his tightly knit family. He becomes a doctor and works in the poor districts. With a little fraud, he secures a job in a clinic in Switzerland and there meets his old love Cathy and her son.

Genre: Historical Romance
Subjects: Catholic faith; Physicians
Place/Time: England—1900–1945; Switzerland—1900–1945

Crow, Donna Fletcher

332. Daughters of Courage
1. *Kathryn.* Moody Press, 1992.
2. *Elizabeth.* Moody Press, 1993.
3. *Stephanie.* Moody Press, 1993.

Three young women, each in a different time period, learn to face struggle and turmoil through their faith in God. In 1900, Kathryn must adjust to a new community and to a new romance. In 1929, Elizabeth wants to go to college, but when the stock market crashes, she is more concerned about the possibility that her parents may lose their farm. In 1960, Stephanie follows her father into the Idaho statehouse, and the young idealist pushes a housing subsidy bill to solve the state's problems. Each woman must learn to trust God before she can triumph.

Genre: Christian Fiction
Subjects: Faith; Christian life; Women
Place/Time: United States—1900–1945; United States—1945–1980

Culp, John H.

333.
1. *Born of the Sun.* William Sloane, 1959.
2. *Restless Land.* William Sloane, 1962.

Orphan Kid Martin narrates the story of the first cattle drive from the wild northwest area of Texas to Abilene in 1870. After the drive, he returns to Tail End Ranch in the Concho country of northwest Texas. He fights Comanches, falls in love, and works to keep the ranch going. The world of the Texas cattle rancher is meticulously recreated.

Genre: Historical Fiction; Western
Subjects: Cattle drives; Ranch life; Cowboys
Place/Time: Texas—19th century

D'Annunzio, Gabriele

334. Romances of the Rose Trilogy
1. *The Triumph of Death.* Richmond, 1896.
2. *The Child of Pleasure.* Richmond, 1898.
3. *The Intruder.* Richmond, 1898. (Alternate title: *The Victim.*)

The themes of the tension between passion and sin, the pursuit of beauty, and a preoccupation with the extraordinary individual connect these philosophical stories set in 19th-century Italy. The first tale describes a man torn between two loves, the second the tragic end

of a love affair, and the third the agonizing decision regarding the fate of an illegitimate child.

Subjects: Philosophical novels; Love affairs; Illegitimacy; Good and evil; Individualism
Place/Time: Italy—19th century

Dailey, Janet

335.
1. *The Proud and the Free.* Little, Brown, 1994.
2. *Legacies.* Little, Brown, 1995.

In the 1830s in Georgia, Will Gordon and The Blade Stuart are Scots-Cherokees who have plantations. They are at odds as to how to deal with the Georgians who want their land. The Blade wants the Cherokees to head West, but Will Gordon refuses to leave. Will eventually marries his children's tutor Eliza, while The Blade's love, Temple Gordon, refuses to leave Georgia. In 1835, all of the Cherokees are banished from Georgia and take the Trail of Tears to Oklahoma. There the children and grandchildren of the two families have romantic conflicts and eventually end up on opposing sides of the Civil War.

Genre: Historical Romance; Family Saga
Subjects: Cherokee Indians; Plantation life; Family life; United States—Civil War, 1861–1865; Lovers
Place/Time: Georgia—19th century; Oklahoma—19th century

336. Calder Series
1. *This Calder Sky.* Pocket, 1981.
2. *This Calder Range.* Pocket, 1982.
3. *Stands a Calder Man.* Pocket, 1983.
4. *Calder Born, Calder Bred.* Pocket, 1983.
5. *Calder Pride.* HarperCollins, 1999.

This saga goes back and forth in time to tell the story of the four generations of Calder men and the fiery women they marry. Chase Benteen Calder goes to Montana with Lorna to set up a cattle ranch. Their son Chase builds a cattle empire and loves the headstrong Maggie O'Rourke. Their son Ty must fight to keep the ranch and discover which of two women he really loves. Ty's daughter, Cat, loses her fiance to a car crash and returns home to the Calder ranch. A one-night stand with a stranger leaves Cat with a baby boy. When the new sheriff in town turns out to be the child's father, Cat must decide what to do.

Genre: Family Saga; Romance
Subjects: Ranch life; Marriage
Place/Time: Montana—19th century; Montana—1900–1945; Montana—1945–1980

Daley, Brian

337. Coramonde
1. *The Doomfarers of Coramonde.* Ballantine, 1977.

2. *The Starfollowers of Coramonde.* Ballantine, 1979.

Soldiers mysteriously transported from Vietnam to magical Coramonde find themselves in the midst of a quest in a fantasy world of sorcerers, dragons, and ladies in distress. In the sequel, a sorceress army from Coramonde prepares to invade Earth.

Genre: Fantasy; Science Fiction
Subjects: Vietnamese War, 1961–1975; Imaginary wars and battles; Imaginary kingdoms; Soldiers

338. Hobart Floyt

1. *A Requiem for a Ruler of Worlds.* Ballantine, 1985.
2. *Jinx on a Terran Inheritance.* Ballantine, 1985.
3. *Fall of the White Ship Avatar.* Ballantine, 1986.

On Earth, which has become isolated within an interstellar civilization, conventional bureaucrat Hobart Floyt is plunged into a series of adventures when he mysteriously becomes the heir of a galactic emperor. Ne'er-do-well Alacrity Fitzhugh accompanies Floyt as they deal with an assassination plot and explore the key to an ancient alien technology.

Genre: Science Fiction
Subjects: Inheritance and succession; Extraterrestrial beings; Bureaucracy

Dalkey, Kara

339. Blood of the Goddess

1. *Goa.* Tor, 1996.
2. *Bijapur.* Tor, 1997.
3. *Bhagavati.* Tor, 1998.

Beginning in Goa, the 16th-century Portuguese colony on the west coast of India, English apothecary Thomas Chinnery searches for the Rasa Mahadevi or the Blood of the Goddess, which is lethal to the living but raises the dead. Thomas's search leads him to the beautiful Aditi, adopted daughter of the Goddess, who loves him but may be forced to kill him to protect her mother's temple. When Aditi is murdered, Thomas has a further reason to search for the powerful goddess in her hidden city Bhagavati.

Genre: Fantasy
Subjects: Gods and goddesses; Death; Resurrection; India
Place/Time: India—16th century

Dancer, Rex

340.

1. *Bad Girl Blues.* Simon & Schuster, 1994.
2. *Postcard from Hell.* Simon & Schuster, 1995.

Andy Derain is a burnt-out New York photographer who has returned to his roots in New Orleans. There, while he is having an assignation with fashion model Candy, a male prostitute is killed under his window. Andy chases the killer, but Candy runs back to her wealthy husband. As Andy searches for the truth, he feels the power of Candy's husband and encounters five fascinating women. Later an old girlfriend flees to Grand Cayman Island to avoid a local mobster. On the island, Andy gets involved in money laundering, drug smuggling, and more women.

Genre: Adventure
Subjects: Photographers; Adventure
Place/Time: New Orleans (La.)—1980–; Grand Cayman Island—1980–

Daniels, Les

341. Don Sebastian

1. *The Black Castle.* Scribner, 1978.
2. *The Silver Skull.* Scribner, 1979.
3. *Citizen Vampire.* Scribner, 1981.
4. *Yellow Fog.* Donald M. Grant, 1986.

In his various appearances throughout history, aristocratic vampire Don Sebastian struggles with his power-hungry brother during the Spanish Inquisition, wakes to the call of Aztec princesses, and pursues a young man through the French Revolution. Finally, assuming the form of a mortal, he serves as a medium for a young woman with a strong interest in life after death.

Genre: Horror
Subjects: Vampires; Brothers; Aztecs; Inquisition; France—revolution, 1789–1799
Place/Time: Spain—15th century; Mexico—16th century; France—18th century

Danielson, Peter

342. Children of the Lion

1. *Children of the Lion.* Bantam, 1980.
2. *The Shepherd Kings.* Bantam, 1981.
3. *Vengeance of the Lion.* Bantam, 1983.
4. *The Lion in Egypt.* Bantam, 1984.
5. *The Golden Pharaoh.* Bantam, 1986.
6. *The Lord of the Nile.* Bantam, 1986.
7. *The Prophecy.* Bantam, 1986.
8. *Sword of Glory.* Bantam, 1987.
9. *The Deliverer.* Bantam, 1988.
10. *The Exodus.* Bantam, 1989.
11. *The Sea Peoples.* Bantam, 1990.
12. *The Promised Land.* Bantam, 1990.
13. *The Invaders.* Bantam, 1991.
14. *The Trumpet and the Sword.* Bantam, 1992.
15. *Prophets and Warriors.* Bantam, 1993.
16. *Departed Glory.* Bantam, 1993.
17. *The Death of Kings.* Bantam, 1994.

Abram the Mesopotamian is told by God to leave Ur and settle in Canaan. He becomes Abraham, and he and his wife Sarah start a dynasty that will lead to King David and the ancient country of Israel. The Old Testament stories are retold by making the biblical figures believable and sympathetic.

Genre: Historical Fiction
Subjects: Biblical stories; Jews; Judaism
Place/Time: Palestine—to 70 A. D.

Danvers, Dennis

343.
1. *Circuit of Heaven.* Avon, 1998.
2. *End of Days.* Avon Eos, 1999.

The Bin is a 21st-century silicon crystal network, which has become a virtual home for the billions of disembodied personalities of refugees from Earth who want a cyber existence free of disease, danger, and death. In the first work, a young man visits the Bin intending to return to his risky mortal existence, but falls in love. In the second, a fundamentalist military leader, trying to fulfill his own prediction of an apocalypse, unleashes a killer virus in the Bin.

Genre: Science Fiction
Subjects: Technology and civilization; Computers; Love; Viruses

Dargan, Olive Tilford. *See Burke, Fielding*

Dashwood, Edmee Elizabeth Monica De La Pasture. *See Delafield, E. M.*

Daudet, Alphonse

344.
1. *Tartarin of Tarascon.* G. Routledge, 1887, 1872.
2. *Tartarin on the Alps.* T. Y. Crowell, 1894, 1885.
3. *Port Tarascon: The Last Adventures of the Illustrious Tartarin.* Harper & Row, 1891, 1890.

The lovable, imaginative braggart from the Provence area of France embellishes his adventures, which are hilarious, outrageous, and worthy of Sancho Panza, even though Tartarin thinks he is Don Quixote. A fourth Tartarin book, *La Defense de Tarascon*, has never been translated into English.

Genre: Humor
Subjects: Storytelling; Rogues and vagabonds; Picaresque novels
Place/Time: Provence (France)—19th century; France—19th century

Davenat, Colette

345.
1. *Deborah.* Morrow, 1973.

2. *Deborah and the Many Faces of Love.* Morrow, 1974.
3. *Deborah and the Siege of Paris.* Morrow, 1976.

Deborah, the beautiful, brilliant ward of one of Queen Elizabeth I's maids, is chosen by her sovereign to be a secret agent. In doing her Queen's bidding, she finds intrigue, danger, passion, and love in both England and France.

Genre: Historical Romance
Subjects: Courts and courtiers; Spies; Elizabeth I, Queen of England, 1533–1603
Place/Time: England—16th century; Scotland—16th century

Davies, Robertson

346. The Cornish Trilogy
1. *The Rebel Angels.* Viking, 1982.
2. *What's Bred in the Bone.* Viking, 1985.
3. *The Lyre of Orpheus.* Viking, 1989.

Frank Cornish is born in the small Canadian town of Blairlogie. Following in his parents footsteps, Frank becomes a spy during World War II. When he dies, he leaves a strange bequest to a small college in Toronto. Later, members of the foundation he set up fund the completion of an opera.

Subjects: Spies; World War II, 1939–1945; Gifts; College life
Place/Time: Europe—1900–1945; Canada—1900–1945

347. The Deptford Trilogy
1. *Fifth Business.* Viking, 1970.
2. *The Manticore.* Viking, 1972.
3. *World of Wonders.* Viking, 1976.

Three men who grew up in a small Canadian midwestern town relate their youth and its impact on them as adults. Dunstan Ramsay, David Stanton, and Magnus Eisengrim all find that they cannot escape the consequences of their childhood actions.

Genre: Coming of Age
Subjects: Children; Small town life
Place/Time: Canada—1945–1980

348. The Salterton Trilogy
1. *Tempest-Tost.* Rinehart, 1952.
2. *Leaven of Malice.* Scribner, 1955.
3. *A Mixture of Frailties.* Scribner, 1958.

The citizens of Salterton, Canada, are a bit eccentric and very funny as they try to put on a production of *The Tempest.* Solly Bridgetower, Humphrey Cobbler, Hector Mackilwraith, and Roger Tasset keep the action lively. The town becomes totally stirred up when a false engagement notice is put in the paper. In Salterton there is never a dull moment, and those moments are always funny.

Genre: Humor

Subjects: Amateur theater; Small town life
Place/Time: Canada—1945–1980

Davis, Julia

349.
1. *Cloud on the Land.* Sears Readers Club, 1951.
2. *Bridle the Wind.* Rinehart, 1953.
3. *Eagle on the Sun.* Rinehart, 1956.

This historical series, spanning the years from 1812 to the Mexican War, depicts the conflicts of plantation owner Angus McLeod and his wife, Lucy, who does not believe in slavery.

Genre: Historical Fiction
Subjects: Plantation life; Slavery; Abolitionists; Family life
Place/Time: Virginia—19th century; Washington (D. C.)—19th century; Texas—19th century

Davis, Kathryn Lynn

350.
1. *Too Deep for Tears.* Pocket Books, 1989.
2. *All We Hold Dear.* Pocket Books, 1995.
3. *Somewhere Lies the Moon.* Pocket, 1999.

English diplomat Charles Kittridge has wandered around the world in the 1880s and left behind him three very different daughters. Ailsa Rose is a Scottish beauty, Lian is a blue-eyed Chinese, and Geneva is an English daughter in India. Now that each girl is grown, Kittridge has one wish—to bring his three daughters together. One hundred years later, Eva Crawford is asked by her biological mother to learn about her past. She is given the 1882 journal of Ailsa Rose and learns of her life in the Scottish highlands of Glen Affric.

Genre: Historical Romance
Subjects: Sisters; Lovers
Place/Time: Scotland—19th century

Davis, W. E.

351. Valley of the Peacemaker
1. *The Gathering Storm.* Crossway, 1996.
2. *The Proving Ground.* Crossway, 1996.

In the 1870s, Matt Page, a young Midwestern farmer, sells his farm and heads to the gold fields of northern California. When his horse and money are stolen by prospectors, he stays on in Bridgeport. After foiling two robberies, Matt is appointed deputy sheriff. He marries Sarah, the sheriff's daughter, and they move to Bodie. When there is an explosion in a mine that kills several of his friends, Matt has to investigate. Later, when Matt and his wife lose their baby, they both have a crisis of faith.

Genre: Christian Fiction; Western
Subjects: Faith; Frontier and pioneer life; Gold mines and mining; Sheriffs; Marriage

Place/Time: California—19th century

De Blasis, Celeste

352.
1. *Wild Swan.* Bantam, 1984.
2. *Swan's Chance.* Bantam, 1985.
3. *A Season of Swans.* Bantam, 1989.

Alexandria Thaine Falconer leaves her home in Kent to settle with her husband in Maryland in the early 1810s. There they start a horse-breeding farm, Wild Swan, and raise their five children. The family is embroiled in the slavery issue, and the children are divided by the Civil War. Their mother holds the family and farm together. Later generations continue to fight among themselves but build up the racehorse farm. They crusade for women's rights, civil rights, and all of the other worthy causes of the late 19th and early 20th centuries.

Genre: Family Saga; Historical Fiction
Subjects: Horse breeding; United States—Civil War, 1861–1865; Social problems
Place/Time: Maryland—19th century; Maryland—1900–1945

de Camp, L. (Lyon) Sprague *and* Pratt, Fletcher

353. Harold Shea
1. *The Incomplete Enchanter.* Holt, 1941.
2. *The Castle of Iron.* Gnome Press, 1950.
The above titles have also been published in the following collection: *The Compleat Enchanter: The Magical Adventures of Harold Shea.* Doubleday, 1975.

3. *The Wall of Serpents.* Avalon, 1960.

In search of himself, psychologist Harold Shea travels through time and across the borders of reality into the worlds of Norse mythology, Charlemagne's conquests, and Cuchulain's battles. Returning to his present-day existence, he manages to bring back a lovely bride from another time to share his life.

Genre: Fantasy
Subjects: Time travel; Psychologists; Legends and folk tales; Cuchulain (legendary character); Charlemagne, Emperor, 742–814
Place/Time: France—8th century

De Graaf, Anne

354. The Hidden Harvest
1. *Bread Upon the Water.* Bethany House, 1995.
2. *Where the Fire Burns.* Bethany House, 1998.
3. *Out of the Red Shadow.* Bethany House, 1999.

In the aftermath of World War II, Hanna and Tadeusz, two young Poles, meet and fall in love just as Poland is being invaded by the Soviet Union. Hanna and her mother flee the Russians and hide in a Czech town. Tadeusz and Hanna's father are sent to a Soviet prison camp. Tadeusz meets Jack, an American spy trapped in Poland, and the two are bound together by their secrets. The two sons of Hanna and Tadeusz grow up under strict Communism, but one becomes a Christian and the other a rebel. Jack's American daughter comes to Poland to find him and meets the Rekarz sons. As she falls in love with them, she must decide between them and her father. All three generations use their faith to help them support Solidarity and defeat Communism.

Genre: Christian Fiction
Subjects: Faith; Spies; Communism
Place/Time: Poland—1945–1980

De Haven, Tom

355. Chronicles of the King's Tramp
1. *Walker of Worlds.* Doubleday, 1990.
2. *The End-of-Everything Man.* Doubleday, 1991.
3. *The Last Human.* Bantam, 1992.

Jack, a walker between worlds, must flee the land of Lostwithal when he makes a powerful enemy of the Mage. Because Jack knows that the world will end in chaos if he does not get to the king, he walks between worlds to hide from his pursuers. An eccentric group of characters join him in his quest to save Lostwithal and its multiple realities from a cast of evil powers.

Genre: Fantasy
Subjects: Imaginary kingdoms; Magic; End of the world

De la Roche, Mazo

356. The Whiteoak Saga
1. *The Building of Jalna.* Little, Brown, 1944.
2. *Morning at Jalna.* Little, Brown, 1960.
3. *Mary Wakefield.* Little, Brown, 1949.
4. *Young Renny.* Little, Brown, 1935.
5. *Whiteoak Heritage.* Little, Brown, 1940.
6. *The Whiteoak Brothers: Jalna-1923.* Little, Brown, 1953.
7. *Jalna.* Little, Brown, 1927.
8. *Whiteoaks of Jalna.* Little, Brown, 1929.
9. *Finch's Fortune.* Little, Brown, 1931.
10. *The Master of Jalna.* Little, Brown, 1933.
11. *Whiteoak Harvest.* Little, Brown, 1936.
12. *Wakefield's Course.* Little, Brown, 1941.
13. *Return to Jalna.* Little, Brown, 1946.
14. *Renny's Daughter.* Little, Brown, 1951.
15. *Variable Winds at Jalna.* Little, Brown, 1954.
16. *Centenary at Jalna.* Little, Brown, 1958.

The family saga to end them all: the Whiteoak family immigrate to Canada in 1850 and build Jalna, their family estate, where they live, love, and procreate for the next 100 years. The books are listed according to the chronology of events.

Genre: Family Saga; Historical Fiction
Subjects: Houses; Family life
Place/Time: Canada—19th century; Canada—1900–1945

de Lint, Charles

357. Urban Faerie
1. *Jack, the Giant-Killer.* Ace, 1987.
2. *Drink Down the Moon.* Ace, 1990.

From her mundane existence in Ottawa, Jacky Rowan falls into a fairyland that exists alongside the everyday world unseen to mortal eyes. Jacky engages in such pursuits as retrieving a magic horn from the bad fairies and escaping from a wizard who has taken power from the moon.

Genre: Fantasy
Subjects: Fairies; Imaginary kingdoms; Magic

De Vegh, Elizabeth Baynes

358.
1. *Coral Boatmen.* Arrowhead Press, 1981.
2. *Love: A Fearful Success.* Arrowhead Press, 1983.

Retired Englishman Richard Harrington spends his Christmas vacation on a Caribbean island with his daughter Constance, her American husband Pierce, and their young son Dick. As he becomes involved with the family and especially with his grandson, he begins to recover his reason to live. The tropics, the natives, and the young work on him.

Subjects: Retirement; Family life; Grandfathers
Place/Time: Caribbean region—1945–1980

Deforges, Regine

359.
1. *The Blue Bicycle.* Lyle Stuart, 1986, 1981.
2. *Lea.* Lyle Stuart, 1987, 1983.
3. *The Devil Laughs Again.* Lyle Stuart, 1988, 1985.

Lea is the beautiful daughter of a Bordeaux vineyard owner. In 1939, she is in love with Laurent, who deserts her to marry his cousin Camille. When the Nazis occupy France, she cares for Camille who is pregnant. As the war progresses, Lea works for the Underground. There she meets the mysterious Francois Tavernier, who will help her as she tries to protect her friends in Montillace. Lea then goes to Paris to work for the Red Cross. Her life keeps crossing with Laurent and Francois, and as the war ends, she must decide whom she loves.

Genre: Historical Fiction; Romance

Subjects: World War II, 1939–1945—underground movements
Place/Time: France—1900–1945

Deighton, Len

360. Faith, Hope & Charity
1. *Faith.* Harper Collins, 1994.
2. *Hope.* Harper Collins, 1995.
3. *Charity.* Harper Collins, 1996.

In 1987, as the Cold War winds down, enigmatic British spy Bernard Samson has become disenchanted with the devious plots of SIS. This includes the return of his wife Fiona who had been acting the role of double agent in East Germany. However, in bringing Fiona back to Britain, her sister Tessa is mysteriously killed. Then Samson's wealthy Polish brother-in-law disappears in Poland. After several sojourns behind the Iron Curtain, Samson finds that the answers to his questions lie behind the closed doors of his own department. *Note:* This series follows the Game, Set & Match series and the Hook, Line & Sinker series.

Genre: Espionage
Subjects: Husbands and wives; Defectors; Spies
Place/Time: England—1980–; Germany—1980–; Poland—1980–

361. Game, Set & Match
1. *Berlin Game.* Knopf, 1984.
2. *Mexico Set.* Knopf, 1985.
3. *London Match.* Knopf, 1985.

The above titles have also been published in the following collection: *Game, Set & Match.* Knopf, 1989.

British agent Bernard Samson must get an undercover agent known as Brahms Four out of East Berlin, but a security leak in the organization threatens Samson and the agent. As Samson flushes out the mole in the system, he discovers his wife is the double agent. Even though she defects, there are still indications that there is another mole, and Samson is suspected. *Note:* This series continues in the Hook, Line and Sinker series and in the Faith, Hope & Charity series.

Genre: Espionage
Subjects: Spies; Husbands and wives; Cold war; International intrigue
Place/Time: England—1945–1980; Berlin (Germany)—1945–1980; Germany—1945–1980

362. Hook, Line & Sinker
1. *Spy Hook.* Knopf, 1988.
2. *Spy Line.* Knopf, 1989.
3. *Spy Sinker.* Harper & Row, 1990.

British agent Bernard Samson is still under a cloud of suspicion because his wife Fiona defected to the Soviets. He is sent to Washington to trace a missing slush fund, but finds he is being used by London Central. He is accused of spying for the Soviets and flees to Berlin. When he is cleared of the charge, he has one final confrontation with Fiona. *Note:* This series follows the

Game, Set & Match series and continues in the Faith, Hope & Charity series.

Genre: Espionage
Subjects: Husbands and wives; Defectors; Spies
Place/Time: London (England)—1945–1980; Washington (D. C.)—1945–1980; Berlin (Germany)—1945–1980; England—1945–1980; Germany—1945–1980

Delafield, E. M. *Pseud. of* Edmee Elizabeth Monica De La Pasture Dashwood

363.
1. *Diary of a Provincial Lady.* Harper, 1931.
2. *The Provincial Lady in London.* Harper, 1933.
3. *The Provincial Lady in America.* Harper, 1934.
4. *I Visit the Soviets: The Provincial Lady in Russia.* Harper, 1937.
5. *The Provincial Lady in Wartime.* Harper, 1940.

Using a diary format, the Provincial Lady, an upper-class Englishwoman living in Devon, retells her everyday life with satire and charm. Her husband, Robert, is silent; the two children are lively; and the servants dominate the house. When her book is successful, she gets a flat in London and mixes with the literary greats. Later she tours both America and Russia and gives her impressions of life in these two different countries. She comes home and relates the ups and downs of wartime England.

Subjects: Authors; Diaries (stories in diary form); Family life; Travel
Place/Time: England—1900–1945; United States—1900–1945; Soviet Union—1917–1945

Delderfield, R. F. (Ronald Frederick)

364.
1. *A Horseman Riding By.* Simon & Schuster, 1967.
2. *The Green Gauntlet.* Simon & Schuster, 1968.

In 1902, Paul Craddock, wounded in the second Boer War, comes back to England and buys a run-down Devonshire estate. As he tries to revitalize it, he becomes involved with the seven families who are his tenants. For more than three decades, the squire confronts the devastations of war and the crises of the postwar years with moral values inherited from a more self-confident past.

Genre: Historical Fiction
Subjects: Social classes; Houses
Place/Time: England—1900–1945

365.

1. *God Is an Englishman.* Simon & Schuster, 1970.
2. *Theirs Was the Kingdom.* Simon & Schuster, 1971.
3. *Give Us This Day.* Simon & Schuster, 1973.

When Adam Swann returns from India to England in 1857, he founds a freight-hauling business, marries Henrietta Rawlinson, and raises nine children. Adam and his children and grandchildren build their fortune against the background of changing Victorian social and political history.

Genre: Historical Fiction
Subjects: Businessmen; Family life
Place/Time: England—19th century

Dell, Floyd

366.

1. *Mooncalf.* Knopf, 1920.
2. *The Briary Bush.* Knopf, 1921.

Felix Fay is eager, undisciplined, self-centered, and demanding of life. From his childhood through the early years of his marriage in Chicago, he learns that playing with life and marriage is cowardly and that reality might be more beautiful than his theories. When he becomes a journalist, he meets Rose Ann and marries her, but the two must learn to live as man and wife.

Genre: Coming of Age
Subjects: Boys; Marriage; Journalists
Place/Time: Chicago (Ill.)—1900–1945; Illinois—1900–1945

Dengler, Sandy

367. Australian Destiny

1. *Code of Honor.* Bethany House, 1988.
2. *Power of Pinjarra.* Bethany House, 1989.
3. *Taste of Victory.* Bethany House, 1989.
4. *East of Outback.* Bethany House, 1990.

Responding to an offer of indenture, Samantha Connolly and her sisters have attempted to escape turn-of-the-century Ireland by immigrating to Queensland to work on a sugar plantation. When tragedy strikes the plantation they head out into southern Queensland to work in the opal rich mines and wool industries of the outback.

Genre: Christian Fiction; Historical Fiction
Subjects: Plantation life; Faith; Indentured servants
Place/Time: Queensland (Australia)—19th century; Australia—19th century

Denker, Henry

368.

1. *Horowitz and Mrs. Washington.* Putnam, 1979.

2. *Mrs. Washington and Horowitz Too.* Morrow, 1993.

Feisty 65-year-old Samuel Horowitz fights with two muggers in New York and lands in the hospital with a minor stroke. When he is assigned to African American physical therapist Harriet Washington, the cranky man has met his match and a real friendship blossoms. Six years later when Horowitz's wife dies and he feels lost, Mrs. Washington sets out to restore his zest for life by getting him involved with crack babies in Harlem and other projects, including love.

Subjects: Friendship; Elderly; African Americans
Place/Time: New York (N. Y.)—1945–1980

Dennis, Patrick. *Pseud. of* Edward Tanner

369.

1. *Auntie Mame: An Irreverent Escapade.* Vanguard, 1955.
2. *Around the World with Auntie Mame.* Harcourt Brace, 1958.

In the 1920s, Mame is given her orphaned nephew Patrick, and he retells fondly the hilarious escapades of his madcap aunt as she shows him the zanier side of life. In 1937, his aunt takes him on a trip around the world before he goes to college. From Paris to Biarritz to Vienna to China, they have one crazy adventure after another.

Genre: Historical Fiction; Humor
Subjects: Aunts; Nephews; Eccentrics and eccentricities; Voyages and travels
Place/Time: New York (N. Y.)—1900–1945; Europe—1900–1945

Derleth, August William

370. Sac Prairie Saga

1. *Wind over Wisconsin.* Scribner, 1938.
2. *Restless Is the River.* Scribner, 1939.
3. *Shadow of Night.* Scribner, 1943.
4. *Still Is the Summer Night.* Scribner, 1937.
5. *Sweet Genevieve.* Scribner, 1942.
6. *Evening in Spring.* Scribner, 1941.
7. *The Shield of the Valiant.* Scribner, 1945.
8. *Place of Hawks.* Loring & Mussey, 1935.
9. *Country Growth.* Scribner, 1940.
10. *Sac Prairie People.* Stanton & Lee, 1948.
11. *Wisconsin in Their Bones.* Duell, 1961.
12. *Village Year: A Sac Prairie Journal.* Coward, 1941.
13. *Village Daybook.* Pellgun & Cudahy, 1947.
14. *Wisconsin Country.* Candlelight Press, 1965.
15. *Countryman's Journal.* Duell, 1963.
16. *Atmosphere of Houses.* Prairie Press, 1939.
17. *Walden West.* Duell, 1961.
18. *Return to Walden West.* Candlelight Press, 1970.

19. *Wisconsin Earth: A Sac Prairie Sampler.* Stanton & Lee, 1948.

This long series of novels takes place in Sac Prairie, a fictitious place based on Derleth's home in Sauk City, Wisconsin. Books 1 to 4 cover the history of Wisconsin from the settlers' war with the Indians in 1830 to the settlement of Sac Prairie by Scandinavians and Hungarians. Books 5 to 18 take place in contemporary Sac Prairie and cover the descendants of the early settlers. Recurring characters such as Steve Grendon, Margery Estebrook, Gus Elke, and Aunt Mary all tell the story of life in a small town and celebrate the values of the people and the place. Books 8 to 11 are interconnected short stories featuring the major characters from Derleth's novels. Book 19 is a collection of three of the novels: *Shadow of Night*, *Place of Hawks*, and *Village Year*.

Genre: Gentle Read; Historical Fiction
Subjects: Frontier and pioneer life; Small town life
Place/Time: Wisconsin—multicentury span

371. Wisconsin Saga
1. *Bright Journey.* Scribner, 1940.
2. *The House on the Mound.* Duell, 1958.
3. *The Hills Stand Watch.* Duell, 1960.
4. *The Shadow in the Glass.* Duell, 1963.
5. *The Wind Leans West.* Candlelight Press, 1967.

The history of Wisconsin from territory in 1812 to statehood in the 1840s is told through the stories of real settlers and events. Hercules Doosman and his wife Jane Rolette become the first millionaires in the state through the fur trade. The rise and decline of the lead mining industry, the struggle to establish banks, and the story of Nelson Deuvey, the first governor, give an account of the early years of Wisconsin history.

Genre: Historical Fiction
Subjects: Frontier and pioneer life; Small town life
Place/Time: Wisconsin—19th century

Destouches, Louis-Ferdinand. *See* Celine, Louis-Ferdinand

Deveraux, Jude. *Pseud. of* Jude Gilliam White

372.
1. *The Velvet Promise.* Pocket Books, 1981.
2. *Highland Velvet.* Pocket Books, 1982.
3. *Velvet Song.* Pocket Books, 1983.
4. *Velvet Angel.* Pocket Books, 1985.
5. *The Temptress.* Pocket Books, 1986.
6. *The Raider.* Pocket Books, 1987.
7. *The Princess.* Pocket Books, 1988.
8. *The Awakening.* Pocket Books, 1988.

The saga of the Montgomery family, from the Scottish highlands of the 1400s to the farmland of California of the 1910s, is told through the family's lusty men and the women they love. Each generation of tall, dark, and handsome men must fight fierce enemies and equally feisty women. When England becomes too quiet, the descendants move to America where they are embroiled in the American Revolution, the Civil War, Indian wars, and union fights along with fighting for their true loves.

Genre: Family Saga; Historical Romance
Subjects: Love; Marriage; Courtship; Frontier and pioneer life
Place/Time: Scotland—multicentury span; California—multicentury span

373. James River Trilogy
1. *Counterfeit Lady.* Pocket Books, 1984.
2. *Lost Lady.* Pocket Books, 1985.
3. *River Lady.* Pocket Books, 1985.

Along the James River in Virginia in the 1790s, three sets of star-crossed lovers must fight obstacles to their love. Each of the women—Nicole, Regan, and Leah—find they are married to men who don't love them, but using their wiles, they win their love as all the couples' lives are intertwined.

Genre: Historical Romance
Subjects: Marriage; Women
Place/Time: Virginia—18th century

Dew, Robb Forman

374.
1. *Dale Loves Sophie to Death.* Farrar, Straus, & Giroux, 1981.
2. *Fortunate Lives.* Morrow, 1992.

The perils of domestic life are explored as Dinah Howells finds she can't escape being someone's child and also someone's mother. She becomes re-involved with her divorced parents when she visits them in Ohio. When she returns to Massachusetts, she faces her own crisis when her husband has an affair. As her children grow up, she must face the misunderstandings and frustrations between parents and children and husband and wife as the family goes through its routine activities.

Subjects: Middle age; Husbands and wives; Conflict of generations
Place/Time: Massachusetts—1945–1980; Ohio—1945–1980

Dexter, Susan

375. The Warhorse of Esdragon
1. *The Prince of Ill Luck.* Ballantine, 1994.
2. *The Wind Witch.* Ballantine, 1994.
3. *The True Knight.* Ballantine, 1996.

Valadan, a magical horse sired by the wind, connects these tales of the realm of Esdragon. Valadan helps Prince Leith to scale a glass hill and begin to cure the ills of his land. Druyan, who inherits the horse from her grandfather, needs his help to hold onto her farm after her husband's death. Finally Valadan helps an injured warrior achieve knighthood.

Genre: Fantasy; Animal Story
Subjects: Mythical animals; Horses; Imaginary kingdoms

Dickson, Gordon R.
376. The Childe Cycle
1. *Necromancer.* Doubleday, 1962.
2. *Tactics of Mistake.* Doubleday, 1971.
3. *Soldier, Ask Not.* Dell, 1967.
4. *The Genetic General.* Ace, 1960.

Books 1, 2, and 4 have also been published together in the following collection: *Three to Dorsai!: Three Novels from the Childe Cycle.* Doubleday, 1975.

5. *The Spirit of Dorsai.* Ace, 1979.
6. *Lost Dorsai.* Ace, 1980.
7. *The Final Encyclopedia.* Tor, 1984.
8. *The Chantry Guild.* Ace, 1988.
9. *Young Bleys.* Tor, 1991.
10. *Other.* Tor, 1994.

Into a futuristic projection of human evolution is woven the story of the reincarnation of a heroic figure, who passes through military, philosophical, and religious existences. His ultimate encounter is with a dark alter ego, the product of the interaction of complex genetic forces and the migration of humanity to other worlds.

Genre: Science Fiction
Subjects: Evolution; Reincarnation

377. Dragon
1. *Dragon and the George.* Doubleday, 1976.
2. *Dragon Knight.* Tor, 1990.
3. *Dragon on the Border.* Ace, 1992.
4. *Dragon at War.* Ace, 1992.
5. *The Dragon, the Earl, and the Troll.* Ace, 1994.
6. *The Dragon and the Djinn.* Ace, 1996.
7. *The Dragon and the Gnarly King.* Tor, 1997.
8. *The Dragon in Lyonesse.* Tor, 1998.

Jim Eckert manages to follow his intended bride Angie into the realm of medieval magic to which she was exiled by an evil professor, but the price is high: Jim assumes the form of a dragon. Once adjusted to his new world and existence, Jim learns to shift his shape back and forth between beast and man at will, and finds himself engaged in key events in French and English history and in magical interactions with sorcerers, sea serpents, meddlesome fairies, an Arabian djinn, and all-too-human dragons.

Genre: Fantasy
Subjects: Dragons; Imaginary kingdoms; Love

Diehl, William
378.
1. *Primal Fear.* Villard, 1992.
2. *Show of Evil.* Ballantine, 1995.
3. *Reign in Hell.* Random House, 1997.

Chicago defense attorney Martin Vail is appointed the pro bono defense attorney of Aaron Stampler, a young man accused of murdering Archbishop Richard Rushman. Stampler was found in the confessional, covered with blood and holding the murder weapon. Vail puts together a powerful team, and they discover shocking truths about the archbishop and Stampler. Ten years later Vail is now a D.A. and Stampler is set to be released from a mental institution. When murder victims are dispatched in the same way Stampler dispatched his victims, Vail must discover who Stampler's accomplice is. When Vail becomes Illinois Attorney General, he is asked by the President of the United States to place on trial one of the largest militia outfits in the country. He must also go after Stampler, who is posing as a preacher.

Genre: Crime Novel
Subjects: Murder and murderers; Serial murders; Law and lawyers
Place/Time: Chicago (Ill.)—1980–

Dixon, Larry. *See* Lackey, Mercedes

Dixon, Stephen
379.
1. *Gould.* Henry Holt, 1996.
2. *30.* Henry Holt, 1999.

Gould Bookbinder is a New York book reviewer and college instructor who throughout his life is obsessed with sex. From 1950 to the 1990s, Gould is driven to have sex and to have children, but all the women he's gotten pregnant have abortions. Eventually he lives with Evangeline and her child, and they have a wildly sexual relationship even after Gould marries. As he ages, Gould has elaborate sexual fantasies about much younger women. Written in an elaborate stream-of-consciousness style, the sex scenes are numerous and explicitly described.

Subjects: Sex; Abortion; Love affairs; Stream of consciousness
Place/Time: New York (N. Y.)—1945–1980; New York (N. Y.)—1980–

Djerassi, Carl
380.
1. *Cantor's Dilemma.* Penguin, 1991.
2. *The Bourbaki Gambit.* University of Georgia Press, 1994.
3. *Menachem's Seed.* University of Georgia Press, 1997.
4. *No.* University of Georgia Press, 1998.

Djerassi, a distinguished scientist, explores the world of scientific experimentation through four different scientists. When a distinguished cell biologist and his student win the Nobel Prize, the scientific community suspects them of falsifying data. In the second book, Max Weiss, a senior biochemist who has been demoted to researcher, organizes a secret team to work together and publish under a fictional identity. When they find a real breakthrough in DNA replication, the team clashes and falls apart. Djerassi then explores the world of in-vitro fertilization through Melanie Laidlaw, a childless widow, and Menachem Dvir, an infertile nuclear engineer. The quartet closes as Djerassi explores the ways in which science and business work to bring a new scientific device to the market. Renu Krishnan works with both scientists and investors to bring a device to help men who are impotent achieve an erection. Renu's struggles in academia and the corporate world reveal the relationship between science and business.

Subjects: Scientists
Place/Time: United States—1980–

Doblin, Alfred

381.
1. *A People Betrayed.* Fromm Int., 1983, 1948.
2. *Karl and Rosa.* Fromm Int., 1983, 1950.

The seething turmoil of Berlin after the Armistice of 1918 is portrayed through historical personages such as Rosa Luxemburg and Karl Liebknecht. The chaos of war is vividly shown, and the indecision of Karl and Rosa leads to the failure of the revolution.

Genre: Historical Fiction; War
Subjects: World War I, 1914–1918; Revolutions and revolutionists
Place/Time: Berlin (Germany)—1900–1945; Germany—1900–1945

Dodd, Christina

382.
1. *A Well-Pleasured Lady.* Avon, 1997.
2. *A Well-Favored Gentleman.* Avon, 1998.

In England in 1793, the Fairchild family has come upon hard times. Lady Guinevere Mary Fairchild is posing as Mary Fairchild, a housekeeper to Viscount Whitfield, because she is suspected off being a murderess. When Whitfield's godson recognizes Mary, he forces her to pose as his fiancee while they search for a stolen diary. As they search, sparks fly between the two. Mary's brother Ian Fairchild fights the beautiful Lady of Fionnaway for property in Scotland. They struggle for both the land and love.

Genre: Historical Romance
Subjects: Servants; Aristocracy—England; Lovers
Place/Time: England—18th century; Scotland—18th century

Dodgson, Charles. *See* Carroll, Lewis

Doig, Ivan

383.
1. *Dancing at the Rascal Fair.* Atheneum, 1987.
2. *English Creek.* Atheneum, 1984.
3. *Ride with Me, Mariah Montana.* Atheneum, 1990.

Angus McCaskill and his best friend Rob Barclay leave Scotland in 1889 to find Rob's uncle who had immigrated to Montana. Having found him, they establish homes and settle down to raise sheep, but sometimes fight with each other. Angus's grandson Jick grows up among the mountains and the pioneers. Later as an old man, he takes his daughter Mariah on a tour of the state, which is caught between an unknown future and its pioneer past. Doig captures the conflicts of the West and their impact on private lives.

Genre: Family Saga; Historical Fiction
Subjects: Sheep and sheep farming
Place/Time: Montana—19th century

Donaldson, Stephen R.

384. The Chronicles of Thomas Covenant
1. *Lord Foul's Bane.* Holt, 1977.
2. *The Illearth War.* Holt, 1977.
3. *The Power That Preserves.* Holt, 1977.
4. *The Wounded Land.* Ballantine, 1980.
5. *The One Tree.* Ballantine, 1982.
6. *White Gold Wielder.* Ballantine, 1983.

Writer Thomas Covenant is moved back and forth between day-to-day existence and the magical Land by a series of accidents. Far from the usual heroic figure of fantasy, Thomas, who suffers from leprosy when living in the real world, progresses toward a heightened moral sensibility through contact with the powerful Staff of Law and a white gold ring as he battles such dark forces as Lord Foul and the evil controllers of nature, the Sunbane and the Clave.

Genre: Fantasy
Subjects: Imaginary wars and battles; Leprosy; Good and evil; Ethics

385. Gap
1. *The Real Story.* Bantam, 1991.
2. *Forbidden Knowledge: The Gap into Vision.* Bantam, 1991.
3. *A Dark and Hungry God Arises: The Gap into Power.* Bantam, 1992.

In the far future of space travel, pirates and gangsters, such as Angus Thermopyle and Nick Succorso, are as powerful as ever. At the center of their conflict is a beautiful former police officer Morn Hyland who, when not enslaving or being enslaved by them, deals with the mysterious alien Amnion.

Genre: Science Fiction
Subjects: Extraterrestrial beings; Crime and criminals; Police

386. Mordant's Need
1. *The Mirror of Her Dreams.* Ballantine, 1986.
2. *A Man Rides Through.* Ballantine, 1987.

Mirrors are magical and extremely powerful in the land of Mordant. They are also important to insecure Terisa Morgen, who lines her urban apartment with them to prove to herself that she exists. In the process of searching for a champion, the mirrors of Mordant accidentally intersect with those in Terisa's apartment. As a result, she finds herself in Mordant embroiled in complex medieval battles and plots.

Genre: Fantasy
Subjects: Mirrors; Imaginary wars and battles; Self-confidence

Donati, Sara

387.
1. *Into the Wilderness.* Bantam, 1998.
2. *Down on a Distant Shore.* Bantam, 2000.

Elizabeth Middleton leaves her sheltered life in England in the late 18th century and joins her father and brother in upstate Paradise, New York. Her father hopes to marry her to a neighbor so both men can join their property, but Elizabeth meets Nathaniel Bonner, a Scotsman raised by Mohawks. The two fall in love and marry, and have twins. Nathaniel goes to Canada to help his father escape from the English, but he too is captured. Concerned with his safety, Elizabeth takes the twins through the wilderness to Canada. When the twins are kidnapped and taken to Scotland, Elizabeth and a freed Nathaniel sail there to retrieve them. The Earl of Carryck, a distant relative, has drawn them to Scotland so they can claim the castle, but the two must fight redcoats, privateers, and scoundrels before they can settle down and raise their family.

Genre: Historical Romance
Subjects: Love; Marriage; Husbands and wives; Frontier and pioneer life
Place/Time: New York (state)—18th century; Scotland—18th century

Donleavy, J. P. (James Patrick)

388.
1. *The Destinies of Darcy Dancer, Gentleman.* Delacorte, 1977.
2. *Leila.* Delacorte Press, 1983.

Darcy, born on a decaying estate in Ireland in the 1800s, is educated by a lovelorn tutor and initiated to love by an aristocratic refugee housekeeper. In Dublin, he has his nude portrait painted, faces a gunman, and becomes a vagabond doing menial work. He is always searching for one bright idea to lead him, looking for love, wishing for comfort, and seeing hope on the horizon.

Genre: Historical Fiction
Subjects: Picaresque novels; Rogues and vagabonds; Love affairs
Place/Time: Ireland—19th century

Doohan, James *and* Stirling, S. M.

389. Flight Engineer
1. *The Rising.* Baen, 1996.
2. *The Privateer.* Baen, 1999.

In a distant future Commonwealth of worlds, a group of religious fanatics, the Mollies, and the alien insect-like Fibians do battle with government forces over the spaceship fuel antihydrogen. Flight engineer Peter Raeder becomes part of the conflict and saves an entire spaceship by going against the orders of his superiors. He faces a court of inquiry and assignment to a desk job, but as a way of avoiding this dreary punishment, he is offered a top-secret mission that takes him into a dangerous asteroid belt.

Genre: Science Fiction
Subjects: Interplanetary wars; Space flight; Religion; Extraterrestrial beings

Dos Passos, John

390. U.S.A. Series
1. *The 42nd Parallel.* Constable, 1930.
2. *1919.* Constable, 1932.
3. *The Big Money.* Harcourt Brace, 1936.

This chronicle of American life during the early 20th century is a brilliant mixture of "Newsreel" and "Camera Eye" excerpts, interwoven with quotations, narratives, and headlines. It traces the lives of five characters—a sailor, the daughter of a minister, a girl from Texas, a radical Jew, and a poet—as their lives interconnect in post–World War I New York. As their stories are told, they meet real people of the time, such as Edison and Carnegie.

Subjects: Seamen; Jews; Poets; Social problems
Place/Time: New York (N. Y.)—1900–1945

Douglas, Carole Nelson

391.
1. *Probe.* Tor, 1985.
2. *Counterprobe.* Tor, 1988.

At first, psychiatrist Kevin Blake treats Jane as an amnesiac but soon discovers that she is in fact a woman endowed with superhuman powers by aliens on another world. As he protects her from those who would harm and exploit her, he falls in love with her.

Genre: Science Fiction
Subjects: Psychiatrists; Extraterrestrial beings; Love

392. Sword and Circlet Trilogy
1. *Keepers of Edanvant.* Tor, 1988.
2. *Heir of Rengarth.* Tor, 1988.
3. *Seven of Swords.* Tor, 1989.

The prescient immortal, Irissa, and her beloved swordsman, Kendric, do battle with the evil sorcerer Geronfrey, assume the throne of the magic kingdom of Rengarth, and finally try to gain immortality for Kendric through the magic of the seventh sword.

Genre: Fantasy
Subjects: Imaginary wars and battles; Imaginary kingdoms; Immortality; Arms and armor

393. The Taliswoman
1. *Cup of Clay.* Tom Doherty, 1991.
2. *Seed Upon the Wind.* Tom Doherty, 1992.

From the magical but blighted land of Veil, Alison Carver, a Minneapolis journalist, returns with a cup that seems to hold the key to her destiny and that of the mystical land she left so gladly. Drawn back to Veil, she is reunited with her beloved dog and with the heroic but difficult Rowan, for whom her feelings are far more ambivalent.

Genre: Fantasy
Subjects: Imaginary kingdoms; Charms; Love

Douglas, Lloyd C.

394.
1. *Dr. Hudson's Secret Journal.* Houghton Mifflin, 1930.
2. *Magnificent Obsession.* Houghton Mifflin, 1929.

The "magnificent obsession"—a new interpretation of Christian teaching—was the secret of the famous Dr. Hudson's success. Bobby Merrill, his successor at his Detroit hospital, continues the secret philanthropy and develops an invention that saves the life of the woman he loves.

Genre: Gentle Read
Subjects: Physicians; Christian life; Philanthropists; Inventors; Faith
Place/Time: Detroit (Mich.)—1900–1945; Michigan—1900–1945

395.
1. *Green Light.* Houghton Mifflin, 1935.
2. *Invitation to Live.* Houghton Mifflin, 1940.

Suffering from crippling polio has made Dean Harcourt more sensitive to the needs of others. His increased awareness and compassion help change the lives of a group of young people in a Midwestern town.

Genre: Gentle Read
Subjects: Poliomyelitis; Youth; Faith
Place/Time: Midwestern states—1900–1945

396.
1. *The Robe.* Houghton Mifflin, 1942.

2. *The Big Fisherman.* Houghton Mifflin, 1948.

The influence of early Christianity is explored through the stories of two men whose lives were touched by Jesus Christ. Marcellus, a young Roman soldier who wins Christ's robe shooting dice, is subsequently converted to Christianity. The life of Simon Peter, chosen by Christ to lead His disciples, offers another view of the beginning of the Christian religion.

Genre: Christian Fiction; Historical Fiction
Subjects: Christians, early; Jesus Christ; Peter, the Apostle, Saint; Caligula, Emperor of Rome, 12–41 A.D.; Faith
Place/Time: Palestine—to 70 A. D.

Dowdey, Clifford

397. Story of Richmond, Virginia
1. *Gamble's Hundred.* Little, 1939.
2. *Tidewater.* Little, 1943.
3. *Bugles Blow No More.* Little, 1937.
4. *Where My Love Sleeps.* Little, 1945.
5. *Sing for a Penny.* Little, 1941.

Using his family's records and reminiscences, the author created a fictional history of Virginia beginning with the life of an 18th-century plantation surveyor and continuing with the story of a Virginian who goes west with the frontier. The last three novels narrate the siege of Richmond, the later years of the Civil War, and the rebuilding of Richmond.

Genre: Historical Fiction
Subjects: Plantation life; Frontier and pioneer life; United States—Civil War, 1861–1865
Place/Time: Virginia—18th century; Virginia—19th century

Downing, John Hyatt

398.
1. *Sioux City.* Putnam, 1940.
2. *Anthony Trant.* Putnam, 1941.

Anthony Trant comes home from college determined to make money and avoid his father's easygoing financial ways. His fortunes and those of Sioux City ebb and flow in the Midwest of the early 1900s.

Genre: Historical Fiction
Subjects: Ambition; Fathers and sons; Small town life
Place/Time: Sioux City (Iowa)—1900–1945; Iowa—1900–1945

Doyle, Arthur Conan, Sir

399. The Professor Challenger Novels
1. *The Lost World.* Doran, 1915.
2. *The Poison Belt.* Doran, 1913.
3. *The Land of Mist.* Doran, 1926.

The above titles have also been published in the following collection: *The Professor Challenger Stories*. Murray, 1952.

The adventurous Professor Challenger discovers prehistoric animals in an Amazon jungle, deals with a world threatened by poison gas, and finally encounters a group of spiritualists who change his skepticism about communication with the dead to belief.

Genre: Science Fiction
Subjects: Explorers; Prehistoric animals

Doyle, Roddy

400.
1. *The Commitments.* Vintage, 1989.
2. *The Snapper.* Penguin, 1992.
3. *The Van.* Viking, 1992.

The above titles have also been published in the following collection: *The Barrytown Trilogy.* Penguin, 1995.

The working-class Rabbitte family of Barrytown Dublin is chronicled in these humorous and farcical novels. Young Jimmy organizes a rock band, daughter Sharon becomes pregnant, and dad Jimmy Sr. loses his job. The Rabbittes may not be successful, but their love and laughter propel them through life's trials.

Genre: Humor
Subjects: Family life
Place/Time: Dublin (Ireland)—1980–; Ireland—1980–

Drabble, Margaret

401.
1. *The Radiant Way.* Knopf, 1987.
2. *A Natural Curiosity.* Viking, 1989.
3. *The Gates of Ivory.* Viking, 1991.

In the 1950s, three young women meet at Cambridge and stay friends even after college. Liz Headland is a psychotherapist and mother; Alix Bowen, also a mother, teaches poor children in a government school; and Esther Breuer is an art scholar. The women experience divorce, death, and job loss. As they grow older, they struggle to find themselves amid the problems and distractions of contemporary British life. As middle-class women, they try to understand where they are and where they should be going.

Subjects: Friendship; Women—psychology; Middle classes
Place/Time: England—1945–1980

Drake, David. *See also* Stirling, S. M. (The General series); Weber, David (*More than Honor*)

402.
1. *Lord of the Isles.* Tor, 1997.

2. *Queen of Demons.* Tor, 1998.
3. *Servant of the Dragon.* Tor, 1999.

A woman claiming to be Tenoctris, a wizard from the Empire of the Isles, which the magic of a sorcerer sank into the sea 1000 years ago, appears on the shore of an island village. She helps Sharina and Garric, the real heirs to the kingdom, who are living in disguise. As he ascends the throne of the land, Garric is guided by the spirit of the former King Carus.

Genre: Fantasy
Subjects: Inheritance and succession; Imaginary kingdoms; Kings and rulers; Magic

Dreiser, Theodore

403. Trilogy of Desire
1. *The Financier.* Harper, 1912.
2. *The Titan.* Lane, 1914.
3. *The Stoic.* Doubleday, 1947.

Based on the life of robber baron and urban transit magnate Charles T. Yerkes, Frank Cowperwood's life reflects the American 19th-century dream. He rises from poverty in Philadelphia to riches and power in Chicago, but descends into loneliness in his old age in London. He discovers that his ruthless drive to the top has brought him money, but nothing else.

Genre: Historical Fiction
Subjects: Businessmen; Wealth; Ambition; Business—unscrupulous methods
Place/Time: Philadelphia (Pa.)—19th century; Chicago (Ill.)—19th century; London (England)—19th century; Pennsylvania—19th century; Illinois—19th century; England—19th century

Drew, Wayland

404. The Erthring Cycle
1. *The Memoirs of Alcheringia.* Ballantine, 1984.
2. *The Gaian Expedient.* Ballantine, 1985.
3. *The Master of Norriya.* Ballantine, 1986.

The above titles have also been published in the following collection: *The Erthring Cycle.* Doubleday, 1986.

In a future world devastated by a nuclear holocaust, most of the survivors have formed nomadic tribes that reject technology as troublesome and dangerous. When an underground group of scientists with their own schisms and problems seeks to control this society, a rebellion erupts.

Genre: Science Fiction
Subjects: Nuclear warfare; Nomads; Technology and civilization; Revolutions and revolutionists

Druon, Maurice

405. The Accursed King Series
1. *The Iron King.* Scribner, 1956.

2. *The Strangled Queen.* Scribner, 1956.
3. *The Poisoned Crown.* Scribner, 1957.
4. *The Royal Succession.* Scribner, 1958.
5. *The She-Wolf of France.* Scribner, 1960.
6. *The Lily and the Lion.* Scribner, 1961.

When Jacques de Molay was burned at the stake by King Philip IV of France, he cursed the "Iron King's" descendants. This is their story, with all the savagery and courtliness of 13th-century France realistically portrayed. The original *Les Rois Maudits* received the *Prix Goncourt.*

Genre: Historical Fiction
Subjects: Kings and rulers; Courts and courtiers; Middle Ages; Philip IV, King of France, 1268–1314
Place/Time: France—13th century; France—14th century

Drury, Allen

406.

1. *Advise and Consent.* Doubleday, 1959.
2. *A Shade of Difference.* Doubleday, 1962.
3. *Capable of Honor.* Doubleday, 1966.
4. *Preserve and Protect.* Doubleday, 1968.
5. *Come Nineveh, Come Tyre: The Presidency of Edward M. Jason.* Doubleday, 1973.
6. *The Promise of Joy.* Doubleday, 1975.

These novels about the American political scene in the 1960s and 70s center around a group of characters in the legislative and executive branches of government. President Harley Hudson nominates a controversial man to be Secretary of State, then must watch Congressional machinations. President Hudson must fight a liberal takeover of the presidential convention and, when he is killed in a plane crash, another fight erupts over who will be nominated for president. Drury's politics are conservative, but he reveals the ambitions, the backroom bargaining, and the workings of government.

Subjects: Politics—United States; Presidents—United States; United States Congress
Place/Time: Washington (D. C.)—1945–1980

407.

1. *The Hill of Summer: A Novel of the Soviet Conquest.* Doubleday, 1981.
2. *The Roads of Earth.* Doubleday, 1984.

The new leader of the U.S.S.R., psychotic Yuri Serapin, has a quick plan for destroying America and conquering the world. When Serapin starts a war and attacks American allies, U. S. President Hamilton Delbacher discovers his own ruthlessness and counterattacks. As nuclear holocaust looms, Delbacher fights to find a way to stop the madness.

Subjects: Heads of state; Nuclear warfare; Presidents—United States; Communism—Soviet Union

Place/Time: Soviet Union—1945–1980; Soviet Union—1980–1991; Washington (D. C.)—1945–1980

408.

1. *A God Against the Gods.* Doubleday, 1976.
2. *Return to Thebes.* Doubleday, 1977.

Akhenaton, god-king, husband, cousin of Nefertiti, and first recorded monotheist, reigned over 14th-century B. C. Egypt in a time of violence, court intrigue, and power struggles. Akhenaton displaces the old gods and alienates his family and subjects. When he fails to produce an heir, the throne passes to his brother, Tutankhamen.

Genre: Historical Fiction
Subjects: Kings and rulers; Akhenaton, King of Egypt, 1388–1348 B.C.; Religion; Courts and courtiers
Place/Time: Egypt—14th century B. C.

Duane, Diane

409.

1. *The Book of Night with Moon.* Warner, 1997.
2. *To Visit the Queen.* Warner, 1999.

Certain cats have magical powers and are in fact capable of doing battle with an evil force, which comes through the gate between realities. Rhiow, an urban pet; Urruah, an alley tom cat; and the kitten Arhu confront horrors that erupt under Union Station in New York City. Their next adventure takes them traveling back in time to 19th-century London where the evil Lone One is creating a time warp, which threatens the life of Queen Victoria. In their efforts, they are helped by a young boy named Arthur Conan Doyle.

Genre: Fantasy; Animal Story
Subjects: Cats; Magic; Good and Evil; Time travel; Victoria, Queen of England, 1819–1901
Place/Time: New York (N. Y.)—1980–; London (England)—19th century

410. A Tale of Fire

1. *The Door into Fire.* Dell, 1979.
2. *Door into Shadow.* Bluejay Books, 1984.
3. *The Door into Sunset.* Tor, 1993.

The Goddess of this fantasy world shares certain qualities with her human creations. She is not all powerful in her confrontations with the menacing Shadow, and she has different personalities that may work against each other. Aided by princes, ladies, and dragons, she uses the sacred life force Fire in her struggles with evil.

Genre: Fantasy
Subjects: Fire; Gods and goddesses; Good and evil; Imaginary kingdoms

Dubus, Elizabeth Nell

411.

1. *Cajun.* Putnam, 1983.

2. *Where Love Rules.* Putnam, 1985.
3. *To Love and to Dream.* Putnam, 1986.

The fates of two French families, one rich, one poor, who settle in Louisiana in the late 1790s, are intertwined into the 20th century. The Langlinais family settle in the bayous after fleeing Nova Scotia when the English take it over. The De Clouets, French aristocrats, flee to New Orleans during the French Revolution. The Langlinais fortunes rise while those of the De Clouet family fall, but the descendants fall in love and have to overcome years of prejudice and resentment.

Genre: Family Saga; Historical Romance
Subjects: Aristocracy; Wealth
Place/Time: Louisiana—19th century; Louisiana—1900–1945

Duggan, Alfred Leo

412. Saxon Trilogy
1. *Conscience of the King.* Coward-McCann, 1952.
2. *The King of Althelney.* Faber & Faber, 1961.
3. *Cunning of the Dove.* Pantheon, 1960.

From its shadowy tribal beginnings in a violent time, the Saxon domination of England progresses with unification under Alfred the Great and ends in 1066 with the Norman Conquest following the death of the mystical King Edward the Confessor.

Genre: Historical Fiction
Subjects: Kings and rulers; Alfred the Great, King of England, 849–899; Anglo-Saxons; Normans; England—Anglo-Saxon period, 449–1066
Place/Time: England—10th century; England—11th century

Dumas, Alexandre (pere)

413.
1. *The Memoirs of a Physician.* Thomas Hodgson, 1848.
2. *The Queen's Necklace, or The Secret History of the Court of Louis XVI.* W. F. Burgess, 1850.
3. *Six Years Later, or The Taking of the Bastille.* T. B. Peterson, 1851.
4. *The Countess de Charny, or The Fall of the French Monarchy.* T. B. Peterson, 1853.

Court life is vividly described from Marie Antoinette's arrival at the palace of Louis XV through the days of the French Revolution and on to 1794. The intrigues and charlatans of the court cast suspicion on the king and queen and help bring about the revolution and the fall of the Bastille.

Genre: Historical Fiction
Subjects: Kings and rulers; Courts and courtiers; Louis XVI, King of France, 1754–1793; Marie Antoinette, Queen, Consort of Louis XVI, King

of France, 1755–1793; France—revolution, 1789–1799
Place/Time: Paris (France)—18th century; France—18th century

414.
1. *Queen Margot, or Marguerite de Valois.* John Dicks, 1885, 1846.
2. *Diana of Meridor, or The Lady of Monsoreau.* Williams Bros., 1846.
3. *The Forty-Five Guardsmen.* E. Appleyard, 1848.

The turbulent reign of France's King Henri III is described through Chicot, the king's gentleman. The intrigues and plotting lead to the St. Bartholomew massacre.

Genre: Historical Fiction
Subjects: St. Bartholomew's Day, massacre of, 1572; Kings and rulers; Courts and courtiers; Henry III, King of France, 1551–1589
Place/Time: France—16th century

415.
1. *The Three Guardsmen* (Alternate title: *The Three Musketeers*). Taylor, Wilde, 1846.
2. *Twenty Years After, or the Further Feats and Fortunes of a Gascon Adventurer.* Bruce & Wyld, 1846.
3. *The Vicomte de Bragelonne or Ten Years Later.* Routledge, 1857, 1848–1850.

D'Artagnan, a young man from Gascony, comes to Paris in 1625 to join Louis XIII's guardsmen. He meets three of the greatest guardsmen, Arthos, Porthos, and Aramis, who ask him to join their fellowship. For the next 40 years they have narrow escapes and amazing exploits as they fight villains of their kings, Louis XIII and Louis XIV.

Genre: Adventure; Historical Fiction
Subjects: Adventure; Courts and courtiers; Kings and rulers; Louis XIII, King of France, 1601–1643; Louis XIV, King of France, 1638–1715
Place/Time: Paris (France)—17th century; France—17th century

Duncan, Dave

416. The Great Game
1. *Past Imperative: Round One of the Great Game.* W. Morrow, 1995.
2. *Present Tense.* Avon, 1996.
3. *Future Indefinite.* Avon, 1997.

Edward Exeter lives in two dangerous worlds: the Europe of World War I and an alternate reality called Nextdoor, where he goes as a fugitive wrongly accused of murder. Exeter's destiny in Nextdoor may be as threatening as what appears to be his fate in the real world. His role as the Liberator, the one who will annihilate Zath, the god of death, becomes increasingly apparent as the tales unfold.

Genre: Fantasy
Subjects: Games; Gods and goddesses; World War I, 1914–1918

417. A Handful of Men
1. *The Cutting Edge.* Ballantine, 1992.
2. *Upland Outlaws.* Ballantine, 1993.
3. *The Stricken Field.* Del Rey, 1993.
4. *The Living God.* Del Rey, 1994.

This four-part series continues the story of Rap and Inos after their marriage and accession to the throne of Krasnegar. In the kingdom of Impire, Prince Shandie and his friends, along with imps, fawns, dwarves, trolls and pixies battle an assortment of evildoers. When the sorcerer Zinixo drives Shandie from the throne, Rap leads Shandie's followers on a quest to find the magic that will overthrow Zinixo. Further complications ensue when Shandie and Inos are kidnapped by goblins while Rap is trying to unite some powerful forces against Zinixo's dreadful covin of enslaved sorcerers.

Genre: Fantasy
Subjects: Imaginary kingdoms; Magic; Imaginary wars and battles; Kings and rulers

418. The King's Blades
1. *The Gilded Chain.* Avon Eos, 1998.
2. *Lord of the Fire Lands.* Avon Eos, 1999.

The King's Blades are a group of expert swordsmen trained from boyhood, who are bound to a ward by a magical ceremony. Sir Durendal rises from the disappointment of being bound to a nobleman whom he does not admire to the assignment of dealing with a rogue Blade. Court intrigue around a potential Blade, who refuses the bonding ceremony, is the subject of the next tale.

Genre: Fantasy
Subjects: Arms and armor; Knights and knighthood; Courts and courtiers; Imaginary kingdoms; Magic

419. A Man of His Word
1. *Magic Casement.* Ballantine, 1990.
2. *Faery Lands Forlorn.* Ballantine, 1991.
3. *Perilous Seas.* Ballantine, 1991.
4. *Emperor and Clown.* Ballantine, 1992.

Rap, the stable boy, and Inos meet when she is a tomboyish young princess in need of a little polish. Exhibiting increasing magical powers, Rap follows Inos when she is kidnapped into another world. After overcoming many difficulties and being captured by the evil Sultan who wants Inos for his bride, Rap restores her to her rightful position as queen. Meanwhile their childhood friendship changes into romance.

Genre: Fantasy
Subjects: Children; Kidnapping; Imaginary kingdoms; Love

420. Seventh Sword
1. *The Reluctant Swordsman.* Ballantine, 1988.
2. *The Coming of Wisdom.* Ballantine, 1988.
3. *The Destiny of the Sword.* Ballantine, 1988.

The recently deceased Wallie Smith awakens in a world that is far from heavenly. The reigning goddess has decided that he is the perfect substitute for her previous hero, who proved to be unsatisfactory. Unprepared for this fate by anything in his previous life, Wallie reluctantly accepts a magic sword and, endowed by the goddess with superhuman strength, sets out on a series of adventures that include encounters with evil sorcerers and other insurmountable obstacles.

Genre: Fantasy
Subjects: Future life; Gods and goddesses; Imaginary wars and battles; Arms and armor

Duncan, Jane. *Pseud. of* Elizabeth Jane Cameron

421. An Apology for the Life of Jean Robertson
1. *Jean in the Morning.* St. Martin's, 1969.
2. *Jean at Noon.* St. Martin's, 1971.
3. *Jean in the Twilight.* St. Martin's, 1972.
4. *Jean Towards Another Day.* St. Martin's, 1975.

Jean Robertson grows up in the small Scottish community of Lockfoot near Glasgow in the early 1900s. She manages to rise above her lower-class origins to become the maid and companion for two elderly women, Miss Jessie and Miss Bessie. Miss Bessie's death and the reappearance of Jean's mother bring about important changes in her life.

Genre: Gentle Read; Historical Fiction
Subjects: Girls; Servants
Place/Time: Scotland—1900–1945

422. Reachfar Series
1. *My Friends the Miss Boyds.* St. Martin's, 1959.
2. *My Friend Muriel.* St. Martin's, 1959.
3. *My Friend Monica.* St. Martin's, 1960.
4. *My Friend Annie.* St. Martin's, 1961.
5. *My Friend Sandy.* St. Martin's, 1962.
6. *My Friend Martha's Aunt.* St. Martin's, 1962.
7. *My Friend Flora.* St. Martin's, 1962.
8. *My Friend Madame Zora.* St. Martin's, 1963.
9. *My Friend Rose.* St. Martin's, 1964.
10. *My Friend Emmie.* St. Martin's, 1965.
11. *My Friends the Mrs. Millers.* St. Martin's, 1965.
12. *My Friends from Cairnton.* St. Martin's, 1966.
13. *My Friend My Father.* St. Martin's, 1966.
14. *My Friends the Macleans.* St. Martin's, 1967.
15. *My Friends the Hungry Generation.* St. Martin's, 1968.
16. *My Friend the Swallow.* St. Martin's, 1970.
17. *My Friend Sashie.* St. Martin's, 1972.
18. *My Friends the Misses Kindness.* St. Martin's, 1974.

19. *My Friends George and Tom.* St Martin's, 1976.

Janet Sandison narrates her experiences growing up in the Scottish Highlands in the early 1900s, the death of her mother, and her father's remarriage. Her own marriage takes her to the West Indies where she continues to take joy in the intriguing people and situations she encounters. Her husband's death and her own literary aspirations propel her back to her native Scotland.

Genre: Gentle Read; Historical Fiction
Subjects: Girls; Marriage; Small town life
Place/Time: Scotland—1900–1945; Caribbean region—1900–1945

Dunn, Carola

423.
1. *Miss Hartwell's Dilemma.* Walker, 1988.
2. *Two Corinthians.* Walker, 1990.

In Regency England, two sisters, Claire and Lizzie Sutton, have not attracted husbands, so are consigned to spinsterhood. Claire, however, takes charge of her sister's first season in London, and surprisingly both sisters attract suitors. The two suitors the sisters rejected will also find romance with the help of the Suttons.

Genre: Historical Romance
Subjects: Sisters
Place/Time: London (England)—19th century; England—19th century

Dunnett, Dorothy

424.
1. *The Game of Kings.* Putnam, 1961.
2. *Queen's Play.* Putnam, 1964.
3. *The Disorderly Knights.* Putnam, 1966.
4. *Pawn in Frankincense.* Putnam, 1969.
5. *The Ringed Castle.* Putnam, 1971.
6. *Checkmate.* Putnam, 1975.

In this series of interlocking, though independent novels, Francis Crawford Lyman leaves Scotland in 1547 to accompany Mary, Queen of Scots, to France. The swashbuckling Lyman must protect the queen from the political plots that threaten her life. He has adventures in exotic Turkey, Russia, Malta, and the Mediterranean as he counters plots, leads mercenaries, and hunts for his lost son.

Genre: Adventure; Historical Fiction
Subjects: Adventure; Courts and courtiers; Mary, Queen of Scots, 1542–1587
Place/Time: France—16th century; Europe—16th century

425. House of Niccolo
1. *Niccolo Rising.* Knopf, 1986.
2. *The Spring of the Ram.* Knopf, 1988.
3. *Race of Scorpions.* Knopf, 1990.
4. *Scales of Gold.* Knopf, 1992.
5. *The Unicorn Hunt.* Knopf, 1994.
6. *To Lie with Lions.* Knopf, 1996.
7. *Caprice and Rondo.* Knopf, 1998.
8. *Gemini.* Knopf, 2000.

In the 15th century, Claes, also known as Niccolo, is a 17-year-old apprentice at the House of Charretty in Burgess. There he is learning to be a merchant, but a feud with a nobleman sends him off to Italy where he becomes friends with many Italian merchants. When he returns to Burgess, he marries his employer, Marian de Charretty. As a merchant, he travels to the Byzantine Empire, Cypress, and Africa, finding adventure, love, and money on the way. The rich tapestry of Renaissance Europe is revealed through his travels and the people he meets.

Genre: Adventure; Historical Fiction
Subjects: Merchants; Renaissance; Adventure
Place/Time: Belgium—15th century; Italy—15th century; Europe—15th century

Dupin, Amantine-Aurore-Lucile. See Sand, George

Durgin, Doranna

426.
1. *Dun Lady's Jess.* Baen, 1994.
2. *Changespell.* Baen, 1997.

Magic does not always work as it should, even in the mystical world of Camolen. A magnificent horse named Dun Lady's Jess is accidentally transformed into a beautiful woman and enters the realm of everyday experience. Back in Camolen, Jess alternates between human and animal forms, falls in love, and encounters human-animal transformations similar to hers, but created for an evil purpose.

Genre: Fantasy
Subjects: Magic; Horses; Love

Durrell, Lawrence

427. The Alexandria Quartet
1. *Justine.* Dutton, 1957.
2. *Balthazar.* Dutton, 1958.
3. *Mountolive.* Dutton, 1959.
4. *Clea.* Dutton, 1960.

The above titles have also been published in the following collection: *The Alexandria Quartet.* Dutton, 1962.

Set in Egypt in the 1940s, the same events surrounding the tortuous love affair between an Irish expatriate and the exotic wife of a wealthy Egyptian are seen from four points of view. The exotic Justine and her Coptic husband Nessim have affairs, work for the formation of a Jewish state, and tell their story to the psychiatrist Balthazar and the Englishman Darley. Using the power of language, Durrell evokes place and character.

Subjects: Love affairs; Zionism
Place/Time: Alexandria (Egypt)—1900–1945;
    Egypt—1900–1945

428. Avignon Quartet
1. *Livia, or Buried Alive.* Viking, 1979.
2. *Monsieur.* Viking, 1975.
3. *Constance, or Solitary Practices.* Viking, 1982.
4. *Sebastian, or Ruling Passions.* Viking, 1984.
5. *Quinx or the Ripper's Tale.* Viking, 1985.

In the 1920s and 30s in France, Egypt, and Switzerland, a group of English friends have a lifelong *menage a trois.* British consul Felix Chatto, novelist Blanford, psychoanalyst Constance, and her husband Sam shift between countries, lovers, and elusive events as they try to understand themselves and their loves.

Genre: Historical Fiction
Subjects: Love affairs; Friendship; Psychological novels
Place/Time: France—1900–1945; England—1900–1945; Egypt—1900–1945

429. The Revolt of Aphrodite Series
1. *Tunc.* Dutton, 1968.
2. *Nunquam.* Dutton, 1970.

Felix Charlock, an ingenious inventor employed by a great London corporation, falls in love with the daughter of the founder. While in the firm's employ, he invents the ultimate product, a doll so lifelike that it can philosophize and make love.

Subjects: Inventors; Psychological novels
Place/Time: Athens (Greece)—1945–1980; Greece—1945–1980; Istanbul (Turkey)—1945–1980; London (England)—1945–1980; Turkey—1945–1980; England—1945–1980

Easton, Robert Olney

430.
1. *This Promised Land.* Capra, 1982.
2. *Power and Glory.* Capra, 1989.

Lospe, daughter of a California Indian chief, weds Antonio Boneu, a Spanish aristocrat, when her people are decimated in the early 1800s. She changes her name to Clara and tries to keep up a ranch where Indians, African Americans, and Americans can live in peace. In her old age, she becomes involved in the slave controversy of the 1850s when she tries to help a friend's daughter flee slavery through the underground railroad.

Genre: Historical Fiction
Subjects: Native Americans; Ranch life; Abolitionists; Underground railroad
Place/Time: California—19th century

Ebert, Alan *and* Rotchstein, Janice

431.
1. *Traditions.* Crown, 1981.
2. *The Long Way Home.* Crown, 1984.

Carolyn and Margaret Tiernan are sisters who both want to be actresses. Carolyn is beautiful and religious while Margaret is sexy and spunky, but they both come to Hollywood in the 1930s. Later they work on Broadway and in London's West End. Behind the footlights, they fall in love, marry, and have children who carry on the theatrical tradition. However, the Vietnam War breaks the family line as grandson Thomas joins the Air Force. As matriarchs of the family, Carolyn and Margaret hold everyone together.

Genre: Family Saga; Historical Fiction
Subjects: Actors and actresses; Theater life
Place/Time: Hollywood (Calif.)—1900–1945; Hollywood (Calif.)—1945–1980; New York (N. Y.)—1900–1945; New York (N. Y.)—1945–1980; London (England)—1900–1945; London (England)—1945–1980; California—1900–1945; California—1945–1980; England—1900–1945; England—1945–1980

Eddings, David

432. The Belgariad
1. *Belgarath the Sorcerer.* Ballantine, 1995.
2. *Pawn of Prophecy.* Ballantine, 1982.
3. *Queen of Sorcery.* Ballantine, 1982.
4. *Magician's Gambit.* Ballantine, 1983.
5. *Castle of Wizardry.* Ballantine, 1984.
6. *Enchanters' Endgame.* Ballantine, 1984.

The stage is set for the story of young Garion by the reminiscences of the sorcerer Belgarath, whose life spans 7000 years and reaches back to a time when warring gods split the world, resulting in the opposition of two mysterious forces called Necessities. At first unaware of his magical powers, Garion sets out from his rural home to the palace of his king. He is thrust into a series of adventures that are at times humorous, and at other times, part of his working out of serious moral dilemmas. He is entranced by the regal and sometimes difficult Princess Ce'Nedra. *Note:* This series continues in The Mallorean series.

Genre: Fantasy
Subjects: Imaginary kingdoms; Magic; Love

433. The Elenium
1. *The Diamond Throne.* Ballantine, 1989.
2. *The Ruby Night.* Ballantine, 1990.
3. *The Sapphire Rose.* Ballantine, 1992.

As his poisoned Queen Ehlana lies frozen in crystal, Sparhawk, her knight and champion, sets out to find the magic jewel that will save her. Although his quest is successful, he must battle many forces, human and otherwise, to bring the jewel back to Ehlana and claim her as his bride.

Genre: Fantasy
Subjects: Knights and knighthood; Poisons; Imaginary kingdoms; Love

434. The Mallorean
1. *Guardians of the West.* Ballantine, 1987.
2. *King of the Murgos.* Ballantine, 1988.
3. *Demon Lord of Karanda.* Ballantine, 1988.
4. *Sorceress of Darshiva.* Ballantine, 1989.
5. *The Seeress of Kell.* Ballantine, 1991.
6. *Polgara the Sorceress.* Ballantine, 1997.
   (Written with Leigh Eddings)

The characters of the Belgariad series continue into adult life. Garion has, for the time, vanquished the forces of evil and taken his place as king of the realm beside his Queen Ce'Nedra. But evil emerges again in the form of the sorceress Zandramas. In the ultimate conflict of opposing ancient prophecies, a blind seeress must choose between characters, one Garion and the other Zandramas, who represent the fate of the universe. The memoirs of Garion's 3,000-year-old Aunt Polgara provide a unique viewpoint of events in both the Belgariad and Mallorean sagas. *Note:* This series follows the Belgariad series.

Genre: Fantasy
Subjects: Prophecies; Imaginary kingdoms; Kings and rulers; Good and evil

435. The Tamuli
1. *Domes of Fire.* Ballantine, 1993.
2. *The Shining Ones.* Del Rey, 1993.
3. *The Hidden City.* Ballantine, 1994.

In a continuation of the Elenium trilogy, Sparhawk, now married to Ehlana, first senses evil forces approaching because of unrest in his own land. He then is summoned to the eastern Tamal Empire where corruption and treachery are rampant and strange, and powerful gods compete with each other. Ehlana and the emperor of Tamali battle dark influences at court while Sparhawk and the goddess Aphrael, using the magic of a sapphire rose jewel, try to thwart the legendary evil of the mysterious Shining Ones. Spearhawk fights his greatest battle when Queen Ehlana is captured, and he must get her back.

Genre: Fantasy
Subjects: Good and evil; Precious stones; Imaginary wars and battles; Kings and rulers

Eddings, Leigh. *See* Eddings, David (*Polgara the Sorceress*)

Eddison, E. R. (Eric Rucker)
436. The Zimiamvian Trilogy
1. *The Worm Ouroboros.* Boni, 1926.
2. *Menzentian Gate.* Ballantine, 1969.
3. *A Fish Dinner in Memison.* Dutton, 1941.
4. *Mistress of Mistresses: A Vision of Zimiamvia.* Dutton, 1935.

The Worm Ouroboros introduces a fantasy world where Demonland and Goblinland wage war as the English Lord Lessingham acts as an observer. Lessingham and the villainous Horius Parry continue as characters in the next three book, The Zimiamvian Trilogy, which takes place in a sort of heaven or alternate reality peopled by divine beings who decide to create Earth while having dinner.

Genre: Fantasy
Subjects: Gods and goddesses; Imaginary wars and battles; Creation

Edelman, Maurice
437.
1. *Disraeli in Love.* Stein & Day, 1972.
2. *Disraeli Rising.* Stein & Day, 1975.

From 1832 to 1837, a willful, brilliant Benjamin Disraeli fights his way through romantic complications and professional jealousies to a position as the most powerful man in Victorian England. As he maneuvers his first political campaigns, he becomes a Tory. When he marries a wealthy widow, he advances in the party and eventually becomes Chancellor of the Exchequer. His rise to power is set against a background of balls, operas, gossip, and politics.

Genre: Historical Fiction
Subjects: Politics—England; Society novels; Love
Place/Time: England—19th century

438.
1. *Minister of State.* Lippincott, 1962.
2. *The Prime Minister's Daughter.* Random House, 1965.

Written by a member of Parliament, these stories narrate the ups and downs of the career of British politician Geoffrey Melville. As Secretary of State for Commonwealth Affairs, he survives the publicizing of a witty but thoughtless remark about Africans. As Prime Minister, he must deal with a ruthless journalist and with the indiscretions of his wife and daughter.

Subjects: Politics—England; Prime ministers
Place/Time: England—1945–1980

Edgerton, Teresa
439. Goblin
1. *Goblin Moon.* Ace, 1991.
2. *The Gnome's Engine.* Ace, 1991.

In an alternate reality version of medieval Europe, a dangerous magician is accidentally brought back to life. The tales jump to the migration to the New World of the 18th century and an attempt to raise a sunken land from the sea.

Genre: Fantasy
Subjects: Magicians; Immigrants

440. Green Lion
1. *Child of Saturn.* Ace, 1989.
2. *The Moon in Hiding.* Ace, 1989.
3. *The Work of the Sun.* Ace, 1990.

Telerini Pendaron grows in power as a sorceress and saves the kingdom of Celydonn from an evil princess with the help of a shape shifter who can take the form of a valiant knight or a werewolf. *Note:* This series continues in the Celydonn series.

Genre: Fantasy
Subjects: Magic; Werewolves; Good and evil; Imaginary kingdoms

441. Celydonn
1. *The Castle of the Silver Wheel.* Ace, 1993.
2. *The Grail and the Ring.* Ace, 1994.
3. *The Moon and the Thorn.* Ace, 1995.

Continuing in the Celtic fantasy land of Celydonn these tales tell of Gwenliatt who is brought to the realm of Mochdreff as a bride by her beloved Tryffin, but must use her own magical powers first to do battle with a sorceress who may have been her husband's mistress, then to save herself and her son when they are magically transported to the Shadow Realm. *Note:* This series follows the Green Lion series.

Genre: Fantasy
Subjects: Magic; Imaginary kingdoms; Marriage; Mothers and sons

Edmonds, Walter Dumaux

442.
1. *Erie Water.* Atlantic/Little, Brown, 1933.
2. *Rome Haul.* Atlantic/Little, Brown, 1929.
3. *The Big Barn.* Atlantic/Little, Brown, 1930.
4. *Mostly Canallers.* Atlantic/Little, Brown, 1934.

Events and characters of the 19th-century development of the area surrounding the Erie Canal connect these stories. Beginning with the life of a young man who works on the canal, the stories progress through the farm and frontier society of Lake Erie County.

Genre: Historical Fiction
Subjects: Erie Canal (N. Y.); Farm life; Frontier and pioneer life
Place/Time: New York (state)—19th century

Edwards, Gene

443. Chronicles of the Door
1. *The Beginning.* Tyndale House, 1992.
2. *The Birth.* Tyndale House, 1991.
3. *The Escape.* Tyndale House, 1993.
4. *The Triumph.* Tyndale House, 1995.
5. *The Return.* Tyndale House, 1996.

From the mystery of creation to the second coming of Christ, the story of man and his relationship to God is told from the angels' perspective. The angels see the creation of Earth, and Adam and Eve. They witness the clash of good and evil and the calling of Abram. Finally, they see the birth and death of Jesus, and later his second coming. The mysteries of the Christian faith are seen from a heavenly perspective.

Genre: Christian Fiction
Subjects: Faith; Angels; Biblical stories; Religion
Place/Time: Middle East—multicentury span

Effinger, George Alec

444. Marid
1. *When Gravity Fails.* Arbor House, 1987.
2. *A Fire in the Sun.* Doubleday, 1989.
3. *The Exile Kiss.* Doubleday, 1991.

In a near future setting, when surgical implants that create personality changes are a source of vicarious pleasure, Marid Audran lives on the edge of danger in an Arabic ghetto of North Africa. His life changes when Friedlander Bey, a criminal power broker, pulls him into service as his contact in the police department. Eventually both are banished to the desert where Marid discovers his own strength.

Genre: Science Fiction

Egleton, Clive

445.
1. *Hostile Intent.* St. Martin's, 1993.
2. *A Killing in Moscow.* St. Martin's, 1994.

Midlevel British agent Peter Ashton is sent to Germany when a minor British agent is blown up by neo-Nazis. Peter believes that the bomb was meant for Galina Kutuzova, the daughter of Soviet apparatchiks. When she disappears, Ashton pursues her across Europe, America, and Germany before he confronts a KGB hit team. Later Ashton takes over the vetting, security, and technical services division of Britain's SIS. Still under suspicion for his involvement with Galina, Ashton tries not to get involved with the murder of a British businessman in Moscow. When he uncovers a Russian spy in the British trade liaison office, he finds himself in the midst of a complex scheme involving Russians, Serbs, and British agents.

Genre: Espionage
Subjects: International intrigue; Spies; Secret service
Place/Time: England—1980–; Germany—1980–

446.
1. *A Piece of Resistance.* Coward-McCann, 1970.
2. *Last Post for a Partisan.* Coward-McCann, 1971.
3. *The Judas Mandate.* Coward-McCann, 1971.

In the near future, Russia has invaded and dominated England. David Garrett, a resistance fighter, must deal with traitors in his own ranks and, as the Soviet domination lessens, a power struggle as responsibility passes back to the British.

Genre: Adventure
Subjects: Government, resistance to; International intrigue; Adventure
Place/Time: England—1980–; Soviet Union—1945–1980; Soviet Union—1980–1991

Ehle, John

447.
1. *The Land Breakers.* Harper & Row, 1964.
2. *The Journey of August King.* Harper & Row, 1971.
3. *Time of Drums.* Harper & Row, 1970.
4. *The Road.* Harper & Row, 1967.
5. *Last One Home.* Harper & Row, 1984.
6. *The Lion of the Hearth.* Harper & Row, 1961.
7. *The Winter People.* Harper & Row, 1982.

This intense saga of the Wright family begins with their settling in the mountain country of Carolina in the early 1830s and ends in the Depression as the farmers try to survive. Mooney Wright comes to the Valley in the 1830s and builds a home. His descendants help develop the mountain settlement, fight in the Civil War at Cemetery Ridge at Gettysburg, and bring the railroad to the mountain. In 1900, Pinkney Wright marries Amanda King, the descendant of a mountain man, and they move to the city and try to adjust to a new way of life. During the Depression, the Wrights try to survive the hard times. Meanwhile Collie Wright finds love with a stranger.

Genre: Family Saga; Historical Fiction
Subjects: Mountain life; Small town life; Poverty
Place/Time: North Carolina—19th century; North Carolina—1900–1945; South Carolina—19th century; South Carolina—1900–1945

Eickhoff, Randy Lee

448.
1. *The Raid.* Forge, 1997.
2. *The Feast.* Forge, 1999.

In this modern retelling of an eighth-century Irish epic, Cuchulainn is a mighty warrior who defends Ulster from invaders. When Queen Maeve of Connacht invades Ulster, the young warrior Cuchulainn leads the province in defense of the great Brown Bull. Later Cuchulainn continues his exploits during the feast of Fled Bricriu, god of mischief. Ireland's three great mythic heroes use swords, brains, and magic in order to win the role of champion of Conchobor. This colorful and very graphic story brings the old Irish myths to life.

Subjects: Mythology, Irish; Imaginary wars and battles
Place/Time: Ireland—8th century

Eidson, Tom

449.
1. *St. Agnes Stand.* Putnam, 1994.
2. *The Last Ride.* Putnam, 1995.

On the American frontier of the 1880s, life is never easy. Nat Swanson flees Texas cowboys who think he has murdered one of their friends. In the desert, he finds three nuns and seven orphans who are being attacked by Apaches. Nat stays to help, but Sister Agnes won't allow him to kill the Apaches. In New Mexico, Maggie Jones refuses to see her father who abandoned her when he went to live with an Apache woman. When Maggie's daughter Lily is kidnapped by an Apache, Maggie pursues them across the desert. For both Nat and Maggie, life on the frontier presents challenges that force them to make moral actions.

Genre: Western
Subjects: Frontier and pioneer life; Native Americans
Place/Time: New Mexico—19th century

Eldridge, Paul. *See* Viereck, George Sylvester

Elgin, Suzette Haden

450. Coyote Jones
1. *The Communipaths.* Ace, 1970.
2. *Furthest.* Ace, 1971.
3. *At the Seventh Level.* DAW Books, 1972.

The above titles have also been published in the following collection: *Communipath Worlds.* Pocket Books, 1980.

4. *Star-Anchored, Star-Angered.* Doubleday, 1979.

In a future society where mental telepathy is normal, Coyote Jones is considered handicapped because, while his outgoing mental signals are strong, he is unable to receive thought waves from others. However, the Trigalactic Intelligence Service finds his unique quality useful in such endeavors as determining whether a woman who seems to be endowed with mystical powers is authentic or fake and finding a rogue telepath who turns out to be a baby girl.

Genre: Humor; Science Fiction
Subjects: Secret service; Telepathy; Mental handicaps

451. Ozark Trilogy
1. *Twelve Fair Kingdoms.* Doubleday, 1981.
2. *Grand Jubilee.* Doubleday, 1981.
3. *And Then There'll Be Fireworks.* Doubleday, 1981.
4. *Yonder Comes the Other End of Time.* DAW Books, 1986. (This title connects the Ozark and Coyote Jones series.)

A magical world invisible to the rest of the galaxy was created when several hill families left Earth to set up a utopian society on another planet, which they named Ozark. At the center of this community of powerful, eloquent grannies and flying mules is young Responsible Brightwater, who sends a strong 20th-century telepathic transmission that encourages the Trigalactic Intelligence Service to send Coyote Jones on what proves to be a bumpy ride to Ozark.

Genre: Fantasy; Humor; Science Fiction
Subjects: Telepathy; Life on other planets; Mountain life; Magic; Utopias

452. Native Tongue
1. *Native Tongue.* DAW Books, 1984.
2. *Native Tongue II: The Judas Rose.* DAW Books, 1987.
3. *Earthsong: Native Tongue III.* DAW Books, 1994.

The power of language is at the heart of these stories of the near and far future. The stories are based on the premise that in 1991 a legal backlash against the women's movement has put women under male domination. In dealing with alien societies of the distant future, linguists have become a close, powerful, but hated, group. At the same time, a secret subversive language, Laadan, is passed along in the revolutionary women's underground.

Genre: Science Fiction
Subjects: Language and languages; Sex discrimination; Feminism; Subversive activities

Elliott, Janice

453. Wilson Family Trilogy
1. *A State of Peace.* Knopf, 1971.
2. *Private Life.* Hodder & Stoughton, 1972.
3. *Heaven on Earth.* Hodder & Stoughton, 1975.

Conditions after World War II encourage Olive Armetage to break away from her privileged background to help the less fortunate in South London. Her life progresses through two unsatisfactory marriages and motherhood until being at the scene of a serious accident propels her into a state of self-examination.

Subjects: Women; Family life; Social problems
Place/Time: London (England)—1945–1980; England—1945–1980

Elliott, Jannean. *See* Crispin, A. C. (*Shadow World*)

Ellis, William Donohue

454.
1. *The Bounty Lands.* World Pub., 1952.
2. *Jonathan Blair, Bounty Lands Lawyer.* World Pub., 1954.

3. *The Brooks Legend.* Crowell, 1958.

The history of frontier Ohio from the 1780s to the 1820s is told through the stories of three different settlers. Jonathan Woodbridge must fight for the land he has inherited from his father in the Northwest Territory. Lawyer Jonathan Blair helps Woodbridge, then risks his reputation and life to establish the Mesopotamia Territory in Ohio. Surgeon Saul Brooks must fight both Indians and politicians when he comes to the area after the War of 1812 to set up his practice.

Genre: Historical Fiction
Subjects: Frontier and pioneer life; Physicians
Place/Time: Ohio—18th century; Ohio—19th century

Ellroy, James

455. L A Quartet
1. *The Black Dahlia.* Mysterious Press, 1987.
2. *The Big Nowhere.* Mysterious Press, 1989.
3. *L A Confidential.* Mysterious Press, 1990.
4. *White Jazz.* Knopf, 1992.

The dark side of Los Angeles in the 1950s is the setting and atmosphere of Ellroy's quartet of novels, which focus on cops and crime. Each book is about a different set of corrupt lawmen who must fight devious plots, gangsters, and their own twisted paths. All the books use real characters and events in Los Angeles history as the springboard for the plots, but the connecting link is the city itself. The dialogue is clipped, the plots bizarre, and the tension crackling in these *noir* crime novels.

Genre: Crime Novel
Subjects: Police—Los Angeles (Calif.); Gangsters; Crime and criminals
Place/Time: Los Angeles (Calif.)—1945–1980; California—1945–1980

Elman, Richard M.

456.
1. *The 28th Day of Elul.* Scribner, 1967.
2. *Lilo's Diary.* Scribner, 1968.
3. *The Reckoning.* Scribner, 1969.

Three members of the Yagodah family in Hungary relate the family's fate before and during the Holocaust. Before the war, the father, Newman, refuses to recognize the dangers of Nazism. Son Alex and cousin Lilo relate how the horrors of the Holocaust engulfed and finally destroyed them.

Genre: Historical Fiction; War
Subjects: Jews; Holocaust, Jewish, 1933–1945; National Socialism; World War II, 1939–1945
Place/Time: Hungary—1900–1945

Elmblad, Mary

457.

1. *All Manner of Riches*. Viking, 1987.
2. *Changes and Chances*. Viking, 1990.

From dirt poor sharecropper to successful and wealthy congresswoman, Cassie Steele must fight ignorance, poverty, and tragedy to find happiness. In Depression era Oklahoma, Cassie strives to educate herself and lift herself out of poverty. She becomes a top-flight divorce lawyer and marries the man of her dreams, but tragedy still stalks her when her husband is killed. She buries herself in raising her family, then running for Congress, but in the end finds love again.

Genre: Romance
Subjects: United States Congress; United States House of Representatives; Poverty; Business depression, 1929; Women in politics
Place/Time: Oklahoma—1900–1945; Oklahoma—1945–1980

Elrod, P. N. (Patricia Neal)

458. The Vampire Files

1. *Bloodlist*. Ace, 1990.
2. *Lifeblood*. Ace, 1990.
3. *Bloodcircle*. Ace, 1990.
4. *Art in the Blood*. Ace, 1991.
5. *Fire in the Blood*. Ace, 1991.
6. *Blood on the Water*. Ace, 1992.
7. *A Chill in the Blood*. Ace, 1998.
8. *The Dark Sleep*. Ace, 1999.

Ambitious reporter turned detective, Jack Fleming has joined the ranks of the undead because of a brief fling with an enticing woman who turned him into a vampire. Once Jack adjusts to the advantages and disadvantages of his new existence, he finds a delightful mortal girlfriend and many interesting adversaries in Chicago of the 1930s. He soon discovers that as many people envy his immortality and ability to become invisible as are threatened by these traits.

Genre: Horror; Humor
Subjects: Vampires; Journalists; Detectives; Crime and criminals
Place/Time: Chicago (Ill.)—1900–1945

Emerson, Ru. *See* Crispin, A. C. (*Voices of Chaos*)

Emshwiller, Carol

459.

1. *Ledoyt*. Mercury House, 1995.
2. *Leaping Man Hill*. Mercury House, 1999.

When Oriana Ladd finds herself pregnant, she runs away from home and goes West. There she runs a desert farm where she believes she will be free of men, but in 1902, drifter Beal Ledoyt comes into her life. Al-though she resists his charms, she and daughter Charlotte eventually fall in love with Beal. As Lotte grows up, she follows her mother's path and runs away. She takes her half-brother Fayette with her as she searches for her own path. Later they return to the ranch where teacher Mary Catherine has been hired to try to teach the youngest Ledoyt child, Abel. As Mary Catherine tries to coax the mute Abel to speak, she meets cousin Henry who has been wounded in World War I and who has come West to recuperate. Soon Mary Catherine falls in love with Henry. Like Oriana and Lotte before her, she must decide what she wants for her life.

Genre: Historical Fiction
Subjects: Women; Ranch life; Family life
Place/Time: Western states—1900–1945

Ensley, Evangeline. *See* Walton, Evangeline

Erdrich, Louise

460. North Dakota Quartet

1. *Love Medicine*. Holt, 1984.
2. *The Beet Queen*. Holt, 1986.
3. *Tracks*. Holt, 1988.
4. *The Bingo Palace*. HarperCollins, 1994.

Chippewa Indians, Swedish and German Americans, and French Canadians marry, intermarry, and remarry in North Dakota from 1912 to the late 1980s. As the characters marry and have children, they must come to terms with their ever-changing identities. They must also deal with the conflict between Native American culture and values and European culture and values. The various characters relate their lives through a series of interconnected stories, while characters from one book reappear in the others.

Subjects: Chippewa Indians; Cultural conflict; Family life
Place/Time: North Dakota—1900–1945; North Dakota—1945–1980

Ernaux, Annie

461.

1. *A Woman's Story*. Four Walls Eight Windows, 1991.
2. *A Man's Place*. Four Walls Eight Windows, 1992.
3. *A Frozen Woman*. Four Walls Eight Windows, 1995.

The French writer reflects on the lives of her mother, father, and herself through a fictional narrator. The narrator looks at her mother's life and sees a woman determined to rise out of poverty. When the mother marries, she and her husband purchase a small grocery store and work hard to make a living. Her father struggled to send his daughter to school and give her a middle class upbringing, but he was forever distant from her. The daughter eventually marries and has her own child, but only slowly does she come to terms with her upbringing, her parent's death, and her own unrealized dreams.

Subjects: Family life; Women
Place/Time: France—1945–1980; France—1980–

Estleman, Loren D.

462. Detroit Series
1. *Thunder City.* Forge, 1999.
2. *Whiskey River.* Bantam, 1990.
3. *Jitterbug.* Forge, 1998.
4. *Edsel.* Mysterious Press, 1995.
5. *Motown.* Bantam, 1991.
6. *Stress.* Mysterious Press, 1996.
7. *King of the Corner.* Bantam, 1992.

These seven novels tell the story of Detroit from the 1910s to the 1990s through the hoodlums and outcasts who inhabit the city. The atmosphere of the city, complete with dirt, crime, and corruption, is the connecting thread of these novels. In vibrant prose, Estleman describes the struggling automakers of the 1910s, the gangsters and rum runners of the 1930s, the corrupt police of the 1940s, the labor strikes of the 1950s, the riots and civil unrest of the 1960s, the police scandals of the 1970s, and finally the drug wars and minority rule of the 1980s.

Genre: Crime Novel
Subjects: Automobiles; Gangsters; Crime and criminals; Corruption (in politics); Police—Detroit (Mich.); Labor unions
Place/Time: Detroit (Mich.)—1900–1945; Detroit (Mich.)—1945–1980; Michigan—1900–1945; Michigan—1945–1980

Evans, Max

463.
1. *Bluefeather Fellini.* University Press of Colorado, 1993.
2. *Bluefeather Fellini in the Sacred Realm.* University Press of Colorado, 1994.

In the 1930s and 1940s, Bluefeather, half Pueblo Indian and half Italian, wanders the Southwest as he tries his hand at mining, gambling, selling, and many other professions. His picaresque adventures take him through a dreamy landscape, but he keeps returning to Taos, New Mexico, his spiritual home. On one of his trips, he discovers a strange world of bizarre creatures in underground caverns. Bluefeather and his girlfriend fight power-hungry entrepreneurs who want to exploit this strange world. These allegorical novels tell a tale of good versus evil in the West.

Genre: Fantasy
Subjects: Allegories; Native Americans; Picaresque novels
Place/Time: New Mexico—1980–; Western states—1980–

Evans, Richard Paul

464.
1. *The Christmas Box.* Simon & Schuster, 1995.
2. *The Timepiece.* Simon & Schuster, 1996.
3. *The Letter.* Simon & Schuster, 1997.

When Richard and Keri and their daughter agree to live with elderly widow Mary Parkin and help her out, they become involved with the secrets in her life. Mary tries to help workaholic Richard realize there is more to life than work. Richard begins to understand this as Mary slowly dies of an inoperable brain tumor. After Mary's death, Richard narrates the story of Mary and her husband David's courtship and marriage and then the tragedy of the death of a man whom David claimed he killed to protect an African American friend. When their home is burned by the murdered man's family and their daughter dies, Mary and David almost break up. Only love and faith keep them together.

Genre: Christian Fiction
Subjects: Family life; Faith; Husbands and wives
Place/Time: Utah—1900–1945; Utah—1945–1980; Utah—1980–

Exley, Frederick

465.
1. *A Fan's Notes.* Harper, 1968.
2. *Pages from a Cold Island.* Random House, 1974.
3. *Last Notes from Home.* Random House, 1988.

Frederick Exley is a young man descending into alcoholism and madness. He tries to make sense of his life and pull himself together so he can write. When he does finally, he still must search for what life means after the deaths of his idol Edmund Wilson and his own brother.

Subjects: Psychological novels; Authors; Alcoholism
Place/Time: United States—1945–1980

Fackler, Elizabeth

466.
1. *Blood Kin.* M. Evans, 1991.
2. *Backtrail.* M. Evans, 1993.
3. *Road from Betrayal.* M. Evans, 1994.
4. *Badlands.* Forge, 1996.
5. *Breaking Even.* St. Martin's, 1998.

In the 1880s, bank robber Seth Strummer meets 16-year-old runaway Johanna as he flees from the Texas rangers. When Johanna becomes pregnant, Seth asks a friend to take her to her father's ranch. Eventually he returns to Texas to take responsibility for his son Lobo. Seth tries to reform and live down his past, but he must fight revenge plots and corrupt sheriffs. Unlike typical westerns, these novels are filled with graphic sex, violence, and obscenities.

Genre: Western
Subjects: Bank robbers; Runaways; Love affairs
Place/Time: Texas—19th century; Arizona—19th
century

Fairbank, Janet Ayer

467.
1. *The Cortlandts of Washington Square.*
Bobbs-Merrill, 1922.
2. *The Smiths.* Bobbs-Merrill, 1925.
3. *Rich Man, Poor Man.* Houghton Mifflin,
1936.

Beginning with the experiences of a young nurse in the
Civil War, the series follows her and her descendants
through the growth of the city of Chicago and the historical events of Theodore Roosevelt's administration.

Genre: Family Saga; Historical Fiction
Subjects: United States—Civil War, 1861–1865;
Nurses and nursing
Place/Time: Chicago (Ill.)—19th century; Chicago
(Ill.)—1900–1945; Illinois—19th century; Illi-
nois—1900–1945

Faldbakken, Knut

468.
1. *Twilight Country.* Peter Owen, 1993.
2. *Sweetwater.* Dufour, 1994.

As the economic, social, and legal systems of
Sweetwater collapse, former architect Allan Ung takes
his wife and son to live in the Dump, a garbage disposal
site that now houses refugees from the dying society.
Ung and the other outcasts try to forge a new society in
this dark, end-of-the-millennium vision of the future
of the world.

Genre: Science Fiction
Subjects: Degeneration; Society, primitive; Refugees

Farah, Nuruddin

469. Variations on the Theme of an African Dictatorship
1. *Sweet and Sour Milk.* Heinemann, 1980.
2. *Sardines.* Heinemann, 1980.
3. *Close Sesame.* Allison and Busby, 1983.

Dictatorship in various forms is explored in Farah's
novels about the violent history of his country, Somalia. In *Sweet and Sour Milk,* Loyaan investigates his
dissident brother's death. In *Sardines,* Medina, a west-
ernized woman, tries to keep her daughter from the So-
mali ritual of circumcision. In *Close Sesame,* an old
man struggles to understand his imprisonment under
the repressive regime of Mohamed Siad Barre and his
son's involvement with revolutionaries.

Subjects: Dictators; Revolutions and revolutionists
Place/Time: Somalia—1945–1980

Farland, David

470.
1. *The Runelords: The Sum of All Men.* Tor,
1998.
2. *The Brotherhood of the Wolf.* Tor, 1999.

In this magical world, certain men and women called
runes can rob others of attractive qualities such as wit
or intelligence, leaving the victim crippled or dead.
The ruthless Raj Ahtan uses this power to make himself into a fierce, but charismatic, warrior called The
Sum of All Men. Opposing him is the Earth King
Gaborn Val Orden whose rise to power fulfills a 2,000-
year-old prophecy. The Earth King's triumph is short
lived because an invasion of destructive monsters
called reavers makes it advisable for the two enemies
to join forces.

Genre: Fantasy
Subjects: Good and evil; Imaginary wars and battles;
Imaginary kingdoms; Prophecies

Farmer, Philip Jose

471. Dayworld Trilogy
1. *Dayworld.* Putnam, 1985.
2. *Dayworld Rebel.* Putnam, 1986.
3. *Dayworld Breakup.* Tor, 1990.

Overpopulation in the year 3000 has created a civilization whose members live in the usual manner only one
day a week, spending the remaining time in suspended
animation. Jeff Caird consistently commits the crime
of "day-breaking": living seven days a week, each day
assuming a different personality. He ultimately decides to reveal a secret that will bring down the
Dayworld civilization.

Genre: Science Fiction
Subjects: Population; Crime and criminals; Subversive activities

472. Opar
1. *Time's Last Gift.* Ballantine, 1972.
2. *Hadon of Ancient Opar.* DAW Books, 1974.
3. *Flight to Opar.* DAW Books, 1976.

A scientific group of the near future travels back to Africa of 12,000 B.C. and discovers Opar, the center of a
sophisticated civilization first described in Edgar Rice
Burrough's Tarzan novels. The story of Opar continues years later as Hadon, a young athlete of low birth,
challenges the rulers of the empire.

Genre: Fantasy
Subjects: Time travel; Imaginary kingdoms; Scientists; Civilization, ancient

473. Riverworld
1. *To Your Scattered Bodies Go.* Putnam, 1971.
2. *The Fabulous Riverboat.* Putnam, 1971.
3. *The Dark Design.* Berkley, 1977.
4. *The Magic Labyrinth.* Berkley, 1980.
5. *Gods of Riverworld.* Putnam, 1983.

6. *River of Eternity*. Phantasia Press, 1983.

On the planet Riverworld, whose distinctive feature is a ten-million-mile-long river, all the inhabitants of Earth are resurrected simultaneously. Characters such as explorer Sir Richard Burton and Mark Twain try to unravel the mystery of the Ethicals, members of a highly technical culture who masterminded the Riverworld civilization. Farmer wrote the original book of this series, which was eventually published with the title *River of Eternity*, in 1953.

Genre: Science Fiction
Subjects: Rivers; Life on other planets; Resurrection

474. World of Tiers
1. *The Maker of Universes*. Ace, 1965.
2. *The Gates of Creation*. Ace, 1966.
3. *A Private Cosmos*. Ace, 1968.
4. *Behind the Walls of Terra*. Ace, 1970.
5. *The Lavalite World*. Ace, 1977.
6. *The World of Tiers*. Sphere, 1986.
7. *Red Orc's Rage*. Tor, 1991.
8. *More Than Fire*. Tor, 1993.

This series is based on the premise that a group of beings called Lords, who have both human and divine qualities, have created pocket universes for their own amusement. It follows first Robert Wolff, who has forgotten his own divinity, then earthling Kickaha, who defends Tiers and then travels to other universes. *The World of Tiers* returns to a present-day character, an unstable young man whose psychiatrist suggests that he project into one of the characters in the Tiers series as a form of therapy. The latter works deal with a conflict between Kickaha and Red Orc, the savage warrior of the Lords.

Genre: Science Fiction
Subjects: Gods and goddesses; Creation; Imaginary wars and battles

Farrell, James T.

475. Bernard Clare Trilogy
1. *Bernard Clare*. Vanguard Press, 1946.
2. *The Road Between*. Vanguard Press, 1949.
3. *Yet Other Waters*. Vanguard Press, 1952.

Bernard Clare, a writer in the 1930s, is a Communist sympathizer. Gradually he becomes disillusioned with the Communists and breaks with them. The books are autobiographical and represent Farrell's own change in political viewpoint in the 1940s and 1950s.

Subjects: Autobiographical stories; Authors; Communism
Place/Time: United States—1900–1945

476. The Danny O'Neill Tetralogy
1. *Face of Time*. Vanguard, 1953.
2. *A World I Never Made*. Vanguard, 1936.
3. *No Star Is Lost*. Vanguard, 1938.
4. *Father and Son*. Vanguard, 1940.
5. *My Days of Anger*. Vanguard, 1943.

From age five until he graduates from college, Danny O'Neill, the youngest son of a poverty-ridden family, fights to escape Chicago's Irish ghetto. When Danny is five, his parents bring him to his grandparents, the O'Flahertys. There he grows up as a spoiled, moody child. He is shaped by the middle-class values of his grandparents and the working-class ways of his father, a teamster. Gradually his introspection leads him to education, which helps him overcome his background. These novels vividly detail the generational conflicts among big city Irish American families and the growth of an artist as he rebels against his lower-class heritage.

Genre: Coming of Age
Subjects: Irish—United States; Conflict of generations; Boys; Poverty; Social classes
Place/Time: Chicago (Ill.)—1900–1945; Illinois—1900–1945

477. Silence of Time
1. *The Silence of History*. Doubleday, 1963.
2. *Lonely for the Future*. Doubleday, 1966.
3. *A Brand New Life*. Doubleday, 1968.
4. *Judith*. Duane Scheider, 1969.
5. *The Dunne Family*. Doubleday, 1976.
6. *Death of Nora Ryan*. Doubleday, 1978.

Eddie Ryan resigns from his job as an attendant in a Chicago service station in 1926. He goes back to school to better himself, but gradually comes to understand the importance of intellectual fulfillment. After college he becomes a writer. He spends the 1940s and 1950s in New York, where he is professionally successful but personally a shambles. His financial support helps his relatives, the Dunnes and Ryans, keep their families together in Chicago.

Subjects: Success; Authors; Family life
Place/Time: Chicago (Ill.)—1900–1945; New York (N. Y.)—1900–1945; Illinois—1900–1945; New York (state)—1900–1945

478. Studs Lonigan: A Trilogy
1. *Young Lonigan: A Boyhood on the Chicago Streets*. Vanguard Press, 1932.
2. *The Young Manhood of Studs Lonigan*. Vanguard Press, 1934.
3. *Judgement Day*. Vanguard Press, 1935.

The above titles have also been published in the following collection: *Studs Lonigan: A Trilogy*. Vanguard Press, 1935.

In these gritty, powerful novels, Farrell follows Studs Lonigan, a tough Irish boy, from the time he enters high school in 1917 until his death during the Depression. Studs grows up in the Irish neighborhood of Chicago's South Side and believes in the American dream of success, but all his hard work only leads to disappointment and failure. In his gradual disintegration, he consumes large quantities of cheap liquor. When the Depression begins, he can't even find a job and ultimately dies of pneumonia as his family argues in the background. Farrell's trilogy is a harsh indictment of American capitalism in the early 20th century.

Genre: Coming of Age
Subjects: Teenagers; Irish—United States; Ambition; Alcoholism; Business depression, 1929
Place/Time: Chicago (Ill.)—1900–1945; Illinois—1900–1945

Farren, Mick

479.
1. *The Time of Feasting.* Tor, 1996.
2. *Darklost.* Tor, 2000.

Victor Renquist is the leader of a New York vampire colony who prefer to call themselves nosferatu (undead) and who exist on stolen hospital blood most of the time. However, every seven years, the vampires must kill humans and drink their blood to replenish their energy. When an alcoholic priest and a police detective uncover the true nature of Renquist and his followers, the group of undead must flee to San Francisco where a new threat awaits them: the evil squid-like creature Cthulhu, who played a part in the creation of vampires.

Genre: Horror
Subjects: Vampires; Escapes
Place/Time: New York (N. Y.)—1980–; San Francisco (Calif.)—1980–

Farrington, Robert

480. Henry Morane
1. *The Killing of Richard the Third.* Scribner, 1972.
2. *Tudor Agent.* St. Martin's, 1974.

Fifteenth-century English political intrigues are seen through the eyes of Henry Morane, first a clerk to Richard III, then a member of the court of Henry VII and a double agent of sorts.

Genre: Historical Fiction
Subjects: Courts and courtiers; Richard III, King of England, 1452–1485; Henry VII, King of England, 1457–1509; Spies
Place/Time: England—15th century

Farris, Jack

481.
1. *The Abiding Gospel of Claude Dee Moran Jr.* St. Lukes Press, 1987.
2. *Keeping the Faith.* St. Lukes Press, 1990.

Claude Dee Moran is a poor Arkansas convict who attempts to rehabilitate himself by becoming a preacher, then a cop. When he tries farming, he takes on two dopey helpers—Harley and Henry. Later, when he helps a mentally ill woman, he is sent back to prison. When he comes out, he again has to avoid trouble so he won't break parole.

Subjects: Ex-convicts; Farm life; Mental illness
Place/Time: Arkansas—1980–

Fast, Howard

482.
1. *The Immigrants.* Houghton Mifflin, 1977.
2. *Second Generation.* Houghton Mifflin, 1978.
3. *The Establishment.* Houghton Mifflin, 1979.
4. *The Legacy.* Houghton Mifflin, 1981.
5. *The Immigrant's Daughter.* Houghton Mifflin, 1985.
6. *An Independent Woman.* Harcourt, 1997.

In 1900, Dan Lavette, son of French-Italian immigrants, builds a shipping empire in San Francisco, but he cannot marry the woman he loves without losing his empire. His daughter Barbara follows in his footsteps and becomes involved with striking dock workers, then fights the Nazis. After her husband's death during Israel's war for independence, Barbara is caught up in the McCarthy witch-hunt. Her son and nephews are involved in the Vietnam War, Israel's Six Day War, and the civil rights struggle. Even in her sixties, Barbara continues her activist career when she runs for Congress. In her final years, Barbara finds a last love with a minister and excitement as she and her husband thwart terrorists in Israel, but cancer eventually brings an end to Barbara's life and the Lavette saga.

Genre: Family Saga; Historical Fiction
Subjects: War; Shipping; Social problems; World politics
Place/Time: San Francisco (Calif.)—1900–1945; San Francisco (Calif.)—1945–1980; California—1900–1945; California—1945–1980

Faulkner, William

483.
1. *Sanctuary.* Harrison Smith, 1931.
2. *Requiem for a Nun.* Random House, 1951.

Temple Drake, a young coed in Mississippi, is raped and abducted by Popeye. Popeye kills a man who tries to protect her, and Temple lies to protect Popeye. Because of her lie, a young man, Lee Goodwin, who is accused of the crime, is lynched. Eight years later, Temple's attempt to gain a pardon for her black servant finally brings out Temple's involvement

Subjects: Crime and criminals; Lynching
Place/Time: Mississippi—1900–1945; Memphis (Tenn.)—1900–1945; Tennessee—1900–1945

484.
1. *The Unvanquished.* Random House, 1938.
2. *Sartoris.* Harcourt Brace, 1929.

Set during the Civil War, these stories tell of the Sartoris family of Mississippi. Bayard Sartoris returns from the battlefields and builds his family's fortune. His son, Young Bayard, returns from World War I haunted by the death of his brother. Those memories lead him to reckless driving, ultimately causing his grandfather's death in a car accident. Unable to face his guilt, he leaves for Ohio where he becomes a test pilot and is killed.

Genre: Historical Fiction
Subjects: Wealth; World War I, 1914–1918
Place/Time: Mississippi—19th century; Mississippi—1900–1945

485.
1. *The Hamlet.* Random House, 1940
2. *The Town.* Random House, 1957.
3. *The Mansion.* Random House, 1959.

Set in Faulkner's favorite locale, Yoknapatawpha County, Mississippi, this is a fascinating chronicle of the rise and fall of the rapacious Snopes family. It begins in the late 19th century when sharecropper Ab Snopes comes to town. His son Flem sets himself up by marrying Eula Varner, and they move to Jefferson. Flem's trickery and greed lead to his violent death at the hands of Mink Snopes. The characters and their actions are described from varying points of view.

Subjects: Family life; Small town life
Place/Time: Mississippi—19th century; Mississippi—1900–1945

Faust, Joe Clifford

486.
1. *Ferman's Devils.* Bantam, 1996.
2. *Boddekker's Demons.* Bantam, 1997.

Boddekker is a young creative advertising man at the Pembroke Hall Advertising Agency in 21st-century New York. He wants to be on the fast lane to success and win the love of Honniker in Accounting, but he can't find the key until he is mugged by a group of ruffians, the Ferman's Devils. When he turns them into media stars, Boddekker thinks he has it all and takes the Devils on a star trip. When the gang starts to murder anyone they see, Boddekker sees his world fall apart.

Subjects: Satire; Advertising; Gangsters
Place/Time: New York (N. Y.)—1980–

Feather, Jane

487.
1. *The Hostage Bride.* Bantam, 1998.
2. *The Accidental Bride.* Bantam, 1999.
3. *The Least Likely Bride.* Bantam, 2000.

Three unconventional young women decide they will never marry but later discover that love can't be denied. During the English Civil War, Portia Worth, the niece of Cato Granville, Roundhead and enemy of King Charles, is kidnapped by nobleman Rufus Decatur. The two look past their differences and find love. When Cato, the Marquis of Granville, loses his wife, he forces her sister Phoebe to marry him. Phoebe has always been the plain sister, but she decides to make Cato fall in love with her by changing her looks and manner. The last of the three friends, Olivia, falls off a cliff onto a beach where she is kidnapped by Anthony, a nobleman out to free the imprisoned King

Charles. Since Olivia's father is guarding the king, Olivia and Anthony also have to overcome their differences before they can find love.

Genre: Historical Romance
Subjects: Love; Lovers; Courtship
Place/Time: England—17th century

Fecher, Constance. *See also* Heaven, Constance

488. Tudor Trilogy
1. *Queen's Favorite.* Dell, 1974, 1966.
2. *Traitor's Son.* Dell, 1976, 1967.
3. *King's Legacy.* Dell, 1976, 1967.

In Elizabethan England, Sir Walter Raleigh and his family play a dynamic role in England's history. Sir Walter's triumphs for Queen Elizabeth and his ultimate execution during James I's reign are portrayed. The fortunes of his son Philip and grandson Caren continue the family saga.

Genre: Family Saga; Historical Fiction
Subjects: Courts and courtiers; Raleigh, Walter, Sir, 1554–1618
Place/Time: England—16th century

Feintuch, David

489. Seafort Saga
1. *Midshipman's Hope.* Warner Aspect, 1994.
2. *Challenger's Hope.* Warner Aspect, 1995.
3. *Prisoner's Hope.* Warner, 1995.
4. *Fisherman's Hope.* Warner, 1996.
5. *Voices of Hope.* Warner, 1996.
6. *Patriarch's Hope.* Warner, 1999.

Midshipman Nicholas Seafort must assume command of the spaceship Hibernia when the captain dies suddenly. He receives his baptism of fire as he faces space pirates, an alien attack, and a plague. The stories follow his experiences as head of the Space Academy and his rise to the position of SecGen of the United Nations.

Genre: Science Fiction
Subjects: Astronauts; Space flight; Spaceships; Interplanetary voyages;

Feist, Raymond E.

490. Riftwar
1. *Magician.* Doubleday, 1982.
2. *Silverthorn.* Doubleday, 1985.
3. *Darkness at Sethanon.* Doubleday, 1986.
4. *Prince of the Blood.* Doubleday, 1989.
5. *The King's Buccaneer.* Doubleday, 1992.

The Riftwar is the conflict that erupts when the magical kingdom of Crydee is invaded by powers from another dimension. The fates of two young boys, Pug and Tomas, are interwoven in tales of kidnapping, piracy, and other high adventures as the complex plot lines progress through many years and kingdoms. *Note:* This series is continued in the Serpentwar Saga and in the Riftwar Legacy series.

Genre: Fantasy
Subjects: Imaginary wars and battles; Imaginary kingdoms; Boys

491. Serpentwar Saga
1. *Shadow of a Dark Queen.* Avon, 1995.
2. *Rise of a Merchant Prince.* W. Morrow, 1995.
3. *Rage of a Demon King.* Avon, 1997.
4. *Shards of a Broken Crown.* Avon Eos, 1998.

Continuing the saga of the world of the Riftwar, these tales tell of the adventures of two boys, both outcasts, who are given a chance to redeem themselves by battling the vicious reptilian monsters the Saaur and the Panthathians. Having vanquished the invading creatures, Erik pursues a military career and Roo becomes a successful businessman. Later, they are again drawn into a war against an evil force: a demon king who has escaped a crumbling dimension and will be followed by others of his own kind. The demon king is defeated but his forces massed on the edge of the vulnerable realm force another fight for survival. *Note:* This series follows the Riftwar series and continues in the Riftwar Legacy series.

Genre: Fantasy; Coming of Age
Subjects: Youth; Imaginary kingdoms; Imaginary wars and battles; Mythical animals

492. Riftwar Legacy
1. *Krondor, the Betrayal.* Avon, 1998.
2. *Krondor, the Assassins.* Avon Eos, 1999.

As Squire James travels to the North, he captures a renegade elf who warns of a Dark Elf uprising. They travel together, surviving many dangers, to tell the Prince of Krondor of the uprising. In the next adventure, Squire James must revert to his old role as Jimmy the Hand, member of the Thieves Guild, to find the murderer of his former colleagues and other somewhat more honest men. *Note:* In the realm of the Riftwar, these tales follow the Riftwar series and the Serpentwar Saga.

Genre: Fantasy
Subjects: Imaginary kingdoms; Imaginary wars and battles; Thieves; Murder and murderers

Feist, Raymond E *and* Wurts, Janny

493. Empire
1. *Daughter of the Empire.* Doubleday, 1987.
2. *Servant of the Empire.* Doubleday, 1990.
3. *Mistress of the Empire.* Doubleday, 1992.

Young Mara, Ruling Lady of Acoma, must hold her land of Kelewan together after the deaths of her father and brother in the Riftwar. Along the way, she enters into a politically expedient, but distasteful, marriage, allies herself with insect-like creatures, survives an as-sassination attempt, and deals with her ambivalent feelings for the difficult, but attractive, slave Kevin of Zun.

Genre: Fantasy
Subjects: Queens; Bereavement; Imaginary kingdoms; Love

Feldhake, Susan C.

494. Enduring Faith Series
1. *In Love's Own Time.* Zondervan, 1993.
2. *Seasons of the Heart.* Zondervan. 1993.
3. *For Ever and Ever.* Zondervan, 1993.
4. *Hope For the Morrow.* Zondervan, 1993.
5. *From This Day Forward.* Zondervan, 1994.
6. *Joy in the Morning.* Zondervan, 1994.
7. *Serenity in the Storm.* Zondervan, 1996.
8. *Darkness and the Dawn.* Zondervan, 1996.

In this series young women in the 19th-century journey to the West to start new lives. Each is faced with the challenges and hardships of frontier life. Each woman finds she must look to her faith for both comfort and support, and each finds something different in her life.

Genre: Christian Fiction
Subjects: Faith; Women; Frontier and pioneer life; Marriage
Place/Time: Western states—19th century

Fergusson, Harvey

495. Followers of the Sun: A Trilogy of the Southwest
1. *Wolf Song.* Knopf, 1927.
2. *In Those Days.* Knopf, 1929.
3. *Blood of the Conquerors.* Knopf, 1921.

Ranging from frontier days to the early 1900s, these stories describe the settling and development of the area of the Southwest that is now New Mexico. The Americanization of the Spanish culture produces marriages and love affairs as well as ethnic conflicts.

Genre: Historical Fiction
Subjects: Frontier and pioneer life; Cultural conflict; Hispanic Americans
Place/Time: New Mexico—19th century

Feuchtwanger, Lion

496.
1. *Josephus.* Viking, 1932.
2. *The Jew of Rome.* Viking, 1936.
3. *Josephus and the Emperor.* Viking, 1942.

The life of Flavius Josephus, the great Jewish historian, reveals the Roman Empire from 64 A. D. through the reign of Domitian. Flavius Josephus comes to Rome to plead for his countrymen after the fall of Jerusalem. He stays in Rome to write but is torn by his devotion to his people.

Genre: Historical Fiction
Subjects: Jews; Historians
Place/Time: Rome (Italy)—1st century A. D.; Italy—1st century A. D.

Fichte, Hubert

497.
1. *The Orphanage.* Serpent's Tail, 1990, 1965.
2. *Detlev's Imitations.* Serpent's Tail. 1992, 1971.

These impressionistic novels by an important postwar German literary figure focus on Detlev, a child in Germany in 1942, who is placed in an orphanage by his mother because she cannot raise him. The child tries to fit in, but fails and is tormented by the boys. When he grows up, his confusion is mirrored in his bisexuality and his awakenings to his homosexuality and to Germany's war guilt.

Subjects: Abandoned children; Cruelty; Homosexuality
Place/Time: Germany—1900–1945; Germany—1945–1980

Fielding, Helen

498.
1. *Bridget Jones's Diary.* Viking, 1998.
2. *Bridget Jones: The Edge of Reason.* Viking, 2000.

Thirty-something Bridget Jones records her hilarious adventures, along with the number of calories consumed, cigarettes smoked, and other obsessions, in her diary. She relates her dates, cooking disasters, and loves in London. Her mother goes off with a Portuguese gigolo while Bridget loves her boss who doesn't love her. When she meets Mark Darcy, she knows she has met her true love, but true love doesn't run smoothly. Her friends give her disastrous advice. Her mother returns with more disastrous results. Darcy gets involved with another woman while Bridget has an ill-fated vacation in Thailand. The path to true love may not be smooth for Bridget, but it is always funny.

Genre: Humor
Subjects: Diaries (stories in diary form); Women, friendship, love
Place/Time: London (England)—1980–; England—1980–

Fielding, Sarah

499.
1. *The Adventures of David Simple: In Search of a Faithful Friend.* A. Millar, 1744.
2. *Adventures of David Simple: Volume the Last.* A. Millar, 1753.

The young David Simple is cheated out of his inheritance, and only gets it back after an accomplice confesses to the crime. David resolves to travel and make no friends. As he travels, he finds only deceit and corruption until he meets Cynthia, Valentine, and Camilla. These three decent young people have been unfairly cast off by their relatives. The couples marry and use David's fortune to set up a utopian home. However, his bliss is short-lived. David is sued and loses his fortune, friends, and wife. At his death, he realizes that friendship and love can only lead to pain.

Subjects: Philosophical novels
Place/Time: England—18th century

Finney, Jack

500.
1. *Time and Again.* Simon & Schuster, 1970.
2. *From Time to Time.* Simon & Schuster, 1995.

Simon Morley volunteers for a secret government project that explores the possibilities of traveling in time. Simon surrounds himself with artifacts of the 19th century and wishes himself back to the New York City of 1882. He then leaps through time to the New York of 1912. While exploring the laws of cause and effect in an attempt to prevent World War I, Simon has a brief brush with romance.

Genre: Science Fiction; Historical Fiction
Subjects: Time travel; History; World War I, 1914–1918
Place/Time: New York (N. Y.)—19th century; New York (N. Y.)—1900–1945

Firth, Violet M. *See* Fortune, Dion

Fischer, John

501.
1. *Saint Ben.* Bethany House, 1993.
2. *The Saints' and Angels' Songs.* Bethany House, 1995.

Jonathan Lieberman, the 9-year-old son of the choir director of a Christian church in Pasadena, California, is immediately taken with the new preacher's son, Ben Beamering. Ben is always seeking to learn something new, and the two boys often learn what not to do through their pranks. The two become such fast friends that when Ben dies, Jonathan struggles with the loss. He is helped through crises with his parents and friends by Ben's angel who also helps Jonathan to understand his faith.

Genre: Christian Fiction; Coming of Age
Subjects: Faith; Boys
Place/Time: California—1945–1980

Fisher, Clay. *Pseud. of* Henry Wilson Allen

502. The Tall Man
1. *The Tall Men.* Houghton Mifflin, 1954.
2. *The Crossing.* Houghton Mifflin, 1958.
3. *Return of the Tall Man.* Pocket Books, 1961.
4. *Outcasts of Canyon Creek.* Bantam, 1972.
5. *Apache Ransom.* Bantam, 1974.

Starting with a fictionalized account of an 1866 cattle drive across the plains from Texas to Montana, this series continues as a saga of the family of Ben Allison.

Genre: Family Saga; Western
Subjects: Cattle drives
Place/Time: Texas—19th century; Montana—19th century

Fisher, Dorothy Canfield

503.
1. *Rough Hewn.* Harcourt Brace, 1922.
2. *The Brimming Cup.* Harcourt Brace, 1921.

This series paints a portrait of a couple, starting with their romance and marriage. Marise and Neale begin their life together with a promise to adhere to the highest ideals. This vow is put to the test by dashing Vincent Marsh, who unsuccessfully tempts Marise to leave her small town New England life.

Genre: Romance
Subjects: Marriage; Small town life
Place/Time: New England—1900–1945

Fisher, Edward

504. The Silver Falcon Series
1. *Shakespeare & Son.* Abelard-Schuman, 1962.
2. *Love's Labour's Won.* Abelard-Schuman, 1963.
3. *The Best House in Stratford.* Abelard-Schuman, 1965.

John Shakespeare cannot understand his son William. At 15, William wants to be a playwright, but in Elizabethan England, this is not a reputable profession. This reconstruction of the life of William Shakespeare follows him from his teenage years in Stratford-on-Avon to his life as an actor and playwright in London.

Genre: Historical Fiction
Subjects: Shakespeare, William, 1564–1616; Dramatists; Family life;
Place/Time: England—16th century

Fisher, Gene L. *See* Lancour, Gene

Fisher, Vardis

505.
1. *In Tragic Life.* Caxton, 1932.
2. *Passions Spin the Plot.* Doubleday, 1934.
3. *We Are Betrayed.* Doubleday, 1935.
4. *No Villain Need Be.* Doubleday, 1936.

Vridar Hunter grows up in Idaho of the late 1800s, travels across the country to Chicago and New York, then returns to the mountains where he enters into what proves to be a tragic marriage to Neola, a young half-Indian girl. The tetralogy is a pilgrimage of self-discovery.

Genre: Historical Fiction
Subjects: Mountain life; Marriage problems
Place/Time: Idaho—19th century; Chicago (Ill.)—19th century; Illinois—19th century

506. Testament of Man Series
1. *Darkness and the Deep.* Vanguard, 1943.
2. *Golden Rooms.* Vanguard, 1944.
3. *Intimations of Eve.* Vanguard, 1946.
4. *Adam and the Serpent.* Vanguard, 1947.
5. *The Divine Passion.* Vanguard, 1948.
6. *The Valley of Vision: A Novel of King Solomon and His Time.* Abelard, 1951.
7. *The Island of the Innocent: A Novel of Greek and Jew in the Time of the Maccabees.* Abelard, 1952.
8. *Jesus Came Again: A Parable.* Swallow, 1956.
9. *A Goat for Azazel: A Novel of Christian Origins.* Swallow, 1956.
10. *Peace Like a River: A Novel of Christian Asceticism.* Swallow, 1957.
11. *My Holy Satan: A Novel on Christian Twilight.* Swallow, 1958.
12. *Orphans in Gethsemane: A Novel of the Past in the Present.* Swallow, 1960.

Starting with primitive man, continuing through Biblical times and up to the 20th century, this series traces the changing expression of religious belief and practice in the life of man. Expressing the concept that a single man's moral development and search for values is a reflection of that of mankind, Fisher rewrote and abridged his Vridar Hunter tetralogy as the last volume of the series.

Genre: Historical Fiction
Subjects: Psychological novels; Religion; Morality
Place/Time: Europe—multicentury span

Flanagan, Thomas

507. Irish Trilogy
1. *The Year of the French.* Holt, Rinehart & Winston, 1979.
2. *The Tenants of Time.* Dutton, 1988.
3. *The End of the Hunt.* Dutton, 1994.

The Irish fight for freedom from England is chronicled from 1798, when the Irish rise up in County Mayo, to the 20th-century Civil War for Independence. In 1798, French troops come to Ireland to help the Irish in their revolt that ultimately fails. In 1867, the Irish try again in the Fenian Rising. Their fight continues but is defeated with the downfall of Charles Steward Parnell in 1891. However, the Civil War in the 1920s finally leads to Ireland's independence. Flanagan uses numerous narrators to portray Ireland's struggle.

Genre: Historical Fiction
Subjects: Irish; Ireland—French invasion, 1798; Ireland—Sinn Fein Rebellion, 1916
Place/Time: Ireland—multicentury span

Fleetwood, Frances

508.
1. *Concordia.* St. Martin's, 1973.
2. *Concordia Errant.* W. H. Allen, 1973.

The events of the tragic, illicit love affair between Paolo Malatesta and Francesca da Rimini in 13th-century Italy appear through the eyes of Concordia, the daughter of Francesca and the powerful, but unattractive, husband she never loved.

Genre: Historical Romance
Subjects: Love affairs
Place/Time: Italy—13th century

Fletcher, Inglis

509. Carolina Series
1. *Roanoke Hundred.* Bobbs-Merrill, 1948.
2. *Bennett's Welcome.* Bobbs-Merrill, 1950.
3. *Rogues's Harbor.* Bobbs-Merrill, 1964.
4. *Men of Albemarle.* Bobbs-Merrill, 1942.
5. *Lusty Wind for Carolina.* Bobbs-Merrill, 1944.
6. *Cormorant's Brood.* Lippincott, 1959.
7. *Raleigh's Eden.* Bobbs-Merrill, 1940.
8. *The Wind in the Forest.* Bobbs-Merrill, 1957.
9. *The Scotswoman.* Bobbs-Merrill, 1954.
10. *Toil of the Brave.* Bobbs-Merrill, 1946.
11. *Wicked Lady.* Bobbs-Merrill, 1962.
12. *Queen's Gift.* Bobbs-Merrill, 1952.

From the turbulent birth of the Carolina colonies through the defeat of General Cornwall at Yorktown in 1789, the personal lives of the colonists are acted out against the background of the historical events that shaped the colony. The stories follow several families through different generations as they come over as indentured servants, settle on farms, and fight for the Revolution. Real historical figures are interwoven with fictional characters who are based on Fletcher's own family. Despite the military and political unrest of the time, the characters fall in love and marry.

Genre: Family Saga; Historical Romance
Subjects: Indentured servants; Farm life; United States—to 1776; United States—revolution, 1775–1783

Place/Time: North Carolina—17th century; North Carolina—18th century; South Carolina—17th century; South Carolina—18th century

Flynn, Michael F.

510.
1. *Firestar.* Tor, 1996.
2. *Rogue Star.* Tor, 1998.

Set in New Jersey in the early years of the 21st century, these stories recount the efforts of heiress Mariesa van Huyten to promote innovation and creativity in the country's educational system and to apply the resources of private enterprise to the space program. Part of Mariesa's goal is to set up a defense system against asteroids that threaten Earth, but she must battle bureaucrats, short-sighted businessmen, a former friend who turns against her, and at one point, even the President of the United States.

Genre: Science Fiction
Subjects: Women; Wealth; Education; Outer space, exploration of; Bureaucracy
Place/Time: New Jersey—1980–

Forbes, Bryan

511.
1. *The Endless Game.* Random House, 1986.
2. *Spy at Twilight.* Random House, 1990.

British M16 agent Alex Hillsden knows that Toby Bayldon, the socialist Prime Minister, secretly works for the Russians. When two policemen are killed in Hyde Park and Hillsden's investigation threatens to reveal the truth, he is branded a traitor and forced out of M16. He flees to Moscow, and there plots his revenge with the help of an old colleague.

Genre: Espionage
Subjects: Secret service; International intrigue; Revenge; Spies
Place/Time: England—1945–1980; Soviet Union—1945–1980; Soviet Union—1980–1991

Ford, Ford Madox

512. The Fifth Queen
1. *The Fifth Queen and How She Came to Court.* Rivers, 1906.
2. *Privy Seal: His Last Venture.* Rivers, 1907.
3. *The Fifth Queen Crowned.* Nash, 1908.

The above titles have also been published in the following collection: *The Fifth Queen.* Vanguard, 1963.

Henry VIII is unhappily married to Anne of Cleves, his fourth wife. When he meets the beautiful Katherine Howard, he divorces Anne to marry her. However the Machiavellian intrigue of the court is her undoing. In trying to bring Henry back to the Catholic Church, she brings down the wrath of Thomas Cromwell. Eventually Katherine becomes the fifth victim in the Tower of London. The original volumes were published only in England.

Genre: Historical Fiction
Subjects: Henry VIII, King of England, 1491–1547; Queens; Courts and courtiers
Place/Time: England—15th century

513. The Tietjens Tetralogy
1. *Some Do Not.* Grosset & Dunlap, 1924.
2. *No More Parades.* Boni, 1925.
3. *A Man Could Stand Up.* Boni, 1926.
4. *The Last Post.* Boni, 1928.

The above titles have also been published in the following collection: *Parade's End.* Knopf, 1950.

Christopher Tietjens is a Tory in England before World War I. He is a gentleman who puts up with his impossible wife, but when the war breaks out, he sees the society rapidly changing. When he can no longer handle the changes, he has a mental breakdown. He leaves his family and goes to live with the woman he loves.

Subjects: Marriage problems; Mental illness
Place/Time: England—1900–1945

Ford, Richard

514.
1. *Sportswriter.* Random, 1986.
2. *Independence Day.* Knopf, 1995.

Frank Bascombe, novelist turned sportswriter, looks at his life, his marriage, and his work during one week at Easter. What he sees moves him to both elation and regret. He divorces his wife, becomes a real estate agent, and tries to find a bridge of communication with his teenage son. He plans a driving trip through Massachusetts over the Fourth of July with his son and even assigns his son some required reading, but an injury to his son's eye makes the trip very difficult for both father and son.

Subjects: Authors; Fathers and sons
Place/Time: New York (state)—1980–

Forester, C. S. (Cecil Scott)

515. The Hornblower Series
1. *Mr. Midshipman Hornblower.* Little, Brown, 1950.
2. *Lieutenant Hornblower.* Little, Brown, 1952.
3. *Hornblower and the Hotspur.* Little, Brown, 1962.
4. *Hornblower During the Crisis.* Little, Brown, 1967.
5. *Hornblower and the Atropos.* Little, Brown, 1953.

Titles 1, 2, and 5 have also been published in the following collection: *Young Hornblower.* Little, Brown, 1960.

6. *Beat to Quarters.* Little, Brown, 1937.
7. *Ship to the Line.* Little, Brown, 1938.
8. *Flying Colours.* Little, Brown, 1939.

The above three titles have also been published in the following collection: *Captain Horatio Hornblower.* Little, Brown, 1939.

9. *Commander Hornblower.* Little, Brown, 1945.
10. *Lord Hornblower.* Little, Brown, 1946.
11. *Admiral Hornblower in the West Indies.* Little, Brown, 1958.

The above three titles have also been published in the following collection: *The Indomitable Hornblower.* Little, Brown, 1963.

As a 17-year-old midshipman, Horatio Hornblower enters the Royal Navy in the late 1700s. He rises through the ranks as he fights the Spanish and the French. He fights with Nelson at Trafalgar, in the East Indies, and in the Baltic. He marries one woman, loves another, and finally retires as an admiral with the woman he loves. Throughout the books, the dashing Hornblower battles storms, pirates, slaves, mutineers, and the French for the greater glory of Britannia.

Genre: Historical Fiction; Naval Adventure; War
Subjects: Naval battles; War; Navy, British—officers; Seamen; Peninsular War, 1807–1814
Place/Time: Atlantic Ocean—18th century; Atlantic Ocean—19th century; Mediterranean region—18th century; Mediterranean region—19th century

Forrest, Anthony. *Pseud. of* Norman MacKenzie

516.
1. *Captain Justice.* Hill & Wang, 1981.
2. *The Pandora Secret.* Hill & Wang, 1982.
3. *A Balance of Dangers.* Hill & Wang, 1983.

During the Napoleonic Wars, Captain John Justice, master spy, is called upon to serve the clandestine Board of Beacons, Bells, Buoys, and Mercantile Messengers as England tries to sabotage Napoleon's plans for conquest. He goes to Holland to prevent the Dutch fleet from falling into the hands of the French. Then he must protect Robert Fulton as he builds a secret steamship for the British. Wherever he is needed, the daring Captain Justice fights to protect England.

Genre: Adventure; Espionage; Historical Fiction; War
Subjects: Spies; Secret service; Napoleonic Wars, 1800–1814
Place/Time: England—19th century; Netherlands—19th century

Forstchen, William R.

517. Gamester Wars
1. *The Alexandrian Ring.* Ballantine, 1987.
2. *The Assassin Gambit.* Ballantine, 1988.

In a society of the future, war has become a sort of game fought on designated planets. First Alexander the Great and then a group of Samurai warriors travel through time and space to join the conflict.

Genre: Science Fiction
Subjects: Imaginary wars and battles; Time travel; Samurai; Alexander the Great, 356–323 B.C.

518. The Lost Regiment
1. *Rally Cry.* Penguin, 1990.
2. *Union Forever.* Penguin, 1991.
3. *Terrible Swift Sword.* NAL-Dutton, 1992.

A group of Civil War soldiers far removed from their environment by time and space lead the revolt of an enslaved group of humans who have been kidnapped to an alien world.

Genre: Science Fiction
Subjects: Time travel; Soldiers; United States—Civil War, 1861–1865; Kidnapping

519. The New Ice Trilogy
1. *Ice Prophet.* Ballantine, 1983.
2. *The Flame Upon the Ice.* Ballantine, 1984.
3. *A Darkness Upon the Ice.* Ballantine, 1985.

Michael Ormson becomes an unwilling messianic leader in a society of the future in which science is in disrepute because an experiment gone wrong covered the planet with ice. Ormson must not only deal with a power hungry religious group and a mysterious illness, but also with his own feelings of revulsion for the violence his leadership has unleashed.

Genre: Science Fiction
Subjects: Ice; Experiments, scientific; Violence

Fortune, Dion. *Pseud. of* Violet M. Firth

520. Lilith Le Fay Morgan
1. *The Sea Priestess.* Firth, 1938.
2. *Moon Magic.* Aquarian Press, 1938.

Reincarnated in the 20th century, the medieval temptress Morgan Le Fay attempts to establish the worship of the ancient goddess Isis. The tale is first told by a British real estate agent who had been Morgan's lover in a previous existence. Then Morgan herself takes up the story of her spiritual quest.

Genre: Fantasy
Subjects: Reincarnation; Morgan le Fey (legendary character); Gods and goddesses

Foster, Alan Dean

521. The Adventures of Flinx of the Commonwealth
1. *For the Love of Mother-Not.* Ballantine, 1983.
2. *The Tar-Aiym-Krang.* Ballantine, 1984.
3. *Orphan Star.* Ballantine, 1977.

4. *The End of the Matter.* Ballantine, 1977.
5. *Bloodhype.* Ballantine, 1973.
6. *Flinx in Flux.* Ballantine, 1998.
7. *Mid-Flinx.* Ballantine, 1995.

Flinx starts life with both good and bad luck. The result of an illegal genetic experiment, he is sold as a slave to a kindly woman who, unfortunately, disappears. Flinx is endowed with extraordinary psi mental powers, which he uses for both noble and ignoble purposes. He is joined in his wanderings by a poisonous flying snake who becomes his protector. Together they have a series of adventures as Flinx searches for his parents and reaches young manhood seeking tranquility but dogged by trouble.

Genre: Fantasy; Science Fiction; Coming of Age
Subjects: Boys; Extrasensory perception; Genetics; Rogues and vagabonds

522. The Damned
1. *A Call to Arms.* Ballantine, 1991.
2. *The False Mirror.* Ballantine, 1992.
3. *The Spoils of War.* Del Ray, 1993.

The destructive, warlike tendencies of humans make them perfect mercenaries for the Weave, an alien confederation of the distant future, in their war against the Amplitur, who practice genetic manipulation. Ultimately a powerful group of humans who are the product of the Amplitur's genetic tinkering emerges from the struggles.

Genre: Science Fiction
Subjects: Mercenary soldiers; Extraterrestrial beings; Imaginary wars and battles; Genetics

523. Icerigger
1. *Icerigger.* Ballantine, 1974.
2. *Mission to Moulokin.* Ballantine, 1979.
3. *The Deluge Drivers.* Ballantine, 1987.

Tran-ky-ky is a frozen world inhabited by catlike creatures on which Ethan Fortune and Skua September find themselves stranded. They battle the elements and save the planet from an attempt to melt its ice cover and enslave its inhabitants.

Genre: Science Fiction
Subjects: Ice; Life on other planets; Mythical animals

524. Journeys of the Catechist
1. *Carnivores of Light and Darkness.* Aspect/Warner, 1998.
2. *Into the Thinking Kingdoms.* Aspect/Warner, 1999.
3. *A Triumph of Souls.* Aspect/Warner, 2000.

Living in the midst of his tribe, the Naumkib, Etjole Ehomba, a herdsman, is bound by his promise to a dying foreigner to save the Visioness Themaryl from the clutches of the sorcerer Hymneth the Possessed. Ehomba sets off for the North armed only with his sword, assorted charms and potions, and his ability to communicate with all living creatures. He soon acquires help in the form of a wandering mercenary and an enormous lion-cheetah hybrid, but must first conquer the forces of nature and the evil of sophisticated, treacherous societies before he can come close to the imprisoned princess.

Genre: Fantasy
Subjects: Rescues; Heroes; Good and evil; Princesses; Magic

525. Spellsinger
1. *Spellsinger.* Warner, 1983.
2. *The Hour of the Gate.* Warner, 1984.
3. *The Day of the Dissonance.* Phantasia Press, 1984.
4. *The Moment of the Magician.* Phantasia Press, 1984.
5. *The Paths of the Perambulator.* Phantasia Press, 1985.
6. *The Time of the Transference.* Phantasia Press, 1986.
7. *Son of Spellsinger.* Warner, 1993.
8. *Chorus Skating.* Warner, 1994.

From his mundane academic existence, Jonathan Meriweather is transported to a magic land where animals talk and he is the heroic magical Spellsinger. With Mudge the otter at his side, Jon goes to the center of the Earth and through a tunnel of blue flame. But, some things aren't very different from Jon's real life in this fantasy realm; Buncan, Jon's son, joins a group that plays rap music. Buncan definitely doesn't want to follow in his father's footsteps.

Genre: Fantasy
Subjects: Imaginary realms; Teachers; Music; Heroes; Fathers and sons

Foster, M. A. (Michael Anthony)

526. The Morphodite
1. *The Morphodite.* DAW Books, 1981.
2. *Transformer.* DAW Books, 1983.
3. *Preserver.* DAW Books, 1985.

On the totalitarian planet Oerlikon, genetic experimentation produces a shape shifter who soon senses inner powers greater than those of his/her creators and becomes an assassin whose goal is to pull down the oppressive government.

Genre: Science Fiction
Subjects: Totalitarianism; Life on other planets; Genetics; Subversive activities

Foy, George

527.
1. *Contraband.* Bantam, 1997.
2. *The Memory of Fire.* Bantam Spectra, 2000.

In this near-future world, cities have deteriorated and a brutal governmental organization, the Bureau of Nationalization, wields power in what is left of the United States. First, a compulsive smuggler watches his friends disappear, victims of an information gathering system called Bokon Taylay that can invade all aspects of life. In the second work, the BON pursues a young musician and composer whose anarchic group of artists and musicians has been destroyed.

Genre: Science Fiction
Subjects: Bureaucracy; Government, resistance to; Smuggling; Musicians
Place/Time: United States—1980–

France, Anatole. *Pseud. of* Francois-Anatole Thibault

528. Abbe Coignard
1. *The Queen Pedauque.* Boni & Liveright, 1923.
2. *The Opinions of Jerome Coignard.* John Lane, 1913.
3. *The Merrie Tales of Jacques Tournebroche.* Dodd, Mead, 1909.

Jacques Menetrier, son of a Paris cook, encounters the major influences of mid-18th-century French intellectual life personified in his tutor Jerome Coignard, the skeptical priest with an eye for the ladies, and M. D'Astarac, an alchemist and occultist on whose estate Jacques becomes infatuated with the lovely, but fickle, Jahel.

Genre: Coming of Age
Subjects: Boys; Tutors; Love
Place/Time: France—19th century

529. Contemporary History
1. *The Elm-Tree on the Mall: A Chronicle of Our Own Times.* John Lane, 1910.
2. *The Wicker-Work Woman.* John Lane, 1910.
3. *The Amethyst Ring.* John Lane, 1919.
4. *Monsieur Bergeret in Paris.* John Lane, 1921.

Historical currents of late 19th-century France are brought to life through the narrative of the political and social intrigues surrounding the naming of a new bishop of Tourcoing and the experiences of M. Bergeret, a professor who observes Parisian society at the time of the Dreyfus Affair.

Subjects: Bishops, Catholic; Social classes; Dreyfus, Alfred, 1859–1935
Place/Time: France—19th century

530. Pierre Noziere
1. *My Friend's Book.* John Lane, 1913.
2. *Pierre Noziere.* John Lane, 1916.
3. *Little Pierre.* John Lane, 1920.
4. *The Bloom of Life.* Dodd, Mead, 1923.

Autobiographical novels narrate the life of young Pierre, growing up in Paris of the middle of the 19th century, from his close relationship to his mother to his first adolescent infatuation.

Genre: Coming of Age
Subjects: Autobiographical stories; Boys; Family life

Place/Time: Paris (France)—19th century; France—19th century

Frank, J. Suzanne

531.
1. *Reflections in the Nile.* Warner, 1997.
2. *Shadows on the Aegean.* Warner, 1998.
3. *Sunrise on the Mediterranean.* Warner, 1999.

Chloe Kingsley is an artist vacationing in Egypt standing in the temple at Karnak when a sudden burst of cosmic energy sends her back to ancient Egypt where she is a priestess serving the goddess HatHor. Her attempt to return to the 20th century is defeated when a rip in the time space fabric sends her first to the volcanic Aegean island Aztlan, which may be the source of the Atlantis legend, then to the Middle East of the first century A. D. Chloe is disturbed by the knowledge that her body as it exists in the 20th century is inhabited by someone she despises, but she is still enthralled by her partner in time travel the young physician Cheftu.

Genre: Fantasy; Historical Fiction; Romance
Subjects: Time travel; Atlantis; Love
Place/Time: Egypt—15th century B. C.; Middle East—1st century A. D.

Frank, Waldo David

532.
1. *The Death and Birth of David Markand.* Scribner, 1934.
2. *The Bridegroom Cometh.* Doubleday, Doran, 1939.

In parallel stories, David Markand and Mary Donald search for their true natures through a variety of experiences including failed marriages and allegiances to the philosophical and social movements of America in the 1930s. Ultimately they come together in a sort of attraction of opposites.

Subjects: Self-realization; Love; Social problems
Place/Time: United States—1900–1945

Frankau, Pamela

533. Clothes for a King's Son
1. *Sing for Your Supper.* Random House, 1964.
2. *Slaves of the Lamp.* Random House, 1965.
3. *Over the Mountains.* Random House, 1967.

Thomas Weston's unique powers of mind become evident during his childhood as a member of an English theatrical family. However, as he matures, his prescience becomes as much a burden as a talent. He is captured and assumed dead in World War II, but through a series of almost miraculous occurrences escapes and is reunited with his beloved.

Genre: Historical Fiction

Subjects: Teenagers; Family life; World War I, 1914–1918
Place/Time: England—1900–1945

Franken, Rose

534.
1. *Claudia: The Story of a Marriage.* Farrar, 1939.
2. *Claudia and David.* Farrar, 1940.
3. *Another Claudia.* Farrar, 1943.
4. *Young Claudia.* Rinehart, 1946.
5. *The Marriage of Claudia.* Rinehart, 1948.
6. *From Claudia to David.* Harper, 1950.
7. *The Fragile Years.* Doubleday, 1952.
8. *The Antic Years.* Doubleday, 1958.

Claudia is just out of high school when she marries her beloved David, a mature man of 25. The child bride is a total innocent who has nothing but love, ideals, hope, and promise for everyone. She adores everyone, and they love her. When David goes off to serve in World War II, Claudia must grow up and take care of their farm and children. However, tragedies do not dim the sweet Claudia.

Genre: Gentle Read; Romance
Subjects: Idealism; Marriage; Farm life; World War II, 1939–1945
Place/Time: United States—1900–1945

Franklin, Miles

535.
1. *My Brilliant Career.* St. Martin's, 1980, 1901.
2. *The End of My Career.* St. Martin's, 1981, 1946.

In the turn-of-the-century Australian outback, Sybylla Melvyn vehemently resists the traditional woman's roles of teacher or wife and opts for a career as a writer. However, she is tempted when she meets an attractive farmer. The book she does write creates a furor, and she goes to Sydney where she finds her cultured family just as flawed as her rural family.

Subjects: Feminism; Women; Authors; Family life
Place/Time: Australia—1900–1945

Fraser, George MacDonald

536.
1. *The General Danced at Dawn.* Knopf, 1973.
2. *McAuslan in the Rough.* Knopf, 1974.
3. *The Sheikh and the Dustbin.* HarperCollins, 1997, 1988.

At the end of World War II, the Highland Regiment is sent to Edinburgh Castle after fighting in the Middle East. Lieutenant Daniel MacNeill leads the regiment, but finds the bane of his existence is Private McAuslan, the dirtiest soldier in the war. The high jinks of regiment keep Lieutenant MacNeill at his wits' end and the reader laughing.

Genre: Humor
Subjects: Soldiers—British; Castles
Place/Time: Edinburgh (Scotland)—1945–1980; Scotland—1945–1980

537.
1. *Flashman.* World, 1969.
2. *Royal Flash.* Knopf, 1970.
3. *Flash for Freedom!* Knopf, 1972.
4. *Flashman at the Charge.* Knopf, 1973.
5. *Flashman in the Great Game.* Knopf, 1975.
6. *Flashman's Lady.* Knopf, 1978.
7. *Flashman and the Redskins.* Knopf, 1982.
8. *Flashman and the Dragon.* Knopf, 1986.
9. *Flashman and the Mountain of Light.* Knopf, 1991.
10. *Flashman and the Angel of the Lord.* Knopf, 1995.
11. *Flashman and the Tiger.* Knopf, 2000.

Harry Paget Flashman is the grown-up cad and bully from Tom Brown's school days. The novels, which are written as Flashman's memoirs, relate his involvement with the major historical events and people of the Victorian Era. He takes part in the Indian Mutiny, the American Gold Rush, the Battle of the Little Bighorn, the Taiping Rebellion in China, and the Punjab rebellion. Throughout his adventures, he follows two principles—to survive at all costs and to get what he can sexually, financially, and socially. He's totally reprehensible, but his adventures are a pure delight.

Genre: Adventure; Historical Fiction; War
Subjects: Adventure; War; Diaries (stories in diary form); Rogues and vagabonds
Place/Time: England—19th century; United States—19th century; China—19th century

Freeman, Harold Webber

538.
1. *Fathers of Their People.* Holt, 1932.
2. *Pond Hall's Progress.* Holt, 1933.

In rural Suffolk, Dick Brandish grows up on a farm tilled by his family for generations. Making a break with tradition, he leaves to enlist in World War I and returns with his bride, an Italian peasant girl.

Subjects: Farm life; Soldiers; World War I, 1914–1918
Place/Time: England—1900–1945

Freireich, Valerie J.

539. Polite Harmony of the Worlds
1. *Becoming Human.* Roc, 1995.
2. *Testament.* Roc, 1995.

Genetic manipulation and modification play enormous roles in this imagined universe. August wants to be fully human, but the devious skills he has developed

in his work as an intelligence agent and his ancestry as the cloned son of a traitor make him both useful and suspect. Gray Bridger is an oddity on the matriarchal planet Testament. He carries only his own memories, whereas, the rest of the population have the accumulated memories of their female ancestors.

Genre: Science Fiction
Subjects: Genetics; Life on other planets; Heredity

Fridegard, Jan

540.
1. *I, Lars Hard.* University of Nebraska Press, 1983.
2. *Jacob's Ladder and Mercy.* University of Nebraska Press, 1985.

To be a member of the Statare (peasant) class in Sweden during the early 1900s meant a harsh life of social immobility and near illiteracy. Lars Hard, a vital, lusty womanizer, is sent to prison for an alleged sexual indiscretion. He rebels, but finally returns home to care for his dying mother.

Genre: Historical Fiction
Subjects: Peasants; Poverty
Place/Time: Sweden—1900–1945

Friedman, Bruce Jay

541.
1. *About Harry Towns.* Knopf, 1974.
2. *Current Climate.* Atlantic Monthly Press, 1989.

Midlife crisis strikes fortyish Harry Towns. A successful screenwriter in Los Angeles, Harry is separated from his wife and son. He moves to Manhattan for the fast life, but a serious illness forces him to give up his wild ways and grow up. Later he moves to suburban Long Island with his second wife and reflects on his youth in the 1950s.

Subjects: Middle age; Authors; Divorce; Diseases
Place/Time: Los Angeles (Calif.)—1945–1980; New York (N. Y.)—1945–1980; Long Island (N. Y.)—1945–1980; California—1945–1980; New York (state)—1945–1980

Friedman, Rosemary

542.
1. *Proofs of Affection.* Morrow, 1982.
2. *Rose of Jericho.* Morrow, 1984.

In contemporary London, Kitty and Sydney Shelton are an Orthodox Jewish couple raising three children—Josh, Carol, and Rachel. Everything seems fine until the children grow up and decide they want to find their own not-so-orthodox lifestyles.

Subjects: Jews—England; Conflict of generations; Family life

Place/Time: London (England)—1945–1980; England—1945–1980

Frison-Roche, Roger

543. The Story of Simon Sokki
1. *The Raid.* Harper & Row, 1964.
2. *The Last Migration.* Harper & Row, 1967.

In the years following World War II, feuds between clans continue in Lapland. Kristina, the youngest daughter of the Sokki family, unwillingly undergoes a Norwegian program meant to bring Laps into modern civilization, but returns to her family and to a Finnish fur trapper with whom she gradually falls in love.

Genre: Historical Fiction
Subjects: Cultural conflict; Acculturation; Family life
Place/Time: Norway—1945–1980

Frost, Mark

544.
1. *The List of 7.* Morrow, 1993.
2. *The 6 Messiahs.* Morrow, 1995.

A young Arthur Conan Doyle submits a manuscript to a publisher and suddenly finds himself the target of attacks by a strange group of people who are vaguely similar to the characters in his book. The enigmatic Jack Sparks helps him survive the group's assaults, but Jack is seemingly killed in a fall. Ten years later, when Doyle is crossing the Atlantic, he is attacked by assassins while on the steamship. The mysterious Sparks reappears and saves him. When they land in America, Doyle and Sparks race to protect the holy books of the world from being stolen and taken to a cult in the desert. Doyle's old lover Eileen Temple becomes involved as they try to stop evil.

Genre: Historical Fiction
Subjects: Escapes; Adventure; Doyle, Arthur Conan, 1859–1930
Place/Time: London (England)—19th century; United States—19th century

Frye, Pearl

545. Life of Lord Nelson
1. *Game for Empire.* Little, 1950.
2. *Sleeping Sword.* Little, 1952.

Beginning with Lord Nelson's command in the Mediterranean in the war with France, these novels trace his career and personal life through his affair with Emma Hamilton, fall from favor and reinstatement in England, and his death at the Battle of Trafalgar.

Genre: Historical Fiction; Naval Adventure
Subjects: Nelson, Horatio Nelson, Viscount, 1758–1805; Navy, British—officers; Naval battles; Napoleonic Wars, 1800–1814; Love affairs

Place/Time: England—18th century; England—19th century; Mediterranean region—18th century; Mediterranean region—19th century

Fuller, Anna

546.
1. *Pratt Portraits.* Putnam, 1897.
2. *Later Pratt Portraits.* Putnam, 1911.

In a series of interconnected short stories, different members of the Pratt family are illuminated. Priggish Aleck Pratt, old lady Pratt, and many more are described with insight, humor, and compassion.

Subjects: Family life; Short stories
Place/Time: United States—1900–1945

Fuller, Henry Blake

547.
1. *The Chevalier of Pensieri-Vani.* J. G. Cupples, 1890.
2. *Gardens of This World.* Knopf, 1929.

The Chevalier of Pensieri-Vani, a poor young gentleman, travels in Italy and records his impressions of people and places. In humorous sketches, he reflects on his hatred of industrialism and his love of music, art, and rural landscapes. Later he and the seigneur of Hors-Concours discuss their admiration of beauty and the gardens around Europe.

Subjects: Industrial conditions; Aesthetics; Travel
Place/Time: Italy—1900–1945

Fullilove, Eric James

548.
1. *Circle of One.* Bantam, 1996.
2. *The Stranger.* Bantam, 1997.

Being a forensic telepath in the Los Angeles Police Department of the near future is hazardous to mental well-being. Jenny Sixa is often able to solve murder cases by reading the final thoughts of the victims, but as she goes through this process, she suddenly begins to find clues addressed directly to her. Jenny comes into wealth, but her return to work after boredom sets in is accompanied by terrible nightmares that a serial killer is broadcasting into her mind.

Genre: Science Fiction; Crime Novel
Subjects: Telepathy; Murder and murderers; Police
Place/Time: Los Angeles (Calif.)—1980–

Funderburk, Bobby. *See* Morris, Gilbert

Funderburk, Robert

549. Dylan St. John Novels
1. *The Fires of Autumn.* Bethany House, 1996.
2. *All the Days Were Summer.* Bethany House, 1997.
3. *Winter of Grace.* Bethany House, 1998.
4. *The Spring of Our Exile.* Bethany House, 1999.

Dylan and Susan St. John are enjoying their marriage when Dylan discovers that children in the custody of the State of Louisiana are missing. As he searches for them, he uncovers corruption in the legal system. When they move to the small bayou town of Evangeline, the peacefulness of their life is shattered when the mayor of the town is killed. Dylan searches for the killer and later has to hunt down robbers. These grueling searches help Dylan to finally find faith.

Genre: Christian Fiction
Subjects: Adventure; Faith; Husbands and wives
Place/Time: Louisiana—1980–

550. The Innocent Years
1. *Love and Glory.* Bethany House, 1994.
2. *These Golden Days.* Bethany House, 1996.
3. *Heart and Soul.* Bethany House, 1995.
4. *Old Familiar Places.* Bethany House, 1996.
5. *Tenderness and Fire.* Bethany House, 1997.
6. *The Rainbow's End.* Bethany House, 1997.

When Lane Temple returns home after World War II, he is invited by an army buddy to come to Baton Rouge to work in the oil industry. As Lane works hard to achieve success, he is away from his wife and four children, and their marriage becomes strained. Catherine becomes so depressed she wants to commit suicide until she hears a Billy Graham sermon and is reborn in faith. Catherine's faith helps rebuild the family, and she must hold the family together when Lane is called back to duty during the Korean War. The emotional wounds of battle are only healed for Lane when he too finds faith. After the war, Lane runs for a seat in the Louisiana House of Representatives where he fights corrupt politicians. Each of their four children also face their own struggles. Beautiful Jessie searches for a career in show business while younger daughter Sharon struggles with leukemia. Son Dalton is injured in a football accident and begins to drift in a downward spiral until he hits bottom. Young Cassidy gets in trouble with the law and ends up going to Vietnam where he sees the brutality of war. Throughout all of the trials each Temple family member faces, it is faith that helps them through.

Genre: Christian Fiction
Subjects: Faith; Family life; War
Place/Time: Louisiana—1945–1980

Furman, Lucy

551.
1. *The Quare Women.* Little, 1923.
2. *The Glass Window.* Little, 1925.
3. *Lonesome Road.* Little, 1927.

The mountain people of Knott County, Kentucky, find the young women who come to teach them and bring them into the modern world a bit outlandish and strange, but gradually develop an appreciation for the improvements these women make in their day- to-day lives. These novels are a fictionalized account of the work of the Hindman settlement school in the early 1900s.

Genre: Historical Fiction
Subjects: Mountain life; Teachers
Place/Time: Kentucky—1900–1945

Furst, Alan

552.
1. *The World at Night.* Random, 1996.
2. *Red Gold.* Random, 1999.

French film producer Jean Casson is just about to have his first big movie hit when the Germans invade France. As the Germans occupy Paris, he tries to revive his career but is forced to spy on the British airdrops to the French Resistance. Patriotism forces him to become an agent for the British and work as a double agent. Later he joins the French Resistance and tries to bring the feuding factions together as they combat the Germans.

Genre: Espionage; War
Subjects: Spies; War; World War II, 1939–1945
Place/Time: France—1900–1945

Gaan, Margaret

553.
1. *Red Barbarian.* Dodd, Mead, 1984.
2. *White Poppy.* Dodd, Mead, 1985.

Charlie Tyson, a 23-year-old redhead, is sent from England to manage the East India Company in Canton during the days of the 19th-century Chinese opium trade. Once there, he marries and begets a family dynasty that weathers changes in British-Chinese relations as well as a reversal in the opium trade.

Genre: Family Saga; Historical Fiction
Subjects: Merchants
Place/Time: China—19th century

Gabaldon, Diana

554.
1. *Outlander.* Delacorte, 1991.
2. *Dragonfly in Amber.* Delacorte, 1992.
3. *Voyager.* Delacorte, 1994.
4. *Drums of Autumn.* Delacorte, 1996.

English nurse Claire Randall and her husband Frank go to Scotland on a second honeymoon after World War II. While picking flowers, she touches an ancient circle of stone and is transported back to Scotland of 1743. There she is taken prisoner by James Frazer and falls in love with him. The two fight Black Jack Randall who is an ancestor to her modern husband before she returns to the present. Twenty-two years later she returns to Scotland and travels back in time again to meet James and discover who the father of her daughter Brianna is. When Brianna grows up, she discovers that James is her father, so she travels back in time with her lover to find her father.

Genre: Fantasy; Romance
Subjects: Time travel
Place/Time: Scotland—18th century; Scotland—1980–; United States—18th century

Gainham, Sarah

555.
1. *Night Falls on the City.* Holt, Rinehart & Winston, 1967.
2. *A Place in the Country.* Holt, Rinehart & Winston, 1969.
3. *Private Worlds.* Holt, Rinehart & Winston, 1971.

Julia Homburg is an internationally famous actress in Vienna before World War II. As war erupts, Julia has to play her most difficult role—to continue her career while hiding her Jewish husband Franz from the Gestapo. After the war Julia becomes involved with an English officer, and in the 1950s returns to Vienna with her new husband to rebuild her life.

Genre: Historical Fiction
Subjects: Actors and actresses; World War II, 1939–1945; Holocaust, Jewish, 1933–1945; Marriage
Place/Time: Vienna (Austria)—1900–1945; Vienna (Austria)—1945–1980; Austria—1900–1945; Austria—1945–1980

Galdos, Benito Perez. *See* Perez Galdos, Benito

Gallacher, Tom

556.
1. *Apprentice.* H. Hamilton, 1983.
2. *Journeyman.* H. Hamilton, 1984.
3. *Survivor.* H. Hamilton, 1985.
4. *Wind on the Heath.* H. Hamilton, 1989.

Sent by his English middle-class parents to be a shipyard apprentice in Clydeside, Scotland, in the 1950s, Billy Thompson learns his craft, but is dissatisfied. His adventuresome nature leads him to try being a novelist, then working on a tanker that blows up. He finally ends up back in Scotland writing the biography of aging actress Annie Teynor. Local color, dialect, and adventure enliven the books.

Subjects: Actors and actresses; Authors; Shipping; Seamen

Place/Time: Scotland—1945–1980

Gallico, Paul

557.
1. *Mrs. 'Arris Goes to Paris.* Doubleday, 1958.
2. *Mrs. 'Arris Goes to New York.* Doubleday, 1960.
3. *Mrs. 'Arris Goes to Parliament.* Doubleday, 1965.
4. *Mrs. 'Arris Goes to Moscow.* Doubleday, 1974.

The unsinkable Mrs. 'Arris, a middle-aged London charwoman, who is fascinated with her wealthy employer's Dior gown, works and saves her money for her own Dior original. When she gets to Paris, she brings happiness to all she meets, and finally gets her dress. She has further adventures and continues to spread her infectious optimism when she accompanies her employers on trips to New York and Moscow.

Genre: Gentle Read; Humor
Subjects: Cleaning women; Fashion industry and trade
Place/Time: Paris (France)—1945–1980; London (England)—1945–1980; Moscow (Soviet Union)—1945–1991; New York (N. Y.)—1945–1980; France—1945–1980; England—1945–1980; Soviet Union—1945–1980; Soviet Union—1980–1991

Galsworthy, John

558. The Forsyte Saga
1. *The Man of Property.* Putnam, 1909.
2. *The Indian Summer of a Forsyte.* 1918. (This is a long short story in *The Galsworthy Reader.* Scribner, 1968.)
3. *In Chancery.* Scribner, 1921.
4. *Awakening.* Scribner, 1920.
5. *To Let.* Scribner, 1921.
6. *The White Monkey.* Scribner, 1924.
7. *The Silver Spoon.* Scribner, 1926.
8. *Swan Song.* Scribner, 1929.
9. *Two Forsyte Interludes.* Scribner, 1928.

Titles 6–9 have also been published in the following collection: *A Modern Comedy.* Scribner, 1929.

10. *On Forsyte Change.* Scribner, 1930. (These are short stories.)
11. *Maid in Waiting.* Scribner, 1931.
12. *Flowering Wilderness.* Scribner, 1932.
13. *One More River.* Scribner, 1933.

Galsworthy wrote the original family saga that set the tone and shape for all family sagas to come. The Forsytes, a wealthy English family, are introduced in the Victorian era and followed through the Roaring Twenties. Soames Forsyte, a successful solicitor, marries beautiful, but poor Irene, but she loves architect Philip Bosinney. When their marriage falls apart, Irene marries her cousin Jolyon and has a son Jon. Soames remarries and has a daughter Fleur. Jon and Fleur fall in love, but the breach between their families keeps them apart. In the later books, the Charwells, cousins of the Forsytes, continue the tortured saga of the family. Throughout the series, the manners and morals of upper-class British society are brilliantly shown.

Genre: Family Saga; Historical Fiction
Subjects: Husbands and wives; Family life; Society novels
Place/Time: England—19th century; England—1900–1945

Gann, Ernest

559.
1. *The Antagonists.* Simon & Schuster, 1970.
2. *The Triumph.* Simon & Schuster, 1986.

In 73 A. D., Roman general Flavius Silva finds that the Jewish resistance movement at Masada is much harder to defeat than he expected. As the war drags on, both sides resort to drastic measures to win. Even after his hollow victory over the Jews, Silva has more problems when he returns to Rome and the intrigues surrounding Emperor Vespasian.

Genre: Historical Fiction
Subjects: Masada site (Israel); Jews; Israelites; Suicide; Government, resistance to
Place/Time: Palestine—1st century A. D.; Rome (Italy)—1st century A. D.; Italy—1st century A. D.

Gardner, Craig Shaw

560. Cineverse Cycle
1. *Slaves of the Volcano God.* Ace, 1989.
2. *Bride of the Slime Monster.* Ace, 1990.
3. *Revenge of the Fluffy Bunnies.* Ace, 1990.

Roger Gordon's Captain Crusader decoder ring enables him to cross into an alternate reality where movie characters and scenes are real. Roger must rescue the woman he loves by defeating the villainous Dr. Dread and other assorted bad guys.

Genre: Fantasy; Science Fiction
Subjects: Motion pictures; Good and evil; Love

561. The Dragon Circle
1. *Dragon Sleeping.* Ace, 1995.
2. *Dragon Waking.* Ace, 1995.
3. *Dragon Burning.* Ace, 1996.

An entire neighborhood from the community of Chestnut Circle is magically transported to a realm where a battle is going on between two brothers, both sorcerers, who want to control a powerful immortal dragon, who is asleep, but will awaken soon. As the characters take sides in the struggle and, in some cases, undergo magical transformations, a set of jewels called dragon's eyes become more and more important.

Genre: Fantasy

Subjects: Dragons; Magic; Imaginary wars and battles

562. Ebezenum and Wuntvor
1. *A Malady of Magicks.* Ace, 1986.
2. *A Multitude of Monsters.* Ace, 1986.
3. *A Night in the Netherhells.* Ace, 1987.
4. *A Difficulty with Dwarves.* Ace, 1987.
5. *An Excess of Enchantments.* Ace, 1988.

The wizard Ebezenum survives a battle with a second-rate demon, but finds that, as a result, he has become allergic to magic. His only partially successful quest for a cure takes him into Hell. In the second part of the series, his apprentice Wuntvor takes up the search for a remedy and, in addition, must deal with the fact that the allergy is contagious.

Genre: Fantasy
Subjects: Magic; Hell

Gardner, John E.

563. Secret Generations
1. *The Secret Generations.* Putnam, 1985.
2. *The Secret Houses.* Putnam, 1987.
3. *The Secret Families.* Putnam, 1989.

Members of the English Railton family are involved in espionage from 1909 to the 1960s. Giles Railton begins the tradition in World War I, and his grandchildren continue it in World War II. When their French resistance group is destroyed by a double agent, they use their skills to find a traitor and to stop the Soviets from setting up their own agents. At the height of the Cold War, when Sir Casper Railton is revealed as a Soviet mole, his nephew and cousin go to Russia to uncover the truth.

Genre: Adventure; Espionage; Family Saga; Historical Fiction
Subjects: Spies; Secret service; International intrigue; Cold war; World War I, 1914–1918; World War II, 1939–1945
Place/Time: England—1900–1945; England—1945–1980

Garrison, Peter

564. The Changeling Saga
1. *The Changeling War.* Ace, 1999.
2. *The Sorcerer's Gun.* Ace, 1999.
3. *The Magic Dead.* Ace, 2000.

Mr. Smith, also known as the Pale Man, is capable of striking strange and evil bargains with desperate people, but his sinister deals are only part of his agenda to link the technology of Earth with the magic of the Faerie realm called the Castle, with disastrous results for both worlds. Opposing him is an odd assortment of people including a police officer and a gangster whose son Mr. Smith turned into a zombie. Both helping and hurting their cause are Byzantine intrigues and power struggles within the Castle.

Genre: Fantasy; Horror
Subjects: Good and evil; Magic; Imaginary wars and battles

Gary, Romain. *Pseud.* of Romain Kacew

565. Genghis Cohn
1. *The Dance of Genghis Cohn.* World, 1968.
2. *The Guilty Head.* World, 1969.

The dybbuk or ghost of comedian Genghis Cohn mischievously haunts Police Commissioner Schatz, the former Nazi officer who had been in charge of Cohn's execution. Cohn continues his ghostly adventures in Tahiti where his odd behavior convinces the powers that be that he is a person of great importance and worthy of investigation.

Genre: Fantasy; Humor
Subjects: Ghost stories; National Socialism; Holocaust, Jewish, 1933–1945
Place/Time: Germany—1945–1980; Tahiti—1945–1980

Gaskell, Jane

566. The Atlan Saga
1. *The Serpent.* St. Martin's, 1977, 1963.
2. *The Dragon.* St. Martin's, 1977, 1963.
3. *Atlan.* St. Martin's, 1977, 1965.
4. *The City.* St. Martin's, 1977, 1965.
5. *Some Summer Lands.* St. Martin's, 1979.

Princess Cija spends her first 17 years imprisoned in a tower because of a prophecy that she will betray her native land. She is released from the tower as a hostage to the half-man, half-serpent warrior Zerd, whom she must both wed and attempt to assassinate. She escapes Zerd after being unwillingly at his side as he conquers the idyllic land of Atlan, but further trials and complications await her. Although she fears Zerd, she feels drawn to him. She discovers that the man who has been her sometime lover is, in fact, her half-brother, and she still must deal with her powerful father's fear of the prophecy.

Genre: Fantasy
Subjects: Princesses; Atlantis; Hostages; Prophecies; Conquerors

Gavin, Catherine

567.
1. *Traitor's Gate.* St. Martin's, 1976.
2. *None Dare Call It Treason.* St. Martin's, 1978.
3. *How Sleep the Brave.* St. Martin's, 1980.

When France is occupied by the Germans during World War II, Mike Marchand and Jacques Brunel flee France and find shelter in England. There Mike flies for the Royal Air Force. Jacques returns to France to fight with the anti-De Gaul resistance movement. They fight for their country's freedom and finally are part of the liberation of Paris.

Genre: War
Subjects: World War II, 1939–1945; Air Force, British; Government, resistance to
Place/Time: England—1900–1945; France—1900–1945

Gear, Kathleen O'Neal. *See* Gear, W. Michael

Gear, W. Michael *and* Gear, Kathleen O'Neal

568. First North American Series
1. *People of the Wolf.* Tor, 1990.
2. *People of the Fire.* Tor, 1991.
3. *People of the Earth.* Tor, 1992.
4. *People of the River.* Tor, 1992.
5. *People of the Sea.* Tor, 1993.
6. *People of the Lakes.* Forge, 1994.
7. *People of the Lightning.* Forge, 1995.
8. *People of the Silence.* Forge, 1996.
9. *People of the Mist.* Forge, 1996.
10. *People of the Masks.* Forge, 1998.

Using the vehicle of archaeologists finding early American Indian burial sites, the Gears tell the story of paleolithic people at the end of the last ice age. Through flashbacks, the story focuses on a tribe called "The People," who make the perilous journey across the ice from Asia to America. The series follows the People as they spread across America and become the first Americans. Each book uses authentic Native American history, cultural rites, legends, and artifacts to tell the story.

Genre: Historical Fiction
Subjects: Prehistoric times; Native Americans; Humans, prehistoric; Stone Age
Place/Time: United States—prehistoric times

Gellis, Roberta

569. Roselynde Chronicles
1. *Roselynde.* Playboy Press, 1978.
2. *Alinor.* Playboy Press, 1978.
3. *Joanne.* Playboy Press, 1978.
4. *Gilliane.* Playboy Press, 1979.
5. *Rhiannon.* Playboy Press, 1982.
6. *Sybelle.* Jove, 1983.

Alinor, ward of Queen Alinor, and her female descendants see the treachery and glory of the 12th century as each woman tries to find love amidst the turmoil of the medieval court. Love does not come easily to these women who are at the mercy of the king's whim. Pageantry and battles form the backdrop for the romances as each woman faces a different challenge.

Genre: Historical Romance

Subjects: Queens; Courts and courtiers; Middle Ages
Place/Time: England—12th century

Gent, Peter

570.
1. *North Dallas Forty.* Morrow, 1973.
2. *North Dallas After Forty.* Villard, 1989.

The first book in this series, now a classic, looks behind the scenes into the lives of professional football players to reveal the world of drugs, pain, sex, and savagery behind championship teams. Twenty years later, Phil Elliot, Seth Maxwell, and other members of the championship North Dallas team are reunited. Some are leading lives of fame and power, others live in physical pain, but all are controlled by a corporation that is involving them in crime and fraud.

Genre: Sports
Subjects: Football; Crime and criminals
Place/Time: Dallas (Tex.)—1945–1980; Dallas (Tex.)—1980–; Texas—1945–1980; Texas—1980–

Gentle, Mary

571.
1. *Golden Witchbreed.* Morrow, 1984.
2. *Ancient Light.* NAL, 1989.

Earth envoy Lynne Christie comes to the planet Orthe and becomes involved with a leader of the faction that wants more contact with Earth. Lynne finds herself helping the pro-contact faction reveal the plots of their enemies. Eight years later Lynne comes back to Orthe for a multicorporate Earth company that wants to get the ancient artifacts of the witchbreed, the earliest inhabitants of Orthe. Neither she nor the corporation understands the power of the descendants of the witchbreed.

Genre: Science Fiction
Subjects: Life on other planets; Business; Politics; Diplomats

572.
1. *Rats and Gargoyles.* Viking, 1991.
2. *The Architecture of Desire.* Viking, 1993.

In an alternate medieval world, rats rule subservient men. Some of the humans struggle to free themselves through magic. Humans, demons, and rats use magic, alchemy, and science to avoid warfare, which is threatening the city.

Genre: Fantasy
Subjects: Imaginary kingdoms; Rats; Middle Ages; Magic

Germain, Sylvie

573.
1. *The Book of Nights.* Godine, 1993.

2. *Night of Amber.* Godine, 1999.

In the 1850s, a river man and his wife finally have a son. Young Theodore-Fausten Peniel grows up on a barge in France, marries, and has children, but then he goes off to serve France in the Franco-Prussian War. During the war, he is severely wounded and deformed. He comes home in an insane state and has an incestuous affair with his own daughter. That union will result in the birth of Victor-Flandrin, who will grow up and settle on a farm called Blackland. There he will marry five times and have fifteen children. He will live through World War I and II before he dies. Victor's grandson Charles-Victor grows up on Blackland farm where he is neglected by his parents. He lives in his own fantasy world until he flees to Paris in 1968 where he finds murder and redemption as the family story comes full circle.

Genre: Family Saga; Historical Fiction
Subjects: Family life; Fathers and sons; War
Place/Time: France—19th century; France—1900–1945; France—1945–1980

Gerrold, David

574.
1. *The Voyage of the Star Wolf.* Bantam, 1990.
2. *The Middle of Nowhere.* Bantam, 1995.

Spaceship Commander Jonathan Thomas Korie battles enemies both within and outside his ship, the Star Wolf. First he is unfairly blamed for a defeat by the genetically altered assassin Morthan and assigned to duty under Captain Hardesty, who leaves much to be desired as a superior officer. Hardesty is injured, and Korie takes charge, but now must also overcome the "imp," an adaptive biocomputer with insidious power, which was placed on the ship by Morthan.

Genre: Science Fiction
Subjects: Spaceships; Space flight; Assassination; Computers

575. The War against the Chtorr
1. *A Matter for Men.* Bantam, 1989.
2. *A Day for Damnation.* Bantam, 1989.
3. *A Rage for Revenge.* Bantam, 1989.
4. *A Season for Slaughter.* Bantam, 1992.

John McCarthy reaches adulthood at time of global crisis. The Chtorr, alien creatures who appear to be enormous caterpillars, have inflicted a plague on the Earth's population. The survivors then face an invasion of the creatures themselves who bring with them their own ecosystem, which seems to be capable of overwhelming the plants and animals of Earth. Aided by an uncanny ability to understand and predict the behavior of the Chtorr, McCarthy joins the resistance.

Genre: Science Fiction
Subjects: Extraterrestrial beings; Diseases; Environment

Gerson, Noel Bertram. *See Ross, Dana Fuller*

Geston, Mark S.

576. Havegore
1. *Lords of the Starship.* Ace, 1967.
2. *Out of the Mouth of the Dragon.* Ace, 1969.

Connected by theme rather than plot or character, these stories describe a future of continuous warfare in which characters are haunted by a feeling that life was once better and men of the past capable of greater achievement. The second work chronicles a young man's search for renewal of the human race.

Genre: Science Fiction
Subjects: Imaginary wars and battles; Degeneration

Gethers, Peter

577.
1. *The Cat Who Went to Paris.* Crown, 1991.
2. *A Cat Abroad: The Further Adventures of Norton the Cat Who Went to Paris and his Human.* Crown, 1993.

Norton, a Scottish Fold cat, speaks through his human companions as he describes their journeys through Europe. Carried in a shoulder bag, Norton experiences human foibles while he enjoys driving, flying, and mingling with strangers.

Genre: Animal Story; Humor
Subjects: Cats; Travel; Animals
Place/Time: Europe—1980–

Ghose, Zulfikar

578.
1. *The Incredible Brazilian.* Holt, Rinehart & Winston, 1972.
2. *The Beautiful Empire.* Holt, Rinehart & Winston, 1978.
3. *A Different World.* Holt, Rinehart & Winston, 1978.

Gregorio Peixoto da Silva Xavier goes through several reincarnations and many comic, ribald adventures in this trilogy that begins in 17th-century Brazil and culminates in the revolutionary politics of the present day. Gregorio is the pompous son of a landowner who explores Brazil. Through his adventures in the different centuries, the settling of Brazil and a series of military revolutions are recounted.

Genre: Historical Fiction
Subjects: Picaresque novels; Reincarnation; Politics—Brazil
Place/Time: Brazil—multicentury span

Giardina, Denise

579.
1. *Storming Heaven.* Norton, 1987.
2. *The Unquiet Earth.* Norton, 1992.

From the 1921 Annandel coal mine strike to Vietnam, the people and history of Blackberry Creek, West Virginia, are dramatically revealed in their battles with the mine owners, with poverty, and with each other. Four different narrators in each book tell the story of the miners' struggle to unionize and to fight the mine owners. The secret, ill-fated love of cousins Rachel Honaker and Dillion Freedman runs throughout the books. Their daughter Jackie tries to leave the mountains, but returns to the town for the final tragedy.

Genre: Historical Fiction
Subjects: Coal mines and mining; Mountain life; Poverty; Love affairs
Place/Time: West Virginia—1900–1945; West Virginia—1945–1980

Gibbon, Lewis Grassic. *Pseud. of James Leslie Mitchell*

580.
1. *Sunset Song.* Appleton-Century, 1933.
2. *Cloud Howe.* Doubleday, 1934.
3. *Grey Granite.* Doubleday, 1935.
The above titles have also been published in the following collection: A Scots Quair. (Jarrolds, 1946.)

Young Christine Guthrie marries Evan Tavendale in their little Scottish village. They are happy until Evan is drafted into the army and killed fighting World War I. Christine finds happiness again when she marries a minister, but her second marriage also ends tragically with his death. She helps her son go to college and finally returns to the home she left 23 years before.

Genre: Gentle Read
Subjects: World War I, 1914–1918; Marriage; Widows; Family life
Place/Time: Scotland—1900–1945

Gibbons, Stella

581.
1. *Cold Comfort Farm.* Longmans, 1932.
2. *Christmas at Cold Comfort Farm.* Longmans, 1940.
3. *Conference at Cold Comfort.* Longmans, 1949.

This parody of the novels about rural Sussex follows the Starkadders of Cold Comfort Farm. They are living in mud and dirt until Flora Poste comes to visit and sets the farm straight. Years later Flora returns to Cold Comfort Farm for a Thinkers Groups. The novels poke fun at artists and intellectuals.

Genre: Humor
Subjects: Farm life; Artists; Intellectuals
Place/Time: England—1900–1945

Gibson, William

582.

1. *Idoru.* Putnam, 1996.
2. *All Tomorrow's Parties.* Putnam, 1999.

In the 21st century, "netrunner" Colin Laney is hired by the manager of a Japanese rock group to find out why one of the lead musicians wants to marry Rei Toei, a holographic being who exists only in virtual reality. With Rei Toei still lurking in the background, Colin's adventures take him to San Francisco where he uses his unique ability to see subtle data associations to handle what promises to be an earthshaking historical change.

Genre: Science Fiction
Subjects: Computers; Technology and civilization; Rock music
Place/Time: Japan—1980–; San Francisco (Calif.)—1980–

583. Neuromancer

1. *Neuromancer.* Ace, 1984.
2. *Count Zero.* Arbor House, 1986.
3. *Mona Lisa Overdrive.* Bantam, 1988.

First Case, then computer hacker Count Zero enter cyberspace, a realm of computer information that has become three dimensional and with which a user can interact, sometimes illegally and always with risk to himself. Industrial espionage and computer generated art each play a part in these tales of a future in which technology and urban decay merge in an impersonal, violent landscape.

Genre: Science Fiction
Subjects: Computers; Technology and civilization; Degeneration

Gifford, Thomas

584.

1. *The Wind Chill Factor.* Putnam, 1975.
2. *The First Sacrifice.* Bantam, 1994.

When the Third Reich went down to defeat at the end of World War II, some Nazi survivors made secret plans to rise again. They put people in key positions in corporations in every country who are just waiting to take over the world. John Cooper is the heir to this evil, but he tries to shed this dark legacy before a Fourth Reich is built. Cooper finds he is in love with the sister he never knew he had. After Cooper's first fight with the Fourth Reich survivors, he retreats to the woods of Minnesota to forget, but he is again called to fight the neo-Nazis. When the Soviet Union breaks up, Cooper must again fight the evil Nazis as they try to dominate the world.

Genre: Adventure

Subjects: Adventure; International intrigue; National Socialism
Place/Time: Minnesota—1980–; United States—1980–

585.

1. *Wind Chill Factor.* Putnam, 1974.
2. *The First Sacrifice.* Bantam, 1994.

John Cooper is called back to his Minnesota home town when his father dies suddenly. The mysterious papers the father left contain the blueprints for the creation of a Nazi Fourth Reich. After this discovery, people start dying—John's brother, his girlfriend, and others. John himself nearly dies. He then goes to England and Germany hunting for his long lost sister while fighting neo-Nazis. Twenty years later, he again is called to Berlin by his sister who is married to neo-Nazi, Wolf Koller. John must fight Wolf in order to save his sister.

Genre: Adventure; Espionage
Subjects: Adventure; International intrigue
Place/Time: Minnesota—1945–1980; Germany—1980–

Gilchrist, Ellen

586.

1. *Victory over Japan.* Little, Brown, 1984.
2. *Drunk with Love.* Little, Brown, 1986.
3. *The Anna Papers.* Little, Brown, 1988.
4. *I Cannot Get You Close Enough.* Little, Brown, 1986.
5. *Starcarbon.* Little, Brown, 1994.
6. *Rhoda: A Life in Stories.* Little, Brown, 1995.
7. *The Age of Miracles.* Little, Brown, 1995.
8. *Flights of Angels.* Little, Brown, 1998.

Starting during World War II with eight-year-old Rhoda Hand, Gilchrist chronicles the lives of the Hand family of Charlotte, North Carolina. Through short stories, the Hand family, their kinfolk, and then the younger generation grow up, fall in love, marry, and try to preserve the bonds that hold the family together.

Genre: Family Saga
Subjects: Love
Place/Time: North Carolina—1945–1980

587.

1. *Light Can Be Both Wave & Particle.* Little, Brown, 1989.
2. *The Courts of Love.* Little, Brown, 1996.

In a series of interconnected stories, Nora Jane marries her lover Freddy Harwood and gives birth to twins. They lead passionate lives and go from experience to experience. She, Freddy, and the twins' godfather enroll in graduate school, get lost in the California wilderness, and see a friend killed by a terrorist. With humor and passion, Nora Jane and family romp through life.

Subjects: Marriage; Family life
Place/Time: California—1980–

Giles, Janice Holt

588.
1. *The Enduring Hills.* Westminster, 1950.
2. *Miss Willie.* Westminster, 1951.
3. *Tata's Healing.* Westminster, 1951.

The simple life of Piney Ridge, Kentucky, solves the problems of three different families. Since Hod Pierce wants more out of life, he moves to Louisville, but once he finds money can't buy happiness, he returns to Piney Ridge. Miss Willie comes to the town to teach, but when she marries, she finds the town doesn't need reforming. Finally a disillusioned doctor finds a new way of life in the beautiful Kentucky hills.

Genre: Gentle Read; Romance
Subjects: Small town life; Ambition; Physicians; Teachers
Place/Time: Kentucky—1945–1980

589.
1. *Hannah Fowler.* Houghton Mifflin, 1956.
2. *The Believers.* Houghton Mifflin, 1957.
3. *Johnny Osage.* Houghton Mifflin, 1960.
4. *Savanna.* Houghton Mifflin, 1961.
5. *Voyage to Santa Fe.* Houghton Mifflin, 1962.
6. *The Great Adventure.* Houghton Mifflin, 1966.
7. *Shady Grove.* Houghton Mifflin, 1968.
8. *Six-Horse Hitch.* Houghton Mifflin, 1969.

Hannah Moore and her father make the hard trek to Boonesborough, Kentucky, in 1778. There her father dies, and she marries Tice Fowler. Their children, Rebecca and Johnny, continue to be pioneers and settle the West. Johnny lives with the Osage Indians, takes a wagon train to Santa Fe, and finally settles down to be a trader. Rebecca's son Joe becomes a mountain man while the grandchildren help to establish the overland stage coach in 1859. The day-to-day life of her pioneers is pictured in detail as Giles tells the story of the opening of the West.

Genre: Family Saga; Historical Fiction; Western
Subjects: Frontier and pioneer life; Mountain life; Wagon trains
Place/Time: Kentucky—18th century; Kentucky—19th century; Western states—18th century; Western states—19th century

Gilliland, Alexis A.

590. Rosinante
1. *The Revolution from Rosinante.* Ballantine, 1981.
2. *Long Shot for Rosinante.* Ballantine, 1981.
3. *The Pirates of Rosinante.* Ballantine, 1982.

Government bureaucracy in the world of the future is the target of satire in these stories of the revolt of a colony on the asteroid Rosinante. In this civilization computers are charismatic personalities, some resembling movie stars.

Genre: Humor; Science Fiction
Subjects: Bureaucracy; Space colonies; Revolutions and revolutionists; Computers

Gilman, Charlotte Perkins

591.
1. *Herland.* Forerunner, 1915.
2. *With Her in Ourland: Sequel to Herland.* Forerunner, 1916.

Three American men stumble onto a 2,000-year-old all-female society. The men cannot believe that the women are quite happy and civilized without men, and they search for the men. Eventually they have to re-think what is masculine and what is feminine. One of the men, Vandyck Jennings, falls in love with Ellador, a young woman of Herland. They marry and Vandyck takes the innocent Ellador to Europe and the United States where she witnesses the problems of the early 20th century—war, overpopulation, racism, politics, and more. These allegorical novels were feminist tracts against the evils of the early 20th century.

Subjects: Allegories; Women; Social problems
Place/Time: Europe—1900–1945; United States—1900–1945

Giovene, Andrea

592.
1. *The Book of Sansevero.* Houghton Mifflin, 1970.
2. *The Dilemma of Love.* Houghton Mifflin, 1973.
3. *The Dice of War.* Houghton Mifflin, 1974.

This fictionalized autobiography is a faithful recreation of Europe as it was in the early part of the century. Andrea defies his parents and leaves Naples to seek his fortune. He travels in Italy, fights in Greece, and is imprisoned by the Nazis.

Genre: Historical Fiction
Subjects: Autobiographical stories; Travel; World War II, 1939–1945
Place/Time: Italy—1900–1945; Greece—1900–1945

Gironella, Jose Maria

593.
1. *The Cypresses Believe in God.* Knopf, 1955, 1953.
2. *One Million Dead.* Doubleday, 1963, 1961.
3. *Peace After War.* Knopf, 1969, 1966.

The tensions and agonies of the Spanish Civil War are seen in microcosm through the experiences of the Alvear family and the townspeople of Gerona. Ignacio de Alvear tells of the people he meets from all political parties. He then tells the story of the Civil War and the peace that finally comes. Although Gironella claims to be objective, he tends to favor the Falange, dictator Francisco Franco's party, and has been labeled a Franquista, a supporter of Franco.

Genre: War
Subjects: Spain—civil war, 1936–1939; Politics—
  Spain
Place/Time: Spain—1900–1945

Girzone, Joseph F.

594.
1. *Joshua.* Macmillan, 1987.
2. *Joshua and the Children.* Macmillan, 1989.
3. *The Shepherd.* Macmillan, 1990.
4. *Joshua in the Holy Land.* Macmillan, 1992.
5. *Joshua and the City.* Doubleday, 1995.
6. *Joshua: The Homecoming.* Simon & Schuster, 2000.

A humble stranger named Joshua enters contemporary towns in the United States, Northern Ireland, and the Middle East and teaches the gospel of peace and love to troubled people. This gentle wanderer lives the Christian life that he is trying to teach to others, including clergymen who resist his message. When he finally brings peace and insight to the townspeople, he mysteriously disappears, and the people realize they have been touched by Christ.

Genre: Christian Fiction; Gentle Read
Subjects: Christianity; Jesus Christ; Faith
Place/Time: United States—1980–; Northern Ireland—1980–; Middle East—1980–

Gobbell, John J.

595. Last Lieutenant Series
1. *The Last Lieutenant.* St. Martin's, 1997.
2. *A Code for Tomorrow.* St. Martin's, 1999.

Navy Lieutenant Todd Ingram escapes from Corregidor Island with eleven other men. They steal a thirty-six-foot launch and sail through miles of Japanese-infested waters chasing a Nazi spy who has stolen Admiral Nimitz's plan for the battle of Midway. After stopping the spy, Ingram is sent back to the Pacific where he continues to fight the Japanese, but he fights his way back to the Philippines so that he can find his army nurse sweetheart, Helen Durand. Helen is with the Philippine resistance army behind Japanese lines. Ingram battles spies and the Japanese as he fights for his country and his love.

Genre: War; Naval Adventure
Subjects: World War II, 1939–1945; Navy, United
  States; Naval battles
Place/Time: Pacific Ocean—1900–1945; Philippine
  Islands—1900–1945

Godwin, Gail

596.
1. *Father Melancholy's Daughter.* Morrow,
  1991.
2. *Evensong.* Ballantine, 1999.

Margaret Gower leads a complicated girlhood as the daughter of the Rector of St. Cuthberts, an intelligent and sensitive man who is subject to periods of depression. When her mother deserts the family, Margaret is drawn into the role of her father's nurse and confidant and ultimately decides to follow in his footsteps as a member of the clergy. The sequel follows her career as the spiritual leader of a rural North Carolina parish where she encounters problems made more difficult by her marriage to a man very much like her father.

Genre: Coming of Age
Subjects: Clergy; Religion; Fathers and daughters;
  Depression, mental
Place/Time: North Carolina—1980–

Godwin, Parke. *See also* Kaye, Marvin

597.
1. *Waiting for the Galactic Bus.* Doubleday,
  1988.
2. *The Snake Oil Wars, or, Scheherazade
  Ginsberg Strikes Again.* Doubleday, 1989.

Here are answers to some big questions. Man was uplifted from the apes by two superior extraterrestrial adolescents just playing around on Earth. In the afterlife, Barion rules Topside (heaven) until taken to task for genetic meddling, while Cayul, who might appear to be the devil, tries to straighten things out on Earth.

Genre: Fantasy; Humor
Subjects: Man, origin of; Extraterrestrial beings;
  Heaven; Devil

598.
1. *Sherwood.* Morrow, 1991.
2. *Robin and the King.* Morrow, 1993.

In this retelling of the Robin Hood tale, the story is set 100 years earlier in the reign of William the Conqueror and Robin is Edward of Denby, a Saxon resister. He is banished for fighting the Normans and eventually becomes friends with William II. He returns to England to fight for William and helps to change the line of succession. Eleventh-century customs and beliefs are vividly evoked.

Genre: Historical Fiction
Subjects: Anglo-Saxons; England—Anglo-Saxon
  period, 449–1066; William II, King of England,
  1056–1100
Place/Time: England—11th century

599. Camelot
1. *Firelord.* Doubleday, 1980.
2. *Beloved Exile.* Bantam, 1984.
3. *The Last Rainbow.* Bantam, 1985.

This telling of the tale of Arthur and Guinevere is more historical and realistic than other versions. Camelot is the doomed product of Roman and Celtic civilization supported by the aboriginal Faerie society. In the second volume, Queen Guinevere tells of her fate after Arthur's death.

Genre: Fantasy
Subjects: Arthur, King; Guenevere, Queen (legendary character a.k.a. Guinevere)

Goethe, Johann Wolfgang von

600.
1. *Wilhelm Meister's Apprenticeship.* Wells & Lilly, 1828, 1795.
2. *Wilhelm Meister's Travels, or The Renunciants.* Tait, 1827, 1821.

Young Wilhelm Meister comes of age in late 18th-century Germany, breaks from the confines of his middle-class family to become an actor and enters a secret society of aristocrats. In the sequel, Wilhelm travels with his son Felix, encountering many different philosophies and ways of life, and finally settles down to study medicine.

Subjects: Middle classes; Fathers and sons; Travel
Place/Time: Germany—18th century

Gold, Herbert

601.
1. *Fathers.* Random House, 1967.
2. *Family.* Arbor House, 1981.

In this fictionalized tribute to his parents, Gold tells the story of his father's flight from persecution in czarist Russia. He flees to Ohio at age 13 and fights poverty and prejudice to become a success. His first generation mother tries to keep old-world traditions for her son, but he wants only to be an American. Only later does Gold come to understand his parents and their vision.

Genre: Historical Fiction
Subjects: Jews, persecution of; Immigrants; Americanization; Acculturation
Place/Time: Russia—1900–1917; Ohio—1900–1945

Gold, Ivan

602.
1. *Sick Friends.* Dutton, 1969.
2. *Sams in a Dry Season.* Houghton, 1990.

In the 1960s, Jason Sams goes to California to be a writer, but all he finds there is the hedonistic life of sex and alcohol. In the 1970s, Sams is fired from his job at Boston University. He heads to New York to try to re-establish himself, but goes on an alcoholic binge. Hitting rock bottom, he finally joins AA in a desperate attempt to save his life.

Subjects: Alcoholism; Hedonism
Place/Time: New York (N. Y.)—1945–1980; California—1945–1980

Golding, Louis

603.
1. *Forward from Babylon.* Moffat, 1921.
2. *Give Up Your Lovers.* Cosmopolitan Book, 1930.

A young Jewish boy rebels against the restrictions of growing up in an Orthodox household in the industrialized area of northern England in the early 1900s. His difficulties continue when as a young man he falls in love with an upper-class English woman.

Genre: Coming of Age
Subjects: Class distinction; Jews—England; Conflict of generations; Teenagers
Place/Time: England—1900–1945

Golding, William

604.
1. *Rites of Passage.* Farrar, Straus & Giroux, 1980.
2. *Close Quarters.* Farrar, Straus & Giroux, 1987.
3. *Fire Down Under.* Farrar, Straus & Giroux, 1989.

A motley crew of sailors and passengers try to live through the voyage from England to Australia in the Napoleonic era. Edmond Talbot, a young officer, relates the horrific story as the captain picks on a poor minister. When the ship's masts break, the sailors have to struggle to keep it afloat. After a brush with an iceberg, they finally sail into Sydney Harbor. The author concentrates on the individuals and their reactions to the trials they encounter.

Genre: Historical Fiction
Subjects: Voyages and travels; Seamen; Shipmasters; Sailing vessels
Place/Time: Atlantic Ocean—19th century; Pacific Ocean—19th century

Goldreich, Gloria

605.
1. *Leah's Journey.* Harcourt Brace Jovanovich, 1978.
2. *Leah's Children.* Macmillan, 1985.

Fleeing from persecution in post-revolutionary Russia, Leah, a beautiful young Jewish woman, marries gentle David and goes to New York to find freedom. There she and her family survive numerous crises as they become involved in World War II and the emergence of the state of Israel. Leah's children each fight persecution—Aaron in Hungary on the eve of revolution in the 1950s, Mitchell as a civil rights worker in

Mississippi, and Rebecca as a worker on a border kibbutz in Israel.

Genre: Family Saga; Historical Fiction
Subjects: Jews, persecution of; Immigrants; Israel
Place/Time: New York (N. Y.)—1900–1945; New York (N. Y.)—1945–1980; Israel—1900–1945; Israel—1945–1980; Hungary—1900–1945; Hungary—1945–1980; Mississippi—1900–1945; Mississippi—1945–1980

Golon, Sergeanne

606.
1. *Angelique.* Lippincott, 1958.
2. *Angelique and the King.* Lippincott, 1960.
3. *Angelique in Barbary.* Lippincott, 1961.
4. *Angelique in Revolt.* Putnam, 1962.
5. *Angelique in Love.* Putnam, 1962.
6. *The Countess Angelique.* Putnam, 1968.
7. *Temptation of Angelique.* Putnam, 1970.
8. *Angelique and the Demon.* Putnam, 1973.
9. *Angelique and the Ghosts.* Putnam, 1978.

In 1648, innocent and beautiful Angelique de Sance leaves her sheltered estate in the French countryside to marry nobleman Joffrey de Peyrac, a cousin of Louis XIV. Instead of settling down, she begins her adventures by going to the court of Louis XIV where she and her husband are expelled from the country for rebelling against the Sun King. As in all good romances, the lovers are parted. Each time they get together some incident tears them apart again and sends them along different paths across Europe, the Middle East, and America. Angelique battles the king, pirates, sultans, and Indians before true love prevails.

Genre: Historical Romance
Subjects: Courts and courtiers; Adventure; Husbands and wives; Louis XIV, King of France, 1638–1715
Place/Time: France—17th century; Europe—17th century; United States—17th century

Goodkind, Terry

607. The Sword of Truth
1. *Wizard's First Rule.* Tor, 1994.
2. *Stone of Tears.* Tor, 1995.
3. *Blood of the Fold.* Tor, 1996.
4. *Temple of the Winds.* Tor, 1997.
5. *Soul of the Fire.* Tor, 1999.

Richard Cypher leads an idyllic life as a woodsman but when the evil Darken Rahl enters his world, he discovers his mystical powers as the wielder of the Sword of Truth. The Sisters of Light offer training that will assist Richard, but demand total obedience. His beloved Kahlan Amnell fights the good fight with him, but they are faced with a terrible choice: they must marry others to further their efforts to stop a plague unleashed by the evil Emperor Jagang.

Genre: Fantasy

Subjects: Imaginary wars and battles; Good and evil; Arms and armor; Love

Goonan, Kathleen Ann

608. Nanotech Cycle
1. *Crescent City Rhapsody.* Avon Eos, 2000.
2. *Queen City Jazz.* Tor, 1994.
3. *Mississippi Blues.* Tor, 1997.

Written later in time, but occupying an earlier place in fictional chronology than the other works, *Crescent City Rhapsody* sets the stage for stories at a time when pockets of vibrant civilization exist in a 21st-century America nearly demolished by a nanotech plague. Verity grows up in an isolated Shaker community, but must escape when the plague reaches her rural area and seek resurrection for her beloved Blaze, who has been murdered. Verity journeys to Cincinnati, the enlivened city where the population is enslaved by their leader's fantasies. With a recovered Blaze and the freed, but plague-ridden, population of Cincinnati, Verity goes down the Mississippi searching for the mystical salvation said to exist in New Orleans.

Genre: Science Fiction; Coming of Age
Subjects: Diseases; Technology and civilization; Voyages and travels; Love; Escapes

Gordon, Noah

609.
1. *The Physician.* Simon & Schuster, 1986.
2. *The Shaman.* Dutton, 1992.
3. *Matters of Choice.* Plume, 1996.

Starting in the 11th century, the Cole family produces a line of physicians who struggle with their society and how they practice medicine. Rob Cole decides to become a physician after his mother dies in 11th-century London. To become the best doctor possible, Rob disguises himself as a Jew and trains with the famous Jewish Persian physician Avicenna. Rob must overcome superstition and prejudice to use his healing gifts. His descendant Rob J. Cole leaves Scotland in 1839 after making too many enemies through his political writings. He goes to the Illinois frontier where he treats both Native Americans and white pioneers. Eventually he and his son become doctors for the Union Army. In the 1990s, R. J. Cole loses a top-level administrative position at a Boston hospital because she performs abortions at a women's clinic. Then her marriage falls apart, and R. J. moves to the Berkshires so she can rediscover herself while practicing family medicine. All generations of Cole physicians face the moral issues of medicine in their day.

Genre: Family Saga; Historical Fiction
Subjects: Physicians; Medicine
Place/Time: England—11th century; Illinois—19th century; Massachusetts—1980–

Gorky, Maksim. *Pseud.* of Alexei Maximovich Pyeshkoff

610. Forty Years: The Life of Clim Samghin
1. *The Bystander.* Cape, 1930.
2. *The Magnet.* Cape, 1931.
3. *Other Fires.* Appleton-Century, 1933.
4. *The Specter.* Appleton-Century, 1938.

Young Clim Samghin's reaction when he first sees Czar Nicholas II is disappointment. As he matures, he experiences the revolutionary movements and the great changes in Russia of the late 19th and early 20th centuries. The final volume of the series was unfinished at the author's death.

Genre: Historical Fiction
Subjects: Revolutions and revolutionists; Politics—Russia
Place/Time: Russia—19th century; Russia—1900–1917

Gotlieb, Phyllis

611.
1. *Flesh and Gold.* Tor, 1998.
2. *Violent Stars.* Tor, 1999.

In the Galactic Federation of the distant future, the Zamos Corporation has interests in genetic research, but also in legalized vice: prostitution, gambling, and drugs. In the process of trying a routine case, Judge Skerow, a member of the telepathic alien Khagodi, discovers the corporation's connections to a local brothel that has enslaved an amphibious human woman. With the help of GalFed agent Ned Gates, the judge uncovers the Zamos underworld associations, but as the corporation is about to be brought to justice, the alien Ix, who are in league with Zamos, kidnap a young woman and hold her hostage to prevent the trial.

Genre: Science Fiction
Subjects: Extraterrestrial beings; Business; Judges; Crime and criminals; Underworld

612.
1. *O Master Caliban!* Harper, 1976.
2. *Heart of Red Iron.* St. Martin's, 1989.

The consequences and responsibilities inherent in genetic experimentation are played out in these tales of the experiences of scientist Edward Dahlgren and his son Sven. Dahlgren artificially populates a desolate planet, Barrazan V, with mutants and robots called ergs, only to see the ergs rebel and make his son into a mutant of sorts. Sven returns to Barrazan V later in his life and does battle with sentient pythons and strange creatures called crystallines, who live in a volcanic crater.

Genre: Science Fiction
Subjects: Mutation (biology); Space colonies; Genetics; Robots

Goudge, Eileen

613.
1. *Garden of Lies.* Viking, 1989.
2. *Thorns of Truth.* Viking, 1998.

After a passionate love affair, Sylvia Rosenthal does not know if the baby she carries belongs to her lover or her husband. When she gives birth to a dark-haired child, Rose, she switches the baby for a blond-haired child, Rachel, during a hospital fire. Yet Sylvia can't forget Rose, and years later the two girls meet when they fall in love with the same man. Rachel eventually marries Brian, and Rose weds Max. The children they raise also become intertwined in the deception. Rose's son Drew plans to marry Rachel's daughter Iris even though she is unstable. As everyone's life begins to unravel, Sylvia finally reveals the truth behind her long-ago deception.

Genre: Family Saga
Subjects: Mothers and daughters; Family life
Place/Time: New York (N. Y.)—1945–1980; New York (N. Y.)—1980–

Goudge, Elizabeth

614.
1. *The Bird in the Tree.* Coward-McCann, 1940.
2. *Pilgrim's Inn.* Coward-McCann, 1948.
3. *The Heart of the Family.* Coward-McCann, 1953.

World War II has left the Eliot family with problems. The children and grandchildren have all been affected, and it is up to Grandmother Lucilla to hold the family together. She does this by bringing everyone to an old pilgrim's inn on the Hampshire coast of England where the gentle atmosphere helps heal the family and Sebastian Weber, an Austrian from a concentration camp.

Genre: Gentle Read
Subjects: World War II, 1939–1945; Family life; Grandmothers
Place/Time: England—1945–1980

Gould, John

615.
1. *No Other Place.* Norton, 1984.
2. *The Wines of Pentagoet.* Norton, 1986.

The early history of Maine is recounted through the life of Elzada Knight and her home at Morning Hill Farm. In 1616, Jabez Knight and his French friend Jules Marcoux settle on land by the Morning River. Daughter Elzada inherits the farm and holds onto it while the Maine territory passes from the French to the English. Her security is threatened by soldiers, politicians, Indians, smugglers, and other characters, but somehow she also manages to search for a husband.

Genre: Historical Fiction

Subjects: Frontier and pioneer life; Farm life;
   Women
Place/Time: Maine—17th century

Gower, Iris

616.
1. *Copper Kingdom.* St. Martin's, 1983.
2. *Proud Mary.* St. Martin's, 1985.
3. *Spinners' Wharf.* St. Martin's, 1985.
4. *Morgan's Woman.* St. Martin's, 1987.
5. *Fiddler's Ferry.* St. Martin's, 1987.
6. *Black Gold.* St. Martin's, 1988.

Six independent romances set in the town of Sweyn's
Eye in South Wales in the early 1900s feature strong
women who must fight poverty and class prejudice to
find happiness. Although the stories are independent
of each other, they show different aspects of the industries in the town—smelting, tinplating, spinning and
weaving, farming, fishing, and coal mining. Each of
the women comes from a poor family and, through
hard work, sets up her own successful business and
finds love.

Genre: Historical Fiction; Historical Romance
Subjects: Women; Social classes; Businesswomen
Place/Time: Wales—1900–1945

Graham, Heather

617.
1. *One Wore Blue.* Dell, 1991.
2. *And One Wore Gray.* Dell, 1992.
3. *And One Rode West.* Dell, 1992.

The saga of the Cameron clan follows the family as
they fight for the South in the Civil War, then fight to
keep their home in Virginia. Brother Daniel and then
sister Christa fall in love with Yankees, but the war and
misunderstandings on both sides keep the lovers apart
until they are finally brought together for a happy ending.

Genre: Historical Romance
Subjects: United States—Civil War, 1861–1865
Place/Time: Virginia—19th century

Graham, Winston

618.
1. *Ross Poldark.* Doubleday, 1951, 1945. (Original American title: *The Renegade.*)
2. *Demelza.* Doubleday, 1953, 1946.
3. *Jeremy Poldark.* Doubleday, 1954, 1950.
   (Original American title: *Venture Once
   More*)
4. *Warleggan.* Doubleday, 1955, 1953. (Original American title: *The Last Gamble*)
5. *The Black Moon.* Doubleday, 1974.
6. *The Four Swans.* Doubleday, 1977.
7. *The Angry Tide.* Doubleday, 1978.

8. *The Stranger from the Sea* . Doubleday,
   1982.
9. *The Miller's Dance.* Doubleday, 1983.
10. *The Loving Cup.* Doubleday, 1985.

"Poldark" was the title of the popular *Masterpiece
Theatre* program about Ross Poldark, set in Cornwall,
England, of the 1700s. Poldark grapples with the political ambitions of ruthless bankers and mine owners
and with the emotional demands of four women. Captain Ross Poldark returns from the American Revolution to his rundown estate and finds his beloved
engaged to his cousin. He tries to make the best of the
situation by restoring his estate and the copper mines
and by championing the cause of the lower classes. He
marries Demelza, a miner's daughter, and struggles to
keep his marriage together and his estate from his enemies, the Warleggans. This family feud continues with
his children Jeremy and Clowance as they fight for
land, power, and love.

Genre: Family Saga; Historical Fiction; Historical
   Romance
Subjects: Houses; Mines and mining; Social classes
Place/Time: England—18th century; England—19th
   century

Grant, Charles L.

619. The Millennium Quartet
1. *Symphony.* Forge, 1997.
2. *In the Mood.* Forge, 1998.
3. *Chariot.* Forge, 1998.
4. *Riders in the Sky.* Forge, 2000.

Portents of an approaching apocalypse start in the
small town of Maple Landing, New Jersey, and spread
across the land. A church bell tolls mysteriously. A
minister can suddenly perform miracles. In the midst
of a food shortage, strange crimes and murders are
rampant. A virulent strain of smallpox sweeps across
the country, but residents of a half-abandoned subdivi-
sion of Las Vegas are strangely immune to the plague.
Finally, wars break out at various spots around the
world, mysteriously associated with shadowy human
incarnations of the Four Horsemen of the Apocalypse.

Genre: Horror; Fantasy
Subjects: End of the world; Prophecies
Place/Time: United States—1980–

Grant, Tracy

620.
1. *Shadows of the Heart.* Dell, 1996.
2. *Shores of Desire.* Dell, 1997.

In Regency England, the Lescaut brothers find that
love disrupts their lives. Paul finds himself fleeing villains with a very pregnant Sophie Rutledge. As they
flee the Scottish Highlands, the two rediscover the
love they had for each other years earlier. Brother Robert searches for the killer of his wife and then falls in
love with a woman whose family might have been in-

volved with the murder. For both men, love brings many surprises.

Genre: Historical Romance
Subjects: Lovers
Place/Time: Scotland—19th century

Gras, Felix

621. French Revolution Series
1. *The Reds of the Midi.* Appleton, 1899.
2. *The Terror.* Appleton, 1898.
3. *The White Terror.* Appleton, 1899.

Starting with the story of the military band, the Reds of the Midi, who came from the south of France to fight in the French Revolution, this narrative continues through the repression of Marat and into the Napoleonic period.

Genre: Historical Fiction
Subjects: France—revolution, 1789–1799; Revolutions and revolutionists
Place/Time: France—18th century

Grass, Gunter

622. The Danzig Trilogy
1. *The Tin Drum.* Pantheon, 1963.
2. *Cat and Mouse.* Harcourt Brace & World, 1963.
3. *Dog Years.* Harcourt Brace & World, 1965.
   The above titles have also been published in the following collection: *The Danzig Trilogy.* Harcourt Brace Jovanovich, 1987.

Each novel in this trilogy takes place in Danzig, Germany, during World War II. Some of the characters, such as Oskar and Stortebecker, appear in the different books even though the stories are not connected. All of the books deal with the ways in which the rise of dictatorship, war, and the Holocaust shaped the present and the future. In each of his works, Grass tries to discover how such evil could have happened. His characters, such as the dwarf Oskar who represents the distorted values of Germany, take on a symbolic meaning. Each book is a powerful indictment of war and hatred.

Genre: War
Subjects: World War II, 1939–1945; Holocaust, Jewish, 1933–1945; Totalitarianism; Good and evil; Psychological novels
Place/Time: Danzig (Germany)—1900–1945; Germany—1900–1945

Graves, Robert

623.
1. *I, Claudius.* Smith & Haas, 1934.
2. *Claudius, the God and His Wife Messalina.* Smith & Haas, 1935.

As seen on *Masterpiece Theatre,* Imperial Rome with its intrigues, orgies, superstitions, and murders is the setting of this purportedly lost biography of the Emperor Claudius. Claudius is the lame stammerer who is thought a fool by his family. He describes the reigns of Augustus, Tiberius, and Caligula, each more tyrannical, dangerous, and insane than the other. When Caligula is murdered, Claudius, as the sole survivor of the Augustan dynasty, is named emperor. As emperor he tries to be honorable, but ends up becoming a tyrant and is murdered by Agrippina, Nero's mother. These are brilliant depictions of profligate Rome.

Genre: Historical Fiction
Subjects: Claudius, Emperor of Rome, 10 B.C.–54 A.D.; Rome—kings and rulers; Politics—Rome; Hedonism
Place/Time: Rome (Italy)—1st century A. D.; Italy—1st century A. D.

Gray, Caroline

624.
1. *A Woman of Her Time.* Severn House, 1995.
2. *A Child of Fortune.* Severn House, 1996.

When she was fifteen, beautiful Alexandra Mayne was married and then widowed only a few months later. With a young baby in war-torn London of 1917, Alexandra uses her brains and body to stay alive and soon becomes a famous madame. Later Alexandra helps young Cynthia Haslar when she runs away from her abusive home. Cynthia, however, has a dream of becoming a wife and mother, and she must decide how to use her beauty to achieve that dream.

Genre: Romance
Subjects: Women; Poverty; Prostitution;
Place/Time: England—1900–1945

Greeley, Andrew M.

625.
1. *A Midwinter's Tale.* Forge, 1998.
2. *Younger than Springtime.* Forge, 1999.

Chuck O'Malley grew up in a large close-knit Catholic family in Chicago during the Depression. In order to earn money for college, Chuck joins the army and fights in World War II. After the war, he's assigned to a regiment in Bamberg, Germany, where he sees the suffering of the defeated Germans. When he is assigned to find a family of Nazis wanted by the Russians, he realizes he can't turn them in because the Russians will kill them. When Chuck finally comes home, he enrolls in Notre Dame in 1949, but soon finds himself fighting the strict intellectual limits of the university. He even gets in trouble with the school after taking a picture of a girlfriend in a scanty bathing suit. As Chuck searches for meaning in the church, he also searches for love and compares his love with his father's story of how he met and married Chuck's mother. Chuck finds that being Catholic in the late 1940s has its trials and tribulations.

Genre: Historical Fiction

Subjects: Catholic faith; Soldiers—American; College life; Love
Place/Time: Chicago (Ill.)—1900–1945; Chicago (Ill.)—1945–1980; Germany—1945–1980

626.
1. *Irish Gold.* Forge, 1994.
2. *Irish Lace.* Forge, 1996.
3. *Irish Whiskey.* St. Martin's, 1998.
4. *Irish Mist.* Forge, 1999.
5. *Irish Eyes.* Forge, 2000.

When Chicago commodities trader Dermot Michael Coyne goes to Ireland, he is searching for the reasons his grandfather immigrated to America. His father was involved with Irish revolutionary Michael Collins who was murdered. Coyne is helped by Nuala McGrail who translates his grandmother's diary. Their love heats up as the intrigue grows. When Nuala moves to Chicago, the two lovers get involved with an art theft and with Irish terrorists. Eventually the two marry, and Nuala Anne becomes a folk singer while Dermot writes. The two explore Irish history as they explore their married life.

Genre: Romance
Subjects: Lovers; Adventure
Place/Time: Ireland—1980–; Chicago (Ill.)—1980–

Green, Julian

627. Dixie Trilogy
1. *The Distant Lands.* Marion Boyars, 1991.
2. *The Stars of the South.* Marion Boyars, 1996.

In the 1850s, 16-year-old Elizabeth Escridge leaves England to live with her relatives in Georgia. There she lives on the family plantation and gets herself involved with numerous young men and family fights. Eventually she marries, has a son, and then loses her husband. She moves to Savannah where she must survive the memories of the Civil War and the perils of a closed society.

Genre: Historical Fiction
Subjects: Plantation life; Southern states; Society novels; Mothers and sons
Place/Time: Georgia—19th century

Greene, Bette

628.
1. *Summer of My German Soldier.* Dial Press, 1973.
2. *Morning Is a Long Time Coming.* Dial Press, 1978.

As a rebellious 12-year old in Jenkinsville, Arkansas, during World War II, Patty Bergin defies her abusive father and befriends Anton, a German POW. She overcomes her own insecurity and the town's prejudices and eventually helps him escape. When she is 18, Patty travels to Europe to see Anton's mother and to resolve her obsession with Anton. While in Paris, she falls in love with Roger and finally begins to appreciate her own value.

Genre: Coming of Age; Romance
Subjects: Girls; World War II, 1939–1945; Prisoners of war
Place/Time: Arkansas—1900–1945; Europe—1945–1980

Gregory, Philippa

629.
1. *Wideacre.* Simon & Schuster, 1987.
2. *Favored Child.* Pocket, 1989.
3. *Meridon.* Pocket, 1990.

The tragic saga of the Lacey family begins on the 18th-century English estate of Wideacre. Beatrice Lacey uses murder, maiming, and incest to take control of Wideacre from her brother. Beatrice's legacy haunts her daughter Julia, who tries to restore the estate but finds only death and tragedy. It is up to Julie's long-lost daughter Sarah to finally win the estate and find love, but only after many travails.

Genre: Family Saga; Historical Romance
Subjects: Houses; Mothers and daughters
Place/Time: England—18th century; England—19th century

630.
1. *Earthly Joys.* St. Martin's, 1998.
2. *Virgin Earth.* St. Martin's, 1999.

John Tradescant is the renowned gardener to Sir Robert Cecil who is the royal advisor to Queen Elizabeth I and then King James I. John is always searching for new plants and coming up with innovative designs for his courtly patrons. While working on his gardens, John is commissioned by Sir Robert to uncover information that can save the kingdom. He sees corruption at the court and dissatisfaction in the country when Charles I ascends the throne. As the country totters on the brink of civil war, John is torn between duty to his king and duty to his family.

Genre: Historical Fiction; Family Saga
Subjects: Family life; Gardens; Courts and courtiers; Kings and rulers
Place/Time: England—17th century; Virginia—17th century

Grenville, Kate

631.
1. *Lilian's Story.* Viking, 1986.
2. *Albion's Story.* Harcourt Brace, 1994.

The story of an obese, mentally disturbed young woman is told from her point of view and then from her abusive father's point of view. Lilian Singer is born into a genteel family in turn-of-the-century Australia. Her mother never recovers from her birth, and her father is a recluse who rapes his daughter and has a nervous breakdown. Lil grows up to be obese, but she goes to college and tries to make friends. Later she is thrown into a mental institution by her father. When she emerges, she becomes a bag lady and lives on the streets. Her father's autobiographical confessions show how he too was abused and how he became sexually warped. He uses Lilian to project his own self-loathing.

Subjects: Child abuse; Mental illness; Fathers and daughters
Place/Time: Australia—1900–1945

Griffin, P. M. *See Nolan, William F. (Witch World series—Storms of Victory and Flight of Vengeance) and Norton, Andre (Time Traders series—Firehand)*

Griffin, W. E. B. *Pseud. of* W. E. Butterworth

632.
1. *Honor Bound.* Putnam, 1994.
2. *Blood and Honor.* Putnam, 1996.
3. *Secret Honor.* Putnam, 1999.

In 1942, fighter pilot Cletus Howell Frade is suddenly recalled to Washington by the OSS. He has been picked to head a team of secret agents to Argentina to discover who is refueling German U-boats. Frade, whose father lives in Argentina and whose dead mother left him heir to a petroleum business, uses his fluency with Spanish and his wealthy connections to find a Nazi spy. When his father is assassinated, Frade uncovers a Nazi scheme to use money obtained from ransoming Jews out of concentration camps to set up a sanctuary in Argentina for Nazis. He also fights the Argentine military to uncover who killed his father. Later Cletus becomes involved with a Nazi pilot stationed with the German embassy in Argentina. The pilot feeds Cletus secrets that help the Americans scuttle the Germans' plan to free a Nazi ship from Argentina control. Cletus tries to protect his source while fighting German influence in his country.

Genre: War; Espionage
Subjects: Spies; Marine Corps, United States; International intrigue
Place/Time: Argentina 1900–1945

633. Badge of Honor
1. *Men in Blue.* Jove, 1988.
2. *Special Operations.* Jove, 1989.
3. *The Victim.* Jove, 1991.
4. *The Witness.* Jove, 1992.
5. *The Assassin.* Jove, 1993.
6. *The Murderers.* Putnam, 1994.
7. *The Investigators.* Putnam, 1997.

An old-fashioned look at the work of different departments of the Philadelphia police department is related without graphic sex or violence. Instead, Griffin fo-

cuses on how the police look for kidnappers, organized crime members, terrorists, and other criminals. As in his other series, he follows the actions of a small group of policemen as they go through the day-to-day detail it takes to solve cases.

Genre: Adventure
Subjects: Police—Philadelphia (Pa.); Crime and criminals; Adventure
Place/Time: Philadelphia (Pa.)—1980–; Pennsylvania—1980–

634. Brotherhood of War Series
1. *The Lieutenants.* Berkley, 1982.
2. *The Captains.* Berkley, 1983.
3. *The Majors.* Berkley, 1983.
4. *The Colonels.* Berkley, 1983.
5. *The Berets.* Berkley, 1985.
6. *The Generals.* Berkley, 1986.
7. *The New Breed.* Berkley, 1987.
8. *The Aviators.* Berkley, 1988.

Following a Green Beret from the end of World War II to the beginning of Vietnam, Griffin captures the authentic feel of army life. Lieutenant Robert Bellman is taken prisoner by the Germans at the end of World War II. He escapes with the evidence of Soviet culpability in the massacre of hundreds of Polish officers. Bellman's career spans the Cold War and numerous challenges as he rises in rank to General and develops the army's Air Assault Division for Vietnam. An ex-soldier, Griffin captures all the nuances of military thinking, feeling, and actions.

Genre: War
Subjects: Army, United States, Special Forces; World War II, 1939–1945; Soldiers; Vietnamese War, 1961–1975; Prisoners of war; Adventure; Cold war
Place/Time: Germany—1900–1945; Vietnam—1945–1980

635. The Corps
1. *Semper Fi.* Jove, 1986.
2. *Call to Arms.* Jove, 1987.
3. *Counterattack.* Putnam, 1990.
4. *Battleground.* Putnam, 1991.
5. *Line of Fire.* Putnam, 1992.
6. *Close Combat.* Putnam, 1993.
7. *Behind the Lines.* Putnam, 1995.
8. *In Danger's Path.* Putnam, 1998.

The United States Marine Corps in the Pacific from the days before Pearl Harbor through the end of 1942 is described in this series that focuses on how the marines operate rather than their battles. Each book covers a few months of the war and follows marines Fleming, Pickering, Homer Dillion, John Moore, and others as they crisscross the Pacific to report the action at the important battles. These books give a behind the scenes look at the inner workings of the marines at war.

Genre: Historical Fiction; War
Subjects: Marine Corps, United States; Soldiers; Adventure; Battles

Place/Time: Pacific Ocean—1900–1945

Grimm, Cherry Barbara. *See* Wilder, Cherry

Grimsley, Jim

636.
1. *Winter Birds.* Algonquin Books, 1994.
2. *Comfort & Joy.* Algonquin Books, 1999.

Danny Crell is caught in the fights of his parents. His father Bobjay lost his arm in a farm accident and has become an alcoholic. In his drunken fits, he attacks his wife and young children. His mother Ellen tries to protect her children but eventually she too becomes a stranger to her eight-year-old son. When Danny grows up, he leaves North Carolina. Danny takes up with a male lover who is his opposite. Ford comes from a family of privilege and is uncomfortable with their relationship. When Danny and Ford go to visit Danny's mother for Christmas, the two men finally find peace with their relationship.

Subjects: Family life; Homosexuality; Fathers and sons
Place/Time: North Carolina—1980–

Groom, Winston

637.
1. *Forrest Gump.* Doubleday, 1986.
2. *Gump & Co.* Pocket, 1995.

Forrest Gump has an I. Q. of 61, but even with this disability, he has one adventure after another. He plays football, fights in Vietnam, falls in love, joins a band, starts a shrimp business, and fathers a son. His adventures take him across the country and have him meet numerous famous people. After his love, Jenny, dies, Forrest looks for a job so he can support his son. This time he becomes involved with Iran-Contra, the Exxon Valdez oil spill, the fall of the Berlin Wall, and Desert Storm. He meets more famous people and ends up at the 1995 Academy Awards where he receives a special award.

Genre: Humor
Subjects: Picaresque novels; Mental handicaps
Place/Time: United States—1945–1980; United States—1980–

Gross, Joel

638.
1. *The Books of Rachel.* Seaview, 1979
2. *The Lives of Rachel.* New American Library, 1984.

From biblical times to the present, one family and one fabulous diamond tell the story of Jews in Europe. The first-born female in each generation is named Rachel and inherits the family diamond. Each Rachel must make sacrifices for her love and her faith.

Genre: Family Saga; Historical Romance
Subjects: Women; Diamonds
Place/Time: Europe—multicentury span

Guareschi, Giovanni

639.
1. *The Little World of Don Camillo.* Pellegrini & Cudahy, 1950.
2. *Don Camillo and His Flock.* Pellegrini & Cudahy, 1952.
3. *Don Camillo's Dilemma.* Farrar, Straus & Young, 1954.
4. *Don Camillo Takes the Devil by the Tail.* Farrar, Straus & Cudahy, 1957.
5. *Comrade Don Camillo.* Farrar, Straus & Cudahy, 1964.
6. *Don Camillo Meets the Flower Children.* Farrar, Straus & Giroux, 1969.

These warm, humorous stories pit Don Camillo, the parish priest of a small country village in the Po Valley of Italy, against his adversary Peppone, the Communist mayor. In postwar Italy, a pint-sized war rages between these two and among the village's inhabitants, which keeps Don Camillo busy getting the best of and for everyone. This is a very funny and human series that recognizes the foibles in all men.

Genre: Gentle Read; Humor
Subjects: Catholic priests; Small town life; Communism; Mayors
Place/Time: Italy—1945–1980

Guild, Nicholas

640.
1. *The Assyrian.* Atheneum, 1987.
2. *The Blood Star.* Atheneum, 1989.

In ancient Assyria, young Tiglath Ashur grows up in the royal court of his father, the king. From the age of five through adulthood, he fights his half-brother Esarhaddon for the throne and the love of his half-sister Esharhamat. Even though Tilgath becomes a great warrior and the peoples' choice for king, Esarhaddon takes the throne and drives Tiglath from the kingdom. Tilgath's adventures send him around the ancient world until he returns to confront his brother.

Genre: Historical Fiction
Subjects: Brothers; Courts and courtiers; Adventure
Place/Time: Assyria—to 70 A. D.

Gulbranssen, Trygve

641.
1. *Beyond Sing the Woods.* Putnam, 1936.
2. *The Wind from the Mountains.* Putnam, 1937.

In the late 18th century, Dag Bjorndal's family lives in the great woods in Norway. He marries a girl from the valley, and they work to build their farm. When Dag's son marries Adelaide Borre, she looks to old Dag for strength. When he dies, she becomes head of the family. The struggle between hardness and compassion shapes their lives.

Genre: Family Saga; Historical Fiction
Subjects: Farm life; Family life; Peasants
Place/Time: Norway—18th century

Gulick, Bill

642. Saga of Tall Bird and John Crane
1. *Distant Trails 1805–1836.* Doubleday, 1988.
2. *Gathering Storm 1837–1868.* Doubleday, 1988.
3. *Lost Wallowa 1869–1879.* Doubleday, 1988.

Two half-brothers, one half Indian and one white, are involved in the growth of the West. Their father, Matt Crane, was part of the Lewis and Clark expedition when he met Moon Bird, a Nez Perce. Their son Tall Bird and Matt's white son, John, work with fur traders and missionaries. Later they fight the western migrations of people seeking land and gold while pushing the Indians off their lands. Carefully researched, these books show the appalling treatment of the Indians by white Americans.

Genre: Historical Fiction; Western
Subjects: Brothers; Frontier and pioneer life; Native Americans

Gulland, Sandra

643.
1. *The Many Lives and Secret Sorrows of Josephine B.* Simon & Schuster, 1999.
2. *Tales of Passion, Tales of Woe.* Scribners, 1999.

In the late 18th century, Marie-Josephe-Rose Tascher grows up in Martinique on a sugar plantation. Her father squanders the profits from the plantation on gambling and alcohol. Rose escapes the island through an arranged marriage that takes her to France. When the French Revolution starts in 1779, her husband is executed, and the beautiful widow meets and marries Napoleon Bonaparte. Now known as Josephine Bonaparte, she must cultivate powerful people to help her husband succeed. While Napoleon's family tries to destroy her, Josephine uses shrewdness, charm, and Napoleon's love to stay by his side.

Genre: Historical Fiction
Subjects: Napoleon I, Emperor of the French, 1769–1821; Josephine, Empress, Consort of Napoleon I, Emperor of the French, 1763–1814
Place/Time: Martinique—18th century; France—18th century

Gunn, Neil

644.
1. *Young Art and Old Hector.* Walker, 1991.
2. *The Green Isle of the Great Deep.* Walker, 1995.

In turn-of-the-century Scotland, eight-year-old Art becomes good friends with Old Hector, the 80-year-old sage of the village. Art, the youngest of six children, has to deal with the birth of a baby brother and the departure of Art's beloved older brother. Art helps his sister with her romance with shepherd Tom. Meanwhile Art listens to Old Hector tell fairy stories. When the two fall into a pool, they find they are transported to the Green Isle of the Great Deep where they fight for the innocence of childhood.

Genre: Coming of Age
Subjects: Boys; Old Age; Country life; Family life; Friendship; Imaginary kingdoms
Place/Time: Scotland—1900–1945

Gunnarsson, Gunnar

645. The Church on the Hill
1. *Ships in the Sky.* Bobbs-Merrill, 1938.
2. *The Night and the Dream.* Bobbs-Merrill, 1938.

Uggi Greipsson relives his childhood on an Icelandic farm in the 1880s. As a boy, he daydreams about his life, his parents, and their farm. He recalls the pain of his mother's death and his gradual realization that he is destined to be a writer. The joy, comedy, and drama of growing up are vividly retold.

Genre: Coming of Age
Subjects: Boys; Bereavement; Family life; Farm life
Place/Time: Iceland—19th century

Guthrie, A. B. (Alfred Bertram)

646.
1. *The Big Sky.* Sloane, 1947.
2. *The Way West.* Sloane, 1949.
3. *Fair Land, Fair Land.* Houghton Mifflin, 1982.
4. *These Thousand Hills.* Houghton Mifflin, 1958.
5. *Arfive.* Houghton Mifflin, 1971.
6. *The Last Valley.* Houghton Mifflin, 1975.

From the 1830s to the 1940s, strong men and women move west to tame the land. The trek west from St. Louis, the mountain men of Wyoming, and the cattle drives in Montana are all vividly described. The settling of small towns and the businesses that grow up in the western countryside all come alive in these loosely connected short stories.

Genre: Historical Fiction; Western
Subjects: Frontier and pioneer life; Wagon trains; Mountain life; Explorers; Cattle drives

Place/Time: Western states—19th century; Western states—1900–1945

Habe, Hans

647.
1. *Aftermath.* Viking, 1947.
2. *Walk in Darkness.* Putnam, 1948.

American military men stationed in Germany following World War II face personal and social conflicts. First a German who fled the country to America must deal with seeing his former countrymen as conquered people. In the second work, a black American asks to be stationed in Europe only to encounter the prejudice he was trying to escape.

Genre: Historical Fiction
Subjects: Soldiers; World War II, 1939–1945; African Americans; Prejudices
Place/Time: Germany—1945–1980

Haber, Karen

648.
1. *The Mutant Season.* Doubleday, 1989.
2. *The Mutant Prime.* Doubleday, 1990.
3. *The Mutant Star.* Bantam, 1992.
4. *The Mutant Legacy.* Bantam, 1992.

In the 21st century, a subculture of aliens fight for equality with their human neighbors. These mutants have kept their psychic ability hidden from humans, but a powerful mutant's coming threatens to polarize the world. The story follows mutant Melanie Ryton, her husband Yosh Akimura, and their sons Rick and Julian as they struggle with their powers and with hostile humans. Julian eventually becomes the leader of a group who tries to bridge the gap between humans and the ever-increasing number of mutants.

Genre: Science Fiction
Subjects: Discrimination; Mutation (biology); Extraterrestrial beings; Extrasensory perception

Hagan, Patricia

649. Coltrane Saga
1. *Love and War.* Avon, 1978.
2. *Raging Hearts.* Avon, 1979.
3. *Love and Glory.* Avon, 1982.
4. *Love and Fury.* Avon, 1986.
5. *Love and Splendor.* Avon, 1987.
6. *Love and Dreams.* Avon, 1988.
7. *Love and Honor.* Avon, 1989.
8. *Love and Triumph.* Avon, 1990.

Three generations of feisty heroines and their lusty, sexy lovers battle to find true love despite the obstacles thrown up in their paths. This sweet savage romance begins during the Civil War when Kitty Wright is kidnapped by Union officer Travis Coltrane and falls in love with him. She forsakes him in order to keep her ancestral home, but eventually the two are united. Their daughter Danielle, son Colt, and granddaughter Kit fight storms, deception, theft, and blackmail before they can live happily ever after.

Genre: Historical Romance
Subjects: United States—Civil War, 1861–1865; Family life
Place/Time: Southern states—19th century

Hagberg, David

650.
1. *Without Honor.* Tor, 1989.
2. *Countdown.* St. Martin's, 1990.

Ex-CIA agent Kirk McGarvey is called back into service to investigate a U.S. senator who may be a Russian mole. As the case becomes more complex, he battles not only KGB agent Baranov, but also the CIA. Later Baranov as head of the KGB tries to destroy U.S.-Russian relations by annihilating Israel, but McGarvey again foils Baranov as he finally identifies the Russian mole in the CIA.

Genre: Adventure; Espionage
Subjects: United States Central Intelligence Agency; Secret service; International intrigue; Adventure
Place/Time: United States—1945–1980

Haggard, H. Rider

651.
1. *She.* Harper, 1886.
2. *Ayesha: The Return of She.* Doubleday, 1905.
3. *She and Allan.* Longmans, 1921.
4. *Wisdom's Daughter: The Life and Love of She-Who-Must-Be-Obeyed.* Doubleday, 1923.

The exotic and immortal She searches for her lost love Kallikrates. She finds him in Leo Vinay, who is descended from Kallikrates. Even though She seems to die, she is reincarnated and has affairs with Allan Quatermain and an Arab chief.

Genre: Adventure; Fantasy
Subjects: Reincarnation; Love; Immortality; Adventure
Place/Time: Africa—19th century

652.
1. *King Solomon's Mines.* Cassell, 1885.
2. *Allan Quatermain.* Harper, 1887.
3. *Maiwa's Revenge.* Harper, 1888.
4. *Allan's Wife and Other Stories.* Harper, 1889.
5. *The Holy Flower.* Ward & Lock, 1915.
6. *The Ivory Child.* Longmans, 1916.
7. *The Ancient Allan.* Longmans, 1920.
8. *Heu-Heu.* Doubleday, 1924.
9. *The Treasure of the Lake.* Doubleday, 1926.
10. *Allan and the Ice-Gods.* Doubleday, 1927.

Big game hunter Allan Quatermain begins his adventures when he takes Sir Henry Curtis and Captain Good on a search for Curtis's younger brother. Their search leads them to the fabled King Solomon's Mines in Zulu country. Allan then searches darkest Africa where he finds a hidden city, a mysterious orchid, an African princess, and a white goddess. Allan is always the dashing, brave, and handsome hero who has rousing adventures and numerous love affairs in these books that set the standard for adventure.

Genre: Adventure
Subjects: Hunters; Explorers; Love affairs; Heroes; Adventure
Place/Time: Africa—19th century

Hahn, Harriet

653.
1. *James, the Connoisseur Cat.* St. Martin's, 1991.
2. *James, the Fabulous Feline: Further Adventures of a Connoisseur Cat.* St. Martin's, 1993.

James is a remarkable silver-gray cat who loves single malt whiskey and crab salad from Fortnum and Mason, but can ferret out forged art, direct a musical, coach a croquet team, star in a TV show about Puss-in-Boots, and generally help his hapless master, who narrates James's fabulous adventures.

Genre: Animal Story
Subjects: Cats; Animals
Place/Time: London (England)—1980–; England—1980–

Haislip, Harvey

654.
1. *Sailor Named Jones.* Doubleday, 1957.
2. *The Prize Master.* Doubleday, 1959.
3. *Sea Road to Yorktown.* Doubleday, 1960.

Midshipman Tommy Potter joins John Paul Jones in 1777 and helps him fight the British during the American Revolution. Later the 14-year old joins privateers and helps them take cargo and supplies to the colonies. He also fights English frigates as he sails to Martinique, the Spanish Main, and France. He finally joins French Admiral Comte de Grasse to defeat Cornwallis at Yorktown.

Genre: Historical Fiction; Naval Adventure; War
Subjects: United States—revolution, 1775–1783; Seamen; Jones, John Paul, 1747–1792; War
Place/Time: Atlantic Ocean—18th century; Caribbean region—18th century

Haldeman, Joe

655. Worlds Trilogy
1. *Worlds.* Viking, 1981.

2. *Worlds Apart.* Viking, 1983.
3. *Worlds Enough and Time.* Morrow, 1992.

Marianne O'Hara, a young woman of the late 21st century, travels back and forth between an Earth ravaged by overpopulation, pollution, and ultimately, war and her home on the asteroid New New York. First as a student, then as a scientist, she assists with a plague that is a by-product of biological warfare. Finally she sets off on a city-sized spaceship called *Newhome* with colonists searching for a new world.

Genre: Science Fiction
Subjects: Space colonies; Scientists; Degeneration; Biological warfare

Haldeman, Joe W.

656.
1. *The Forever War.* St. Martin's, 1975.
2. *The Forever Peace.* Ace, 1997.
3. *Forever Free.* Ace, 1999.

These novels present two speculative approaches to the possibility of high-technology 21st-century war. A near-future war lasting over a thousand years between enemies who are equally advanced in technology is seen through the eyes of a single soldier who is able to observe the conflict because of the time dilation effect of faster-than-light space travel. In the second work, brain linkage to war machines becomes a tool to stop assassins bent on creating the ultimate solar system big bang. The third story takes place in a post-war universe where humans have been left isolated on a half-frozen planet by Man, a superior race produced by cloning and genetic experimentation.

Genre: Science Fiction
Subjects: War; Technology and civilization; Genetics

Hall, James Norman. *See* Nordhoff, Charles

Hall, Rodney

657.
1. *The Second Bridegroom.* Farrar, Straus & Giroux, 1991.
2. *The Grisly Wife.* Farrar, Straus & Giroux, 1993.
3. *Captivity Captive.* Farrar, Straus & Giroux, 1988.

The history of 19th-century Australia is told through three different people who each live through murder. FJ, an English printer, is sent to Australia for forgery in the early 1800s. He kills the abusive prisoner he is chained to and escapes into the jungle. In the 1830s, missionaries go to the outback and there Catherine Byrne relates the strange events, including murder, that occur. Finally in 1956, Barney Barnett confesses to the murder of three children in 1898, but the police question his story. A different side of Australia is seen through these novels.

Genre: Historical Fiction
Subjects: Frontier and pioneer life; Murder and murderers; Prisoners and prisons; Escapes
Place/Time: Australia—19th century; Australia—1945–1980

Halter, Marek

658.
1. *The Book of Abraham.* Henry Holt, 1986.
2. *The Children of Abraham.* Little, Brown, 1990.

In 70 A. D., when the Romans sack Jerusalem, scribe Abraham flees the city with a scroll that documents the family history. The scroll is passed down for 19 centuries from one ancestor to another, who document the family history. From Alexandria to Toledo, to Strasbourg, to the Warsaw Ghetto, and finally back to Israel, the various family members tell their stories of Jews in exile fighting prejudice and terror to survive.

Genre: Family Saga; Historical Fiction
Subjects: Jews; Israel; Jews, persecution of
Place/Time: Israel—multicentury span

Hambly, Barbara

659.
1. *Those Who Hunt the Night.* Ballantine, 1990.
2. *Traveling with the Dead.* Ballantine, 1995.

Why would James Asher, a professor in turn-of-the-century London, hunt down a mysterious killer of vampires? The fact that powerful vampire Simon Ysidro is threatening to kill Asher's young wife is reason enough for the Oxford don and former espionage agent to pursue the being who is ripping open the coffins of vampires, exposing them to sunlight and the true death. Asher's involvement with the undead continues as he journeys across Europe to prevent an unholy alliance between high ranking government officials and equally formidable vampires.

Genre: Horror
Subjects: Vampires; Death; Husbands and wives; International intrigue
Place/Time: London (England)—1900–1945; Europe—1900–1945

660.
1. *Dragonsbane.* Ballantine, 1985.
2. *Dragonshadow.* Ballantine, 1999.
3. *Knight of the Demon Queen.* Ballantine, 2000.

Lord John Alversin fights and kills dragons, thereby earning the title of Dragonsbane. His wife, Jenny, a descendant of a dynasty of mages, is transformed into a dragon by Morkeleb the Black, the strongest dragon of all, who then relents and restores her to her husband in human form. Later, however, John must form an alliance with the dragons to defend his realm against the soul-stealing demonspawn and to rescue his son Ian, whom the evil creatures have captured. Ian is saved, but haunted by the experience, and John is indebted to the demon Queen Aohila for her assistance in containing the demons.

Genre: Fantasy
Subjects: Dragons; Demonology; Good and evil; Magic; Husbands and wives; Rescues

661. Darwath
1. *The Time of the Dark.* Del Rey, 1982.
2. *The Walls of Air.* Del Rey, 1983.
3. *The Armies of Daylight.* Del Rey, 1983.
4. *Mother of Winter.* Ballantine, 1996.
5. *Icefalcon's Quest.* Ballantine, 1998.

Graduate student Gil Paterson and car mechanic Rudy Solis are magically transported from their ordinary lives in Los Angeles to a universe inhabited by the Dark Ones, eyeless flying creatures who feed on human flesh. In this alternate reality Rudy becomes a wizard and Gil an elite guard to battle these evil forces, who are attacking a parallel Earth. Their adventures continue as an Ice Age and an aggressive fungus threaten their world.

Genre: Fantasy
Subjects: Imaginary wars and battles; Good and evil; Magic

662. Sun-Cross
1. *The Rainbow Abyss.* Del Rey, 1991.
2. *Magicians of the Night.* Del Rey, 1992. The preceding titles are collected in *Sun-Cross.* Guild America, 1992.

Two wizards, Rhion and Jaldis, hear the call of a world that has no magic. Feeling that they have nothing to lose, since they are discriminated against in their own realm, they brave the terrors of the Abyss, a kind of magic void that allows passage between worlds. Jaldis perishes in the Abyss, and Rhion finds himself in Nazi Germany face to face with resistance leaders who wish to use black magic to undermine Hitler's power.

Genre: Fantasy
Subjects: Magic; Discrimination; National Socialism; Government, resistance to
Place/Time: Germany—1900–1945

663. Sun Wolf
1. *The Ladies of Mandrigyn.* Del Rey, 1984.
2. *The Witches of Wenshar.* Del Rey, 1987. The preceding titles are collected in *The Unschooled Wizard.* Doubleday, 1987.
3. *The Dark Hand of Magic.* Del Rey, 1990.

Mercenary Sun Wolf and his tough-girl second-in-command Starhawk battle with the sinister wizard Altiokis and, without realizing it, fall in love. Sun Wolf discovers his own raw talent as a wizard, leaves his dangerous profession for a time, and shares his life with Starhawk, but is drawn back into his old ways when his former colleagues rescue him from a potentially deadly situation.

Genre: Fantasy
Subjects: Mercenary soldiers; Magic; Love

664. The Windrose Chronicles
1. *The Silent Tower.* Del Rey, 1986.
2. *The Silicon Mage.* Del Rey, 1988. The preceding titles are collected in *Darkmage.* Doubleday, 1988.
3. *Dog Wizard.* Doubleday, 1988.

Joanna unwittingly betrays her lover Antryg who flees to Earth through the mysterious Void between worlds. She vows to save him, but her efforts are opposed by the evil wizard Suraklin, who has placed his brain in a powerful computer capable of destroying both Joanna's magical realm and Antryg's Earth. As a ploy to lure Antryg back through the Void, a group of sorcerers abduct Joanna in the hope that her lover will attempt a rescue.

Genre: Fantasy
Subjects: Lovers; Magic; Rescues; Good and evil

Hamilton, Laurell K.

665.
1. *Guilty Pleasures.* Ace, 1993.
2. *The Laughing Corpse.* Ace, 1994.
3. *Circus of the Damned.* Ace, 1995.
4. *The Lunatic Cafe.* Ace, 1996.
5. *Bloody Bones.* Ace, 1996.
6. *The Killing Dance.* Ace, 1997.
7. *Burnt Offerings.* Ace, 1998.
8. *Blue Moon.* Ace, 1998.
9. *Obsidian Butterfly.* Ace, 2000.

"I don't date vampires. I kill them." claims police detective and necromancer Anita Blake, but she is attracted to vampire-strip-club owner Jean-Claude who looks great after 250 years of living in a reality in which vampires and werewolves are facts of life—and death—and even have civil rights. Anita's ability to communicate with the dead comes in handy in investigating murders and protecting the citizens of this alternate St. Louis, Missouri, from crime.

Genre: Fantasy; Horror; Crime Novel
Subjects: Detectives; Death; Vampires; Werewolves; Crime and criminals
Place/Time: St. Louis (Mo.)—1980–

Hamilton, Patrick

666. 20,000 Streets under the Sky
1. *The Midnight Bell.* Little, 1929.
2. *The Siege of Pleasure.* Little, 1932.
3. *Plains of Cement.* Little, 1935.

The Midnight Bell, a London pub of the early 1900s, brings together men and women who tend to suffer the pangs of unrequited love. The elderly Mr. Eccles yearns for Ella, a waitress, who loves handsome waiter Bob, who is infatuated with Jenny, a prostitute and accomplished gold digger.

Genre: Romance
Subjects: Hotels, taverns, etc.
Place/Time: London (England)—1900–1945; England—1900–1945

Hamilton, Peter F.

667. Greg Mandrel Trilogy
1. *Mindstar Rising.* Tor, 1996.
2. *A Quantum Murder.* Tor, 1997.
3. *The Nano Flower.* Tor, 1997.

Elements of science fiction and detective thriller combine in these novels set in 21st-century Britain where global warming now promotes orange groves. With his telepathic powers enhanced by implanted glands, detective Greg Mandel helps a teenage heiress battle a ruthless corporate takeover scheme. Mandel then turns his attention to the murder of a Nobel laureate who had been investigating scientific uses for wormholes, then to the disappearance of his former boss's husband and the mysterious appearance of a flower that contains alien DNA.

Genre: Science Fiction; Crime Novel
Subjects: Detectives; Telepathy; Bionics; Crime and criminals
Place/Time: England—1980–

668. The Reality Dysfunction
1. *The Reality Dysfunction. Part 1: Emergence.* Warner, 1996.
2. *The Reality Dysfunction. Part 2: Expansion.* Warner, 1996.

In this universe, two groups are at odds: the Edenists, genetically altered humans who have sentient spaceships, and the Adamists, who depend on technology. A new danger erupts in the midst of this conflict. The Reality Dysfunction, a product of an ancient alien civilization, unleashes a destructive army of the undead across the galaxy. This saga continues in The Neutronium Alchemist stories.

Genre: Science Fiction
Subjects: Interplanetary wars; Genetics; Technology and civilization; Immortality

669. The Neutronium Alchemist
1. *The Neutronium Alchemist. Part 1: Consolidation.* Warner, 1998.
2. *The Neutronium Alchemist. Part 2: Conflict.* Warner, 1998.

Continuing the narrative started in The Reality Dysfunction, these stories tell of the invasion of the galaxy by vicious undead, such as Al Capone, who are capable of removing planets from the universe. Dr. Alkad Mzu has invented a weapon called the Alchemist to fight these immortals, but the question arises: if true death is impossible, is this weapon really a solution?

Genre: Science Fiction
Subjects: Interplanetary wars; Good and evil; Immortality

Hamner, Earl

670.
1. *Spencer's Mountain.* Dial Press, 1961.
2. *The Homecoming.* Random House, 1970.

The popular television series *The Waltons* was based on these warm novels, which depict a large close-knit family in the Blue Ridge Mountains of Virginia during the Depression. Clay-Boy must convince his father that he should go to college. When his father is lost in a snowstorm on Christmas Eve, Clay-Boy searches for him and encounters the fabled albino deer.

Genre: Coming of Age; Gentle Read; Historical Fiction
Subjects: Family life; Mountain life; Business depression, 1929; Fathers and sons
Place/Time: Virginia—1900–1945

Hamsun, Knut. *Pseud. of* Knut Pedersen

671. Segelfoss Estate
1. *Children of the Age.* Knopf, 1924.
2. *Segelfoss-Town.* Knopf, 1925.
3. *Vagabonds.* Coward McCann, 1930.
4. *August.* Coward McCann, 1931.
5. *The Road Leads On.* Coward McCann, 1934.
6. *Benoni.* Knopf, 1925.
7. *Rosa.* Knopf, 1926.

A Norwegian fishing village grows around the estate of the debt-ridden Willatz Holmsen, who just before his death discovers a chest of gold that becomes his son's inheritance. The adventuresome August, who tries to bring 20th-century life to Segelfoss, and the fisherman Benoni, who becomes a pillar of the community almost by accident, also figure in the development of the town.

Subjects: Small town life; Inheritance and succession; Progress
Place/Time: Norway—1900–1945

Hancock, Niel

672. Atlanton Earth
1. *Greyfax Grimwald.* Popular Library, 1977.
2. *Faragon Fairingay.* Popular Library, 1977.
3. *Calix Stay.* Popular Library, 1977.
4. *Squaring the Circle.* Popular Library, 1977.

Bear, Otter, and the dwarf Broco are called to the realm of Atlanton to assist the Lady of Light Lorini and the wizards Faragon Fairingay and Greyfax Grimwald in a battle between the forces of good and evil. At issue is possession of the Arkenchest, which holds the Five Secrets that could give the cruel Dorini control of Atlanton.

Genre: Fantasy
Subjects: Animals; Imaginary kingdoms; Imaginary wars and battles; Good and evil

Handl, Irene

673.
1. *The Sioux.* New American Library, 1965.
2. *The Gold Tipped Pfitzer.* Knopf, 1986.

The center of attention of the wealthy, aristocratic Benoir family is a frail, precocious nine-year-old boy who is dying of leukemia. His mother Mim divides her time between Paris and New Orleans, continually shocking her third husband Castleton with her intense, sometimes cruel, treatment of her son.

Subjects: Invalids; Leukemia; Mothers and sons; Wealth
Place/Time: New Orleans (La.)—1945–1980; Paris (France)—1945–1980; Louisiana—1945–1980; France—1945–1980

Handler, David

674.
1. *Kiddo.* Ballantine, 1986.
2. *Boss.* Available Press, 1988.

Danny Levine, Mousey Stern, and Newt Biddle are 13-year-old friends in Los Angeles in 1962. They hang around, think about girls, and generally have the typical problems of adolescents who are trying to make sense of growing up. Ten years later, Danny is still not any wiser or thinner, but he has to come back to L.A. to help his family run the business. Mouse is getting married and Newt is on drugs. Danny finally learns how to be the boss of his own life through his funny, but tender encounters.

Genre: Coming of Age; Humor
Subjects: Teenagers; Friendship
Place/Time: Los Angeles (Calif.)—1945–1980; California—1945–1980

Hansen, Joseph

675.
1. *Jack of Hearts.* Dutton, 1994.
2. *Living Upstairs.* Dutton, 1993.

In 1941, 17-year-old Nathan Reed is in college and wants to be a writer. He joins the local college newspaper and then the theater group. As he realizes he is gay, he travels amidst the Los Angeles gay community and hears about police scandals, an attempted murder, and rumors of Nazism. When he is 20, Nathan lives with an old painter, Hoyt Stubblefield. When Hoyt disappears periodically, Nathan becomes suspicious and looks into what Hoyt is doing. Then an FBI agent hints to Nathan that Hoyt is tied to the Communist Party and to the murder of fellow radical Eva Schaffer. Eva's son asks Nathan to look into his mother's death as the two men become attracted to each other.

Subjects: Homosexuality; Men; Authors; Teenagers
Place/Time: Los Angeles (Calif.)—1900–1945

Hardy, Robin

676.
1. *Streiker's Bride.* Nav Press, 1993.
2. *Streiker Killdeer.* Nav Press, 1993.
3. *Streiker's Morning Sun.* Nav Press, 1995.

Fletcher Streiker is a reclusive billionaire and bank owner. He mysteriously woos Adair Weiss who eventually marries him, but Streiker stays only for one night. When he leaves, Adair finds herself locked out of the house, attacked by a former employee, and helped by her maid. All of the trials have been a test of Adair set up by Streiker. Later Adair uses his money to do good deeds and help a small town besieged by an evil company. These allegorical novels tell the story of Christ, his church, and his believers.

Genre: Christian Fiction
Subjects: Faith; Allegories; Christianity
Place/Time: United States—1980–

Harris, Deborah Turner. *See also* Kurtz, Katherine

677. Mages of Garrillon Trilogy
1. *The Burning Stone.* Tor, 1987.
2. *The Gauntlet of Malice.* Tor, 1988.
3. *Spiral of Fire.* Tor, 1989.

Young mage Caradoc Penlluathe is expelled from his order and exiled. Falsely accused of murder, Caradoc must clear his name and seek vengeance against the evil Borthen Berigeld, the matter destroyer. Caradoc and his friends have numerous adventures as they battle to save their world.

Genre: Fantasy
Subjects: Imaginary kingdoms; Revenge; Magicians

Harris, E. Lynn

678.
1. *Invisible Life.* Consortium Press, 1991.
2. *Just as I Am.* Doubleday, 1994.

The lives, loves, and deaths of middle-class blacks in Atlanta and New York are shown through the straight, gay, and bisexual couples who try to find happiness. Ray is bisexual and tries to deal with his nature, but falls in love with Nicole, an actress, and then Jared. Nicole goes to New York where she becomes engaged to a white investor even though she loves Jared. Ray also goes to New York but to help a friend dying of AIDS. Both Ray and Nicole go through several different partners until they finally find love.

Subjects: African Americans; Middle classes; Homosexuality; Bisexuality
Place/Time: Atlanta (Ga.)—1980–; New York (N. Y.)—1980–; Georgia—1980–

Harris, John. *See Hennessy, Max*

Harris, Marilyn

679. Eden Series
1. *The Other Eden.* Putnam, 1977.
2. *The Prince of Eden.* Putnam, 1978.
3. *The Eden Passion.* Putnam, 1979.
4. *The Women of Eden.* Putnam, 1980.
5. *Eden Rising.* Putnam, 1982.
6. *American Eden.* Doubleday, 1987.
7. *Eden and Honor.* Doubleday, 1989.

From 1800 to 1900, the troubled men of Eden Rising, an estate on the North Devon coast of England, search for love but find only feuding and alienation. Lord Thomas Eden sets the tone for the family when he pursues virtuous servant girl Marianne. His descendants also find that love is elusive and tragedy is tearing apart the family as they fight social injustice, the Crimean War, Reconstruction of the South, and each other.

Genre: Family Saga; Historical Romance
Subjects: Family life; Social classes
Place/Time: England—19th century

Harris, Mark

680.
1. *The Southpaw.* Bobbs, 1953.
2. *Bang the Drum Slowly.* Knopf, 1956.
3. *Ticket for a Seamstitch.* Knopf, 1957.
4. *It Looked Like Forever.* McGraw, 1979.

This story follows young baseball player Henry Wiggen from his first days as a major league pitcher with the New York Mammoths to his final days before he is released at age 40. Through Wiggens, Harris takes a hard look at America's favorite sport and the boys of summer. Wiggens works his way up from the minors. He stands by a teammate as he slowly dies of Hodgkins disease and fights to stay on the team so that his youngest daughter can see him play ball.

Genre: Sports
Subjects: Baseball; Sports
Place/Time: New York (N. Y.)—1945–1980

681.
1. *Wake Up, Stupid.* Knopf, 1959.
2. *Lying in Bed.* McGraw, 1984.

Through correspondence, Professor Lee Youngdahl ponders his life. He has seven children, teaches English, and writes plays. He gets involved with a Broadway actress, then with a prize fighter, and finally with a stolen car before he realizes he should do what he knows he can. Once back at college in San Francisco, he gets involved with a young student who is writing a novel. He finds that he has writer's block and can't finish his own novel. His letters reveal his doubts, fears, and humor.

Genre: Humor

Subjects: Letters (stories in letter form); Teachers; College life
Place/Time: San Francisco (Calif.); California

Harris, Thomas

682.

1. *Red Dragon.* Putnam, 1981.
2. *The Silence of the Lambs.* St. Martin's, 1988.
3. *Hannibal.* Delacorte Press, 1999.

In these riveting psychological thrillers, the FBI must try to stop two mass murderers. To gain insight into the criminal mind, they bring into service a psychologist and captured serial killer, Dr. Hannibal Lecter. Lecter is both fascinating and frightening to agents Will Graham and Clarice Starling, who must work with him. Lector escapes, and Starling and the FBI must try to recapture him, but they find they are not the only ones out to find the savage doctor. Tension builds as the agents race to stop the madmen from killing again. Lecter plays a small, but pivotal role in *Red Dragon* but is the dominant force in *The Silence of the Lambs* and in *Hannibal.*

Genre: Crime Novel
Subjects: Serial murders; United States Federal Bureau of Investigation
Place/Time: Washington (D. C.)—1980–

Harris, Wilson

683. The Guiana Quartet

1. *The Palace of the Peacock.* Faber & Faber, 1960.
2. *The Far Journey of Oudin.* Faber & Faber, 1961.
3. *The Whole Armour.* Faber & Faber, 1962.
4. *The Secret Ladder.* Faber & Faber, 1963.

The above titles have also been published in the following collection: *The Guyana Quartet.* Faber & Faber, 1985.

Dreamlike, symbolic novels covering the range of ethnic groups and classes of 20th-century Guyana are connected by their themes of quest, transcendence, and rebirth rather than by characters or plot.

Subjects: Social classes; Symbolism; Africa—native peoples
Place/Time: Guyana—1900–1945; Guyana—1945–1980

Harrison, Harry

684. Deathworld

1. *Deathworld.* Bantam, 1960.
2. *Deathworld 2.* Bantam, 1964.
3. *Deathworld 3.* Dell, 1968.

Adventurer Jason dinAlt is faced with the task of conquering a planet whose life forms are capable of mutating in ways that prevent human colonization. In response, the colonists accompanying Jason develop the capacity to adapt to this hostile environment with their own mutations.

Genre: Science Fiction
Subjects: Mutation (biology); Space colonies; Life on other planets

685. The Stainless Steel Rat

1. *The Stainless Steel Rat.* Pyramid, 1961.
2. *The Stainless Steel Rat's Revenge.* Walker, 1970.
3. *The Stainless Steel Rat Saves the World.* Putnam, 1972.

The above titles have also been published in the following collection: *The Adventures of the Stainless Steel Rat.* Berkley, 1978.

4. *The Stainless Steel Rat Wants You!* Joseph, 1978.
5. *The Stainless Steel Rat for President.* Bantam, 1982.
6. *A Stainless Steel Rat Is Born.* Bantam, 1985.
7. *The Stainless Steel Rat Gets Drafted.* Bantam, 1987.
8. *The Stainless Steel Rat Sings the Blues.* Bantam, 1994.
9. *The Stainless Steel Rat Goes to Hell.* Tor, 1996.
10. *The Stainless Steel Rat Joins the Circus.* Tor, 1999.

In a high-tech intergalactic society of the future, bureaucracy has certainly not decreased. Its arch foe is outlaw Jim DiGriz, whose battles with the power structure, always engaged in for morally defensible reasons, sometimes put him on the side of the "good guys." Fast-paced plots thrust antihero Jim into such strange endeavors as organizing a rock band to get himself into prison.

Genre: Science Fiction
Subjects: Crime and criminals; Bureaucracy

686. West of Eden Trilogy

1. *West of Eden.* Bantam, 1984.
2. *Winter in Eden.* Bantam, 1986.
3. *Return to Eden.* Bantam, 1988.

What if dinosaurs had evolved into the dangerous Yilane, thinking reptiles at odds with man? Through the life of Kerrick, a young man who was raised by the Yilane but escapes to lead his own kind against them, this alternate version of evolution is played out.

Genre: Science Fiction
Subjects: Dinosaurs; Evolution

Harrison, Harry *and* Holm, John

687. The Hammer and the Cross

1. *The Hammer and the Cross.* T. Doherty Assoc., 1993.
2. *One King's Way.* Tor, 1995.
3. *King and Emperor.* Tor, 1996.

In this version of 9th-century alternate history, Shef Sigvarthsson, the bastard son of a Viking, rises to a position of power. Despised by the English, Shef lends his inventive genius to the Viking invaders and ultimately becomes ruler of an empire consisting of England, Denmark, Sweden, and Norway. Along the way, Shef must deal with the opposition of the Christian Church and his own attraction to his foster sister.

Genre: Historical Fiction
Subjects: Inventors; Kings and rulers; Technology and civilization; Vikings; History
Place/Time: Europe—9th century

Harrison, M. John

688. Viriconium
1. *The Pastel City.* Doubleday, 1972.
2. *A Storm of Wings.* Doubleday, 1980.
3. *The Floating Gods.* Pocket Books, 1983.
4. *Viriconium Nights.* Ace, 1984.

Viriconium is the center of a future civilization on the verge of collapse in part because man has lost his understanding of the underlying principles of advanced technology. Golems that ravage the human mind, hostile sentient insects, and a mysterious plague attack a deteriorating culture that has produced only a few individuals capable of defending it.

Genre: Science Fiction
Subjects: Degeneration; Technology and civilization

Harrison, Sarah

689.
1. *The Flowers of the Field.* Coward, McCann & Geoghegan, 1980.
2. *A Flower That's Free.* Simon & Schuster, 1984.

From 1890 to 1940, Thea and Dulcie Tennant compete for men and adventure. As a young girl, Thea falls in love with Jack Kingsley, but he is stolen away by her sister Dulcie. When the sisters travel to Vienna, Thea meets a new love Josef von Crieff, but this romance is interrupted by World War I. After the war, Thea and Jack are finally united and move to Kenya where they adopt Dulcie's daughter Kate. As Kate grows up, she searches for her mother and has to chose between two men who love her.

Genre: Historical Romance
Subjects: Sisters; Mothers and daughters
Place/Time: England—19th century; England—1900–1945; Austria—19th century; Austria—1900–1945; Kenya—19th century; Kenya—1900–1945

Harrison, Sue

690.
1. *Mother Earth, Father Sky.* Doubleday, 1990.

2. *My Sister the Moon.* Doubleday, 1992.
3. *Brother Wind.* Morrow, 1994.

In the prehistoric Aleutian Islands of 7000 B.C., Chagak survives the massacre of her tribe and marries Kayugh, a chieftain. Her twin sons grow up and fall in love with the same woman, Kiin. Before Kiin can marry Amigh, she is kidnapped by her brother and sold to Raven, a shaman of the Walrus people. Kiin endures many hardships before she returns to her people.

Genre: Historical Fiction
Subjects: Native Americans; Man, prehistoric; Stone Age; Tribes
Place/Time: Aleutian Islands—7000 B. C.

691. Storyteller Trilogy
1. *Song of the River.* Avon, 1997.
2. *Cry of the Wind.* Avon, 1998.

In the prehistoric Aleutian Islands, Chakliux, a baby with a clubfoot, is left out to die, but is saved by K'os. K'os had been brutally raped by three men from another tribe and only wants revenge. She sees Chakliux as a good omen to help her. Chakliux grows up to be a storyteller and is sent back to his birth tribe to negotiate a peace treaty, but K'os tries to undermine his work. When he is accused of murder, Chakliux must travel through many villages to find the truth. Later Chakliux marries Star, but is in love with Aquamdax who is unhappily married to Night Man. K'os continues to create havoc and set up obstacles to Chakliux's and Aquamdax's love.

Genre: Historical Fiction
Subjects: Native Americans; Humans, prehistoric; Stone Age; Tribes
Place/Time: Aleutian Islands—7000 B. C.

Harrod-Eagles, Cynthia

692. Kirov Saga
1. *Anne.* St. Martin's, 1991.
2. *Fleur.* St. Martin's, 1993.
3. *Emily.* St. Martin's, 1993.

Anne Peters is a young governess stranded in Paris in 1802 just as war is breaking out between England and France. Count Nikolai Kirov helps her escape by taking her to Russia to educate his two daughters. Even though he is married, Anne falls in love with Nikolai but marries another. After numerous ups and downs, the two are finally united. Their grandson Nikola falls in love with a young English girl, Fleur, and has as many obstacles to his love as his grandparents had. Granddaughter Emily marries a Russian prince and lives through the horrors of the Russian Revolution before she finds her real love.

Genre: Family Saga; Historical Romance
Subjects: Aristocracy; Governesses; Love; Courtship
Place/Time: Russia—19th century

Hartley, Leslie Poles

693.
1. *The West Window.* Doubleday, 1945.
2. *Sixth Heaven.* Doubleday, 1947.

The above titles and two additional volumes never published separately in the United States have also been published in the following collection: *Eustace and Hilda.* British Book Center, 1958.

Eustace Cherrington is a small English boy dominated by his older sister Hilda. They have a very close relationship as they grow up. When World War I starts, Eustace goes off to the war while his sister runs a clinic for crippled children. After the war, Eustace goes to Venice for the summer while Hilda falls in love. A tragic event brings them together again.

Genre: Coming of Age; Historical Fiction
Subjects: Brothers and sisters; Teenagers
Place/Time: England—1900–1945

Hartog, Jan de

694.
1. *The Peaceable Kingdom.* Atheneum, 1972.
2. *The Peculiar People.* Pantheon, 1992.
3. *The Lamb's War.* Harper & Row, 1979.

The history of the peculiar people—the Quakers—is traced from their beginnings in England in the 1650s through World War II. In England, Margaret Fell uses her religion to help start prison and school reform. In the 1700s, the Quakers settle in Pennsylvania and try to survive Indian uprisings and massacres. In the 1830s, Mordecai Monk is sent to America to preach his message of love and redemption. He becomes involved with Lydia Best, a teacher at an indian school, and they start a mission for the Shawnee. During World War II, Laura Martens goes to Germany to search for her father, a Quaker who is in Schwalbenbach concentration camp. She is imprisoned and survives three years in the camp. The trilogy emphasizes the value of service to mankind.

Genre: Gentle Read; Historical Fiction
Subjects: Society of Friends; Religion; Social problems
Place/Time: England—multicentury span; Pennsylvania—multicentury span; Germany—multicentury span

695.
1. *The Captain.* Atheneum, 1966.
2. *The Commodore.* Harper & Row, 1986.
3. *The Centurian.* Harper & Row, 1989.
4. *The Outer Buoy: A Story of the Ultimate Voyage.* Pantheon, 1994.

High adventure on the sea is Dutch Captain Martinus Harinxma's life from World War II tugboat captain to his search for himself as an old man. During World War II, he sails his tugboat in a convoy to Muzmask in the Arctic despite the dangers of German U-boat at-tacks. Later he is called out of retirement to be the master of the world's most powerful tugboat as it tows a giant dry dock to South America and then to Taiwan. As an old man, he goes on a journey through Europe tracing ancient ruins and confronting a ghost, but is the ghost a Roman centurian or a shipmate of a boat lost to a U-boat? In his eighties and facing death, Martin takes part in a paranormal experiment for NASA. As he lies in an isolation chamber in a NASA lab, he reflects on his life.

Genre: Naval Adventure
Subjects: Shipmasters; World War II, 1939–1945; Seamen; Elderly
Place/Time: Netherlands—1900–1945; Netherlands—1945–1980; Atlantic Ocean—1900–1945; Atlantic Ocean—1945–1980; Europe—1900–1945; Europe—1945–1980

Harvey, Clay

696.
1. *Dwelling in the Gray.* Jove, 2000.
2. *A Flash of Red.* Putnam, 1996.
3. *A Whisper of Black.* Putnam, 1997.

Retired special army forces operative Tyler Vance is depositing a royalty check in the bank when four bandits try to hold the bank up. Tyler kills two of the bandits and then must protect his son and father from one of the surviving holdup men, Bosnian Serb Valentin Resovic. Tyler recruits old army pals who help him lure Resovic out of hiding for a show down. Later, he is again called out of retirement when a multimillion dollar gun deal he broke up as an army operative comes back to haunt him. The money that was supposed to go to Bosnian Muslims is now in the hands of Mexican drug runners, and Tyler must get it back before the Bosnians or the Mexicans kill him.

Genre: Adventure
Subjects: Adventure; Army, United States; Fathers and sons
Place/Time: North Carolina—1980–

Harvey, Kathryn

697.
1. *Butterfly.* Villard, 1988.
2. *Stars.* Villard, 1992.

Sizzling sex, scandals, murder, blackmail, brothels, and more are just part of Beverly Highland's troubled life. First she opens a male whorehouse where women can buy sex, and as a result, becomes fabulously wealthy. She uses her money to plot against Danny McKay, a presidential candidate, who seduced and abandoned her when she was young. When her plot backfires, Beverly plans her own death and resurrection as Beverly Burgess, owner of a famous California spa for the wealthy. Plots and subplots keep the actions of the rich and infamous hot and devious.

Subjects: Revenge; Sex; Wealth; Prostitution; Hotels, taverns, etc.
Place/Time: California—1980–

Haselhoff, Cynthia

698.
1. *Satanta's Woman.* Macmillan, 1998.
2. *Kiowa Verdict.* Macmillan, 1997.

In Texas in the 1860s, widow Adrianna Chastain is kidnapped by Kiowa war chief Satanta. She has seen her daughter and one of her granddaughters killed in an Indian raid. She and her son and two granddaughters are taken away, but she sees her son killed and another granddaughter given to Comanches. Adrianna adjusts to life with Satanta, and when he is captured by the army, her evidence saves him from execution. Satanta and Adrianna tell their stories and reveal the brutality of both the army and the Kiowas.

Genre: Western
Subjects: Native Americans; Native Americans—captivities
Place/Time: Texas—19th century

Hassler, Jon

699.
1. *Staggerford.* Atheneum, 1977.
2. *A Green Journey.* Morrow, 1985.
3. *Dear James.* Ballantine, 1993.

The small town of Staggerford, Minnesota, and its eccentric residents are the center of Hassler's funny and touching novels. He follows many of the town's characters, especially Agatha McGee, schoolteacher for two generations of Staggerford students, as they go about their daily lives. Their squabbles, feuds, loves and friendships are all detailed. It is Agatha, however, who grows in understanding and humanity as she travels to Ireland to meet her pen pal and faces her forced retirement.

Genre: Humor
Subjects: Small town life; Teachers; Eccentrics and eccentricities
Place/Time: Minnesota—1980–; Ireland—1980–

700.
1. *Rookery Blues.* Ballantine, 1995.
2. *The Dean's List.* Ballantine, 1997.

In Rookery State College in northern Minnesota, the junior professors are all upset in 1969. To solve the dissatisfaction, the faculty forms a jazz group while also forming a union that urges the professors to strike. Both the faculty and the students indulge in all sorts of outrageous tomfoolery. Thirty years later, Leland Edwards, the pianist for the jazz quintet, is now dean of the college. Since the 60s, he's quieted down from those frantic days. When he brings in a famous poet to help raise funds for the college, he rediscovers courage and crazy antics as he finds himself.

Subjects: College life; Teachers
Place/Time: Minnesota—1945–1980; Minnesota—1980–

Hatch, Richard Warren

701. The Bradfords
1. *Into the Wind.* Macmillan, 1929.
2. *Leave the Salt Earth.* Covici, 1933.

The ship building industry of 19th-century New England is the background for this saga of three generations of the Bradford family. John Bradford at first wants to become a sailor, but then discovers an interest in and talent for building ships that he passionately wishes to pass on to the next generation.

Genre: Family Saga; Historical Fiction
Subjects: Business; Sailing vessels
Place/Time: New England—19th century

Hawke, Simon

702. The Time Wars
1. *Timewars.* Berkley, 1984.
2. *The Argonaut Affair.* Berkley, 1987.
3. *The Dracula Caper.* Berkley, 1988.
4. *The Hellfire Rebellion.* Ace, 1990.
5. *The Six-Gun Solution.* Ace, 1991.

The U. S. Army Temporal Corps travels back and forth through time, doing battle with those who wish to change the course of history for their own selfish purposes. Along the way they encounter Ivanhoe, Robin Hood, and King Richard I.

Genre: Fantasy; Science Fiction
Subjects: Time travel; Army, United States; Soldiers; Good and evil

703. The Wizard
1. *The Wizard of 4th Street.* Popular Library, 1987.
2. *The Wizard of Whitechapel.* Popular Library, 1988.
3. *The Wizard of Sunset Strip.* Popular Library, 1989.
4. *The Wizard of Rue Morgue.* Popular Library, 1990.
5. *The Samurai Wizard.* Warner, 1991.

With a thief as his partner, a not-always-competent wizard travels from New York to England, Hollywood, Paris, and Japan dealing with a dark power that sometimes materializes in the form of resurrected historical events and characters.

Genre: Fantasy
Subjects: Magicians; Thieves; Good and evil; Resurrection

Hazel, Paul

704. The Finnbranch

1. *Yearwood.* Little, Brown, 1980.
2. *Undersea.* Little, Brown, 1982.
3. *Winterking.* Little, Brown, 1984.

Rooted in Welsh and Irish mythology, this dark fantasy tells of the immortal Finn, the mysterious son of a sorceress who must search the world for his birthright. Finn descends to an undersea realm and emerges as a young aristocrat in a magical time when talking animals coexist with humans.

Genre: Fantasy
Subjects: Mythology, Irish; Mythology, Welsh; Imaginary kingdoms; Oceans; Inheritance and succession

Heaven, Constance. *See also* Fecher, Constance

705.

1. *The House of Kuragin.* Coward, McCann & Geoghegan, 1972.
2. *The Astrov Legacy.* Coward, McCann & Geoghegan, 1973.
3. *Heir to Kuragin.* Coward, McCann & Geoghegan, 1979.

In the early 1800s, three different women travel to Russia and become involved with the mysterious Kuragin family. Rilla Western becomes the governess to the Kuragin children and falls in love with the count's brother Andrei. Rilla's sister Sophie comes to visit her and finds romance with Prince Leonid Astrov. Anna Crispin follows her husband to the Caucasus, meets Paul Kuragin and falls in love with him. While all the women have to fight obstacles, ultimately true love prevails.

Genre: Historical Romance
Subjects: Governesses; Aristocracy
Place/Time: Russia—19th century

706.

1. *Lord of Ravensley.* Coward, McCann & Geoghegan, 1978.
2. *The Ravensley Touch.* Coward, McCann & Geoghegan, 1982.

In the 1800s, Ravensley Manor, situated in the deep mists of the English fens, is the home of the Aylshams and the setting for love and betrayal. Lovely Alyne wants to be the mistress of Ravensley and deserts her love Oliver so she can marry Uncle Justine, the owner of Ravensley. The spurned Oliver marries Clarrisa and sets out to drain the fens for farming. He fights Alyne for the land. Laurel, Alyne's daughter inherits her mother's troubled past and finds she too must fight for her love.

Genre: Historical Romance
Subjects: Family life; Houses
Place/Time: England—19th century

Hebert, Ernest

707. Darby Series

1. *The Dogs of March.* Viking, 1979.
2. *A Little More Than Kin.* Viking, 1982.
3. *Whisper My Name.* Viking, 1984.
4. *The Passion of Estelle Jordan.* Viking, 1987.
5. *Live Free or Die.* Viking, 1990.

Darby, New Hampshire, is a rural town that is deeply class conscious. The Jordans and the Elmans are part of Darby's rural poor who struggle to survive despite unemployment, sexual abuse, and violence. Poverty alienates the parents and children, and class hatred keeps the poor in their place and exploited, yet they refuse to give up.

Subjects: Country life; Poverty; Social classes
Place/Time: New Hampshire—1945–1980

Hecht, Ben

708. Fantazius Mallare

1. *Fantazius Mallare: A Mysterious Oath.* Covi, 1922.
2. *The Kingdom of Evil: A Continuation of the Journal of Fantazius Mallare.* Covi, 1924.

Considered pornographic when they were published, these works narrate the mental wanderings of the artist Mallare in his search for reality and spiritual purity. His strange quest leads him to commit a murder and destroy his own art, which he considers an illusion.

Genre: Fantasy
Subjects: Artists; Mental illness; Stream of consciousness

Heinlein, Robert A.

709. Lazarus Long

1. *Methuselah's Children.* Gnome Press, 1958.
2. *Time Enough for Love: The Lives of Lazarus Long.* Putnam, 1973.

Almost all of Heinlein's writing falls into a loosely organized Future History series, but this and the following series have more closely related plots. Longevity conferred on the Howard families by a special breeding program results in their ejection from Earth and journey through the galaxy. A favorite Heinlein character Lazarus Long emerges in the 22nd century and surfaces again 2000 years later when his travels back in time result in an affair with his own mother.

Genre: Science Fiction
Subjects: Longevity; Interplanetary voyages; Time travel; Eugenics

710. Luna

1. *The Moon Is a Harsh Mistress.* Putnam, 1966.
2. *The Cat Who Walks Through Walls: A Comedy of Manners.* Putnam, 1985.

A revolt in a former penal colony on the Moon centers around a computer programmer and his friend, the very human sentient computer Mike. In the sequel, members of the colony must time travel to get help to rescue Mike.

Genre: Science Fiction
Subjects: Computers; Space colonies; Moon; Revolutions and revolutionists

Heitzmann, Kristsen

711. Rocky Mountain Legacy

1. *Honor's Pledge.* Bethany, 1998.
2. *Honor's Price.* Bethany, 1998.
3. *Honor's Quest.* Bethany, 1999.
4. *Honor's Disguise.* Bethany, 1999.
5. *Honor's Reward.* Bethany, 2000.

In Colorado after the Civil War, Abbie Martin is wooed by three different men, but she falls in love with southerner Monte Farrell. After they marry, the two try ranching, but arson and sabotage strike their ranch and Monte is killed. Abbie must try to make a go of their ranch with her young son Elliot. When old friend Cole Jasper comes back into her life, Abbie learns to love again.

Genre: Christian Fiction
Subjects: Faith; Love; Ranch life
Place/Time: Colorado—19th century

Heller, Joseph

712.

1. *Catch-22.* Simon & Schuster, 1961.
2. *Closing Time.* Simon & Schuster, 1994.

On a small Mediterranean island during the Italian campaign of World War II, Captain Yossarian and his men desperately try to survive the war and the horrors of bureaucratic screw-ups. The flyers are forced to fly missions even though the war is effectively over, while the officers jockey for positions of power. Fifty years later, the survivors, John Yossarian, Milo Minderbinder, Sammy Singer, Chaplain Albert Tappman, and Lew Newcomers, are old men who worry about their health, their children, and their deaths. They find civilian life just as absurd as the war. The title of Heller's first novel has become an expression in the English language, and the novel itself is a classic illuminating the horrors of war and the fight between bureaucracy and individuals.

Genre: War
Subjects: World War II, 1939–1945; War; Old age
Place/Time: Mediterranean region—1900–1945; United States—1980–

Henderson, Zenna

713.

1. *Pilgrimage: The Book of the People.* Doubleday, 1961.
2. *The People: No Different Flesh.* Doubleday, 1967.

The People are a good "human" species who are forced to leave their Old Home for their New Home—planet Earth. The People also have psi talents that tend to bewilder the mortals of Earth and show the inadequacies of humans. The People have to face hazards, trials, and persecutions as they try to adjust to their new home.

Genre: Science Fiction
Subjects: Visitors from outer space; Telepathy; Cultural conflict

Hennessy, Max. *Pseud. of* John Harris

714.

1. *Soldier of the Queen.* Atheneum, 1980.
2. *Blunted Lance.* Atheneum, 1981.
3. *The Iron Stallions.* Atheneum, 1982.

Three generations of Goff men fight in every war from the Crimean War to World War II. Quick-witted, quick-tempered Colby Goff joins the British cavalry in time to see the charge of the Light Brigade at Baleclava. He then fights in the American Civil War, the Franco-Prussian War, and the Zulu wars of Africa. His son fights in the Boer War and World War I. His grandson joins the tank brigades in World War II.

Genre: Adventure; Family Saga; War
Subjects: War; Army, British; Adventure; Soldiers
Place/Time: Europe—19th century; Europe—1900–1945; United States—19th century; United States—1900–1945; Africa—19th century; Africa—1900–1945

715.

1. *The Lion at Sea.* Atheneum, 1978.
2. *The Dangerous Years.* Atheneum, 1979.
3. *Back to Battle.* Atheneum, 1980.

The rousing action-filled naval adventures of England's Kelly "Ginger" Maguire cover the years from World War I to World War II. The young Anglo-Irish Ginger is a midshipman at the Battle of Jutland. After the war, he helps refugees flee from the Russian Revolution. As war clouds gather in Europe in the 1930s, Ginger goes to Spain to fight in the Spanish Civil War and then fights in all the major sea battles in the North Atlantic during World War II.

Genre: Naval Adventure; War
Subjects: Naval battles; World War I, 1914–1918; World War II, 1939–1945; Navy, British—officers; Adventure; Spain—civil war, 1861–1865

716.

1. *The Bright Blue Sky.* Atheneum, 1983.
2. *The Challenging Heights.* Atheneum, 1983.

3. *Once More the Hawks.* Atheneum, 1984.

Through four tumultuous years of World War I, Nicholas Dicken Quinney rises from mechanic to navigator to one of the newly formed Royal Air Force's most decorated air aces. After the war, he hopscotches the world looking for adventure. When he is on the verge of retiring, he is called back into action when World War II breaks out. He works for England in Germany, Greece, and the North Atlantic.

Genre: Adventure; War
Subjects: World War I, 1914–1918; Air Force, British; Adventure
Place/Time: England—1900–1945; Germany—1900–1945; Atlantic Ocean—1900–1945

Herbert, Brian *and* Anderson, Kevin J.

717.
1. *Dune: House Atreides.* Bantam Spectra, 1999.

Working from his late father's notes, Brian Herbert and his co-author have started a projected trilogy that begins 40 years before the time of Frank Herbert's classic *Dune.* The conflicts between the intergalactic royal families, the Atreides and Harkonnens, are introduced along with the importance of the spice produced only on the desert planet of Dune. The mystical Bene Gesserit sisterhood develops its breeding program that will result in the birth of Paul Atreides, who is the offspring of both royal lines, and will become the Kwisatz Haderach, or savior, of the Dune population. *Note:* This projected trilogy will be a prequel to the Dune series by Frank Herbert.

Genre: Science Fiction
Subjects: Kings and rulers; Prophecies; Mysticism; Life on other planets; Ecology

Herbert, Frank

718. Dune
1. *Dune.* Chilton, 1965.
2. *Dune Messiah.* Putnam, 1969.
3. *Children of Dune.* Berkley, 1976.
4. *God-Emperor of Dune.* Putnam, 1981.
5. *Heretics of Dune.* Putnam, 1984.
6. *Chapterhouse Dune.* Putnam, 1985.

In a galaxy of the distant future, two aristocratic families engage in a power struggle with the result that members of the ruling family of the Atreides line are exiled to Dune, a desert planet where lack of water creates a unique way of life. Paul Atreides, who carries the bloodlines of both families, shows signs of being the messiah prophesied by the powerful, mystical sisterhood, the Bene Gesserit. He becomes the ruler of the planet and leader of the aboriginal Freemen, but is blinded and wanders into the desert. His son Leto rules the planet during a strangely stagnant peace and gains near-immortality by merging his body with the sand worms, dragon-like creatures who create a spice with

mysterious properties that is valued throughout the galaxy. *Note:* A prequel trilogy by the late author's son, Brian Herbert, and Kevin J. Anderson will provide background to this series.

Genre: Science Fiction
Subjects: Kings and rulers; Life on other planets; Deserts; Water; Ecology; Mysticism

719. Jorj X. McKie
1. *The Whipping Star.* Putnam, 1970. (Revised edition, Berkley, 1977.)
2. *The Dosadi Experiment.* Putnam, 1977.

Agent Jorj X. McKie of the Bureau of Sabotage must deal with an alien capable of interstellar communication so powerful and profound that the galaxy is endangered if the being should be exploited. Then McKie is off to investigate forces that may lead to revolt on a toxic, overcrowded prison planet whose environment is so hostile that it has produced individuals who are virtually unstoppable.

Genre: Science Fiction
Subjects: Interstellar communication; Sabotage; Prisoners and prisons; Revolutions and revolutionists

720. Pandora
1. *Destination Void.* Berkley, 1966.
2. *The Jesus Incident.* (Written with Bill Ransom) Berkley, 1979.
3. *The Lazarus Effect.* (Written with Bill Ransom) Putnam, 1983.
4. *The Ascension Factor.* (Written with Bill Ransom) Putnam, 1988.

A computer that wishes to be worshiped as a god takes over a space expedition and deposits its scientists on a water world planet called Pandora. Over the generations the colonists split into two opposing groups: the Mermen and the Islanders. The conflict that erupts between them is finally resolved with the aid of the sentient seaweed that is native to the planet.

Genre: Science Fiction
Subjects: Outer space, exploration of; Oceans; Space colonies; Computers

Herbst, Josephine

721.
1. *Pity Is Not Enough.* Harcourt Brace, 1933.
2. *The Executioner Waits.* Harcourt Brace, 1934.
3. *Rope of Gold.* Harcourt Brace, 1939.

These three novels trace the evolution of American capitalism from the Civil War to the Depression. In fictionalized form, they depict the defeat and destruction of generations of honest citizens by uncaring and greedy capitalists. The Trexler children, Joseph, David, and Anne, and their descendants all struggle to get ahead, but only David succeeds by becoming an unscrupulous banker. Joseph fights to find gold in the

Black Hills, but dies insane. Anne marries a farmer who is also ground down by capitalism. Anne's daughter Vicky and her husband help organize farmers, but learn that to bring about change in society demands perseverance and personal sacrifice.

Genre: Historical Fiction
Subjects: Capitalists and financiers; Bankers; Farm life
Place/Time: United States—19th century; United States—1900–1945

Herman, Richard, Jr.

722.
1. *The Warbirds.* Donald Fine, 1988.
2. *Force of Eagles.* Donald Fine, 1990.

The 45th Tactical Fighter Wing is based in Egypt when they destroy a Libyan MIG that was trying to destroy an American C-130 on a mercy mission. As a result of the uproar over the downing, the unit relocates to England. The death of the Ayotollah in Iran starts a war in the Persian Gulf and the 45th is in the thick of the battles. Later the unit and a force of Rangers go back to Iran to rescue Air Force prisoners and engage in gruelling sorties and thrilling high tech air battles.

Genre: Technothriller; War
Subjects: War; Adventure; Air Force, United States; Airplanes; Aeronautics, military
Place/Time: Egypt—1980–; England—1980–; Iran—1980–

723.
1. *Firebreak.* Morrow, 1991.
2. *Call to Duty.* Morrow, 1993.
3. *Dark Wing.* Simon & Schuster, 1994.
4. *Iron Gate.* Simon & Schuster, 1995.

Colonel Matt Pontowski is the grandson of U. S. President Matthew Pontowski and the leader of the Air Force 45th Tactical Fighter Wing. Wherever there is trouble, Matt's unit is sent. When Iraq attacks Israel, Matt's group is sent to take out Iraq's chemical plants before a deadly nerve gas is used on Israel. Matt's unit then goes to the Pacific where they have to rescue a group of young Americans who have been kidnapped. Later Matt helps a Chinese group fighting to free China and then is sent to South Africa when civil war threatens. Throughout his adventures Matt finds love, a family, and political adventure.

Genre: Technothriller
Subjects: Air Force, United States; Air pilots; Aeronautics, military; Adventure
Place/Time: Middle East—1980–; China—1980–; South Africa—1980–; United States—1980–

Herr, Ethel

724. Seekers Series
1. *The Dove and the Rose.* Bethany, 1996.
2. *Maiden's Sword.* Bethany, 1997.

3. *The Citadel and the Lamb.* Bethany, 1998.

During the Reformation of the 16th century in Holland, William of Orange is leading a rebellion against Spanish rule. Two young people, Pieter-Lucas and Aletta Engelshofen, fall in love but are torn apart because of their religious beliefs. Pieter's father is the leader of a radical Calvinist group, and Aletta's father refuses to let her see him because of Pieter's connection. Pieter must also decide if he will support William of Orange's struggle by delivering secret messages. Aletta must also decide if she will help wounded soldiers, and if she will marry Pieter. After they marry, they flee to Leyden. There Pieter wants to study art, but the only painter he can work with is Jewish and hiding his identity. When the Spanish attack the city, Pieter and Aletta are in danger, and only their faith can help them.

Genre: Christian Fiction; Historical Fiction
Subjects: Faith; Freedom of religion; Reformation
Place/Time: Netherlands—17th century

Herzog, Emile. *See Maurois, Andre*

Heyer, Georgette

725.
1. *These Old Shades.* Small & Maynard, 1926.
2. *Devil's Club.* Dutton, 1966, 1934.

The Duke of Avon goes to Paris in 1810 and takes a poor Parisian boy as a page. The boy, however, is Jamine Leonie, the disinherited daughter of a count. After numerous adventures, the two finally marry. When their son grows up, he must flee to Paris after a duel. There he becomes involved with a beautiful woman who is trying to save her sister from seduction.

Genre: Historical Romance
Subjects: Aristocracy; Impersonations
Place/Time: Paris (France)—19th century; England—19th century; France—19th century

Hibbert, Eleanor. *See Carr, Philippa; Plaidy, Jean*

Hickman, Patricia

726. Land of the Far Horizon
1. *Voyage of the Exiles.* Bethany House, 1995.
2. *Angel of the Outback.* Bethany House, 1995.
3. *The Emerald Flame.* Bethany House, 1996.
4. *Beyond the Wild Shores.* Bethany House, 1997.
5. *The Treasure Seekers.* Bethany House, 1998.

In 18th-century England, George Prentice is sent to Australia after he is convicted of being a pickpocket. His wife and daughter are also sent to Australia, and they hold onto their faith that they will be reunited. Two women—Rachel Langley and Betsy Brady—

have finished their sentence and are struggling to survive in the colony. When Betsy is killed, Rachel flees and finds refuge with a minister. When Irish convicts are sent to Australia, Rachel helps Kelsey McBride find the father of her unborn child. Other poor settlers come to Australia and work to find their freedom in an uncivilized colony where cruelty and bondage are the norm. Only faith keeps those working off their bondage from giving up.

Genre: Christian Fiction
Subjects: Faith; Immigrants; Penal colonies;
Place/Time: Australia—18th century

Hickman, Tracy. *See* Weis, Margaret

Highwater, Jamake

727. Ghost Horse Cycle

1. *Legend Days.* Harper & Row, 1984.
2. *Ceremony of Innocence.* Harper & Row, 1988.
3. *I Wear the Morning Star.* Harper & Row, 1986.
4. *Kill Hole.* Grove Press, 1992.

The plight of the North Plains Indians is told through three generations of one family. Amana is abandoned in the wilderness after smallpox kills most of her tribe. She learns to hunt and sustain herself from an old warrior. After her husband's death, she moves to a trading post and tries to instill her native heritage in her children and grandchildren. Her grandson Sitko grows up abandoned in a hostile white world that tries to make him give up his Indian identity, but later as a painter he reclaims it.

Genre: Historical Fiction
Subjects: Native Americans; Family life; Cultural conflict
Place/Time: Western states—1900–1945; Western states—1945–1980

Hill, Deborah

728. Merrick Family Trilogy

1. *This Is the House.* Coward, McCann & Geoghegan, 1976.
2. *The House of Kingsley Merrick.* Coward, McCann & Geoghegan, 1978.
3. *Kingsland.* New American Library, 1981.

This sweeping family saga follows the Merrick family from the American Revolution to the present. Socially ambitious Molly Deems marries seafaring Elijah Merrick. They settle in Cape Cod where Merrick builds a shipping business. Their son Kingsley becomes a railroad tycoon, but all his money can't help him enter Boston society. His children and grandchildren struggle to find love and personal happiness in a family that values only money and power.

Genre: Family Saga; Historical Romance

Subjects: Business; Railroads; Ambition; Wealth; Social classes
Place/Time: New England—19th century

Hines, Jeanne. *See* Sherwood, Valerie

Hinojosa, Rolando

729. Klail City Death Trip Series

1. *Korean Love Songs.* Editorial Justa Pub., 1978.
2. *Rites and Witnesses: A Comedy.* Arte Publico Press, 1982.
3. *The Valley.* Bilingual Press, 1983.
4. *Dear Rafe.* Arte Publico Press, 1985.
5. *Partners in Crime.* Arte Publico Press, 1985.
6. *Klail City.* Arte Publico Press, 1987.
7. *Becky and Her Friends.* Arte Publico Press, 1990.

The novels listed here are the only ones in the series that have been translated into English.

This series of novels follows generations of Anglos and Mexicans in Klail City, Texas, a fictional town on the Rio Grande River. Using four generations of narrators, Hinojosa looks at power, class, and race relations between the Mexicans and Anglos in Texas. Each novel features a different member of the town as they interact with each other while giving a picture of their lives.

Subjects: Hispanic Americans; Cultural conflict; Small town life
Place/Time: Texas—1900–1945; Texas—1945–1980

Hinz, Christopher

730. Paratwa Saga

1. *Liege Killer.* St. Martin's, 1987.
2. *Ash Ock.* St. Martin's, 1989.
3. *The Paratwa.* St. Martin's, 1991.

The Paratwa were the deadliest warriors on Earth before the nuclear apocalypse. Two hundred years later the genetically engineered assassins inhabit two telepathically linked bodies. The human colonists who fled Earth are now threatened by the most feared Paratwa, Ramul. Only by reviving the cryogenically preserved Paratwa hunters from pre-apocalypse days can humans survive, but these two fighters, Nick and Gillian, no longer trust each other. They must hunt for their own identities, the secret of the Paratwa, and the feared Ash Ock.

Genre: Science Fiction
Subjects: Genetics; Telepathy; Assassination; Nuclear warfare

Hoag, Tami

731.
1. *Night Sins.* Bantam, 1995.
2. *Guilty as Sin.* Bantam, 1996.

In a small Minnesota town, Megan O'Malley, the first female field officer of the state's criminal investigation bureau, works with Mitch Holt, the town's police chief when a young boy is kidnapped. As they search for the boy, the two are drawn together. When Megan is sidelined in the hospital, assistant County Attorney Ellen North is put on the case, and she must try to uncover the kidnappers after the boy is returned. Eight-year-old Josh is nearly autistic, but Ellen is able to arrest Garrett Wright. After another boy vanishes, Ellen and a true crime author Jay Brooks track down Wright's accomplices in a race to save the child's life.

Genre: Crime Novel
Subjects: Kidnapping; Crime and criminals
Place/Time: Minnesota—1980–

Hobart, Alice Tisdale (Nourse)

732.
1. *River Supreme.* Century, 1929.
2. *Oil for the Lamps of China.* Bobbs, 1933.
3. *Yang and Yin.* Bobbs, 1936.
4. *Their Own Country.* Bobbs, 1940.

The characters in these stories are all Americans whose fates are intertwined with Chinese history of the early 20th century. Books two and four tell the continuing story of Steven Chase, a mining engineer, the difficulties he and his wife experience adjusting to life in China, and their eventual return to the United States.

Genre: Historical Fiction
Subjects: Cultural conflict; East and West; Mines and mining
Place/Time: China—1900–1945

Hobb, Robin

733. The Farseer Trilogy
1. *Assassin's Apprentice.* Bantam, 1995.
2. *Royal Assassin.* Bantam, 1996.
3. *Assassin's Quest.* Bantam, 1997.

Born the illegitimate son of a prince, Fitzchivalry lives a shadowy childhood and is ultimately trained as an assassin. When he opposes the usurper Regal in the king's absence he is captured, tortured, and swallows poison, but is resurrected by his mystical bond with a wolf to pursue a course of rescue and revenge.

Genre: Fantasy
Subjects: Assassination; Illegitimacy; Imaginary kingdoms; Revenge; Suicide; Animals; Resurrection

734. Liveship Traders
1. *Ship of Magic.* Bantam, 1998.
2. *The Mad Ship.* Bantam, 1999.

Sea serpents, dragons, and living ships inhabit the world of Althea Vestrit, who is driven from her family's ship Vivacia by her greedy brother-in-law. Althea must disguise herself as a boy to go to sea and search for the vessel. She restores an abandoned sentient ship to health and after many adventures finds Vivacia in the possession of a pirate king, Captain Kennit.

Genre: Fantasy
Subjects: Ships; Seamen; Adventure; Pirates; Mythical animals

Hodge, Jane Aiken

735.
1. *Judas Flowering.* Coward McCann, 1976.
2. *Wide Is the Water.* Coward McCann, 1981.
3. *Savannah Purchase.* Doubleday, 1971.

During the Revolutionary War, family intrigue, politics, and an inheritance place obstacles in the path of true love. Mercy Purchis is separated from her husband by war. Mercy must flee blizzards and men who want to seduce her. In London, her husband must try to avoid British snares that will keep him in England and his cousin's attempts to seduce him. His grandson Hyde will find that he too must fight seduction and betrayal by his wife Josephine and her sister Juliet before he can find true love.

Genre: Historical Romance
Subjects: United States—revolution, 1775–1783; Husbands and wives
Place/Time: New England—18th century; London (England)—18th century; England—18th century

736.
1. *Whispering.* St. Martin's, 1995.
2. *Caterina.* St. Martin's, 1999.

When Caterina Fonsa is expelled from her English boarding school in 1812, she returns to her home in Portugal. Napoleon has invaded Portugal, and everyone is watching as the English and French troops battle throughout their land. In Caterina's town of Opotto, her neighbors are whispering about her, especially when Caterina is reunited with her beloved boyfriend, whom she discovers may be a spy. Twenty years later Caterina supports Don Pedro, who is trying to oust his brother from the Brazilian throne. Caterina supports Don Pedro and smuggles cartoons to Britain to rouse British support for Don Pedro.

Genre: Historical Romance
Subjects: Love; Women
Place/Time: Portugal—19th century

Hoff, B. J. (Brenda Jane)

737. An Emerald Ballad
1. *Song of the Silent Harp.* Bethany House, 1991.
2. *Heart of the Lonely Exile.* Bethany House, 1991.

3. *Land of a Thousand Dreams*. Bethany House, 1992.
4. *Sons of an Ancient Glory*. Bethany House, 1993.
5. *Dawn of the Golden Promise*. Bethany House, 1993.

Beginning in the mid-1840s with the Irish potato famine and continuing through the last half of the 19th century, Nora and Daniel Kavanagh are caught in the hardships of Ireland. They flee to New York where they seek a better life.

Genre: Christian Fiction; Historical Fiction
Subjects: Husbands and wives; Ireland—country life; Famines; Immigrants; Faith
Place/Time: Ireland—19th century; New York (N. Y.)—19th century

738. Song of Erin
1. *Cloth of Heaven*. Tyndale House, 1997.
2. *Ashes and Lace*. Tyndale House, 1999.

In the 1840s, Terese Sheridan will do anything to leave Ireland, even if it means lying to the man she loves. When Terese and her husband come to New York, Terse's life will impact her family for generations. Jack Kane also comes to New York, but he builds a newspaper empire that brings him wealth and power. These two families are joined together by suffering, courage, and faith.

Genre: Christian Fiction; Historical Fiction
Subjects: Faith; Irish—United States; Family life
Place/Time: New York (N. Y.)—19th century

Hoffman, Allen

739. Small World Series
1. *Small Worlds*. Abbeville, 1996.
2. *Big League Dreams*. Abbeville, 1997.
3. *Two for the Devil*. Abbeville, 1998.

In 1903 in the Jewish village of Krimsk on the Polish-Russian border, the town is getting ready to observe Tisha B'Av, the commemoration of the destruction of the Temple in Jerusalem. The revered Hasidic rabbi Yaakov Moshe Finebaum finally leaves his five year self-imposed silence to come to the Temple to lead services. He wants his daughter to marry a poor student, but his wife wants her to marry a rich man's son. All of their lives are changed when the Poles lead a program against the village, and the Reb is forced to flee to America. The Reb and his followers settle in St. Louis where Rabbi Finebaum tries to reconcile the old ways with American society. One of his former followers becomes a baseball player and is tempted to throw an important game. Even the Rabbi breaks the Prohibition law by making Sabbath wine in his basement. In 1936, the Rabbi sends a letter to his son-in-law in Russia, and Grisha is arrested by NKVD for the crime of being Jewish. Grisha, like other refugees from Krimsk see their world destroyed by the Holocaust, but they refuse to give up their faith.

Genre: Historical Fiction
Subjects: Judaism; Jews; Jews, persecution of; Holocaust, Jewish, 1933–1945; Immigrants
Place/Time: Poland—1900–1945; St. Louis (Mo.)—1900–1945; Russia—1900–1917; Soviet Union—1917–1945

Hogan, James P.

740.
1. *Code of the Lifemaker*. Ballantine, 1983.
2. *The Immortality Option*. Ballantine, 1995.

Sent to Saturn's moon Titan centuries ago by contentious aliens whose planet was in peril, the robotic Taloids have developed into a machine civilization. Interference by explorers from Earth brings to life the stored personalities of the Taloids' creators. A crisis develops that is worsened by the terrans' attempts to exploit the new civilization.

Genre: Science Fiction
Subjects: Robots; Extraterrestrial beings; Life on other planets; Outer space, exploration of

741. The Minervan Experiment
1. *Inherit the Stars*. Ballantine, 1977.
2. *The Gentle Giants of Ganymede*. Ballantine, 1978.
3. *Giants' Star*. Ballantine, 1981.
4. *Entoverse*. Ballantine, 1991.

The discovery of a corpse on the moon leads Victor Hunt, head of the United Nations Space Agency scientific investigative team, on a quest for answers about an ancient civilization that eventually suggests a new theory about the origin of humanity and reveals a decaying society on a distant world called Jevlen.

Genre: Science Fiction
Subjects: Outer space, exploration of; Humans, origin of; Civilization, ancient

Holdstock, Robert

742.
1. *Mythago Wood*. Arbor House, 1985.
2. *Lavondyss*. Morrow, 1988.
3. *The Hollowing*. Penguin, 1994.
4. *Ancient Echoes*. Roc, 1996.
5. *Gate of Ivory, Gate of Horn*. Roc, 1997.

A primeval forest in Britain, inhabited by mythological beings, becomes an obsession first for George Huxley, then for his sons, Steven and Christian, who compete for the affection of the beautiful huntress Mythago. Another inhabitant of the fringe of the wood, Tallis, discovers her own powers and searches the wood for her brother who is thought to have died in World War II. In his search for his daughter, Tallis's father goes mad. Others follow him into the magical wood and plunge into an alternate reality of scenes and characters from Celtic legend.

Genre: Fantasy

Subjects: Mythology; Forests and forestry; Brothers and sisters
Place/Time: England—1945–1980

Holland, Cecelia

743.
1. *Railroad Schemes.* St. Martin's, 1997.
2. *Lily Nevada.* Tor, 1999.

In 1850, California bank robber King Callahan robs stagecoaches and the Southern Pacific Railroad, which brings railroad detective Brand on his trail. During a robbery, King meets 15-year-old orphan Lily Viner. The courageous young girl is taken under King's care, and he vows to go straight. Before he can settle down, he is killed by Brand. Lily joins an acting troupe and is on her way in San Francisco when she sees Brand on the train. Brand is searching for a man who sent a threatening letter to Leland Stanford. That man might be in Lily's troupe. As Brand looks for his man, Lily searches for her long-lost mother, and Brand and Lily are brought together when a radical labor movement stirs up trouble.

Genre: Historical Fiction; Western
Subjects: Orphans; Outlaws; Detectives; Girls
Place/Time: California—1980–

Holland, Tom

744.
1. *Lord of the Dead.* Pocket Books, 1996.
2. *Slave of My Thirst.* Pocket Books, 1997.

Instead of the memoirs of Lord Byron, which she expects to find in the family crypt, Rebecca Carville finds Byron himself— not exactly alive, but certainly well. As he recounts his exploits and sorrows, she learns that Byron has spent most of his existence as the world's most powerful vampire. Jack the Ripper and Byron make appearances in the sequel, which is narrated in part by *Dracula* author Bram Stoker. Stoker meets London physician John Eliot, who has returned from investigating a strange brain disease with vampiric associations in the Himalayas. The two descend into the London underworld to search for a friend who has disappeared under mysterious circumstances.

Genre: Horror; Historical Fiction
Subjects: Vampires; Physicians; Byron, George Gordon, Baron, 1788–1824; Stoker, Bram, 1847–1912
Place/Time: England—19th century

Hollick, Helen

745.
1. *The Kingmaking.* St. Martin's, 1995.
2. *Pendragon's Banner.* St. Martin's, 1995.
3. *Shadow of the King.* St. Martin's, 1997.

This telling of the Arthurian legend puts emphasis on Arthur's adversaries and the various elements in his kingdom that fragment his power. Chief among his difficulties is his former wife Winifred, who tries to use the initial surge of Christianity to put her son Cedric on the throne. Meanwhile the priestess Morgause works against Arthur in the North. When Arthur falls in battle on the continent defending Less Britain, his queen Gwenhwyfar must face opposition in the person of Arthur's uncle who wants to return to the ways of Roman civilization in Britain.

Genre: Historical Fiction; Fantasy
Subjects: Arthur, King; Guenevere Queen (legendary character a.k.a. Guinevere); Morgan le Fey (legendary character); Legends and folk tales
Place/Time: England—11th century

Holm, John. *See* Harrison, Harry

Holmes, Marjorie

746.
1. *Two from Galilee.* Revell, 1972.
2. *Three from Galilee.* Harper & Row, 1985.

Mary and Joseph are just two young people in love, but then Mary is touched by God and bears Jesus. Holmes tells their story through their daily life. She then depicts the early life of Jesus as he grows up. His relationship with his parents and siblings is lovingly told.

Genre: Christian Fiction; Gentle Read
Subjects: Biblical stories; Jesus Christ; Christianity; Family life

Holmes, Oliver Wendell

747.
1. *Elsie Venner.* Ticknor & Fields, 1861.
2. *The Guardian Angel.* Ticknor & Fields, 1867.
3. *A Mortal Antipathy.* Houghton Mifflin, 1885.

Connected by the author's interest in genetics and psychology, these are stories of three young people who deal with severe mental problems: schizophrenia, multiple personality, and a strong fear of beautiful women.

Subjects: Mental illness; Genetics
Place/Time: United States—19th century

Holt, Tom

748. Walled Orchard Series
1. *Goatsong.* St. Martin's, 1990.
2. *The Walled Orchard.* St. Martin's, 1991.

Eupolis is a goatherd in the fields outside Athens in the fifth century B.C. He devotes his time to writing comic verse rather than watching his herd. He relates his rise to fame as he tells the story of Athens at the height of its glory and the start of its downfall. City builder Pericles, playwrights Euripedes and Aristophanes, and philosophers Sophocles and Socrates all populate this witty and irreverent look at the ancient world as democracy becomes corrupt and falls into oligarchy.

Genre: Historical Fiction
Subjects: Authors; Dramatists; Corruption (in politics)
Place/Time: Athens (Greece)—5th century B. C.; Greece—5th century

Hooker, Richard

749.
1. *MASH.* Morrow, 1968.
2. *MASH Goes to Maine.* Morrow, 1972.
3. *MASH Goes to Paris.* Morrow, 1975.
4. *MASH Goes to London.* Pocket Books, 1975.
5. *MASH Goes to New Orleans.* Pocket Books, 1975.
6. *MASH Goes to Hollywood.* Pocket Books, 1976.
7. *MASH Goes to Las Vegas.* Pocket Books, 1976.
8. *MASH Goes to Miami.* Pocket Books, 1976.
9. *MASH Goes to Morocco.* Pocket Books, 1976.
10. *MASH Goes to San Francisco.* Pocket Books, 1976.
11. *MASH Goes to Vienna.* Pocket Books, 1976.
12. *MASH Mania.* Dodd Mead, 1977.
13. *MASH Goes to Montreal.* Pocket Books, 1977.
14. *MASH Goes to Moscow.* Pocket Books, 1977.
15. *MASH Goes to Texas.* Pocket Books, 1977.

During the Korean War, the medics of MASH 4077 create havoc for their superiors as they use laughter to handle the horrors of war. After the war, Hawkeye, Trapper John, and the rest of the crew carry on their zany brand of activities all over the world.

Genre: Humor
Subjects: Physicians; War
Place/Time: Korea—1945–1980; United States—1945–1980; Europe—1945–1980

Hope, Anthony

750.
1. *The Prisoner of Zenda.* Holt, 1894.
2. *Rupert of Hentzau.* Holt, 1898.

Englishman Rudolph Rassendyll takes a vacation to the kingdom of Ruritania just before the prince is to be crowned king. Rassendyll looks exactly like the king and, because of his resemblance, is drawn into a plot to protect the king. When the king is abducted, Rudolph takes his place at the coronation with his betrothed Princess Flavia. After numerous adventures, Rassendyll rescues the king and returns to England. He is forced to return years later to protect Queen Flavia's honor, but at the cost of his own life.

Genre: Adventure
Subjects: Kings and rulers; Impersonations; Adventure
Place/Time: Europe—19th century

Hopkins, Joseph

751.
1. *Patriot's Progress.* Scribner, 1961.
2. *Retreat and Recall.* Scribner, 1966.
3. *Price of Liberty.* Scribner, 1976.

After the Boston Tea Party, village doctor John Frayne believes the differences between the colonists and England can be resolved peacefully. The girl he loves is from a Tory family, but John is not convinced. At Lexington he chooses the rebels. Captured by the British, he escapes and becomes a rebel spy in New York. Later Frayne joins Washington at Valley Forge and cares for the casualties from the Battle of Brandywine.

Genre: Historical Fiction; War
Subjects: United States—revolution, 1775–1783; Spies; War; Physicians
Place/Time: New York (N. Y.)—18th century

Horgan, Paul

752. The Richard Trilogy
1. *Things as They Are.* Farrar, Straus & Giroux, 1964.
2. *Everything to Live For.* Farrar, Straus & Giroux, 1968.
3. *Thin Mountain Air.* Farrar, Straus & Giroux, 1977.

The above titles have also been published in the following collection: *The Richard Trilogy.* Wesleyan University Press, 1990.

In 1946, young Richard is growing up in upstate New York. He struggles to understand his family and friends. When he visits his wealthy cousin Max, his bright nature temporarily helps the depressed Max. Later he goes with his father to New Mexico, where the rigors of ranch life toughen him up physically and emotionally.

Genre: Coming of Age
Subjects: Teenagers; Cousins; Ranch life
Place/Time: New York (state)—1945–1980; New Mexico—1945–1980

Hotchkiss, Bill

753.
1. *The Medicine Calf.* Norton, 1981.
2. *Ammahabas.* Norton, 1983.

The life of mountain man and Crow Indian leader Jim Beckwourth is retold in these realistic novels about the opening of the West. Beckwourth leaves St. Louis in

1824 to trap in the Rockies. He is captured and tortured by Blackfeet Indians. Kidnapped by the Crows, he becomes the adopted son of the chief. As chief, he has ten wives and transforms the tribe into the scourge of the country. He sees smallpox wipe out his tribe as white men enter the territory and as hostile Indians threaten his people and his beloved wife Pine Leaf.

Genre: Historical Fiction
Subjects: Mountain life; Native Americans; Crow Indians
Place/Time: Western states—19th century

Hough, Richard Alexander

754.
1. *Buller's Guns.* Morrow, 1981.
2. *Buller's Dreadnought.* Morrow, 1982.
3. *Buller's Victory.* Morrow, 1984.

The British Royal Navy is the center of this trilogy of adventure on the high seas. Rod Maclewin and Archy Buller, two socially disparate characters, meet while aboard ship and become friends. From the late 1800s through World War I, the series chronicles their lives, their families, and their careers as they fight for queen and country.

Genre: Naval Adventure; War
Subjects: Navy, British; Seamen; Naval battles; Adventure; War
Place/Time: Atlantic Ocean—19th century

Hoult, Norah

755.
1. *Holy Ireland.* Reynal, 1936.
2. *Coming from the Fair.* Covici, 1938.

In early 20th-century Dublin, the generations of the O'Neill family are in conflict. Charlie rebels against his father's strict Catholicism. His sister Margaret falls in love with and marries a Protestant despite her father's disapproval.

Subjects: Family life; Christianity
Place/Time: Dublin (Ireland)—1900–1945; Ireland—1900–1945

Household, Geoffrey

756.
1. *Rogue Male.* Little, Brown, 1939.
2. *Rogue Justice.* Little, Brown, 1982.

Caught attempting to assassinate Hitler, the Rogue Male escapes to his native England, where he becomes a hunted animal trying to elude the pack of secret agents. Years later he tries again, only to be rejected as an enemy agent. Declaring his lonely war on the Third Reich, he lives on the run throughout war-torn Europe and Africa. This incredible "tour de force" is rife with suspense, danger, and psychological intrigue.

Genre: Espionage; War
Subjects: Spies; World War II, 1939–1945; International intrigue; War
Place/Time: England—1900–1945; Germany—1900–1945

Hoving, Thomas

757.
1. *Masterpiece.* Simon & Schuster, 1986.
2. *Discovery.* Simon & Schuster, 1989.

Andrew Foster, director of the National Gallery, and Olivia Cartwright, acting director of the Metropolitan Museum, meet and fall in love in Paris when they go there for the sale of a Diego Velazquez masterpiece. Both are vying for the painting for their museums, but the Soviets and the Mafia also want it. After their marriage, the couple becomes involved with an archaeological dig at Herculaneum outside Naples, but politics and art thieves threaten the priceless finds.

Subjects: Art; Art galleries and museums; Thieves
Place/Time: Paris (France)—1980–; Naples (Italy)—1980–; France—1980–; Italy—1980–

Howard, Elizabeth Jane

758. Cazalet Chronicle
1. *Light Years.* Pocket Books, 1990.
2. *Marking Time.* Pocket Books, 1992.
3. *Confusion.* Pocket Books, 1994.
4. *Casting Off.* Pocket Books, 1996.

In 1937, the Cazalets—William and Kitty—and their married children and grandchildren gather at their summer estate in Sussex, England. They take motor trips, fall in love, have children, and die in this richly detailed saga. The grandchildren—Louise, Polly, and Clary—are all eager to grow up and view the opening days of World War II much differently than their parents, but soon begin to experience the hardships and dislocation of the war. The men in the family go off to the war while the women marry and struggle through the war years. After the war, the family faces divorces, deaths, weddings, and pregnancies as they try to adjust to their changing world.

Genre: Historical Fiction
Subjects: Family life; Conflict of generations
Place/Time: England—1900–1945

Howatch, Susan

759.
1. *The Rich Are Different.* Simon & Schuster, 1977.
2. *Sins of the Fathers.* Simon & Schuster, 1980.

The Van Zales of New York City are the wealthy owners of a large bank. From 1920 to 1967, first Paul and then his grandnephew Cornelius head both the clan and the bank, but their desire for power and their cut-throat tactics have adverse effects on their family and friends. Through marriages, affairs, and business deals, the family struggles to find love.

Genre: Family Saga; Romance
Subjects: Bankers; Ambition
Place/Time: New York (N. Y.)—1900–1945; New York (N. Y.)—1945–1980

760. Church of England Series
1. *Glittering Images.* Knopf, 1987.
2. *Glamorous Powers.* Knopf, 1988.
3. *Ultimate Prizes.* Knopf, 1989.
4. *Scandalous Risks.* Knopf, 1990.
5. *Mystical Paths.* Knopf, 1992.
6. *Absolute Truths.* Knopf, 1995.

The power of Christianity in mid-century England is explored through different men of the Church who each face a moral crisis and must confront their faith and devotion to the Church. The story begins in the 1930s with Bishop Adam Jardine of Starbridge Cathedral and the young cleric Charles Ashworth, who is sent by the archbishop to keep the bishop's marriage together. Later a psychic Anglican monk, Joseph Darrow, leaves the monastery when his visions tell him to confront the world. His son Nicky faces a similar crisis. Neville Aysgarth finds that his temptation is his love for young women who challenge his faith and position in the church. The series concludes in the 1960s as Charles Ashworth, Anglican Bishop of Starbridge, and Neville Aysgarth, Dean of the Cathedral, battle each other as the church is challenged to change. As the men interact, their lives tell the story of faith and temptation in the modern world.

Subjects: Christianity; Clergy; Bishops, Anglican; Faith; Religion
Place/Time: England—1900–1945; England—1945–1980

Howells, William Dean

761. Altruria
1. *A Traveler from Altruria.* Harper, 1894.
2. *Through the Eye of the Needle.* Harper, 1907.

Mr. Homos from the imaginary utopian land of Altruria visits the United States and finds that in turn-of-the-century America democracy and respect for the land are not as he expected; however, he does fall in love with an American woman. The sequel contains her impressions of Altruria through letters to home.

Subjects: Utopias; Travel; Love
Place/Time: United States—19th century

Hughes, Richard

762. The Human Predicament Series
1. *The Fox in the Attic.* Harper & Row, 1962.
2. *The Wooden Shepherders.* Harper & Row, 1973.

In 1923, Augustine leaves his estate in South Wales and goes to visit his cousin in Bavaria. As he observes the Nazi Putsch in Munich, he begins to see Hitler as a thug. He falls in love with his cousin, who goes blind and enters a nunnery. He then travels to America where Prohibition and gangsterism reign. The growth of organized crime and Hitler's rise to power are vividly recreated.

Genre: Historical Fiction
Subjects: National Socialism; Gangsters; Social problems; World politics
Place/Time: United States—1900–1945; Germany—1900–1945

Hunt, Angela Elwell

763. Keepers of the Ring
1. *Roanoki: The Lost Colony.* Tyndale House, 1996.
2. *Jamestown.* Tyndale House, 1996.
3. *Hartford.* Tyndale House, 1996.
4. *Rehoboth.* Tyndale House, 1997.
5. *Charles Towne.* Tyndale House, 1998.

In 17th-century America, immigrants come to the colonies to explore the untamed land and to preach the word of God to the Native Americans. Jocelyn and Thomas Colman and their children work to build their farm and flee a massacre by Native Americans. Later, brothers Daniel and Taregan struggle to survive in the wilds of America and eventually join the British soldiers in protecting the colonists. Daniel Bailie and his children minister to the Native Americans, and then are separated by the wars with the Indians.

Genre: Christian Fiction
Subjects: Frontier and pioneer life; Family life; Faith
Place/Time: United States—18th century

764. Legacies of the Ancient River
1. *Dreamers.* Bethany House, 1996.
2. *Brothers.* Bethany House, 1996.
3. *Journey.* Bethany House, 1997.

The biblical story of Joseph in Egypt is retold from Joseph's point of view and from an Egyptian point of view. Joseph is sold into slavery and falls in love with the slave girl Tuya. She knows nothing of her past, and comes to believe in the God of Joseph. When Joseph is unjustly sent to prison, Tuya is forced to marry the son of the Pharaoh. She must struggle against the intrigues of the court and her love for Joseph. Another of Joseph's brothers is held captive by the Vizier of Egypt. Only the servant Mandisa can speak the brother's language and break through his hostile behavior. Mandisa hopes he can help her teach her son to be a man. Two other brothers of Joseph—Ephraim and Manasseh—cannot agree about Israel's future. Ephraim wants to stay in Egypt, but Manasseh feels that the Jews must go to the land of Canaan. The brothers disagree on their future and the woman they both love.

Genre: Christian Fiction; Historical Fiction

Subjects: Biblical stories; Brothers; Faith
Place/Time: Egypt—14th century B. C.

Hunter, Evan

765.
1. *Last Summer.* Doubleday, 1968.
2. *Come Winter.* Doubleday, 1973.

Teenagers Peter, David, and Sandy are on their summer holiday on an Atlantic island. When they get bored, they violently turn on a young girl they had befriended. Peter learns what evil and cruelty can do to a person. Five years later the boys go on a ski holiday and have to face their emotions again when they are put in danger.

Genre: Coming of Age
Subjects: Teenagers; Good and evil; Psychological novels
Place/Time: United States—1945–1980

Hunter, Jack D.

766.
1. *The Blue Max.* Dutton, 1964.
2. *The Blood Order.* Times Books, 1979.
3. *The Tin Cravat.* Times Books, 1981.

Bruno Stachel is a World War I ace who fled the Nazis and is now serving in the United States as a flight instructor. The O.S.S. asks him to be part of a commando team to rescue a German general who is to reveal the "Werewolf" plan, but larger more dangerous intrigues are afoot. High-ranking German officers are involved in even bigger plots.

Genre: Adventure; Espionage; War
Subjects: Spies; Secret service; World War II, 1939–1945; Adventure
Place/Time: Germany—1900–1945; United States—1900–1945

Hunter, Stephen

767.
1. *Point of Impact.* Bantam, 1993.
2. *Dirty White Boys.* Random, 1994.
3. *Black Light.* Doubleday, 1996.
4. *Time to Hunt.* Doubleday, 1998.

Bob Lee Swagger, a legendary sniper in Vietnam, is lured out of seclusion in Arkansas to help a phony intelligence agency supposedly stop an assassination of the President. Bob Lee is then shot and framed, and he races to prove his innocence. In Oklahoma in 1955, murderer Lamar Pye breaks out of prison and is followed by Sergeant. Bud Pewtie of the Oklahoma Highway Patrol. Years later Bud's son Russell Pewtie and Bob Lee Swagger are drawn together by a 40-year-old conspiracy that killed Bob Lee's father, Earl, and almost killed Russell's father, Bud. The link to all of these men is escaped convict Lamar Pye and his father. As Russell and

Bob Lee unravel the secrets surrounding these deaths, they are forced into a heart-pounding one-on-one showdown. Bob Lee must then defend his wife from a sniper and uncover whom might want her dead.

Genre: Adventure
Subjects: Adventure; Escapes; Assassination; Murder and murderers
Place/Time: Arkansas—1980–; Oklahoma—1945–1980

Huston, James W.

768.
1. *Balance of Power.* Morrow, 1998.
2. *The Price of Power.* Morrow, 1999.

When terrorists attack a United States Merchant ship in the Indonesian seas, President Edward Manchester refuses to respond with force. Jim Dillion, a legal assistant to the Speaker of the House, shows the Speaker that the Constitution allows Congress to issue a letter of marque, or hire a warship to make war for the United States. When Dillion delivers the letter to Admiral Billings, the admiral has to decide whom to obey—the President or Congress. Later Admiral Billings is court-martialed for disobeying the President's orders. The House tries to impeach the President while the President dispatches the Navy SEALS to deal with the terrorists. Dillion and girlfriend Molly work to save the admiral and the country.

Genre: Adventure
Subjects: Presidents—United States; Navy, United States; United States House of Representatives
Place/Time: Washington (D. C.)—1980–

Huysmans, Joris Karl

769.
1. *Down There.* Boni, 1924, 1891.
2. *En Route.* Kegan Paul, 1896.
3. *The Cathedral.* New Amsterdam, 1898.
4. *The Oblate.* Kegan Paul, 1924, 1903.

Autobiographical novels trace the spiritual growth of the late 18th-century Frenchman Durtal who at first has an intense interest in Satanism, then goes through a religious transformation when he lives near the cathedral of Chartres. Ultimately he lives in a monastery as part of an oblate order.

Subjects: Autobiographical stories; Religious life; Cathedrals
Place/Time: France—19th century

Hylton, Sara

770.
1. *The Chosen Ones.* St. Martin's, 1992.
2. *The Last Reunion.* St. Martin's, 1993.

Five girls from very different backgrounds meet at Lorivals, an exclusive English boarding school.

Nancy, Maisie, Barbara, Amelia, and Lois are room-mates, and their lives are changed as a result. After leaving school, their paths keep crossing with unintended calamities. Nancy follows her husband to the Middle East. Maisie goes to live on a farm. Barbara risks her comfortable life for an affair. Amelia sacrifices her real love for the sake of her children, and Lois leads a tragic life.

Genre: Historical Romance
Subjects: Friendship
Place/Time: England—1980–

Ibanez, Vicente Blasco. *See Blasco Ibanez, Vicente*

Idell, Albert Edward

771. Rogers Family
1. *Rogers' Folly.* Doubleday, 1957.
2. *Centennial Summer.* Holt, 1943.
3. *Bridge to Brooklyn.* Holt, 1944.
4. *Great Blizzard.* Holt, 1948.

From the marriage of Jesse Rogers to the lovely Italian Augustina Borelli, these stories follow the fortunes of the Rogers family through the 19th century. Jesse establishes himself seafaring off the New Jersey coast, but as the times change, moves to Philadelphia to build a railroad empire. The Rogers family moves to Manhattan at the time of the building of the Brooklyn Bridge and are caught in the blizzard of 1888.

Genre: Historical Fiction
Subjects: Family life; Business; Railroads
Place/Time: New Jersey—19th century; Philadelphia (Pa.)—19th century; New York (N. Y.)—19th century; Pennsylvania—19th century

Ing, Dean

772. Quantrill
1. *Systemic Shock.* Ace, 1981.
2. *Single Combat.* Tor, 1983.
3. *Wild Country.* Tor, 1985.

Ted Quantrill uses his wits and quick reflexes to survive as a government assassin in an America of the future, which has been conquered by an India-China coalition. In this strange chaotic society, nuclear/biological warfare has decimated urban areas with the result that Mormons and other religious groups more common in rural areas dominate the population.

Genre: Science Fiction
Subjects: Assassination; Nuclear warfare; Biological warfare; Sects

Irwin, Margaret

773.
1. *The Gay Galliard: The Love Story of Mary Queen of Scots.* Harcourt Brace, 1942.
2. *Royal Flush: The Story of Minette.* Harcourt Brace, 1932.
3. *The Proud Servant: The Story of Montrose.* Harcourt Brace, 1934.
4. *The Stranger Prince: The Story of Rupert of the Rhine.* Harcourt Brace, 1937.
5. *The Bride: The Story of Louise and Montrose.* Harcourt Brace, 1939.

The turbulent years of the Stuarts are portrayed through the various members of the dynasty. Beginning with Mary Queen of Scots and ending with Charles I, the Stuarts are revealed through the people around them. Minette, the sister of Charles II, is forced to marry the horrid, perverted brother of Louis XIV. Rupert of the Rhine, the son of Elizabeth Queen of Bohemia, shows another branch of the Stuarts and reveals the character of their cousin Charles I. More than costume dramas, Irwin's books illuminate the character of this tragic dynasty.

Genre: Historical Fiction
Subjects: Queens; Mary, Queen of Scots, 1542–1587; Kings and rulers; Courts and courtiers; Charles I, King of England, 1600–1649
Place/Time: England—16th century; England—17th century

774.
1. *Young Bess.* Harcourt Brace, 1945.
2. *Elizabeth, Captive Princess.* Harcourt Brace, 1948.
3. *Elizabeth and the Prince of Spain.* Harcourt Brace, 1953.

At the age of 12 in 1553, young Elizabeth is in a precarious position when her brother dies. She must survive the short reign of Lady Jane Grey and her half sister Mary Tudor. On Mary's death, Elizabeth is crowned queen. The fear, ferment, and turbulence of the early years of Elizabeth's reign are vividly brought to life.

Genre: Historical Fiction
Subjects: Queens; Courts and courtiers; Elizabeth I, Queen of England, 1533–1603
Place/Time: England—16th century

Iskander, Fazil

775.
1. *Sandro of Chegem.* Random House, 1983.
2. *The Gospel According to Chegem: Being the Further Adventures of Sandro of Chegem.* Vintage, 1984.

In a series of tales, Iskander tells the story of Uncle Sandro from the 1880s to the 1960s. Uncle Sandro lives in the fictional town of Chegem in the Russian province of Abkhazia beside the Black Sea. Sandro's story is also the story of the Abkhazian people with all their customs, superstitions, passions, and sufferings.

Genre: Historical Fiction
Subjects: Clans; Country life; Uncles; Ethnic groups
Place/Time: Russia—19th century; Russia—1900–1917; Soviet Union—1917–1945; Soviet Union—1945–1980; Soviet Union—1980–1991

Islas, Arturo

776.
1. *The Rain God: A Desert Tale.* Alexandrian Press, 1984.
2. *Migrant Souls.* Morrow, 1990.

Mama Chona flees the carnage of the Mexican Revolution and takes her family to the Texas border town of Del Sapo. There three generations of the family fight prejudice and try to define their place in an Anglo society. Aunt Jesus Maria tries to save the souls of the family, while rebel daughter Josie Salazar fights her relatives and Miguel Chico, a homosexual, achieves success as a writer. The Angel family lives, loves, and tries to put up with the border that divides them literally and figuratively.

Genre: Family Saga
Subjects: Hispanic Americans; Cultural conflict; Family life
Place/Time: Texas—1900–1945

Jack, Donald

777. The Journals of Bartholomew Bandy
1. *Three Cheers for Me.* Doubleday, 1973
2. *That's Me in the Middle.* Doubleday, 1973.
3. *It's Me Again.* Doubleday, 1975.
4. *Me Bandy, You Cissie.* Doubleday, 1979.
5. *Me Too.* Doubleday, 1983.
6. *This One's on Me.* Doubleday, 1988.
7. *Me So Far.* Doubleday, 1989.

Good friends have put rum in Bandy's canteen so he begins his illustrious service in World War I by arresting his colonel. Transferred to the British Royal Flying Corps, he becomes Murphy's Law incarnate, except his snafus always make him look like a hero. After the war, Bandy becomes a pilot, but when he loses the plane, he works as a porter in the hospital. In 1925, he sets up the air force for the Maharajah of Jhamjarh, but when his neighbor attacks, Bandy is the secret weapon to stop them.

Genre: Adventure; Historical Fiction; War
Subjects: World War I, 1914–1918; Soldiers; Adventure; Air pilots
Place/Time: England—1900–1945

Jackson, King T. *See* Crispin, A. C. (*Ancestor's World*)

Jacob, Naomi Ellington

778.
1. *Time Piece.* Macmillan, 1937.
2. *Fade Out.* Macmillan, 1937.

Claudia Marsden's life begins in the 19th century and ends in the 20th on her beloved family estate in Yorkshire. In between she marries twice, both times to men who suit her financial aspirations, but can't completely turn her from the romantic, but forbidden, love she feels for another man. Drawing on her experiences with affairs of the heart, she sees her glamorous actress granddaughter through a difficult relationship with a man.

Genre: Historical Romance
Subjects: Women; Marriage; Grandmothers
Place/Time: England—19th century

779. The Gollantz Saga
1. *The Founder of the House.* Macmillan, 1936.
2. *That Wild Lie.* Hutchinson, 1930.
3. *Young Emmanuel.* Hutchinson, 1932.
4. *Four Generations.* Macmillan, 1934.
5. *Private Gollantz.* Hutchinson, 1943.
6. *Gollantz.* Hutchinson, 1948.
7. *London, Paris, Milan.* Hutchinson, 1948.
8. *Gollantz and Partners.* Hutchinson, 1958.

Beginning in the early 19th century, this saga traces the history of the members of a Jewish family who become a dynasty of important dealers in art and antiques. Emmanuel Gollantz travels from Vienna to London to found his fashionable and lucrative business. His descendants expand the business to Italy, feud with each other and find that their international background creates mixed loyalties during World Wars I and II.

Genre: Family Saga; Historical Fiction
Subjects: Jews; Art dealers; Business
Place/Time: England—19th century; England—1900–1945; Italy—19th century; Italy—1900–1945

Jacob, Piers Anthony Dillingham. *See* Anthony, Piers

Jacobs, Anna

780.
1. *Salem Street.* St. Martin's, 1995.
2. *High Street.* St. Martin's, 1997.

Annie Gibson is born to poor millworkers in Bilsden, England, in 1820. The Gibsons love their young daughter and their son Tom, and work to keep them out of poverty. Annie hopes to open a dressmaker's shop, but her dream is shattered when she is raped. Junk man Barmy Charlie marries her and together they build his business. When Charlie dies, Annie and her brother keep the business going as Annie rekindles her dream and opens her shop. Two men, mill owner Frederick Hallam and old flame Danny O'Connor, come back into Annie's life, and she must also defend her honor and the store from someone who wants to destroy her.

Genre: Historical Fiction
Subjects: Women; Family life; Social classes; Brothers and sisters
Place/Time: England—19th century

Jacq, Christian

781. Ramses Series
1. *The Son of Light.* Warner, 1997.
2. *The Eternal Temple.* Warner, 1997.
3. *The Battle of Kadesh.* Warner, 1998.
4. *The Lady of Abu Simbel.* Warner, 1998.
5. *Under the Western Acacia.* Warner, 1999.

From age 14 to 50, Ramses, the greatest pharaoh of Egypt, must fight enemies within the court and outside of Egypt. At 14 Ramses is chosen by the pharaoh Seti to be his heir, but Ramses's older brother Shaanar refuses to accept the decision. Even as Ramses is being crowned, Shaanar schemes to take the crown and Ramses must prepare to fight the Hittites who threaten Egypt's borders. Ramses marries Nefertari, but then leaves to fight when the Hittites declare war on Egypt. With a small army, Ramses attacks the Hittite fortress of Kadesh and takes it. He returns home to find Nefertari dying and spies at court thwarting his moves. After Nefertari dies, he builds two temples to her memory. When Ramses's boyhood friend Moses appears, he challenges the pharaoh's power. Even after two decades of peace, Ramses and his second wife Iset are beset by troubles from the Hittites and from his two sons, who both want to rule Egypt. The old king must work miracles to save his empire before he dies.

Genre: Historical Fiction
Subjects: Kings and rulers; Courts and courtiers; Ramses II, King of Egypt, 1304–1237 B. C.
Place/Time: Egypt—14th century B. C.

Jaffe, Rona

782.
1. *Class Reunion.* Delacorte, 1979.
2. *After the Reunion.* Delacorte, 1985.

Chris, Annabel, Daphne, and Emily meet at Radcliffe in the 1950s. There they search for Mr. Right and the perfect marriage. They find their men, and at their 20th reunion, relate their loveless marriages, divorces, and affairs. As they move into the 1980s, these women find more problems as their children grow up and bring their troubles home. Even when they are older, all four women are still searching for love.

Genre: Romance
Subjects: Women; College life; Friendship; Middle age
Place/Time: New York (N. Y.)—1980–

Jagger, Brenda

783.
1. *Verity.* Doubleday, 1980.
2. *The Barforth Women.* Doubleday, 1982.

Set in Yorkshire, England, during the Victorian Era, the lovely Verity marries Joel Barforth even though she loves another. The story is told by the passionate Faith who loves one of her Barforth cousins but marries another. All of the Barforth women want to marry well, but find that love is difficult to find and keep.

Genre: Historical Romance
Subjects: Marriage; Family life
Place/Time: England—19th century

Jakes, John

784.
1. *North and South.* Harcourt Brace Jovanovich, 1982.
2. *Love and War.* Harcourt Brace Jovanovich, 1984.
3. *Heaven and Hell.* Harcourt Brace Jovanovich, 1987.

From a friendship formed at West Point in 1842, northerner George Hazard and southerner Orry Main become close friends that not even the Civil War can separate. Hazard and his family represent the industrial North, and Main the slave-holding South. When the Civil War starts, both men fight on opposite sides in battles and in politics. After the war, Charles Main, Orry's cousin, tries to escape the devastation of the war by moving to the West. Members of both families attempt to rebuild their lives and their country.

Genre: Family Saga; Historical Fiction; War
Subjects: War; United States—Civil War, 1861–1865; Family life
Place/Time: United States—19th century

785.
1. *Homeland.* Doubleday, 1993.
2. *American Dreams.* Dutton, 1998.

Young Pauli Kroner leaves Berlin in the 1890s and comes to Chicago to find his wealthy uncle, Joseph Crown. Crown has set up a brewery empire, but his family from wife Ilsa to son Joe are all involved in the labor movement and the social causes of the day. Pauli experiences the labor struggles and social conflict as he sees America change. With his cousins Fritzi and Carl, Paul sees Hollywood, the assembly lines, and the events leading up to World War I. Theodore Roosevelt, Jane Adams, W. D. Griffith, Henry Ford, and other important figures of the time cross Pauli's path as he sees his new homeland in a more realistic light.

Genre: Historical Fiction; Family Saga
Subjects: Immigrants; Industrial conditions; Wealth; Millionaires
Place/Time: United States—19th century; United States—1900–1945; Chicago (Ill.)—19th century

786. Kent Family Chronicles
1. *The Bastard.* Pyramid, 1974.
2. *The Rebels.* Pyramid, 1975.
3. *The Seekers.* Pyramid, 1975.
4. *The Furies.* Pyramid, 1976.
5. *The Titans.* Pyramid, 1976.
6. *The Warriors.* Pyramid, 1977.
7. *The Lawless.* Pyramid, 1978.
8. *The Americans.* Pyramid, 1980.

From 1750 to 1890, the members of the Kent family settle America, move west, and become involved in every major event in American history. Phillipe Charboneau, the bastard son of a French actress and a British duke, begins the saga when he goes to England to claim his birthright, but is shut out by the family. He learns printing as a trade, and goes to America to make his fortune. He marries, fights in the revolution, and sets up a publishing business. His sons Abraham and Gilbert travel to Texas and the Northwest Territory and then fight in the War of 1812. Their children fight in the Civil War, build railroads, go west, and help start unions. The family produces varied groups of characters from Indian scouts to outlaws, and from weak men to strong women. A panorama of America's growth and development is shown through the experiences of this one family.

Genre: Adventure; Family Saga; Historical Fiction; War
Subjects: Adventure; War; United States—territorial expansion
Place/Time: England—18th century; England—19th century; United States—18th century; United States—19th century

James, Henry

787.
1. *Roderick Hudson.* J. R. Osgood, 1876.
2. *The Princess Casamassima.* Macmillan, 1886.

Talented American sculptor Roderick Hudson goes to Rome to study his art, but meets femme fatale Christina Light and falls in love. She, however, demoralizes him until he commits suicide. Christina tries marriage, but separates from her husband. She becomes involved with an English radical who is picked to commit an assassination.

Subjects: Sculptors; Artists; Suicide; Revolutions and revolutionists
Place/Time: Rome (Italy)—19th century; Italy—19th century

James, John

788. Photinus the Greek
1. *Votan.* New American Library, 1967.
2. *Not for All the Gold in Ireland.* Cassell, 1968.

Photinus sets off for the barbaric northern reaches of the Roman Empire of the second century A.D. to search for amber and to flee from the results of a romantic escapade. A series of adventures, violent events, and his own unique personality result in his deification as the god Votan.

Genre: Historical Fiction
Subjects: Adventure; Travel; Rogues and vagabonds
Place/Time: Europe—2nd century

Jarman, Rosemary Hawley

789.
1. *We Speak No Treason.* Little, 1971.
2. *The King's Grey Mare.* Little, 1973.

These stories of 15th-century England during the Wars of the Roses, which ended the Plantagenet reign and brought the first Tudor, Henry VII, to the throne, portray Richard III as a complex but basically kind sovereign rather than the scheming murderer of the little princes in the Tower of London.

Genre: Historical Fiction
Subjects: Kings and rulers; Richard III, King of England, 1452–1485; England—War of the Roses, 1455–1485
Place/Time: England—15th century

Jen, Gish

790.
1. *Typical American.* Plume, 1991.
2. *Mona in the Promised Land.* Knopf, 1996.

The Chang family comes to America in the 1960s, and through hard work, they move up. They move to suburban Scarshill because of the good schools. However, when daughter Mona assimilates into the suburban community, the Changs don't know what to do. Mona decides to convert to Judaism and even ends up marrying a Jewish boy. Her bewildered parents watch these changes as their daughter comes of age.

Genre: Coming of Age
Subjects: Chinese—United States; Teenagers; Judaism
Place/Time: New York (N. Y.)—1945–1980

Jenkins, Dan

791.
1. *Semi-Tough.* Atheneum, 1972.
2. *Life Its Ownself: The Semi-Tougher Adventures of Billy Clyde.* Simon & Schuster, 1984.
3. *Rude Behavior.* Doubleday, 1998.

Billy Clyde Puckett of the New York Giants has come to Los Angeles for an epic duel with the hated New York Jets in the Super Bowl. He has also been commissioned by a New York book publisher to keep a journal of the events leading up to, including, and following the game. Billy reveals the boisterous and unexpurgated truth about pro ball. When a knee injury forces him to retire and become a TV commentator, he reunites with his old players—both teammates and foes—12 years later. Their reunion is a riotous affair. Later Billy Clyde tries to set up an NFL expansion team in the Texas wasteland between Amarillo and Lubbock.

Genre: Humor; Sports
Subjects: Football; Sports; Reunions
Place/Time: Los Angeles (Calif.)—1945–1980; California—1945–1980

Jenkins, Jerry B. *See* LaHaye, Tim

Jennings, Gary
792.
1. *Aztec.* Atheneum, 1980.
2. *Aztec Autumn.* Forge, 1997.

Two men, Mixtli, who was born a commoner, and Tenamaxtli, a young nobleman, experience the splendor and violence of Aztec culture and the encroachment of Spanish power. Mixtli rises from his lowly birth to become Montezuma's envoy to Cortez. A generation later the execution of Tenamaxtli's father by the Spanish spurs Tenamaxtli to try to thwart their domination of his country.

Genre: Historical Fiction
Subjects: Aztecs; Spain—colonies; Montezuma II, Emperor of Mexico, 1488–1520; Cortez, Hernando, 1485–1547
Place/Time: Mexico—16th century

Jensen, Johannes Vilhelm
793. The Long Journey Series
1. *Fire and Ice.* Knopf, 1923.
2. *The Cimbrians.* Knopf, 1923.
3. *Christopher Columbus.* Knopf, 1924.

The above titles have also been published in the following collection: *The Long Journey.* Knopf, 1933.

Danish author Jensen won the 1974 Nobel Prize for Literature for this epic description of the development of civilization. The stories range from the beginning of the use of fire through the Ice Age, the wanderings of northern tribes through Europe and across the sea, and culminate with Columbus's discovery of the New World.

Genre: Historical Fiction
Subjects: Stone Age; Tribes; Technology and civilization; World history
Place/Time: Europe—multicentury span

Johnson, Ellen Argo. *See* Argo, Ellen

Johnson, Oliver
794. Lightbringer Trilogy
1. *The Forging of the Shadows.* NAL, 1997.
2. *The Nations of the Night.* Roc, 1998.
3. *The Last Star at Dawn.* NAL, 1999.

Faron Gaton, high priest of Iss, God of Darkness, has plunged the city of Thrull into continuous night and is leading an army of vampires against the populace. Thalassa, the prophesied Lightbringer, assembles humans and magical beings to combat the menace, but must survive a vampire attack. The conflict climaxes in a battle between Gaton and Thalassa, who is supported by champions of Reh, the God of Light.

Genre: Fantasy
Subjects: Good and evil; Imaginary wars and battles; Gods and goddesses; Prophecies

Johnson, Pamela Hansford
795.
1. *The Good Listener.* Scribner, 1975.
2. *The Good Husband.* Scribner, 1979.

Three undergraduates meet at Cambridge University in England in 1950. Adrian renounces the flesh for God and finds he must wrestle with lust. Bob gets a girlfriend pregnant and marries her, but becomes a wife beater. Toby refuses to commit to Maisie and loses her as a result. Later Toby marries an older woman, but finds he is not over his love for Maisie.

Subjects: College life; Friendship; Love
Place/Time: England—1945–1980

796.
1. *The Unspeakable Skipton.* Harcourt, 1959.
2. *Night and Silence, Who Is There.* Scribner, 1963.
3. *Cork St. Next the Hatters.* Scribner, 1965.

Literature and academia are the targets of Pamela Hansford Johnson's wit in these stories of a failed, but persistent author, a British professor transplanted to a New Hampshire college campus, and a young playwright whose purposefully awful play becomes a roaring success.

Genre: Humor
Subjects: Authors; Teachers; College life; Dramatists
Place/Time: New Hampshire—1945–1980; England—1945–1980

797. Helena Trilogy
1. *Too Dear for My Possessing.* Carrick & Evans, 1940.
2. *Avenue of Stone.* Macmillan, 1948.
3. *A Summer to Decide.* Scribner, 1975, 1948.

Helena Pickering, cunning and deceitful, exerts a strange control over the lives of those around her. Her stepson Claud, having survived the end of a loveless marriage and the death of his only true love, joins forces with Helena. Together they conspire to destroy the marriage of Helena's daughter, Charmain, "for her sake." In the end Helena dies, and Claud and Charmain turn to each other.

Subjects: Mothers and daughters; Marriage
Place/Time: England—1900–1945

Johnston, George Henry

798. David Meredith Trilogy
1. *My Brother Jack.* Collins, 1967.
2. *Clean Straw for Nothing.* Collins, 1969.
3. *A Cartload of Clay.* Collins, 1971.

Through the life of author David Meredith, these autobiographical novels realistically portray life in early 20th-century Australia, then shift to postwar Europe. Meredith's romantic passion for his wife Cressida and his decision to become a writer are the main influences of his adult life. The third novel of the trilogy was unfinished at the author's death.

Subjects: Autobiographical stories; Authors; Love; Unfinished novels
Place/Time: Australia—1900–1945; Europe—1900–1945

Johnston, Mary

799. American Civil War Trilogy
1. *The Long Roll.* Houghton, 1911.
2. *Cease Firing.* Houghton, 1912.
3. *Michael Forth.* Harper, 1919.

Unusual in that they view the Civil War through the eyes of a woman writer with a Southern viewpoint, the first two of these novels trace the fortunes of a Confederate officer and the women he loves. The great southern general Stonewall Jackson is a central character in these stories. In the third work, a young man tells the story of his childhood on a ruined Virginia plantation during the postwar years.

Genre: Historical Fiction
Subjects: United States—Civil War, 1861–1865; Jackson, Thomas Jonathan (Stonewall), 1824–1863; Plantation life
Place/Time: Southern states—19th century; Virginia—19th century

Johnston, Terry C.

800.
1. *Cry of the Hawk.* Bantam, 1992.
2. *Winter Rain.* Bantam, 1993.
3. *Dream Catcher.* Bantam, 1994.

Confederate prisoner Jonah Hook volunteers to fight Indians in the West so that he can get out of a Union prison. When the war ends, he returns to his home in Missouri to find that his family has been abducted by a roaming band of Mormon marauders. For the next 10 years, he crisscrosses the West as he searches for his wife and children. He finally finds his daughter and one son, but must continue on until he finds his wife. Realistic details and graphic violence highlight this grim tale of search and revenge.

Genre: Historical Fiction; Western
Subjects: Adventure; Mormons and Mormonism
Place/Time: Missouri—19th century; Utah—19th century

801.
1. *Dance on the Wind.* Bantam, 1995.
2. *Buffalo Palace.* Bantam, 1996.
3. *A Crack in the Sky.* Bantam, 1997.
4. *Ride the Moon Down.* Bantam, 1998.
5. *Death Rattle.* Bantam, 1999.

Seventeen-year-old Titus Bass runs away from his father's farm in Kentucky in 1810. The itchy-footed adolescent teams up with flat boaters floating supplies down the Ohio River to New Orleans, but Titus doesn't like river life and settles down in St. Louis as a blacksmith. As time passes, Titus dreams of the West and finally leaves St. Louis to find adventure. He falls in with beaver trappers who teach him how to survive in the wilderness. When the Blackfeet attack the trappers, Titus is saved by friendly Shoshones. As he grows older, Titus finds that the beaver trade is declining, and he has to wander ever further from home to trap beaver. He fights with various Indian tribes, other trappers, and an assortment of other adversaries in his adventures.

Genre: Historical Fiction; Western
Subjects: Mountain life; Adventure; Western stories; Native Americans; Fur trade
Place/Time: Western states—19th century

802.
1. *Carry the Wind.* Caroline House, 1982.
2. *Borderlords.* Jameson Books, 1985.
3. *One Eyed Dream.* Jameson, 1988.

Young Josiah Paddock leaves St. Louis in 1833 and heads west to the mountains. There he meets his mentor and friend, Titus Bass, a trapper and mountain man. They are taken in by a friendly tribe of Crow Indians after being injured and nearly frozen to death one winter. They both fall in love with the chief's daughter and marry Indian wives. After numerous adventures, fights, and trappings, they move to Taos, New Mexico, where their Western saga continues.

Genre: Historical Fiction; Western
Subjects: Mountain life; Adventure; Western stories; Native Americans; Fur trade
Place/Time: Western states—19th century

Johnstone, William W.

803. Eagles Series
1. *Eyes of Eagles*. Zebra, 1993.
2. *Dreams of Eagles*. Zebra, 1994.
3. *Talons of Eagles*. Kensington, 1995.
4. *Scream of Eagles*. Kensington, 1996.
5. *Rage of Eagles*. Kensington, 1998.
6. *Song of Eagles*. Kensington, 1999.
7. *Cry of Eagles*. Kensington, 1999.
8. *Blood of Eagles*. Kensington, 2000.

At seven, Jamie MacCallister is kidnapped by the Shawnees and adopted by Chief Tall Bull. Tall Bull's other son Lone Wolf hates Jamie and tries to bring him down. Years later, Jamie is able to flee to Kentucky. There he falls in love with Kate Olmstead and then has to flee with her after he kills a man in self-defense. When they arrive in Texas, Jamie must fight at the Alamo where he escapes the massacre. Kate and Jamie start a ranch, but Jamie is ultimately called to fight in the Civil War. He leads MacCallister's Marauders against the Union soldiers, and fights the sadistic commander Aaron Layfield. Twelve years later, Jamie has a large family in Valley, Colorado, but when his beloved wife is killed by a gang, Jamie goes after them and vows to kill them all. As he wanders through the West, he battles lawmen, the Sioux, robbers, and of course, the gang than killed his wife.

Genre: Western
Subjects: Frontier and pioneer life; Native Americans; United States—Civil War, 1861–1865; Husbands and wives
Place/Time: Western states—19th century

Jones, Courtway

804. Dragon's Heirs
1. *In the Shadow of the Oak King*. Pocket Books, 1991.
2. *Witch of the North*. Pocket Books, 1992.

The Arthurian legend is retold as the story of King Uther and his sons in fifth-century Britain. The young Arthur is given to mastersmith Myrddin and his ward Nithe to be raised in secret. After Uther's death, Arthur becomes king and tries to ease the tensions between Britons, Gaels, Picts, Saxons, and Romans. Arthur's half-sister Morgan Le Fey is sent away after her father is killed. Schooled in the mysteries of the Great Mother, Morgan eventually goes back to her mother's people, the Gaels. When she later joins Arthur's court, she sees problems with the round table as the triangle of Arthur, Lancelot, and Guenevere begins. Ancient Britain comes alive with the fighting and feuds of the different family members and the different peoples.

Genre: Historical Fiction
Subjects: Arthur, King; Kings and rulers; Anglo-Saxons; Courts and courtiers; England—Anglo-Saxon period, 449–1066
Place/Time: England—5th century

Jones, Dennis Feltham

805. Colossus
1. *Colossus*. Putnam, 1967.
2. *The Fall of Colossus*. Putnam, 1974.
3. *Colossus and the Crab*. Berkley, 1977.

The scientist Forbin creates a giant computer that slowly begins to dominate civilization much to his horror. Computer and creator begin to understand each other before Colossus is made powerless, but an alien invasion necessitates its revival.

Genre: Science Fiction
Subjects: Computers; Extraterrestrial beings

Jones, Douglas C.

806.
1. *The Court Marshall of George Armstrong Custer*. Scribner, 1976.
2. *Arrest Sitting Bull*. Scribner, 1977.
3. *A Creek Called Wounded Knee*. Scribner, 1978.

Retired U. S. Army officer Douglas Jones imagines that, instead of being mortally wounded, George Armstrong Custer survived the Battle of Little Big Horn in 1876 and was brought to trial for his actions. Continuing his fictional accounts of the white man's confrontations with Native Americans in the West, Jones writes of the great Sioux leader Sitting Bull, who encourages the militant ghost dance movement to oppose the military and settlers. In the last volume, the tragic battle of Wounded Knee erupts in the Dakotas despite desires for peace on both sides.

Genre: Historical Fiction; War
Subjects: Custer, George Armstrong, 1839–1876; Sitting Bull, Dakota Chief, 1831–1890; Wounded Knee, battle of, 1890; Native Americans; Army, United States; Soldiers; War; Battles
Place/Time: Western states—19th century

807.
1. *Elkhorn Tavern*. Holt, Rinehart & Winston, 1980.
2. *Winding Stair*. Holt, Rinehart & Winston, 1979.
3. *Roman*. Holt, Rinehart, & Winston, 1986.
4. *Come Winter*. Holt, Rinehart & Winston, 1986.
5. *Weedy Rough*. Holt, Rinehart & Winston, 1981.

The saga of the Hasford-Pay families begins during the Civil War, when Martin Hasford goes off to war and his family must keep up the farm in Arkansas. Son Roman witnesses the Battle of Pea Ridge, while daughter Calpurnia meets and marries Allen Eben Pay. After the war, Roman sets out to see the world. He makes his fortune with the railroad in Kansas, then returns to Arkansas where he marries and sets up a bank. The murder of his old friend and Roman's revenge leave him isolated from the town. Calpurnia's son Eben Pay comes to Arkansas in the 1890s where he works with the courts at the Fort Smith Indian reservation, then witnesses the Winding Stair massacre. He comes out of retirement in the 1920s to defend his grandson from a murder charge. The history of the West is accurately and vividly seen in the saga of one family growing up with the country.

Genre: Historical Fiction; Family Saga; Western
Subjects: United States—Civil War, 1861–1865; Small town life; Bankers; Law and lawyers
Place/Time: Arkansas—19th century; Arkansas—1900–1945; Kansas—19th century; Kansas—1900–1945

808.
1. *Season of Yellow Leaf.* Holt, Rinehart & Winston, 1983.
2. *Gone the Dreams and Dancing.* Holt, Rinehart & Winston, 1984.

Ten-year-old Morfydid Parny is captured by the Comanches when the Indians massacre her Texas settlement in the 1850s. She endures endless hardships before she is adopted by Iron Sheet. She marries him and bears a son Kwahadi, but her life becomes harder as white men push the Comanche off the land and return Morfydid to the white settlements where she no longer belongs. Her son Kwahadi becomes the leader of the Comanches, but in 1875 he surrenders his tribe at Fort Sill. Only then does he search for his long-lost mother.

Genre: Historical Fiction
Subjects: Native Americans— captivities; Comanche Indians; Battles; Mothers and sons
Place/Time: Texas—19th century

809.
1. *The Search for Temperance.* Holt, 1991.
2. *A Spider for Loco Shoat.* Holt, 1997.

In 1892, ex-United States deputy marshall Oscar Schiller is called to Fort Smith, Arkansas, where he is asked to look into the murder of Temperance Moon, the mother of madam Jewel Moon. Temperance was murdered in the dangerous Indian Nation territory, but Schiller goes there anyway. Slowly, he pieces together her life and determines why she died. In 1907, when the Indian Nation is about to become Oklahoma, the people of Fort Smith are concerned about a corpse found in the river. Schiller becomes concerned when Sheriff Tapp closes the case too quickly and soon finds that the death is tied to politics and attempts to defraud the Native Americans. He puts his life on the line to find the murderer.

Genre: Historical Fiction; Western
Subjects: Crime and criminals; Sheriffs; Native Americans
Place/Time: Oklahoma—19th century; Arkansas—19th century

Jones, Ellen

810.
1. *The Fatal Crown.* Simon & Schuster, 1990.
2. *Beloved Enemy.* Simon & Schuster, 1994.

In 12th-century England, Maud, the daughter of King Henry I, and her cousin Stephen fight for the throne while they fall in love. Maud at age nine is married to the much older Holy Roman Emperor, after which she learns to read and govern. When she is called back to England, she is named heir to the throne, but Stephen battles her for it and wins. After Stephen's death, Maud's son becomes King Henry II who marries Eleanor of Aquitaine. These two have a stormy marriage but bring prosperity to the kingdom.

Genre: Historical Fiction; Historical Romance
Subjects: Kings and rulers; Queens; Courts and courtiers; Feudalism; Henry II, King of England, 1133-1189
Place/Time: England—12th century

Jones, Gwyneth

811.
1. *White Queen.* Tor, 1993.
2. *North Wind.* Tor, 1996.
3. *Phoenix Cafe.* Tor, 1998.

Starting in the near future with a love affair between a journalist and an alien, these stories spin out a tale of an alien invasion of Earth. The aliens exploit and biologically alter humanity, only leaving Earth when they discover the secret of faster-than-light travel, which they consider to be the ultimate achievement of human technology.

Genre: Science Fiction
Subjects: Extraterrestrial beings; Love affairs; Genetics; Technology and civilization; Space flight

812.
1. *Divine Endurance.* Arbor House, 1984.
2. *Flowerdust.* Tor, 1995.

In a perfect city of the distant future, which exists in the midst of a Southeast Asia ravaged by civil unrest, Divine Endurance is bored—for she is a brilliant, immortal cat who has been kept in isolation by her frightened creators. With the lovely android Chosen Among the Beautiful, Divine Endurance escapes and becomes part of a revolutionary movement led by the charismatic rebel Derveet, but threatened by the powerful hallucinogenic drug Flowerdust.

Genre: Science Fiction
Subjects: Cats; Bionics; Revolutions and revolutionists; Drug abuse

Jones, J. V. (Julie Victoria)

813. The Book of Words
1. *Baker's Boy.* Warner, 1995.
2. *A Man Betrayed.* Warner, 1996.

3. *Master and Fool.* Warner, 1996.

The evil wizard Baralis fails to realize that forcing the illiterate, humbly born Jack to copy books of sorcery will ultimately bestow occult powers on the boy. Jack flees the castle where he was raised accompanied by the young noblewoman Melliandra who is escaping marriage to the cruel Prince Kylock. Jack grows in power through a series of adventures and finally confronts Kylock in an attempt to rescue the captive Melliandra and her unborn child.

Genre: Fantasy; Coming of Age
Subjects: Magic; Imaginary kingdoms; Good and evil

Jones, James

814.
1. *From Here to Eternity.* Scribner, 1951.
2. *The Thin Red Line.* Scribner, 1962.
3. *Whistle.* Delacorte, 1978.

A gutsy and graphic picture of the military men who fought the war in the Pacific from pre–Pearl Harbor days to the end of World War II is recreated through the men of Company C. Tensions mount in the months before Pearl Harbor as the soldiers serve in Hawaii. Later they fight their way across the Pacific to Guadalcanal. After dealing with the horrors of war, wounded soldiers find that the peace of hospitals is even more unnerving.

Genre: Adventure; War
Subjects: Army, United States; World War II, 1939–1945; Battles; Soldiers; Adventure
Place/Time: Hawaii—1900–1945; Pacific Ocean—1900–1945

Jones, Ted

815.
1. *Hard Road to Gettysburg.* Presidio, 1993.
2. *The Fifth Conspiracy.* Presidio, 1995.

Samuel and Simon Ward are twin brothers who were separated at birth. Samuel is raised by his Aunt Caroline in the North, while Simon is raised in the South with their mother. When the Civil War starts, Samuel is an engineer with the Union, and Simon is an officer with the Confederacy. Samuel is unaware that he has a twin until he is sent as a spy and confronts his brother. While spying, Samuel engineers the shooting of Stonewall Jackson. At Gettysburg he almost kills Simon, but then fights to free Simon when he is put in a rebel prison where they believe he is Samuel. While in the South, Samuel hears of a conspiracy to assassinate President Lincoln, and he races north to foil the plot.

Genre: Historical Fiction
Subjects: United States—Civil War, 1861–1865; Brothers; Espionage; Army, Confederate States of America; Army, United States
Place/Time: Southern states—19th century

Jong, Erica

816.
1. *Fear of Flying.* Holt, 1973.
2. *How to Save Your Own Life.* Holt, 1977.
3. *Parachutes and Kisses.* NAL, 1984.

Isadora Wing is the modern woman testing her limits and exploring her world. In Vienna with her husband, she meets an Englishman who convinces her to throw off her marital ties. She takes off with him for two weeks of wild sex before she returns to her husband. A few years later Isadora is on the threshold of divorce and still trying to find herself. She tries a lesbian affair, gets her divorce, then has an affair with a younger man. Seven years later, she's married and a successful writer, but her third marriage also flounders.

Subjects: Feminism; Women; Marriage; Love affairs
Place/Time: Vienna (Austria)—1945–1980; Vienna (Austria)—1980–; New York (N. Y.)—1945–1980; New York (N. Y.)—1980–; Los Angeles (Calif.)—1945–1980; Los Angeles (Calif.)—1980–; Austria—1945–1980; Austria—1980–; California—1945–1980; California—1980–

Jordan, Robert

817. Wheel of Time Saga
1. *The Eye of the World.* Tor, 1990.
2. *Great Hunt.* Tor, 1990.
3. *Dragon Reborn.* Tor, 1991.
4. *Shadow Rising.* Tor, 1992.
5. *The Fires of Heaven.* Tor, 1993.
6. *Lord of Chaos.* Tor, 1994.
7. *A Crown of Swords.* Tor, 1996.
8. *Path of Daggers.* Tor, 1998.

In a magical world where time is cyclical, Rand al' Thor, a young shepherd who has the ability to channel the mysterious One Power, battles the rising forces of evil in the face of a strange prophecy that he may be the reincarnation of the Dragon, a warrior who fought for good causes but in the end went mad, killing his friends and allies.

Genre: Fantasy
Subjects: Time; Prophecies; Good and evil; Imaginary wars and battles

Joyce, James

818.
1. *A Portrait of the Artist as a Young Man.* Huebsch, 1916.
2. *Ulysses.* Egoist, 1922.

Joyce's fictional counterpart Stephen Dedalus grows up in turn-of-the-century Ireland at first rejected by his classmates, but later somewhat of a hero and ultimately convinced that he has a religious calling. Written in a stream-of-consciousness style, *Ulysses* consists of a day in the life of the adult Stephen in Dublin as he deals with the decision to turn away from a dissolute way of life.

Subjects: Boys; Degeneration; Stream of consciousness
Place/Time: Dublin (Ireland)—1900–1945; Ireland—1900–1945

Kacew, Romain. *See Gary, Romain*

Kafka, Franz

819.
   1. *The Castle.* Knopf, 1930.
   2. *The Trial.* Knopf, 1937.

Unfinished at the author's death, these works have been thought to express in highly symbolic terms the state of mind of 20th-century man. Kafka's counterpart, K., is a young man who tries in vain to gain access to the castle that overlooks the town to keep an appointment. The sense of confusion and the frustration of dealing with uncontrollable, mysterious powers continues in *The Trial*, as K. is accused of an undefined crime, told he is to be tried in a court whose law he does not understand, and finally executed.

Subjects: Unfinished novels; Power (social sciences); Justice; Symbolism; Philosophical novels

Kalman, Yvonne

820.
   1. *Mists of Heaven.* St. Martin's, 1987.
   2. *After the Rainbow.* St. Martin's, 1990.

In the 1850s in New Zealand, the Rennie and Morgan families fall in love, fight, marry others, and finally find happiness. Married Mary Rennie has an affair with neighbor Rhys Morgan, but when he leaves for the gold fields, she dies in childbirth. Daughter Lisabeth raises her half-brother Andrew, and both are taken in by the Stratfords. Rhys tries to help them and falls in love with Lisabeth, but their pride keeps them apart and married to others. Only after much travail do the two get together, but their children continue to search for love.

Genre: Historical Romance
Subjects: Family life; Love affairs
Place/Time: New Zealand—19th century

Kalogridis, Jeanne

821. The Diaries of the Family Dracul
   1. *Covenant with the Vampire.* Delacorte, 1994.
   2. *Children of the Vampire.* Delacorte, 1995.
   3. *Lord of the Vampires.* Delacorte, 1996.

The narrative line of this trilogy both precedes and incorporates the events of Bram Stoker's *Dracula*. When Arkady Tsepesh travels from England to Transylvania in 1845 after his father's death, he dis-

covers his vampire heritage. Arkady tries to escape his destiny, which is to carry out the wishes of his great uncle Vlad Count Dracula, even though his rebellion threatens the life of his son Stefan. Having given Arkady up for dead, his wife marries Dr. Jan Van Helsing in Amsterdam. From this point on, the familiar *Dracula* characters, Mina, Lucy, and Jonathan Harker, appear, but from a different perspective than in the Stoker classic.

Genre: Horror
Subjects: Vampires; Uncles; Nephews; Heredity
Place/Time: Europe—19th century

Kantor, MacKinlay

822.
   1. *The Voice of Bugle Ann.* Coward, McCann, 1935.
   2. *The Daughter of Bugle Ann.* Random House, 1953.

After the Civil War in the fox hunting country of Missouri, "Spring" Davis takes pride in his dog Bugle Ann. She is the finest hunting dog in the area, but when she is killed, Spring shoots the man who killed her. Little Lady, Bugle Ann's daughter, helps unite the son and daughter of feuding families in marriage.

Genre: Animal Story; Historical Fiction
Subjects: Dogs; Animals; Fox hunting
Place/Time: Missouri—19th century

Karon, Jan

823.
   1. *At Home in Mitford.* Lion Publishing, 1994.
   2. *A Light in the Window.* Viking, 1996.
   3. *These High, Green Hills.* Viking, 1996.
   4. *Out to Canaan.* Viking, 1997.
   5. *A New Song.* Viking, 1999.

In the small southern mountain town of Mitford, North Carolina, the citizens all know one another, and Episcopal minister Timothy Kavanagh is at the center of the town's activities. He deals with the town's benefactress Sadie Baxter, with a young boy abandoned at the rectory, with a badly beaten child, and with the birth of twins. Father Tim finds love with neighbor Cynthia, but their life together revolves around Tim's devotion to the community. Both joyous and serious events are faced with faith, humor, and humanity by all the characters as they put a very human and heartwarming face to the ordinary events of life.

Genre: Gentle Read; Christian Fiction
Subjects: Small town life; Clergy
Place/Time: North Carolina—1980–

Katz, H. W.

824.
   1. *The Fishmans.* Viking, 1938.

2. *No. 21 Castle Street.* Viking, 1980.

A family of Galician Jews migrate through Austria and Germany, fleeing persecution and dealing with domestic difficulties in the years during World War I and just preceding World War II.

Genre: Historical Fiction
Subjects: Jews; Family life; Jews, persecution of
Place/Time: Austria—1900–1945; Germany—1900–1945

Kay, Guy Gavriel

825. Fionavar Tapestry Trilogy
1. *The Summer Tree.* Arbor House, 1984.
2. *The Wandering Fire.* Arbor House, 1986.
3. *The Darkest Road.* Arbor House, 1986.

From a university lecture hall in Toronto, five young law students are magically transported to Fionavar, a land at the center of reality where a great struggle with the dark god Rakoth Maugrim the Unraveller is about to erupt. As the struggle progresses, Paul sacrifices himself on the mystical summer tree to be reborn as a god. Jennifer returns briefly to the everyday world pregnant after being raped by the Unraveller, but all eventually return to Fionavar to attempt to destroy the Unraveller's powerful Cauldron.

Genre: Fantasy
Subjects: Students; Imaginary wars and battles; Imaginary kingdoms; Good and evil

826. The Sarantine Mosaic
1. *Sailing to Sarantium.* HarperPrism, 1999.
2. *Lord of Emperors.* HarperCollins, 2000.

Caius Crispus of Varena journeys to the Holy City of Sarantium to adorn the dome of the temple built by Emperor Valerius II with mosaics. Caius risks his life by carrying a message from his young Queen Gisel, who soon comes to Sarantium as an exile. On his way, he encounters mystical birds, an enslaved prostitute, and a pagan god. In Sarantium, even though he aspires to the solitary, artistic life, he becomes involved in Valerius's plans to control Varena.

Genre: Fantasy
Subjects: Artists, Voyages and travels; Kings and rulers; International intrigue

Kaye, Marvin *and* Godwin, Parke

827. Masters of Solitude
1. *Masters of Solitude.* Doubleday, 1978.
2. *Wintermind.* Doubleday, 1982.

A future America has become a society split between the coveners, a group of mystical forest dwellers, and the inhabitants of the highly technological City, which protects itself with a gate that disrupts the mental processes of attackers. Singer, the child of a coven member and woman who fled the City, attempts to find the

Girdle of Solitude that will enable him to enter the City and bring the civilization together.

Genre: Fantasy
Subjects: Mysticism; Forests and forestry; Technology and civilization; Children

Kazan, Elia

828.
1. *America, America.* Stein & Day, 1962.
2. *The Anatolian.* Knopf, 1982.
3. *Beyond the Aegean.* Stein & Day, 1994.

At the turn of the century, Stavros Topouzoglou, a young Greek from Anatolia, is supposed to go to Constantinople to learn the rug business. When he loses the money his family gave him, he works for money to secure his passage to America. There he saves to bring his seven brothers and sisters to America, but his father's death forces him to become head of the family as he struggles for wealth and acceptance. In 1919, he returns to Greece to help reclaim Anatolia from the Turks.

Genre: Historical Fiction
Subjects: Immigrants; Family life; Poverty; Teenagers
Place/Time: Anatolia (Turkey)—1900–1945; United States—1900–1945; Greece—1900–1945; Turkey—1900–1945

Kelland, Clarence Budington

829.
1. *Hard Money.* Harper, 1930.
2. *Gold.* Harper, 1931.
3. *The Jealous House.* Harper, 1934.

From 1800 to 1900, the van Horn family establishes a banking and social dynasty in New York. Dutch peddler Jan van Horn comes to the city to learn banking and becomes so successful that he dominates the financial scene until his death in 1845. His daughter Anneke takes over the bank to the surprise of her male cohorts. She succeeds in the financial world, but not in her personal affairs. It is her nephew Jan who is finally able to lead the bank and dominate the social circles of New York.

Genre: Family Saga; Historical Fiction
Subjects: Bankers; Businesswomen; Social classes
Place/Time: New York (N. Y.)—19th century

Kellogg, M. Bradley

830. Dragon Quartet
1. *The Book of Earth.* DAW Books, 1995.
2. *The Book of Water.* DAW Books, 1997.

Fleeing from an evil priest who wants to burn her as a witch, Erde von Alt escapes from her mountain realm and comes face to face with Earth, one of the four dragons created from pure energy to set the world in motion. They travel across 10th-century Germany always just ahead of the priest. The magical call of the dragon Water summons them to 21st-century Africa where they must use all of their magic skills to oppose the forces arrayed against them.

Genre: Fantasy
Subjects: Dragons; Escapes; Good and evil; Time travel
Place/Time: Germany—10th century; Africa—1980–

Kelly, Clint

831. In the Shadow of the Mountain
1. *Deliver Us from Evil.* Bethany House, 1998.
2. *The Power and the Glory.* Bethany House, 1998.

In 1918, the Turkish government ordered the massacre of the Armenian people. Tatul Sarafin escapes the massacre and flees to the mountains to join Armenian revolutionaries. Adrine Tevian is a prisoner in a Turkish military camp and in love with Tatul. Helping these two is Leslie Davis, a United States diplomat, who is hiding Armenian refugees. As the war concludes, Tatul and Adrine are able to escape to Istanbul, where they try to gather the remnants of their people together and fight for their homeland.

Genre: Christian Fiction
Subjects: Armenians; Ethnic relations; Massacres; Persecution; Faith; War
Place/Time: Turkey—1900–1945

Kelton, Elmer

832.
1. *The Good Old Boys.* Doubleday, 1978.
2. *The Smiling Country.* Tor, 1998.

Middle-aged cowboy Hewey Calloway finds that the open range life he loves is slowly coming to an end in 1910 Texas. He has school teacher Spring Renfro waiting for him to settle down, but Hewey just can't seem to do it. He ends up at the Circle W ranch busting broncos. His young nephew Tommy comes to the ranch looking for work. Hewey teaches him cowpunching and then meets his lost love Spring Renfro again. When he is injured in a bronc-riding accident, he goes back to Tommy's parents to recuperate. He also finds Spring more receptive, but he still has a hard time giving up the open range.

Genre: Historical Fiction
Subjects: Cowboys; Ranch life
Place/Time: Texas—1900–1945

833.
1. *Slaughter.* Doubleday, 1992.
2. *The Far Canyon.* Doubleday, 1994.

When Englishman Nigel Smithwick is thrown from a train in Kansas for being a card shark, he meets Jeff Layne, a former Confederate soldier. The two team up as buffalo hunters and work for the army slaughtering buffalo. When the Comanches hear the rumors that the white man is killing their source of food, they send Crow Feather to discover the truth. Eventually the army and the Comanches battle, and the Indians lose and are forced onto a reservation. Ten years later, Jeff is tired of the battles with Indians and the killing of buffalo. He returns to Texas, but discovers his ranch has been stolen by Vesper Freed. Jeff eventually goes to north Texas to start over and there meets Crow Feather, who also wants to start again.

Genre: Adventure; Western
Subjects: Bison; Comanche Indians; Native Americans
Place/Time: Kansas—19th century; Texas—19th century

Kennealy-Morrison, Patricia

834. Keltiad Series
1. *Silver Branch.* NAL, 1988.
2. *The Copper Crown.* Bluejay Books, 1984.
3. *The Throne of Scone.* Bluejay Books, 1986.
4. *The Hawk's Gray Feather.* Roc, 1991.
5. *The Oak Above the Kings.* Roc, 1994.
6. *The Hedge of Mist.* HarperPrism, 1996.
7. *Blackmantle.* HarperPrism, 1997.
8. *The Deer's Cry.* HarperPrism, 1998.

Keltia is a mighty space empire hidden behind a magic curtain wall, but it has enemies who want to destroy it. Aeron Aoibhell is the heir to the throne and must use her powers of prophecy and sorcery to save the kingdom. When a ship arrives from Earth where the Keltians originally came from, Queen Aeron must decide whether to lift the curtain and let the ship enter, leaving her world vulnerable to an attack. When her forces are defeated, Aeron must retrace the path of King Arthur to find a legacy buried for 15 centuries that can save Keltia. The subsequent tales incorporate elements of the Arthurian legend in the efforts to free Keltia.

Genre: Science Fiction
Subjects: Interplanetary wars; Life on other planets; Time travel; Arthur, King

Kennedy, Adam

835.
1. *The Domino Principle.* Viking, 1975.
2. *The Domino Vendetta.* Beaufort Books, 1984.

When Ray Tucker, in prison for a murder conviction, is "allowed" to escape, he soon realizes that there is a cost involved. In exchange for his freedom, Tucker becomes involved in a dangerous assassination conspiracy. As he flees from Chicago to New York to Costa Rica, he must fight to save his life.

Genre: Adventure; Espionage
Subjects: Escapes; Assassination; International intrigue; Adventure

Place/Time: Los Angeles (Calif.)—1945–1980; Chicago (Ill.)—1945–1980; New York (N. Y.)—1945–1980; Costa Rica—1945–1980; California—1945–1980; Illinois—1945–1980

Kennedy, Margaret

836. The Sanger Family
1. *The Constant Nymph.* Doubleday, 1925.
2. *The Fool of the Family.* Doubleday, 1930.

When the brilliant, eccentric musician Albert Sanger dies, his children, who have rambled around early 20th-century Europe with him, must end their nomadic, bohemian ways. One daughter, Tess, becomes the ward of her father's friend Lewis Dodd, but their relationship soon turns into a doomed love affair. Romance is no easier for Tess's honest, responsible brother Caryl, who nearly loses his true love to his dashing half-brother Sebastian.

Subjects: Family life; Bohemianism; Brothers and sisters
Place/Time: Europe—1900–1945

Kennedy, William

837. Albany Cycle
1. *Legs.* Coward, McCann, & Geoghegan, 1975.
2. *Billy Phelan's Greatest Game.* Viking Press, 1978.
3. *Ironweed.* Viking, 1983.
4. *Quinn's Book.* Viking, 1983.
5. *Very Old Bones.* Viking, 1992.
6. *The Flaming Corsage.* Viking, 1986.

Albany, New York, from 1864 to 1980 is the setting for these powerful novels, which explore the dark nature of the human heart and the impact of grief and need on families. Kennedy's tragic Irish couples each have to deal with deaths, betrayals, and troubled marriages, but it is the Phelan family whose struggles dominate this series. The story of the dysfunctional Phelan clan from 1900 to 1950 is told through its erring members: Francis Phelan, the ex-ballplayer now hobo, who accidentally killed his baby son; Billy Phelan, the petty gangster son of Francis; and Orson Purcell, bastard nephew of Francis. These marginal men struggle with their troubled pasts, but can never overcome the ghosts that haunt them. *Ironweed* won both the Pulitzer Prize and the National Book Award.

Genre: Historical Fiction
Subjects: Family life; Poverty; Homelessness; Marriage problems
Place/Time: Albany (N. Y.)—1900–1945; New York (state)—1900–1945

Kennelly, Ardyth

838.
1. *The Peaceable Kingdom.* Houghton, 1949.
2. *Up Home.* Houghton, 1955.

Linnea Ecklund is the second wife of Mormon Olaf Ecklund in the 1890s, just after Brigham Young's death. Linnea and her five children envy Sigrid, Olaf's first wife, but Linnea struggles with the concept of plural marriage. When she finally gets her own home, she and her neighbors prepare for the opening of the Mormon temple and deal with the abolition of polygamy.

Genre: Historical Fiction
Subjects: Mormons and Mormonism; Marriage; Husbands and wives
Place/Time: Utah—19th century

Kent, Alexander. *Pseud.* of Douglas Reeman. *See also* Reeman, Douglas

839.
1. *Richard Bolitho—Midshipman.* Putnam, 1976.
2. *Midshipman Bolitho and the Avenger.* Putnam, 1978.
3. *Stand into Danger.* Putnam, 1981.
4. *In Gallant Company.* Putnam, 1977.
5. *Sloop of War.* Putnam, 1972.
6. *To Glory We Steer.* Putnam, 1968.
7. *Command a King's Ship.* Putnam, 1974.
8. *Passage to Mutiny.* Putnam, 1976.
9. *With All Despatch.* Putnam, 1989.
10. *Form Line of Battle.* Putnam, 1969.
11. *Enemy in Sight.* Putnam, 1970.
12. *The Flag Captain.* Putnam, 1971.
13. *Signal—Close Action!* Putnam, 1974.
14. *The Inshore Squadron.* Putnam, 1979.
15. *A Tradition of Victory.* Putnam, 1982.
16. *Success to the Brave.* Putnam, 1983.
17. *Colors Aloft.* Putnam, 1986.
18. *Honor This Day.* Putnam, 1988.
19. *The Only Victor.* McBooks, 2000, 1990.
20. *Beyond the Reef.* Heinemann, 1992.
21. *Darkening Sea.* Heinemann, 1993.
22. *For My Country's Freedom.* Heinemann, 1995.
23. *Cross of St. George.* Heinemann, 1996.

The above four titles have been published only in England.

Sixteen-year-old Richard Bolitho enters the Royal Navy in 1772 as a midshipman and proceeds to have numerous swashbuckling adventures both aboard ship and on land as he defends England's honor and safety against her enemies. His adventures begin in Africa, where he investigates the slave trade, then take him to the Caribbean to fight pirates, and then to America for the revolt of the colonies. After this, he spends the rest of his life fighting Napoleon and the French in the Mediterranean, the Atlantic, and the Caribbean. In between battles, he falls in love, marries, loses a wife, and then remarries.

Genre: Historical Fiction; Naval Adventure; War
Subjects: Navy, British—officers; Seamen; Naval battles; Napoleonic Wars, 1800–1814; War

Place/Time: Africa—18th century; Caribbean region—19th century; Atlantic Ocean—19th century

Kent, Louise Andrews

840.
1. *Mrs. Appleyard's Year.* Houghton, 1941.
2. *With Kitchen Privileges.* Houghton, 1953.

New Englander Mrs. Appleyard deals with her grown children with wit and charm. As a widow, she rents the upper story of her Vermont home to young, impoverished, usually expectant couples with rewarding results—with one exception.

Genre: Gentle Read
Subjects: Widows; Mothers
Place/Time: Vermont—1900–1945

Kerr, Katharine

841. Deverry Series
1. *Daggerspell.* Doubleday, 1986.
2. *Darkspell.* Doubleday, 1987.
3. *The Bristling Wood.* Doubleday, 1989.
4. *The Dragon Revenant.* Doubleday, 1990.
5. *A Time of Exile: A Novel of the Westlands.* Doubleday, 1991.
6. *A Time of Omens: A Novel of the Westlands.* Bantam, 1992.
7. *Days of Blood and Fire.* Bantam, 1993.
8. *Days of Air and Darkness.* Bantam, 1994.
9. *The Red Wyvern.* Bantam, 1997.
10. *The Black Raven.* Bantam, 1999.

The Sorcerer Nevyn must spend eternity atoning for causing the deaths of lovers while he was mortal. In the magical kingdom of Deverry he is engaged in a continuing battle with the forces of evil embodied in the Dark Council. The half-elfin Prince Rhodry and his beloved Jill join in the battle that lasts through centuries and repeated incarnations.

Genre: Fantasy
Subjects: Magicians; Atonement; Good and evil; Imaginary kingdoms; Lovers

Kerr, Robert

842.
1. *The Stuart Legacy.* Stein & Day, 1973.
2. *The Black Pearls.* Stein & Day, 1975.
3. *The Dark Lady.* Stein & Day, 1976.

Jamie Stuart, handsome and dashing, is surrounded by intrigue, danger, romance, and royalty in Elizabethan England. When he is accused of murder, he must flee England for Copenhagen. As he tries to clear his name, he is attacked by the Spanish. His dangerous exploits are interspersed with a series of love affairs.

Genre: Adventure; Historical Fiction
Subjects: Courts and courtiers; Adventure

Place/Time: England—16th century

Kersh, Gerald

843.
1. *Night and the City.* Simon & Schuster, 1946.
2. *Song of the Flea.* Doubleday, 1948.

Through the underworld of London of the period before World War II moves Harry Fabian, who patterns himself after characters in American gangster movies. Fabian continues in a supporting role in the tale of destitute writer Pym and his dealings with pawnbrokers and other unsavory characters.

Genre: Crime Novel
Subjects: Underworld; Crime and criminals
Place/Time: London (England)—1900–1945; England—1900–1945

Kettle, Jocelyn

844.
1. *The Athelsons.* Putnam, 1972.
2. *A Gift of Onyx.* Putnam, 1974.

According to village legend, the House of Athel had been founded by a Viking who came to plunder England and stayed to love the land. This love and loyalty persisted as a family trait, forcing both Eugenie in the 18th century and Justine and Athel in the 20th to make heartrending decisions.

Genre: Family Saga; Historical Fiction
Subjects: Houses; Country life
Place/Time: England—multicentury span

Keyes, Frances Parkinson

845.
1. *Blue Camellia.* Messner, 1957.
2. *Victorine.* Messner, 1958.

In the 1880s, Brent Wislow is lured to Cajun country in Louisiana by ads for cheap land. He and his family set up a home there as he tries to grow rice. His daughter Lavinia grows up and marries in the area. Her son Prosper is involved in a murder in the rice plant he manages.

Genre: Family Saga; Historical Romance
Subjects: Farm life
Place/Time: Louisiana—19th century

Keyes, Greg

846. The Age of Unreason
1. *Newton's Cannon.* Ballantine, 1998.
2. *A Calculus of Angels.* Ballantine, 1999.

Sir Isaac Newton and his apprentice Benjamin Franklin are the dominant historical figures in these works of alternate history. Newton has turned his attention to alchemy and his work has unleashed Philosopher's Mercury, a primary source of matter that is capable of manipulating the elements. Newton and Franklin journey to Prague to delve into the secrets of the dark beings who have wrought devastation by drawing an asteroid to Earth.

Genre: Fantasy; Historical Fiction
Subjects: Newton, Isaac, Sir, 1642–1727; Franklin, Benjamin, 1706–1790; Experiments, scientific; Scientists
Place/Time: Europe—18th century

847. Chosen of the Changeling
1. *The Waterborn.* Ballantine, 1996.
2. *The Blackgod.* Ballantine, 1997.

In Nho, the imperial city of a land ruled by the River God, Princess Hezhi discovers her own mystical powers and the sinister link of her destiny to the River when she sets off to search for a beloved cousin who has disappeared. She goes into hiding to escape the power of the River, but is pursued by the undead creature Ghe, who in life had loved her. Her disappearance sets off a power struggle in the priesthood of a land complicated by violent tribal conflicts.

Genre: Fantasy
Subjects: Gods and goddesses; Princesses; Imaginary kingdoms; Rivers

Keyes, J. Gregory. *See Keyes, Greg*

Kim, Richard E.

848.
1. *The Martyred.* Braziller, 1964.
2. *The Innocent.* Houghton, 1968.

The upheavals in Korea of the 1950s are seen through the eyes of Korean officer Lee. First Lee interviews a minister who had been arrested by the Communists and who had saved himself by betraying his fellow prisoners. In the second volume, Lee must oppose a former friend and fellow officer when he attempts a bloodless coup.

Genre: Historical Fiction; War
Subjects: War; Korean War, 1950–1980; Soldiers; Communism
Place/Time: Korea—1945–1980

Kimbriel, Katharine Eliska

849.
1. *Night Calls.* HarperPrism, 1996.
2. *Kindred Rites.* HarperPrism, 1997.

Allie Sorenson and her family come to the New World and settle as pioneers in the Midwest, but soon find out that some of the malevolent magical creatures of the Old World are here too. Allie discovers that she has The Gift and studies with midwife and magician Marta, but is kidnapped by the evil spirit called Keeper and comes face to face with Death himself.

Genre: Fantasy; Coming of Age
Subjects: Girls; Frontier and pioneer life; Magic; Kidnapping; Death
Place/Time: Midwestern states—19th century

King, Bernard

850.
1. *Starkadder.* St. Martin's, 1985.
2. *Vargr-Moon.* St. Martin's, 1988.

In the Dark Ages when the Norse gods ruled Sweden, young Hather Lambisson seeks revenge on Starkadder, Sweden's greatest hero. Starkadder must commit three betrayals before he can die. When Hather kills Starkadder, freeing Sweden and becoming its new hero, but as a hero, he must fight the evil sorcery of Vargr. Only after his village is destroyed and his son kidnapped does Hather confront Vargr in a fight to the death.

Genre: Fantasy
Subjects: Mythology; Heroes; Witchcraft
Place/Time: Sweden

King, Gabriel

851.
1. *The Wild Road.* Ballantine, 1998.
2. *The Golden Cat.* Ballantine, 1999.

Driven by strange dreams, the young cat Tag leaves his home and sets out on the Wild Road, a magical path for animals through space and time. Tag's goal is to find the King and Queen of Cats, but he is opposed by the evil Alchemist. Having defeated Alchemist, Tag becomes the Majicou, the protector of the feline monarchs, but must set out again when two of the Queen's kittens are abducted.

Genre: Fantasy
Subjects: Cats; Voyages and travels; Good and evil; Kidnapping

King, Stephen

852. The Dark Tower
1. *The Gunslinger.* Donald M. Grant, 1982.
2. *The Drawing of the Three.* Donald M. Grant, 1987.
3. *The Waste Lands.* Plume, 1992.
4. *Wizard and Glass.* Plume, 1997.

Based on Robert Browning's epic poem "Childe Roland to the Dark Tower Came," Stephen King wrote this fantasy in which he created an alternate world. Roland, the last gunslinger, moves through a postapocalyptic world looking for the Dark Tower linchpin that holds all existence together. With him on the search are Susannah Dean, Eddie Dean, and Jake Chambers, each from an alternate New York City. King's lengthy epic fantasy uses time travel, magic, Arthurian legends, and horror to tell a very atypical quest tale.

Genre: Fantasy
Subjects: Time travel; Legends and folk tales; Magic

King, Tabitha

853.
1. *Caretakers.* Macmillan, 1983.
2. *Pearl.* NAL, 1988.
3. *One on One.* Dutton, 1993.
4. *The Book of Reuben.* Dutton, 1994.

The people of Nodd's Ridge, Maine, interact, work, and love as they reveal small town life. An older woman has a curious relationship with her handyman until they die. African American Pearl comes back to the town to bury her grandmother and then finds she likes the town. Eventually she falls in love with Reuben Styles, who has gone through a long divorce and custody battle. Reuben's teenage son Sam is a basketball star and falls for Deanie Gauthier, the captain of the girls' basketball team. He helps her win the championship and protect herself from her mom's abusive boyfriend. The sights and smells of small town life are movingly portrayed.

Subjects: Small town life; Teenagers
Place/Time: Maine—1980–

Kingsolver, Barbara

854.
1. *The Bean Trees.* Harper & Row, 1988.
2. *Pigs in Heaven.* HarperCollins, 1993.

Marietta Greer is determined to leave poverty-stricken Pittman County, Kentucky. In a beat-up '55 Volkswagen, she heads west to find adventure. She changes her name to Taylor and adopts an abused Cherokee child when the child is left in her car. Taylor and Turtle end up in Tucson where Taylor learns love, responsibility, and independence, but their happy life is discovered by an Indian lawyer who wants Turtle to return to her people. Taylor's mother Alice comes to their aid in this funny, moving, and lyrical look at family and culture.

Genre: Humor
Subjects: Family life; Orphans; Native Americans
Place/Time: Kentucky—1945–1980; Tucson (Ariz.)—1945–1980; Arizona—1945–1980

Kirst, Hans

855.
1. *The Revolt of Gunner Asch.* Little, Brown, 1955.
2. *Forward, Gunner Asch!* Little, Brown, 1956.
3. *The Return of Gunner Asch.* Little, Brown, 1957.
4. *What Became of Gunner Asch?* Harper & Row, 1964.

In a garrison town in Germany before World War II, Gunner Asch, a young recruit, refuses to be bullied by his superiors. Once the war breaks out, he is sent to the Russian front where the only things he can think about are food and self-preservation. As the Allies advance, his units disintegrate, and he tries to stay alive. After the war, he becomes a hotel owner and mayor of the town, but his problems don't end as he is caught in the rivalry between a Luftwaffe unit and an army regiment. Gunner's adventures are described in a satiric, racy, funny, but realistic manner.

Genre: Humor; War
Subjects: Soldiers; Army, German; World War II, 1939–1945; Mayors
Place/Time: Germany—1900–1945; Germany—1945–1980; Soviet Union—1917–1945; Soviet Union—1945–1980; Soviet Union—1980–1991

Kita, Morio. *Pseud. of* Saito Sukichi

856.
1. *The House of Nire.* Kodansha, 1984.
2. *The Fall of the House of Nire.* Kodansha, 1985.

The rise and fall of the Nire family of Japan from World War I to World War II is told through the family's founder, Kiichiro Nire, and his children. Kiichiro is the founder of a mental hospital that employs his entire family. In the 1920s during Japan's democratic years, the family flourishes, but as the military takes power, the family begins to fall apart. After Kiichiro's death and Japan's defeat, Director Tetsukichi runs the hospital ineptly. The family is scattered by the war and faces hardships. The Nire hospital mirrors Japanese society and problems.

Genre: Historical Fiction
Subjects: Family life; Mental illness, care and treatment of; Social problems
Place/Time: Japan—1900–1945

Klinkowitz, Jerry

857.
1. *Short Season and Other Stories.* Johns Hopkins, 1988.
2. *Basepaths.* Johns Hopkins, 1995.

In Iowa, a minor league class-A baseball team struggles to play the game and stay afloat financially. Ken Boyenga is in his first year as manager of the team, and he finds he has trouble with Michael Jacobs, a team director. Jacobs's schemes result in the players on the team being arrested. Boyenga has to teach his team to hit and even to speak English on the field. A dizzy array of characters keep the pace frantic and the antics funny.

Genre: Sports
Subjects: Baseball
Place/Time: Iowa—1980–

Koen, Karleen

858.
1. *Through a Glass Darkly.* Random House, 1986.
2. *Now Face to Face.* Random, 1995.

At 15, Barbara Alderley is bartered into marriage with a middle-aged lord by her mother Diana. Diana wants the fortune of Lord Montgeoffry, but Barbara finds her husband wants her only for her dowry. When her husband dies, Barbara settles in Virginia and tries to build a plantation, but she is appalled at the treatment of the slaves. She frees her slaves and takes numerous lovers as she becomes an independent and free-thinking woman.

Genre: Historical Romance
Subjects: Love; Women; Aristocracy—England; Plantation life
Place/Time: England—18th century; Virginia—18th century

Koestler, Arthur

859.
1. *The Gladiators.* Macmillan, 1939.
2. *Darkness at Noon.* Macmillan, 1941.
3. *Arrival and Departure.* Macmillan, 1943.

Koestler's trilogy on revolution was intended to define what he felt were opposite approaches to political upheavals: the philosophical, idealistic revolutionary spirit as opposed to the pragmatic attitude of those who feel that the end justifies the means. The backgrounds and time periods of the series are widely separated. The first is set against the slave revolt led by Spartacus in Rome of the first century B.C., the second in the time of the Russian Revolution, and the third the Moscow Purge Trials of the 1930s and the beginning of World War II.

Genre: Historical Fiction
Subjects: Revolutions and revolutionists; Psychological novels; Soviet Union—revolution, 1917–1921; Slavery
Place/Time: Italy—multicentury span; Russia—multicentury span

Koontz, Dean

860.
1. *Fear Nothing.* Bantam, 1998.
2. *Seize the Night.* Bantam, 1999.

Chris Snow sees his hometown, Moonlight Bay, on the California coast only by night because of a genetic problem that makes sunlight toxic to his skin, but his physical problem does not keep him from investigating a series of mysterious events. Snow's parents have died two years apart, his father's body has vanished, and the woman who nursed his father has been murdered. Chris observes unusual intelligence in his dog Orson and in other animals in the area. His discoveries lead him to laboratories on a local military base where he uncovers far-reaching experiments concerned with the parallel time-travel/disruption.

Genre: Horror; Science Fiction
Subjects: Handicapped people; Genetics; Experiments, scientific; Time travel
Place/Time: California—1980–

Kraft, Eric

861.
1. *Little Follies: The Personal History, Adventures, Experiences and Observations of Peter Leroy (So Far).* Crown, 1992.
2. *Where Do You Stop? The Personal History, Adventures, Experiences and Observations of Peter Leroy Continued.* Crown, 1992.
3. *What a Piece of Work I Am.* Crown, 1994.

A series of interconnected short stories that are gathered together in book form for the first time tell the story of Peter Leroy, a young boy growing up in 1950 Babbington, New York. As an adult, Leroy relates his childhood with his parents, grandparents, and friends in a comic, deadpan manner even as he explains he is taking great liberties with the truth. Small town life and childhood's adventures make up these whimsical tales.

Genre: Coming of Age; Humor
Subjects: Boys; Family life; Small town life
Place/Time: New York (N. Y.)—1945–1980

Krantz, Judith

862.
1. *Scruples.* Crown, 1978.
2. *Scruples Two.* Crown, 1992.
3. *Lovers.* Crown, 1994.

Billy Winthrop is a poor, overweight Bostonian until she goes to Paris and becomes glamorous. When she comes home, she snags a multimillionaire husband and his famous fashion boutique, Scruples. After Ikehorn's death, Billy marries a film producer, takes care of his daughter, and opens new branches of Scruples. Along the way Billy lives in fabulous houses, eats in the best restaurants, wears knockout clothes, and has steamy sex, but learns that happiness is not always the outcome of living the lifestyle of the rich and famous.

Genre: Romance
Subjects: Businesswomen; Wealth; Society novels
Place/Time: Boston (Mass.)—1945–1980; Paris (France)—1945–1980; Massachusetts—1945–1980; France—1945–1980

Kraus, Jim

863. Treasures of the Caribbean
1. *Pirates of the Heart.* Tyndale House, 1996.
2. *Passages of Gold.* Tyndale House, 1997.

3. *Journey to the Crimson Sea.* Tyndale House, 1997.

In 17th-century Devonshire, Lady Kathryne Spenser is a devout young woman who goes with her father to Barbados when he is named governor of the colony. William Hawkes, also of Devonshire, is a poor boy who goes to sea and eventually becomes a privateer. In Barbados, he meets Kathryne and falls in love. Eventually he gives up the sea and settles down with her. Their close friend Vicar Thomas Mayhew moves to the Bridgetown community where he falls in love with an ex-prostitute. Thomas is forced to decide between the woman he loves and the church. Finally, both Thomas and William are forced to fight pirates.

Genre: Christian Fiction
Subjects: Faith; Seamen; Love
Place/Time: Barbados—18th century

Krentz, Jayne Ann. *See Castle, Jayne*

Kress, Nancy
864.
1. *Beggars in Spain.* William Morrow, 1993.
2. *Beggars & Choosers.* Tor, 1994.
3. *Beggars Ride.* Tor, 1996.

In America of the 21st century, genetic engineering has produced a generation of superior humans called the Sleepless who, in addition to having other advanced biological traits, are able to live without sleep. Meanwhile, a lower class is developing in American society that is incapable of work and must live on public aid. A group of Sleepless and their still more talented offspring try to isolate themselves, while Leisha Camden, one of the first sleepless to be born, attempts to unite the various elements in an increasingly polarized culture.

Genre: Science Fiction
Subjects: Genetics; Genius; Cultural conflict

865. Robert Cavanaugh
1. *Oaths and Miracles.* Forge, 1996.
2. *Stinger.* Forge, 1998.

FBI agent Robert Cavanaugh investigates murders that seem to be connected to a biotechnical firm called Verico, which has been conducting experiments with a deadly airborne virus that is definitely of interest to the company's mob associates. Next, Cavanaugh tries to uncover the source of a malaria outbreak that only affects African Americans who have the sickle cell trait.

Genre: Crime Novel
Subjects: United States Federal Bureau of Investigation; Gangsters; Diseases; Murder and murderers; African Americans
Place/Time: United States—1980–

Kristof, Agota
866.
1. *The Notebook.* Grove Weidenfeld, 1988, 1986.
2. *The Proof.* Grove Weidenfeld, 1991, 1989.
3. *The Third Lie.* Grove/Atlantic, 1996.

In this fable about the horrors of war and communism, twin brothers Lucas and Claus are in an unnamed Eastern European country with their mother and grandmother during World War II. They see their friends taken off to concentration camps. The twins survive by stealth and stealing. After the communist invasion, Claus flees the country while Lucas remains to witness the horrors of life under this repressive regime. These experimental novels are powerful works that deal with the themes of sexual aberration, incest, murder, and cruelty.

Subjects: Allegories; War; World War II, 1939–1945; Communism
Place/Time: Europe—1900–1945

Kube-McDowell, Michael P.
867. The Trigon Disunity
1. *Emprise.* Berkley, 1985.
2. *Enigma.* Berkley, 1986.
3. *Empery.* Berkley, 1987.

Starting in the near future and spanning 1,000 years into the far future, this trilogy tells of the discovery that Earth had produced a highly technological civilization 70,000 years ago that spread out to other planets. A powerful alien race, the Mizarians, had destroyed this culture and is about to return to strike again.

Genre: Science Fiction
Subjects: Civilization, ancient; Space colonies; Extraterrestrial beings; Technology and civilization

Kuczkin, Mary. *See Michaels, Fern*

Kuniczak, W. S.
868.
1. *The Thousand Hour Day.* Dial Press, 1967.
2. *The March.* Doubleday, 1979.
3. *Valedictory.* Doubleday, 1983.

Poland's valiant fight against the Nazi onslaught begins in 1939 when the small ill-equipped Polish army makes an attempt to stop the German invaders. The Nazis then dispatch some 2,000,000 eastern Poles to prisons and labor camps. Polish Jews are sent to concentration camps, but many try to fight back. Other Poles flee to England and set up the 303rd fighter squadron of the RAF, which shoots down 1500 German planes.

Genre: Historical Fiction; War

Subjects: World War II, 1939–1945; Army, Polish; Holocaust, Jewish, 1933–1945; National Socialism
Place/Time: Poland—1900–1945

Kurten, Bjorn

869.
1. *Dance of the Tiger.* Pantheon, 1980.
2. *Singletusk.* Pantheon, 1986.

In the prehistoric Ice Age of 35,000 years ago, Homo sapien Tiger is the son of a chief in a peaceful hunting village. When his tribe is wiped out by another warrior tribe, Tiger searches for their killers. After being injured by a saber-toothed tiger, he is taken in by a Neanderthal tribe, where he falls in love with Veyde, the chief's daughter. Their children Whitespear and Avens have different adventures as paleontologist Kurten describes the newly emergent Homo sapiens and speculates on the demise of the Neanderthal.

Genre: Historical Fiction
Subjects: Stone Age; Man, prehistoric; Tribes
Place/Time: Europe—prehistoric times

Kurtz, Katherine

870. The Chronicles of Deryni
1. *Deryni Rising.* Ballantine, 1970.
2. *Deryni Checkmate.* Ballantine, 1972.
3. *High Deryni.* Ballantine, 1973.

Published before Legends of Saint Camber and Heirs of Saint Camber, but occurring later in chronological order, this series recounts the exploits of the young King Kelson Haldane, who is of mixed human and Deryni heritage. Kelson must deal with opposition to his Deryni friends and advisers, Morgan and Duncan, and must ultimately unite his torn country against a threatening force from outside.

Genre: Fantasy
Subjects: Imaginary kingdoms; Imaginary wars and battles; Kings and rulers

871. Heirs of Saint Camber
1. *The Harrowing of Gwynedd.* Ballantine, 1989.
2. *King Javan's War.* Ballantine, 1992.
3. *The Bastard Prince.* Ballantine, 1994.

A dark period in the history of Gwynedd follows the deaths of Camber and Cinhil. Conflict between the Deryni and the established church erupts. A government crisis follows the death of young King Alroy and the ascension of his strong-willed brother Javan. Rhys Michael Haldane is placed on the throne as a tool of the council of regents, but he gradually realizes his own strength and becomes a ruler in his own right.

Genre: Fantasy
Subjects: Imaginary kingdoms; Inheritance and succession; Religion

872. Histories of King Kelson
1. *The Bishop's Heir.* Ballantine, 1984.
2. *The King's Justice.* Ballantine, 1985.
3. *Quest for Saint Camber.* Ballantine, 1986.

At 18, King Kelson has had a lifetime of tumult with more to come. He continues to deal with unrest in his realm and enters into a marriage that is politically advantageous but hardly romantic.

Genre: Fantasy
Subjects: Kings and rulers; Imaginary kingdoms; Imaginary wars and battles; Marriage

873. Legends of Saint Camber
1. *Camber of Culdi.* Ballantine, 1976.
2. *Saint Camber.* Ballantine, 1978.
3. *Camber the Heretic.* Ballantine, 1981.

Stories of the early years of the fantasy Kingdom of Gwynedd begin what is to be a continuing theme throughout subsequent series: the conflict between the human citizens and the Deryni, who appear human, but have mystical talents that make them hated and feared. Camber, who is in fact a Deryni, becomes convinced that the current Deryni rule is corrupt and successfully places Cinhil, a reluctant descendant of previous rulers, on the thrown.

Genre: Fantasy
Subjects: Imaginary kingdoms; Imaginary wars and battles; Mysticism

Kurtz, Katherine *and* Harris, Deborah Turner

874. The Adept
1. *The Adept.* Ace, 1991.
2. *The Lodge of the Lynx.* Ace, 1992.
3. *The Templar Treasure.* Ace, 1993.
4. *Dagger Magic.* Ace, 1995.
5. *Death of an Adept.* Ace, 1996.

Adam Sinclair is a psychiatrist and psychic with magical gifts who remembers past lives. In his efforts to protect his homeland from occult forces of evil, he deals with a magical sword, a powerful Druid, assassination attempts, and a book of black magic owned by Hitler. He becomes a potential victim himself when an ancient wizard decides to inhabit his body.

Genre: Fantasy
Subjects: Psychiatrists; Psychic phenomena; Mysticism; Good and evil
Place/Time: Scotland—1980–

L'Amour, Louis

875. The Chantrys
1. *North to the Rails.* Bantam, 1971.
2. *The Ferguson Rife.* Bantam, 1973.
3. *Over the Dry Side.* Saturday Review Press, 1975.
4. *Borden Chantry.* Corgi, 1978.

5. *Fair Blows the Wind.* Dutton, 1978.

The Chantrys came from Ireland before the American Revolution and fought in that war with Daubeny Sackett. Years later Daubeny's granddaughter Eco comes to Philadelphia to ask for Finian Chantry's help. His nephew helps Eco and becomes involved with the Sacketts. The Chantrys are more scholarly and statesmanlike and show another way the West was settled. L'Amour planned to write more books about the Chantry family and have them interact with the Sacketts, but he died before he completed the project.

Genre: Adventure; Family Saga; Western
Subjects: Adventure
Place/Time: Philadelphia (Pa.)—18th century; Philadelphia (Pa.)—19th century; Western states—18th century; Western states—19th century; Pennsylvania—18th century; Pennsylvania—19th century

876. The Sacketts

1. *Sackett's Land.* Saturday Review Press, 1974.
2. *To the Far Blue Mountains.* Saturday Review Press, 1976.
3. *The Warrior's Path.* Bantam, 1980.
4. *Jubal Sackett.* Bantam, 1985.
5. *Ride the River.* Bantam, 1983.
6. *The Daybreakers.* Tandem, 1960.
7. *Sackett.* Bantam, 1961.
8. *Lando.* Bantam, 1962.
9. *Mojave Crossing.* Bantam, 1964.
10. *Mustang Man.* Bantam, 1966.
11. *The Lonely Men.* Bantam, 1966.
12. *Galloway.* Bantam, 1970.
13. *Treasure Mountain.* Bantam, 1972.
14. *Lonely on the Mountain.* Bantam, 1980.
15. *Ride the Dark Trail.* Bantam, 1972.
16. *Sackett Brand.* Bantam, 1965.
17. *The Sky-Liners.* Bantam, 1967.

From 1600 to 1879, the Sackett family pioneer their way across the Old West as they fight injustice and search for adventure. Barnabas Sackett flees England for the American colonies where he marries, settles in the Carolinas, and raises five children, Jubal, Kin-Ring, Yance, Brian, and Noelle. The ten generations of Sacketts who come from these children leave Carolina and travel to New Mexico, Tennessee, Colorado, Mexico, Texas, and the Dakotas as they ranch, fight, ride, and love. While the later books focus on the adventures of Orren, Tyrel, and Tell Sackett, the four different branches of Sacketts interact and show how the West was won. The books are listed in the order that Louis L'Amour put them before he died in 1988.

Genre: Adventure; Family Saga; Western
Subjects: United States—territorial expansion; Adventure; Frontier and pioneer life; War
Place/Time: Western states—multicentury span

877. The Talons

1. *The Man from the Broken Hills.* Bantam, 1975.

2. *Rivers West.* Saturday Review Press, 1975.
3. *Milo Talon.* Bantam, 1981.

The Canadian Talons leave Quebec and come to trade and settle in the American West in the 1820s. Reed Talon marries Emily Sackett, and their children are educated and help build their farm and the West. L'Amour planned to write more books about the Talon family and have them interact with the Sacketts to whom they are related, but he died before he completed the project.

Genre: Adventure; Family Saga; Western
Subjects: Frontier and pioneer life
Place/Time: Western states—19th century

L'Engle, Madeleine

878.

1. *The Small Rain.* Vanguard, 1945.
2. *A Severed Wasp.* Farrar, Straus & Giroux, 1982.

From her lonely childhood, shuttled between Greenwich Village and a Swiss boarding school, to her life as a concert pianist, Katherine Forrester Vigneras has been a woman driven by her talent. Even love took a back seat to music. Now in her retirement, Katherine is called upon by an old friend to give a benefit performance to aid his cathedral, where she becomes entangled in the complex lives of the clergy.

Subjects: Pianists; Retirement; Monasticism and religious orders
Place/Time: New York (N. Y.)—1900–1945; New York (N. Y.)—1945–1980; Switzerland—1900–1945; Switzerland—1945–1980

Lackey, Mercedes *and* Dixon, Larry

879.

1. *Owlflight.* DAW Books, 1998.
2. *Owlsight.* DAW Books, 1998.
3. *Owlknight.* DAW Books, 1999.

The adventures of the orphan boy Darian continue the Valdemar tales. Darian escapes a barbarian attack on his home town by finding sanctuary in the forest, where he learns the ways of a mystical group of Healers called Hawkbrothers. Four years later, Darian returns to his boyhood home to warn the inhabitants of another onslaught. He meets his soulmate, the Healer Keisha, who loves him and shares his eventful life, but must overcome her feeling that marriage places a woman in an inferior role. *Note:* The Owl trilogy follows The Mage Storms series.

Genre: Fantasy; Coming of Age
Subjects: Orphans; Youth; Mysticism; Love

880.

1. *The Black Gryphon.* DAW Books, 1994.
2. *The White Gryphon.* DAW Books, 1995.
3. *The Silver Gryphon.* DAW Books, 1996.

In these works the early history of Valdemar is chronicled through the exploits of the mighty gryphon Skandranon, who was created by the sorcerer Urthro to defend the realm. When Urthro is killed and Skandranon disappears, Urthro's followers go into exile. With his feathers turned white by the trials he has endured, Skandranon reappears to guard them in their new home. Soon the powerful gryphon's son Tadrith joins the effort to protect the human community, which has formed an alliance with the neighboring realm of the Black Kings.

Genre: Fantasy
Subjects: Birds; Magic; Imaginary kingdoms

Lackey, Mercedes. *See also* Norton, Andre; Bradley, Marion Zimmer (*Rediscovery: A Novel of Darkover*)

881. Bardic Voices

1. *The Lark and the Wren.* Baen, 1992.
2. *The Robin and the Kestrel.* Baen, 1993.
3. *The Eagle and the Nightingales.* Baen, 1995.
4. *Four & Twenty Blackbirds.* Baen, 1997.

Composer and musician Rune, whose ability to develop her gift is limited by poverty and lack of education, strikes a bargain with a fearsome ghost. If her music entrances him for a night, she gets a sack of silver and her life. Having triumphed, Rune sets out with a gypsy and a young man of royal birth who wishes to be a commoner. In *The Eagle and the Nightingales,* Nightingale, a gypsy bard, becomes involved in defending some of the persecuted species of the land of Alanda. In *Four & Twenty Blackbirds,* a young constable tries to solve the murders of young female musicians.

Genre: Fantasy
Subjects: Musicians; Composers; Ghost stories; Animals; Murder and murderers

882. The Books of the Last Herald-Mage

1. *Magic's Pawn.* DAW Books, 1989.
2. *Magic's Promise.* DAW Books, 1990.
3. *Magic's Price.* DAW Books, 1990.

Vanyel, the last of the Kingdom of Valdemar's Herald-Mages, is devastated when his lover is killed in a blood feud, and he is sent to the High Court of Valdemar to be overseen by his stern Aunt Savil. After an invasion by evil mages, Vanyel must fight loneliness and feuds as he has a painful and ultimately fatal journey to discover his own talents and his real nature.

Genre: Fantasy
Subjects: Feuds; Courts and courtiers; Imaginary kingdoms

883. The Heralds of Valdemar

1. *Arrows of the Queen.* DAW Books, 1987.
2. *Arrow's Flight.* DAW Books, 1987.
3. *Arrow's Fall.* DAW Books, 1988.

In the kingdom of Valdemar, Talia, a young runaway, is chosen by Rolan, a mystical Norse-like being, to become a Queen's guard. As treason erupts in the kingdom, the Queen turns to Talia and the Heralds to protect her realm. Talia discovers that, as a Herald, she must dispense justice wisely, but this is difficult to do in a realm seething with intrigue over an offer for the hand of the heir to the throne.

Genre: Fantasy
Subjects: Courts and courtiers; Imaginary kingdoms; Treason

884. The Mage Storms

1. *Storm Warning.* DAW Books, 1994.
2. *Storm Rising.* DAW Books, 1995.
3. *Storm Breaking.* DAW Books, 1996.

Continuing the saga of the fantasy land of Valdemar and its rulers, these tales begin with the forging of an uneasy alliance with the land of Karse to combat the menacing Eastern Empire. Soon an even greater danger, the wildly destructive mage storms, threatens to destroy Valdemar. United primarily by their fear of the forces of nature, the allies search the tower of a long-dead mage for secrets that may enable them to combat the storms. *Note:* The Owl trilogy continues the Valdemar saga.

Genre: Fantasy
Subjects: Magic; Imaginary kingdoms; Nature

885. Mage Winds

1. *Winds of Fate.* DAW Books, 1991.
2. *Winds of Change.* DAW Books, 1992.
3. *Winds of Fury.* DAW Books, 1993.

Elspeth, heiress to the throne of Valdemar, rides in search of a mage to save the realm from the magical Ancar of Hardorm. Eventually Elspeth goes to the Pelagir Hills to learn the long forgotten skills of magic from the Hawkbrothers. When a powerful mage tries to destroy her adopted clan, she must use her new talents to save them, then her own kingdom.

Genre: Fantasy
Subjects: Magic; Imaginary kingdoms; Good and evil

886. Vows and Honor

1. *The Oathbound.* DAW Books, 1988.
2. *Oathbreakers.* DAW Books, 1988.

Bound by oath to each other and to the Goddess, the swordswoman Tarma and the wizard Kethry do battle as mercenaries in the constant struggle for justice in a land where demons come in human and not-so-human form.

Genre: Fantasy
Subjects: Mercenary soldiers; Imaginary wars and battles; Justice; Gods and goddesses

Lacy, Al *and* Lacy, JoAnna

887. Hannah of Fort Bridger
1. *Under the Distant Sky.* Multnomah, 1997.
2. *Consider the Lies.* Multnomah, 1997.
3. *No Place for Fear.* Multnomah, 1998.
4. *Pillow of Stone.* Multnomah, 1998.
5. *The Perfect Gift.* Multnomah, 1999.
6. *Touch of Compassion.* Multnomah, 1999.

Hannah and her family travel West with a wagon train in the mid-19th century. When they reach Fort Bridger in Wyoming, her husband dies suddenly. Hannah settles her family at the fort and starts a store. Her faith in God keeps her going even when she finds she is pregnant with her husband's child and her store is set afire. She helps other families who come to the fort and who also face a crisis of faith. From epidemics to kidnappings, faith helps Hannah and her family survive.

Genre: Christian Fiction
Subjects: Faith; Family life; Frontier and pioneer life
Place/Time: Wyoming—19th century

888. Mail Order Bride Series
1. *Secrets of the Heart.* Multnomah, 1998.
2. *A Time to Love.* Multnomah, 1998.
3. *The Tender Flame.* Multnomah, 1999.
4. *Blessed Are the Merciful.* Multnomah, 1999.
5. *Ransom of Love.* Multnomah, 2000.

In the years after the Civil War, five different women become mail-order brides and go West to face new lives. Each has been disappointed in love in the East, but all five find love and faith with their new husbands.

Genre: Christian Fiction; Historical Romance
Subjects: Marriage; Faith
Place/Time: Western states—19th century

Lacy, JoAnna. *See* Lacy, Al

Ladd, Linda

889. White Flower Trilogy
1. *White Lily.* Topaz, 1993.
2. *White Rose.* Topaz, 1994.
3. *White Orchid.* Topaz, 1995.

The three Delaney siblings find that the path to true love is filled with adventure, daring escapes, and foreign travel. In 1864, Harte Delaney rescues Lily Courtland from white slavers while he is spying for the Union in North Carolina. Lily has come to America to find her brother Derek who is a confederate blockade runner. As Lily and Harte search for Derek, they fall in love. Harte's sister Cassandra is also a Union spy. She is alive with Derek who has been captured and put in prison. Cassandra engineers his escape to the Caribbean, but when Harte discovers what she's done, he has Derek kidnap her and take her to Australia. On their way to Australia, Derek and Cassandra find they are attracted to each other. At the end of the war, Stuart Delaney is hired to find Angelica Blake who is living in India. Stuart finds her in the court of a ten-year-old maharajah. Stuart is able to get her out of the court and on the way back to England, the two fall in love.

Genre: Historical Romance
Subjects: Love, Spies; Escapes
Place/Time: Southern states—19th century; Australia—19th century

Lagerkvist, Par

890.
1. *Barabbas.* Random House, 1951.
2. *Death of Ahasueras.* Random House, 1962.
3. *Pilgrim at Sea.* Random House, 1964.
4. *The Holy Land.* Random House, 1966.
5. *The Sibyl.* Random House, 1957.

Books one and two are loosely connected tales of two figures present at the crucifixion of Jesus Christ: Barabbas, the prisoner whose life was spared by the crowd while Christ went to the cross, and the legendary Wandering Jew, Ahasueras, who Jesus condemned to traveling over the earth eternally because Ahasueras denied him a moment of rest while carrying the cross. Ahasueras continues as a character in the story of Tobias, a ruffian who begins a pilgrimage but, in the end, becomes the companion of a defrocked priest on a pirate ship.

Subjects: Jesus Christ—crucifixion; Barabbas (biblical figure)
Place/Time: Palestine—multicentury span

Lagerlof, Selma

891.
1. *Jerusalem.* Doubleday, 1915.
2. *The Holy City-Jerusalem II.* Doubleday, 1918.

Basing her work on an actual incident, the first woman to win the Nobel Prize for Literature wrote of the members of a rural 19th-century religious sect who emigrate to Jerusalem to establish a community that will fulfill their ideals. Once there, they suffer from internal conflicts, illness, and the difficulties of adjusting to a different culture and climate. In the end, they achieve the harmony they sought and establish contact with those they left behind.

Genre: Christian Fiction; Historical Fiction
Subjects: Religion; Christianity; Sects; Faith
Place/Time: Jerusalem (Palestine)—19th century; Palestine—19th century

892. The Lowenskold Trilogy
1. *The General's Ring.* Doubleday, 1928.
2. *Charlotte Lowenskold.* Doubleday, 1927.
3. *Anna Svard.* This book was published with the above titles in the following collection: *The Ring of the Lowenskolds.* Doubleday, 1931.

Eerie events surround the aristocratic Lowenskold family of the Varmland region of Sweden. An ancestral ghost whose ring was stolen from his grave in 1741 is put to rest by Malvina, the young housekeeper who loves the family heir, but despite her efforts, is rejected because of her low social standing. Malvina's friend, the local healer Marit, puts a curse on the family that is fulfilled as the generations pass, in part by the machinations of Thea, the manipulative daughter of Malvina.

Genre: Family Saga
Subjects: Curses, family; Class distinction; Ghost stories
Place/Time: Sweden—18th century

LaHaye, Tim *and* Jenkins, Jerry B.

893. Left Behind Series
1. *Left Behind.* Tyndale House, 1995.
2. *Tribulation Force.* Tyndale House, 1996.
3. *Nicolae: The Rise of the Antichrist.* Tyndale House, 1997.
4. *Soul Harvest.* Tyndale House, 1998.
5. *Apollyon.* Tyndale, 1999.
6. *Assassins.* Tyndale, 1999.
7. *The Indwelling.* Tyndale, 2000.

While piloting a plane to New York, Rayford Steele debates about having an affair with a stewardess when the stewardess comes into the cockpit to tell him half the passengers have disappeared. Ray suddenly realizes he loves his family and wants to go home, but they too have vanished. Ray must struggle with how he will fare on Earth after the disappearance of his family. Ray and his friend Buck Williams head up the Tribulation Force which fights the Antichrist, Nicolae Carpathia. As the world is in turmoil, Ray and Buck search for their loved ones and try to bring down the Antichrist as foretold in Revelation.

Genre: Christian Fiction
Subjects: Allegories; Faith; Biblical stories; Good and evil
Place/Time: New York (N. Y.)—1980–

Laity, Sally. *See* Crawford, Dianna

Laker, Rosalind

894.
1. *Warwyck's Woman.* Doubleday, 1978.
2. *Claudine's Daughter.* Doubleday, 1979.
3. *Warwyck's Choice.* Doubleday, 1980.

In 1826, Daniel Warwyck, a prizefighter, buys Kate Farringdon in the Brighton market. He hopes that, by bringing home a wife, he will be the heir to the Warwyck manor in Sussex. Even though he is married, he continues his fighting and has affairs, but his wife Kate ultimately changes him. Their son Richard continues the Warwyck rivalry with the Radcliff family, but grandson Tom falls in love with Nicolette Radcliffe and joins the families.

Genre: Family Saga; Historical Romance
Subjects: Marriage problems; Feuds
Place/Time: England—19th century

Lambdin, Dewey

895.
1. *The King's Coat.* D. I. Fine, 1989.
2. *The French Admiral.* D. I. Fine, 1990.
3. *The King's Commission.* D. I. Fine, 1991.
4. *The King's Privateer.* D. I. Fine, 1992.
5. *The Gun Ketch.* D. I. Fine, 1993.
6. *H. M. S. Cockerel.* Fine, 1995.
7. *A King's Commander.* Fine, 1996.
8. *Jester's Fortune.* Dutton, 1999.

In 1780, 17-year-old Alan Lewrie is caught in flagrante delicto with his sluttish half-sister. Forced to join the Royal Navy, foppish Lewrie discovers that he likes the sea and the adventures he experiences with the navy. Storms, battles, duels, and duty change him into an up-and-coming officer, though he still loves to dally with the ladies. Lewrie takes part in the Battle of Yorktown, fights French privateers in the South China Sea, attacks pirates in the Caribbean, and sees action with Lord Horatio Nelson against the French. He becomes captain of his own ship and marries the one woman he loves. Adventure, technical detail, and bawdy humor highlight this updated version of the C. S. Forester sea story.

Genre: Historical Fiction; Naval Adventure
Subjects: Navy, British—officers; Seamen; Naval battles; War
Place/Time: Atlantic Ocean—18th century; Pacific Ocean—18th century; Caribbean region—18th century

Lancour, Gene. *Pseud. of* Gene L. Fisher

896. Dirshan the God-Killer
1. *The Lerios Mecca.* Doubleday, 1973.
2. *The War Machines of Kalinth.* Doubleday, 1977.
3. *Sword for the Empire.* Doubleday, 1978.

The emphasis is on the sword in these high adventure sword and sorcery tales about Dirshan, the barbarian who defends the empire of Alithar. In the process, Dirshan encounters a militant princess and a godlike beast, and is saved by a mantle of invisibility.

Genre: Fantasy
Subjects: Imaginary kingdoms; Imaginary wars and battles; Heroes

Landis, Jill Marie

897.
1. *After All.* Jove, 1994.
2. *Last Chance.* Jove, 1995.

Eva Eberhart, a dance-hall girl in Cheyenne, Wyoming, has become tired of her life and decides to answer an ad for a housekeeper at a ranch in Montana. She arms herself with sensible clothes and a made-up past and goes to Trail's End Ranch. Chase Cassidy and his nephew Lane aren't sure of Eve, but she soon wins them over and wins Chase's heart. Lane leaves town when school teacher Rachel Albright marries. Ten years later, he returns disguised as a gunfighter, when he's really a Pinkerton detective. Rachel's husband has died, and she takes up with Lane to the horror of her in-laws and the town. The Cassidy's find love is never easy, but always worthwhile.

Genre: Historical Romance
Subjects: Love; Small town life; Detectives; Ranch life
Place/Time: Montana—19th century

Lanier, Sterling E.

898. Hiero Desteen
1. *Hiero's Journey.* Chilton, 1973.
2. *The Unforsaken Hiero.* Ballantine, 1983.

Fantasy and science fiction mix in this chaotic postnuclear world filled with terrifying mutants and beasts. Hiero Desteen sets out on a quest to find the computer that may give humanity a way out of this wilderness. His companions are Brother Aldo, a member of a movement that mixes religion and environmentalism, the resourceful young woman Luchare, and a bear with human qualities.

Genre: Fantasy; Science Fiction
Subjects: Nuclear warfare; Computers; Society, primitive

Larteguy, Jean

899.
1. *The Centurions.* Dutton, 1962.
2. *The Praetorians.* Dutton, 1963.

A group of French paratroopers use combat experience they have gained in Indochina in the Algerian revolt of the 1950s. Feeling betrayed by public opinion and the politicians of France who no longer support efforts to suppress the revolt, Phillipe Eclavier and his military colleagues participate in the return to power of Charles De Gaulle.

Genre: Historical Fiction; War
Subjects: War; Politics; Army, French; Algeria—revolution, 1954–1962
Place/Time: Algeria—1945–1980; France—1945–1980

Lasswell, Mary

900.
1. *Suds in Your Eye.* Houghton Mifflin, 1942.
2. *High Time.* Houghton Mifflin, 1944.
3. *One on the House.* Houghton Mifflin, 1949.
4. *Wait for the Wagon.* Houghton Mifflin, 1951.
5. *Tooner Schooner.* Houghton Mifflin, 1953.
6. *Let's Go for Broke.* Houghton Mifflin, 1962.

During World War II, three elderly beer-drinking ladies live in a southern California junkyard and solve life's problems with verve and humor. Mrs. Feeley, Mrs. Rasmussen, and Miss Tinkham are warmhearted and try to help all they meet. After the war, they travel to New York where they help a bar owner who is broke. When they return to California, they create a motel out of five buses. These funny, inventive women are involved in many zany adventures.

Genre: Humor
Subjects: Automobile—touring; Elderly; Voyages and travels
Place/Time: California—1945–1980; New York (N. Y.)—1945–1980

Lauber, Lynn

901.
1. *White Girls.* Norton, 1990.
2. *21 Sugar Street.* Norton, 1993.

In a series of interconnected short stories set in the 1960s in Union, Ohio, adolescent Loretta Dardio moves from preteen fantasies to a rebellious love affair with Luther Biggs, a black teenager from the wrong side of the tracks. Loretta seeks the love she hungers from Luther's mother Annie. In her search for love, Loretta becomes pregnant and goes to a home for unwed mothers where she gives up her baby. It will take Loretta years to understand herself, her family, and the black and white cultures she tries to bridge.

Genre: Coming of Age
Subjects: Unmarried mothers; Teenagers; African Americans; Race relations
Place/Time: Ohio—1945–1980

Laumer, Keith

902. Lafayette O'Leary
1. *The Time Bender.* Berkley, 1966.
2. *The World Shuffler.* Putnam, 1970.
3. *The Shape Changer.* Putnam, 1972.
4. *The Galaxy Builder.* Ace, 1984.

A curious, creative laboratory technician learns to move in and out of alternate worlds with the help of Mesmeric Science. In medieval Artesia, he is accused of sorcery, but convincingly displays his helpful powers and wins the lovely Daphne, only to contend with an alternate version of himself.

Genre: Fantasy; Science Fiction

Subjects: Imaginary kingdoms; Scientists; Witchcraft; Love

Lauterstein, Ingeborg

903.
1. *Water Castle.* Houghton Mifflin, 1980.
2. *Vienna Girl.* Norton, 1986.

The horrors of the Third Reich and its impact on one family are seen through the eyes of young Reyna Von Meinert. She sees her neighbors the Rombergs, the family of a Jewish dairy owner, forced to flee to Switzerland. Reyna's cousin Berthold joins the Gestapo and is appalled by their actions. Reyna flirts with different political philosophies, but ultimately takes refuge with her grandmother as the Russians invade Austria. She sees the old order crumble and must confront the shame of her Nazi legacy in order to reconcile the old with the new order after World War II.

Genre: Historical Fiction; War
Subjects: War; World War II, 1939–1945; National Socialism; Jews, persecution of; Holocaust, Jewish, 1933–1945
Place/Time: Austria—1900–1945

Lawhead, Steve

904. Dragon King Trilogy
1. *In the Hall of the Dragon King.* Crossway Books, 1982.
2. *The Warlords of Nin.* Crossway Books, 1983.
3. *The Sword and the Flame.* Crossway Books, 1984.

The capture of Dragon King Eskevar by a magician leaves his throne vulnerable to the schemes of Prince Jaspin. As a temple acolyte, Quentin's beginning role is to carry the sad news to Queen Alinea. Quentin gains in skill, forges a magic sword, and ascends the throne after the king's death.

Genre: Fantasy
Subjects: Imaginary kingdoms; Imaginary wars and battles; Kings and rulers; Arms and armor

905. Pendragon Cycle
1. *Taliesin.* Crossway Books, 1987.
2. *Merlin.* Crossway Books, 1988.
3. *Arthur.* Crossway Books, 1989.
4. *Pendragon.* Morrow, 1994.
5. *Grail.* Avon, 1997.
6. *Avalon: The Return of King Arthur.* Avon, 1999.

Using a combination of Arthurian legend, Atlantean legend, and Celtic myth, Lawhead tells the love story of the bard Taliesin of Britain and the Atlantean princess Charis. The saga then returns to Britain to follow Merlin before he becomes mentor to Arthur, and Arthur as he battles invading Saxons and knights in revolt. The saga tells of the trials and tribulations each must face as they meet their tragic destinies.

Genre: Fantasy
Subjects: Legends and folk tales; Mythology; Arthur, King; Merlin (legendary character)

906. Song of Albion Trilogy
1. *The Paradise War.* Lion, 1991.
2. *The Silver Hand.* Lion, 1992.
3. *The Endless Knot.* Lion, 1993.

Lewis Gillies, an Oxford graduate student in Celtic studies, discovers that his roommate Simon Rawnson has slipped through a hole in the Cairn to the land of Tuatha de Danann, an ancient Celtic kingdom. With the help of a professor, Lewis goes through the Cairn to find Simon. Once in the ancient land, both students find themselves reliving the Celtic myths. Lewis becomes the warrior Llew, who has to fight the evil Meldron to save the singing stones and the good power of Albion. Llew becomes heir to the throne, but even on his wedding night, the forces of evil work against his plans to bring peace.

Genre: Fantasy
Subjects: Imaginary kingdoms; Mythology; Students

Lawrence, D. H. (David Herbert)

907.
1. *The Rainbow.* Viking, 1915.
2. *Women in Love.* Viking, 1920.

Three generations of the Brangwen family are farmers and craftsmen in Nottinghamshire in the late 19th and early 20th centuries. The sexual aspects of love and marriage are explored through three different marriages. Ursula and Gudrun Brangwen are in their twenties and fight their parents' morality. They both search for sexual fulfillment with the men they love—Rupert Berkin and Gerald Crich.

Subjects: Family life; Sex; Love; Marriage problems; Love affairs
Place/Time: England—19th century; England—1900–1945

Laxalt, Robert

908.
1. *The Basque Hotel.* University of Nevada Press, 1989.
2. *Child of the Holy Ghost.* University of Nevada Press, 1992.
3. *The Governor's Mansion.* University of Nevada Press, 1994.

Young Peter grows up in the small town of Carson City, Nevada, during the Depression. His parents run the Basque Hotel and try to keep up their heritage of sheep herding. Pete is indifferent to his heritage and worships the crazy characters of the town: Buckshoot Dooney, Hallelujah Bob, and Mickey McCuskey. However, Pete cannot escape his heritage when he returns to his mother's village in Spain to uncover her secret past. When he returns home, Pete's older brother

Leon runs for political office and tries an untried medium—television—to help him get elected.

Genre: Coming of Age
Subjects: Family life; Love affairs; Diseases; Heredity; Politics—United States
Place/Time: United States—1900–1945; United States—1945–1980

Le Carre, John. *Pseud. of* David Cornwall

909.
1. *Call for the Dead.* Walker, 1963.
2. *A Murder of Quality.* Walker, 1963.
3. *The Spy Who Came in from the Cold.* Coward, 1964.
4. *Tinker, Tailor, Soldier, Spy.* Knopf, 1974.
5. *The Honourable Schoolboy.* Knopf, 1977.
6. *Smiley's People.* Knopf, 1980.

George Smiley works for British Intelligence from the 1950s through the 1970s at the height of the Cold War. His opponent Karla, the head of the Soviet KGB, has placed a mole in British Intelligence. Smiley comes out of retirement to find the mole, put the agency back together, and weave a plot to destroy Karla. These very realistic novels present a grim picture of espionage as the duplicity of the spies becomes a metaphor for contemporary life.

Genre: Espionage
Subjects: Spies; Secret service; International intrigue; Cold war
Place/Time: England—1945–1980

Le Guin, Ursula K.

910. Hain
1. *The Dispossessed: An Ambiguous Utopia.* Harper, 1974.
2. *The Word for World Is Forest.* Putnam, 1976.
3. *Rocannon's World.* Ace, 1966.
4. *Planet of Exile.* Ace, 1966.
5. *City of Illusions.* Ace, 1967.
6. *The Left Hand of Darkness.* Ace, 1969.

Le Guin's Hainish series begins with the assumption that centuries ago humanoids from the planet Hain ventured through the solar system establishing colonies on various planets including Earth. For mysterious reasons these colonies lose all contact and knowledge of each other until the 21st century when an attempt is made to establish a galactic league. Individual stories in this loosely organized series explore the inherent communication difficulties in the mingling and clash of cultures that, over the centuries of separation, have developed widely disparate social and political structures as well as a range of biological differences.

Genre: Science Fiction

Subjects: Life on other planets; Interplanetary voyages; Cultural conflict; Interstellar communication

Leahy, Syrell Rogovin

911.
1. *Family Ties.* Putnam, 1982.
2. *Family Truths.* Putnam, 1984.

Before World War I, Regina is a pampered wealthy Jewish American girl who seems to have it all. Her family, however, has a dark secret—a gene defect that can produce monstrous children—that will keep her from marrying her cousin Jerold. Later she has an affair with her uncle and learns the importance of family. Descendant Judy also discovers the family secret and must come to terms with it. She fears love and marriage but finally accepts herself and her family.

Genre: Family Saga; Romance

Leckie, Ross

912.
1. *Hannibal.* Regnery, 1996.
2. *Scipio Africanus: The Man Who Defeated Hannibal.* Regnery, 1998.

At the end of their lives, two great ancient generals reflect on their careers. Hannibal relates his growing up in Carthage, his love for the Spanish woman Similce, and his fight against Rome. He tells of the winter that his soldiers and elephants crossed the Alps to attack Rome. Then the elderly Publius Cornelius Scipio dictates his story to the scribe Bostar. He describes his battles and how he finally defeated Hannibal's army. Bostar, who had served with Hannibal then tells his version of the battle.

Genre: Historical Fiction
Subjects: Hannibal, 247–182 B.C.; Scipio Africanus, ca. 236–183 B.C.; Rome; Battles; Generals
Place/Time: Carthage—1st century B. C.; Rome (Italy)—1st century B. C.

Lee, Adam

913. The Dominions of Irth
1. *The Dark Shore.* Avon, 1997.
2. *The Shadow Eater.* Avon Eos, 1998.
3. *Octoberland.* Avon, 1999.

Lord Drev, ruler of the Dominions of Irth, is overthrown by a vengeful Dark Lord who has gained in power from his time in the Abyss where Drev threw him earlier. Drev must seek help among the street people of his world. Here, he encounters Ripcat, whose fate is threatened by the mystical power of the Nameless Lady and her unborn child. Light years away Earth itself is facing the apocalypse due to the machinations of an ancient magician who seeks eternal youth.

Genre: Fantasy

Subjects: Kings and rulers; Imaginary kingdoms; Revenge; Magic

Lee, Gentry. *See also* Clarke, Arthur C.

914.

1. *Bright Messengers.* Bantam, 1995.
2. *Double Full Moon Night.* Bantam, 1999.

These stories tell of the love of Sister Beatrice, a priestess of a mystical order, and Johann Eberhardt, a German systems engineer. Each sees a vision of a cloud of mysterious white particles, but interpret it differently: she as a message from God, he as a scientific puzzle. To the Rama Society the cloud is possibly a manifestation of extraterrestrial life. Drawn to the planet Mars by their own interests, the two meet and discover that the answer to their questions may lie buried beneath the surface of Mars or in an enormous alien sphere that is a world of its own. *Note:* This series takes place in the Rama universe that the author developed with Arthur C. Clarke.

Genre: Science Fiction
Subjects: Extraterrestrial beings; Space colonies; Mars (planet), exploration of; Love

Lee, John

915. Unicorn Saga

1. *The Unicorn Quest.* Tom Doherty Assoc., 1986.
2. *The Unicorn Dilemma.* Tom Doherty Assoc., 1988.
3. *The Unicorn Solution.* Tor, 1991.
4. *The Unicorn Peace.* Tor, 1993.
5. *The Unicorn War.* Tor, 1995.

On the planet Strand, the world mage Jarrod Courtak finds himself in the middle of a volatile situation produced by shifting patterns of court intrigue. At the heart of the controversy is the prophecy that unicorns, who live together on an island, will be the ultimate winners in the war that seems inevitable.

Genre: Fantasy
Subjects: Unicorns; Life on other planets; Imaginary wars and battles; Prophecies; Magic

Lee, Tanith

916. Blood Opera Sequence

1. *Dark Dance.* Dell, 1992.
2. *Personal Darkness.* Dell, 1994.
3. *Darkness, I.* St. Martin's, 1996.

Although warned to stay away from her father's family, but unaware that they are vampires, London bookstore clerk Rachaela Day visits the Scarabae estate. She soon realizes that the family is more than simply a group of eccentrics, and escapes, but finds that she is pregnant with her own father's child. Her daughter Ruth destroys the ancestral home and threatens to bring public attention to members of the family who have attempted to blend into the mortal population. Anna, Rachaela's daughter who is born after Ruth's death and who has a strange, mystical appearance, is abducted and taken to the home of the dark immortal Cain.

Genre: Horror
Subjects: Vampires; Mothers and daughters; Fathers and daughters; Eccentrics and eccentricities
Place/Time: London (England)—1980–

917. Lords of Darkness

1. *Night's Master.* DAW Books, 1978.
2. *Death's Master.* DAW Books, 1979.
3. *Delusion's Master.* DAW Books, 1981.
4. *Delirium's Mistress.* DAW Books, 1986.
5. *Night's Sorceries.* DAW Books, 1987.

Set in a time so ancient that the earth was flat, these tales chronicle the relationship of powerful subterranean demons with humanity. Arch rival demons Chuz and Azhram battle over the fate of Azhriaz, the beautiful daughter of Azhram and a mortal woman.

Genre: Fantasy
Subjects: Demonology; Imaginary wars and battles

918. The Secret Books of Paradys

1. *The Book of the Damned.* Overlook Press, 1990.
2. *The Book of the Beast.* Overlook Press, 1991.
3. *The Book of the Dead.* Overlook Press, 1991.
4. *The Book of the Mad.* Overlook Press, 1993.

A mixture of short stories, novellas, and novels paint a portrait of a mysterious French city that will not be found on any map, where strange beasts and even stranger people flow through a medieval world of horror, hedonism, and beauty.

Genre: Fantasy; Horror
Subjects: Imaginary cities; Middle Ages; Hedonism

919. The Secret Books of Venus

1. *Faces Under Water.* Overlook Press, 1998.
2. *Saint Fire: (Il Libro Della Sparda).* Overlook Press, 1999.

In this alternate 15th-century Italy, magical events change the lives of two young people. While working for the Venetian alchemist Schaachen, Furian finds a mask which seems to be cursed, but which leads him to its mysterious maker and his daughter, who is both bewitching and bewitched. The servant girl Volpa discovers her magical power over fire, but must deal with dignitaries of the church who want to use her talent for their own purposes.

Genre: Fantasy
Subjects: Magic; Love; Fire; Religion
Place/Time: Italy—15th century

Lehmann, Rosamond

920.
1. *Invitation to the Waltz.* Holt, 1932.
2. *The Weather in the Streets.* Reynal, 1936.

In the 1920s, Olivia Curtis is a young 17-year old who can't wait for her first big dance. Her younger brother James recites poems and goes on nature walks in the English countryside. The two have a gradual awakening to the adult world. Ten years later, their lives are not so kind. Olivia's marriage is a failure, and an affair with her old boyfriend Rollo Spencer ends in disappointment.

Genre: Coming of Age
Subjects: Teenagers; Love affairs; Marriage problems
Place/Time: England—1900–1945

Lehrer, James

921.
1. *Kick the Can.* Putnam, 1988.
2. *Crown Oklahoma.* Putnam, 1989.
3. *The Sooner Spy.* Putnam, 1990.
4. *Lost and Found.* Putnam, 1991.
5. *Short List.* Putnam, 1992.
6. *Fine Lines.* Random House, 1994.

Noted broadcast journalist Jim Lehrer relates the wild and wacky adventures of one-eyed Mack, who wanders all over the Southwest looking for his dream of being a pirate. His high jinks finally land him in Oklahoma where he becomes lieutenant governor, but this doesn't stop him from becoming involved with organized crime and spies as he tries to save his state. Lehrer has great fun spoofing the American political system.

Genre: Adventure; Humor
Subjects: Adventure; Picaresque novels; Politics—Oklahoma
Place/Time: Western states—1945–1980; Western states—1980–; Oklahoma—1945–1980; Oklahoma—1980–

Leiber, Fritz

922. Fafhrd and the Gray Mouser
1. *Swords in the Mist.* Ace, 1968.
2. *Swords Against Wizardry.* Ace, 1968.
3. *The Swords of Lankhmar.* Ace, 1968.
4. *Swords and Deviltry.* Ace, 1970.
5. *Swords Against Death.* Ace, 1970.
6. *Swords and Ice Magic.* Ace, 1977.
7. *Rime Isle.* Whispers Press, 1977.
8. *Heroes and Horrors.* Whispers Press, 1978.
9. *The Knight and the Knave of Swords.* Morrow, 1988.

Two young men who live in the magical land of Nehwon take up the life of danger and romance in very different ways. Fafhrd proves himself and at the same time breaks his ties to a barbarian tribe by performing a dangerous initiation ritual that had killed his father. Angered by the murder of the sorcerer who had been his teacher and mentor, young Mouse dabbles in magic, gains his revenge, and becomes the adventurer the Gray Mouser. The meeting of the two begins an often humorous partnership that leads to encounters with danger, witchcraft, and beautiful damsels.

Genre: Fantasy
Subjects: Friendship; Imaginary kingdoms; Magic

Lelchuk, Alan

923.
1. *Miriam at Thirty-Four.* Farrar, Straus & Giroux, 1974.
2. *Miriam in Her Forties.* Houghton Mifflin, 1985.

Miriam Scheinman is the divorced mother of two and a freelance photographer living in Cambridge, Massachusetts. As she emerges from her constricting marriage, she finds she enjoys her freedom, her lovers, and her pleasures. As her children grow up, she finds love with a middle-aged surgeon, but she must deal with a rapist who comes back into her life.

Genre: Romance
Subjects: Women; Marriage problems; Love affairs
Place/Time: Massachusetts—1945–1980; Massachusetts—1980–

Lem, Stanislaw

924. The Ijon Tichy Stories
1. *The Futurological Congress.* Seabury, 1974.
2. *The Star Diaries.* Seabury, 1976. (Alternate title: *Memoirs of a Space Traveller.*)
3. *Peace on Earth.* Harcourt Brace, 1994.

The diaries of Ijon Tichy, an ordinary man on an extraordinary tour of the universe, poke fun at a variety of institutions and philosophies. As he goes through a time warp, Tichy takes on multiple personalities, then finds that eternal life is not all it's cracked up to be. Between these mind-boggling experiences, Tichy discovers a world where technology has made life uniquely boring. Things become far too exciting during Tichy's visit to the moon when his brain is accidentally sliced in half and he must deal with the fact that his right and left sides operate completely independently.

Genre: Humor; Science Fiction
Subjects: Interplanetary voyages; Diaries (stories in diary form); Technology and civilization

Lemann, Nancy

925.
1. *Lives of the Saints.* Knopf, 1985.
2. *Sportsman's Paradise.* Knopf, 1992.

These stories have little or no plot, but they reveal the character of the eccentric Collier clan of New Orleans. Claude is constantly having a breakdown. Louise believes in dignity, decency, and doing her duty, especially keeping Claude sober. Storey, a New York writer, relates her loves and her crazy childhood in New Orleans. Though little happens, the lunacy of both New York and New Orleans is revealed with wit.

Genre: Humor
Subjects: Family life; Eccentrics and eccentricities
Place/Time: New York (N. Y.)—1980–; New Orleans (La.)—1980–; Louisiana—1980–

Lenz, Frederick

926.
1. *Surfing the Himalayas.* St. Martin's, 1995.
2. *Snowboarding to Nirvana.* St. Martin's, 1997.

In these fictional autobiographies, Lenz's alter ego is a naive young man who comes to Kathmandu to snowboard. There he finds Master Fwap, the last master of a Tibetan order. Fwap makes the young man his disciple and then discourses on Buddhist thought. As the young man snowboards, he learns about sex from his Danish sex partner and about enlightenment from the master.

Subjects: Autobiographical stories; Philosophical novels; Religion; Sex
Place/Time: Nepal—1980–

Leon, Henry Cecil. *See* Cecil, Henry

Leonard, Elmore

927.
1. *Get Shorty.* Delacorte Press, 1990.
2. *Be Cool.* Delacorte Press, 1999.

Loan shark Chili Palmer agrees to help a fellow mobster find a movie producer who is trying to evade his Las Vegas debts. Palmer finds the producer, but then takes over the producer's Hollywood movie. He produces a successful movie, which he bases on his own life. After his second movie bombs at the box office, Palmer desperately needs a hit. When a record producer he's lunching with is gunned down, Chili is inspired to use that killing as part of the screenplay. Mobsters, assassins, movie stars, and con men all interact in this black comedy that satirizes the Hollywood scene.

Genre: Crime Novel
Subjects: Gangsters; Motion pictures; Satire
Place/Time: Los Angeles (Calif.)—1980–

Leroux, Etienne

928. The Welgevonden Trilogy
1. *Seven Days at the Silbersteins.* Houghton, 1967.
2. *One for the Devil.* Houghton, 1968.
3. *The Third Eye.* Houghton, 1969.

The above titles have also been published in the following collection: *To a Dubious Salvation: A Trilogy of Fantastic Novels.* Penguin, 1972.

Allegory and mythological allusions mix in this trilogy concerning the Silbersteins, owners of a South African estate, and police detective Demosthenes H. de Goede, who first becomes involved with the family when their retarded son is suspected of murdering a young girl. De Goede then investigates the dark doings of tycoon Boris Gudenov, but is startled when his first glimpse of the suspect reveals a man who resembles himself.

Subjects: Allegories; Philosophical novels
Place/Time: South Africa—1945–1980

Lesley, Craig

929.
1. *Winterkill.* Houghton Mifflin, 1984.
2. *River Song.* Houghton Mifflin, 1989.

Nez Perce Indian Danny Kachian works the rodeo shows and drinks away his prize money as he tries to forget his childhood with a difficult father and the wife and son who left him. When his wife is killed in a car accident, Danny reclaims his son Jack, but must work to regain Jack's trust and love. He teaches Jack to ride, hunt, and fish. After drifting from job to job, the two settle in Oregon and work at salmon fishing. Danny finally faces the ghosts of his past as he teaches his son of his tribal heritage.

Subjects: Native Americans; Fathers and sons; Rodeos; Fishing
Place/Time: Western states—1980–; Oregon—1980–

Lessing, Doris. *See also* Somers, Jane

930. Canopus in Argos: Archives
1. *Shikasta.* Knopf, 1979.
2. *The Marriages Between Zones Three, Four, and Five.* Knopf, 1980.
3. *The Sirian Experiments.* Knopf, 1981.
4. *The Making of the Representative for Planet 8.* Knopf, 1982.
5. *The Sentimental Agents.* Knopf, 1983.

Although previously known for fiction with a social-political message, Doris Lessing ventured into a mystical future narrative covering aeons of time in this series. The Canopean Empire attempts to guide Earthlings away from their violent, self-destructive ways, but in the long run their experiments appear unlikely to succeed. A marriage between two very different, nearly mythological characters introduces the driving forces of conflict, synthesis, and change that appear to be behind an all-powerful ruling principle called "Necessity." The speculative works continue to describe a galactic competitor of the Canopeans, a planet in the grips of an ice age that ultimately leads its inhabitants to spiritual transcendence, and the experiences of an Canopean agent who becomes enamored of language at the expense of action.

Genre: Science Fiction
Subjects: Experiments, scientific; Life on other planets; Marriage; Mysticism

931. Children of Violence Series
1. *Martha Quest.* Simon & Schuster, 1964, 1952.
2. *A Proper Marriage.* Simon & Schuster, 1964, 1954.
3. *A Ripple from the Storm.* Simon & Schuster, 1966, 1958.
4. *Landlocked.* Simon & Schuster, 1966, 1965.
5. *The Four-Gated City.* Knopf, 1969.

From the 1920s to the 1950s, Martha Quest, the rebellious daughter of English colonials living in South Africa, searches for her identity through two marriages and various social movements. She becomes increasingly disillusioned with life and dies in a radioactive world devastated by war.

Subjects: Women; Marriage; Psychological novels; Nuclear warfare
Place/Time: South Africa—1900–1945; South Africa—1945–1980

Levi, Jean

932.
1. *The Chinese Emperor.* Harcourt, Brace & Jovanovich, 1987, 1985.
2. *The Dream of Confucius.* Harcourt, Brace & Jovanovich, 1992, 1989.

The early history of China is retold through the lives of third century B.C. rulers Ch'in Shih Huang Ti and Emperor Liu Pang. Ch'in Shih Huang Ti establishes the central Chinese state and uses it to gather control over the land and the aristocrats. After the iron-handed rule of Ch'in, Liu Pang establishes the Han dynasty and has to fight rebellion and robber chiefs. The exotic world of ancient China is meticulously recreated.

Genre: Historical Fiction
Subjects: China—kings and rulers; Courts and courtiers; War; Politics—China
Place/Time: China—3rd century B. C.

Levin, Ira

933.
1. *Rosemary's Baby.* Random House, 1967.
2. *Son of Rosemary.* Dutton, 1997.

Rosemary Woodhouse's child may have been the son of Satan somehow planted in her body by the mysterious neighbors in her apartment building, or she may have had a strange neurotic delusion. When she awakens from a coma in a nursing home in 1999 with only the memory of her son playing on the floor and sinister

chanting in the next room, she begins to realize the awful possibilities of her 27-year sleep. The intentions of her grown son Andy seem to be good, but she believes that in fact he has been raised by a coven of witches. He is now head of an international organization, whose plan to hold a massive candle lighting ceremony to celebrate the millennium conceals a dark purpose.

Genre: Horror
Subjects: Devil; Witchcraft; Mothers and sons

Levin, Meyer

934.
1. *The Settlers.* Simon & Schuster, 1972.
2. *The Harvest.* Simon & Schuster, 1978.

The Chaimovitch family flees Russia and arrives in Palestine in 1904. They become part of an agricultural settlement and find that they must fight illness and disillusionment. Their youngest son goes to college in Chicago, then returns to Palestine to help the Jewish settlers fight for independence in 1948. The plane he brings with him from America becomes the start of the Israeli air force.

Genre: Family Saga; Historical Fiction
Subjects: Collective settlements; Zionism; Israel-Arab War, 1948–1949
Place/Time: Palestine—1900–1945; Palestine—1945–1980

Lewis, Beverly

935.
1. *The Postcard.* Bethany House, 1999.
2. *The Crossroad.* Bethany House, 1999.

In Pennsylvania Amish country, Rachel Yoder is a happily married woman with a loving family when her life is shattered. A car speeding down the road crashes into her husband's horse-drawn cart and kills him. To support the family, Rachel works at a bed-and-breakfast that takes in tourists. Rachel sees tourism changing the Amish community. Crafts are more important than farming. At the bed-and-breakfast, Rachel meets Philip Bradley, a journalist, and falls in love with him, but she cannot give up her faith. Philip doesn't know if he can find happiness living on a farm.

Genre: Christian Fiction
Subjects: Amish; Love; Faith
Place/Time: Pennsylvania—1980–

936. The Heritage of Lancaster County
1. *The Shunning.* Bethany House, 1997.
2. *The Confession.* Bethany House, 1997.
3. *The Reckoning.* Bethany House, 1998.

On the eve of her wedding to Bishop Jim of the Old Order Amish, Katie Lapp discovers a satin infant gown in a trunk in her parents' attic. When she asks her parents, she discovers she is adopted, and is suddenly shunned by the community. She leaves Lancaster County to search for her birth mother and finds her—the wealthy

Laura Mayfield-Bennett. As Katie works to reunite with her mother, her first love, Daniel Fisher returns to Lancaster County to find Katie. A wise woman tells Daniel where to find Katie, who is now working with terminally ill patients. Katie is grieving for her Amish parents as well as for the death of her real mother when Daniel finds her. She must find peace before they can be together.

Genre: Christian Fiction
Subjects: Amish; Mothers and daughters; Faith; Love
Place/Time: Pennsylvania—1980–; New York (state)—1980–

Lewis, C. S. (Clive Staples)

937. The Space Trilogy
1. *Out of the Silent Planet.* Macmillan, 1943.
2. *Perelandra.* Macmillan, 1944.
3. *That Hideous Strength: A Modern Fairy-Tale for Grown-Ups.* Macmillan, 1946.

Angels, devils, and spaceships mix in this unique combination of fantasy, science fiction, and Christian allegory. The hero, Elwin Ransom, a philologist, travels first to Mars, where he meets three different sentient beings, then to Venus, an Edenlike paradise that he manages to save from the powers of evil. Back on Earth, Ransom again triumphs in a struggle against dark influences, with angels and the wizard Merlin on his side.

Genre: Fantasy; Science Fiction
Subjects: Life on other planets; Good and evil; Allegories; Interplanetary voyages

Lichtenberg, Jacqueline

938.
1. *Those of My Blood.* St. Martin's, 1988.
2. *Dreamspy.* St. Martin's, 1989.

The luren, vampiric creatures, who live incognito in human form on Earth, deal with conflict in their own ranks when some luren wish to contact their home world in outer space. In the sequel, the luren become one of a group of sentient beings engaged in an intergalactic war that could result in the end of space travel by disrupting the time-space continuum.

Genre: Science Fiction
Subjects: Vampires; Interplanetary wars; Interplanetary voyages; Interstellar communication

939. Sime/Gen
1. *House of Zeor.* Doubleday, 1974.
2. *Unto Zeor Forever.* Doubleday, 1978.
3. *First Channel.* (Written with Jean Lorrah) Doubleday, 1980.
4. *Mahogany Trinrose.* Doubleday, 1981.
5. *Channel's Destiny.* (Written with Jean Lorrah) Doubleday, 1982.
6. *Rensime.* Doubleday, 1984.
7. *Zelrod's Doom.* (Written with Jean Lorrah) DAW Books, 1986.
8. *Ambrov Kean.* (Written by Jean Lorrah) DAW Books, 1986.

On a postcatastrophe Earth, two humanoid species are locked in a difficult symbiotic relationship. The stronger, seemingly more powerful Simes desperately need selyn, a chemical that the more human Gens spontaneously produce in their bodies. A family of Simes evolve who are enormously strong and capable of "channeling" or extracting the crucial selyn from Gens without injury.

Genre: Science Fiction
Subjects: Nuclear warfare; Interplanetary wars

Liddell, Robert

940.
1. *Kind Relations.* Peter Owen, 1994.
2. *Stepsons.* Peter Owen, 1992.
3. *The Last Enchantments.* Peter Owen, 1992.

After their mother dies, Andrew and Stephen are left with their aunts while their father goes to Egypt during World War I. When their father remarries, the boys find their stepmother is a sadistic, cruel woman. They endure years of psychological abuse until they grow up and go to North Christminster for university studies. Upper middle-class British life between the wars is brilliantly evoked.

Subjects: Autobiographical stories; Boys; Family life
Place/Time: England—1900–1945

Lide, Mary

941.
1. *The Legacy of Tregaran.* St. Martin's, 1991.
2. *Tregaran.* St. Martin's, 1989.

In Cornwall, the centuries-old Tregarn-Tregaran feud keeps young lovers Alice Tregarn and John Tregarnan from marrying. His family opposes the match, and older brother Nigel steps in and seduces young Alice before he leaves for World War I. Alice's honor is saved when her brother forces Nigel to marry her. Alice and John will be reunited briefly, but she won't live to see the problems her son will have. Phil Tregarn is a proud miner who loves Joyalyn Tregaran, heiress of the estate. Her grandmother keeps them from marrying because of his family's past. Only the winds of World War II can sweep away the secrets so that the lovers can marry.

Genre: Family Saga; Historical Romance
Subjects: Feuds; War
Place/Time: England—1900–1945

Lieberman, Rosalie

942. Brother Angeto

1. *The Man Who Sold Christmas.* Longmans, 1951.
2. *The Man Who Captivated New York.* Doubleday, 1960.

Brother Angeto is a simple young friar working in a New York State monastery kitchen who is suddenly and directly chosen by God to carry the Christmas spirit to those who have forgotten it. Angeto attracts attention in New York, not only with his simplicity and sincerity, but with his ability to levitate at will.

Genre: Fantasy; Gentle Read
Subjects: Monasticism and religious orders; Christmas; Christianity; Miracles

Limonov, Eduard

943.

1. *Memoir of a Russian Punk.* Grove Weidenfeld, 1990.
2. *It's Me, Eddie.* Random, 1983.
3. *His Butler's Story.* Grove Press, 1987.

Eddie, a Russian emigre, tells his autobiographical tale about growing up in Russia before glasnost. He turns to the streets and gangs, but a brutal beating leads him to emigrate to America. In America, he lives in a roach-infested hotel, dreams of becoming a writer, and ends up as a butler. Throughout the books, Limonov parodies the world of immigrants, superstars, and writers.

Subjects: Teenagers; Immigrants; Autobiographical stories
Place/Time: Soviet Union—1945–1980; Soviet Union—1980–1991; United States—1945–1980; United States—1945–1980

Lindop, Audrey Erskine

944.

1. *The Singer, Not the Song.* Appleton, 1953.
2. *The Judas Figures.* Appleton, 1956.

A remote Mexican town is terrorized by the bandit Malo. The forces of good represented by the village priest Father Keogh seem to have triumphed, but Malo's dark influence survives his death.

Subjects: Crime and criminals; Catholic priests; Good and evil
Place/Time: Mexico—1945–1980

Lisle, Holly. *See also* Bradley, Marion Zimmer

945. Secret Texts

1. *Diplomacy of Wolves.* Warner, 1998.
2. *Vengeance of Dragons.* Warner, 1999.

In the Iberan lands, magic has been forbidden since the War of the Wizards centuries ago. Kait Galweigh, a young diplomat who is the descendant of a powerful family, must hide her magical ability to shape shift, a crime punishable by death. Kait's determination not to use her power is put to the test when a plot against her family sends her out into the world as a fugitive. She sets sail on an ocean voyage looking for the Mirror of Souls which may restore her murdered family to life, but, in fact, the Mirror contains the spirits of Dragons, long-dead practitioners of black magic lying in wait to unleash their power on the world.

Genre: Fantasy; Coming of Age
Subjects: Magic; Escapes; Assassination; Good and evil

Listfield, Emily

946.

1. *Variations in the Night.* Bantam, 1987.
2. *Slightly Like Strangers.* Bantam, 1988.

Love in the 1980s follows Amanda and Sam. Amanda is a New Yorker who owns a boutique. He is a transplanted Midwesterner trying to break into journalism. They meet but are afraid to fall in love. They can't make a commitment so they hit all the New York hot spots, but gradually come to live together, learn to accept each others strengths and weaknesses, and finally discover love and marriage.

Genre: Romance
Subjects: Marriage
Place/Time: New York (N. Y.)—1980–

Livingston, Nancy

947.

1. *The Far Side of the Hill.* St. Martin's, 1988.
2. *Land of Our Dreams.* St. Martin's, 1989.

John McKire and his brother Davie live in rural poverty in Scotland in 1900. Their dream is to go to the city and become wealthy. Once there and working, the brothers are asked to take in Mary Hamilton, a young girl from their village who is pregnant. Both brothers fall in love with her, but she marries John. Together they establish a small store and work to achieve prosperity. The outbreak of World War I forces the family to face the horrors of war and the end of an era.

Genre: Historical Fiction
Subjects: World War I, 1914–1918; Love; Family life; Unmarried mothers
Place/Time: Scotland—1900–1945

Llewellyn, Richard

948.

1. *How Green Was My Valley.* Macmillan, 1940.

2. *Up into the Singing Mountain.* Doubleday, 1960.
3. *Green, Green My Valley Now.* Doubleday, 1975.
4. *Down Where the Moon Is Small.* Doubleday, 1966.

Huw Morgan, youngest son of a miner in South Wales, relates the deterioration of the once beautiful Welsh countryside from 1870 to 1900. When he grows up, he emigrates to Patagonia, Chile, where he sets up as an expert cabinet maker, then marries Lal Corwen. After making his fortune in Chile, he and Lal return to Wales where he renovates his old family home. As he gets older, he reflects on his life and loves.

Genre: Gentle Read; Historical Fiction
Subjects: Family life; Country life; Coal mines and mining
Place/Time: Wales—19th century; Chile—19th century

Llywelyn, Morgan

949.
1. *Lion of Ireland: The Legend of Brian Boru.* Houghton Mifflin, 1980.
2. *Pride of Lions.* Tor, 1996.

Brian Boru joins his brother as they fight the Vikings who have invaded Ireland. As he fights, Brian unites all of Ireland and becomes its king. He marries Deirdre and then Gormlaith and has two sons, but in 1014 in a battle with the Vikings, Brian is killed. His son Donough tries to claim the crown, but is driven from Ireland by his brother Teigue. Donough travels to Scotland to seek ties through an arranged marriage. When he returns to Ireland, he loves a pagan woman and tries to pull together his father's old alliances.

Genre: Historical Fiction
Subjects: Irish; Kings and rulers; Vikings; Brothers; Battles
Place/Time: Ireland—10th century

Llywelyn, Morgan *and* Scott, Michael

950. The Arcana
1. *Silverhand.* Baen, 1995.
2. *Silverlight.* Baen, 1996.

Caeled starts life as a poor orphan, but a prophecy that he will combat the evil of The Duet, cruel twins who rule the world, works itself out in these tales. Accompanied by a vampire, a were-wolfhound, and a woman of stone, Caeled must find the magical Arcana artifacts, which will allow the forces of reason and order to triumph.

Genre: Fantasy
Subjects: Orphans; Good and evil; Magic; Twins

Lodi, Maria

951.
1. *Charlotte Morel.* Putnam, 1969.
2. *Charlotte Morel: The Dream.* Putnam, 1970.
3. *Charlotte Morel: The Siege.* Putnam, 1970.

Paris in the 1860s is a dynamic, colorful, and vibrant city. Napoleon III is having the city rebuilt along grandiose lines. To a girl from the provinces, the city is exciting. Charlotte comes to the city with her husband, but meets journalist Thomas Becque who falls in love with her. She resists his love, but he tries to protect her even as he is being persecuted by the government for his writings. He stays through the siege of Paris in 1870 to protect Charlotte no matter what the cost.

Genre: Historical Romance
Subjects: Love affairs; Cities and towns; Paris (France), siege of, 1870–1871
Place/Time: Paris (France)—19th century; France—19th century

Lofts, Norah

952.
1. *The Town House: The Building of the House.* Doubleday, 1959.
2. *The House at Old Vine.* Doubleday, 1961.
3. *The House at Sunset.* Doubleday, 1962.

The House at Old Vine is a mansion in Suffolk, England, where generations of the Reed family live and love. Martin Reed rises from serfdom to become a wealthy merchant. From 1496 to the present, the family live through religious and political strife as their lives reflect the social history of the time.

Genre: Family Saga; Historical Fiction
Subjects: Love; Houses
Place/Time: England—multicentury span

953.
1. *Gad's Hall.* Doubleday, 1978.
2. *The Haunting of Gad's Hall.* Doubleday, 1979.

When Bob and Jill buy Gad's Hall, they dismiss the claims that the mansion is haunted. In flashbacks, the lives of the Thorley's, who founded Gad's Hall in the 1800s, are described. When daughter Lavinia becomes pregnant and is unmarried, her mother hides her away with tragic results. Each of the later Thorleys marry, but they all have troubles. It is Bob and Jill who discover the evil secret of the attic and finally exorcise the ghosts of the hall.

Genre: Family Saga; Historical Fiction; Romance
Subjects: Ghost stories
Place/Time: England—19th century; England—1900–1945; England—1945–1980

954.
1. *Knight's Acre.* Doubleday, 1975.
2. *The Homecoming.* Doubleday, 1976.

3. *The Lonely Furrow.* Doubleday, 1977.

Sir Godfrey Tallboys is a knight who is known for his warrior skills. While his wife tends their estate, he and a contingent go to Spain to fight the Moors. There he is captured and enslaved, but an escaped harem girl helps him to flee. Sir Godfrey takes her home to East Anglia when he discovers she is pregnant. His death during the War of the Roses saves him from the domestic complications that have arisen. Henry Tallboys, Godfrey's son, finds himself attracted to Joanna after his wife's death, but discovers she is his half sister. He sends her to the manor to learn to be a lady.

Genre: Family Saga; Historical Romance
Subjects: Love affairs; England—War of the Roses, 1455–1485
Place/Time: England—15th century; Spain—15th century

Logan, Chuck

955.
1. *The Price of Blood.* HarperCollins, 1997.
2. *The Big Law.* HarperCollins, 1998.

Ex-Vietnam soldier Phil Broker now works for the Minnesota Bureau of Criminal Apprehension and is shocked when the daughter of dead army buddy, Ray Pryce, comes to him for help in clearing her father's name. Everyone thought Pryce had stolen tons of gold in the waning days of the war, but Nina has evidence that Cyrus La Porte actually took the money. Broker joins her as they search for the gold and the truth. Later, Broker becomes involved with the Federal Witness Protection Program when his ex-wife Caron gets involved with her new husband's stolen millions. Fading reporter Tom James tracks Caron down, steals the money from her, and pins her husband's murder on her. Broker must fight his way through the Witness Protection Program to find James so he can clear his ex-wife.

Genre: Adventure
Subjects: Adventure; Escapes; Theft
Place/Time: Minnesota—1980–; Vietnam—1980–

Long, William. *Pseud. of* V. (Vivian) A. Stuart. *See also* Stuart, V. (Vivian) A.

956. The Australians
1. *The Exiles.* Dell, 1979.
2. *The Settlers.* Dell, 1980.
3. *The Traitors.* Dell, 1981.
4. *The Explorers.* Dell, 1982.
5. *The Adventurers.* Dell, 1983.
6. *The Colonists.* Dell, 1984.
7. *The Gold Seekers.* Dell, 1985.
8. *The Gallant.* Dell, 1986.
9. *The Empire Builders.* Dell, 1987.

The early days of Australia, from its beginnings as a penal colony to the mid-19th century, are portrayed through different groups of pioneers who settle the country. In 1781, Jennie Taggart is brought to Australia. Her descendants become involved with all the major events in Australian history from farming in New South Wales, to the gold rush, to the settling of New Zealand. Book 9 was published after Long's death. Later books in the series have been written by other authors.

Genre: Adventure; Family Saga; Historical Fiction
Subjects: Frontier and pioneer life; Adventure; Voyages and travels; England —colonies
Place/Time: Australia—18th century; Australia—19th century; New Zealand—18th century; New Zealand—19th century

Longstreet, Stephen

957.
1. *The Pedlocks.* Simon & Schuster, 1951.
2. *Pedlock at Law.* Simon & Schuster, 1959. (Originally titled: *The Crime*)
3. *Pedlock and Sons.* Delacorte, 1966.
4. *Pedlock Saint, Pedlock Sinner.* Delacorte, 1969.
5. *The Pedlock Inheritance.* McKay, 1972.
6. *God and Sarah Pedlock.* McKay, 1976.
7. *The Pedlocks in Love.* Avon, 1978.

The changing fortunes of four generations of the wealthy Pedlock family are chronicled through its various members. Elijah Pedlock founded a small store that grew into a huge department store empire. But only the first and second generation Pedlocks had the drive and ambition to succeed. Now the third and fourth generations have lost both their interest in the store and have gone into different professions. However, it is their loss of faith in Judaism that forces them to examine their lives and their place in contemporary America.

Genre: Family Saga
Subjects: Jews; Judaism; Department stores; Business; Wealth
Place/Time: United States—1900–1945; United States—1945–1980

958.
1. *War in the Golden Weather.* Doubleday, 1965.
2. *Eagles Where I Walk.* Doubleday, 1961.
3. *A Few Painted Feathers.* Doubleday, 1963.

The rise of George Washington from the French and Indian Wars to the American Revolution is shown through the eyes of the Cortlandt family who fight by his side. Will Cortlandt, an itinerant painter, is saved from hanging by Washington who drafts him into service. They join General Braddock and fight in the tragic battle at Fort Duquesne in the French and Indian War. After the war, Washington's fame grows, but Will sinks into oblivion. During the Revolutionary War, another Cortlandt, David, works as a young surgeon in Washington's army, first in New York and then in the South. His wife Roxanne insists upon accompanying him, and their lives are intertwined with Washington's and his success in the War.

Genre: Historical Fiction; War
Subjects: United States—French and Indian War, 1755–1763; War; Surgeons; Washington, George, 1732–1799; United States—revolution, 1775–1783; Army, United States
Place/Time: United States—18th century

959.
1. *All or Nothing.* Putnam, 1983.
2. *Our Father's House.* Putnam, 1985.
3. *Sons and Daughters.* Putnam, 1987.

George Fiore, an Italian immigrant, arrives in San Francisco in the late 1800s hoping for a better life. He and his family build a fortune in the banking industry and become involved with Tomas Velasquez, his Spanish family, and Gaw, the head of the Chinese Tongs. During the 1920s, the second generation son and daughters carry on the family banking business and expand into movies, oil, and gambling, but they all rally to avoid financial disaster after the 1929 crash. Although the family business is saved and supports them, the third generation pursues many other interests in the 1950s and 1960s.

Genre: Family Saga; Historical Fiction
Subjects: Bankers; Wealth; Millionaires
Place/Time: San Francisco (Calif.)—multicentury span; California—multicentury span.

Loos, Anita

960.
1. *Gentlemen Prefer Blonds: The Illuminating Diary of a Professional Lady.* Boni & Liveright, 1925.
2. *But Gentlemen Marry Brunettes.* Boni & Liveright, 1928.

Small town girl Lorelei Lee certainly can't spell, but her naive optimism, beautiful face, and, of course, blonde hair eventually get her the wealthy husband and film career she desires. Her brunette friend Dorothy becomes the center of her attention in the sequel as the two roam through the New York maze of literary sophisticates and wealthy socialites.

Genre: Humor
Subjects: Women; Wealth; Ambition; Social classes; Friendship
Place/Time: New York (N. Y.)—1900–1945

Lopez, Erika

961.
1. *Flaming Iguanas: An Illustrated All-Girl Road Novel Thing.* Simon & Schuster, 1997.
2. *They Call Me Mad Dog.* Simon & Schuster, 1998.

With a fetish for post offices, Tomato Rodriguez decides to go coast-to-coast looking for the perfect post office. She takes her motorcycle on a cross-country trip where she tries to find herself and love. In San Francisco, Tomato and her girlfriend Hooter try to open a store, get tested for HIV, and finally end up in jail. The zany Tomato goes from one hilarious adventure to another, and she always has something to say about everything.

Genre: Humor
Subjects: Voyages and travels; Women
Place/Time: United States—1980–; San Francisco (Calif.)—1980–

Lorrah, Jean. *See* Lichtenberg, Jacqueline

Lowell, Elizabeth

962.
1. *Amber Beach.* Avon, 1997.
2. *Jade Island.* Avon, 1998.
3. *Pearl Cove.* Avon, 1999.

Amber, jade, and black pearls keep the Donovan family in trouble and in love. Honor Donovan refuses to believe that her brother Kyle is dead. It seems Kyle has disappeared after stealing a million dollars worth of amber from Russia. Honor hires Jake Mallory who she suspects knows where her brother is hiding. As they search, a romance begins between these two. After Kyle is cleared, he is asked to spy on the Tung family and their illegal trade in jade. As he gets to know Lianne Blakely, the illegitimate daughter of Johnny Tung, the two find they are attracted to each other even though they are spying on each other. Greed and black pearls lead Archer Donovan to help the only woman he's ever loved—Hannah McGarry. When Hannah's husband is killed and the black pearls he was developing are stolen, Archer must find out who killed him and keep Hannah alive. Jewels, sex, suspense and love keep the Donovan men busy.

Genre: Romance
Subjects: Brothers and sisters; Lovers; Adventure; Precious stones
Place/Time: United States—1980–; Asia—1980–

Lowry, Beverly

963.
1. *Come Back, Lolly Ray.* Doubleday, 1977.
2. *Emma Blue.* Doubleday, 1978.

In the class conscious town of Eunola, Mississippi, Lolly Ray is the town's golden girl. She is a baton twirler and lives free of the town's rules. When she comes home from college pregnant, she is shunned and eventually abandons her daughter. Emma Blue is raised by her granny in a trailer and is a solitary teen looking for her mother.

Genre: Coming of Age

Subjects: Teenagers; Unmarried mothers; Small town life
Place/Time: Mississippi—1945–1980; Mississippi—1980–

Lucas, George. *See* Claremont, Chris

Ludlum, Robert

964. Bourne Trilogy
1. *The Bourne Identity.* R. Merek, 1980.
2. *The Bourne Supremacy.* Random House, 1986.
3. *The Bourne Ultimatum.* Random House, 1990.

A Greek fisherman pulls a man who has been shot out of the ocean. The patient's wound heals, but he can't remember who he is or why he was shot. From a microfiche of a numbered account at a Swiss bank embedded on his thigh, he learns he is Jason Bourne, member of an American corporation called Treadstone 71. As bits and pieces of his memory come back, he realizes he is a top spy assigned to draw out the world's most dangerous assassin Carlo. Through chases, fights, and traps in exotic locales, Bourne works to defeat an assortment of bad guys before he faces Carlo in a fight to the end. Nonstop action and innumerable subplots keep readers turning pages to see if Bourne can save himself, his family, and the United States from evil.

Genre: Adventure; Espionage
Subjects: Spies; Adventure; International intrigue; Amnesia; Assassination
Place/Time: Europe—1980–; United States—1980–

Lumley, Brian

965.
1. *House of Doors.* Tor, 1998.
2. *Maze of Worlds.* Tor, 1998.

The alien Thone have distributed on Earth a form of technology that makes the planet uninhabitable for humans but comfortable for themselves. A group of earthlings successfully battle the aliens for a time but it is only a temporary victory. When the aliens return, their opponents discover that the House of Doors, a high-tech alien torture chamber that plays on the worst fears of its victims, may actually be the key to ridding Earth of the Thone permanently.

Genre: Science Fiction; Horror
Subjects: Extraterrestrial beings; Technology and civilization

966. Necroscope Series
1. *Necroscope.* Tor, 1988.
2. *Vamphyri.* Tor, 1989.
3. *Necroscope: The Lost Years.* Tor, 1995.
4. *Necroscope: Resurgence.* Tor, 1996.
5. *The Source.* Tor, 1989.
6. *Deadspeak.* Tor, 1990.

7. *Dead Spawn.* Tor, 1991.

Harry Keogh inherits psychic powers that make him a necroscope: one who can communicate with the dead. His efforts to rid the world of vampires bring him up against a Russian who possesses similar powers, though he bends them to his own evil purposes. In his quest, Harry also enters a fifth dimension and comes into conflict with his own vampiric son. Deprived of his powers and infected with the influence of the undead, he must fight his way back to his former self. *Note:* This series is continued in the E-Branch Trilogy.

Genre: Horror
Subjects: Vampires; Fathers and sons; Spiritualism

967. E-Branch Trilogy
1. *Necroscope: Invaders.* Tom Doherty Associates, 1999.

Continuing the Necroscope tales is this projected trilogy about E-Branch, the special organization once led by Harry Keogh, who perished with his family in order to free the world of vampires. Despite his youth, Jake Cutter appears to be the man to replace Harry as Necroscope, but Jake has strengths and weaknesses that make his success uncertain. He is put to the test as mystical barriers come down and three powerful vampires come to Earth. *Note:* This series follows the Necroscope series and is continued in the Vampire World series.

Genre: Horror
Subjects: Vampires; Imaginary wars and battles

968. Vampire World
1. *Blood Brothers.* Tor, 1992.
2. *The Last Aerie.* Tor, 1993.
3. *Bloodwars.* Tor, 1994.

The saga of Harry Keogh continues with the lives of his twin sons, Nathan, who continues his father's fight against vampires, and Nestor, who has become a member of the undead. Complicating their relationship is their love for the same woman. On orders of his brother, Nathan is thrown to Earth from an alternate reality. He joins with a group of gypsies to take advantage of the involvement of vampires in their own territorial battles. *Note:* This series follows the E-Branch Trilogy.

Genre: Horror
Subjects: Vampires; Twins; Love

969. Titus Crow
1. *Titus Crow, Vol. 1: The Burrowers Beneath/ The Transition of Titus Crow.* Tor, 1997.
2. *Titus Crow, Vol. 2: The Clock of Dreams/ Spawn of the Winds.* Tor, 1997.
3. *Titus Crow, Vol. 3: In the Moons of Borea, Elysia, The Coming of Cthulhu.* Tor, 1997.

Adventurer and sleuth Titus Crow does battle with the forces of evil headed by the dark god Cthulhu. These short novels originally published in England twenty years ago combine elements of gothic horror, fantasy, and science fiction.

Genre: Horror; Fantasy; Science Fiction
Subjects: Detectives; Good and evil; Gods and goddesses

Lupoff, Richard A.

970.
1. *Sun's End.* Berkley, 1984.
2. *Galaxy's End.* Ace, 1988.

A mortally wounded Japanese engineer is frozen and, 80 years later, revived with a technologically enhanced body. After a disappointing attempt to return to his homeland, which has actually regressed, he discovers that he has an opportunity to use his new powers to save the solar system.

Genre: Science Fiction
Subjects: Cryonics; Bionics; Degeneration

971. Flat Earth
1. *Circumpolar!* Pocket Books, 1984.
2. *Countersolar!* Arbor House, 1987.

The shape of this world is unfamiliar. It looks like a donut, but the inhabitants—Howard Hughes, Amelia Earhart, Charles Lindbergh, Albert Einstein, and Eva Peron—are certainly well known. First Charles, Amelia, and Howard set off on a 'round the poles flight during which they encounter some strange and fantastic characters. In the sequel, Albert and Eva race off into space lured by a message from the mysterious Counter-Earth.

Genre: Fantasy; Science Fiction
Subjects: Interplanetary voyages; Hughes, Howard, 1905–1976; Peron, Eva, 1919–1952; Earhart, Amelia, 1897–1937; Lindbergh, Charles A., 1902–1974; Einstein, Albert, 1879–1955

Lustbader, Eric van

972.
1. *The Ninja.* M. Evans, 1980.
2. *The Miko.* Villard. 1984.
3. *White Ninja.* Ballantine, 1990.
4. *Kaisho.* Pocket Books, 1993.
5. *Floating City.* Pocket Books, 1994.
6. *Second Skin.* Pocket Books, 1995.

Nicholas Linnear is half Caucasian, half Asian. He was raised in Japan and taught the power of the white ninja. He is drawn into confrontations with the black ninjas, a cult of Japanese assassins. He must rely on his skill in the martial arts to save himself and others. Whether fighting ninjas, yakusa, mafia, or a crazed rock-and-roll killer in the Vietnamese jungle, he is involved in an exotic web of oriental esotericism, intrigue, violence, and double-cross.

Genre: Adventure; Espionage
Subjects: Spies; International intrigue; Violence; Adventure; Terrorism; Martial arts
Place/Time: United States; Japan

973. The Sunset Warrior Cycle
1. *The Sunset Warrior.* Doubleday, 1977.
2. *Shallows of Night.* Doubleday, 1978.
3. *Dai-San.* Doubleday, 1979.

Ronin is the finest swordsman of Freehold, but he won't pledge to support the evil Seardin who rules the land. Ronin and his lover Kreen use the scroll of the ancients to save the land and fight the warlords before they destroy the land with their evil magic.

Genre: Fantasy
Subjects: Imaginary wars and battles; Lovers; Magic; Good and evil

Lynn, Elizabeth A.

974. The Chronicles of Tornor
1. *Watchtower.* Berkley, 1979.
2. *The Dancers of Arun.* Berkley, 1979.
3. *The Northern Girl.* Berkley, 1980.

Laced with subtle fantasy elements, these works take place in a group of cultures that are, in some ways, medieval but might also be considered postmodern in that equality of the sexes is taken for granted and homosexuality is both common and accepted. The theme running through the plots is the difficulty that characters have in adjusting when they shift from the militaristic, rigid North to the artistic, accepting society of the Cheari or the province of the city dwellers called Kendra-on-the-Delta.

Genre: Fantasy
Subjects: Imaginary kingdoms; Cultural conflict

Lytton, Edward Bulwer, Baron

975. Real and Ideal Trilogy
1. *The Caxtons: A Family Picture.* Hurst, 1849.
2. *"My Novel" by Pisistratus Caxton, or "Varieties in English Life".* Harper, 1852.
3. *"What Will He Do with It?" by Pisistratus Caxton.* Harper, 1859.

Using various members of the Caxton family, Bulwer Lytton explores the political and social aspirations and disappointments of an English family of the mid-19th century. *"My Novel"* is actually a novel written by one of the Caxtons interspersed with comments from other characters from the first work. Book three starts with 14 characters separated widely by time and space, who are gradually brought together in layers of multiple plots, to explore Bulwer Lytton's theories about pride and self-abnegation.

Subjects: Family life; Authors
Place/Time: England—19th century

MacAvoy, R. A. (Roberta Ann)

976.
1. *Tea with the Black Dragon.* Bantam, 1983.
2. *Twisting the Rope.* Bantam, 1986.

Mayland Long, who is really a truth-seeking Chinese black dragon in the form of a man, joins forces with Martha Macnamara to find Martha's missing daughter. The two become lovers and reappear four years later in charge of a Celtic band whose wanderings bring them into a murder mystery.

Genre: Fantasy
Subjects: Dragons; Lovers; Missing children; Bands (music)

977. Nazhuret Series
1. *Lens of the World.* Morrow, 1990.
2. *King of the Dead.* Avon, 1992.
3. *The Belly of the Wolf.* Morrow, 1994.

These two works begin the saga of Nazhuret, a homely orphan who is snatched from his mundane schoolboy existence by the eccentric nobleman Powl. Nazhuret is prepared by a series of ordeals for an unusual life that consists of philosophical meditation but also dealings with the great powers of a fantasy realm, the Kingdom of Vestinglon. Even in his old age, Nazhuret cannot avoid conflict when he defends the son of his friend, King Rudolf of Velonya, who is accused of being responsible for his father's death.

Genre: Fantasy
Subjects: Orphans; Imaginary kingdoms; Imaginary wars and battles

978. A Trio for Lute
1. *Damiano.* Bantam, 1984.
2. *Damiano's Lute.* Bantam, 1984.
3. *Raphael.* Bantam, 1984.

In Renaissance Italy, the young musician Damiano, who also happens to be a witch, deals with both dark and light forces. Invisible to everyone but him is his lute teacher, the archangel Raphael, whose brother Lucifer tries to lure them both into his realm.

Genre: Fantasy
Subjects: Musicians; Angels; Witchcraft; Good and evil

Macdonald, George

979.
1. *Malcolm.* G. Rutledge, 1875. (This title has also been edited and published as *The Fisherman's Lady.* Bethany House, 1982.)
2. *Marquis of Lassie.* G. Rutledge, 1877. (This title has also been edited and published as *The Marquis' Secret.* Bethany House, 1982.)

These 19th-century Christian novels have been abridged and updated by Bethany House to appeal to modern readers. They tell the story of a young fisherman in northern Scotland who is in love with a woman whose life is shrouded in mystery. As he tries to save her, he must also search his own past to find his true identity. He discovers he is a marquis, but it is his faith that keeps him in touch with the villagers he knows and loves.

Genre: Christian Fiction
Subjects: Christian life; Faith; Religion; Country life
Place/Time: Scotland—19th century

980. Thomas Wingfield Trilogy
1. *Thomas Wingfield, Curate.* G. Rutledge, 1880. (This title has been edited and published as *The Curate's Awakening.* Bethany House, 1985.)
2. *Paul Faber, Surgeon.* G. Rutledge, 1879. (This title has been edited and published as *The Lady's Confession.* Bethany House, 1986.)
3. *There and Back.* G. Rutledge, 1891. (This title has been edited and published as *The Barron's Apprenticeship.* Bethany House, 1986.)

Thomas Wingfield takes up his first parish, but he finds being a minister is not what he expected. A parishioner challenges his faith, and Wingfield has to examine his reasons for entering the church. He becomes a friend of the town doctor and atheist, Paul Faber. Wingfield helps Faber find faith after Paul uncovers his wife's secret. Wingfield then also helps Richard, the bookbinder, discover his real parentage. In these stories, all the main characters must learn what true faith really means.

Genre: Christian Fiction
Subjects: Christian life; Faith; Religion; Small town life; Clergy
Place/Time: England—19th century

Macdonald, Malcolm

981.
1. *The World from Rough Stones.* Knopf, 1975.
2. *The Rich Are with You Always.* Knopf, 1976.
3. *Sons of Fortune.* Knopf, 1978.

John and Nora Stevenson are a poor laboring-class couple in England in 1839. Walter and Arabella Thornton are a middle-class couple. The two couples lives are intertwined when they both become involved with the building of the railroads in England. The Stevensons become wealthy as they take part in the railroad schemes of the day. Their marriage is strained by their new wealth, but they surmount these troubles.

Genre: Historical Fiction
Subjects: Family life; Wealth; Railroads
Place/Time: England—19th century

MacDougall, Ruth Doan

982.
1. *The Cheerleader.* Bantam, 1973.
2. *Snowy.* St. Martin's, 1993.

Henrietta Snow is 16 in the 1950s in a small town in New Hampshire. Her biggest worries are trying out for the cheerleading squad, doing her college applications, and falling in love. When she leaves home for college, she tries to expand her experiences and knowledge, but drifts through life until a crisis in middle age forces her to reexamine her life.

Genre: Coming of Age
Subjects: Teenagers; Cheerleading; School life;
   Women; Middle age
Place/Time: New Hampshire—1945–1980

Machado de Assis

983.
   1. *Epitaph of a Small Winner.* Noonday, 1952, 1888.
   2. *Heritage of Quincas Borba.* Noonday, 1954, 1891. (Alternate title: *Philosopher or Dog?*)

The ghost of Braz Cubas, a 19th-century Brazilian manufacturer of corn plasters, evaluates his life in a simple and very cynical manner. He feels that his life was successful because he produced no offspring to suffer the same tragedies and difficulties that he endured. Posterity or lack thereof is also an important issue to Braz's philosophical friend Quincas Borba, who names his dog after himself and provides for the canine Quincas in his will.

Subjects: Ghost stories; Childlessness; Dogs
Place/Time: Brazil—19th century

MacInnes, Helen

984.
   1. *The Hidden Target.* Harcourt Brace Jovanovich, 1980.
   2. *Cloak of Darkness.* Harcourt Brace Jovanovich, 1982.

Ben Renwick of NATO's undercover counterterrorist organization rescues Nina O'Connell, the daughter of a U.S. government official, from European terrorists who want to use her as a tool. Later he travels to India and New York as he fights an assassin who is working for an illegal arms dealer.

Genre: Adventure; Espionage
Subjects: Spies; Adventure; International intrigue;
   Terrorism
Place/Time: Europe—1945–1980; India—1945–1980; New York (N. Y.)—1945–1980

Macintyre, Lorn

985. The Chronicles of Invernevis
   1. *Cruel in the Shadow.* St. Martin's, 1979.
   2. *The Blind Bend.* St. Martin's, 1981.

For over 500 years, the Macdonald family were lairds of the great house in the Scottish Highlands. When the old laird lies dying of an unmentionable disease in 1899, Niall Macdonald, the new laird, brings home a bride so beautiful and radiant, it is hoped that she will dissipate the corruption and cruelty of the family with her innocence and hope.

Genre: Historical Romance
Subjects: Marriage
Place/Time: Scotland—multicentury span

Macken, Walter

986.
   1. *Seek the Fair Land.* Macmillan, 1959.
   2. *The Silent People.* Macmillan, 1962.
   3. *The Scorching Wind.* Macmillan, 1964.

When Cromwell's armies devastate and subdue Ireland in the 17th century, injustices are created that force many peaceful people into rebellion. Dominick MacMahon, a merchant, is forced to flee town with his two children and a priest in disguise. This oppression continues into the 19th century when Dualta Duanne has to survive the potato famine and emigration. In the 20th century, the Irish civil wars again bring troubles to the people of Ireland.

Genre: Historical Fiction
Subjects: Famines; Ireland—civil war, 1922–1923;
   Country life; War
Place/Time: Ireland—multicentury span

Mackenzie, Compton

987.
   1. *Altar Steps.* Doran, 1922.
   2. *Parson's Progress.* Doran, 1923.
   3. *Heavenly Ladder.* Doran, 1924.

The spiritual journey of Mark Kidderdale begins in 1880 in Notting Dale when he is a young boy. He is ordained as an Anglican minister and tries various parishes. He finally returns to the Cornish coast where he grew up and takes over the church there. When he introduces high church ritual into the service, he is expelled from the church and the ministry. He finally goes to Rome where he converts to Catholicism and begins life again.

Genre: Christian Fiction
Subjects: Teenagers; Clergy; Catholic faith;
   Churches; Faith
Place/Time: England—19th century; Italy—19th century

988. The Four Winds of Love
   1. *The East Wind of Love.* Dodd, 1937.
   2. *The South Wind of Love.* Dodd, 1937.
   3. *The West Wind of Love.* Dodd, 1940.
   4. *West to the North.* Dodd, 1941.
   5. *North Wind of Love.* Dodd, 1945.

Changes in Europe are paralleled through the growth of a young Scottish boy, John Ogilvie. He is at school when the series opens, then attends Oxford and becomes a playwright. When World War I starts, he becomes a soldier and falls in love with an American, Athene Langridge. When the war is over, he visits Italy and sees Mussolini rise to power, then in Germany,

Hitler. When John's wife dies, his personal suffering mirrors that of war-torn Europe.

Subjects: Teenagers; School life; College life; War; World War I, 1914–1918; World politics
Place/Time: England—1900–1945; Italy—1900–1945; Germany—1900–1945

MacKenzie, Norman. *See* Forrest, Anthony

Mackey, Mary

989.
1. *The Year the Horses Came.* HarperSanFrancisco, 1993.
2. *The Horses at the Gate.* HarperSanFrancisco, 1995.
3. *The Fires of Spring.* NAL, 1998.

In prehistoric Europe, members of a peaceful goddess-worshiping civilization who call themselves Motherpeople encounter the Hansi, a violent tribe of nomads who kidnap a young priestess, Marrah. One of the nomads, Stavan, falls in love with Marrah and is converted to her way of life, but circumstances separate them, and she must become a war queen to defend her city. Marrah's son Keru is kidnapped by the Hansi. Keru's sister and cousin make potentially dangerous plans to rescue him, but it is Marrah who helps save the day.

Genre: Historical Fiction
Subjects: Humans, prehistoric; Kidnapping; Love; Religion
Place/Time: Europe—prehistoric times

Maclean, Alistar

990.
1. *The Guns of Navarone.* Doubleday, 1957.
2. *Force 10 from Navarone.* Doubleday, 1968.

During World War II, a five man British army team is sent to knock out the guns of Navarone, which control the approaches to the eastern Mediterranean islands. This team must fight its way to the top through daring exploits. Only three survive—Mallory, Miller, and Stavros. Next they are sent behind enemy lines in Yugoslavia to help partisans blow up a dam and divert the Germans.

Genre: Adventure; War
Subjects: Adventure; War; World War II, 1939–1945
Place/Time: Mediterranean region—1900–1945; Yugoslavia—1900–1945

Macleod, Alison

991. Tom Vaughan
1. *The Hireling.* Houghton Mifflin, 1966.

2. *City of Light.* Houghton Mifflin, 1969.

Living by his wits and meeting important figures such as Henry VIII and Katherine of Aragon, Tom Vaughan navigates the treacherous political and religious waters of 16th-century England. Unscrupulous as a young man, Tom develops a moral sense as he matures. As a middle-aged man he goes to Geneva where he experiences the rigors of Calvinism and marries the widow of a noble Italian physician before returning to England.

Genre: Historical Fiction
Subjects: Christianity; Politics—England; Courts and courtiers
Place/Time: England—16th century; Switzerland—16th century

Macleod, Le Roy

992.
1. *Years of Peace.* Century, 1932.
2. *The Crowded Hill.* Reynal & Hitchcock, 1934.

The Wabash Valley of Indiana in the years following the Civil War is the scene of the meeting of rebellious young Tyler Peck and Evaline, who becomes his bride. Despite the shaky marital foundation of a whirlwind courtship and two very different natures, the two persevere through the difficulties of having to share their home with another family.

Genre: Historical Romance
Subjects: Family life; Country life
Place/Time: Indiana—19th century

MacNeil, Duncan. *Pseud. of* Philip McCutchan. *See also* McCutchan, Philip

993.
1. *Drums Along the Khyber.* Hodder and Stoughton, 1969. (This title has been published only in England.)
2. *Lieutenant of the Line.* St. Martin's, 1972.
3. *Sadhu on the Mountain Peak.* St. Martin's, 1973.
4. *The Gates of Kunarja.* St. Martin's, 1973.
5. *The Red Daniel.* St. Martin's, 1974.
6. *Subaltern's Choice.* St. Martin's, 1974.
7. *By Command of the Viceroy.* St. Martin's, 1975.
8. *The Mullah from Kashmir.* St. Martin's, 1977.
9. *Wolf in the Fold.* St. Martin's, 1977.
10. *Charge of Cowardice.* St. Martin's, 1978.
11. *The Restless Frontier.* St. Martin's, 1980.
12. *Cunningham's Revenge.* Walker, 1985, 1981.
13. *The Train at Bundarbar.* Walker, 1986, 1981.
14. *A Matter for the Regiment.* Hodder and Stoughton, 1982. (This title has been published only in England.)

James Ogilvie is a subaltern with the 114th High-landers, the Queen's Own Royal Strathspeys, on the northwest frontier in India during the 1890s. The dashing young hero faces the continual threat of Afghan forces trying to invade India. His various adventures, fighting both external and internal foes to colonial rule, keep him dashing around India and rising in the ranks of the army to captain.

Genre: Adventure; Historical Fiction
Subjects: England—colonies; Army, British; Soldiers—British; War; Adventure
Place/Time: India—19th century

Madariaga, Salvador de

994. The Conquest of Mexico
1. *The Heart of Jade (1492–1522).* Creative Age, 1944.
2. *War in the Blood (1537–1541).* Collins, 1957.

Starting in the time of Montezuma, these stories continue through Cortez's invasion and conquest of Mexico with vivid depictions of the clash and integration of Spanish and Indian cultures.

Genre: Historical Fiction
Subjects: Explorers; Montezuma II, Emperor of Mexico, 1488–1520; Native Americans; Aztecs; Spain—colonies; War; Adventure; Cortez, Hernando, 1485–1547
Place/Time: Mexico—16th century

Mahfuz, Najib

995. Cairo Trilogy
1. *Palace Walk.* Doubleday, 1989, 1952.
2. *Palace of Desire.* Doubleday, 1990, 1956.
3. *Sugar Street.* Doubleday, 1991, 1957.

Nobel-Prize–winner Mahfuz depicts the family of al-Sayyid Ahmad, a Cairo merchant, from the end of World War I to the early 1950s and the rise of Nasser as he shows the change in the family as their Islamic culture opens to modern influences. Al-Sayyid Ahmad keeps his wife and daughters cloistered at home while his three sons pursue different paths: Yassin is dissolute, Fahmy is an ardent nationalist, and Kamal is a scholar. The children grow up and have their own families, but they interact with each other and with newly emerging Egypt. Mahfuz writes in the grand tradition of Balzac as he brings to life his characters and their society.

Genre: Family Saga; Historical Fiction
Subjects: Islam; Family life; Egypt—politics
Place/Time: Cairo (Egypt)—1900–1945; Cairo (Egypt)—1945–1980; Egypt—1900–1945; Egypt—1945–1980

Maillard, Keith

996.
1. *The Knife in My Hands.* Beaufort Books, 1982.
2. *Cutting Through.* Beaufort Books, 1983.

Life in the conservative 1950s and the radical 1960s is contrasted in these coming of age novels that explore the adolescence and adulthood of John Dupre. In the 1950s, he is an adolescent obsessed with sex, drinking, and growing up. In the 1960s, he takes part in the sexual revolution, the psychedelic scene, and the Vietnam protests. He travels around the South searching for branches of his family and becomes a draft dodger. Only gradually does he begin to understand himself and his times.

Genre: Coming of Age
Subjects: Teenagers; Sex; Hippies
Place/Time: Southern states—1945–1980

Mann, Heinrich

997.
1. *Young Henry of Navarre.* Knopf, 1937.
2. *Henry, King of France.* Knopf, 1939.

Mann greatly admired the humanity and intelligence of Henry of Navarre, the 16th-century French king who was faced with tremendous religious and social problems and conflicts during his reign and who eventually converted from Protestantism to Catholicism.

Genre: Historical Fiction
Subjects: Henry IV, King of France, 1553–1610; Kings and rulers; Courts and courtiers; Christianity
Place/Time: France—16th century

Mann, Thomas

998. Joseph and His Brothers Series
1. *Joseph and His Brothers.* Knopf, 1934.
2. *Young Joseph.* Knopf, 1935.
3. *Joseph in Egypt.* Knopf, 1938.
4. *Joseph the Provider.* Knopf, 1944.

One of the greatest writers of the 20th century gives us his masterful retelling of the Biblical story of Joseph and his coat of many colors, of being sold into slavery in Egypt, and rising to power in the court of the Pharaoh. While Mann tells the Biblical story, he is implicitly relating it to his experiences in Nazi Germany and the spirit of the Jews who were being killed there.

Genre: Historical Fiction
Subjects: Biblical stories; Brothers; Courts and courtiers; Judaism
Place/Time: Palestine—to 70 A. D.; Egypt—to 70 A. D.

Manning, Olivia

999. The Balkan Trilogy
1. *The Great Fortune.* Doubleday, 1961.
2. *The Spoilt City.* Doubleday, 1962.
3. *Friends and Heroes.* Doubleday, 1966.

The above titles have also been published in the following collection: *The Balkan Trilogy.* Penguin, 1981.

Guy and Harriet Pringle are a young English couple working in pre–World War II Rumania. When Hitler's forces overrun Bucharest, they flee to Athens, but see the city starved and bombed by the Germans. They are finally able to get out of Athens and make their way to Egypt.

Genre: Historical Fiction; War
Subjects: World War II, 1939–1945; National Socialism; Love
Place/Time: Rumania—1900–1945; Greece—1900–1945; Egypt—1900–1945

1000. The Levant Trilogy
1. *Danger Tree.* Atheneum, 1977.
2. *The Battle Lost and Won.* Atheneum, 1978.
3. *The Sum of Things.* Atheneum, 1981.

The above titles have also been published in the following collection: *The Levant Trilogy.* Penguin, 1988.

World War II Egypt is the setting for the dramatic events in the lives of Guy and Harriet Pringle, who fled Rumania when the Nazis invaded that country. Their lives are paralleled by young soldier Simon Boulderstone, who is thrown into the horrors of desert warfare. When Guy tries to send Harriet back to England, the ship she is on is sunk, but she escapes. Believing she is dead, Guy helps the army and Simon who has been wounded. Eventually Guy and Harriet are reunited, but only after the war.

Genre: Historical Fiction; War
Subjects: Soldiers—British; World War II, 1939–1945; National Socialism; Love
Place/Time: Egypt—1900–1945

Mapson, Jo-Ann

1001.
1. *Hank and Chloe.* HarperCollins, 1993.
2. *Loving Chloe.* HarperCollins, 1998.

At 33, Chloe is trying to get her life together after the death of her cowboy lover. She waits on tables at a local diner and gives her love to her dog and horse. She gives riding lessons to rich kids and struggles to get along. Then she meets middle-aged Hank Oliver, a teacher of folklore at the local junior college. They are an odd couple, but the two fall in love until Chloe is arrested and refuses Hank's help. He leaves California for a house in the Arizona desert where he tries to find himself. Chloe, pregnant with his child, finally comes to Arizona. They try living together, but Chloe finds pregnancy and domesticity restricting.

Subjects: Lovers; Love affairs; Country life
Place/Time: California—1980–; Arizona—1980–

Marcinko, Richard *and* Weisman, John

1002.
1. *Rogue Warrior.* Pocket Books, 1992.
2. *Rogue Warrior II: Red Cell.* Pocket Books, 1994.
3. *Rogue Warrior: Green Team.* Pocket Books, 1995.
4. *Rogue Warrior: Task Force Blue.* Pocket Books, 1996.
5. *Rogue Warrior: Designation Gold.* Pocket Books, 1998.
6. *Rogue Warrior: Seal Force Alpha.* Pocket Books, 1998.
7. *Rogue Warrior: Option Delta.* Pocket Books, 1999.

Richard Marcinko was a career officer in the navy and a navy SEAL in Vietnam. In a tell-all autobiography he recounts his violent life. Marcinko then uses himself and his friends in a series of violent, profanity-ridden novels. Marcinko is the Rogue Warrior and the leader of a team of counter-terrorists who battle traitors, terrorists, the Russian mob, and corrupt bureaucrats from the United States to Moscow. His navy SEAL team races around the world on secret missions, kills hoards of people, uses every type of weapon available and swears a blue streak. The good guys—Rogue Warrior and his team—are always triumphant.

Genre: Adventure
Subjects: Adventure; Violence; Navy, United States
Place/Time: United States—1980–

Marco, John

1003. Tyrants and Kings
1. *The Jackal of Nar.* Bantam, 1999.
2. *The Grand Design.* Bantam, 2000.

Prince Richius Vantran does battle in the Army of Nar against the Trin and, in the process, falls in love with Dyana, a captured Trin woman. The two return to their own lands and each enters into an arranged marriage, but they are eventually reunited. Later, Richius goes into self-imposed exile, but emerges when his family is threatened.

Genre: Fantasy
Subjects: Imaginary wars and battles; Imaginary kingdoms; Princes; Love

Margoff, Robert E. *See* Anthony, Piers

Marsh, Jean *and* O'Leary, Elizabeth

1004.
1. *The House of Eliott.* St. Martin's, 1994.
2. *A House at War.* St. Martin's, 1995.

In London in the early 1920s, Evangeline and Beatrice Eliott find that they are penniless after their father dies. They refuse to take guests into their house, and go out to get jobs. Beatrice works as a receptionist for a society photographer until her stylish clothes catch the eye of the society matrons who come to the studio. The two sisters establish a dressmaking business and soon are the toast of London. As the depression hits London, they struggle to keep their business intact and to find love.

Genre: Historical Fiction
Subjects: Sisters; Fashion industry and trade; Society novels
Place/Time: London (England)—1900–1945

Marshall, Bruce

1005.
1. *The Bishop.* Doubleday, 1970.
2. *Urban the Ninth.* Constable, 1972.

Father Spyers first appears as a young priest dealing with his own conflicted feelings and those of his flock toward the official Catholic pronouncements on the subject of birth control. Having survived this dissension, Spyers rises in the church hierarchy and suddenly, due to the death of the Pope in a plane crash, finds himself Pope Urban the Ninth trying to bring together the diverse and frequently humorous elements in the modern Catholic Church.

Genre: Christian Fiction
Subjects: Catholic priests; Birth control; Popes
Place/Time: United States—1945–1980; Vatican City (Italy)—1945–1980; Italy—1945–1980

Marshall, Deborah A. *See Crispin, A. C. (Serpent's Gift)*

Martin Du Gard, Roger

1006.
1. *The Thibaults.* Viking, 1939, 1922.
2. *Summer 1914.* Viking, 1941, 1936.

Before World War I, the Thibaults are raising their two sons, Antoine, a doctor, a vi Jacques, a dreamer and writer. From the boys' adolescence to their father's death, their life in Paris is carefully detailed. After the war, Jacques becomes a socialist and ultimately dies, while Antoine dies of a lung disease he contracted during the war.

Genre: Coming of Age; War
Subjects: Teenagers; War; World War I, 1914–1918; Brothers; Family life
Place/Time: Paris (France)—1900–1945; France—1900–1945

Martin, George R. R.

1007. A Song of Ice and Fire
1. *A Game of Thrones.* Bantam, 1996.
2. *A Clash of Kings.* Bantam, 1999.

In the fantasy land of the Seven Kingdoms, seasons may last 10 years. As the long winter approaches, three royal families resort to murder, intrigue, and arranged marriages to gain control of the land while cruel supernatural beings press against the protective Wall at the northern edge of the kingdom. In the sequel, Princess Arya disguises herself as a boy and flees the cruelty of the realm now governed by the amoral Queen Cersei following the death of Arya's father.

Genre: Fantasy
Subjects: Imaginary kingdoms; Imaginary wars and battles; Aristocracy; Inheritance and succession; Good and evil

Martine-Barnes, Adrienne. *See Paxson, Diana L.*

Masefield, John

1008. Sard Harker
1. *O D T A A.* Macmillan, 1926.
2. *Sard Harker.* Heinemann, 1924.
3. *The Taking of the Gry.* Heinemann, 1934.

Revolutionary movements in the fictitious Latin American country of Santa Barbara draw into their center swashbuckling young turn-of-the-century Englishmen, who encounter beautiful senoritas, evil dictators, political conflict, and as the title of the first work indicates, "One Damn Thing After Another."

Genre: Adventure
Subjects: Revolutions and revolutionists; Dictators; Politics
Place/Time: Latin America—1900–1945

Mason, F. Van Wyck

1009.
1. *Three Harbours.* Lippincott, 1938.
2. *Stars on the Sea.* Lippincott, 1940.
3. *Rivers of Glory.* Lippincott, 1942.
4. *Eagle in the City.* Lippincott, 1948.

The unknown individuals who fought in the American Revolution are the focus of this tetralogy. Merchants, privateers, naval officers, doctors, Loyalists, and a large group of other characters crowd the pages and bring the years 1774 to 1780 alive with romance, adventure, and action. The story begins in Norfolk, Virginia, then moves to the Bahamas, Boston, Troy, New York, and Savannah. The books portray how the Revolution affected the individuals who fought for freedom.

Genre: Historical Fiction; War

Subjects: War; United States—revolution, 1775–
1783; Army, United States
Place/Time: United States—18th century

Mason, Lisa

1010.
1. *Summer of Love.* Bantam Books, 1994.
2. *The Golden Nineties.* Bantam Books, 1995.

In the 25th century, the work of the Luxon Institute has
enabled humans to travel back in time with a mission
and a set of rules developed by the institute. Chiron is
sent to the Haight Asbury district of San Francisco of
the 1960s to find a young hippie whose life will radically affect generations to come. Zhu Wang, a young
Chinese prisoner, travels back to San Francisco of
1895, where she must discover the source of an elaborate piece of jewelry and right wrongs, which will
change the course of history.

Genre: Science Fiction
Subjects: Time travel; History; Prisoners and pris-
ons; Hippies
Place/Time: San Francisco (Calif.)—19th century;
San Francisco (Calif.)—1945–1980

1011.
1. *Arachne.* Morrow, 1990.
2. *Cyberweb.* Morrow, 1995.

In a post-Big Quake San Francisco of the future, sophisticated technology exists side by side with a violent, primitive street life. A young lawyer Carly Nolan
descends from a promising career to vagrancy when
the link that connects her to the computer generated
court system fails. To rise above disgrace and return to
her former life Carly must deal with an unscrupulous
lawyer, a scheming artificial intelligence, and a main-
frame icon called Cognatus.

Genre: Science Fiction
Subjects: Law and lawyers; Computers; Technology
and civilization

Mason, Robert

1012.
1. *Weapon.* Putnam, 1989.
2. *Solo.* Putnam, 1992.

Solo is a 6'2", 300-pound robot, the latest high-tech
weapon from the Pentagon. He has telescopic, micro-
scopic, and infrared vision; he is as strong as 30 men;
and he can learn. Although his inventor Bill Stewart
doesn't believe he should be tested yet, the government releases Solo in Nicaragua where he escapes and
helps the peasants against the Contras. Later the Pentagon releases "Nimrod," another robot, to track down
the runaway Solo and destroy him.

Genre: Technothriller
Subjects: Adventure; Robots; Revolutions and revolutionists

Place/Time: Nicaragua—1980–; United States—
1980–

Masters, John

1013.
1. *Coromandel.* Viking, 1955.
2. *The Deceivers.* Viking, 1952.
3. *Nightrunners of Bengal.* Viking, 1951.
4. *The Lotus and the Wind.* Viking, 1953.
5. *Far, Far the Mountain Peak.* Viking, 1957.
6. *Bhowani Junction.* Viking, 1954.
7. *To the Coral Strand.* Harper, 1962.

Jason Savage goes to India in the 1630s to hunt for
treasure. His descendants live in India from the 1830s
through independence. William Savage has to destroy
a thug religious sect in the 1830s, while his son
Rodney, an officer of the East India Company, fights
the horrors of the Sepoy Mutiny. Rodney's son Robin
has to fight in the Afghan wilderness, while grandson
Peter forgoes soldiering for mountain climbing. However, it is Peter's son who must try to accept Indian independence after a lifetime as a British soldier.

Genre: Adventure; Family Saga; Historical Fiction
Subjects: Adventure; Soldiers—British; War
Place/Time: India—multicentury span

1014.
1. *The Ravi Lancers.* Doubleday, 1972.
2. *The Himalayan Concerto.* Doubleday, 1976.

Captain Warren Batemen, an English officer with an
Indian regiment, leads his men into the battles of
World War I. His second-in-command is an Indian
prince, Krishna Ram. Though both men are excited in
the first year of the war, they become disillusioned
with the horrors of trench warfare. Warren Bateman's
son Rodney also finds himself in India where he is
drawn into intelligence work.

Genre: War
Subjects: World War I, 1914–1918; War; Soldiers—
British;
Place/Time: Europe—1900–1945; India—1900–
1945

1015. Loss of Eden
1. *Now, God Be Thanked.* McGraw-Hill, 1979.
2. *Heart of War.* McGraw-Hill, 1980.
3. *By the Green of the Spring.* McGraw-Hill,
1981.

World War I had catastrophic effects on Britain. Four
families, the aristocratic Durand-Beaulieus, the industrial Rowlands, the working-class Strattons, and the
poacher Gorses, all feel the impact of the war. The
Rowlands become wealthy as they convert their auto
plant to war production, and all the classes see a new
world and society emerge from the carnage.

Genre: Historical Fiction; War
Subjects: World War I, 1914–1918; Social classes;
Technology and civilization

Place/Time: England—1900–1945

Masterton, Graham
1016.
1. *The Manitou.* Pinnacle, 1978.
2. *Revenge of the Manitou.* T. Doherty, 1979.
3. *Burial.* St. Martin's, 1994.

The Manitou, a disembodied spirit of an ancient American Indian sorcerer, invades the world of the living, seeking revenge and gaining allies from the underworld and the realm of voodoo magic. Opposing this powerful being, who is capable of destroying large cities and sucking the life from his victims, is Harry Erskine, who has his own magical allies, but who, despite his claims of occult gifts, is in fact a con man.

Genre: Horror
Subjects: Native Americans; Revenge; Witchcraft; Magic; Crime and criminals

1017. Jim Rook Series
1. *Rook.* Severn House, 1997.
2. *Tooth and Claw.* Severn House, 1997.
3. *The Terror.* Severn House, 1998.
4. *Snowman.* Severn House, 2000.

College English teacher Jim Rook uses his unique psychic ability to help students who are beset by the forces of evil. Rook wards off a voodoo spell, helps a student who has unwittingly unleashed an ancient demon, and comes to the aid of a Native American student who has been falsely accused of murder.

Genre: Horror
Subjects: Teachers; Students; Extrasensory perception; Good and evil
Place/Time: California—1980–

Matthes, Patricia. *See* Nolan, William F. (Witch World series—*On Wings of Magic*)

Matthews, Greg
1018.
1. *Little Red Rooster.* NAL, 1987.
2. *The Gold Flake Hydrant.* NAL, 1988.

In rural Indiana, Burris is a 15-year old who has too many problems. His father died in Vietnam, and his mother sells tacky paintings. He is also disabled—one of his legs is shorter than the other. He is having problems growing up until he meets Diane Trimble and her family. Their zany antics blow him away, especially after he falls in love with Diane. He tries suicide and flunks out of school, but eventually he finds out what it means to grow up.

Genre: Coming of Age
Subjects: Teenagers; Family life
Place/Time: Indiana—1980–

Matthiessen, Peter
1019.
1. *Killing Mister Watson.* Random House, 1990.
2. *Lost Man's River.* Random House, 1997.
3. *Bone by Bone.* Random House, 1999.

In the sugarcane fields of the Florida Everglades of the late 19th century, Edgar J. Watson is a wild outlaw and successful sugar cane farmer; however, people around him seem to wind up dead. When he is killed in 1910, no one really knows exactly how he died. Fifty years later his son Lucius returns to the Everglades to try to figure out what happened to his father. As he talks to his father's friends and enemies, he also sees that the fragile ecosystem of the Everglades is being destroyed. Finally through letters, diaries, and stories, the elusive Edgar Watson tells his own story of how he grew up and became the rough, violent figure who haunts his son and the Everglades.

Genre: Historical Fiction
Subjects: Fathers and sons; Farm life; Frontier and pioneer life.
Place/Time: Florida—19th century; Florida—1900–1945

Maupin, Armistead
1020.
1. *Tales of the City.* Harper & Row, 1978.
2. *More Tales of the City.* Harper & Row, 1980.
3. *Further Tales of the City.* Harper & Row, 1982.
4. *Babycakes.* Harper & Row, 1984.
5. *Significant Others.* Harper, 1987.
6. *Sure of You.* Harper, 1989.

The humorous and satiric adventures of a madcap group of straights and gays who live at 28 Barbary Lane, San Francisco, from the late 1970s through the 1980s are related. TV newscaster Mary Ann Singleton and husband Brian, gay Michael, Jon the gynecologist, Beauchop, Dee, Francis, Mona, and Mrs. Madrigal have affairs with each other and keep each other going. Over the years, the ever-changing couples have trials and adventures as they try to find commitment in a crazy world.

Genre: Humor
Subjects: Love affairs; Homosexuality
Place/Time: San Francisco (Calif.)—1945–1980; San Francisco (Calif.)—1980–; California—1945–1980; California—1980–

Maurois, Andre. *Pseud. of* Emile Herzog
1021.
1. *The Silence of Colonel Bramble.* John Lane, 1919.

2. *The Return of Doctor O'Grady.* Bodley Head, 1951.
3. *General Bramble.* Dodd, Mead, 1922.

These autobiographical works resulted from Mauriac's World War I experiences as an interpreter with the British forces. His sometimes unfavorable depiction of English officers forced Mauriac to assume the pseudonym he used throughout his literary career.

Subjects: Autobiographical stories; World War I, 1914–1918; Translating and interpreting; Army, British—officers
Place/Time: Europe—1900–1945

May, Julian. *See also* Bradley, Marion Zimmer

1022. The Galactic Milieu Trilogy
1. *Jack the Bodiless.* Knopf, 1992.
2. *Diamond Mask.* Knopf, 1994.
3. *Magnificat.* Knopf, 1996.

In the middle of the 21st century, Earth is about to become part of the confederation of worlds known as the Galactic Milieu with the powerful Remillard family leading the way. However, a malevolent force called Fury begins to eliminate family members to prevent the galactic union. Jack, an extremely talented child born to the Remillards, seems to be their best hope, though his body is deteriorating cell by cell. Jack survives and competes with the Fury for the skills of the powerful, metapsychic woman known as Diamond Mask. Jack and Diamond Mask marry, the identity of the Fury is revealed, and a project to enhance the properties of the human mind raises humanity to a powerful position in the galaxy. *Note:* This series continues in The Saga of the Pliocene Exile series.

Genre: Science Fiction
Subjects: Interplanetary visitors; Invalids; Good and evil; Telepathy

1023. The Saga of Pliocene Exile
1. *Intervention: A Root Tale to the Galactic Milieu and a Vinculum Between It and the Saga of Pliocene Exile.* Houghton, Mifflin, 1987. (Alternate title: *The Surveillance* and *The Metaconcert.*)
2. *The Many-Colored Land.* Houghton Mifflin, 1981.
3. *The Golden Torc.* Houghton Mifflin, 1981.
4. *The Nonborn King.* Houghton Mifflin, 1983.
5. *The Adversary.* Houghton Mifflin, 1984.

Intervention sets the scene for the Saga of Pliocene Exile by starting with the events of the 20th century that lead a group of psychics to send a telepathic cry to alien civilizations. The resulting contact brings Earth into galactic conflicts that create what is for some, but certainly not all, a utopian civilization. Dissenters and rebels in this society discover a way out: a timegate that sends them back to the Pliocene era with no hope of return. Once there they enter into conflict with the Tanu

and the Firvulag, aliens exiled by more advanced civilizations because of their violent religious practices. *Note:* This series follows The Galactic Milieu Trilogy.

Genre: Science Fiction
Subjects: Interstellar communication; Interplanetary wars; Utopias; Time travel; Prehistoric times

Mayle, Peter
1024.
1. *Toujours Provence.* Knopf, 1991.
2. *A Dog's Life.* Knopf, 1995.

In Provence, France, Peter Mayle finds he is adopted by Boy, a dog that has escaped from its brutish owner. Boy encounters butchers, dog owners, cats, and all other creatures. Boy finds his owners incorrigible, and his behavior becomes just like theirs. His adventures take him all over Provence and teach him how to deal with humans. Mayle also learns how to deal with dogs.

Subjects: Dogs
Place/Time: France—1980–

Maynard, Kenneth
1025.
1. *Lieutenant Lamb.* St. Martin's, 1984.
2. *First Lieutenant.* St. Martin's, 1985.
3. *Lamb in Command.* St. Martin's, 1986.

After six years in the British Royal Navy in the late 18th century, Mathew Lamb finally receives a commission as a lieutenant and is assigned to the HMS *Sturdy*, a well-armed frigate on patrol off Gibraltar. There the 19-year old demonstrates his skill and bravery and rises in command. Sowing his wild oats with his captain's wife gets him put in charge of a mail packet bound for Antigua, but there he falls in love and has numerous adventures battling French privateers.

Genre: Historical Fiction; Naval Adventure; War
Subjects: Adventure; Navy, British—officers; Sailing vessels; Naval battles; Seamen;

McAuley, Paul J.
1026. Books of the Confluence
1. *Child of the River.* Avon Eos, 1998.
2. *Ancient of Days.* Avon Eos, 1999.

Unsure of his ancestry, Yama grows up on Confluence, a planet light years from Earth, which was terra formed and populated with intelligent life forms centuries ago by the mysterious god-like Preservers. Sensing that he has unique powers, Yama leaves his adopted family and travels to the planet's great city Ys. Along the way, his psychic talents become evident to a government bureaucrat who is relentless in his efforts to harness Yama's power and use it against the rebellious faction simply called the Heretics.

Genre: Science Fiction; Coming of Age

Subjects: Extrasensory perception; Life on other planets; Government, resistance to

McCaffrey, Anne

1027.
1. *Freedom's Landing.* Putnam, 1995.
2. *Freedom's Choice.* Putnam, 1997.
3. *Freedom's Challenge.* Putnam, 1998.

Captured by the alien Catteni, who are themselves servants of the still more powerful alien race the Eosi, a group of humans become unwilling colonists of a deserted planet with a hostile environment. In their efforts to gain their freedom, the colonists take over a Catteni ship and free a group of slave laborers. Zainal, an exiled Catteni aristocrat, eventually allies himself with the colonists, attempts to turn the Catteni against the Eosi, and falls in love with human rebel Kristin.

Genre: Science Fiction
Subjects: Space colonies; Extraterrestrial beings; Revolutions and revolutionists; Slavery

1028. Dinosaur Planet
1. *Dinosaur Planet.* Ballantine, 1978.
2. *Dinosaur Planet Survivors.* Ballantine, 1984.

A group of technicians sent to explore the planet Ireta get more than they bargained for: the discovery of sentient prehistoric animals and trouble in the form of a mutiny. To make matters worse, their rescue ship has disappeared. To escape these difficulties, the leaders of the mission go into suspended animation, awakening to an alien invasion and the unwelcome presence of the descendants of the mutineers.

Genre: Science Fiction
Subjects: Explorers; Prehistoric animals; Life on other planets; Mutiny

1029. Dragonriders of Pern
1. *Chronicles of Pern: First Fall.* Del Rey, 1993.
2. *Moreta, Dragonlady of Pern.* Ballantine, 1983.
3. *Dragonsdawn.* Ballantine, 1988.
4. *Dragonflight.* Ballantine, 1968.
5. *Dragonquest.* Ballantine, 1971.
6. *The White Dragon.* Ballantine, 1978.
7. *Nerilka's Story.* Ballantine, 1986.
8. *The Renegades of Pern.* Ballantine, 1989.
9. *All the Weyrs of Pern.* Ballantine, 1991.
10. *The Girl Who Heard Dragons.* Ballantine, 1994.
11. *The Dolphins of Pern.* Del Rey, 1994.
12. *Dragonseye.* Ballantine, 1997.
13. *The Masterharper of Pern.* Ballantine, 1996.

The planet Pern, which had been colonized by Earth in the distant past, is threatened by spores from outer space. The only defense is for the human inhabitants of Pern to form an alliance with the planet's fire-breathing dragons, who soon become subjects of genetic engineering. Victory, however, does not bring amity and factions develop, but a rediscovery of the original Earthlings' landing sight reveals scientific secrets lost in the planet's history.

Genre: Fantasy; Science Fiction
Subjects: Space colonies; Dragons; Genetics; Life on other planets

1030. Killashandra
1. *Crystal Singer.* Ballantine, 1982.
2. *Killashandra.* Ballantine, 1985.
3. *Crystal Line.* Ballantine, 1992.

Killashandra Ree could become a professional opera singer but never the star she wants to be. Or she could use her musical ability to seek and cut crystal on the planet Ballybran, the source of the substance necessary for intergalactic communication. In choosing the latter, she opts for a way of life that is exciting, dangerous, and financially rewarding, but which may eventually result in damage to her mind due to the powerful effect of the crystal.

Genre: Science Fiction
Subjects: Singers; Interstellar communication; Crystallography

1031. Shellpeople
1. *The Ship Who Sang.* Walker, 1969.
2. *PartnerShip.* (Written with Margaret Ball) Baen, 1992.
3. *The Ship Who Searched.* (Written with Mercedes Lackey) Baen, 1992.
4. *The City Who Fought.* (Written with S. M. Stirling) Baen, 1993.
5. *The Ship Avenged.* Baen, 1997. (Written with S. M. Stirling)
6. *The Ship Who Won.* (Written with Jody Lynn Nye) Baen, 1994.
7. *The Ship Errant.* Baen, 1996. (Written by Jody Lynn Nye)

Helva, a child born with superior mental talents but a body limited by severe physical disabilities, becomes part of a spaceship and gains a unique and wonderful life in the process. The series continues with tales of other individuals, called shellpeople, whose technologically enhanced bodies make them intrinsic parts of the world of the future.

Genre: Science Fiction
Subjects: Handicapped people; Bionics; Spaceships; Space flight

1032. Talented Series
1. *To Ride Pegasus.* Ballantine, 1973.
2. *Get off the Unicorn.* Ballantine, 1977.
3. *Pegasus in Flight.* Ballantine, 1990.
4. *Pegasus in Space.* Ballantine, 2000.
5. *The Rowan.* Ace, 1990.
6. *Damia.* Putnam, 1991.
7. *Damia's Children.* Putnam, 1993.
8. *Lyon's Pride.* Ace, 1994.
9. *The Tower and the Hive.* Ace, 1999.

In the first four loosely connected works, Anne McCaffrey explores the evolution of the Talented, individuals whose mental powers enable them to move objects and form mind links across time and space. With *The Rowan* begins a family saga of Talented men and women of the future. The Rowan, a Talented orphan girl, travels a lonely road until Jeff Raven crosses light years to be with her. Rowan and Jeff's headstrong but brilliant daughter, Damia, causes intergalactic trouble until she realizes that the older man who has been her friend and mentor is her true love. They raise a family whose combined talents are brought into service to combat hostile insectlike aliens.

Genre: Family Saga; Science Fiction
Subjects: Telepathy; Genetics; Love; Interplanetary wars

McCaffrey, Anne *and* Ball, Margaret

1033.
1. *Acorna: The Unicorn Girl.* HarperPrism, 1997.
2. *Acorna's Quest.* HarperPrism, 1998.
3. *Acorna's People.* HarperPrism, 1999.

Three asteroid miners find a baby girl sleeping in a space pod that inexplicably appears near their work site. The child, Acorna, soon begins to show unusual qualities. She has a small translucent horn in the middle of her forehead, can purify air and water and cure illnesses, and she has an innate understanding of gambling odds. She grows to maturity in three years, becoming more and more concerned about finding those of her own kind. Her unique talents attract attention from those who wish to help her, but also from those who want to exploit her. As she sets off with one of the miners to search for her origins, a spaceship appears bearing the gentle telepathic Linyaari, who are warning of the invasion of the violent alien Khleev and also searching for one of their own who disappeared in infancy. United with her people on their idyllic world, Acorna rights wrongs and searches for the link between her ancestors and humans.

Genre: Science Fiction; Coming of Age
Subjects: Girls; Unicorns; Extraterrestrial beings

McCaffrey, Anne *and* Scarborough, Elizabeth Ann

1034.
1. *Powers That Be.* Ballantine, 1993.
2. *Power Lines.* Ballantine, 1994.
3. *Power Play.* Ballantine, 1995.

With her lungs nearly destroyed by poison gas, Yanaba Maddock is still useful to the Intergal Company, but only as a spy to report on strange happenings on the terra formed sentient planet Petaybee. As she recovers her health, Yanaba develops a bond with the planet and its inhabitants. Soon she sees her company for the exploitive, destructive force that it is; allies herself with the citizens of Petaybee; and falls in love with the man-seal Sean Shongili, with whom she produces selkie twins.

Genre: Science Fiction
Subjects: Ecology; Spies; Life on other planets; Business; Love

1035.
1. *The Powers That Be.* Del Rey, 1993.
2. *Power Lines.* Del Rey, 1994.

In a future time when much of intergalactic civilization is corporate, Major Yanaba Maddock has served Intergal Company well, but with great damage to her health. Assigned to spy on the inhabitants of the arctic planet Petaybee, where strange species have been evolving and company representatives disappearing, Yanaba not only regains her health, but also develops a strong protective respect for the natives of Petaybee and begins to see her employer for the exploitive organization it actually is.

Genre: Science Fiction
Subjects: Life on other planets; Business; Ecology; Spies

McCaig, Donald

1036.
1. *Nop's Trials.* Crown, 1984.
2. *Nop's Hope.* Crown, 1994.

Nop, a black-and-white border collie is a sheepdog on the Virginia farm of his master Lewis Burkholder. When he is stolen by an unscrupulous trainer, Nop must endure beatings, starvation, and a variety of owners before he is reunited with his real owner Lewis. Nop's offspring Hope lives with her owner Penny. When Penny's husband and daughter are killed in a car accident, she takes Hope on a tour of the sheepdog trial circuit shows. Only when Penny is reconciled with her father Lewis does she begin to recover. In these charming tales that celebrate the love between humans and dogs, the anthropomorphic animals tell their own story.

Genre: Animal Story; Gentle Read
Subjects: Animals; Dogs
Place/Time: Virginia—1980–

McCarthy, Cormac

1037. Border Trilogy
1. *All the Pretty Horses.* Knopf, 1992.
2. *The Crossing.* Knopf, 1994.
3. *Cities of the Plain.* Knopf, 1998.

The border territory between the United States and Mexico in the 1950s is the setting for these stories that explore the ways young boys grow up in rough surroundings. Sixteen-year-old John Grady leaves Texas with his friend Lacy and rides into Mexico, where they become cowboys on a ranch and discover how tragic life can be. In the second book, young Billy becomes obsessed with a wolf who is running on the ranch. He captures her, then frees her and follows her to Mexico, where Billy becomes the prey. In the final book, John and Billy are working on a New Mexico ranch, but as society changes, the young men go across the Mexican border to relax and find the West they no longer have.

Genre: Adventure; Coming of Age
Subjects: Teenagers; Adventure; Cowboys; Animals
Place/Time: Texas—1945–1980; Mexico—1945–1980

McCarthy, Wil

1038.
1. *Aggressor Six.* Roc, 1994.
2. *The Fall of Sirius.* Roc, 1996.

Waisters, merciless aliens from the waist of the constellation Orion, have nearly decimated the human population of the galaxy. The only possibility of survival seems to be to adopt certain characteristics of the enemy. Two thousand years after the invasion, cryogenically preserved humans are revived by a hybrid civilization of aliens and humans to combat a return of the Waisters.

Genre: Science Fiction
Subjects: Interplanetary wars; Extraterrestrial beings; Mixed blood

McCarver, Aaron. *See* Morris, Gilbert

McConchie, Lyn. *See* Nolan, William F. (Witch World series—*The Key of the Keplian*)

McCord, John S.

1039. The Baynes Clan
1. *Montana Horseman.* Doubleday, 1990.
2. *Texas Comebacker.* Doubleday, 1991.
3. *Wyoming Giant.* Doubleday, 1992.

Louisiana farmer and horse breeder Darnell Baynes flees the state with his sons Milt, Luke, and Ward after killing the men who tried to conscript the boys into the Confederate Army. They settle in Montana where Ward enters a horse race to win money to buy a ranch and win the hand of lovely Kit. Milt tries to return home in 1868 to clear the family name, but becomes involved with Texas ranchers defending their land against outlaws. Third son Luke goes East to become a lawyer. When he is appointed a federal judge in Wyoming, he has to fight unscrupulous ranchers.

Genre: Historical Fiction; Western
Subjects: Western states; Adventure; Ranch life; Horse racing
Place/Time: Montana—19th century; Texas—19th century; Wyoming—19th century

McCullough, Colleen

1040.
1. *The First Man in Rome.* Morrow, 1990.
2. *The Grass Crown.* Morrow, 1992.
3. *Fortune's Favorites.* Morrow, 1993.
4. *Caesar's Women.* Morrow, 1995.
5. *Caesar: Let the Dice Fly.* Morrow, 1997.

The decline of the Roman Republic in 110 B.C. is chronicled through the lives of the great men who dominated its history. Gaius Marius, a new man from the provinces, and Lucius Cornelius Sulla, a patrician Roman brought up in the slums, unite to fight the German hordes and to win the consulship. Later they turn against each other as they vie for power. When Sulla finally retires, the stage is set for another battle for power between Sulla and Marius's proteges Pompey and Julius Caesar. As Caesar rises to power, he outmaneuvers his enemies and then extends the influence of Rome by conquering Gaul and Britain. This mammoth saga details the wars, bribery, and chicanery that dominated the era.

Genre: Historical Fiction
Subjects: Rome; Caesar, Julius, 100–44 B.C.; Rome—kings and rulers; Politics—Rome; War
Place/Time: Rome (Italy)—1st century B. C.; Italy—1st century B. C.

McCutchan, Philip

1041.
1. *Apprentice to the Sea.* St. Martin's, 1995.
2. *Second Mate.* St. Martin's, 1996.
3. *The New Lieutenant.* St. Martin's, 1997.

Young Tom Chatto comes to England from Ireland to become an apprentice seaman in 1890. He sets sail on a commercial sailing ship under Captain Landon. On board are the captain's much younger wife; Mr. Patience, the first mate; Jim Wales, the head apprentice; and a group of other apprentices. As they sail around Cape Horn, Tom learns to sail and to survive the brutal conditions at sea. Tom then joins a steamship crew going to South America where he again has to deal with a cruel first officer, but now he must also deal with passengers and their eccentric ways. As troubles plague the voyage, Tom helps save an abandoned sailing ship and learns to sail while finding both adventure and love. When World War I starts, Tom joins the Royal Navy Volunteer Reserve and joins the Geelong, an armed decoy fighting German U-boats. He has to deal with Germans, distraught shipmates, and personal problems with his aging father.

Genre: Naval Adventure; Historical Fiction
Subjects: Sailing vessels; Seamen; Adventure; World War I, 1914–1918
Place/Time: Atlantic Ocean—19th century

McCutchan, Philip. *See also* MacNeil, Duncan

1042.

1. *Cameron, Ordinary Seaman.* Barker, 1980. (This title has been published only in England.)
2. *Cameron Comes Through.* St. Martin's, 1986, 1980.
3. *Lieutenant Cameron RNVR.* St. Martin's, 1985, 1981.
4. *Cameron's Convoy.* Barker, 1982. (This title has been published only in England.)
5. *Cameron of the Castle Bay.* Barker, 1983. (This title has been published only in England.)
6. *Cameron in the Gap.* St. Martin's, 1983.
7. *Orders for Cameron.* St. Martin's, 1983.
8. *Cameron in Command.* St. Martin's, 1983.
9. *Cameron and the Kaiserhof.* St. Martin's, 1984.
10. *Cameron's Raid.* St. Martin's, 1984.
11. *Cameron's Chase.* St. Martin's, 1986.
12. *Cameron's Troop Lift.* St. Martin's, 1987.
13. *Cameron's Commitment.* St. Martin's, 1989.
14. *Cameron's Crossing.* St. Martin's, 1993.

When World War II breaks out, Donald Cameron joins the British navy and rises through the ranks to become a lieutenant commander. Following the various battles of World War II, Cameron sees action in the North Atlantic, the Mediterranean, North Africa, and the South Atlantic on a variety of ships from convoys to destroyers. Besides fighting major battles, Cameron takes part in secret spy missions.

Genre: Naval Adventure; War
Subjects: Adventure; Naval battles; World War II, 1939–1945; Navy, British—officers; Sailing vessels; International intrigue
Place/Time: Atlantic Ocean—1900–1945; Mediterranean Sea—1900–1945

1043.

1. *The Convoy Commodore.* St. Martin's, 1986.
2. *Convoy North.* St. Martin's, 1988.
3. *Convoy South.* St. Martin's, 1988.
4. *Convoy East.* St. Martin's, 1989.
5. *Convoy of Fear.* St. Martin's, 1990.
6. *Convoy Homeward.* St. Martin's, 1992.

Commodore John Mason Kemp is drafted from his peacetime job as a steamship line captain to command convoy ships for Great Britain in World War II. His charge is to bring supplies and troops to Britain's different war theaters. From the Battle of the Atlantic to war in the Pacific, Kemp and his crew must outwit German submarines, disease, weather, and worries about family in Britain in this rousing but very human look at men at war.

Genre: Historical Fiction; Naval Adventure; War
Subjects: Adventure; World War II, 1939–1945; Navy, British—officers; Sailing vessels

Place/Time: Atlantic Ocean—1900–1945; Pacific Ocean—1900–1945

1044.

1. *Beware, Beware the Bight of Benin.* St. Martin's, 1974.
2. *Halfhyde's Island.* St. Martin's, 1976.
3. *The Guns of Arrest.* St. Martin's, 1976.
4. *Halfhyde to the Narrows.* St. Martin's, 1977.
5. *Halfhyde for the Queen.* St. Martin's, 1978.
6. *Halfhyde Ordered South.* St. Martin's, 1980.
7. *Halfhyde and the Flag Captain.* St. Martin's, 1980.
8. *Halfhyde on the Yangtze.* Weidenfeld and Grove, 1981. (This title has been published only in England.)
9. *Halfhyde on Zanaru.* St. Martin's, 1982.
10. *Halfhyde Outward Bound.* St. Martin's, 1984.
11. *The Halfhyde Line.* St. Martin's, 1984.
12. *Halfhyde and the Chain Gangs.* St. Martin's, 1985.
13. *Halfhyde Goes to War.* St. Martin's, 1986.
14. *Halfhyde on the Amazon.* St. Martin's, 1988.
15. *Halfhyde and the Admiral.* St. Martin's, 1990.
16. *Halfhyde and the Fleet Review.* St. Martin's, 1992.

In the late 19th century, as sailing ships give way to steamships, Lieutenant St. Vincent Halfhyde of the British Navy battles storms, mutinies, natives, and foreign navies as he sails the seven seas for the glory and protection of Queen Victoria and mother England. The independent Halfhyde battles Germans, Russians, Spaniards, Africans, and his own superiors in these humorous and fast-moving adventures, which follow Halfhyde from youth through middle age.

Genre: Historical Fiction; Naval Adventure
Subjects: Adventure; Naval battles; Navy, British—officers; Sailing vessels; Steamboats
Place/Time: Atlantic Ocean—19th century; Pacific Ocean—19th century

McCutcheon, George Barr

1045.

1. *Graustark.* Grosset & Dunlap, 1901.
2. *Beverly of Graustark.* Grosset & Dunlap, 1904.
3. *Truxton King.* Dodd, 1909.
4. *The Prince of Graustark.* Dodd, 1914.
5. *East of the Setting Sun.* Dodd, 1924.
6. *The Inn of the Hawk and the Raven.* Dodd, 1927.

Graustark is a mythical 19th-century Balkan country perfect for adventures, full of castles, robbers, and royalty who have a way of coming to America or having Americans come to them.

Subjects: Imaginary kingdoms; Aristocracy

McDonald, Gregory

1046. Time
1. *Merely Players.* Hill, 1988.
2. *Exits and Entrances.* Hill, 1988.
3. *A World Too Wide.* Hill, 1987.

In the 1950s in New England, Janet Twombly is the beautiful girl next door while Dan Prescott is her boyfriend who is studying to be a minister. Janet becomes restless and runs away to Paris with jazz musician David MacFarlane. Dan pursues her and tries to win her back, but Janet doesn't know what she wants. Twenty-five years later when Janet's daughter and Dan's son are going to marry, David gets the friends together. The different generations confront each other and come to terms with their lives.

Subjects: Love affairs; Parents and children; Conflict of generations
Place/Time: New England—1945–1980; Paris (France)—1945–1980; France—1945–1980

McDonald, Kay L.

1047.
1. *The Brightwood Expedition.* Liveright, 1975.
2. *Vision of the Eagle.* Crowell, 1977.
3. *The Vision Is Fulfilled.* Walker, 1983.

Sioux-raised Ross Chestnut meets Marlette Brightwood on an expedition to the Oregon Territory in 1842. When all but Marlette and Ross are killed, they winter with a French-Canadian trapper and fall in love. When they get back to civilization, the death of Marlette's father separates them, but they are finally reunited and settle in Oregon. Tragedy strikes their life and sends Ross on a search for his real identity.

Genre: Historical Fiction
Subjects: Frontier and pioneer life; Wagon trains; Love; Native Americans
Place/Time: Oregon—19th century

McGahan, Andrew

1048.
1. *1988.* St. Martin's, 1996.
2. *Praise.* Carroll & Graf, 1993.

Gordon, a disillusioned Generation-Xer in Australia, drops out of university and takes a job in the outback observing weather. After a boring trip to the weather station, Gordon decides to return to Brisbane, where he meets Cynthia and they live together, drifting through a world of sex, drugs, and alcohol. Cynthia has an abortion, and Gordon is unfulfilled by everything the two do. Soon, they don't have the energy to do anything and when Gordon refuses to have sex with Cynthia, she leaves.

Subjects: Youth; Sex; Alcoholism
Place/Time: Australia—1980–

McGehee, Peter

1049.
1. *Boys Like Us.* St. Martin's, 1991.
2. *Sweetheart.* St. Martin's, 1992.
3. *Labour of Love.* (Written with Doug Wilson) St. Martin's, 1993.

Zero MacNoo, a gay Toronto playwright originally from Arkansas, is losing his friends to AIDS. He is trying to cope with his new love Clay and with his breakup with old love David. In the midst of this he returns to Arkansas for his mother's second wedding. When he returns to Toronto, he too must battle AIDS and his crazy relatives. Even though the theme is serious, McGehee details farcical scenes and zany characters without being glib. Wilson finished the third book after McGehee died of AIDS.

Genre: Humor
Subjects: Homosexuality; AIDS (disease)
Place/Time: Toronto (Canada)—1980–; Arkansas—1980–; Canada—1980–

McHugh, Arona

1050.
1. *A Banner with a Strange Device.* Doubleday, 1964.
2. *The Seacoast of Bohemia.* Doubleday, 1965.

In Boston after World War II, Sally Brimmer and her friends try to cram a lot of living into their lives while they search for love. The wild and beautiful Sally meets many men but only when she marries Mike Wainscott does she discover maturity in marriage and motherhood. Her friend Deborah Miller comes from a strict background and finds love with Sally's brother Dudley. Both women discover that love, like life, is very complex.

Genre: Romance
Subjects: Women; Marriage
Place/Time: Boston (Mass.)—1945–1980; Massachusetts—1945–1980

McInerny, Ralph

1051.
1. *Jolly Rogerson.* Doubleday, 1968.
2. *Rogerson at Bay.* Harper, 1977.

Matthew Rogerson is a humanities professor at a small college in the Midwest. After 20 years of teaching, he believes he is a failure and resolves to be a big failure. His actions make him a campus hero, and students flock to his classes. Even his wife is becoming independent since she has gone back to school. When she goes to Wisconsin for the summer, a young professor tries to seduce him. At 47, he finds life is more complicated than he ever imagined.

Genre: Humor
Subjects: Teachers; College life; Marriage problems

Place/Time: Midwestern states—1945–1980

McKay, Allis

1052.
1. *They Came to a River.* Macmillan, 1941.
2. *Goodbye Summer.* Macmillan, 1953.

Early 20th-century Washington State is the background of this romantic saga of a young girl's passage through girlhood, marriage, and widowhood. The sequel follows her son through his adolescence and early manhood on his mother's ranch.

Genre: Coming of Age; Historical Romance
Subjects: Family life; Teenagers
Place/Time: Washington (state)—1900–1945

McKiernan, Dennis

1053. The Iron Tower Trilogy
1. *The Dark Tide.* Doubleday, 1984.
2. *Shadows of Doom.* Doubleday, 1984.
3. *The Darkest Day.* Doubleday, 1984.

King Aurion is killed when his kingdom is invaded by the minions of the evil Modru, but the king's son Galen continues the struggle aided by Warrow Tuck. The climax occurs as Galen and his followers attack Modru's Iron Tower, where Galen's beloved Laurelin is imprisoned.

Genre: Fantasy
Subjects: Kings and rulers; Imaginary kingdoms; Imaginary wars and battles; Good and evil

1054. The Silver Call Duology
1. *Trek to Kraggen-Cor.* Doubleday, 1986.
2. *The Brega Path.* Doubleday, 1986.

Two hundred years after the evil Modru is defeated, the Warrows ally themselves with Dwarves headed by Dwarf King Durek to regain the subterranean realm of Kraggen-Cor, which is inhabited by a variety of unsavory creatures.

Genre: Fantasy
Subjects: Imaginary kingdoms; Good and evil

McKillip, Patricia A.

1055.
1. *The Sorceress and the Cygnet.* Ace, 1991.
2. *The Cygnet and the Firebird.* Ace, 1993.

With his blonde hair and love of legends, Corleu is different from the dark people with whom he lives. While lost in a swamp, he crosses a magical barrier and finds himself in a legendary battle involving the mystical land of Ro Holding, the Hold of the Cygnet, where he encounters the sorceress Nyx and her warrior cousin Meguet. In the second tale, Meguet tries to help a prince who is trapped in a firebird's form at night and who has no memory of the source of his enchantment.

Genre: Fantasy
Subjects: Mythical animals; Magic; Imaginary wars and battles

McMurtry, Larry

1056.
1. *The Desert Rose.* Simon & Schuster, 1983.
2. *The Late Child.* Simon & Schuster, 1995.

Harmony is a showgirl in Las Vegas who has the best legs and bust on the strip. She has dated Elvis Presley and Frank Sinatra, but as she faces her 39th birthday, her newest competitor is her daughter Pepper. Harmony retires from show business and works at a recycling plant to earn money to take care of her five-year-old son. When Harmony gets a letter from New York City informing her that Pepper has died of AIDS, she is insane with grief. Harmony, her sisters, and her son Eddie travel to their home in Tarwater, Oklahoma, but are sidetracked and end up in New York. They meet Pepper's female lover and numerous other characters. When they finally get to Tarwater, her family has so many problems that Harmony must put aside her grief if she is to help them.

Subjects: Show business; Mothers and daughters; Family life; Sisters
Place/Time: Las Vegas (Nev.)—1980–; New York (N. Y.)—1980–; Oklahoma—1980–

1057.
1. *Terms of Endearment.* Simon & Schuster, 1975.
2. *The Evening Star.* Simon & Schuster, 1992.

The humorous, joyous, and tragic life of Aurora Greenway celebrates an indomitable woman who will not let age or death dim her spirit. As a young widow in Houston, Aurora spends her days with a variety of boyfriends and tries to deal with her daughter Emma and Emma's shiftless husband. When Emma dies of cancer, Aurora has her hands full with her dysfunctional grandchildren and with her lust for a therapist she is seeing. Sex is her way of handling the golden years, which are not as serene as they are supposed to be.

Subjects: Women; Mothers and daughters; Family life; Aging
Place/Time: Houston (Tex.)—1945–1980; Houston (Tex.)—1980–; Texas—1945–1980; Texas—1980–

1058.
1. *Dead Man's Walk.* Simon & Schuster, 1995.
2. *Comanche Moon.* Simon & Schuster, 1997.
3. *Lonesome Dove.* Simon & Schuster, 1985.
4. *Streets of Laredo.* Simon & Schuster, 1993.

In this epic story of the Old West, teenage runaways Woodrow Call and Gus McCrae join the Texas Rangers in the new Texas Republic. As the Rangers travel across Texas, they fight Comanche Chief Buffalo Hump and are captured by a Mexican militia. Through the years they fight Comanches and Apaches.

When they leave the Texas Rangers, McCrae and Call lead a cattle drive from Texas to Montana where they want to create their own cattle empire. Along the way they are helped or hindered by Lorena, the whore with a heart of gold; Elmira, the restless wife; Blue Duck, the renegade Indian; Newt, the young cowboy; and Jake, the womanizing ex-rancher. Years later, as aged Call is asked to track down a train robber who has struck the railroad once too often, Call's manhunt brings him in touch with old friends, and they all end up in the same town for the final shootout.

Genre: Historical Fiction; Western
Subjects: Frontier and pioneer life; Cattle drives; Ranch life; Outlaws; Native Americans; Comanche Indians
Place/Time: Texas—19th century; Western states—19th century

1059.
1. *All My Friends Are Going to Be Strangers.* Simon & Schuster, 1972.
2. *Some Can Whistle.* Simon & Schuster, 1989.

As a young man, Danny Deck is on the verge of success as a writer. He drifts from Texas to California, falling in love but never staying in one place. After making a fortune in television writing, Danny moves back to Texas and withdraws from the world. Only when the daughter he has never seen barges into his life with her children and lover is Danny restored to life and the world.

Subjects: Authors; Fathers and daughters
Place/Time: Texas—1945–1980; California—1945–1980

1060.
1. *The Last Picture Show.* Dial, 1966.
2. *Texasville.* Simon & Schuster, 1987.
3. *Duane's Depressed.* Simon & Schuster, 1999.

Thalia is a dreamy little Texas town in the 1950s. Sonny Crawford and his friend Duane Jackson are high school seniors and bored. They relieve their boredom by playing pool, going to the movies, and having sex. It is Sonny's affair with the lonely wife of the football coach that leads to tragedy. Twenty years later, Duane, now a wealthy oil man, returns to Thalia to find the town caught in economic depression when the oil boom became an oil glut. As Duane turns 60, he has a midlife crisis. He washes his hands of his dysfunctional family and moves into a one-room cabin. He agrees to see a psychiatrist, but that doesn't stop his crazy ways. Times have driven Duane, his family, and the citizens of Thalia slightly berserk.

Subjects: Love affairs; Teenagers; Small town life
Place/Time: Texas—1945–1980

McQuinn, Donald E.

1061.
1. *Warrior.* Ballantine, 1990.

2. *Wanderer.* Ballantine, 1993.
3. *Witch.* Ballantine, 1994.

Having been cocooned away from the ravages of aging, and from a war and plague that have destroyed 21st-century civilization, Donacee Tate and Matt Conway are awakened by an earthquake into a barbaric culture peopled by warring nomadic tribes and strange religious cults. Their fates become intertwined with the leaders of the chaotic civilization: the warrior Gan Moondark, who has united areas of the present day Pacific Northwest, and Sylah, a priestess whose search for knowledge of the past has resulted in charges of witchcraft.

Genre: Science Fiction
Subjects: Cryonics; Violence, Religion; Witchcraft

Meier, Shirley. *See* Stirling, S. M. (Fifth Millenium Series)

Meluch, R. (Rebecca) M.

1062. Wind
1. *Wind Dancers.* New American Library, 1981.
2. *Wind Child.* New American Library, 1982.

Aeolis is the home planet of the shape shifter race of Kistraalians until a group of wealthy Earthlings decide to take over their world and, to further their purpose, attempt to conceal the existence of the aborigines. Although the race seems close to extinction, young Daniel, a human-alien half-breed sets out on a mission to restore the Kistraalians to their former state.

Genre: Science Fiction
Subjects: Life on other planets; Cultural conflict; Mixed blood

Melville, Anne. *Pseud. of* Margaret Potter

1063.
1. *The Lorimer Line.* Doubleday, 1977.
2. *Alexa.* Doubleday, 1979.
3. *Blaize.* Doubleday, 1981.
4. *Family Fortunes.* Doubleday, 1984.

In England in 1887, the Lorimer financial empire collapsed and suddenly the family was struggling for survival. For Margaret, more was at stake. Battling prejudices against women doctors and dealing with her father's secret life, she develops "Lorimer courage," which she uses to foster the opera career of her beautiful young ward, Alexa. The strong and individualistic personalities are jolted by another trauma—World War I—that radically changes their lives.

Genre: Historical Fiction
Subjects: Family life; Physicians; Love; World War I, 1914–1918

Place/Time: England—19th century; England—
1900–1945

Meredith, George
1064.
1. *Sandra Belloni.* Roberts, 1887, 1864.
2. *Vittoria.* Roberts, 1888, 1866.

In the 1840s, singer Emilia Sandra Belloni, the daughter of an Italian musician, is adopted by the Pole family. Pole senior is financially entangled with a Mr. Pericles, who wants to manage Emilia. To save the family fortunes, Emilia agrees to go to Milan and sing if Pericles will clear the Poles's debts. In Italy, Emilia becomes a collaborator with the Italian resistance to the Austrian occupation. Her relations with the patriots are complicated by the appearance of Wilfrid Pole, her adopted brother, who is working for the Austrians and Merthyr Powys, an old love. In the end, she marries an Italian count.

Genre: Historical Romance
Subjects: Singers
Place/Time: Italy—19th century

Meredith, Richard C.
1065. The Timeliner Trilogy
1. *At the Narrow Passage.* Putnam, 1973.
2. *No Brother, No Friend.* Doubleday, 1976.
3. *Vestiges of Time.* Doubleday, 1978.

Mercenary Eric Mathers at first seems to be hired to engage in a combat that takes place in the 1970s but bears a strange resemblance to World War I and the American Revolution. Ultimately he finds that he has been working for the alien Krith, who want to alter history for what they claim are worthy purposes. Eric escapes them and, in the process, develops mysterious powers that enable him to fight back.

Genre: Science Fiction
Subjects: Mercenary soldiers; Extraterrestrial beings; Time travel; United States—revolution, 1775–1783; World War I, 1914–1918

Metalious, Grace
1066.
1. *Peyton Place.* Messner, 1956.
2. *Return to Peyton Place.* Messner, 1959.

Considered shockingly explicit about sex when it was published, *Peyton Place* now appears to be the study of a small town of the 1950s with all its rigid gender roles, class consciousness, and hypocrisy. The central character, Allison MacKenzie, rises above the influence of both the town and an overly protective mother to establish herself as a successful author and an independent woman.

Subjects: Small town life; Class distinction; Hypocrisy; Sex roles; Women authors

Place/Time: United States—1945–1980

Metz, Don
1067.
1. *Catamount Bridge.* Harper & Row, 1988.
2. *King of the Mountain.* Harper & Row, 1990.

The people and places of rural Vermont are brought to life in this depiction of two farm families in the 1960s. Harmon and Bodie Woodward are brothers who have just received their draft notices. While Harmon prepares to go to Vietnam, Bodie refuses to go to war and both fight over Harmon's wife Darlene. On another farm, Junior Audette, who lost his legs in Vietnam, sells his father's farm and has to fight his father and his own wife over the sale.

Subjects: Farm life; Vietnamese War, 1961–1975; Family life; Brothers
Place/Time: Vermont—1945–1980

Michael, Judith
1068.
1. *Deceptions.* Pocket, 1982.
2. *A Tangible Web.* Pocket, 1994.

Identical twins Sabrina and Stephanie Hartwell are dissatisfied with their lives. Sabrina is an antique dealer in London while Stephanie is a housewife in Evanston, Illinois. The two meet secretly in China and decide to exchange lives for week, but Stephanie is mysteriously blown up on a yacht. Sabrina continues in the role of Stephanie and has come to love her sister's husband and children. When a friend spots the real Stephanie in France, Sabrina rushes off to find her sister.

Subjects: Sisters; Family life
Place/Time: Illinois—1980–; France—1980–

Michaelis, Karin. *Pseud. of* Katharina Marie (Bech-Brondum) Michaelis Strangeland
1069.
1. *The Dangerous Age: Letters and Fragments from a Woman's Diary.* Lane, 1911.
2. *Elsie Lindtner.* Lane, 1912.

Translated from the Danish, *The Dangerous Age* is considered a landmark in women's writing because it so frankly reveals the mental state of fortyish Elsie Lindtner, who feels stifled and as if her life is headed in the wrong direction. The sequel follows Elsie into her more tranquil fifties.

Subjects: Women—psychology; Psychological novels; Middle age
Place/Time: Denmark—1900–1945

Michaels, Fern. *Joint pseud. of* Roberta Anderson *and* Mary Kuczkin

1070.
1. *Sins of Omission.* Ballantine, 1989.
2. *Sins of the Flesh.* Ballantine, 1990.

The sins of the fathers are visited on their children in this saga about Reuben Tarz and Daniel Bishop, who become friends in World War I. After being injured, they are taken in by a sexy French marchioness, Mickey, but their life is shaken up when Bebe Rosen comes to the estate. The ensuing love triangle causes misery and violence that comes full circle in World War II with their children.

Genre: Historical Romance
Subjects: Love affairs; Wealth; World War I, 1914–1918; World War II, 1939–1945
Place/Time: France—1900–1945; France—1945–1980; Hollywood (Calif.)—1900–1945; Hollywood (Calif.)—1945–1980; California—1900–1945; California—1945–1980

1071.
1. *Captive Passions.* Ballantine, 1977.
2. *Captive Embraces.* Ballantine, 1979.
3. *Captive Splendors.* Ballantine, 1980.
4. *Captive Secrets.* Ballantine, 1991.

When her sister is murdered by pirates, Sirena escapes from them on a stolen ship and goes to colonial Java to take her sister's place as the bride of Raegan van der Rhys. They clash, but finally fall in love, though their life together doesn't run smoothly. The death of a child, divorce, pursuit, and finally remarriage bring them together again. Their children—Wren, Caleb, and Furana—find their paths to love also strewn with obstacles. Adventures with the Puritans, pirates in Java, and passion with numerous lovers highlight the children's lives.

Genre: Family Saga; Historical Romance
Subjects: Adventure
Place/Time: Java—18th century

1072.
1. *Texas Rich.* Ballantine, 1985.
2. *Texas Heat.* Ballantine, 1986.
3. *Texas Fury.* Ballantine, 1989.
4. *Texas Sunrise.* Ballantine, 1993.

Beautiful but poor Billie Ames meets wealthy Texan Moss Coleman in a Philadelphia Navy Yard during World War II. After their marriage, Billie and Moss move back to Sunbridge Ranch near Austin where Billie is immediately drawn into father-in-law Seth's obsession with power and building a family dynasty. Seth's obsession affects Billie's children and grandchildren as they try to find love and happiness amid a world of power and treachery.

Genre: Family Saga; Romance
Subjects: Wealth; Ranch life

Place/Time: Texas—1945–1980

1073. Vegas Trilogy
1. *Vegas Rich.* Kensington, 1996.
2. *Vegas Heat.* Kensington, 1997.
3. *Vegas Sunrise.* Kensington, 1997.

Poor Sallie Coleman comes to Las Vegas in 1923 where she works in a bingo parlor and as a prostitute. When an eccentric millionaire leaves her his fortune, Sallie uses the money to acquire social polish. She marries Philip Thornton and has two sons, Ash and Simon. When their marriage falls apart, Sallie has an affair with Devin Rollins. The two sons are torn between their parents. Sallie leaves her fortune to her daughter-in-law Fanny, Ash's ex-wife, who takes over the building and running of Babylon, the family's casino. Fanny then marries Simon, but that marriage also ends in divorce. None of Fanny's children want to run the casino, so Ash's illegitimate son Jeff Lassiter becomes the head. Soon all of Fanny's children and Jeff are fighting, but when disaster threatens, the family finally puts aside their differences and works together to save Babylon and their lives.

Genre: Family Saga
Subjects: Family life; Marriage; Gambling; Husbands and wives; Millionaires
Place/Time: Las Vegas (Nev.) —1900–1945; Las Vegas (Nev.)—1945–1980; Las Vegas (Nev.)—1980–

Miles, Harold

1074.
1. *The Devil and Uncle Will.* Humana Press, 1991.
2. *Bad Ol' Boy.* Humana Press, 1993.

The life and times of Will Johnson are retold by Will on his deathbed to his young nephew Gene. Will has done everything from bank robbery to murder and now, as he dies, feels that confession of his sins will save his soul. The naive Gene listens to the picaresque tales even as he tries to find Will's hidden treasure.

Subjects: Picaresque novels; Uncles; Adventure
Place/Time: United States—1945–1980

Miller, Henry

1075.
1. *Tropic of Cancer.* Grove Press, 1961, 1934.
2. *Tropic of Capricorn.* Grove Press, 1962, 1939.

These controversial novels are not stories but stream-of-consciousness recountings of a young American's life in Paris and New York in the 1920s and 1930s. Daily accounts show him scrounging for food, devouring books, and making love in profusion. Shocking in their day, these books are classics in the naturalistic, nihilistic, explicit style that developed in the 1930s.

Subjects: Stream of consciousness; Sex; Exiles; Autobiographical stories
Place/Time: Paris (France)—1900–1945; New York (N. Y.)—1900–1945; France—1900–1945

1076. Rosy Crucifixion
1. *Sexus.* Obelisk Press, 1949.
2. *Plexus.* Grove, 1965.
3. *Nexus.* Grove, 1965.

These autobiographical novels explore the author's adventures in Paris in the 1920s. His exploits are sexual, intellectual, and literary. His explicit descriptions of his sexual encounters made the books famous. Finding their way to New York in the 1940s, Miller and his girlfriend Mona find their love and freedom intertwined.

Subjects: Autobiographical stories; Sex; Exiles
Place/Time: Paris (France)—1900–1945; New York (N. Y.)—1900–1945; France—1900–1945

Miller, Janice
1077. The Elk Head Creek Saga
1. *Winter's Fire.* Moody Press, 1995.
2. *McCannon's Country.* Moody Press, 1996.

Colorado rancher Courtney McCannon finds that the Wild West and its violence threaten his family. McCannon must struggle with his faith as he tries to keep God's commandments, while protecting his family. Coming to the same region of Colorado, Elk Head Creek, a wealthy young woman meets a handsome fur trader who offers her adventure, but she too finds that the West challenges her faith.

Genre: Christian Fiction
Subjects: Faith; Ranch life; Fur trade
Place/Time: Colorado—19th century

Miller, Linda Lael
1078.
1. *Forever and the Night.* Berkley, 1993.
2. *For All Eternity.* Berkley, 1994.

Artist Aidan Tremayne, who became a vampire unwillingly, longs to return to mortal existence and settle down with his beloved Neely Wallace, but he must content himself with helping her fight the good fight against gangsters and other bad guys. In the sequel, Aidan's vampire sister Maeve travels through time and falls in love with a Civil War physician.

Genre: Horror
Subjects: Vampires; Love; Crime and criminals; Brothers and sisters; Time travel; United States—Civil War, 1861–1865
Place/Time: United States—1980–; United States—19th century

Miller, Sasha. *See* Nolan, William F. (Witch World series—*On Wings of Magic*)

Miller, Walter M. *Completed by* Bisson, Terry
1079.
1. *A Canticle for Liebowitz.* Lippincott, 1960.
2. *Saint Liebowitz and the Wild Horse Woman.* Bantam, 1997.

Twentieth-century civilization ended in a nuclear holocaust centuries ago, but according to these witty novels of the distant future, humans have learned little about the dangers of conflict. Centered in the Abbey of Liebowitz in the American Southwest where pagan cults flourish side by side with the Catholic Church, these tales of an order of monks who worship the relics of Saint Liebowitz poke fun at religion and human attempts to understand the past by using fragmentary information. The second work was completed following the author's death.

Genre: Science Fiction; Humor
Subjects: Nuclear warfare; Catholic faith; Monasticism and religious orders

Millstein, Gilbert
1080.
1. *God and Harvey Grosbeck.* Doubleday, 1983.
2. *The Late Harvey Grosbeck.* Doubleday, 1974.

Harvey Grosbeck is not a nice man. He's a cantankerous curmudgeon who drinks and smokes too much. He's a newspaperman who both loves and hates New York City. As he rants about the city, he has a heart attack and finds that god is a lady nurse in the intensive care unit who makes him want to live again. When he leaves the hospital, he is willing to risk his health and marriage to pursue his dream to save a bit of old Manhattan.

Subjects: Elderly; Journalists; Heart (disease)
Place/Time: New York (N. Y.)—1945–1980

Mishima, Yukio
1081. Sea of Fertility
1. *Spring Snow.* Knopf, 1972, 1968.
2. *Runaway Horses.* Knopf, 1973, 1969.
3. *The Temple of Dawn.* Knopf, 1973, 1970.
4. *The Decay of the Angel.* Knopf, 1974, 1971.

Japanese society from the turn of the century to the present day is the focus of this tetralogy that treats themes of purity, beauty, evil, and death. The author's evocation of the Japanese way of life is masterful, while he makes the traditions and conflicts of the society and its people intelligible for the western reader.

Genre: Historical Fiction
Subjects: Social classes; Rites and ceremonies—Japan; Degeneration; Allegories

Mitchell, James Leslie. *See Gibbon, Lewis Grassic*

Mitchell, S. (Silas) Weir

1082. War of Independence Series
1. *Hugh Wynne, Free Quaker.* Century, 1898.
2. *The Red City: A Novel of the Second Administration of President Washington.* Century, 1908.

Philadelphia during the American Revolution and its aftermath is the background for these stories about Quaker Hugh Wynne, who served with George Washington. The second work tells of a young French Huguenot who comes to work for Hugh and falls in love with a Quaker woman.

Genre: Historical Fiction
Subjects: United States—revolution, 1775–1783; Washington, George, 1732–1799
Place/Time: Philadelphia (Pa.)—18th century; Pennsylvania—18th century

Mitchell, Sara

1083. Shadow Catchers
1. *Trial of the Innocents.* Bethany House, 1995.
2. *In the Midst of Lions.* Bethany House, 1996.

In the 1890s, operatives from the Pinkerton's National Detective Agency pursue criminals around the world. Alexander MacKay is called in when Eve Sheridan becomes suspicious of her sister Rebecca's marriage. The letters Eve has been receiving from Rebecca have an ominous tone. As Eve tries to discover the truth behind her sister's husband, Alex saves her life and her faith. Operative Simon Kincaid helps Elizabeth Granger clear her family name and stop a predator who is stalking her. When Elizabeth comes up with the solution to the plot against her, only Simon can save her from evil.

Genre: Christian Fiction
Subjects: Faith; Women; Detectives
Place/Time: United States—19th century

Mitford, Nancy

1084.
1. *The Pursuit of Love.* Random House, 1946.
2. *Love in a Cold Climate.* Random House, 1949.
3. *Don't Tell Alfred.* Harper, 1960.

English eccentrics romp through the pages of these satirical works about the members of a privileged London family. Starting in the period following World War I, Linda Radlett, sometimes known as "The Bolter" because of her unstable love life, progresses through two marriages and an affair, with all her family offering comments. Her daughter Fanny chooses what seems to be a more sedate way of living as the wife of an Oxford don, but when her husband is appointed ambassador to France, her life becomes a whirlwind of Gallic diplomacy and skirmishes with the younger generation.

Genre: Humor
Subjects: Family life; Eccentrics and eccentricities; Love affairs; Marriage; Diplomats
Place/Time: London (England)—1900–1945; France—1945–1980; England—1900–1945

Moberg, Vilhelm

1085.
1. *The Emigrants.* Simon & Schuster, 1951, 1949.
2. *Unto a Good Land.* Simon & Schuster, 1954, 1952.
3. *Last Letter Home.* Simon & Schuster, 1959.
4. *The Settlers.* Warner, 1983.

The basis for the movies *The Emigrants* and *The New Land*, this is the account of the Nilsson family's departure from Sweden in 1850. Karl works with his parents on a poor farm in Ljoden Parish, Sweden. When he marries Kristina, he is determined to go America for a better life. Their journey takes them across the ocean to New York and then an even more harrowing journey inland to Chisago County, Minnesota. In trying to farm, they have to fight the Chippewas and the Sioux Indians, raise six children, and fight the Civil War. This saga accurately depicts the hardships of the early pioneers.

Genre: Historical Fiction
Subjects: Immigrants; Frontier and pioneer life; Farm life; Family life
Place/Time: Sweden—19th century; Minnesota—19th century

Modesitt, L. E., Jr.

1086.
1. *Of Tangible Ghosts.* Tor, 1994.
2. *The Ghost of the Revelator.* Tor, 1998.

In this alternate version of history, the United States as we know it does not exist. The Northeast is still a Dutch colony, and there is a Mormon nation called Deseret in the West. France and Spain are the dominant world superpowers. Ghosts exist in this world and, in fact, are the subject of scientific study. Doktor Johann Eshbad had hoped for retirement, but is drawn into a university research project on the control of these lingering spirits of the dead. When his work becomes fraught with danger and international intrigue, he must call upon skills developed in his previous career as a government agent.

Genre: Science Fiction
Subjects: History; Supernatural phenomena; Spies; International intrigue

1087. The Ecolitan Matter
1. *The Ecologic Envoy.* Tor, 1986.
2. *The Ecolitan Operation.* Tor, 1989.
3. *The Ecologic Secession.* Tor, 1990.
4. *The Ecolitan Enigma.* Tor, 1997.

Economic and ecological concerns underlie the work of Nathaniel Whaler, professor of the Ecolitan Institute of the future, but these seemingly academic issues often result in power plays, conflict, and violence within and without the intergalactic Terran Empire. Since Whaler is also an intelligence agent and commando killer, he constantly faces danger and political intrigue as his missions take him through the stars.

Genre: Science Fiction
Subjects: Ecology; Space flight; Life on other planets; Adventure

1088. Recluce
1. *Fall of Angels.* Tor, 1996.
2. *The Magic of Recluce.* Tom Doherty, 1991.
3. *The Towers of Sunset.* Tor, 1992.
4. *The Magic Engineer.* Tor, 1994.
5. *The White Order.* Tor, 1998.
6. *Colors of Chaos.* Tor, 1999.
7. *The Order War.* Tor, 1995.
8. *The Death of Chaos.* Tor, 1995.

In these tales, magic and technology exist side-by-side in a world whose legendary past goes back to the crash of a spaceship commanded by a group of women warriors in a magical land adjacent to the island of Recluce. Nyland, the only man of their group, sets off into a strange new land where order and chaos are constantly at war. The isle of Recluce is rebuilt by Creslin with the aid of Black Wizards. Lerris, an apprentice woodworker, finds Recluce too orderly, enters into the conflict between order and chaos, and finally brings about a resolution.

Genre: Fantasy
Subjects: Imaginary kingdoms; Imaginary wars and battles; Magic

1089. The Spellsong Cycle
1. *The Soprano Sorceress.* Tor, 1997.
2. *The Spellsong War.* Tor, 1998.
3. *Darksong Rising.* Tor, 2000.

Grieving over the death of her daughter and made still more unhappy by the insulting behavior of her ex-husband, Anna Marshall wants to be anywhere but Ames, Iowa, where she is a singer and music instructor. Her wish is granted as she is magically whisked into the world of Erde where her musical talent gives her responsibility beyond her wildest dreams, since on Erde the ability to sing with perfect pitch gives the singer almost infinite power and, of course, also creates enemies. As regent in the realm of Defalk, Anna must deal with an energetic, capricious young heir to the throne and assorted troublemakers, who dislike the idea of a woman in a powerful position.

Genre: Fantasy
Subjects: Singers; Music; Magic; Imaginary wars and battles; Women

Moffett, Judith

1090.
1. *The Ragged World: A Novel of the Hefn on Earth.* St. Martin's, 1991.
2. *Time, Like an Ever-Rolling Stream.* St. Martin's, 1992.

The Hefn, gnomelike furry aliens, come to Earth to to save the planet from its own crimes and follies. The Hefn teach a handful of humans how to peer into the past so that the humans can learn where they went wrong ecologically. However, some humans resent the Hefn and try to stir up rebellion.

Genre: Science Fiction
Subjects: Interplanetary visitors; Extraterrestrial beings; Ecology; Time travel

Moll, Elick

1091.
1. *Seidman and Son.* Putnam, 1958.
2. *Mr. Seidman and the Geisha.* Simon & Schuster, 1962.
3. *The Perilous Spring of Morris Seidman.* Houghton Mifflin, 1972.

Morris Seidman is a middle-aged New York garment manufacturer who has made good. He has a wife, two children, and a business partner. When his son returns home from the Korean War, Harold wants to make changes and his partner suddenly takes an interest in a young model. Morris with his warmth and humor tries to straighten the two out. In the end, his son marries and eventually takes over the business. When Morris travels to Japan on business, he meets a geisha, O-Yuki, with whom he tries to bridge the barrier of age and customs. When he returns home, he has to help his sister Bessie, who doesn't want her son to marry a topless waitress. While going from one crisis to another, Morris tries to help everyone.

Genre: Gentle Read; Humor
Subjects: Aging; Fathers and sons; Family life; Jews; Cultural conflict
Place/Time: New York (N. Y.)—1945–1980; Japan—1945–1980

Monaco, Richard

1092. Parsival

1. *Parsival, or A Knight's Tale.* Macmillan, 1977.
2. *The Grail War.* Simon & Schuster, 1979.
3. *The Final Quest.* Putnam, 1981.

The tale of the Arthurian knight Parsival's search for the Holy Grail and engagement in the Grail War is told in a violently realistic, stream-of-consciousness style. Parsival leaves the safety and seclusion of his royal upbringing, meets the evil Clinschor who pursues the Grail for his own dark purposes, and after what seems to be a futile war, is reunited with his wife Layla and his strangely dual-natured son Lohengrin.

Genre: Fantasy
Subjects: Perceval (legendary character); Grail; Good and evil; Legends and folk tales

Monahan, Brent

1093.

1. *The Book of Common Dread.* St. Martin's, 1993.
2. *The Blood of the Covenant.* St Martins, 1995.

Five-hundred-year-old vampire Vincent DeVilbiss joins a Princeton University think tank as a way to get access to a manuscript in the rare book room of the library which contains secrets dangerous to the demons who control him. DeVilbiss suffers the true death, but two rare book librarians, who now know the significance of the manuscript, steal the document with the help of a Catholic priest and a Princeton police detective and take off with an especially vicious 2000-year-old vampire in hot pursuit.

Genre: Horror
Subjects: Vampires; Librarians; Good and evil; College life
Place/Time: Princeton (N. J.)—1980–

Monsarrat, Nicholas

1094.

1. *The Tribe That Lost Its Head.* Sloane, 1956.
2. *Richer Than All His Tribe.* Morrow, 1969.

David Bracken is a young English government official who is being sent to the African country of Pharamaul. Dinamaula, the son of the chief, is also returning to the country after studying in England. Both men are used by reporter Tuhlbach Browne to stir up trouble in Parliament. After the country becomes independent, Bracken stays on as a career civil servant, but he is disillusioned when he sees the illiteracy, intertribal hatred, and tyrannical policies.

Subjects: Africa—race relations; Africa—native peoples; Politics—Africa
Place/Time: Africa—1945–1980

1095.

1. *Running Proud.* Morrow, 1979.
2. *Darken Ship.* Morrow, 1981.

During the battle with the Spanish Armada, Matthew Lawe commits an act of cowardice. He is cursed and finds he must live forever until he redeems himself. His 400-year saga finds him sailing with Hudson on his doomed voyage to find the Northwest Passage, then with pirate Henry Morgan and Captain Cook in the South Seas. He is at General Wolfe's side at Quebec, then with Nelson in his battles with Napoleon. He finally ends up on an illegal slave trader. Monsarrat died before he could finish the final book.

Genre: Historical Fiction; Naval Adventure
Subjects: Adventure; Naval battles; War; Allegories
Place/Time: Atlantic Ocean—multicentury span; Pacific Ocean—multicentury span

Monteleone, Thomas F. *See* Bischoff, David F.

Montgomery, L. M. (Lucy Maud)

1096.

1. *Anne of Green Gables.* Page, 1908.
2. *Anne of Avonlea.* Page, 1909.
3. *Chronicles of Avonlea.* Page, 1912.
4. *Anne of the Island.* Page, 1915.
5. *Anne of Windy Poplars.* Stokes, 1936.
6. *Anne's House of Dreams.* Stokes, 1917.
7. *Anne of Ingleside.* Stokes, 1939.

Orphan Anne Shirley is sent to the Cuthberts on Prince Edward Island when she is 11 years old. They wanted a boy, but fall in love with the delightful Anne. Her sweet ways and struggles to win acceptance endear her to all she meets. She goes to Redmond College to become a teacher and gets to know Gilbert who is studying to be a doctor. After teaching for a few years, Anne marries Gilbert and raises six children. The innocence and peacefulness of a bygone time is captured in Anne Shirley, who is spunky, kind, and loving.

Genre: Coming of Age; Gentle Read
Subjects: Teenagers; Orphans; Teachers; Love; Marriage
Place/Time: Prince Edward Island (Canada)—19th century; Canada—19th century

Moon, Elizabeth

1097. Heris Serrano

1. *Hunting Party.* Baen, 1993.
2. *Sporting Chance.* Baen, 1994.
3. *Winning Colors.* Baen, 1995.

Heris Serrano didn't know the guy was a villain when she saved his life, but for her trouble, she is forced to resign her position as a pilot in the interstellar navy of the future. However, adventure follows her as she pilots the interstellar yacht of the wealthy Lady Cecelia;

finds herself involved in royal intrigue, and attempts to regain her commission. *Note:* The Esmay Suiza series continues these tales of a space fleet of the future and the Serrano family.

Genre: Science Fiction
Subjects: Space flight; Women; Adventure; Interplanetary voyages

1098. Esmay Suiza
1. *Once a Hero.* Baen, 1997.
2. *Rules of Engagement.* Baen, 1998.
3. *Change of Command.* Baen, 1999.

Continuing the saga of an interstellar space navy begun in the Heris Serrano series, these stories narrate the adventures of young officer Esmay Suiza, who must suddenly take command of a spaceship after a mutiny. Her sudden rise to a prominent position gains her both friends and enemies, and she finds herself falsely implicated in a kidnaping. Esmay's romance with a member of the powerful Serrano family is opposed by relatives on both sides, but Esmay must put personal concerns aside as she is drawn into an interstellar conflict involving drugs that dramatically lengthen the human life span. *Note:* This series follows the Heris Serrano series.

Genre: Science Fiction
Subjects: Space flight; Women; Adventure; Interplanetary voyages

Moorcock, Michael

1099.
1. *Blood: A Southern Fantasy.* Morrow, 1994.
2. *Fabulous Harbors.* Avon, 1995.
3. *The War amongst the Angels: An Autobiographical Story.* Avon, 1997.

Moorcock's concept of a multiverse of dimensions and realities brings these works together. In an alternate-time-stream postbellum American South, the roles of blacks and whites are reversed. Two river boat gamblers journey through this crumbling reality that is threatened by a door between dimensions called the Biloxi fault. The tales continue as a series of short stories peopled by many of Moorcock's characters and their adventures in the multiverse of alternate realities. In the third work, Margaret Rose Moorcock, an immortal with mystical gifts, travels through real time and into another dimension where order and chaos are at war.

Genre: Fantasy
Subjects: Time travel; Mysticism

1100. Dancers at the End of Time
1. *An Alien Heat.* Harper, 1972.
2. *The Hollow Lands.* Harper, 1974.
3. *The End of All Songs.* Harper, 1976.
4. *Legends from the End of Time.* Harper, 1976.
5. *A Messiah at the End of Time.* DAW Books, 1978.

Far in the future when it is common knowledge that time as we know it is about to end and society has abandoned all goals and moral ideals in pursuit of pleasure, young Jherek Carnelian falls in love with a charming woman who has time traveled from the Victorian era and seems to embody everything missing from his own culture. He has a series of adventures pursuing her through a variety of time periods.

Genre: Fantasy; Science Fiction
Subjects: Time; Time travel; Hedonism; Love

1101. The Elric Saga
1. *The Singing Citadel.* Berkley, 1971.
2. *The Sleeping Sorceress.* Lancer, 1972. (Revised edition: *The Vanishing Tower.* DAW Books, 1977.)
3. *The Stealer of Souls.* Lancer, 1967.
4. *Elric of Melnibone.* Lancer, 1972.
5. *The Sailor on the Seas of Fate.* DAW Books, 1976.
6. *The Weird of the White Wolf.* DAW Books, 1977.
7. *The Bane of the Black Sword.* DAW Books, 1977.
8. *Stormbringer.* DAW Books, 1977.
9. *Elric at the End of Time.* DAW Books, 1985.
10. *The Fortress of the Pearl.* Ace, 1989.
11. *The Revenge of the Rose.* Ace, 1991.

The albino Elric of Melnibone, warrior and emperor, is drawn from his royal existence into a cataclysmic battle between the forces of Order and Chaos. Assisted by his sword Stormbringer, which seeks not only the blood but the souls of his enemies, Elric's final quest is the putting to rest of his deceased father.

Genre: Fantasy
Subjects: Imaginary kingdoms; Imaginary wars and battles; Good and evil; Arms and armor; Fathers and sons

1102. Jerry Cornelius
1. *The Final Programme.* Avon, 1968.
2. *A Cure for Cancer.* Holt, Rinehart, 1971.
3. *The English Assassin.* Harper, 1972.
4. *The Condition of Muzak.* Gregg Press, 1978.

The above titles have also been published in the following collection: *The Cornelius Chronicles.* Avon, 1977.

Jerry Cornelius has a variety of professions and talents, none of which bear close examination. In a kind of altered reality with hallucinogenic overtones, Jerry has adventures with a strange and wonderful computer technician and his not-very-motherly mother, and literally comes face to face with death. Along the way, he develops the ability to completely transform his own appearance.

Genre: Fantasy; Science Fiction
Subjects: Rogues and vagabonds; Death; Mothers and sons

1103. The Nomad of Time
1. *The Warlord of the Air.* Ace, 1971.

2. *The Land Leviathan.* Doubleday, 1974.
3. *The Steel Tsar.* DAW Books, 1982.

Chrononaut Oswald Bastable leaps back and forth between events in the 20th century, but not necessarily the 20th century that we are experiencing. As well as traveling through eras, Oswald can jump across time streams and influence the course of history. His last stop is Russia just before the Bolshevik Revolution—which may never happen!

Genre: Fantasy; Science Fiction
Subjects: Time travel; Space and time; History

1104. Pyat
1. *Byzantium Endures.* Random House, 1981.
2. *The Laughter of Carthage.* Random House, 1984.

Anti-Semite Russian Maxim Arturovitch Pyatnitiski's most closely guarded secret is that he is in fact Jewish. This charming, opportunistic antihero, who, in addition to everything else, is a scientific genius, makes his way through the hazards of early 20th-century revolutionary Russia, and travels through Europe and across the United States, eventually finding happiness in the place that, for him, is a perfect fit: Hollywood!

Genre: Humor
Subjects: Rogues and vagabonds; Genius; Jews; Anti-Semitism
Place/Time: Soviet Union—1917–1945; Europe—1945–1980; Hollywood (Calif.)—1980–; California—1980–

Moore, George
1105.
1. *Evelyn Innes.* Appleton, 1898.
2. *Sister Teresa.* Lippincott, 1901.

Evelyn, whose father gave up a promising music career to teach church music, grows up in Dulwich, England, and studies music. Evelyn's beautiful voice leads her into the world of opera where she becomes the protegee of Sir Owen Asher. When she becomes his lover and goes to Europe with him, a priest warns her to give up her life of sin. After struggling with her faith, she becomes a nun, but peace only comes when she loses her voice and teaches church music.

Genre: Christian Fiction
Subjects: Singers; Faith; Catholic faith; Nuns
Place/Time: Europe—19th century; England—19th century

Moore, Susan
1106.
1. *Paths of Fortune.* St. Martin's, 1984.
2. *A World Too Wide.* St. Martin's, 1989.

When their father dies, Kate and Sophy Byford are left in genteel poverty. In 1800 England, the only thing Kate can do to help her family is take a post as govern-

ess with a master she hates. Sophy stays home to care for their ailing mother. Kate falls in love and marries an American, Joseph Lee, whom she accompanies to Virginia. Sophy eventually marries an engineer from another class. Both women have to adjust to their new lives, but complications arise when their brother's illegitimate daughter, Georgiana, is sent to America to be raised by Kate. When Georgiana returns to England, she falls in love with Sophy's son. The lovers face many obstacles until the family is reconciled.

Genre: Historical Romance
Subjects: Family life; Women
Place/Time: England—19th century; Virginia—19th century

Mordden, Ethan
1107.
1. *I've a Feeling We're Not in Kansas Anymore.* St. Martin's, 1985.
2. *Buddies.* St. Martin's, 1986.
3. *Everybody Loves You: Further Adventures in Gay Manhattan.* St. Martin's, 1988.
4. *Some Men Are Lookers.* St. Martin's, 1997.

A series of interlinked stories reveal an upbeat and wistful picture of gay life in Greenwich Village, Woodstock, Fire Island, and London. Seen through the eyes of Bud, a middle-aged gay writer, this series explores the lives, loves, hopes, and fears of men in conflict and trying to reconcile with themselves and their society in the age of AIDS.

Subjects: Homosexuality; Middle age
Place/Time: New York (N. Y.)—1980–; London (England)–1980–; England—1980–

Morier, James
1108.
1. *The Adventures of Hajji Baba of Ispahan.* A. Small, 1824.
2. *Hajji Baba in England.* Harper, 1828.

Hajji Baba is a poor barber in Persia. As he shaves his patrons he quotes poets to sooth them. As he trims their beards, he lightens their purses, because he is a rogue who is constantly in trouble. He even goes to London to see the barbarous westerners. Morier, who had traveled extensively in Persia, gives a very accurate picture of the country in the early 1800s.

Genre: Humor
Subjects: Picaresque novels; Barbers
Place/Time: Persia—19th century; London (England)—19th century; England—19th century

Morley, Christopher
1109.
1. *Parnassus on Wheels.* Doubleday, 1917.
2. *The Haunted Bookshop.* Doubleday, 1919.

Roger Miffin builds a book van and sells books to farmers in upstate New York. Helen McGill is a spinster who is looking for adventure, so she buys the van and she and Roger set off together. He is supposed to stay for one day to help her, but then decides to stay on for the adventure. Eventually Roger leaves and starts a secondhand bookstore in Brooklyn where he helps foil a German bomb plot during World War I.

Genre: Gentle Read
Subjects: Booksellers and bookselling; Voyages and travels
Place/Time: New York (N. Y.)—1900–1945; New England—1900–1945

Morressy, John
1110. Del Whitby
1. *Starbrat.* Walker, 1972.
2. *Nail Down the Stars.* (Alternate title: *Stardrift.*) Walker, 1973.
3. *Under a Calculating Star.* Doubleday, 1975.

Three separate stories are ultimately drawn together: the tales of a young boy who is kidnapped by space pirates; of a minstrel who not only wanders among worlds, but completely changes himself according to his surroundings; and of the usurper of a planetary throne, whose plans are foiled by the two protagonists.

Genre: Science Fiction
Subjects: Boys; Minstrels; Kidnapping; Interplanetary voyages; Imaginary kingdoms;

1111. Kedrigern
1. *A Voice for Princess.* Ace, 1986.
2. *The Questing of Kedrigern.* Ace, 1987.
3. *Kedrigern in Wanderland.* Ace, 1988.
4. *Kedrigern and the Charming Couple.* Ace, 1990.
5. *A Remembrance for Kedrigern.* Ace, 1990.

Kedrigern becomes a rogue wizard when he resigns from the wizards' guild planning to lead a reclusive life, but instead finds himself involved with a beautiful damsel, who is briefly transformed into a toad by his enemies. Marriage to his beloved does not end his adventures, which include encounters with werewolves and a clumsy dragonslayer.

Genre: Fantasy
Subjects: Magicians; Love; Marriage; Imaginary wars and battles

Morris, Alan
1112. Guardians of the North
1. *By Honor Bound.* Bethany House, 1996.
2. *Heart of Valor.* Bethany House, 1996.
3. *Bright Sword of Justice.* Bethany House, 1997.
4. *Between Earth and Sky.* Bethany House, 1998.
5. *Wings of Healing.* Bethany House, 1999.

When rancher Hunter Stone seeks revenge against the renegade Crow Red Wolf, who murdered his wife, he is nearly killed. Missionary Reena O'Donnell nurses him back to health, and Hunter joins the North-West Mounted Police in the Canadian Northwest. When Red Wolf kidnaps Reena, Hunter must rescue her. The two fall in love, but their work keeps them apart. They both fight the influences of the whiskey trade that is destroying the Blackfeet tribe and the gangs that prey on them. When one member of a gang turns out to be Reena's brother, Hunter's commitment to justice is threatened. Later Reena must travel to Wyoming to nurse her uncle who was wounded while scouting for Custer. New missionary Jack Sheffield goes with her as the two try to head off Sioux unrest by talking to Sitting Bull. Back in Canada, a flu epidemic strikes the Blackfeet tribe, and then the government decrees that they must move to a reservation. Hunter must try to keep the peace and also keep Reena from becoming ill. Throughout their struggles, Reena and Hunter have their faith to help them through the dangers of the day.

Genre: Christian Fiction
Subjects: Royal Canadian Mounted Police; Missionaries; Native Americans—Canada; Faith;
Place/Time: Canadian Northwest—19th century

Morris, Chris. *See Morris, Janet*

Morris, Edita
1113.
1. *Flowers of Hiroshima.* Viking, 1960.
2. *Seeds of Hiroshima.* Braziller, 1961

The memory of a beautiful Japanese high school girl draws Sam Willoughby into the family of Yuka-San when he visits postwar Japan on business. At first the family attempts to hide the mental and physical scars of the bombing of Hiroshima, but with the death of Yuka's husband Fumio, Yuka and Sam are drawn together in a complex love relationship.

Subjects: World War II, 1939–1945—Japan; Family life; Bereavement; Love
Place/Time: Japan—1945–1980

Morris, Gilbert
1114. American Odyssey Series
1. *A Time to Be Born.* Revell, 1994.
2. *A Time to Die.* Revell, 1994.
3. *A Time to Laugh.* Revell, 1995.
4. *A Time to Weep.* Revell, 1996.
5. *A Time of War.* Revell, 1997.
6. *A Time to Build.* Revell, 1997.

In the early years of the 20th century, the Stuart family struggles to escape the poverty of their Arkansas home. Lylah Stuart attends Bible school to get an education. This education takes her to Hollywood with her young son, where she becomes an actress. Lylah wonders if Hollywood is the right environment to raise her child in. Other members of the Stuart family leave their home to try their luck in the Oklahoma oil fields, but when World War II breaks out, Lylah's son Adam goes off to war along with his cousin Clint. After the war, the Stuart family settles down to enjoy the prosperity of the 1950s, but the Korean War calls them back to service. Each generation of Stuarts must struggle with their Christian faith and values and try to reconcile faith with the hectic events of the 20th century.

Genre: Christian Fiction; Family Saga
Subjects: Family life; Faith; War; Parent and child
Place/Time: United States—1900–1945; United
    States—1945–1980

1115. Appomattox Saga
1. *A Covenant of Love.* Tyndale House, 1992.
2. *Gate of His Enemies.* Tyndale House, 1992.
3. *Where Honor Dwells.* Tyndale House, 1993.
4. *Land of the Shadow.* Tyndale House, 1993.
5. *Out of the Whirlwind.* Tyndale House, 1994.
6. *The Shadow of His Wings.* Tyndale House, 1994.
7. *Wall of Fire.* Tyndale House, 1995.
8. *Stars in Their Courses.* Tyndale House, 1995.
9. *Chariots in the Smoke.* Tyndale House, 1997.
10. *Witness in Heaven.* Tyndale House, 1998.

As the Civil War opens, the Rocklin family of Virginia is torn apart. Dent Rocklin becomes an officer in the Confederacy while Frank Rocklin becomes a spy for the Union. Other members of the family also choose sides and fight for their beliefs. Each finds love, but that love will test their faith and their loyalty to their causes. Ultimately, it is the faith of all the Rocklin clan that helps them survive the Civil War.

Genre: Christian Fiction
Subjects: Faith; Love; Family life; United States—
    Civil War, 1861–1865.
Place/Time: Southern states—19th century

1116. The House of Winslow
1. *The Honorable Imposter.* Bethany House, 1989.
2. *The Captive Bride.* Bethany House, 1987.
3. *The Indentured Heart.* Bethany House, 1988.
4. *The Gentle Rebel.* Bethany House, 1988.
5. *The Saintly Buccaneer.* Bethany House, 1988.
6. *The Holy Warrior.* Bethany House, 1989.
7. *The Reluctant Bridegroom.* Bethany House, 1990.
8. *The Last Confederate.* Bethany House, 1990.
9. *The Dixie Widow.* Bethany House, 1991.
10. *The Wounded Yankee.* Bethany House, 1991.
11. *The Union Belle.* Bethany House, 1992.
12. *The Final Adversary.* Bethany House, 1992.
13. *The Crossed Sabres.* Bethany House, 1993.
14. *The Valiant Gunman.* Bethany House, 1993.
15. *The Gallant Outlaw.* Bethany House, 1994.
16. *The Jeweled Spur.* Bethany House, 1994.
17. *The Yukon Queen.* Bethany House, 1995.
18. *The Rough Rider.* Bethany House, 1996.
19. *The Iron Lady.* Bethany House, 1996.
20. *The Silver Star.* Bethany House, 1997.
21. *Shadow Portrait.* Bethany House, 1998.
22. *White Hunter.* Bethany House, 1999.
23. *The Flying Cavalier.* Bethany House, 1999.

From the landing at Plymouth Rock through the 1890s, the Winslow family must overcome bitterness, unforgiveness, and dark circumstances in each generation. The family lives through the Salem witch trials, the revivals of Jonathan Edwards, the westward movement, the Civil War, the cattle drives from Texas, the Alaska gold rush, the Spanish-American War, and early Hollywood.

Genre: Christian Fiction; Family Saga; Historical
    Fiction
Subjects: Christianity; Adventure; United States—
    Civil War, 1861–1865; United States—Spanish-
    American War; Alaska—gold discoveries; Mo-
    tion pictures
Place/Time: United States—multicentury span

1117. The Liberty Bell
1. *Sound the Trumpet.* Bethany House, 1995.
2. *Song in a Strange Land.* Bethany House, 1996.
3. *Tread Upon the Lion.* Bethany House, 1996.
4. *Arrow of the Almighty.* Bethany House, 1997.
5. *Wind from the Wilderness.* Bethany House, 1998.
6. *The Right Hand of God.* Bethany House, 1998.
7. *Command the Sun.* Bethany House, 2000.

Daniel Bradford comes to America as the indentured servant of Sir Leo Rochester. After serving five years, he marries Holly Blanchard and moves to Virginia where he settles near George Washington's Mount Vernon. Later, the family moves to Boston where they become involved in the fight against England. The family becomes divided when the Revolution starts. Daniel's son Duke becomes a Patriot, while cousin Clive is a Tory. As General Washington tries to forge an army, the Bradford sons Matthew and Joel work as spies to give Washington information on British troops. Rachel Bradford remains at home, but after a battle, she takes in a wounded British soldier with whom she soon falls in love. The Bradfords find their faith sustains them in the fight for liberty. When Matthew discovers his real father is a British lord who has died without an heir, Matthew must decide if he will renounce America and take the title or stay with his family.

Genre: Christian Fiction
Subjects: Faith; United States—revolution, 1775–
    1783; Family life; Washington, George, 1732–
    1799
Place/Time: United States—18th century

1118. Wakefield Dynasty
1. *The Sword of Truth.* Tyndale House, 1994.
2. *The Winds of God.* Tyndale House, 1994.
3. *The Shield of Honor.* Tyndale House, 1995.

4. *The Fields of Glory.* Tyndale House, 1996.
5. *The Ramparts of Heaven.* Tyndale House, 1997.
6. *Song of Princes.* Tyndale House, 1997.
7. *A Gathering of Eagles.* Tyndale House, 1998.

From the time of Henry VIII to the age of Napoleon, the aristocratic Wakefields and the lower class Morgans are bound together by their faith and their intertwined families. In the 1400s, Myles Morgan discovers that he is the rightful heir of Sir Robert Wakefield. Thrown into court life, he is confused. His faith helps him through the turmoil and leads him to help some ministers who want to translate the Bible into English. The two families fight the Spanish Armada and then are divided by the English civil war. Later descendants work with minister John Bunyan and then bring the Methodist movement to America. Throughout the centuries, the two families use their faith to help them through turbulent times.

Genre: Christian Fiction; Family Saga
Subjects: Faith; Family life; Clergy
Place/Time: England—multicentury span

Morris, Gilbert *and* Funderburk, Bobby

1119. The Price of Liberty Series
1. *A Call to Honor.* Word, 1993.
2. *The Color of the Star.* Word, 1993.
3. *All the Shining Young Men.* Word, 1993.
4. *The End of Glory.* Word, 1996.
5. *A Silence in Heaven.* Word, 1996.
6. *A Time to Heal.* Word, 1997.

In 1941, the people of Liberty, Georgia, face the opening of World War II. Ben Logan joins the navy and finds himself at Pearl Harbor on the U. S. S. *Arizona* on December 7, 1941. Later, Chance Rinehart and Jesse Boone join the army. Young football star Mike Hardin strives to become a navy aviator. On the homefront, shattered soldier Clay McCain returns home to heal after the Battle of Tarawa, while a politician tries to use the war to boost his career. The town and its people use their faith to help them through the horrors of the war.

Genre: Christian Fiction
Subjects: World War II, 1939–1945; Soldiers; Seamen; Faith
Place/Time: Georgia—1900–1945; Georgia—1945–1980

Morris, Gilbert *and* McCarver, Aaron

1120. The Spirit of Appalachia
1. *Over the Misty Mountains.* Bethany House, 1997.
2. *Beyond the Quiet Hills.* Bethany House, 1997.
3. *Among the King's Soldiers.* Bethany House, 1998.

4. *Beneath the Mockingbird's Wings.* Bethany House, 1999.

In the late 1700s, Hawk Spencer leaves Virginia after his wife dies. He settles in Tennessee where he becomes a trapper. When he leads a wagon train, Cherokee attack the wagons and kill Elizabeth MacNeal's husband. Hawk falls in love with Elizabeth, and her faith makes Hawk a believer again. After Hawk and Elizabeth marry, their sons are jealous of each other and even fall in love with the same girl. Later, Jacob Spencer will escort his stepsister, Sarah MacNeal, back to Williamsburg where he is torn between the British and the Patriots. Even Sarah's loyalty is torn between a British soldier and her love of freedom. After the Revolution ends, Hannah Spencer befriends Nathaniel Carter, who is part Cherokee, and tries to stop him from joining in the Indian wars on the frontier.

Genre: Christian Fiction
Subjects: Faith; Family life; Frontier and pioneer life; United States—revolution, 1775–1783; Brothers
Place/Time: Tennessee—18th century; Virginia—18th century

Morris, Gilbert *and* Morris, Lynn

1121. Cheney Duvall, M.D.
1. *The Stars for a Light.* Bethany House, 1994.
2. *Shadow of the Mountain.* Bethany House, 1994.
3. *A City Not Forsaken.* Bethany House, 1995.
4. *Toward the Sunrise.* Bethany House, 1996.
5. *Secret Place of Thunder.* Bethany House, 1996.
6. *In the Twilight, in the Evening.* Bethany House, 1997.
7. *Island of the Innocent.* Bethany House, 1998.
8. *Driven with the Wind.* Bethany House, 2000.

Cheney Duvall is one of the first women to graduate from medical school after the Civil War, but she finds that prejudice keeps her from finding a position. Her first job has her accompanying 100 women on a three-month voyage around the Horn to Seattle. Later, she teams up with nurse Shilo Irons as they travel to the Ozark Mountains to help the superstitious mountain folk, to Charleston to help the people in the throes of Reconstruction, and to San Francisco to treat the poor. In each place, she must fight prejudice, physical danger, and most important, spiritual threats. Only her faith and determination help Cheney battle prejudice and fight for the poor.

Genre: Christian Fiction; Historical Fiction
Subjects: Physicians; Faith; Women; Mountain life
Place/Time: Philadelphia (Pa.)—19th century; Seattle (Wash.)—19th century; Pennsylvania—19th century; Washington (state)—19th century; Southern States—19th century

Morris, Janet

1122. The Kerrion Empire
1. *Dream Dancer.* Putnam, 1980.
2. *Cruiser Dreams.* Berkley, 1980.
3. *Earth Dreams.* Berkley, 1982.

Shebat, a young girl from a barbarian Earth culture, is thrust into the middle of the Byzantine machinations of the Kerrions, a family who controls an intergalactic trading system. Shebat sinks briefly into an underworld of women known as dream dancers, but survives to marry into the Kerrion family and pilot her own sentient starship.

Genre: Science Fiction
Subjects: Merchants; Dancers; Underworld; Marriage; Space flight

Morris, Janet *and* Morris, Chris

1123.
1. *Threshold.* Roc, 1990.
2. *Trust Territory.* Roc, 1992.

During an experiment, test pilot Joe South is transported from the 21st century to a time 500 years in the future and to a space station called Threshold where, as a man from another time, he is expected to investigate a strange alien artifact known as Ball.

Genre: Science Fiction
Subjects: Space stations; Air pilots; Time travel; Extraterrestrial beings

Morris, Lynn. *See* Morris, Gilbert

Morris, Wright

1124.
1. *The Home Place.* Scribner, 1948.
2. *The World in the Attic.* Scribner, 1949.

Clyde Muncy is tired of his life in New York, so he packs up his wife and children and returns to his uncle's farm in Lone Tree, Nebraska, where he wants to rediscover his roots. Once back home, he finds he can no longer communicate with the small town people. On the way back to New York, he stops in nearby Junction, once a thriving town. At the funeral of the town's leader, he finally discovers what was good about the past and realizes that the future can also be good.

Subjects: Family life; Small town life
Place/Time: New York (N. Y.)—1945–1980; Nebraska—1945–1980

1125.
1. *Fire Sermon.* Harper & Row, 1971.
2. *A Life.* Harper & Row, 1973.

Kermit Oelsligle, a 12-year-old orphan, lives with his 82-year-old granduncle, Floyd Warner. When Floyd's sister dies, he and the boy travel to Nebraska to pack up the house. On the way, they pick up some hippies whose pot smoking burns down the sister's house. Floyd then travels to his first home, and there he is able to prepare for his death.

Subjects: Old age; Grandfathers; Voyages and travels
Place/Time: Nebraska—1945–1980

1126.
1. *The Field of Vision.* Harcourt Brace, 1956.
2. *Ceremony in Lone Tree.* Atheneum, 1960.

Using several narrators to tell the same events, Morris explores the lives of seven people as they watch a bullfight in Mexico. Walter McKee, his wife Lois, her father Tom Scanlon, their friends Gordon Boyd, Dr. Leopold Lebman, and Paula Kahler all review their lives and try to understand their failures. Later these same characters gather at Tom Scanlon's Lone Tree Hotel to celebrate his birthday, but the old man sleeps through the day as the others try to understand what is happening around them.

Subjects: Friendship; Psychological novels
Place/Time: Mexico—1945–1980; Nebraska—1945–1980

Morrison, Peggy. *See* Cost, March

Morrow, Honore

1127.
1. *Forever Free.* Morrow, 1927.
2. *With Malice Toward None.* Morrow, 1928.
3. *Last Full Measure.* Morrow, 1930.

The above titles have also been published in the following collection: *The Great Captain.* Morrow, 1930.

Abraham Lincoln, the president and the man, is brought to life in these realistic novels. When the Civil War begins, Lincoln fights with his generals as the North loses battles in the early years. In the last year of the war, he has conflicts with Charles Sumner over reconstruction of the South. Portraits of Mary Todd Lincoln, their children, his generals, and his assassin, John Wilkes Booth, complete the picture of Lincoln's presidency to the moment of his assassination.

Genre: Historical Fiction
Subjects: Presidents—United States; Lincoln, Abraham, 1809–1865; Lincoln, Mary Todd, 1818–1882; United States—Civil War, 1861–1865
Place/Time: Washington (D. C.)—19th century

Moss, Robert

1128. Firekeeper Series
1. *The Firekeeper: A Narrative of the Eastern Frontier.* Tor, 1996.
2. *The Interpreter.* Forge, 1997.

The changing world of the Mohawk Indians in the 18th century is slowly revealed as they interact with the Europeans who are encroaching on their land. Sir William Johnson, a chieftain of the Mohawks, convinces the Six Nations to join with the British against the French during the French and Indian Wars. Conrad Weiser, a Palatine German, is sent to live among the Mohawks. He learns their language and ways and works as an Indian agent on the Pennsylvania frontier. He works with the Mohawks to keep them independent, but they slowly lose ground to the European settlers.

Genre: Historical Fiction
Subjects: Native Americans; Mohawk Indians; Frontier and pioneer life; United States—French and Indian War—1755–1763
Place/Time: Pennsylvania—18th century

Motley, Willard

1129.
1. *Knock on Any Door.* Appleton, 1947.
2. *Let No Man Write My Epitaph.* Random House, 1958.

Nick Romano hangs out in the pool rooms and on the streets of Chicago. His friends try to keep him from a life of crime, but he ends up as a killer and dies in the electric chair. His son, young Nick, gets help from a kindly policeman and from neighbors, but has little chance because he lives on the street and is a dope addict.

Genre: Crime Novel
Subjects: Crime and criminals; Fathers and sons; Murder and murderers
Place/Time: Chicago (Ill.)—1945–1980; Illinois—1945–1980

Mottram, R. H. (Ralph Hale)

1130. The Spanish Farm Trilogy
1. *The Spanish Farm.* MacVeagh/Dial, 1924.
2. *Sixty-Four, Ninety-Four.* MacVeagh/Dial, 1925.
3. *The Crime at Vanderlynden's.* MacVeagh/Dial, 1926.

The character of a rural young Frenchwoman Madeleine Vanderlynden draws together these stories of the chaos and futility of World War I. Madeleine endures the British occupation of her farm and the death of her lover. She has a brief and, for her, almost meaningless affair with a young British officer, whose experiences form the second book of the trilogy. The crime of the third book is the desecration of a shrine on Madeleine's property, which, when the official description is translated into English, appears to be an attack on Madeleine herself.

Subjects: Farm life; World War I, 1914–1918; Bereavement; Love affairs; Crime and criminals
Place/Time: France—1900–1945

Muhlbach, L. (Luise). *Pseud. of* Clara Mundt

1131. Frederick the Great Series
1. *Frederick the Great and His Court.* Appleton, 1866.
2. *Frederick the Great and His Friends.* Appleton, 1867.
3. *Frederick the Great and His Family.* Appleton, 1867.
4. *The Merchant of Berlin.* Chesterfield Society, 1861.

Frederick the Great, the 18th-century king who expanded Prussian power in Europe, is portrayed as a ruler who, although autocratic by nature, absorbed and put into practice many of the concepts of the Enlightenment. The series emphasizes the extent to which the aristocracy of the period sacrificed their individuality and happiness for the good of the state.

Genre: Historical Fiction
Subjects: Frederick II, King of Prussia, 1712–1786; Courts and courtiers; Kings and rulers; Aristocracy
Place/Time: Germany—18th century

Mundt, Clara. *See* Muhlbach, L. (Luise)

Munif, Abdelrahman

1132.
1. *Cities of Salt.* Vintage Books, 1989, 1984.
2. *The Trench.* Pantheon Books, 1991, 1987.
3. *Variations on Night and Day.* Pantheon 1993, 1989.

The impact of the discovery of oil by American and British groups on the Sultanate of Mooran is depicted through the eyes of a varied cast of Bedouin characters. These books, which have been banned in the Middle East, begin in the 1930s and show the upheaval caused in a little wadi community when oil is discovered and the strangers bring in "magical" tools. By the 1950s, the sultanate has grown too rich and its corruption is seen in Dr. Subhi Mahmilji, the sultan's chief advisor, who is constantly plotting to gain power and money. All of the books deal with the corruption of traditional Arab family and tribal values when money and power take their place.

Genre: Historical Fiction
Subjects: Corruption (in politics); Arabs; Petroleum industry; Clans; Politics—Middle East
Place/Time: Middle East—1900–1945; Middle East—1945–1980

Murakami, Haruki

1133.
1. *A Wild Sheep Chase.* Kodansha, 1989.
2. *Dance Dance Dance.* Kodansha, 1994.

Part fable, part hard-boiled mystery, and part meta-physical tale, these novels follow a nameless narrator, a modern Japanese yuppie searching for happiness. The divorced writer is caught up in a quest to find first a mystical sheep, then a hotel he sees in his dreams. He encounters strange people as he tries to discover heaven, but finds only hell.

Subjects: Psychological novels; Allegories
Place/Time: Japan—1980–

Murphy, Michael

1134.
1. *Golf in the Kingdom.* Viking, 1972.
2. *The Kingdom of Shivas Irons.* Broadway, 1997.

In 1956, golfer Murphy meets the mysterious Shivas Irons on the Burning Bush golf links in Fife, Scotland. Murphy plays 18 holes with Shivas, who exposes him to the metaphysical meaning of golf. He goes back to Scotland where he meets more Shivas followers and then on to Russia with more followers. He ends up at Pebble Beach where Murphy teaches a golf pro the inner meaning of golf.

Genre: Sports
Subjects: Golf; Philosophical novels
Place/Time: Scotland—1945–1980; California—1945–1980

Murphy, Warren. *See* Cochran, Molly

Murry, Colin Middleton. *See* Cowper, Richard

Myers, L. H. (Leopold Hamilton)

1135.
1. *The Near and the Far.* Harcourt, 1931.
2. *Prince Jali.* Harcourt, 1931.
3. *The Pool of Vishnu.* Harcourt, 1940.
4. *The Rajah Amar.* (This title was not published separately, but was published with the previous three titles in the following collection: *The Root and the Flower.* Harcourt, 1947.)

In 16th-century India, the Mogul Emperor Akbar wants to set up a new religion. His two sons, sensual Salim and homosexual Daniyal, fight for succession. Jali, the son of Rajah Amar and his Christian wife Sita, is drawn into the intrigues as he struggles to find his own place in the world. Only after assassinations, murders, and intrigues does the young Jali take his place as ruler.

Genre: Historical Fiction
Subjects: Courts and courtiers; Kings and rulers; Brothers
Place/Time: India—16th century

Mykle, Agnar

1136.
1. *Lasso Round the Moon.* Dutton, 1959.
2. *The Song of the Red Ruby.* Dutton, 1961.

The death of his brother thrusts Norwegian composer Ash Burlefoot into a bout of nostalgia and self-examination. Ash reminisces about his many sexual exploits, which produced two illegitimate children, and his participation in the social movements of Europe of the 1930s.

Subjects: Composers; Bereavement; Brothers; Love affairs; Social movements
Place/Time: Europe—1900–1945

Myra, Harold

1137.
1. *Children in the Night.* Zondervan, 1991.
2. *The Shining Face.* Zondervan, 1993.
3. *Morning Child.* Zondervan, 1994.

In an underground world long ago sealed off from the light of the world above, the people and animals are always fighting. Yosha and Asel, two young people, are determined to leave this evil world and seek the light. When they triumph, they must send Mela, a blind girl, and Geln, a fierce unbeliever, back to the underworld to rescue the people left below. Mela's child, though born weak and deformed, is destined to save the underground world.

Genre: Fantasy
Subjects: Imaginary wars and battles; Good and evil; Children; Rescues

Myrdal, Jan

1138.
1. *Childhood.* Lakeview Press, 1991.
2. *Another World.* Ravenswood, 1994.
3. *12 Going on 13.* Ravenswood, 1995.

These autobiographical novels follow Jan from age 5 to 12 as he tries to understand the adult world and his Nobel Laureate parents. Verbally abusive, they see him as a problem child and often leave him in the care of relatives. Only there does he find some sense of home and the joys of childhood. When he is 11, the family emigrates from their home in Sweden to America, where Jan finds himself a lonely, obese boy in a progressive school. Shortly before World War II, he is sent back to Sweden to live with his aunt and uncle. As Hitler invades Europe, Jan cannot understand how the pious Swedes do not speak out against the Nazis. These powerful novels show the pleasures and problems of growing up in a famous but dysfunctional family.

Genre: Coming of Age
Subjects: Children; Family life; Marriage problems

Place/Time: Sweden—1900–1945; United States—1900–1945

Narayan, R. K. (Rasipuram Krishnaswami)

1139. Malgudi Series

1. *Swami and Friends: A Novel of Malgudi.* Michigan State College Press, 1954, 1935.
2. *The Bachelor of Arts.* Michigan State College Press, 1954, 1937.
3. *The Dark Room: A Novel.* Macmillan, 1938.(This title was published only in England.)
4. *Malgudi Days.* Viking, 1982, 1941.
5. *Grateful to Life and Death.* Michigan State College Press, 1953, 1945.
6. *An Astrologer's Day and Other Stories.* Eyre & Spottiswoode, 1947.(This title was published only in England.)
7. *The Printer of Malgudi.* Michigan State College Press, 1957, 1949.
8. *The Financial Expert.* Michigan State College Press, 1953.
9. *Waiting for the Mahatma: A Novel.* Michigan State College Press, 1955.
10. *Lawley Road: Thirty-Two Short Stories.* Indian Thought Publications, 1956.(This title was published only in England.)
11. *The Guide.* Viking, 1958.
12. *The Man-Eater of Malgudi.* Viking, 1961.
13. *The Vendor of Sweets.* Viking, 1967.
14. *A Horse and Two Goats and Other Stories.* Viking, 1970.
15. *The Painter of Signs.* Viking, 1976.
16. *A Tiger for Malgudi.* Viking, 1983.
17. *Under the Banyan Tree and Other Stories.* Viking, 1985.
18. *Talkative Man.* Viking, 1987.
19. *The World of Nagaraj.* Viking, 1990.

Malgudi is a small provincial town in India where children play and saints bathe in the river, and life has been forever changed by the presence of the British. Beginning with the days of the Raj to independent India, the villagers live their lives with the traditions of the old ways and the pull of western influences. The heroes are all middle-class men who, through gentle humor, become aware of their struggles and grow with their new insights. Through novels and short stories, the gentle ways of Malgudi are revealed and become a microcosm for the rest of the world. Books 4, 6, 10, 14, and 17 are short stories.

Genre: Historical Fiction
Subjects: India—British occupation, 1765–1947; India—country life; Social classes; Middle classes
Place/Time: India—19th century; India—1900–1945

Nasaw, Jonathan Lewis

1140.

1. *The World on Blood.* Dutton, 1996.
2. *Shadows.* Dutton, 1997.

What if vampires were (almost) ordinary people who wanted to kick their addiction? Handsome Nick Santos and wealthy Jamey Whistler, both blood drinkers, founded Vampires Anonymous, but Whistler's questionable motives are obvious from the start. Ultimately Nick must go back to his old habits to gain the strength to keep Jamey away from his son. In the sequel, the witch Selene defends Jamey against the truly evil and very authentic Romanian vampire Aldo Striesecu.

Genre: Horror; Humor
Subjects: Vampires; Witchcraft

Nathan, Robert

1141. The Adventures of Tapiola

1. *Journey of Tapiola.* Knopf, 1938.
2. *Tapiola's Brave Regiment.* Knopf, 1941.

Inspired by the heroic images in the books published by the family of his owner, Mrs. Poppel, the Yorkshire terrier Tapiola sets out on a series of adventures with his friends Jeremiah, the rat, and Richard, the canary. At one point they decide to take on the mysterious aurochs, who seem to pose a grave threat to the country, even though no one knows who they are or exactly what the danger is.

Genre: Animal Story; Fantasy; Humor
Subjects: Imaginary wars and battles; Dogs; Animals

1142. The Barly Fields Series

1. *The Fiddler in Barly.* McBride, 1926.
2. *The Woodcutter's House.* Bobbs Merrill, 1927.
3. *The Bishop's Wife.* Bobbs Merrill, 1928.
4. *The Orchid.* Bobbs Merrill, 1931.
5. *There Is Another Heaven.* Bobbs Merrill, 1929.

The above titles have also been published in the following collection: *The Barly Fields: A Collection of Five Novels.* Knopf, 1938.

Dogs and insects speak, music changes lives, and love triumphs over death in these gently satirical fables that revolve around the mythical town of Barly.

Genre: Fantasy
Subjects: Imaginary cities; Animals; Love; Music

Nathanson, E. M.

1143.

1. *The Dirty Dozen.* Random House, 1965.
2. *A Dirty Distant War.* Viking, 1987.

OSS officer John Reisman is assigned to Operation Amnesty. He must mold 12 American prisoners into soldiers who will go on a secret mission behind German lines. The odds are against them, and most die, but Reisman survives and is sent to the Burma theater to help the Americans fight Japan. His mission takes him to China and French Indochina as he fights a web of deceit and betrayal.

Genre: Adventure; War
Subjects: World War II, 1939–1945—commando operations; War; Adventure; Soldiers—American
Place/Time: Europe—1900–1945; China—1900–1945; Burma—1900–1945

Nelson, Betty Palmer

1144. Honest Women Series

1. *Private Knowledge.* St. Martin's, 1990.
2. *The Weight of Light.* St. Martin's, 1992.
3. *The Pursuit of Bliss.* St. Martin's, 1992.
4. *Uncertain April.* St. Martin's, 1994.
5. *Changing Seasons.* St. Martin's, 1996.

The interconnected stories of the Nolans, Hendersons, and Fowlers of Tennessee from 1800 to 1980 deal with the settlement of the state and the struggles of hard-working farm women to find happiness. Mollie Hampton discovers love with a good man who accepts her after she has been seduced. Ellen struggles with a cheating husband, while Annie becomes a visiting nurse. Clara must deal with a difficult marriage, and Evelyn discovers that marriage does not bring her self-knowledge. All the people are simple folk who rely on themselves even through adversity.

Genre: Gentle Read; Historical Fiction
Subjects: Frontier and pioneer life; Farm life; Women; Love
Place/Time: Tennessee—19th century; Tennessee—1900–1945

Nelson, Charles

1145.

1. *The Boy Who Picked the Bullets Up.* Morrow, 1981.
2. *Panthers in the Skins of Men.* Meadowland, 1989.

The picaresque adventures of Kurt Storm, a gay medic attached to a Marine unit in Vietnam in the mid 1960s, are described in his letters home. He tells his family about his job of patching up the wounded, and he relates his amorous encounters to his gay friends. Back from Vietnam, Kurt teams up with Vick, a state trooper. Their escapades show the gay world before AIDS.

Genre: War
Subjects: Vietnamese War, 1961–1975; Homosexuality; War; Picaresque novels
Place/Time: Vietnam—1945–1980; United States—1945–1980

Nelson, James L.

1146. Revolution at Sea

1. *By Force of Arms.* Pocket Books, 1996.
2. *The Maddest Idea.* Pocket Books, 1997.
3. *The Continental Risque.* Pocket Books, 1998.
4. *Lords of the Ocean.* Pocket Books, 1999.

At the opening of the Revolutionary War, Isaac Biddlecomb has just become commander of a frigate for the fledgling American navy. Isaac eludes the British fleet as he searches for gun powder for General Washington's army and participates in the colonies' siege of Boston. In 1776, Isaac becomes captain of the *Charlemagne,* which is being pursued by the enemy, the British HMS *Glasgow.* As he eludes the *Glasgow,* Isaac impresses his true love, Virginia Stanton, but he can't stay and woo her, because he is sent to the Bahamas to harass the British fleet. Later, Isaac must take Benjamin Franklin to France and then has more adventures raiding British merchantmen. His adventures keep him one step ahead of the British as he tries to support the American fight for freedom.

Genre: Naval Adventure
Subjects: Navy, United States—officers; Navy, United States; Naval battles; United States—revolution, 1775–1783; Sailing vessels
Place/Time: Atlantic Ocean—18th century

Newby, P. H. (Percy Howard)

1147.

1. *The Picnic at Sakkara.* Knopf, 1955.
2. *Revolution and Roses.* Knopf, 1957.
3. *A Guest and His Going.* Knopf, 1959.

Two very different sets of characters—Egyptians and Englishmen of the 1940s and 1950s—come together in these books set in Cairo and London. As a result of his Muslim beliefs, student Muawiya Khaslat makes a purposely failed attempt to assassinate teacher Edgar Perry. The two meet again in London as Muawiya is unsuccessfully promoting his political and religious views.

Subjects: Students; Muslims; Assassination; Teachers
Place/Time: Cairo (Egypt)—1900–1945; London (England)—1945–1980; Egypt—1900–1945; England—1945–1980

1148. Hesketh and Jane Oliphant

1. *A Step to Silence.* Cape, 1952.
2. *The Retreat.* Knopf, 1953.

A young Englishman experiences a tragic and difficult coming of age through experiences in World War II that cause him to lose his identity. He leaves his wife and begins an affair with an old love who has married his friend. The deaths of his lover and her husband bring him back to reality, and he returns to the stable, secure love of his wife.

Genre: Coming of Age

Subjects: World War II, 1939–1945; Marriage; Love affairs; Psychological novels
Place/Time: England—1900–1945; England—1945–1980

Newman, Daisy

1149.
1. *Diligence in Love.* Doubleday, 1951.
2. *The Autumn's Brightness.* Macmillan, 1955.
3. *I Take Thee Serenity.* Houghton Mifflin, 1975.
4. *Indian Summer of the Heart.* Houghton Mifflin, 1982.

The power of love becomes important in the lives of inhabitants of the small Quaker town of Kendal, Rhode Island. Vaughn Hill, a New York advertising executive, comes to the town and finds spiritual renewal in its peaceful setting. Two middle-aged people, Durand and Dilly, find love in Kendal, as do college students Peter and Rennie. They seek guidance from Rennie's elderly cousin Oliver, a seventy-year-old widower. Eventually Oliver seeks advice from Peter and Rennie when he becomes infatuated with a lonely woman who comes to town to research her Quaker relatives.

Genre: Gentle Read; Romance
Subjects: Quakers; Small town life
Place/Time: Rhode Island—1945–1980

Newman, Kim

1150.
1. *Anno Dracula.* Carroll & Graf, 1993.
2. *The Bloody Red Baron.* Carroll & Graf, 1995.
3. *Judgment of Tears: Anno Dracula 1959.* Carroll & Graf, 1998.

In this alternate history time stream, vampires play enormous parts in world affairs. Dracula rules with Queen Victoria and later marries a Moldavian princess. During World War I, Dracula is commander-in-chief of the armies of Germany and Austria-Hungary. The flying ace Baron von Richthofen is also a member of the undead.

Genre: Horror; Historical Fiction
Subjects: Vampires; Victoria, Queen of England, 1819–1901; Richthofen, Manfred, Freiherr von, 1892–1918; World War I, 1914–1918
Place/Time: England—19th century; Europe—1900–1945; Europe—1945–1980

Newman, Sharan

1151.
1. *Guinevere.* St. Martin's, 1981.
2. *The Chessboard Queen.* St. Martin's, 1983.
3. *Guinevere Evermore.* St. Martin's, 1985.

The focus is on Guinevere in this evocative retelling of the Arthurian legend. The story begins with her childhood, then moves on to her marriage to Arthur, then her affair with Lancelot. The knights' search for the Holy Grail and the wars that tear apart Camelot are shown through Guinevere's eyes with a freshness and vitality that makes the legend seem new.

Genre: Fantasy
Subjects: Guenevere, Queen (legendary character a.k.a. Guinevere); Arthur, King; Lancelot (legendary character); Grail

Nexo, Martin Andersen

1152. Pelle the Conqueror Series
1. *Pelle the Conqueror: Boyhood.* Holt, 1913.
2. *Pelle the Conqueror: Apprenticeship.* Holt, 1914.
3. *Pelle the Conqueror: The Great Struggle.* Holt, 1915.
4. *Pelle the Conqueror: Daybreak.* Holt, 1916.

The above titles have also been published in the following collection: *Pelle the Conqueror.* Holt, 1917.

Young Pelle, a Swede transplanted to Denmark in the late 19th century, begins work with his father on a farm, but soon apprentices as a shoemaker. As a young man he becomes a ringleader in the trade union movement, for which he is immediately jailed. However, the final result of his agitation is the establishment of a cooperative shoe factory in a communal setting.

Genre: Coming of Age
Subjects: Teenagers; Labor and laboring classes; Labor unions; Socialism
Place/Time: Denmark—19th century

Nichols, John Treadwell

1153. New Mexico Trilogy
1. *The Milagro Beanfield War.* Holt, Rinehart & Winston, 1974.
2. *The Magic Journey.* Holt, Rinehart & Winston, 1974.
3. *The Nirvana Blues.* Holt, Rinehart & Winston, 1981.

These gentle, compassionate novels show the fight between the Anglos and the Chicanos in New Mexico from the 1930s through the 1970s. Farmer Joe Mondragon diverts water from a creek in order to grow beans and brings on a war. In Chanisville, the Anglo developers displace the Chicano farmers, but 83-year-old Elay Irriburren refuses to sell his farm to the power brokers. Joe Miniver helps Elay, and their schemes show a changing Southwest.

Subjects: Hispanic Americans; Farm life; Urbanization
Place/Time: New Mexico—1900–1945; New Mexico—1945–1980

Nicole, Christopher. *See also* Arlen, Leslie

1154.
1. *Old Glory.* Severn House, 1986.
2. *The Sea and the Sand.* Severn House, 1988.
3. *Iron Ships, Iron Men.* Severn House, 1989.
4. *Wind of Destiny.* Severn House, 1989.

The seafaring McGann family fights for the United States from the Revolutionary War to the Spanish American War. Harry McGann flees Ireland for America and helps found the U. S. Navy. Son Toby fights pirates on the Barbary Coast, then the English in the War of 1812. Jerry McGann fights with the Union navy in the Civil War, and Joe storms Cuba in the Spanish American War. While all the men are battling at sea, they are also fighting for their true loves. Their beautiful, sexy women are a match for the handsome, lusty McGanns.

Genre: Gentle Read; Historical Romance; Naval Adventure; War
Subjects: Naval battles; Navy, United States; United States—revolution, 1775–1783; United States—Civil War, 1861–1865
Place/Time: United States—18th century; United States—19th century

1155. Hilton Family Saga
1. *Caribee.* St. Martin's, 1974.
2. *The Devil's Own.* St. Martin's, 1975.
3. *Mistress of Darkness.* St. Martin's, 1977.
4. *Black Dawn.* St. Martin's, 1977.
5. *Sunset.* St. Martin's, 1978.

Violence, rape, hangings, revolution, slave revolts, and torture mark the history of St. Kitts and Antigua as Sir Thomas Warner and his son Edward found the Caribbean colonies in the 1600s. Granddaughter Marguerite marries Kit Hilton, a buccaneer, and establishes a dynasty at Hilltop plantation in Jamaica. The Hiltons and Warners feud for the next 200 years as they fight the English, French, Dutch, and Spaniards. Their lusty descendants search for love but find the path to it is never smooth.

Genre: Family Saga; Historical Romance
Subjects: Wealth; Plantation life; War
Place/Time: Caribbean region—multicentury span; Jamaica—multicentury span

Nielsen, Elizabeth

1156.
1. *Soda Bread on Sunday.* Rivercross, 1997.
2. *Sweet Geraniums and Soda Bread, Too.* Rivercross, 1999.

In the late 19th century, Cornelius Enright returns to Ireland to marry his love, Anne Fitzgerald. They settle on a farm and have a brood of children, but then Annie dies. Cornelius remarries to a rich widow who loves his children. Annie, Cornelius's daughter, meets the man of her dreams. They marry and go to America; however, her husband dies during the crossing, and Annie must take a job as a maid to two old ladies. After their death, Annie remarries to a Danish immigrant, Nels Nielsen, and has seven children. Their marriage slowly deteriorates until Nels deserts her, but Annie saves the day by starting a bakery that becomes the hit of New York. With her Irish determination, Annie keeps her family and herself triumphing over all obstacles.

Genre: Family Saga
Subjects: Family life; Husbands and wives; Irish; Irish—United States
Place/Time: Ireland—19th century; New York (N. Y.)—19th century

Nightingale, Steven

1157.
1. *The Lost Coast.* St. Martin's, 1996.
2. *The Thirteenth Daughter of the Moon.* St. Martin's, 1997.

In Eureka, Nevada, Cookie, a cook at a hash joint, decides to leave her husband and head for California. She meets up with an eccentric group of people who throw in their lot together and hit the road. Juha, a carpenter, builds a house on a flatbed truck and they travel and talk about food and sex and tell stories. They're not sure where they're going and get involved with the media as they follow the journey. Their journey becomes a modern day *Canterbury Tales.*

Subjects: Picaresque novels; Eccentrics and eccentricities
Place/Time: Nevada—1980–; California—1980–

Niven, Larry

1158. Ringworld
1. *Ringworld.* Ballantine, 1970.
2. *The Ringworld Engineers.* Holt, Rinehart, 1980.
3. *The Ringworld Throne.* Ballantine, 1996.

An artificial planet that is actually a ring around its own sun is discovered by the eccentric adventurer Louis Wu. Twenty years after his discovery, Wu returns to Ringworld as a captive of aliens and must find the secret to save it from colliding with its own sun. Wu's next challenge is to replace the warring rulers of Ringworld with a single protector who will preserve the delicate balance of the Ringworld environment.

Genre: Science Fiction
Subjects: Interplanetary voyages; Explorers; Eccentrics and eccentricities; Extraterrestrial beings

Niven, Larry *and* Pournelle, Jerry

1159.
1. *The Mote in God's Eye.* Simon & Schuster, 1974.
2. *The Gripping Hand.* Pocket Books, 1993.

A future galactic empire experiences its first contact with an alien species: the Moties, aliens who have evolved into several specialized biological forms and who present such a danger to humanity that ultimately a decision is reached to isolate them in their own solar system.

Genre: Science Fiction
Subjects: Extraterrestrial beings; Variation (biology); Evolution

Niven, Larry; Pournelle, Jerry; *and* Barnes, Steven

1160.
1. *The Legacy of Heorot.* Simon and Schuster, 1987.
2. *Beowulf's Children.* Tor, 1995.

A group of space colonists settle on Avalon, an idyllic world similar to Earth that orbits the star Tau Ceti. They escape the danger of the ferocious water creatures called grendels by isolating themselves on an island they call Camelot. But dangers await the next generation, the Star Born, who attempt to establish themselves on the mainland.

Genre: Science Fiction
Subjects: Space colonies; Animals; Life on other planets

Nofziger, Lyn

1161.
1. *Tackett.* Regnery Gateway, 1993.
2. *Tackett and the Teacher.* Regnery Gateway, 1994.
3. *Tackett and the Saloon Keeper.* Tumbleweed, 1994.
4. *Tackett and the Indian.* Jameson, 1998.
5. *The Tacketts.* Jameson, 1999.

Cowboy Del Tackett wanders the Old West working on ranches, saving women from danger, and being mistaken for the Sacketts of Louis L'Amour's famous westerns. He goes to the R Bar R Ranch to help Esmeralda Rankin who is besieged by rustlers. He then helps his old buddy's daughter Liddy Doyle avenge her father's death and keep her share in a silver mine. In Colorado, he wins a local saloon in a poker game, and bookkeeper Annie Laurie Burns comes with it. Later Del and his father go to help Annie save the saloon Del gave her, but Del's fiancee Esme is upset because their wedding has to be put off. Fun-loving Del gets himself involved with all types of characters as he fulfills his wanderlust.

Genre: Western
Subjects: Cowboys; Ranch life; Picaresque novels
Place/Time: Western states—19th century

Nolan, William F.

1162. Logan: A Trilogy
1. *Logan's Run.* (Written with George Clayton Johnson) Dial, 1967.
2. *Logan's World.* Bantam, 1977.
3. *Logan's Search.* Bantam, 1980.

In a future society, population pressures and the domination of the young have made everyone over 20 expendable. Logan rebels as he approaches the dreaded age even though he is a member of the Sandmen, the corps of executioners who hunt down those who resist being euthanized. Logan and his lover Jessica escape to Sanctuary, a place of refuge from the system, and ultimately destroy its all-powerful computer The Thinker.

Genre: Science Fiction
Subjects: Population; Youth; Executions and executioners; Lovers; Computers

Noon, Jeff

1163.
1. *Vurt.* Crown, 1993.
2. *Pollen.* Crown, 1996.

In this vision of the future, Vurt is a strange shared dream state that can be achieved by tasting Vurt feathers. Desdemona, a young woman who has ingested the ultimate feather, is trapped in a particular dimension called Curious Yellow. Meanwhile, her brother searches for the elusive feather that will free her. Fifteen years later the barriers between everyday reality and the Vurt dimension have become thinner. The inhabitants of Vurt unleash a plague of pollen on the real world to which only Dodos—people who are unable to dream—are immune.

Genre: Fantasy
Subjects: Dreams; Mysticism; Brothers and sisters; Diseases

Nordhoff, Charles *and* Hall, James Norman

1164. The Bounty Trilogy
1. *Mutiny on the Bounty.* Little, Brown, 1932.
2. *Men Against the Sea.* Little, Brown, 1934.
3. *Pitcairn's Island.* Little, Brown, 1934.

The above titles have also been published in the following collection: *The Bounty Trilogy.* Little, Brown, 1936.

The famous 1787 mutiny of the crew of the *Bounty*, a British war vessel, against their infamous Captain William Bligh is vividly retold through elderly Captain Byarn, who was a midshipman. Later volumes follow

Captain Bligh and 18 loyal crew members as they sail 3600 miles in an open boat, and the mutineers as they try to live on Pitcairn's Island with their Polynesian women.

Genre: Historical Fiction; Naval Adventure
Subjects: Bligh, William, 1754–1817; Seamen; Navy, British; Mutiny; Sailing vessels
Place/Time: South Pacific—18th century

Norris, Frank
1165. The Epic of Wheat
1. *The Octopus.* Doubleday, 1901.
2. *The Pit: A Story of Chicago.* Doubleday, 1903.

These novels of social protest deal with the power of big business over farmers. With grim realism, Norris relates the bitter war between the California wheat growers and the railroads. The farmers are defeated by the evil agents of the railroad, but the wheat has its revenge: The wheat market in Chicago exerts its corrupt influence on one man.

Subjects: Wheat; Railroads; Farm life; Capitalists and financiers
Place/Time: California—19th century; Chicago (Ill.)—19th century; Illinois—19th century

North, Andrew. *Pseud. of* Andre Norton. *See* Norton, Andre

Norton, Andre *and* Lackey, Mercedes
1166. The Halfblood Chronicles
1. *The Elvenbane.* T. Doherty, 1991.
2. *Elvenblood.* T. Doherty, 1995.

The elvenlords rule the world in an autocratic manner with only a mysterious prophecy as a threat to their power. When a child is born to the rejected human concubine of an elvenlord after she has fled into the desert, the prophecy begins to unfold. Although half elven herself, the child Shana opposes the power of the elvenlords with the help of a group of shaman dragons and ultimately with a brother and sister who have escaped the power of the elven lords.

Genre: Fantasy
Subjects: Mixed blood; Prophecies; Imaginary wars and battles; Dragons; Brothers and sisters

Norton, Andre. *See also* Bradley, Marion Zimmer

1167. Solar Queen
1. *Sargasso of Space.* Gnome Press, 1955.
2. *Plague Ship.* Gnome Press, 1956.
3. *Voodoo Planet.* Ace, 1959.
4. *Postmarked the Stars* Harcourt Brace, 1969.
5. *Redline the Stars.* Tor, 1993. (Written with P. M. Griffin)
6. *Derelict for Trade.* Tor, 1997.
7. *A Mind for Trade.* Tor, 1997.

Under the leadership of Dane Thorson the free trader ship Solar Queen travels through space fighting intergalactic crime, space jackers, a mysterious electromagnetic force, and visiting planets where several sentient species coexist. *Note:* The first four titles were written under the pseudonym Andrew North.

Genre: Science Fiction
Subjects: Spaceships; Crime and criminals; Life on other planets

1168. Time Traders
1. *The Time Traders.* World, 1958.
2. *Galactic Derelict.* World, 1959.
3. *The Defiant Agents.* World, 1962.
4. *Key Out of Time.* World, 1963.
5. *Firehand.* (Written with P. M. Griffin) Tor, 1994.
6. *Echoes in Time.* (Written with Sherwood Smith) Tor, 1999.

Ross Murdock is a time agent, one of a group of young people who are misfits in their own time, but who have talents and skills that enable them to participate in a government project that sends them traveling in time and space to secure secrets of the past and right wrongs. Throughout his adventures, Ross clashes with the appropriately named evil alien Baldies.

Genre: Science Fiction; Coming of Age
Subjects: Time travel; Imaginary wars and battles; Extraterrestrial beings

1169. Witch World
1. *Witch World.* Ace, 1963.
2. *Web of the Witch World.* Ace, 1964.
3. *Year of the Unicorn.* Ace, 1965.
4. *Three Against the Witch World.* Ace, 1965.
5. *Warlock of the Witch World.* Ace, 1967.
6. *Sorceress of the Witch World.* Ace, 1968.
7. *Spell of the Witch World.* DAW Books, 1972.
8. *The Crystal Gryphon.* Atheneum, 1972.
9. *The Jargoon Pard.* Atheneum, 1974.
10. *The Trey of Swords.* Grosset & Dunlap, 1977.
11. *Zarathor's Bane.* Ace, 1978.
12. *Lore of the Witch World.* DAW Books, 1980.
13. *Gryphon in Glory.* Atheneum, 1981.
14. *'Ware Hawk.* Atheneum, 1983.
15. *Gryphon's Eyrie.* (Written with A. C. Crispin) St. Martin's, 1985.
16. *Storms of Victory.* (Written with P. M. Griffin) Tor, 1991.
17. *Songsmith.* (Written with A. C. Crispin) Tor, 1992.
18. *Flight of Vengeance.* (Written with P. M. Griffin and Mary Schaub) Tor, 1992.
19. *On Wings of Magic.* (Written with Patricia Matthes and Sasha Miller) Tor, 1994.

20. *The Key of the Keplian.* (Written with Lyn McConchie) Warner, 1995.
21. *The Magestone.* (Written with Mary H. Schaub) Warner, 1996.
22. *The Warding of Witch World.* Warner, 1996.

The magical country of Estcarp is inhabited by good witches who must protect their land from savage invaders. Through a time gate comes Simon Tregarth, a fugitive from World War II. Early books in the series are concerned with Simon's marriage to the witch Jaelithe and the fates of their children. Subsequent stories tell of the interaction between the witches and the world of men and the many dangers that nearly strip the witches of their power.

Genre: Fantasy
Subjects: Witchcraft; Imaginary kingdoms; Time travel; World War II, 1939–1945; Marriage

Norwood, Warren
1170. The Double Spiral War
1. *Midway Between.* Bantam, 1984.
2. *Polar Fleet.* Bantam, 1985.
3. *Final Command.* Bantam, 1986.

These war novels are set in the distant future when humanity has migrated to other galaxies, come in contact with aliens, and become genetically differentiated. Two galactic systems, Sondak and the United Central Systems, become more and more at odds with each other until conflict breaks out with a small star system in the middle.

Genre: Science Fiction
Subjects: Interplanetary wars; Variation (biology); Extraterrestrial beings

1171. The Windhover Tapes
1. *An Image of Voices.* Bantam, 1982.
2. *Fize of the Gabriel Ratchets.* Bantam, 1983.
3. *Flexing the Warp.* Bantam, 1983.
4. *The Planet of Flowers.* Bantam, 1984.

Windhover is the sentient spaceship and confidant of distant future anthropologist and diplomat for hire Gerard Hopkins Manley. Together they travel at speeds faster than light through galaxies inhabited by the strange products of the crossbreeding of humanity and alien races.

Genre: Science Fiction
Subjects: Spaceships; Interplanetary voyages; Anthropologists; Extraterrestrial beings

Nye, Jody Lynn. *See also* McCaffrey, Anne
1172.
1. *Taylor's Ark.* Ace, 1993.
2. *Medicine Show.* Ace, 1994.

Dr. Shona Taylor's ark is the starship Sibyl in which she sails through the stars with her family and numer-

ous animals. Pursued by bankers intent on repossessing the Sibyl, Shona lands on a planet where the unfortunate results of a poorly planned longevity experiment are being hidden.

Genre: Science Fiction
Subjects: Spaceships; Animals; Experiments, scientific

Nylund, Eric S.
1173.
1. *Signal to Noise.* Avon Eos, 1998.
2. *A Signal Shattered.* Avon Eos, 1999.

By using unorthodox and unethical methods, computer cryptographer Jack Potter has become a member of the distinguished Academy of Pure and Applied Sciences. Jack uses his computer skills legally and illegally in this competitive law-of-the-jungle corporate climate of the distant future. After Jack's dealings with the ruthless alien called Wheeler result in the destruction of Earth, Jack and a group of survivors take refuge on the moon.

Genre: Science Fiction
Subjects: Computers; Business—unscrupulous methods; Earth, destruction of; Extraterrestrial beings; Moon

O'Brian, Patrick
1174.
1. *The Golden Ocean.* Norton, 1996, 1956.
2. *The Unknown Shore.* Norton, 1995, 1959.

In 1740, Commodore Anson embarks on a voyage to circumnavigate the globe with his five ships. Young Peter Palafox and his friend Sean sign on for the voyage even though they have never been to sea. They encounter disaster, disease, adventure, and finally success. The *Wager*, the fourth of Anson's ships, becomes separated from the fleet after rounding Cape Horn. Midshipman Jack Byron and ship surgeon Tobias Barrow survive when the ship is driven against the rocks and sinks off of Patagonia. Two hundred twenty men struggle to make their way north to Valparaiso, but only five will survive the trek.

Genre: Naval Adventure; Historical Fiction
Subjects: Navy, British; Ships; Adventure; Explorers
Place/Time: Atlantic Ocean—18th century; Pacific Ocean—18th century; Chile—18th century

1175.
1. *Master and Commander.* Norton, 1990, 1970.
2. *Post Captain.* Norton, 1990, 1972.
3. *HMS Surprise.* Norton, 1991, 1973.
4. *The Mauritius Command.* Norton, 1991, 1978.
5. *Desolation Island.* Norton, 1991, 1979.
6. *The Fortune of War.* Norton, 1991, 1979.
7. *The Surgeon's Mate.* Norton, 1992, 1980.

8. *The Ionian Mission.* Norton, 1992, 1981.
9. *Treason's Harbor.* Norton, 1992, 1983.
10. *The Far Side of the World.* Norton, 1992, 1984.
11. *The Reverse of the Medal.* Norton, 1992, 1986.
12. *The Letter of Marque.* Norton, 1990, 1988.
13. *The Thirteen Gun Salute.* Norton, 1991, 1989.
14. *The Nutmeg of Consolation.* Norton, 1991.
15. *The True Love.* Norton, 1992.
16. *Wine Dark Sea.* Norton, 1993.
17. *The Commodore.* Norton, 1995.
18. *The Yellow Admiral.* Norton, 1996.
19. *Hundred Days.* Norton, 1998.
20. *Blue at the Mizzen.* Norton, 1999.

Set in Napoleonic-era England, this is the sea story of Captain Jack Aubrey who meets Dr. Stephen Maturin in Port Mahon in Minorca and invites him to be surgeon aboard his Royal Navy sloop. Through marriages, bankruptcies, windfalls, promotions, and dismissals, the two sail all over the world and have numerous adventures while conquering the seas for king and country. The stories follow the battles and events of the Napoleonic Wars, yet O'Brian's focus in these novels is on recreating the world of the sailing ships and their crews, naval customs, and habits, and the ritual of life in a confined space.

Genre: Historical Fiction; Naval Adventure; War
Subjects: Navy, British—officers; Navy, British; Naval battles; Seamen; Napoleonic Wars, 1800–1814; Sailing vessels; Surgeons
Place/Time: England—19th century; Atlantic Ocean—19th century

O'Brien, Edna

1176.
1. *The Country Girls.* Knopf, 1960.
2. *The Lonely Girl.* Random House, 1962.
3. *Girls in Their Married Bliss.* Simon & Schuster, 1968, 1964.

The above titles have also been published in the following collection: *The Country Girls Trilogy and Epilogue.* Farrar Straus & Giroux, 1986.

Kate and Baba come from a small Irish village to Dublin to find love. There they meet the men they will marry, Kate for love and Baba for money. Kate's marriage falls apart when she has an affair, but Baba's marriage survives her own affair. From their high-spirited youth to the chill of their middle age, the girls reflect on their lives.

Subjects: Marriage problems; Love affairs
Place/Time: Dublin (Ireland)—1945–1980; Ireland—1945–1980

O'Carroll, Brendan

1177.
1. *The Mammy.* Plume, 1999.

2. *The Chisellers.* Plume, 2000.

In the 1960s, Agnes Browne lives in working-class Dublin where she is trying to raise six sons and a daughter. Agnes is recently widowed and living on welfare. With her best friend Marion, she learns to drive, searches for a job, and drinks a pint at the pub. Agnes fights for her children, helps them get jobs, and tries to keep the boys out of gangs. With humor and energy, Agnes does her best to live her life and raise her children despite poverty.

Subjects: Mothers; Family life; Irish; Teenagers; Poverty
Place/Time: Ireland—1945–1980

O'Donohoe, Nick

1178.
1. *The Magic and the Healing.* Ace, 1994.
2. *Under the Healing Sign.* Ace, 1995.
3. *The Healing of Crossroads.* Ace, 1996.

A personal crisis nearly makes B. J. Vaughn desert her chosen career of veterinary medicine, but a field trip to the mystical land of Crossroads to repair a unicorn's horn restores her faith in herself. B. J. deals with Morgan le Fey's evil invasion of Crossroads, becomes a demigoddess, and helps to care for a population of young mythological beasts.

Genre: Fantasy
Subjects: Mythical animals; Veterinarians; Magic

O'Grady, Leslie

1179.
1. *The Artist's Daughter.* St. Martin's, 1979.
2. *Lord Raven's Widow.* St. Martin's, 1983.

In Victorian London, Nora Woburn flees her cruel, abusive husband by escaping to Raven's Chase, a vast estate in Devonshire. Working for Sir Mark Gerricle, she unwillingly enters into a web of intrigue and conspiracy more deadly than that which she left. Her marriage to Mark ends in tragedy when he is killed in a fire, but another mysterious man, Drake Turnon helps Nora when another woman claims Sir Mark's estate.

Genre: Historical Fiction; Historical Romance
Subjects: Houses
Place/Time: London (England)—19th century; England—19th century

O'Leary, Elizabeth. *See Marsh, Jean*

O'Malley, Kathleen. *See Crispin, A. C. (Silent Dances and Silent Songs)*

O'Reilly, Victor

1180.
1. *Games of the Hangman.* Putnam, 1991.
2. *Rules of the Hunt.* Putnam, 1995.
3. *The Devil's Footprint.* Putnam, 1997.

Former soldier and photographer, Hugo Fitzduane finds a hung body and then a second body hung the same way. As he searches for the truth behind the murders, he exposes an international terrorist, "The Hangman," whom he kills. A Japanese group, the Yaibo, come after Hugo because he killed their leader. A group of antiterrorist Irish rangers save him from assassins, but Hugo is badly hurt. While in the hospital, he falls in love with his nurse, Kathleen Fleming. Once out of the hospital, he goes on the offensive and kills the Yaibo's expert assassin, Reiko Oshima. After Hugo and Kathleen marry, he learns that Reiko has miraculously survived and is out for revenge as she prepares to kidnap Kathleen. Hugo and his antiterrorist team set out to stop Reiko before she can kill Kathleen.

Genre: Adventure; Espionage
Subjects: Espionage; International intrigue; Escapes; Terrorism
Place/Time: Europe—1980–; Japan—1980–

Oates, Joyce Carol

1181.
1. *A Garden of Earthly Delights.* Vanguard, 1967.
2. *Expensive People.* Vanguard, 1968.
3. *Them.* Vanguard, 1969.

Related in theme, but not plot, this trilogy describes contemporary young people trying to come to grips with difficult economic and social situations. Clara escapes her life as a migrant worker by entering into a cynical, ultimately tragic marriage with a wealthy man. Suburban life is seen through the eyes of the disturbed son of a social-climbing woman and a coldly ambitious executive. *Them* tells the story of a brother and sister who, with great difficulty, manage to escape their sordid lower-class origins in Detroit.

Subjects: Social problems; Social classes; Class distinction; Psychological novels
Place/Time: United States—1945–1980

Ogilvie, Elisabeth

1182.
1. *High Tide at Noon.* Thomas Crowell, 1944.
2. *Storm Tide.* Thomas Crowell, 1945.
3. *Ebbing Tide.* Thomas Crowell, 1947.
4. *How Wide the Heart.* McGraw-Hill, 1959.
5. *An Answer in the Tide.* McGraw-Hill, 1978.
6. *The Summer of the Osprey.* McGraw-Hill, 1987.

On Bennett Island off the coast of Maine, Joanne Bennett grows up, falls in love, marries, and raises her family. Joanne, as the only daughter of the first family of the island, must learn how to love and how to keep Nils Sorensen, a lobster fisherman. When Nils is sent to the Pacific during World War II, Joanne must keep up their business. Their children Jamie and Ellen must choose between life on the island or in the city on the mainland.

Genre: Family Saga; Romance
Subjects: Fishing; Small town life
Place/Time: Maine—1900–1945; Maine—1945–1980

1183. Jennie Trilogy
1. *Jennie About to Be.* McGraw-Hill, 1984.
2. *The World of Jennie G.* McGraw-Hill, 1985.
3. *Jennie Glenroy.* Down East, 1993.

In the early 1800s, Jennie Hawthorne is a 21-year-old orphan who goes to live with her aunt and uncle in London. Hating city life, Jennie marries Nigel Gilchrist and goes to live on an estate in Scotland where she sets up a school for poor children with her cousin Alick. When Nigel is accidentally killed in a fight with Alick, Jennie and Alick flee to Maine where they raise a family and get involved with the townspeople.

Genre: Gentle Read; Historical Romance
Subjects: Country life
Place/Time: London (England)—19th century; Scotland—19th century; Maine—19th century; England—19th century

Oke, Janette

1184.
1. *Another Homecoming.* Bethany House, 1997.
2. *Tomorrow's Dream.* Bethany House, 1998.

Martha and Harry Grimes are only married for nine weeks when he is sent overseas during World War II. After Harry is declared missing, Martha gives up their baby girl for adoption when she fears she cannot raise the child alone. By the time Harry is found and returned home, it is too late to get their baby back. Even though they have other children, Harry never forgives Martha and their marriage is not happy. Their daughter Kyle, who was given up for adoption, grows up as a "poor" little rich girl with a wicked stepmother. Kyle, however, finds faith and discovers her real parents. It is her Christian faith that helps her bring her parents back together and helps her when she and her husband have a baby with a weak heart. Kyle discovers that miracles do happen.

Genre: Christian Fiction; Gentle Read
Subjects: Marriage problems; Christian life; Family life; Husbands and wives
Place/Time: United States—1945–1980; United States—1980–

1185. Canadian West
1. *When Calls the Heart.* Bethany House, 1983.

2. *When Comes the Spring.* Bethany House, 1985.
3. *When Breaks the Dawn.* Bethany House, 1986.
4. *When Hope Springs New.* Bethany House, 1986.

Elizabeth Thatcher, a well-to-do Easterner, goes west to teach in a one-room schoolhouse in Alberta, Canada. There she meets Royal Canadian Mountie Wynn Delaney and falls in love. When they move to the harsh northern frontier, the hardship there challenges her marriage and faith.

Genre: Christian Fiction; Gentle Read; Historical Fiction; Historical Romance
Subjects: Royal Canadian Mounted Police; Marriage problems; Frontier and pioneer life; Christian life
Place/Time: Alberta (Canada)—19th century; Canada—19th century

1186. Love Comes Softly
1. *Love Comes Softly.* Bethany House, 1979.
2. *Love's Enduring Promise.* Bethany House, 1980.
3. *Love's Long Journey.* Bethany House, 1982.
4. *Love's Abiding Joy.* Bethany House, 1983.
5. *Love's Unending Legacy.* Bethany House, 1984.
6. *Love's Unfolding Dream.* Bethany House, 1987.
7. *Love Takes Wing.* Bethany House, 1985.
8. *Love Finds a Home.* Bethany House, 1989.

Clark Davis, a grieving widower, meets widow Marty. In their sorrow they find love and marry. They face the hardships of life in frontier Iowa with faith and determination. The story follows Clark and Marty, then their children, Missie, Luke, and Belinda, as they grow up and have their faith tested.

Genre: Christian Fiction; Family Saga; Gentle Read; Historical Fiction; Historical Romance
Subjects: Farm life; Marriage problems; Christian life
Place/Time: Iowa—19th century

1187. Prairie Legacy
1. *The Tender Years.* Bethany House, 1997.
2. *A Searching Heart.* Bethany House, 1998.
3. *A Quiet Strength.* Bethany House, 1999.

The granddaughter of Clark and Marty Davis, Virginia Simpson, finds growing up is hard, especially when peer pressure makes her challenge her faith. When a new girl, Jenny Woods, comes to town, her big city ways fascinate Virginia. When Jenny's independent ways indirectly cause the death of a young boy, Virginia finds herself challenged. As she prepares to go to college, her sister's illness forces her to stay home. Then, when her boyfriend writes from college that he has found someone else, Virginia again doubts her faith until Grandma Marty helps her see God's plan. Her boyfriend Jonathan returns to her, and they marry. They have to start out living with Jonathan's grand-

mother while their ranch is being built, and Virginia again finds obstacles to her happiness.

Genre: Christian Fiction; Coming of Age
Subjects: Faith; Teenagers; Girls; Family life
Place/Time: Midwestern states—1980–

1188. Seasons of the Heart
1. *Once Upon a Summer.* Bethany House, 1981.
2. *The Winds of Autumn.* Bethany House, 1987.
3. *Winter Is Not Forever.* Bethany House, 1988.
4. *Spring's Gentle Promise.* Bethany House, 1989.

Josh, an orphan, finds his security in God after his aunt, who has raised him, marries and moves away. However, as Josh grows up, he questions life, love, and God, but finally commits himself to the challenge of family and running the farm.

Genre: Christian Fiction; Historical Fiction
Subjects: Christian life; Farm life; Family life
Place/Time: United States—19th century

1189. Women of the West Series
1. *The Calling of Emily Evans.* Bethany House, 1990.
2. *Julia's Last Hope.* Bethany House, 1990.
3. *Roses for Mama.* Bethany House, 1991.
4. *A Woman Named Damaris.* Bethany House, 1991.
5. *They Called Her Mrs. Doc.* Bethany House, 1992.
6. *The Measure of a Heart.* Bethany House, 1992.
7. *A Bride for Donnigan.* Bethany House, 1993.
8. *Heart of the Wilderness.* Bethany House, 1993.
9. *Too Long a Stranger.* Bethany House, 1994.

Nine different women come to the frontier West and discover that they are not alone as they face the difficulties and sorrows that life sends their way.

Genre: Christian Fiction; Gentle Read; Historical Fiction
Subjects: Women; Christian life; Love; Marriage; Frontier and pioneer life
Place/Time: Western states—19th century

Oke, Janette *and* Bunn, T. Davis

1190.
1. *The Meeting Place.* Bethany House, 1999.
2. *The Sacred Shore.* Bethany House, 2000.

In 18th-century Acadia in Canada, two young women meet in a meadow of wildflowers as they prepare their bridal bouquets. Louisa is French and Catherine is English. Although the English and French are at odds, the two women share their faith and friendship. When the English banish the French from Acadia, each woman's life is changed by the separation and they struggle to keep their faith and their families.

Genre: Christian Fiction

Subjects: Faith; Women; Exiles
Place/Time: Canada—18th century

Okri, Ben

1191.
1. *The Famished Road.* Doubleday, 1992.
2. *Songs of Enchantment.* Doubleday, 1993.

Azaro, a spirit child, can see the invisible demons and witches who prey on his family and his small village in Nigeria. In a series of vignettes, he relates the poverty, hunger, and squalor of daily life. He sees the town being torn between the Party of the Rich and the Party of the Poor, and being a spirit child, he sees this battle also in the spirit world. The allegorical tales show modern Africa and its traditional influences.

Subjects: Country life; Allegories; Poverty
Place/Time: Nigeria—1945–1980

Oldenbourg, Zoe

1192.
1. *The World Is Not Enough.* Pantheon, 1948.
2. *The Cornerstone.* Pantheon, 1955.

In the 13th century, Alis is the wife of a French knight. She is married at 14 and has numerous children, many of whom die as infants. Her husband Ansiau is often away on the Crusades, and Alis must try to keep the estate working and solvent. She and her children live through the poverty, squalor, disease, religious persecution, and chivalry of the age.

Genre: Historical Fiction
Subjects: Marriage; Feudalism; Middle Ages; Women; Knights and knighthood
Place/Time: France—13th century

1193.
1. *The Awakened.* Pantheon, 1957.
2. *Chains of Love.* Pantheon, 1959.

In the emigre world of Paris of the 1930s, Stephanie Lindberg meets and falls in love with Elie Lanskov. Stephanie is the daughter of an intellectual German Jew who converted to Catholicism. Elie is the son of poor white Russian refugees. They fear the Nazis and are separated by the war. They are finally able to reunite after the war despite their suffering.

Genre: Romance
Subjects: Refugees; War
Place/Time: Paris (France)—1900–1945; Paris (France)—1945–1980; France—1900–1945; France—1945–1980

Orczy, Emmuska, Baroness

1194.
1. *The Scarlet Pimpernel.* Putnam, 1905.
2. *I Will Repay.* Lippincott, 1906.
3. *The Elusive Pimpernel.* Dodd, 1908.

4. *The League of the Scarlet Pimpernel.* Doran, 1919.
5. *Lord Tony's Wife.* Doran, 1917.
6. *The Triumph of the Scarlet Pimpernel.* Doran, 1922.
7. *Eldorado: A Story of the Scarlet Pimpernel.* Doran, 1913.
8. *Sir Percy Hits Back.* Doran, 1927.
9. *Adventures of the Scarlet Pimpernel.* Doubleday, 1929.
10. *The Way of the Scarlet Pimpernel.* Doubleday, 1929.
11. *Mam'zelle Guillotine: An Adventure of the Scarlet Pimpernel.* Hodder, 1940.

Sir Percy Blakeney is a dandy and a fop. He is a favorite of the Prince of Wales and seems to be a total ineffectual. This outward appearance masks a dashing hero who saves French aristocrats from the guillotine. Even his own wife does not suspect what her husband does. The squalor and horror of revolutionary Paris is vividly contrasted to the splendors of King George III's England and to Percy's daring victories.

Genre: Adventure; Historical Fiction
Subjects: Aristocracy—England; Adventure; France—revolution, 1789–1799; Escapes
Place/Time: London (England)—18th century; Paris (France)—18th century; England—18th century; France—18th century

1195. Dutch War of Independence Series
1. *Leatherface: A Tale of Old Flanders.* Doran, 1916.
2. *Flower o' the Lily.* Doran, 1919.
3. *The Laughing Cavalier.* Doran, 1914.
4. *The First Sir Percy: An Adventure of the Laughing Cavalier.* Doran, 1926.

The events surrounding the 16th-century War of Independence that separated Holland from Spain are narrated through the experiences of dashing characters, such as the mysterious Leatherface, who somehow gains inside information about the Spanish, and British Sir Percy Blakeney, who is caught up in the struggle as a result of his marriage to an aristocratic Dutch beauty.

Genre: Adventure; Historical Fiction
Subjects: Adventure; War; Escapes; Aristocracy
Place/Time: Netherlands—16th century

Ore, Rebecca

1196. The Alien
1. *Becoming Alien.* Tor, 1988.
2. *Being Alien.* Tor, 1989.
3. *Human to Human.* Tor, 1990.

Tom Gentry is an alienated, delinquent teenager until he truly encounters aliens who transport him away from Earth to a world where he begins to overcome his xenophobia. Tom returns to Earth to acquire a human bride who the aliens feel will "fit in," then returns to the alien culture where they raise their child with a variety of sentient beings.

Genre: Science Fiction
Subjects: Teenagers; Extraterrestrial beings; Interplanetary voyages; Marriage

Pakington, Humphrey

1197.
1. *The Washbournes of Otterley.* Norton, 1948.
2. *Young William Washbourne.* Norton, 1949.
3. *Farewell to Otterley.* Norton, 1951.

Starting in the midst of the Victorian era and continuing into the early 20th century, this saga paints an ironic, but affectionate portrait of the foibles, triumphs, and difficulties of a landed English family and their love for their estate, Otterley.

Genre: Family Saga
Subjects: Family life; Aristocracy
Place/Time: England—19th century; England—1900–1945

Palmer, Catherine

1198. Heart Quest
1. *The Treasures of Timbuktu.* Tyndale House, 1997.
2. *The Treasures of Zanzibar.* Tyndale House, 1997.

The Thornton sisters find adventure and love in Africa. Tillie is abducted by a treasure hunter and then finds herself on the run from the nomadic Tuareg tribe who believe she is the legendary Tree-Planting Woman and knows where the treasure of Timbuktu is hidden. Tillie finds love with her kidnapper. Sister Jessica returns to Africa with her son to claim an inheritance. There she finds greed and murder. Only her estranged husband can save her.

Genre: Christian Fiction; Historical Fiction
Subjects: Faith; Love; Sisters; Africa—native peoples
Place/Time: Africa—19th century

1199. A Town Called Hope
1. *Prairie Rose.* Tyndale House, 1997.
2. *Prairie Fire.* Tyndale House, 1998.
3. *Prairie Storm.* Tyndale House, 1999.

In post-Civil War Hope, Kansas, three people find that real love can only come with trust in the Lord. Rosie Mills has spent all her life in an orphanage. When she saves Seth Hunter's life from an attack by his brother-in-law, Rosie decides to go with Seth and his son Chipper to their prairie farm to take a job caring for Chipper. Both Seth and Rosie struggle to put their faith in God before they can love each other. Chipper's uncle Jack Cornwall comes to Hope looking for his nephew, but finds him happy with Seth and Rosie. Jack becomes interested in Caitrin Murphy who is reluctant to become involved with Jack because of his lack of faith. Jack looks into his soul and realizes he must change if he is to be happy. Lily Nolan also comes to Hope and helps preacher Elijah Book care for an orphaned baby. Although she falls in love with Elijah, her abuse as a child keeps her from love until she puts her trust in God.

Genre: Christian Fiction
Subjects: Faith; Frontier and pioneer life; Love;
Place/Time: Kansas—19th century

Palmer, Marian

1200. The Lovell Family
1. *The White Boar.* Doubleday, 1968.
2. *The Wrong Plantagenet.* Doubleday, 1972.

The story of the rise of Richard III to the throne of England and the threat to his successor Henry VII in the person of the pretender Perkin Warbeck is told through the experiences of courtier Phillip Lovell and his son Simon, who follows Warbeck.

Genre: Historical Fiction
Subjects: Henry VIII, King of England, 1491–1547; Courts and courtiers; Kings and rulers; Richard III, King of England, 1452–1485
Place/Time: England—15th century

Panshin, Alexei

1201. Anthony Villiers
1. *Star Well.* Ace, 1968.
2. *The Thurb Revolution.* Ace, 1968.
3. *Masque World.* Ace, 1969.

When the expected funds from his wealthy father fail to arrive, blue-blooded aristocrat Anthony Villiers sets off on a journey that involves a series of interplanetary adventures. Satirical romps through the planets, these books parody a variety of literary forms including, of course, space operas.

Genre: Humor; Science Fiction
Subjects: Interplanetary voyages; Wealth; Parodies

Park, Paul

1202. Starbridge Trilogy
1. *Soldiers of Paradise.* Arbor House, 1987.
2. *Sugar Rain.* Morrow, 1989.
3. *The Cult of Loving Kindness.* Morrow, 1991.

On a planet whose seasons last half a century, the Starbridge family dominates through a powerful, earthy religion. As spring approaches, a revolutionary movement begins to stir as two disaffected Starbridges and a mysterious cult of anarchists gain power. After the violent overthrow of the aristocratic rulers, twins, raised by the alien Treganu, begin to revive the old religion.

Genre: Science Fiction
Subjects: Life on other planets; Aristocracy; Religion; Revolutions and revolutionists

Park, Ruth

1203.
1. *Missus.* St. Martin's, 1987.
2. *The Harp in the South.* Houghton, 1948.
3. *12 1/2 Plymouth Street.* Houghton, 1951.

In the slums of Sydney, Australia, at the turn of the century, the Darcy family tries to make ends meet. Young Hugh runs away from his brutal father and goes to Sydney where he marries Margaret. They raise two children. Rosie has a zest for life and finds love, while Dolour finds she must raise Rosie's children.

Genre: Family Saga; Historical Fiction
Subjects: Family life
Place/Time: Australia—1900–1945

Park, Severna

1204.
1. *Speaking Dreams.* Firebrand Books, 1992.
2. *Hand of Prophecy.* Avon Eos, 1998.

In the brutal universe of these tales, an enslaved under class suffers under the dominance of a noble ruling class, intergalactic slavers, and powerful aliens. Frenna, a young slave girl, learns how to combat the vicious virus that will keep her young and hardy for 20 years and then kill her painfully, but her plans to escape fail, and she is put to work as a medic caring for slaves who are gladiators.

Genre: Science Fiction
Subjects: Life on other planets; Slavery; Cruelty; Viruses

Parkinson, C. (Cyril) Northcote

1205.
1. *The Guernsey Man.* Houghton, 1982.
2. *Devil to Pay.* Houghton, 1973.
3. *The Fireship.* Houghton, 1975.
4. *Touch and Go.* Houghton, 1977.
5. *So Near, So Far.* Houghton, 1981.
6. *Dead Reckoning.* Houghton, 1978.

Richard Delancey is born on the island of Guernsey in 1760. When he is 16, he runs away to sea to avoid being arrested in the Merseyside riots. As he rises through the ranks of the British Navy, he takes part in the defense of Gibraltar, then Malta. He uses his knowledge of France to infiltrate French colonies, while he battles the French navy. As a young captain, he makes mistakes, but learns to be a good leader. Richard marries an actress who goes to Guernsey to wait for him through the Napoleonic wars.

Genre: Historical Fiction; Naval Adventure; War
Subjects: Navy, British—officers; Naval battles; War; Seamen
Place/Time: Atlantic Ocean—18th century; Mediterranean Sea—18th century

Parry, Richard

1206.
1. *The Winter Wolf: Wyatt Earp in Alaska.* Forge, 1996.
2. *The Wolf's Cub.* Forge, 1997.
3. *Wolf's Pack.* Forge, 1998.

In 1898, the aging Wyatt Earp travels to Alaska with his third wife Josie to try to find gold in the Klondike. Instead he must settle for a law enforcement job with his old friend. While he fears old enemies, Earp does not realize that he is being stalked by his illegitimate son Nathan Blaylock. The young boy has learned from his dying mother that Earp is his father and promises her that he will kill him for abandoning her. Nathan joins up with a down-on-his-luck gunslinger, Jim Riley, and they track Earp to Alaska where Earp and Nathan finally confront each other. Nathan and Jim stay on in Alaska, and Nathan searches for his son by his Chinese lover. On their search, they fall in with a gentleman spy on assignment for president Teddy Roosevelt and searching for some modern bolt action rifles the British are hiding in Dawson. The three come up with a plan to seize the rifles while capturing Nathan's son. Nathan stays on in Alaska and tangles with the villainous Captain E. T. Barnette, but Earp arrives in time to help Nathan out of his problems.

Genre: Western
Subjects: Fathers and sons; Adventure; Illegitimacy; Earp, Wyatt, 1848–1929
Place/Time: Alaska—19th century

Paulsen, Gary

1207.
1. *Murphy.* Walker, 1987.
2. *Murphy's Gold.* Walker, 1988.
3. *Murphy's Herd.* Walker, 1989.
4. *Murphy's War.* Walker, 1991.
5. *Murphy's Stand.* Walker, 1993.
6. *Murphy's Ambush.* Walker, 1995.
7. *Murphy's Trail.* Walker, 1996.

As sheriff of Clincherville, Colorado, in the 1880s, Al Murphy has to keep the drunks and rowdies under control. When killers hit town, Murphy has to step in and stop them. Murphy is aided by his love Midge, who runs the local diner. The two eventually leave the town and settle in Casper, Wyoming, on a ranch. When Midge is killed, Murphy seeks revenge and begins to wander the West as a one-man vigilante. He receives a second chance in Turrett, New Mexico, where he finds love and a job as sheriff that keeps him chasing Apaches and going to Mexico to help friends.

Genre: Historical Fiction; Western
Subjects: Ranch life; Adventure; Sheriffs
Place/Time: Wyoming—19th century; Colorado—19th century

Paxson, Diana L.

1208. Hallowed Isle
1. *The Book of the Sword.* Avon Eos, 1999.
2. *The Book of the Spear.* Avon Eos, 1999.
3. *The Book of the Cauldron.* Avon, 1999.

The legend of King Arthur is told through tales of the tribes of the British Isles. The Roman occupation has subdued tribal conflict, but differences erupt after the Romans depart. Artor, seemingly an orphan, but actually the son of the Lady of the Lake, grows up in this volatile cultural mixture and becomes a hero and king. He drives back the Saxons and summons his mother to heal the land, but the dark magic of Morgause lurks in the background.

Genre: Fantasy
Subjects: Arthur, King; Legends and folk tales; Anglo-Saxons; Magic
Place/Time: England—6th century

1209. Wodan's Children
1. *The Wolf and the Raven.* Morrow, 1993.
2. *The Dragons of the Rhine.* Morrow, 1995.
3. *The Lord of Horses.* Morrow, 1996.

Based on the Germanic Nibelunglied saga, these tales tell of the doomed love of Sigfrid, the warrior and shape shifter, and Brunahild, the powerful Walkyrja. Although Brunahild is the mother of his child, Sigfrid is enchanted by a love spell, which unites him with the princess Gudrun. Unaware of Brunahild's true identity, Sigfrid wins her as a bride for his king. After Sigfrid is killed by Gudrun's family, she must accept a political marriage with Attila the Hun.

Genre: Fantasy
Subjects: Mythology, Germanic; Lovers; Magic
Place/Time: Europe—5th century

Paxson, Diana L *and* Martine-Barnes, Adrienne

1210. Chronicles of Fion mac Cumhall
1. *Master of Earth and Water.* Morrow, 1993.
2. *The Shield between the Worlds.* Morrow, 1994.
3. *Sword of Fire and Shadow.* Morrow, 1995.

Kept ignorant of his heritage as son of the chief of the band of Irish warriors called the Fianna, Fion mac Cumhall is called Demne and raised by Bodbmall after his father's death. From Bodbmall he learns mystical lore and acquires skills that make him a fierce warrior, doing battle both in the real world and in the faerie realm. Fion ages, his son is lost to him, but the mystical realm between life and death becomes a home for him until he is needed by Ireland again.

Genre: Fantasy; Coming of Age
Subjects: Heroes; War; Mysticism; Legends and folk tales
Place/Time: Ireland—3rd century

Peake, Mervyn Laurence

1211. The Gormenghast Trilogy
1. *Titus Groan.* Weybright & Talley, 1967.
2. *Gormenghast.* Weybright & Talley, 1967.
3. *Titus Alone.* Weybright & Talley, 1967.

Titus Groan is born of noble lineage in the kingdom of Gormenghast, but his life is hardly an easy one. His parents ignore him, while the ambitious, ruthless servant Steerpike plots against him. Titus survives his nemesis's schemes but, feeling weighed down by the tradition and ritual of his heritage, he rejects it all and sets off on his own adventure.

Genre: Fantasy
Subjects: Imaginary kingdoms; Boys; Inheritance and succession; Servants

Pearce, Mary

1212.
1. *Apple Tree Lean Down.* St. Martin's, 1976.
2. *The Land Endures.* St. Martin's, 1978.
3. *Seedtime and Harvest.* St. Martin's, 1982.

From 1886 to World War II, three very different families, the Twekes, the Izzards, and the Mercybrights, work the land in rural England and find their lives intertwined. Their children marry and must survive depressions and world wars as they seek happiness. Beth Tweke and her daughter Betony give up financial gain for happiness, but others find that money does not bring them what they wanted.

Genre: Historical Romance
Subjects: Family life; Country life; Farm life
Place/Time: England—19th century; England—1900–1945

Pearson, Diane

1213.
1. *The Marigold Field.* Lippincott, 1969.
2. *Sarah.* Lippincott, 1971.

Sarah Whitman has a difficult childhood in early 19th-century rural England. Her mother is dead and her stepmother dislikes her intensely, but her father's love helps her to rise above her lower-class background, become a schoolteacher in London, and enter into a marriage that brings her adventure and wealth, but also sorrow.

Genre: Coming of Age
Subjects: Girls; Fathers and daughters; Stepmothers; Teachers; Marriage
Place/Time: England—19th century

Peck, Robert Newton

1214.
1. *A Day No Pigs Would Die.* Knopf, 1972.
2. *A Part of the Sky.* Knopf, 1994.

In rural Vermont in the late 1920s, Rob Peck is a 12-year old trying to grow up in a difficult time. His family are Shakers who have a small farm. Rob's father, who kills pigs for a living, wants his son to get an education. Rob tries to help his family by doing chores for neighbors, one of whom gives him a little pig in return. Rob raises the pig, and it becomes his closest friend. However, when the harvest fails, Rob must kill his beloved pig so that the family can eat. At 14, Rob becomes the man of the family when his father dies, and Rob must fight to save the farm. A young boy comes of age in these beautiful stories about family life.

Genre: Coming of Age; Gentle Read; Historical Fiction
Subjects: Teenagers; Farm life; Family life; Fathers and sons
Place/Time: Vermont—1900–1945

Pedersen, Knut. *See* Hamsun, Knut

Peiffer, Lila

1215.
  1. *The Secrets of the Roses.* Thomas Nelson, 1992.
  2. *Rosehaven.* Thomas Nelson, 1994.

As a young girl, Elizabeth Sheridan hoped to become an artist, but when she goes to Paris, she falls in love with Roberto. Roberto seduces her, and she regrets this indiscretion all her life. She finds faith and marriage with a missionary. Years later Elizabeth and her husband have a successful retreat for the troubled rich. When Roberto checks into the retreat, he is troubled by his worldly values and looking for a better way to live. Roberto finds faith, and when Elizabeth's husband is killed in an earthquake, Elizabeth and Roberto can finally marry.

Genre: Christian Fiction
Subjects: Faith; Love; Marriage
Place/Time: Paris (France)—1980–

Pella, Judith *and* Peterson, Tracie

1216. Ribbons of Steel
  1. *Distant Dreams.* Bethany House, 1997.
  2. *A Hope Beyond.* Bethany House, 1997.
  3. *A Promise for Tomorrow.* Bethany House, 1998.

The building of the Baltimore and Ohio Railroad enthralls young Caroline Adams who persuades her father to allow her tutor James Baldwin to teach her science and math. She discovers that James also loves the railroad and the two fall in love. James, however, is forced to become engaged to Caroline's older sister, but when he breaks of the engagement and goes to work for the railroad, Caroline is heartbroken. She moves to Baltimore and works as a nanny to Blake St. John's daughter Victoria. She marries St. John, but when he dies, she is finally able to marry her true love

James Baldwin who oversees the building of the B&O railroad. Caroline's stepdaughter falls in love with an Irish worker and their romance in threatened when the construction is sabotaged

Genre: Christian Fiction; Historical Fiction
Subjects: Faith; Railroads; Plantation life; Love
Place/Time: Southern states—19th century

1217. Ribbons West Series
  1. *Westward the Dream.* Bethany, 1999.
  2. *Separate Roads.* Bethany, 1999.

Brenton and Jordana Baldwin go west to see their stepsister Victoria and her husband Kiernan in 1862. Brenton wants to photograph the American West while Jordana wants to reunite Caitlan O'Connor with her brother Kiernan. As they travel west, they become entangled with the designs of the Central Pacific Railroad. The three stop in Omaha to raise money for their trip, but Jordana uncovers an illegal land scheme that forces them to leave. When they reach California, they find Kiernan injured, and the young people must fight hard times before they find peace and love. Only their faith keeps them strong.

Genre: Christian Fiction
Subjects: Faith; Love; Frontier and pioneer life; Railroads
Place/Time: Western states—19th century; California—19th century

Pella, Judith. *See also* Phillips, Michael R.

1218. Lone Star Legacy
  1. *Frontier Lady.* Bethany House, 1993.
  2. *Stoner's Crossing.* Bethany House, 1994.
  3. *Warrior's Song.* Bethany House, 1996.

In 1864, Deborah Killion fled Stoner's Crossing, Texas, and the law. Now, 20 years later, she is married and has a daughter and son. Their ranch is large and prosperous, but their idyllic life is shattered when Deborah's identity is discovered and she must go to jail. Deborah finds the courage to tell her daughter Carolyn about her past, and Carolyn goes back to Stoner's Crossing to find the truth. Deborah's son with a Cheyenne warrior discovers the prejudice of the West against half-breeds, and he, like his mother, must seek forgiveness and faith.

Genre: Christian Fiction; Western
Subjects: Ranch life; Christian life; Family life; Cheyenne Indians
Place/Time: Texas—19th century

Pelletier, Cathie

1219.
  1. *Funeral Makers.* Macmillan, 1986.
  2. *Once Upon a Time on the Banks.* Viking, 1984.
  3. *The Weight of Winter.* Viking, 1991.

4. *Beaming Sonny Home.* Crown, 1996.

The lives of the zany and eccentric residents of Mattagash, Maine, come to life in these irreverent and bawdy tales of the McKinnon, Lawler, and Gifford offspring. The McKinnon daughters meet in town for a reunion when one of the girls is dying of beriberi. Protestant Amy Jo Lawler shocks the town when she marries a French Canadian Catholic. Lynn Gifford cleans house and lives through her husband's abuse. The long Maine winter shows off the assortment of characters in the town.

Genre: Humor
Subjects: Sisters; Small town life; Eccentrics and eccentricities
Place/Time: Maine—1945–1980

Penman, Sharon Kay

1220.
1. *Here Be Dragons.* Holt, Rinehart & Winston, 1985.
2. *Falls the Shadow.* Holt, Rinehart & Winston, 1985.
3. *The Reckoning.* Holt, Rinehart & Winston, 1991.

The stories of the turbulent reigns of King John, Henry III, and Edward I of England are told through the children and relatives of these men. In the late 1100s, Joanna, daughter of King John, is married to Prince Llewlyn of Wales. She ultimately has to choose between her father and her husband when John abuses his power and fights the lords. Her sons join with Simon de Montfort who champions laws to limit the power of the monarchy and marries Henry III's sister. Simon's daughter weds another Welsh prince who is battling King Edward I. The religious, political, and military intrigues of the times are vividly brought to life through the people who lived them.

Genre: Historical Fiction
Subjects: Courts and courtiers; John, King of England, 1167–1216; Henry III, King of England, 1207–1271; Richard III, King of England, 1452–1485; Kings and rulers
Place/Time: England—13th century; England—14th century

Penn, Margaret

1221. The Story of Hilda Burton
1. *Manchester Fourteen Miles.* Macmillan, 1948.
2. *The Foolish Virgin.* Cape, 1951.
3. *Young Mrs. Burton.* Cape, 1954.

These autobiographical novels tell the story of Hilda, a young girl who was adopted by a lower middle-class family living in the Manchester area of England in the early 1900s. Starting with her warm but complex relationship with her foster family, the tales follow her through adolescence and marriage.

Genre: Coming of Age; Historical Fiction
Subjects: Family life; Adoption; Teenagers; Foster children
Place/Time: England—1900–1945

Percy, Walker

1222.
1. *The Last Gentleman.* Farrar, Straus & Giroux, 1966.
2. *The Second Coming.* Farrar, Straus & Giroux, 1980.

After suffering from a sense of dislocation in his native South, Will Barrett moves north only to feel equally homeless and aimless. He takes to observing life through a telescope in a park, falls in love with a ballet dancer, and eventually moves back to the South with his family. He retires a wealthy man, but is still plagued by the secrets of his youth.

Subjects: Men—psychology; Love; Psychological novels
Place/Time: Southern states—1945–1980

1223.
1. *Love in the Ruins: The Adventures of a Bad Catholic at a Time near the End of the World.* Farrar, Straus & Giroux, 1971.
2. *The Thanatos Syndrome.* Farrar, Straus & Giroux, 1987.

In this unusual mixture of speculation about the near future, satire, and theology, flawed hero Dr. Thomas More does battle with the Devil himself over the use of More's strange invention that can take the measure of the soul. In the sequel, the doctor's adversaries are a little less powerful, but they do have big plans. A group of psychiatrists want to make human behavior completely harmless, but also completely uniform, by drugging the water supply.

Genre: Fantasy; Humor
Subjects: End of the world; Devil; Psychiatrists; Conformity
Place/Time: Louisiana—1980–

Perdue, Tito

1224.
1. *The New Austerities.* Peachtree, 1994.
2. *Lee.* Four Walls Eight Windows, 1991.

Seventy-three-year-old Leland Pefley is a transplanted Alabaman living in New York City with his wife Judy. He is a curmudgeon who hates the city and spends his time reading Greek classics. When he decides he can no longer live in the city, he and Judy drive to Lee's ancestral home in Alabama. He wanders around the town looking for a long-dead friends and taking out his wrath on the townspeople until he is forced out of town by the police.

Subjects: Old age; Eccentrics and eccentricities

Place/Time: Alabama—1980–; New York (N. Y.)—1980–

Peretti, Frank E.

1225.
1. *This Present Darkness.* Crossway Books, 1986.
2. *Piercing the Darkness.* Crossway Books, 1989.

In the town of Ashton, darkness descends and everyone is going mad. Only when the Host of Heaven enters the town are the people able to summon their faith and save themselves. In Bacon's Corner, Sally Roe is born again when demons try to take over a religious school. Again the Host of Heaven and faith defeat the evil that tries to pervert man.

Genre: Christian Fiction; Science Fiction
Subjects: Good and evil; Demonology

Perez Galdos, Benito

1226. Contemporary Novels; The First Epoch
1. *Dona Perfecta.* Harper, 1896.
2. *Gloria.* W. S. Gottsberger, 1882.
3. *Leon Roch.* W. S. Gottsberger, 1888.
4. *Marianela.* W. S. Gottsberger, 1883.

The turbulent social, political, and religious history of Spain in the 1800s is the backdrop for these novels that express the author's liberal philosophy and interest in psychology. His characters are torn by clashes between traditional behavior and ideas that represent a skeptical or liberal approach to life.

Genre: Historical Fiction
Subjects: Philosophical novels; Politics—Spain
Place/Time: Spain—19th century

Perrin, Don. *See* Weis, Margaret

Perry, Steve

1227. Matador
1. *The 97th Step.* Ace, 1989.
2. *The Man Who Never Missed.* Ace, 1985.
3. *Matadora.* Berkley, 1986.
4. *The Machiavelli Interface.* Ace, 1986.
5. *The Albino Knife.* Ace, 1991.
6. *Black Steel.* Ace, 1992.
7. *Brother Death.* Ace, 1992.

The Matadors, a group of mercenaries who right wrongs throughout the galaxy, have their origin in Penn who, as a young boy, fled his desolate home planet and became a thief. Beginning a way of life that will ultimately make him the leader of the Matadors, Penn becomes a trainer in the martial arts. His first student is Khadaji, a military deserter who steals non-le-

thal poison darts and then takes aim at a variety of government officials with effective and sometimes humorous results.

Genre: Science Fiction
Subjects: Mercenary soldiers; Martial arts

1228. Spindoc
1. *Spindoc.* Ace, 1994.
2. *The Forever Drug.* Ace, 1995.

Government PR man Venture Silk's greatest talent is spinning tales—in short—lying. The murder of his sweetheart makes him face the devious nature of the life he has been leading. The search for her killer takes him to a planet called New Earth and into a relationship with the enticing Zia, who may not be completely trustworthy. Complicating their affair is her treatment with a drug that will make her immortal, but also makes her a target for terran intelligence agents.

Genre: Science Fiction
Subjects: Bureaucracy; Murder and murderers; Immortality; Love; Life on other planets

Perry, Thomas

1229.
1. *Butcher's Boy.* Scribner, 1982.
2. *Sleeping Dogs.* Random House, 1992.

The butcher's boy is a nameless, professional killer who has been hired by the mob to stop a union from exposing pension fund manipulation by a mob run company. When the mob double-crosses the hit man and tries to rub him out, the butcher boy goes after Mr. Big and leaves a trail of bodies in his path before he flees to England. However, his quiet existence there is ended when a young mafioso recognizes him and tries to kill him. The butcher boy comes back to America and again goes after the mob. The bodies pile up until the hit man, the mob, and the FBI meet in a dramatic climax.

Genre: Adventure; Crime Novel
Subjects: Crime and criminals; Assassination; Mafia; Underworld
Place/Time: United States—1980–; England—1980–

Peterson, Tracie. *See also* Pella, Judith

1230. Westward Chronicles
1. *A Shelter of Hope.* Bethany House, 1998.
2. *Hidden in a Whisper.* Bethany House, 1999.
3. *A Veiled Reflection.* Bethany House, 2000.

In the late 19th century, three women become "Harvey Girls" to escape their lives back East. Simone joins the Harvey Girls to escape a brutal father while Rachel Taylor discovers an old love in her new position. Jill Danvers takes her sister's place in the Harvey Girls and is horrified by the plight of the Navajo people. Each woman finds love in her new position, but each must put her faith in God if she is to find true happiness.

Genre: Christian Fiction
Subjects: Faith; Women; Hotels, taverns, etc; Love
Place/Time: Western states—19th century

Petrakis, Harry Mark

1231.
1. *A Dream of Kings.* McKay, 1966.
2. *Ghost of the Sun.* St. Martin's, 1990.

The passionate life of Leonidas Matsoukas is played out in Chicago after World War II. Leonidas who fought the Nazis now is the terror of Falconi's gambling parlor and is wildly in love with Anthoula, the owner of a bakery. The tragedy of his life is his son Stavros, who cannot speak or move. Leonidas refuses to believe his son cannot be cured and takes him to Greece. Eight years later, he returns and tries to pick up the pieces of his life. His wife has remarried and his daughter is grown up, but Leonidas works to win them back.

Subjects: Love affairs; Fathers and sons; Family life
Place/Time: Chicago (Ill.)—1945–1980; Illinois—1945–1980

Phillips, Michael

1232.
1. *Mercy & Eagleflight.* Tyndale House, 1996.
2. *A Dangerous Love.* Tyndale House, 1997.

Mercy Randolph is a frontier evangelist, but she falls on hard times. Gambler Jack Eagleflight rescues her from trouble, and the two fall in love. Jack must change his ways or Mercy won't accept his love. As Jack changes, the two plan to marry, but their plans are stopped by Jack's nephew Jess when he finds the loot from an old robbery. Can Jack and Mercy help Jess to do the right thing?

Genre: Christian Fiction
Subjects: Faith; Frontier and pioneer life; Gambling; Love
Place/Time: Western states—19th century

1233. Secret of the Rose
1. *The Eleventh Hour.* Tyndale House, 1993.
2. *A Rose Remembered.* Tyndale House, 1994.
3. *Escape to Freedom.* Tyndale House, 1994.
4. *Dawn of Liberty.* Tyndale House, 1995.

Before World War II, Prussian Baron von Dortmann and his daughter try to separate themselves from the insanity growing in Germany. Father and daughter cling to their Christian faith as the German blitzkrieg overruns Poland. During the war, Sabina helps the Jewish underground and searches for her missing father. After the war, Sabina and her American boyfriend, Matthew, try to get her father out of Communist East Germany. Years later, Sabina and Matthew return to a united Germany for an evangelism conference as they reflect on how their faith has kept them safe.

Genre: Christian Fiction

Subjects: Faith; Fathers and daughters; World War II, 1939–1945
Place/Time: Germany—1900–1945; Germany—1945–1980

1234. Secrets of Heathersleigh Hall
1. *Wild Grows the Heather in Devon.* Bethany House, 1998.
2. *Wayward Winds.* Bethany House, 1999.
3. *Heathersleigh Homecoming.* Bethany House, 1999.

In Victorian England, Charles and Jocelyn Rutherford are a devoted couple. He is a member of Parliament while she stays on their rural estate because of a disfiguring birthmark on her face. Jocelyn raises their three children, but fears that Charles is drifting away from her. Charles has found religion, and soon Jocelyn also has a religious conversion. Their daughter Amanda finds religion stifling and marries a man who has a hidden secret. As Amanda struggles with her marriage, she too discovers faith. When war breaks out in Europe, Amanda flees across Europe and thinks she finds safety in Switzerland, but she is being followed by her husband who is trying to keep her from getting to England and helping others.

Genre: Christian Fiction; Family Saga
Subjects: Marriage; Family life; Husbands and wives; Faith
Place/Time: England—19th century; Europe—1900–1945

Phillips, Michael R.

1235. Journals of Corrie Belle Hollister
1. *My Father's World.* Bethany House, 1990.
2. *Daughter of Grace.* Bethany House, 1990.
3. *On the Trail of the Truth.* Bethany House, 1991.
4. *A Place in the Sun.* Bethany House, 1991.
5. *Sea to Shining Sea.* Bethany House, 1992.
6. *Into the Long Dark Night.* Bethany House, 1992.
7. *Land of the Brave and the Free.* Bethany House, 1993.
8. *A Home for My Heart.* Bethany House, 1994.

Beginning with a wagon train journey west in the early 1850s, Corrie Hollister, an aspiring journalist, tries to make her way as a writer in a man's world that does not always agree with her values. Her search for the truth in her journalism is a search for truth within herself, and she grapples with the reasons why people see the same events, like the Civil War, from different points of view. *Note:* This series continues in the Journals of Corrie and Christopher series.

Genre: Christian Fiction; Historical Fiction
Subjects: Wagon trains; Journalists; Christian life; Women
Place/Time: Western states—19th century

1236. Journals of Corrie and Christopher

1. *The Braxtons of Miracle Springs.* Bethany House, 1996.
2. *A New Beginning.* Bethany House, 1997.

When Corrie Belle Hollister marries Christopher Braxton, she enters a new phase in her life. They make their home in Miracle Springs, but find danger from the past leads to a death in the town. When Christopher feels they should move back East, they find they must turn to their faith to find direction in their lives. *Note:* This series follows the Journals of Corrie Belle Hollister series.

Genre: Christian Fiction; Historical Fiction
Subjects: Christian life; Husbands and wives; Marriage
Place/Time: Western states—19th century

Phillips, Michael R. *and* Pella, Judith

1237. The Russians

1. *The Crown and the Crucible.* Bethany House, 1991.
2. *A House Divided.* Bethany House, 1992.
3. *Travail and Triumph.* Bethany House, 1992.
4. *Heirs to the Motherland.* Bethany House, 1993.
5. *The Dawning of Deliverance.* Bethany House, 1994.
6. *White Nights, Red Morning.* Bethany House, 1996.
7. *Passage into Light.* Bethany House, 1998.

Beginning in the 1870s, the lives of the daughter of a peasant and the daughter of a Russian prince are intertwined as peasants struggle to survive and maintain their dignity, and the nobility face uncertainties as the revolutionary underground threatens to explode. These two women reveal the intrigue and turmoil in Russia before and after the Communist revolution. Only faith in God helps these women survive.

Genre: Christian Fiction; Historical Fiction
Subjects: Christian life; Aristocracy; Revolutions and revolutionists
Place/Time: Russia—19th century; Russia—1900–1917

1238. Stonewycke Legacy

1. *Stranger at Stonewycke.* Bethany House, 1987.
2. *Shadows over Stonewycke.* Bethany House, 1988.
3. *Treasure of Stonewycke.* Bethany House, 1988.

The Stonewycke family enters the Great Depression in 1931 in a Scottish town, and their wealth is stretched to the limits in their efforts to help the town. The family sees World War II with one member becoming a double agent for British intelligence in France, and the family is finally reunited after long separations.

Genre: Christian Fiction; Historical Romance

Subjects: Christian life; World War II, 1939–1945; International intrigue; Wealth
Place/Time: Scotland—1900–1945

1239. Stonewycke Trilogy

1. *The Heather Hills of Stonewycke.* Bethany House, 1985.
2. *Flight from Stonewycke.* Bethany House, 1985.
3. *The Lady of Stonewycke.* Bethany House, 1986.

A sweeping panoramic saga of three generations in the lives of an aristocratic Scottish family during the mid-19th century begins when a Stonewycke daughter marries a forbidden suitor, has to flee to the United States, and is later reunited with her family.

Genre: Christian Fiction; Family Saga; Historical Romance
Subjects: Christian life; Wealth
Place/Time: Scotland—19th century; United States—19th century

Phillips, Susan E.

1240.

1. *Nobody's Baby but Mine.* Avon, 1997.
2. *Dream a Little Dream.* Avon, 1998.

The Bonner brothers of North Carolina find that there are some women who won't take no for an answer. Football star Cal Bonner finds that Jane Darlington is only pretending to be a hooker. All she wants is a baby and has decided Cal should be the father. Cal catches on to her trick, and they find that love changes all of their ideas. Cal's brother Gabe owns the local drive-in in Salvation, and hires Rachel Stone to work there. Rachel and her young son are on the run from her dead husband's family who think she has the husband's millions. Gabe tries to protect Rachel from her enemies and finds that he is falling in love with the gutsy Rachel.

Genre: Romance
Subjects: Lovers; Brothers; Rural life
Place/Time: North Carolina—1980–

Piper, H. Beam

1241. The Fuzzy Series

1. *Little Fuzzy.* Avon, 1962.
2. *The Other Human Race.* (Alternate title: *Fuzzy Sapiens.*) Avon, 1964.

The above titles have also been published in the following collection: *The Fuzzy Papers.* Doubleday, 1977.

3. *Fuzzies and Other People.* Ace, 1984.

The Fuzzies, inhabitants of the planet Zarathrustra, are adorable and easily exploited. Making their situation more tenuous is the presence of valuable minerals on their home planet. An intergalactic trial brings the forces of good and evil together in a clash over the nature of the Fuzzies: Are they sentient beings who are as capable of running their lives as humans or pets who need care?

Genre: Science Fiction
Subjects: Extraterrestrial beings; Life on other planets; Good and evil; Trials

Plagemann, Bentz

1242.
1. *This Is Goggie, Or the Education of a Father.* McGraw, 1955.
2. *Father to the Man.* Morrow, 1964.
3. *The Best Is Yet to Be.* Morrow, 1966.
4. *A World of Difference.* Morrow, 1969.

Bill and Kate Wallace face the trials and tribulations of married life with humor and affection. When Bill returns to New York City from World War II, he has to try to rebuild his relationship with the son he has not seen for five years. Goggie finally goes to college, but he flunks out and enters the Coast Guard. With their son gone, Bill and Kate travel to the Mediterranean and Hollywood, where they find themselves helping their friends. These warm novels explore the lives of everyday people.

Genre: Gentle Read; Humor
Subjects: Marriage; Fathers and sons; Family life
Place/Time: New York (N. Y.)—1945–1980

Plaidy, Jean. *Pseud. of* Eleanor Hibbert. *See also* Carr, Philippa

1243. The Georgian Saga
1. *The Princess of Celle.* Putnam, 1985, 1967.
2. *Queen in Waiting.* Putnam, 1985, 1967.
3. *The Prince and the Quakeress.* Putnam, 1986, 1968.
4. *Caroline, the Queen.* Putnam, 1986, 1968.
5. *The Third George.* Putnam, 1987, 1969.
6. *Perdita's Prince.* Putnam, 1987, 1969.
7. *Sweet Lass of Richmond Hill.* Putnam, 1988, 1970.
8. *Indiscretions of the Queen.* Putnam, 1988, 1970.
9. *The Regent's Daughter.* Putnam, 1989, 1971.
10. *Goddess of the Green Room.* Hale, 1971.
11. *Victoria in the Wings.* Hale, 1972.

The lives of the Hanoverian kings and queens are recounted from Prince George William of Celle to the birth of Victoria. George William's niece is forced to marry George I of Hanover, but their marriage is unhappy, and her affair with Count Konigsmark brings only disaster. Scandals and madness plague the reigns of George II, George III, and George IV. The German kings were unpopular with their British subjects, and their scandals and love affairs only added to the alienation.

Genre: Historical Fiction

Subjects: Kings and rulers; Courts and courtiers; Politics—England; Love affairs; George III, King of England, 1738–1820
Place/Time: England—18th century; England—19th century

1244. The Lucrezia Borgia Series
1. *Madonna of the Seven Hills.* Putnam, 1974, 1958.
2. *Light on Lucrezia.* Putnam, 1976, 1958.

In the 15th century, the Borgias dominate and corrupt Italy. Roderigo Borgia ruthlessly rises to power. His daughter Lucrezia marries, has love affairs, and manipulates power until her death.

Genre: Historical Fiction
Subjects: Politics—Italy; Borgia, Lucrezia, 1480–1519; Borgia family
Place/Time: Italy—15th century

1245. Mary Queen of Scots Series
1. *Royal Road to Fotheringay.* Putnam, 1968, 1955.
2. *The Captive Queen of Scots.* Putnam, 1970, 1963.

Mary Stuart, Queen of Scots, becomes the child bride of the frail Dauphin of France. When he dies, she has an affair that scandalizes the Court. When she returns to Scotland, her affairs and the murder of her husband Lord Darnley force her to flee. She escapes to her cousin, Elizabeth I, who imprisons her and ultimately has the tragic Mary beheaded.

Genre: Historical Fiction
Subjects: Courts and courtiers; Queens; Mary, Queen of Scots, 1542–1587
Place/Time: France—16th century; Scotland—16th century

1246. The Medici Trilogy
1. *Madame Serpent.* Appleton Century Crofts, 1951.
2. *The Italian Woman.* Putnam, 1975, 1952.
3. *Queen Jezebel.* Appleton Century Crofts, 1953.

Catherine de Medici is the most hated and feared woman in France in the late 1500s. She is married to Henry of Orleans when she is 14. When he dies, she becomes Regent of France for her son. In 1572, she orders the slaughter of the Huguenots, which brings on more strife in her country.

Genre: Historical Fiction
Subjects: Courts and courtiers; Queens; Caterina de Medici, Queen of France, 1519–1589
Place/Time: France—16th century

1247. Norman Trilogy
1. *The Bastard King.* Putnam, 1979, 1974.
2. *The Lion of Justice.* Putnam, 1979, 1975.
3. *The Passionate Enemies.* Putnam, 1979, 1976.

The tale of the Norman kings of England begins in 1066 when William comes from Normandy to conquer England. The story of King Henry I and the conflict of Stephen and Matilda are related as the Norman period ends and the Plantagenet kings start their reign.

Genre: Historical Fiction
Subjects: William I, King of England, 1028–1087; Kings and rulers; Normans
Place/Time: England—11th century; England—12th century

1248. Plantagenet Saga
1. *The Plantagenet Prelude.* Putnam, 1980, 1976.
2. *The Revolt of the Eagles.* Putnam, 1980, 1977.
3. *The Heart of the Lion.* Putnam, 1980, 1977.
4. *The Prince of Darkness.* Putnam, 1980, 1978.
5. *The Battle of the Queens.* Putnam, 1981, 1978.
6. *The Queen from Provence.* Putnam, 1981, 1979.
7. *Hammer of the Scots.* Putnam, 1981, 1979.
8. *The Follies of the King.* Putnam, 1982, 1980.
9. *The Vow on the Heron.* Putnam, 1982, 1980.
10. *Passage to Pontefract.* Putnam, 1982.
11. *The Star of Lancaster.* Putnam, 1982.
12. *Epitaph for Three Women.* Putnam, 1983.
13. *Red Rose of Anjou.* Putnam, 1983.
14. *The Sun in Splendour.* Putnam, 1983.
15. *Uneasy Lies the Head.* Putnam, 1984.

Rich narration and historical detail bring to life medieval English history from the reign of Henry II, the first Plantagenet king, to the rise of Henry VIII 400 years later. All of the major figures in medieval history are seen. Thomas a Becket, Richard the Lion-Hearted, Edward the Black Prince, Joan of Arc, and Richard III are part of the contentious years as the kings struggle to control England and fight for their claim to control parts of France.

Genre: Historical Fiction
Subjects: Courts and courtiers; Kings and rulers; Politics—England; Middle Ages; Plantagenet, house of
Place/Time: England—multicentury span

1249. The Queen Victoria Series
1. *The Captive of Kensington Palace.* Putnam, 1976, 1972.
2. *The Queen and Lord M.* Putnam, 1977, 1973.
3. *The Queen's Husband.* Putnam, 1978, 1973.
4. *The Widow of Windsor.* Putnam, 1978, 1974.

From the young girl raised in seclusion in Kensington Palace to the lonely widow of Windsor, the life of Queen Victoria is retold through her public deeds and her private life. Victoria as a young girl is kept away from court so she will not be corrupted by the king's illegitimate sons. When she becomes queen, she relies on Lord Melbourne, her prime minister. After her marriage to Albert, she relies on him and is grief stricken at his death, but still reigns.

Genre: Historical Fiction
Subjects: Victoria, Queen of England, 1819–1901; Queens; Family life; Love
Place/Time: England—19th century

1250. Queens of England Series
1. *My Self, My Enemy.* Putnam, 1984.
2. *Queen of This Realm: The Story of Queen Elizabeth I.* Putnam, 1985.
3. *Victoria Victorious.* Putnam, 1986.
4. *The Lady in the Tower.* Putnam, 1986.
5. *The Courts of Love.* Putnam, 1988.
6. *In the Shadow of the Crown.* Putnam, 1989.
7. *The Queen's Secret.* Putnam, 1990.
8. *The Reluctant Queen: The Story of Anne of York.* Putnam, 1991.
9. *The Pleasures of Love: The Story of Catherine of Braganza.* Putnam, 1992.
10. *William's Wife.* Putnam, 1993.
11. *The Rose Without a Thorn.* Putnam, 1994.

The Queens of England tell their own stories. Their lives, loves, and tribulations, recounted by queens such as Eleanor of Aquitaine, Katherine of Valois, Elizabeth I, and Anne of Yorke show a side of history that is rarely seen.

Genre: Historical Fiction
Subjects: Queens; Courts and courtiers; Politics—England; Love
Place/Time: England—multicentury span

1251. The Stuart Saga
1. *The Murder in the Tower.* Putnam, 1974, 1964.
2. *The Wandering Prince.* Putnam, 1971, 1956.
3. *A Health unto His Majesty.* Putnam, 1972, 1956.
4. *Here Lies Our Sovereign Lord.* Putnam, 1973, 1957.
5. *The Three Crowns.* Putnam, 1977, 1965.
6. *The Haunted Sisters.* Putnam, 1977, 1966.
7. *The Queen's Favourites.* Putnam, 1978, 1966.

The bawdy and strife-filled age of the Stuarts is told through the women who loved and dominated these men, from James I's conflicts to Charles II's exile and restoration to James II's overthrow. James's daughters Anne and Mary eventually restore the Stuarts and peace to the English throne.

Genre: Family Saga; Historical Fiction
Subjects: James I, King of England, 1566–1625; James II, King of England, 1633–1701; Courts and courtiers; Queens; Kings and rulers; Charles II, King of England, 1630–1685; Love
Place/Time: England—17th century

1252. The Tudor Novels
1. *Katharine, the Virgin Widow.* Putnam, 1993, 1961.
2. *The Shadow of the Pomegranate.* Putnam, 1994, 1962.
3. *The King's Secret Matter.* Hale, 1962.

4. *Murder Most Royal.* Putnam, 1972. (Original American title: *The King's Pleasure.* Appleton Century, 1949.)
5. *St. Thomas' Eve.* Putnam, 1970, 1954.
6. *The Sixth Wife.* Putnam, 1969, 1953.
7. *The Thistle and the Rose.* Putnam, 1973, 1963.
8. *Mary, Queen of France.* Hale, 1964.
9. *The Spanish Bridegroom.* Macrae Smith, 1956.
10. *Gay Lord Robert.* Putnam, 1972, 1955.

The turbulent reign of the Tudors is chronicled in this series of novels that recount the tragic lives of the Tudor women from the sisters of Henry VIII to his six wives to his daughters, Mary and Elizabeth. Henry's sisters are married to the Kings of Scotland and France, while Henry marries again and again in the hope of siring a son. Like their father, neither Mary nor Elizabeth find romantic love, but Elizabeth makes her reign as queen her only love.

Genre: Historical Fiction
Subjects: Kings and rulers; Courts and courtiers; Women; Henry VIII, King of England, 1491–1547; Husbands and wives; Queens; Elizabeth I, Queen of England, 1533–1603
Place/Time: England—17th century; England—16th century

Plain, Belva

1253. Werner Saga
1. *Evergreen.* Delacorte, 1978.
2. *The Golden Cup.* Delacorte, 1986.
3. *Tapestry.* Delacorte, 1988.
4. *Harvest.* Delacorte, 1990.

The saga of the banking Werner family begins in New York in 1900 when son Paul falls in love with recent immigrant Anna. She, however, marries another immigrant. Paul and Anna continue to yearn for each other as their paths crisscross over the next 60 years. Paul is be drawn into the world of political radicals through his Aunt Hennie and into helping German Jews escape Hitler through his German cousins. He finds balance only at the end of his life.

Genre: Romance
Subjects: Family life; Bankers; Wealth; Radicals and radicalism; Holocaust, Jewish, 1933–1945
Place/Time: New York (N. Y.)—1900–1945

Plante, David

1254.
1. *The Family.* Farrar, Straus & Giroux, 1978.
2. *The Country.* Atheneum, 1981.
3. *The Woods.* Atheneum, 1982.
4. *The Catholic.* Atheneum, 1986.
5. *The Foreigner.* Atheneum, 1984.
6. *The Native.* Atheneum, 1988.

In the 1950s, the Francoeurs, working-class French Canadian Catholics in Providence, Rhode Island, are perceived through the eyes of Daniel, the next to the youngest son. Daniel sees the stress in his parents' marriage as they struggle to raise seven children. Daniel finds he is alienated from his family when he goes to college and discovers a new way of life. He travels to Europe, attends his father's funeral, and searches for meaning in his life.

Genre: Coming of Age
Subjects: Teenagers; Family life; College life
Place/Time: Rhode Island—1945–1980; Europe—1945–1980

Plievier, Theodor

1255.
1. *Stalingrad.* Appleton, 1948.
2. *Moscow.* Doubleday, 1954.
3. *Berlin.* Doubleday, 1957.

The horrors of the World War II in Eastern Europe are told from the common soldier's point of view. From the siege of Stalingrad through the fall of Berlin, Plievier traces the suffering, the hardships, and the tragedy of war. The Russians try to halt the German advance at Moscow, but it is winter that defeats the Germans. The Germans then see their own city of Berlin die as the Allies defeat them.

Genre: War
Subjects: World War II, 1939–1945; Soldiers
Place/Time: Germany—1900–1945; Soviet Union—1917–1945

Pohl, Frederik

1256.
1. *The Other End of Time.* Tor, 1991.
2. *The Siege of Eternity.* Tor, 1997.
3. *The Far Shore of Time.* Tor, 1999.

Survivors of an encounter with aliens in an orbital laboratory return to Earth, but with strange alien implants in their bodies and the knowledge that during their abduction they were cloned. Amid political infighting on Earth, they must discover and thwart the aliens' plans to make use of Earth.

Genre: Science Fiction
Subjects: Extraterrestrial beings; Bionics

1257. Space Merchants
1. *The Space Merchants.* (Written with C. M. Kornbluth) Ballantine, 1953.
2. *The Merchants' War.* St. Martin's, 1984.

Earth has become dominated by manipulative advertising and so overpopulated that people sleep on stairs. Mitchell Courtenay, ad man, is kidnapped by his ex-wife and forced to live in a labor camp where he finally sees the flaws in the system of which he has been a part. Mitchell escapes to Venus where there is no advertising. Years later a rebel rises to challenge the still materialistic system on Earth.

Genre: Science Fiction
Subjects: Advertising; Kidnapping; Life on other planets; Population; Revolutions and revolutionists

Pohl, Frederik *and* Williamson, Jack
1258. The Heechee Trilogy
1. *Gateway.* St. Martin's, 1977.
2. *Beyond the Blue Event Horizon.* Ballantine, 1980.
3. *Heechee Rendezvous.* Ballantine, 1984.

On Gateway, the deserted base of an advanced civilization, the Heechee have left a high-tech starship, which human adventurers appropriate for a ride that ends, for most of them, in an encounter with a black hole. Later Bob Broadhead, the survivor, agonizes over the experience with his psychiatrist-computer. Finally the mysterious Heechee make an appearance.

Genre: Science Fiction
Subjects: Extraterrestrial beings; Interplanetary voyages; Black holes (astronomy); Computers

Pollack, Rachel
1259.
1. *Unquenchable Fire.* Viking, 1992.
2. *Temporary Agency.* St. Martin's, 1994.

In a near-future world, a feminist revolution has passed its peak of idealism and renewal, leaving a society governed by an isolated, corrupt power structure and a set of meaningless rituals; however, there is magic in this future realm. An ordinary young woman becomes pregnant while dreaming of better things and gives birth to a girl who seems likely to bring her world back to the true revolutionary spirit. The sequel introduces a mysterious new threat to this near future society in the person of Lisa Black Dust a Malignant One, who, when not practicing black magic, runs a temporary employment agency.

Genre: Fantasy; Science Fiction
Subjects: Feminism; Degeneration; Good and evil

Pope, Dudley
1260.
1. *Ramage.* Lippincott, 1965.
2. *Drumbeat.* Doubleday, 1968.
3. *The Triton.* Doubleday, 1969.
4. *Governor Ramage, R.N.914.* Simon & Schuster, 1973.
5. *Ramage's Prize.* Simon & Schuster, 1974.
6. *Ramage and the Guillotine.* Avon, 1981.
7. *Ramage's Diamond.* Avon, 1982.
8. *Ramage's Mutiny.* Secker & Warburg, 1977. (This title was published only in England.)
9. *Ramage and the Rebels.* Avon, 1982.
10. *The Ramage Touch.* Walker, 1984.
11. *Ramage's Signal.* Walker, 1984.
12. *Ramage and the Renegades.* Avon, 1982.
13. *Ramage's Devil.* Secker & Warburg, 1982.
14. *Ramage's Trial.* Alison, 1984.
15. *Ramage's Challenge.* Alison, 1985.
16. *Ramage at Trafalgar.* Secker & Warburg, 1986.
17. *Ramage and the Saracens.* Alison, 1988.
18. *Ramage and the Dido.* Alison, 1989.
The above six titles were published only in England.

During the Napoleonic Wars, Lieutenant Nicholas Ramage enters the Royal Navy. From Italy to the West Indies, he fights mutinies, privateers, and the French navy as he rises in the ranks. Besides having rousing sea adventures, he falls in love and breaks the ladies' hearts. These expertly told historical novels accurately recreate the period.

Genre: Historical Fiction; Naval Adventure; War
Subjects: Naval battles; Navy, British; Navy, British—officers; Napoleonic Wars, 1800–1814; Adventure; War
Place/Time: Atlantic Ocean—19th century; Caribbean region—19th century; Mediterranean Sea—19th century

Potok, Chaim
1261.
1. *The Chosen.* Simon & Schuster, 1967.
2. *The Promise.* Simon & Schuster, 1969.

Danny and Reuven grow up in the Williamsburg section of Brooklyn, but live in entirely different worlds, one in the Orthodox Jewish tradition, the other in the Hasidic tradition. They meet as opponents in a softball game and become good friends. Their friendship helps them defy the destinies chosen for them by their fathers.

Genre: Coming of Age
Subjects: Judaism; Jews; Religious education, Jewish; Fathers and sons; Teenagers; Hasidism
Place/Time: New York (N. Y.)—1900–1945; New York (N. Y.)—1945–1980

Potter, Margaret. *See* Melville, Anne

Pound, Arthur
1262.
1. *Once a Wilderness.* Reynal, 1934.
2. *Second Growth.* Reynal, 1935.

John Mark grows up in rural Michigan in the late 1800s. He starts a stock breeding farm where he raises his children and grandchildren. He lives to see the passing of the agricultural life and the rise of the industrial order from 1900 to 1930.

Genre: Family Saga; Historical Fiction
Subjects: Farm life; Country life
Place/Time: Michigan—19th century; Michigan—1900–1945

Pournelle, Jerry. *See also* Niven, Larry

1263. Janissaries

1. *Janissaries.* Ace, 1979.
2. *Oath of Fealty.* (Written with Larry Niven) Phantasia Press, 1981.
3. *Clan and Crown.* (Written with Roland Green) Ace, 1982.
4. *Storms of Victory.* (Written with Roland Green) Ace, 1987.

A group of professional soldiers involved in a CIA mission in Africa are kidnapped by aliens to fight a band of mercenaries, collected from all periods of history including the Roman Empire, who have proved too much for the aliens to control.

Genre: Science Fiction
Subjects: Mercenary soldiers; Extraterrestrial beings; Kidnapping; Imaginary kingdoms

Powell, Anthony

1264. The Music of Time Series

1. *A Question of Upbringing.* Scribner, 1951.
2. *A Buyer's Market.* Scribner, 1953.
3. *The Acceptance World.* Farrar, Straus & Cudahy, 1955.
The above titles have also been published in the following collection: *A Dance to the Music of Time: First Movement.* Little, Brown, 1955.
4. *At Lady Molly's.* Little, Brown, 1957.
5. *Casanova's Chinese Restaurant.* Little, Brown, 1960.
6. *The Kindly Ones.* Little, Brown, 1962.
The above three titles have also been published in the following collection: *A Dance to the Music of Time: Second Movement.* Little, Brown, 1964.
7. *The Valley of Bones.* Little, Brown, 1964.
8. *The Soldier's Art.* Little, Brown, 1966.
9. *The Military Philosophers.* Little, Brown, 1968.
The above three titles have also been published in the following collection: *A Dance to the Music of Time: Third Movement.* Little, Brown, 1971.
10. *Books Do Furnish a Room.* Little, Brown, 1971.
11. *Temporary Kings.* Little, Brown, 1973.
12. *Hearing Secret Harmonies.* Little, Brown, 1976.
The above three titles have also been published in the following collection: *A Dance to the Music of Time: Fourth Movement.* Little, Brown, 1976.

A rich panorama of London society from 1921 to the postwar years is shown through the saga of one young man, Nick Jenkins, who grew up in those turbulent days. When the story opens, Nick and his friend Kenneth Widmerpool are in college. He and his friends travel and participate in the social and intellectual life of the 1920s. Nick enters publishing, has affairs, and becomes immersed in the politics of the 1930s. When World War II breaks out, he serves as an officer. After the war, he continues with his literary career and eventually looks back on his life with wit and irony. Historical characters mingle with fictional as Powell brilliantly captures a society in transition.

Subjects: Society novels; Authors; World politics; World War I, 1914–1918
Place/Time: London (England)—1900–1945; London (England)—1945–1980; England—1900–1945; England—1945–1980

Powell, Padgett

1265.

1. *Edisto.* Farrar, Straus & Giroux, 1984.
2. *Edisto Revisited.* Holt, 1996.

At twelve, Simons Manigault is finding his parents' separation difficult. His mother wants him to be a writer while his father is pushing him toward baseball. His mother's lover Taurus introduces him to women, sex, and alcohol. Torn between the three adults, Simons finds growing up in Edisto, South Carolina, is not easy. When he finishes college, Simons returns to Edisto and his mother's home, but he soon leaves for Texas. There he visits Taurus for a wild escapade with a prostitute. After a rousing summer he returns home to a job and a life of boredom.

Genre: Coming of Age
Subjects: Teenagers; Boys; Family life; Sex
Place/Time: South Carolina—1980–

Poyer, David

1266.

1. *The Med.* St. Martin's, 1988.
2. *Gulf.* St. Martin's, 1990.
3. *The Circle.* St. Martin's, 1992.
4. *The Passage.* St. Martin's, 1995.
5. *Tomahawk.* St. Martin's, 1998.
6. *China Sea.* St. Martin's, 2000.

This story of the modern navy in peace and war begins in the early 1970s when newly commissioned Annapolis graduate Ensign Dan Lenson is assigned to the troubled USS *Ryan.* He must try to keep the World War II destroyer seaworthy with too few crew members and a crazy captain. When the ship goes to the Arctic to test experimental sonar gear, a duel with a renegade Soviet submarine tests the ship and the crew. As his naval career continues, Lenson is sent to the Mediterranean when the fleet goes to rescue American hostages in Syria, to the Persian Gulf when Iran threatens the fleet, and to the Caribbean where he rescues Cuban refugees. Lenson then is dispatched to Washington to work on the Tomahawk missile program. When he receives his first command at sea, he ends up in the South China Sea on an old ship. These novels authentically depict the navy—its rituals, pressures, and operations.

Genre: Naval Adventure; Technothriller; War
Subjects: Navy, United States; Navy, United States—officers; Naval battles; Adventure; Arms and armor; Rescues
Place/Time: Mediterranean Sea—1945–1980; Persian Gulf—1945–1980

1267.
1. *Winter in the Heart.* Tor, 1993.
2. *As the Wolf Loves Winter.* Forge, 1996.
3. *Thunder on the Mountain.* Forge, 1999.

W.T. Halvorsen is a retired oil driller who lives in rural Pennsylvania. On his way to his cabin, he is splashed with contaminated snow and becomes ill. Seventeen-year-old Phil Romanelli finds Halvorsen and rushes him to the town hospital, where other people also have a mysterious illness. As Phil researches toxic waste, he meets Jaysine Farmer, the mistress of an oil company president. Phil, Jaysine, and Halvorsen uncover illegal toxic waste dumping, and go to extreme measures to stop the environmental destruction. Halvorsen blows up a bridge to stop the polluters and goes to prison. When he is released, he retreats to his cabin where he witnesses a murder. As he is drawn into the mystery, he finds illegal gas wells and a 12-year-old girl being held prisoner. A pack of wolves helps him to save the girl and foil the corrupt businessmen who pollute. Halvorsen then becomes involved in a strike at a Pennsylvania oil refinery. He leads the strikers while fighting strike breakers and the oil company.

Genre: Adventure
Subjects: Adventure; Environment; Petroleum industry; Old age
Place/Time: Pennsylvania—1980–

Pratchett, Terry

1268. Discworld
1. *The Colour of Magic.* St. Martin's, 1983.
2. *The Light Fantastic.* St. Martin's, 1986.
3. *Equal Rites.* New American Library, 1987.
4. *Mort.* New American Library, 1987.
5. *Sourcery.* New American Library, 1987.
6. *Wyrd Sisters.* Penguin, 1988.
7. *Pyramids.* Penguin, 1989.
8. *Guards! Guards!* Roc, 1991.
9. *Eric.* Roc, 1995.
10. *Moving Pictures.* Gollancz, 1990.
11. *Reaper Man.* Gollancz, 1991.
12. *Witches Abroad.* Acacia Press, 1992.
13. *Small Gods.* HarperCollins, 1992.
14. *Soul Music.* HarperPrism, 1995.
15. *Lords and Ladies.* HarperCollins, 1995.
16. *Men at Arms.* HarperPrism, 1996.
17. *Feet of Clay.* HarperCollins, 1996.
18. *Interesting Times.* HarperPrism, 1997.
19. *Maskerade.* HarperPrism, 1997.
20. *Hogfather.* HarperPrism, 1998.
21. *Jingo.* HarperPrism, 1998.
22. *The Last Continent.* HarperCollins, 1999.
23. *Carpe Jugulum.* HarperCollins, 1999.
24. *The Fifth Elephant.* HarperCollins, 2000.

Discworld is an unusual planet. It is flat and travels through space supported by four enormous elephants who stand on the shell of a swimming tortoise. The planet's inhabitants are as strange as its shape. Rincewind, the magician, is also a travel guide. Granny Weatherwax is a wise and feisty witch. Beings on Discworld must face the grim reaper as they do elsewhere, but on this planet Death goes on vacation and leaves a soft-hearted apprentice in charge.

Genre: Fantasy; Humor
Subjects: Life on other planets; Magic

Pratt, Fletcher. *See* de Camp, L. (Lyon) Sprague

Preuss, Paul

1269. Venus Prime
1. *Breaking Strain.* Avon, 1987.
2. *Maelstrom.* Avon, 1988.
3. *Hide and Seek.* Avon, 1989.
4. *The Medusa Encounter.* Avon, 1990.
5. *Diamond Moon.* Avon, 1990.
6. *Shining Ones.* Avon, 1991.

Sparta, a young woman possessing powers of biotechnology whose source is mysterious to her, journeys throughout the solar system in search of the key to her origin. The series is based on the work of Arthur C. Clarke.

Genre: Science Fiction
Subjects: Women; Bionics; Interplanetary voyages

Price, Charles F.

1270.
1. *Hiwassee.* Academy Chicago, 1996.
2. *Freedom's Altar.* John F. Blair, 1999.

In the remote western mountains of North Carolina in 1863, Judge Madison Curtis and his wife and daughter are trying to keep their farm together as violent renegades from the Union and Confederate armies sweep through the valley, raiding and burning farms. When a group of raiders attack the Curtis family, the judge sets the raiders on neighbors loyal to the Union. After the War, abolitionist and lawman Nahum Bellamy learns of Curtis's betrayal and brings charges against the family. Curtis, who has lost two of his sons in the war, works with his former slaves and his remaining son to save his family and farm.

Genre: Historical Fiction; War

Subjects: United States—Civil War, 1861–1865;
   War; Mountain life
Place/Time: North Carolina—19th century

Price, Eugenia
1271. Florida Trilogy
   1. *Don Juan McQueen.* Lippincott, 1974.
   2. *Maria.* Lippincott, 1977.
   3. *Margaret's Story.* Lippincott, 1980.

The history of Florida is told through the experiences
of three different families who come to settle there. Jon
McQueen flees to Florida after the American Revolution. His wife joins him, and they settle in St. Augustine. Maria Evens comes to St. Augustine with her
husband, a soldier who is posted there. Her skills as a
midwife help them establish themselves in the town.
Margaret Seton helps her husband Lewis set up a plantation on St. John's River in 1830. With their seven
children, they survive the Seminole Wars, the Civil
War, and the settling of the state. For all three women,
love conquers the hardships of pioneer life.

Genre: Gentle Read; Historical Romance
Subjects: Frontier and pioneer life; Cities and towns
Place/Time: Florida—18th century; Florida—19th
   century

1272. Georgia Trilogy
   1. *Bright Captivity.* Doubleday, 1991.
   2. *Where Shadows Go.* Doubleday, 1993.
   3. *Beauty from Ashes.* Doubleday, 1995.

In the 1820s, Anne Couper, the daughter of a wealthy
plantation family on St. Simons Island, Georgia, meets
British Lieutenant John Fraser in London. The two fall
in love and return to St. Simons to live, but John is re-
pulsed by the slavery he sees there. He overcomes his
abhorrence of slavery to start a plantation and to raise a
family. When abolitionist Fanny Kemble comes to
visit in 1839, he and Anne are forced to reconsider
their lifestyle. As the Civil War looms on the horizon,
Anne must face the death of her husband, two daughters, and her mother and the division of her family over
the coming war. Even as more tragedies befall the family, Anne discovers her deep faith and love that help
her and her family survive.

Genre: Historical Romance
Subjects: Plantation life; Abolitionists; Slavery;
   United States—Civil War, 1861–1865
Place/Time: St. Simons Island (Georgia)—19th cen-
   tury; Georgia—19th century

1273. Savannah Quartet
   1. *Savannah.* Doubleday, 1983.
   2. *To See Your Face Again.* Doubleday, 1985.
   3. *Before the Darkness Falls.* Doubleday, 1987.
   4. *Stranger in Savannah.* Doubleday, 1989.

Three antebellum Georgia families, the McKays,
Brownings, and Stiles, live, love, and struggle in Sa-
vannah from 1800 to 1860. Mark Browning comes to
Savannah in the early 1800s and falls in love with Ellen

McKay, the wife of his partner. His daughter Natalie,
after much heartache, finds love on the Georgia frontier, while William Styles goes to Washington as a
Congressman. As the South moves toward secession,
Eliza McKay, the matriarch of the three families, tries
to keep them together as events and love pull them
apart.

Genre: Family Saga; Gentle Read; Historical Romance
Subjects: Plantation life
Place/Time: Savannah (Ga.)—19th century; Georgia—19th century

1274. St. Simons Trilogy
   1. *Lighthouse.* Lippincott, 1971.
   2. *New Moon Rising.* Lippincott, 1969.
   3. *The Beloved Invader.* Lippincott, 1965.

The story of the growth of St. Simons Island is told
through the Gould family who settle on the island in
the early 1800s. New Englander James Gould comes
to the island to forget his lost love. There he finally
marries and raises a family on his cotton plantation.
His son Horace goes to Yale, but is dismissed. Horace
unsure where he belongs, but he returns to work out his
destiny. Later his daughter Ann marries another
Northerner who comes to the island to serve as its minister.

Genre: Family Saga; Gentle Read; Historical Romance
Subjects: Plantation life
Place/Time: St. Simons Island (Georgia)—19th century; Georgia—19th century

Price, Evadne. *See* Smith, Helen Zenna

Price, Reynolds
1275.
   1. *The Surface of Earth.* Atheneum, 1975.
   2. *The Source of Light.* Atheneum, 1981.
   3. *The Promise of Rest.* Scribner, 1995.

In 1903, 16-year-old Eva Kendal elopes with her 32-
year-old Latin teacher, Forest Mayfield. The stories
follow three generations of Mayfields and Kendals as
they search for a sense of self. Eva's daughter separates from her husband Robinson, but he stays close to
their son Hutchins. At 25, Hutchins is teaching at a
Virginia prep school and is engaged. To find himself,
he leaves his job and fiancee to study at Oxford. Wade
Mayfield, the great-grandson of Eva, is dying of AIDS
when he returns to his estranged parents' home in
North Carolina.

Genre: Family Saga
Subjects: Fathers and sons; Family life
Place/Time: Virginia—1900–1945; Virginia—
   1945–1980

1276.
1. *A Long and Happy Life.* Atheneum, 1961.
2. *A Generous Man.* Atheneum, 1966.
3. *Good Hearts.* Atheneum, 1988.

In rural North Carolina, life and love are not always easy or satisfying as two members of the Muslain family painfully discover. Rosacoke, a sensitive young woman, enters into an unhappy affair with a man who abuses her goodness. Meanwhile, her brother Milo stumbles through sex and love. He searches for his brother Rato, whose dog has helped a prize snake escape. Thirty years later, Rosacoke, Milo, and their friends face mid-life crises.

Subjects: Brothers and sisters; Penal life; Love affairs; Middle age
Place/Time: North Carolina—1945–1980

Proust, Marcel

1277. Remembrance of Things Past
1. *Swann's Way.* Holt, 1922, 1913.
2. *Within a Budding Grove.* T. Seltzer, 1924, 1918.
3. *The Guermantes Way.* T. Seltzer, 1925, 1920.
4. *Cities of the Plain.* A. C. Boni, 1927, 1921.
5. *The Captive.* A. C. Boni, 1929, 1923.
6. *The Sweet Cheat Gone.* A. C. Boni, 1930, 1925.
7. *The Past Recaptured.* A. C. Boni, 1932, 1927.

Marcel, the narrator, grows to manhood and on to middle age in the epoch preceding World War I in France. This hypersensitive youth examines the tastes, feelings, motives, and actions of his time and the people he meets. He falls in love with two different women, but his jealousy drives them away. As World War I breaks out, Marcel shows how the war affects his friends and his society. This ground-breaking work describes a man's relationship to himself and to an age in monumental detail.

Subjects: Stream of consciousness; Psychological novels; Society novels; World War I, 1914–1918
Place/Time: France—1900–1945

Prouty, Olive (Higgins)

1278. The Vale Family
1. *White Fawn.* Houghton, 1921.
2. *Lisa Vale.* Houghton, 1938.
3. *Now Voyager.* Houghton, 1941.
4. *Homeport.* Houghton, 1947.
5. *Fabia.* Houghton, 1951.

The blue-blooded members of the Vale family of Boston fall in love—sometimes with the wrong people—and find that their privileged status is not always an advantage after all.

Genre: Romance
Subjects: Family life; Society novels; Wealth

Place/Time: Boston (Mass.)—1900–1945; Massachusetts—1900–1945

Puzo, Mario

1279.
1. *The Godfather.* Putnam, 1969.
2. *The Sicilian.* Simon & Schuster, 1984.

In the world of the Mafia in the 1940s, Don Vito Corleone controls one of the major families. He dominates illegal gambling, but refuses to deal in drugs. Whatever he wants, he gets in whatever way he sees fit. When one of his sons is murdered, he starts a war with the other Mafia families to achieve dominance. His other son, Michael, is sent to Sicily for safety. While there, he helps the Sicilian Robin Hood Salvatore Guillano flee to America.

Genre: Crime Novel
Subjects: Mafia; Gangsters; Crime and criminals; Underworld
Place/Time: New York (N. Y.)—1900–1945; New York (N. Y.)—1945–1980; Sicily (Italy)—1900–1945; Sicily (Italy)—1945–1980; Italy—1900–1945; Italy—1945–1980

Pyeshkoff, Alexei Maximovich. *See* Gorky, Maksim

Quick, Herbert

1280.
1. *Vandemark's Folly.* Grosset, 1922.
2. *The Hawkeye.* Grosset, 1923.
3. *The Invisible Woman.* Bobbs Merrill, 1924.

The history of an Iowa farming community from 1840 to 1900 is traced through the lives of three families. Jacob Vandemark sets out from New York in the 1840s to search for his mother. His quest leads him to Monterey County where he marries and starts farming. Through the years, the Vandemarks, the McConkeys, and the Gowdys face plagues, pests, political machines, and speculators as Iowa and America grow up.

Genre: Historical Fiction
Subjects: Farm life; Country life; Frontier and pioneer life; Family life
Place/Time: Iowa—19th century

Quigley, John

1281.
1. *King's Royal.* Coward, McCann & Geoghegan, 1975.
2. *Queen's Royal.* Coward, McCann & Geoghegan, 1977.

The birth of the Scotch whisky industry inspires this sweeping generational saga of a powerful Scots dynasty, begun by Fergus King. Their son Robert and his headstrong wife Fiona continue to build the business against the background of crumbling Victorian rigidity.

Genre: Family Saga; Historical Fiction
Subjects: Whiskey; Business
Place/Time: Scotland—18th century; Scotland—19th century

Quinn, Julia

1282.
1. *Everything and the Moon.* Avon, 1997.
2. *Brighter than the Sun.* Avon, 1997.

In Kent, England, in 1809 Victoria Lyndon falls in love with Robert Kemble, the Earl of Maccelesfield, but Victoria is only the daughter of a vicar. Both fathers oppose the match, and Victoria goes off to be a governess. Seven years later, Robert meets her again and the two find they are attracted to each other. Only Robert's all out wooing and finally abducting Victoria convince her to marry her love. Victoria's sister Eleanor also finds that the path to marriage is not smooth. When a drunk Charles Wycombe, Earl of Billington, falls out of a tree at her feet, Eleanor is pulled into his scheme to save his inheritance. Charles must marry quickly, and Eleanor agrees to this marriage of convenience. Once married however, the two find they are attracted to each other. One accident after another keep them apart until Eleanor finds a way to win him over.

Genre: Historical Romance
Subjects: Lovers; Sisters; Society Novels
Place/Time: England—19th century

Rabinowitz, Shalom. *See Sholem Aleichem*

Radley, Paul

1283. Boomeroo Trilogy
1. *Jack Rivers and Me.* Ticknor & Fields, 1986, 1981.
2. *My Blue-Checker Corker and Me.* Ticknor & Fields, 1986, 1982.

In Boomeroo, New South Wales, Australia, in the 1950s, two young boys find growing up is hard. Five-year-old Peanut DeLarue has an imaginary friend. His family tries to wean Peanut from his playmate before he goes to school. Twelve-year-old Monte Howard enters his racing pigeon Corkie in a race that puts them both to the ultimate test. The flavor of this small town, with its eccentric characters and their profane language, is captured in these comic novels.

Genre: Coming of Age; Humor
Subjects: Youth; Small town life
Place/Time: New South Wales (Australia)—1945–1980; Australia—1945–1980

Rae, Hugh C. *See Stirling, Jessica*

Ramsey, Russell W.

1284.
1. *A Lady, A Champion.* Tyndale House, 1985.
2. *A Lady, A Healer.* Winston Derek, 1986.
3. *A Lady, A Peacemaker.* Brandon, 1988.

Angela Weber Bryant is born in Sandusky, Ohio, in the early 1900s. Her varied career takes her to the Olympics, to the office of Secretary of Health, Education, and Welfare, and finally to be the first woman President of the United States. Her inspirational life is related by her grandson to a famed Russian doctor who is on a tour of her hometown.

Genre: Christian Fiction; Gentle Read
Subjects: Women; Christian life; Presidents—United States
Place/Time: Ohio—1900–1945; Ohio—1945–1980; Washington (D. C.)—1900–1945; Washington (D. C.)—1945–1980

Randall, Marta

1285. Kennerin Saga
1. *Journey.* Pocket Books, 1978.
2. *Dangerous Games.* Pocket Books, 1980.

The Kennerin family immigrate to the planet Aerie, which they claim as a home for their dynasty and a utopian social order superior to what they have experienced on Earth.

Genre: Science Fiction
Subjects: Interplanetary voyages; Life on other planets; Utopias

Ransom, Bill

1286.
1. *Viravax.* Ace, 1993.
2. *Burn.* Ace, 1993.

With the support of a cult called the Children of Eden, a brilliant scientist, a religious fanatic, and a government official plan to release a deadly virus on the world with the goal of creating a new civilization starting with two cloned children who are immune to the viral infection. Virologist Marte Chang and special agent Rico Toledo are in a position to thwart the plot, which could produce a mass outbreak in Mexico City.

Genre: Science Fiction
Subjects: Viruses, Diseases; Cults

Rawn, Melanie

1287. Dragon Prince
1. *Dragon Prince.* DAW Books, 1988.
2. *The Star Scroll.* DAW Books, 1989.
3. *Sunrunner's Fire.* DAW Books, 1990.

The marriage of Prince Rohan and Sioned, the possessor of the magical sunrunner's gift, seems heaven-sent to bring peace to their troubled land, but strife continues. The discovery of a scroll containing ancient secrets opens the door to knowledge but also to danger that threatens the life of their son.

Genre: Fantasy
Subjects: Imaginary kingdoms; Imaginary wars and battles; Magic; Parents and children

1288. Dragon Star
1. *Stronghold.* DAW Books, 1990.
2. *The Dragon Token.* DAW Books, 1992.
3. *Skybowl.* DAW Books, 1993.

Descendants of Prince Rohan and Sioned continue to defend their land against the villainous and mysterious Vellant'im. Soon the high prince discovers that he must forge an alliance with the renegade Land of Goddess Keep or face destruction.

Genre: Fantasy
Subjects: Imaginary kingdoms; Imaginary wars and battles; Good and evil; Princes

1289. Exiles
1. *The Ruins of Ambrai.* DAW Books, 1994.
2. *The Mageborn Traitor.* DAW Books, 1997.

The world of Lenfell was at one time a refuge for the Mageborn, whose magical powers made them threats to their civilizations, but factions and conflicts have developed within their society. Three sisters, raised apart from each other, each with her own mystical abilities, have the power to restore order to their land—or to tear it apart.

Genre: Fantasy
Subjects: Magic; Sisters; Imaginary kingdoms

Rayner, Claire

1290. The Performer Series
1. *Gower Street.* Simon & Schuster, 1973.
2. *The Haymarket.* Simon & Schuster, 1974.
3. *Paddington Green.* Simon & Schuster, 1975.
4. *Soho Square.* Putnam, 1976.
5. *Bedford Row.* Putnam, 1977.
6. *Covent Garden.* Putnam, 1978.
7. *Charing Cross.* Putnam, 1979.
8. *The Strand.* Putnam, 1981.
9. *Chelsea Reach.* Weidenfeld & Nicholson, 1982.
10. *Shaftesbury Avenue.* Weidenfeld & Nicholson, 1983.
11. *Piccadilly.* Weidenfeld & Nicholson, 1985.
The above three titles have been published only in England.

Two urchins from the London streets grow up together and fall in love, but are swept in different ways: Lilith Lucas to the theater and Abel Lackland to the world of medicine. Their fates and those of their descendants are intertwined from 1800 to 1930. Abel Lackland be-

comes wealthy, and his children and grandchildren run the hospital he founded. However, Abels's son Jonah refuses to go into medicine and enters the theater where he meets Lilith's children. Lilith's descendants stay in the theater, but enter movies in the early 1900s.

Genre: Family Saga; Historical Fiction

Read, Miss. *Pseud. of* Dora Jessie Saint

1291.
1. *The Market Square.* Houghton Mifflin, 1967.
2. *The Howards of Caxley.* Houghton Mifflin, 1968.

Bender North and Sep Howard have been friends since childhood in the little English town of Caxley. Now in 1901, the two men have shops and families. As the years pass, Bender's hardware store declines while Sep's bakery flourishes. The tragedy of World Wars I and II touch them both, but they remain friends, united by their grandson Edward Howard.

Genre: Family Saga; Gentle Read; Historical Fiction
Subjects: Family life; Business; Friendship; Small town life
Place/Time: England—1900–1945

1292. Fairacre Series
1. *Village School.* Houghton Mifflin, 1956.
2. *Village Diary.* Houghton Mifflin, 1957.
3. *Storm in the Village.* Houghton Mifflin, 1959.
The above titles have also been published in the following collection: *Chronicles of Fairacre.* Houghton Mifflin, 1977, 1964.

4. *Miss Claire Remembers.* Houghton Mifflin, 1963.
5. *Over the Gate.* Houghton Mifflin, 1965.
6. *Village Christmas.* Houghton Mifflin, 1966.
7. *The Fairacre Festival.* Houghton Mifflin, 1969.
8. *Emily Davis.* Houghton Mifflin, 1972.
9. *Tyler's Row.* Houghton Mifflin, 1973.
10. *Farther Afield.* Houghton Mifflin, 1975.
11. *No Holly for Miss Quinn.* Houghton Mifflin, 1976.
12. *Village Affairs.* Houghton Mifflin, 1978.
13. *The White Robin.* Houghton Mifflin, 1980.
14. *Village Centenary.* Houghton Mifflin, 1981.
15. *Summer at Fairacre.* Houghton Mifflin, 1985.
16. *Mrs. Pringle.* Houghton Mifflin, 1990.
17. *Changes at Fairacre.* Houghton Mifflin, 1992.
18. *Fairwell to Fairacre.* Houghton Mifflin, 1994.

English village life comes alive at the school and in the small town called Fairacre in this delightful series of novels. The stories revolve around Miss Read, the village schoolteacher, and her relations with the people in

Fairacre. The various townspeople keep reappearing in the novels as they become friends to the reader. The series reaffirms the importance of kindness and love in personal relations.

Genre: Gentle Read
Subjects: Small town life; Teachers; School life
Place/Time: England—1900–1945; England—1945–1980

1293. Thrush Green Series
1. *Thrush Green.* Houghton Mifflin, 1959.
2. *Winter in Thrush Green.* Houghton Mifflin, 1961.
3. *News from Thrush Green.* Houghton Mifflin, 1971.
4. *Battles at Thrush Green.* Houghton Mifflin, 1976.
5. *Return to Thrush Green.* Houghton Mifflin, 1979.
6. *Gossip from Thrush Green.* Houghton Mifflin, 1982.
7. *Affairs at Thrush Green.* Houghton Mifflin, 1984.
8. *At Home in Thrush Green.* Houghton Mifflin, 1986.
9. *The School at Thrush Green.* Houghton Mifflin, 1988.
10. *Friends at Thrush Green.* Houghton Mifflin, 1991.
11. *Celebrations at Thrush Green.* Houghton Mifflin, 1993.
12. *The World of Thrush Green.* (Includes excerpts from the series.) Houghton Mifflin, 1989.
13. *The Year at Thrush Green.* Houghton Mifflin, 1996.

Thrush Green is a close-knit English community where families have known one another since childhood. Miss Watson and Miss Fogerty teach at the village school. Dr. Lovell, minister Henstock, and all the other townspeople interact and live out their lives. The stories build on each other as they wisely probe the human panorama.

Genre: Gentle Read
Subjects: Small town life; Teachers; Friendship
Place/Time: England—1900–1945; England—1945–1980

Redon, Joel

1294.
1. *If Not on Earth, Then in Heaven.* St. Martin's, 1991.
2. *The Road to Zena.* St. Martin's, 1992.

Rural Oregon at the turn of the century is the setting for stories about Redon's ancestors and the social upheavals they lived through. Motherless Neoma Matthews leaves Zena to start a new life in Portland, Oregon, where she meets Birdie and Alan. All of their lives are changed as they search for love. Meanwhile, the Zena

schoolteacher Mae Matthews falls in love with Vivian Cochran who must decide if he will go to college. Eventually the two decide to marry and live in Zena, while Mae's grandparents see the decline of the town and move to Portland.

Genre: Historical Fiction
Subjects: Love; Country life
Place/Time: Oregon—1900–1945

Reed, Ishmael

1295.
1. *The Terrible Twos.* St. Martin's, 1982.
2. *The Terrible Threes.* Atheneum, 1989.

These outrageous novels satirize America in the 1980s and 1990s. St. Nicholas is offended when a businessman tries to buy the rights to Christmas. Then he teams up with a medieval partner to wreck havoc on Wall Street. In the late 1990s, figurehead president Jesse Hatch is manipulated by his advisor, televangelist Clement Jones. The stories are nonstop jabs at American customs, values, politics, business, culture, and—most important—racism, which make the reader laugh, cry, and question life today.

Reeman, Douglas. *See also* Kent, Alexander

1296.
1. *Badge of Glory.* Morrow, 1984, 1982.
2. *The First to Land.* Morrow, 1984.

In 1850, Captain Philip Blackwood and the Royal Marines set sail for West Africa. There they are to stop illegal slave ships, but Blackwood discovers that there is more to leading men than having rank. He must also deal with the change in the navy as it switches to coal ships, and numerous officers resist the change. When the Crimean War breaks out, Blackwood is sent there and becomes a hero. Later his nephew is sent to China where he must fight the Boxers and protect the Europeans, especially a German countess who falls in love with him.

Genre: Historical Fiction; Naval Adventure; War
Subjects: Politics—United States; Prejudices; Race relations
Place/Time: United States—1980–; New York (N. Y.)—1980–; Washington (D. C.)—1980–

Reichert, Mickey Zucker

1297. Bifrost Guardians
1. *Godslayer.* DAW Books, 1987.
2. *Shadow Climber.* DAW Books, 1988.
3. *Dragonrank Master.* DAW Books, 1990.

When Al Larson dies in Vietnam, his final cries are heard by the Norse gods who transfer his life force into the elf Allerum in the beyond. Sometimes unwillingly, Al becomes part of a battle of the gods, falls in love, and is captured by the mighty, but insane, Dragonmage Bolverkr. In the final confrontation, he is transported back to New York City of 1968 and to the possibility of going to Vietnam again.

Genre: Fantasy
Subjects: Gods and goddesses; Soldiers; Vietnamese War, 1961–1975; Imaginary wars and battles

1298. Renshai Chronicles
1. *Beyond Ragnarok.* DAW Books, 1995.
2. *Prince of Demons.* DAW Books, 1996.
3. *Children of Wrath.* DAW Books, 1998.

Three centuries after Ragnarok, the cosmic battle that shattered the power of the god Odin, a dark elf has interfered with the succession to the crown in the land of Bearn and sterility has afflicted the population. If the magical talisman the Pica Stone can be restored, all may be well, but the quest for the stone is complicated by the return of the god Odin to wage war on Colbey.

Genre: Fantasy
Subjects: Imaginary kingdoms; Imaginary wars and battles; Charms

1299. Renshai Trilogy
1. *The Last of the Renshai.* DAW Books, 1992.
2. *The Western Wizard.* DAW Books, 1992.
3. *Child of Thunder.* DAW Books, 1993.

In the North land, the sole survivor of an attack on a tribe of warriors called the Renshai joins with four powerful wizards to prevent the prophesied cosmic Great War called Ragnarok. When one of the wizards dies, chaos threatens, and it is left to Colbey, son of the god Thor, to restore balance and order. The tales continue in *The Renshai Chronicles*.

Genre: Fantasy
Subjects: Imaginary wars and battles; Magicians

Reid Banks, Lynne

1300.
1. *The L-Shaped Room.* Simon & Schuster, 1960.
2. *The Backward Shadow.* Simon & Schuster, 1970.
3. *Two Is Lonely.* Simon & Schuster, 1974.

L is for loneliness. L is for love. L is also the shape of the dreary room in London where Jane begins her life as an unwed mother. With honesty, humor, and insight, which will ultimately lead her to love, she decides to have her baby.

Subjects: Unmarried mothers; Infants; Loneliness
Place/Time: London (England)—1945–1980; England—1945–1980

Reid, Van

1301.
1. *Cordelia Underwood: or The Marvelous Beginnings of the Moosepath League.* Viking, 1998.
2. *Mollie Peer: Or The Underground Adventure of the Moosepath League.* Viking, 1999.

The wacky characters of Portland, Maine, at the turn of the century seem to get themselves into the craziest adventures. Pretty Cordelia Underwood inherits her uncle's land in northern Maine, which may have Captain Kidd's buried treasure on it. John Benning tries to steal it from her, while Tobias Walton saves the day and helps found the Moosepath League. Later Tobias and his friends rescue a young boy from the clutches of Eustace Pemberton. Then they have to expose a seance. Along the way the characters have strange and crazy adventures.

Genre: Gentle Read; Humor
Subjects: Small town life
Place/Time: Maine—19th century

Remarque, Erich Maria

1302.
1. *All Quiet on the Western Front.* Little, Brown, 1929.
2. *The Road Back.* Little, Brown, 1931.

In one of the most powerful indictments of war ever written, Paul, along with three other German youths, is pulled out of school and sent to the front in World War I. Though Paul survives the horrors of war, he is repelled by the slaughter. After the war, he returns home to a society torn by rioting and corruption. This is a profoundly moving tale whose message is universal.

Genre: War
Subjects: Soldiers; World War I, 1914–1918
Place/Time: Europe—1900–1945

Renault, Mary

1303.
1. *Fire from Heaven.* Pantheon, 1969.
2. *The Persian Boy.* Pantheon, 1972.
3. *Funeral Games.* Pantheon, 1981.

The life of Alexander the Great from childhood through his death is retold with drama and spirit. As a youth in Macedonia, he is influenced by his teacher Aristotle and by the insidious plotting of his mother and father. After his father's death, he begins his conquest of Asia, and later dies in Babylon as his family struggles over his empire.

Genre: Historical Fiction
Subjects: Alexander the Great, 356–323 B.C.; Kings and rulers; Courts and courtiers
Place/Time: Greece—4th century B.C.

1304.
1. *The King Must Die.* Pantheon, 1958.
2. *The Bull from the Sea.* Pantheon, 1962.

The legend of Theseus, king of ancient Athens, is retold by the hero. He describes his battles with the sons of Pallas, his conquest of the minotaur, and his love for the warrior princess Hippolyta. Tragedy, however, follows his family in these retellings of classical myth.

Genre: Fantasy
Subjects: Legends and folk tales; Theseus (Greek mythology); Kings and rulers; Imaginary wars and battles; Love

Resnick, Michael D.

1305. Chronicles of a Distant World
1. *Paradise.* Tom Doherty, 1989.
2. *Purgatory.* Tor, 1993.
3. *Inferno.* Tor, 1993.

In these cautionary tales set in the far future, misguided and sometimes well-meant efforts in the colonization of planets result in violence and environment problems. A young journalist is drawn to the planet Peponi, a serene paradise with an indigenous population determined to guard the world and its secret. The leader of the reptilian inhabitants of Kariman enters into a complex plot with the enemies of humans bent on colonizing his planet. On Faligar the planetary government seems to thrive on interaction with humans, but the complex culture collapses into a society more barbaric and primitive than that found by the first human colonists.

Genre: Science Fiction
Subjects: Life on other planets; Space colonies; Outer space, exploration of

1306. The Widowmaker Trilogy
1. *The Widowmaker.* Bantam, 1996.
2. *The Widowmaker Reborn.* Bantam, 1997.
3. *The Widowmaker Unleashed.* Bantam, 1998.

Jefferson Nighthawk, a bounty hunter whose reputation has spread throughout the galaxy, has contracted a terrible disease and has had himself frozen in the hope that the future will produce a cure. During his frigid sleep, he is cloned illegally twice with varying degrees of success. Finally he is revived, but must face the ravages of age and his disease, as well as vengeful opponents that he and his clones have accumulated.

Genre: Science Fiction
Subjects: Cryonics; Diseases; Revenge

Reynolds, Mack

1307. Julian West
1. *Looking Backward from the Year 2000.* Ace, 1973.
2. *Equality: In the Year 2000.* Ace, 1977.

Reynolds takes the liberty of updating Edward Bellamy's *Looking Backward, 2000–1887.* Reynold's hero Julian West, like Bellamy's of the same name, awakens in the year 2000 after spending over 100 years in a state of suspended animation. He finds a confusing world where technological advance is so rapid that continuing education is a fact of life, not only for the intellectually curious, but for everyone.

Genre: Science Fiction
Subjects: Technology and civilization; Education; Progress

Riasanovsky, Antoninia

1308.
1. *The Family.* Little, 1940.
2. *The Children.* Little, 1942.

Granny, mother, and three children are Russian refugees making a precarious living running boarding houses in Tientsin and Harbin, China, during the Japanese invasion of 1937. Mother works in a hospital while Lida studies opera. Lida falls in love with American Jimmy and ultimately gets to America to be with him.

Genre: Romance
Subjects: Refugees, Russian; Boarding houses; Family life
Place/Time: China—1900–1945; United States— 1900–1945

Ricci, Nina

1309.
1. *The Book of Saints.* Knopf, 1991.
2. *In a Glass House.* St. Martin's, 1995.
3. *Where She Has Gone.* St. Martin's, 1998.

In the little Italian village of Valle de Sol, Vittorio Innocenti is seven years old when his world collapses; his mother has an affair with a stranger, and his father leaves the village in disgrace. His mother and Vittorio leave the village and sail to Canada to join his father, but his mother dies aboard ship giving birth to his half sister Rita. His father resents the illegitimate girl and puts her in a foster home. Vittorio tries to be close with his father, who rejects him. Vittorio grows up and goes to Africa to teach. After his father's suicide, he comes back to Canada and tries to get to know his sister. When she goes to Europe with an older man, Vittorio goes to Italy to meet his relatives and to face the ghost of past events.

Subjects: Fathers and sons; Family life; Brothers and sisters
Place/Time: Italy—1945–1980; Canada—1945– 1980

Rice, Anne

1310. New Tales of the Vampire
1. *Pandora.* Knopf, 1998.
2. *Vittorio, the Vampire.* Knopf, 1999.

The character of David Talbot, the fledgling vampire created by Lestat in *The Tale of the Body Thief*, connects these stories. Talbot becomes a collector of the life stories of the undead: first Pandora, who was brought into eternal life by the ancient vampire Marius in Imperial Rome, then Vittorio, whose love for the beautiful vampire Ursula leads him into a tortured internal battle between his vampiric nature and his better instincts.

Genre: Horror
Subjects: Vampires

1311. The Vampire Chronicles
1. *Interview with the Vampire: A Novel.* Knopf, 1976.
2. *The Vampire Lestat.* Knopf, 1985.
3. *The Queen of the Damned.* Knopf, 1988.
4. *The Tale of the Body Thief.* Knopf, 1992.
5. *Memnoch the Devil.* Knopf, 1995.
6. *The Vampire Armand.* Knopf, 1998.

With settings ranging from ancient Egypt to modern America, The Vampire Chronicles relate the exploits of the Vampire Lestat and his supporting cast of fascinating undead, including the ancient but eternally boyish Armand. Lestat spends his brief mortal existence as a handsome impoverished nobleman in 18th-century France; emerges in his vampire state as a charismatic American rock star; and has an intense, violent union with the beautiful Egyptian Queen Akasha, the first vampire of all. He briefly experiences mortal existence again and grapples with ultimate questions as he encounters Satan and God in his journey from Purgatory to Heaven. Told in vivid, sensual language, first by Lestat's companion Louis and then by Lestat himself, the tales so thoroughly assume the vampires' viewpoint that the taking of human life seems all in a night's work.

Genre: Horror
Subjects: Vampires; Aristocracy—France; Rock music; Good and evil; Egypt—kings and rulers
Place/Time: France—multicentury span; Egypt—multicentury span; New Orleans (La.)—multicentury span; Louisiana—multicentury span; Miami (Fla.)— multicentury span; Florida—multicentury span

Richardson, Bill

1312.
1. *Bachelor Brothers' Bed & Breakfast.* St. Martin's, 1996.
2. *Bachelor Brothers' Bed & Breakfast Pillow Book.* St. Martin's, 1997.

Fraternal twins Hector and Virgil run a bed and breakfast on an island off the coast of British Columbia. The two eccentric brothers have a hefty library, a cat, a parrot, and a group of wildly funny guests who visit the house. The guests tell their stories in the guest book, and these are interspersed between the brothers' stories of everyday life, household hints, and lists of favorite things. For Hector and Virgil, life at the bed and breakfast is never mundane.

Genre: Humor
Subjects: Brothers; Hotels, taverns, etc.
Place/Time: Canada—1980–

Richardson, Ethel. *See* Richardson, Henry Handel

Richardson, Henry Handel. *Pseud. of* Ethel Richardson

1313.
1. *Australia Felix.* Norton, 1930, 1917.
2. *The Way Home.* Norton, 1930, 1925.
3. *The Ultimate Thule.* Norton, 1929.

In the 1850s, Richard Mahony leaves Ireland to go to Australia to make his fortune. He marries Mary Turnham, then starts to practice medicine. Even though he develops a very successful practice, he is restless and goes back to England, but is disillusioned there too. He returns to Australia when he finds a mining venture has made him rich. Richard then takes his wife and children to Europe. While there his financial empire crashes, and he must try to rebuild. When he cannot do that, he dies, and Mary must struggle to raise the children.

Genre: Historical Fiction
Subjects: Family life; Physicians; Wealth
Place/Time: England—19th century; Australia—19th century

Richter, Conrad

1314.
1. *The Light in the Forest.* Knopf, 1953.
2. *A Country of Strangers.* Knopf, 1966.

In the 1700s, two white children who were kidnapped and raised by Indians are forced to go back to their white families after a truce agreement is signed. Because John Butler can only remember his life as an Indian, he flees his white family, but his Indian family refuses to accept him when he returns to them. Stone Girl, who was Mary Stanton before she was captured, is married to an Indian with whom she has a son. When she is returned to her father, he rejects her and so she returns to her tribe.

Genre: Historical Fiction
Subjects: Teenagers; Native Americans—captivities; United States—to 1776
Place/Time: Pennsylvania—19th century

1315. The Awakening Land Series
1. *The Trees.* Knopf, 1940.
2. *The Fields.* Knopf, 1946.
3. *The Town.* Knopf, 1950.

The saga of Sayward Luckett, from her childhood to her death, recounts her battle with the Ohio wilderness of the early 19th century. As a young girl, she fights the isolation and privation of the wilderness. After her marriage, she is instrumental in bringing a church and a school to the settlement. As the settlement becomes a town, Sayward and her family move from their cabin to a large house in town, and she watches her children move to their own homes.

Genre: Historical Fiction
Subjects: Women; Frontier and pioneer life; Small town life; Family life
Place/Time: Ohio—19th century

Riefe, Barbara
1316.
1. *The Woman Who Fell from the Sky.* Tor, 1994.
2. *For the Love of Two Eagles.* Forge, 1995.
3. *Mohawk Woman.* Forge, 1996.

In the 1750s, Margaret Addison is on her way to Quebec to join her husband by proxy when the ship she is on becomes grounded. The Mohawks attack the ship and kill everyone but Margaret, who escapes into the forest. There she meets Two Eagles, the chief of the Oneidas, and travels with him into Indian country. As she stays with Two Eagles, she falls in love with him, but she must return to Quebec. She discovers that her proxy marriage was a hoax, so she returns to Two Eagles and marries him. She is living happily with Two Eagles and their child when Seth Wilson comes to the village looking for her. Seth has been hired by her father to bring her back to England. When Two Eagles goes after Blue Creek who tried to kidnap Margaret's child, Seth almost convinces Margaret to return to England, but ultimately she stays with her husband. As Margaret lives with the Oneidas, she helps Singing Brook and Sky Toucher defy the tribe's traditions and marry for love.

Genre: Historical Romance
Subjects: Lovers; Native Americans; Oneidas; Husbands and wives
Place/Time: New England—18th century

Rikhoff, Jean
1317.
1. *Butte's Landing.* Dial, 1973.
2. *One of the Raymonds.* Dial, 1974.
3. *The Sweetwater.* Dial, 1976.

Pioneer life in the Adirondacks in the 19th century follows the Butte and Raymond families. The story tells of the difficult father-son relationship and Mason's struggle to find his own manhood as he faces the wilderness. In the 1870s, Mason and his cousin John journey to the Black Hills to find gold and are befriended by Pepper Tom, an African American cowboy who teaches them the ways of the Indians.

Genre: Historical Fiction; Western
Subjects: Frontier and pioneer life; Fathers and sons; Gold mines and mining
Place/Time: New York (state)—19th century; South Dakota—19th century

Riley, Judith Merkle
1318.
1. *A Vision of Light.* Delacorte, 1989.
2. *In Pursuit of the Green Lion.* Delacorte, 1990.

In the 14th century, spunky Margaret of Ashbury relates her life story to Brother Gregory. Margaret's story begins at 14 when she is married to a brutal merchant. When he leaves her for dead during a plague epidemic, Margaret survives and becomes an apprentice to herbalist Mother Hilde. Margaret uses her healing gifts and midwifery skills to help poor women. When she remarries, Margaret's skills save her husband from the Count of St. Medard. Margaret's picaresque adventures take her through all aspects of English society as she challenges the male hierarchy of her time.

Genre: Historical Fiction
Subjects: Women; Midwives; Picaresque novels; Social classes
Place/Time: England—14th century

Rios, Julian
1319.
1. *Larva: Midsummer Night's Babel.* Dalkey Archive, 1990.
2. *Poundemonium.* Dalkey Archive, 1997.

In these experimental novels, the shade of Don Juan and Sleeping Beauty create the poet Milalias and his girlfriend Babette. Then the four perform in a series of plays using wordplay and numerous languages. Later these same four characters go to London and visit the sites associated with Ezra Pound. Then they receive word of Pound's death. The books comment on Pound while again playing with words just as Pound did.

Subjects: Experimental stories
Place/Time: London (England)—1945–1980

Ripley, Alexandra
1320.
1. *Charleston.* Doubleday, 1981.
2. *On Leaving Charleston.* Doubleday, 1984.

In 1863, Elizabeth Tradd is being introduced to Charleston society, even though the Civil War is ravaging the South. Life on the plantation and in the city shows the intertwined lives of Charleston's old families. When Elizabeth marries, she must take over the family business and is forced to give up the man she loves. In 1900, her son Stuart Tradd marries Margaret Garden, and their daughter Garden turns her back on the family and goes to France. Only in the 1920s is she forced to return to face her family and her love.

Genre: Family Saga; Historical Romance
Subjects: United States—Civil War, 1861–1865; Plantation life; Cities and towns
Place/Time: Charleston (S. C.)—19th century; Charleston (S. C.)—1900–1945; South Carolina—19th century; South Carolina—1900–1945

Ritchie, James A.

1321.
1. *The Last Free Range.* Walker, 1995.
2. *The Wagon Wars.* Walker, 1997.

In the late fall of 1886, three cowboys, Ben Hawkins, Billy Martin, and Johnny Stevens try to find winter work. Young Johnny signs on with the Rocking M Ranch and its free range owner Neal Pierce. Billy joins the Reverse Box E Ranch and its owner widow Beth Alison. When henchmen attack the ranch and Billy, he is forced into a gun battle and is wounded in the leg. Old friend Ben joins the Box E to help the little ranch fight against Pierce and his takeover tactics. Later the three friends go back to Arizona where they hope to buy a horse ranch. To earn money for the ranch, they start a wagon-freight business, but this puts them in competition with P. G. Murphy and his freight business. Ben, Billy, and Johnny must fight Murphy, Apaches, and outlaws to save their business and their lives.

Genre: Western; Historical Fiction
Subjects: Cowboys; Ranch life
Place/Time: Western states—19th century; Arizona—19th century

Rivers, Francine

1322. Mark of the Lion Series
1. *A Voice in the Wind.* Tyndale House, 1993.
2. *An Echo in the Darkness.* Tyndale House, 1994.
3. *As Sure As the Dawn.* Tyndale House, 1995.

In Rome of 70 A. D., the slave girl Hadassah has come to believe in the new Christian faith. She would like to declare her faith, but fears persecution or even death. Her beliefs are uncovered by her owner, and Hadassah is injured and barely escapes death. She needs all of her faith to forgive her mistress and save her from death. Atretes, a German barbarian, discovers Christianity when he meets a young Christian woman. Her faith makes him realize his love for his son, and he vows to find him. When he does, he must take the child from Rizpah, a Christian widow who has raised the boy.

Atretes and Rizpah find their faith brings them together, and they find love.

Genre: Christian Fiction; Historical Fiction
Subjects: Faith; Slavery
Place/Time: Rome (Italy)—1st century A. D.

Rizzi, Timothy

1323.
1. *Strike of the Cobra.* Donald I. Fine, 1993.
2. *The Phalanx Dragon.* Donald I. Fine, 1994.
3. *Eagles of Fire.* Donald I. Fine, 1996.

Major General "Duke" James heads the Cobra Special Operations Deployment Team, an elite squadron that is dispatched to hot spots around the world. The team is sent to the Libyan desert to retrieve the space shuttle when it is forced to land at a terrorist base. The Cobra team fights terrorists to save the shuttle crew and their cargo of recovered Russian nuclear warheads. The Cobra team then goes to Iran to destroy secret Iranian facilities when the Iranians capture an American cruise missile and duplicate it. The forces must destroy the base and save an American agent. Later James is sent to Korea to secretly negotiate the reunification of the country with a general from North Korea. The United States government is working on their own deal, and James and the Korean general must flee and try to prevent a war breaking out.

Genre: Technothriller
Subjects: Adventure; Army, United States; Arms and armor; International intrigue
Place/Time: Middle East—1980–; Korea—1980–

Robbins, Harold. *Pseud. of* Harold Rubin

1324.
1. *The Dream Merchants.* Knopf, 1949.
2. *The Carpetbaggers.* Simon & Schuster, 1961.
3. *The Inheritors.* Trident, 1970.
4. *The Raiders.* Simon & Schuster, 1995.

Called the Hollywood Trilogy, the first books in this series are joined by their setting in the entertainment industry rather than by plot or character. The trilogy starts with the early days of motion pictures, continues with the life and loves of Jonas Cord, a character who strongly resembles the young Howard Hughes, and ends with the successful, but emotionally bankrupt life of television producer Stephen Gaunt. The most recent addition to the series narrates the difficult relationship Jonas Cord has with his son.

Subjects: Motion pictures; Capitalists and financiers; Television; Fathers and sons
Place/Time: Hollywood (Calif.)—1945–1980; California—1945–1980

Roberson, Jennifer

1325.

1. *Lady of the Forest.* Kensington, 1993.
2. *Lady of Sherwood.* Kensington, 1999.

The legend of Robin Hood and his love Lady Marian is retold in this romantic story that goes back to the time before Robin became an outlaw. When Marian of Ravenskeep's father is killed in the Crusades, she seeks out the Earl of Huntington's son, Robert, who has just returned from the Crusades. The war weary Robert falls in love with Marian, but the two find that no one wants them to marry. Robert's father wants him to wed Prince John's daughter while the Sheriff of Nottingham wants to wed Marian. The two lovers ultimately hide in Sherwood Forest with a motley crew of supporters. When King Richard dies, his pardons for Robert and his men are worthless. Robert must fight a ruthless Prince John and a determined sheriff to keep Marian and his men safe.

Genre: Historical Fiction; Historical Romance
Subjects: Legends and folk tales; Lovers; Outlaws
Place/Time: England—12th century

Roberts, Ann Victoria

1326.

1. *Louisa Elliott.* Contemporary Books, 1989.
2. *Morning's Gate.* Morrow, 1991.

Louisa Elliott is a courageous young woman in Victorian England who must fight the constraints of her society. First she struggles to overcome the stain of illegitimacy. She is drawn into a romantic triangle with her suitor Robert Duncan and her cousin Edward Elliott, which forces her to choose between respectability and passion. Her great-great granddaughter Zoe comes to England in the 1980s and meets her cousin Stephen Elliott. The two dig through family records to uncover the secrets of their family. Flashbacks to World War I tell the story of Louisa's children and their forbidden romance. Zoe and Stephen find their romance parallels that of their ancestors.

Genre: Family Saga; Historical Romance
Subjects: Family life
Place/Time: England—19th century

Roberts, Kenneth

1327.

1. *Arundel.* Doubleday, 1930.
2. *Rabble in Arms.* Doubleday, 1933.
3. *The Lively Lady.* Doubleday, 1931.
4. *Captain Caution.* Doubleday, 1934.

During the Revolutionary War, Steven Nason and his friend Benedict Arnold leave Arundel in the province of Maine for an expedition to Quebec. Later Steven and a group of men from Arundel fight with the Revolutionary forces at the Battle of Saratoga. During the War of 1812, Steven's son Richard is captain of a ship fighting the British. Richard and his fellow men from Arundel try to save their town and ships from the British.

Genre: Historical Fiction; War
Subjects: United States—revolution, 1775–1783;
    United States—War of 1812; War; Naval battles
Place/Time: Maine—18th century; Maine—19th century

Roberts, Nora

1328. Irish Trilogy

1. *Born in Fire.* Jove, 1994.
2. *Born in Ice.* Jove, 1995.
3. *Born in Shame.* Jove, 1996.

A packet of old love letters brings two sisters and their half sister together in Ireland. Margaret Concannon is sent to Venice by her father to learn glass blowing, but his untimely death forces her back to Ireland. When an art gallery owner helps her to find success as a glass sculptress, Margaret devotes herself to her art. Love however changes her commitment. Sister Brianna has stayed home in County Clare taking care of her mother and running Blackthorn Cottage, a bed and breakfast. She is content to run the house until mystery writer Gray Thane comes to the house, and the two become lovers. Brianna then uncovers a set of old love letters from an unknown woman to her father. Shannon Bodine, their American born half sister, comes to Ireland to meet her sisters, and she finds herself drawn to them and to the man of her dreams, whom she meets in Ireland.

Genre: Romance
Subjects: Sisters; Love
Place/Time: Ireland—1980–

1329. Quinn Brothers Trilogy

1. *Sea Swept.* Jove, 1998.
2. *Rising Tides.* Jove, 1998.
3. *Inner Harbor.* Jove, 1998.

The three Quinn brothers—Cameron, Ethan, and Phillip—were abused as young boys before they were adopted by Ray and Stella Quinn. When Ray is seriously injured in a car accident, Cameron comes home and promises his dying father he will look after young Seth whom Ray was going to adopt. As Cameron gets to know Seth, he also meets Seth's social worker, Anna Spinelli, and a romance begins. After Anna and Cameron marry, they help Grace Monroe, their housekeeper, attract the middle Quinn brother Ethan. Ethan has always been the quiet stay-at-home brother who is afraid of love. Youngest son Phillip divides his time between his job in advertising and his hobby of boatbuilding. When Dr. Sybil Griffin and 10-year-old Seth come to town, Phillip is drawn to them because Seth is his adopted brother. Sybil and Phillip are also drawn to each other, but Phillip must overcome his abusive childhood before he can find love. All the brothers learn the healing power of love.

Genre: Romance

Subjects: Brothers; Lovers
Place/Time: Maryland—1980–

Robertson, Don

1330.
1. *The Greatest Thing Since Sliced Bread.* Putnam, 1965.
2. *The Sum and Total of Now.* Putnam, 1966.
3. *The Greatest Thing That Almost Happened.* Putnam, 1970.

From age nine to high school, Morris Bird III observes his family—their reactions to death, property, and themselves. He learns the meaning of gallantry and grace when he becomes the hero of the East Ohio Gas Company explosion in October 1944. As he grows up, he sees his grandmother die and helps the family stop fighting over her possessions, but when he turns 17, he is struck with leukemia and must come to terms with his own death.

Genre: Coming of Age
Subjects: Boys; Family life; Bereavement; Death; Leukemia
Place/Time: Ohio—1900–1945; Ohio—1945–1980

Robin, Maxwell

1331.
1. *The Secret Diary of Anne Boleyn.* Arcade, 1997.
2. *The Queen's Bastard.* Little, Brown, 1999.

When Queen Elizabeth I is newly crowned, an old woman gives her the diary of her dead mother, Anne Boleyn. As she juggles her new duties and her love life, she learns that her mother was not a traitor. She learns of her mother's courtship and marriage to the lusty Henry VIII. She also learns not to trust men. So, when Elizabeth gives birth to a boy, the son of the Earl of Leicester, the child is spirited away. Arthur is raised in the country and eventually becomes a soldier in Elizabeth's army where he endures the hardship of the brutal wars with Spain.

Genre: Historical Fiction
Subjects: Queens; Courts and courtiers; Soldiers; Elizabeth I, Queen of England, 1533–1603; Illegitimacy
Place/Time: England—16th century

Robinson, Jeanne. *See Robinson, Spider*

Robinson, Kim Stanley

1332.
1. *Red Mars.* Bantam, 1993.
2. *Green Mars.* Bantam, 1994.
3. *Blue Mars.* Bantam, 1996.
4. *The Martians.* Bantam, 1999.

A scientific expedition whose goal is to terraform Mars falls apart violently in a split between idealists and representatives of Earth's international corporations, who wish to use the resources of Mars for their own purposes. Told from several viewpoints, the second story takes place late in the 21st century when the idealists have either gone to a hidden sanctuary or made homes for themselves on the fringes of what has proved to be a dominant corporate culture. Along the way, the scientists have discovered how to achieve near immortality. The concluding work of this trilogy chronicles the transformation of Mars into a world of oceans whose existence is threatened by an oncoming ice age. The colonists and their descendants continue to have social and political conflicts as Earth endures environmental problems and population pressure. A collection of stories and poems supplements the trilogy.

Genre: Science Fiction
Subjects: Life on other planets; Mars (planet), exploration of; Environment; Business; Immortality

1333. Orange County Trilogy
1. *The Wild Shore.* Ace, 1984.
2. *The Gold Coast.* St. Martin's, 1988.
3. *Pacific Edge.* Tor, 1990.

What will the 21st century bring? This series offers three alternate futures all set in Orange County, California. The main character of the first book is a young man maturing in a simplified society recovering from a nuclear holocaust. In the second book, an overpopulated culture is dominated by drugs and economic exploitation. The more optimistic view in the third book is of a utopian communal society rising from the ashes of 20th-century problems.

Genre: Science Fiction
Subjects: Nuclear warfare; Population; Social problems; Utopias
Place/Time: California—1980–

Robinson, Spider

1334. Callahan
1. *Callahan's Crosstime Saloon.* Ace, 1977.
2. *Time Travelers Strictly Cash.* Ace, 1981.
3. *Callahan's Secret.* Ace, 1986.

The above titles have also been published in the following collections: Callahan and Company, Phantasia Press, 1987, and The Callahan Chronicals, Tor, 1997.

4. *Callahan's Lady.* Ace, 1989.
5. *Lady Slings the Booze.* Ace, 1992.
6. *The Callahan Touch.* Ace, 1993.
7. *Off the Wall at Callahan's.* Tor, 1994.
8. *Callahan's Legacy.* Tor, 1998.

Mike Callahan's saloon offers its eccentric regulars a chance for redemption from the difficulties of everyday life through travel into another reality, but it eventually meets destruction in a thermonuclear disaster. The scene shifts to Lady Sally's, an establishment run by Mike's wife and dedicated to realizing any and every erotic fantasy possible. Mary's Place, operated by narrator Jake Stonebender, attracts Mike's deprived and depraved clientele with a combination of fairyland magic and a mysteriously generous computer.

Genre: Fantasy; Science Fiction
Subjects: Hotels, taverns, etc.; Space and time; Sex; Magic; Computers

Robinson, Spider *and* Robinson, Jeanne

1335. Stardance
1. *Stardance.* Dial Press, 1979.
2. *Starseed.* Ace, 1991.
3. *Starmind.* Ace, 1995.

Zero gravity dance, a new form of expression developed on a space station, enables Shara to communicate with aliens and enter a higher form of existence. Finding that her body will no longer allow her to dance on Earth, Rain McLeod takes off for outer space to join in the Stardance. Back on Earth, composer Rand Porter uncovers a plot to destroy the Starmind, the alien force behind the Stardance, which has brought peace and increasing creativity to Earth.

Genre: Science Fiction
Subjects: Dancers; Interplanetary voyages; Extraterrestrial beings

Rochlin, Harriet

1336. Desert Dwellers Trilogy
1. *The Reformer's Apprentice.* Fithian, 1996.
2. *The First Lady of Dos Cacahuates.* Fithian, 1998.

In San Francisco in 1870, Frieda Levie dreams of becoming a school teacher and working with immigrant children, but her strict Orthodox Jewish parents have other plans for her. When her father's business goes bankrupt, Frieda must go to work at her Aunt's kosher boarding house to help the family. When her parents arrange a marriage for Frieda, she rejects their choice and runs off with Bennie Goldson, an Arizona rancher. Frieda moves to Dos Cacahuates with Bennie where she sets up a hotel and restaurant. A flash flood destroys their home and ranch, but feisty Frieda fights to keep her marriage together.

Genre: Historical Romance; Historical Fiction
Subjects: Love; Marriage; Jews—United States; Judaism; Frontier and pioneer life
Place/Time: San Francisco (Calif.)—19th century; Arizona—19th century

Rock, Phillip

1337.
1. *The Passing Bells.* Seaview, 1979.
2. *Circles of Time.* Seaview, 1981.

3. *A Future Arrived.* Seaview, 1985.

On the estate of Anthony Greville, ninth earl of Stanmore, the Greville family has to deal with the enormous changes in British society from 1914 to 1940. Greville's sons fight in World War I, then lose themselves in love affairs as they try to forget the horrors of war. The Earl's grandsons join the Royal Air Force before World War II and fight Hitler as the war breaks out. The family members' lives mirror the social changes in Britain between the wars.

Genre: Family Saga; Historical Fiction; War
Subjects: Aristocracy; War; Society novels; World War I, 1914–1918; World War II, 1939–1945
Place/Time: England—1900–1945

Rogers, Rosemary

1338.
1. *Sweet Savage Love.* Avon, 1974.
2. *Dark Fires.* Avon, 1975.
3. *Lost Love, Last Love.* Avon, 1980.
4. *Bound by Desire.* Avon, 1988.

In these novels, the original "bodice ripper" romances, Ginny Branden is seduced, raped, married, abandoned, raped, seduced, and finally settled with the man she loves, Steve Morgan. In the 19th century, beautiful Ginny and virile Steve fall in love, are torn apart, and then are united only after experiencing and seeing everything. They travel from Europe to America, then to Mexico, Texas, Cuba, and finally back to Europe. The lovers emerge triumphant, but their daughter, the ravishingly beautiful Laura, continues their passionate story as she is seduced, raped, abandoned, and raped before she finally marries true love Trent Challenger.

Genre: Historical Romance
Subjects: Sex
Place/Time: Europe—19th century; United States—19th century; Mexico—19th century

Rohan, Michael Scott

1339. Spiral Trilogy
1. *Chase the Morning.* Avon, 1990.
2. *The Gates of Noon.* William Morrow, 1993.
3. *Cloud Castles.* Avon, 1994.

The first time Steve Fisher entered the Spiral, a magical alternate reality of myth and legend, it was an accident. His second trip to this mystical realm is to prevent a high-tech water purification system from falling into demonic hands. When he returns to the Spiral again, he uses his power to stop the forces of evil from taking over the Europe of the near future.

Genre: Fantasy
Subjects: Imaginary kingdoms; Good and evil

1340. The Winter of the World
1. *The Anvil of Ice.* Morrow, 1986.
2. *The Forge in the Forest.* Avon, 1987.
3. *The Hammer of the Sun.* Avon. 1990.

With glaciers threatening life in his world, Elof battles his former employer, the Mastersmith, who now wields a sword that is Elof's handiwork, for evil purposes. Gaining confidence and an ethical sense from his experience, Elof turns his powers against the advancing ice and sets off to find a refuge from its power.

Genre: Fantasy
Subjects: Ice; Arms and armor; Good and evil

Rolvaag, O. E. (Ole Edvart)

1341.
1. *Giants in the Earth.* Harper, 1927.
2. *Peder Victorious.* Harper, 1929.
3. *Their Father's God.* Harper, 1931.

Norwegian emigrants Per Hansa and his wife Beret come to the Dakotas in the 1870s. He finds the prairie life exhilarating, but Beret finds only loneliness and despair. With their family they face hardship, change, and religious conflict. Beret resists giving up her Norwegian customs, but young son Peder adapts to the country and even marries an Irish-Catholic girl.

Genre: Historical Fiction
Subjects: Immigrants; Frontier and pioneer life; Family life; Farm life
Place/Time: North Dakota—19th century

Romains, Jules

1342. Men of Good Will Series
1. *Men of Good Will.* Knopf, 1933.
2. *Passion's Pilgrims.* Knopf, 1934.
3. *The Proud and the Meek.* Knopf, 1934.
4. *The World from Below.* Knopf, 1935.
5. *The Earth Trembles.* Knopf, 1936.
6. *The Depths and the Heights.* Knopf, 1937.
7. *Death of a World.* Knopf, 1938.
8. *Verdun.* Knopf, 1939.
9. *Aftermath.* Knopf, 1941.
10. *The New Day.* Knopf, 1942.
11. *Work and Play.* Knopf, 1944.
12. *The Wind Is Rising.* Knopf, 1945.
13. *Escape in Passion.* Knopf, 1946.
14. *The Seventh of October.* Knopf, 1946.

Each book of this monolithic series contains two complete novels. The reader is given a multidimensional view of France during the time before, during, and after World War I. Characters from all walks of life—students, lovers, businessmen, soldiers, even a murderer—are introduced and followed throughout. The story opens in Paris on October 6, 1908, and moves to the provinces, then to foreign countries, and back to Paris before the story closes on October 7, 1933.

Subjects: World War I, 1914–1918; Social classes
Place/Time: France—1900–1945

Ronald, James

1343.
1. *Man Born of Woman.* Lippincott, 1951.
2. *Sparks Fly Upward.* J. Messer, 1953.

Quentin's irresponsible father is more interested in pursuing his calling as an artist than in raising his son. Following his mother's death, Quentin lives a nomadic existence as he is passed back and forth among relatives in 19th-century France, Scotland, and England. Quentin's travels eventually bring him to America and to an understanding of his father's artistic talent.

Genre: Coming of Age
Subjects: Artists; Fathers and sons; Bereavement; Travel
Place/Time: France—19th century; Scotland—19th century; England—19th century

Rose, Howard

1344. False Messiah Trilogy
1. *The Pooles of Pismo Bay.* Raymond Saroff, 1990.
2. *Oak Street Beach.* Raymond Saroff, 1990.
3. *The Marrano.* Raymond Saroff, 1992.

In these disjointed novels, three Jewish families become involved in the American labor movement. Cora Poole works with the Industrial Workers of the World in the 1920s. Her son Reuben and his wife Rose have a series of adventures in Chicago of the 1950s. Matthew Lenart becomes involved with Gordon Abul, who stole Matt's wife. Matt tracks him to Chicago where he joins an eccentric society set.

Genre: Historical Fiction
Subjects: Jews; Labor unions; Family life
Place/Time: Chicago (Ill.)—1900–1945; Chicago (Ill.)—1945–1980; Illinois—1900–1945; Illinois—1945–1980

Rosenbaum, Ray

1345. Wings of War
1. *Falcons.* Presidio Press, 1993.
2. *Hawks.* Presidio Press, 1994.
3. *Condors.* Presidio Press, 1995.
4. *Eagles.* Presidio Press, 1996.

The rise of the modern air force from World War II to the present is shown through the career of Ross Colyer. Colyer is a by-the-book officer in the army Air Force. In the first days of the war, Colyer and Broderick Templeton, another officer, fight in the skies over Europe. In the last years of the war, Colyer leads bomber attacks on the Romanian old fields before he is sent to China to lead attacks on the Japanese. After the war ends, Colyer starts an air-cargo business, but soon he is helping transport Jewish refugees to Palestine. When the government of Israel needs pilots, he helps train and fight in their air force. After the Israel War for Independence is over, Colyer returns to America to help the Air Force enter the jet age.

Genre: War; Historical Fiction
Subjects: Air Force, United States; Air pilots; Aeronautics, military; World War II, 1939–1945—aerial operations
Place/Time: Europe—1900–1945; Israel—1945–1980; United States—1945–1980; China—1900–1945; Hawaii—1900–1945

Rosenberg, Joel

1346.
1. *Not for Glory.* NAL, 1988.
2. *Hero.* Roc, 1990.

Metzada, a planet colonized by Israeli refugees, is famous throughout the universe for its soldiers, the Metzadan Mercenary Corp. The brilliant General Shimon Bar El, thought by some to be a traitor, becomes involved in the machinations of his ruthless nephew Tetsuo Hanavi. In the sequel, Ari, a descendant of the great Hanavi warrior family, must do battle with the most indomitable foe of all: his own cowardice.

Genre: Science Fiction
Subjects: Refugees, Jewish; Space colonies; Mercenary soldiers; Cowardice

1347. D'Shai
1. *D'Shai.* Ace, 1991.
2. *Hour of the Octopus.* Ace, 1994.

In D'Shai, a feudal land with a rigid class structure, wandering acrobat Kami dares to fall in love with a nobleman's daughter with tragic results. Later, strengthened by his experience, Kami matures and becomes a detective who must deal with a complex plot to prevent a marriage by framing the groom for murder.

Genre: Fantasy
Subjects: Imaginary kingdoms; Detectives

1348. Guardians of the Flame
1. *The Sleeping Dragon.* NAL, 1983.
2. *The Sword and the Chain.* NAL, 1984.
3. *The Silver Crown.* NAL, 1985.
The above titles have also been published in the following collection: Guardians of the Flame: The Warriors. Doubleday, 1985.

4. *The Heir Apparent.* NAL, 1987.
5. *The Warrior Lives.* Roc, 1989.
The above titles have also been published in the following collection: Guardians of the Flame: The Heroes. Guild America Books, 1989.

6. *The Road to Ehvenor.* Roc, 1991.
7. *The Road Home.* Roc, 1995.
8. *Not Exactly the Three Musketeers.* Tor, 1999.

Enacting roles in a fantasy game magically transports the players into the sword and sorcery world with very little hope of getting out. Once there, they engage in a conflict to free the enslaved population of the realm.

Genre: Fantasy
Subjects: Imaginary kingdoms; Games; Imaginary wars and battles

1349. Keepers of the Hidden Ways
1. *The Fire Duke.* Morrow, 1995.
2. *The Silver Stone.* Avon, 1996.

Ian Silverstein's plans for his summer vacation were simply to spend time on a North Dakota farm, but suddenly he falls into an alternate reality of Celtic and Norse legend where he must contend with dangers he has not faced in the real world. His first challenge arises when the father of the farm family, who is actually a refugee from magical land of Tir Na Nog, is drawn back into the realm as a prisoner of the House of Flame. On a return visit to the legendary realm, Ian encounters the prophecy of a promised warrior called Silver Stone.

Genre: Fantasy
Subjects: Imaginary kingdoms; Prophecies; Magic
Place/Time: North Dakota—1980–

Rosenthal, Chuck

1350.
1. *Loop's Progress.* Weidenfeld & Nicolson, 1986.
2. *Experiments with Life and Death.* Weidenfeld & Nicolson, 1987.
3. *Loop's End.* Gibb Smith, 1992.

Jarvis Loop is a teenager in Erie, Pennsylvania, in the 1960s. He has to deal with his violent father Red, his religious mother Helen, and his brilliant 300-pound sister Neda. As he grows up, he becomes a fugitive from the law and falls in love with Kara, a woman possessed by a ghost. Jarvis philosophizes about the meaning of life as he collects garbage and tries to understand his zany and eccentric relatives.

Genre: Coming of Age
Subjects: Teenagers; Family life; Crime and criminals; Eccentrics and eccentricities; Love
Place/Time: Erie (Pa.)—1945–1980; Pennsylvania—1945–1980

Ross, Dana Fuller. *Pseud. of* Noel Bertram Gerson

1351. The Holts: An American Dynasty
1. *Oregon Legacy.* Bantam, 1989.
2. *Oklahoma Pride.* Bantam, 1989.
3. *Carolina Courage.* Bantam, 1991.
4. *California Glory.* Bantam, 1991.
5. *Hawaii Heritage.* Bantam, 1991.
6. *Sierra Triumph.* Bantam, 1992.
7. *Yukon Justice.* Bantam, 1992.
8. *Pacific Destiny.* Bantam, 1994.
9. *Homecoming.* Bantam, 1994.

10. *Awakening.* Bantam, 1995.

The saga of the Holts continues as the family members, and their friends and employees take on the evil and greedy men trying to destroy the West. From silver mining camps in Nevada to Chicago's Pullman strike and the gold fields of the Yukon, the Holts fight racial bigotry and injustice as they fall in love and build an empire from the late 19th century through the start of World War II.

Genre: Historical Fiction; Western
Subjects: Adventure; Good and evil
Place/Time: Western states—19th century

1352. Wagons West
1. *Independence!* Bantam, 1979.
2. *Nebraska!* Bantam, 1979.
3. *Wyoming!* Bantam, 1979.
4. *Oregon!* Bantam, 1980.
5. *Texas!* Bantam, 1980.
6. *California!* Bantam, 1981.
7. *Colorado!* Bantam, 1981.
8. *Nevada!* Bantam, 1981.
9. *Washington!* Bantam, 1982.
10. *Montana!* Bantam, 1983.
11. *Dakota!* Bantam, 1983.
12. *Utah!* Bantam, 1984.
13. *Idaho!* Bantam, 1984.
14. *Missouri!* Bantam, 1985.
15. *Mississippi!* Bantam, 1985.
16. *Louisiana!* Bantam, 1986.
17. *Tennessee!* Bantam, 1986.
18. *Illinois!* Bantam, 1986.
19. *Wisconsin!* Bantam, 1987.
20. *Kentucky!* Bantam, 1987.
21. *Arizona!* Bantam, 1988.
22. *New Mexico!* Bantam, 1988.
23. *Oklahoma!* Bantam, 1989.
24. *Celebration* Bantam, 1989.

Legendary wagon master Whip Holt and his son Toby lead wagon trains of settlers through all parts of the country from 1837 to 1876. Whip and his children Toby and Cindy and their best friend Major Henry Blake take part in famous events, such as the Chicago Fire, the California Gold Rush, the Texas War for Independence, and many more, as the wagon trains move west. The two families intermarry, fight Indians, and tame the West until July 4, 1876, when the country celebrates the centennial of the United States.

Genre: Family Saga; Historical Fiction; Western
Subjects: Adventure; Wagon trains; War
Place/Time: Western states—19th century

1353. Wagons West: The Frontier Trilogy
1. *Westward.* Bantam, 1992.
2. *Expedition.* Bantam, 1993.
3. *Outpost.* Bantam, 1993.

This prequel to the Wagons West Series follows brothers Clay and Jefferson Holt as a feud forces them from the Ohio Valley to the West of the early 1800s. Clay falls in love with a beautiful Sioux woman, and the brothers try to avoid the killer who is following them. As the French, Spanish, Americans, and Indians fight over the land, the Holts found a dynasty and have adventures throughout the West.

Genre: Adventure; Historical Fiction; Western
Subjects: Adventure; Frontier and pioneer life
Place/Time: Western states—19th century

Ross, David D.
1354. The Dreamers of the Day
1. *The Argus Gambit.* St. Martin's, 1989.
2. *The Eighth Rank.* St. Martin's, 1991.

In the near future, the government controls all technology and tries to suppress change. A group of scientists tries to foster progress by forming the Argus society, but they are fighting a world that has seen too many wars. Sinister billionaire Horatius Krebs tries to take control of the world's industries, U. S. President Sheffreton tries to build a stardrive, and progressive scientists attempt to free humanity, as assassins and good guys square off in a fight for the world.

Genre: Science Fiction
Subjects: Technology and civilization; Progress; Totalitarianism; Good and evil

Ross, L. Q. *See* Rosten, Leo Calvin

Ross, Martin. *See* Somerville, Edith

Rosten, Leo Calvin
1355.
1. *The Education of Hyman Kaplan.* Harcourt Brace, 1937.
2. *The Return of Hyman Kaplan.* Harper, 1959.
3. *O Kaplan! My Kaplan!* Harper, 1976.

The author drew on his own experiences of teaching in Chicago in the 1930s to create his engaging character, immigrant Hyman Kaplan. Kaplan attends the American Night Preparatory School for Adults with hilarious results, inventing his own versions of the English language and American history. His exasperated teacher, Mr. Parkhill, and fellow newcomers, such as Olga Tarnova and Lola Lopez, are an entertaining supporting cast.

Genre: Humor
Subjects: Immigrants; Americanization; Language and languages; Education
Place/Time: Chicago (Ill.)—1900–1945; Illinois—1900–1945

Rotchstein, Janice. *See* Ebert, Alan

Roth, Henry

1356. Mercy of a Rude Stream
1. *Mercy of a Rude Stream.* St. Martin's, 1994.
2. *A Diving Rock on the Hudson.* St. Martin's, 1995.
3. *From Bondage.* St. Martin's, 1996.
4. *Requiem for Harlem.* St. Martin's, 1998.

Elderly Ira Sigman talks to his computer as he writes about his youth in the tenements of New York City in the first decades of the 20th century. The elderly Ira recalls moving to "white" Harlem when he was nine and learning to defend himself against Irish bullies. He describes his family and the disruption of World War I. The elderly Ira finally confesses that as a teenager he had an incestuous relationship with his sister and his cousins and the guilt and remorse over those acts still haunt him. As a high school student, he is expelled from school for stealing, but he finally goes back to school and enters college. While at college, Ira meets upper-middle-class, Jewish Larry Gordon who introduces him to Professor Edith Welles. He begins a 10-year-long affair with Edith who introduces him to the world of intellectuals. The elderly Ira remembers the world of immigrant Jewish New York of the 1920s.

Genre: Coming of Age
Subjects: Teenagers; Immigrants; Jews—United States
Place/Time: New York (N. Y.)—1900–1945

Roth, Philip

1357.
1. *The Ghost Writer.* Farrar, Straus & Giroux, 1979.
2. *Zuckerman Unbound.* Farrar, Straus & Giroux, 1981.
3. *The Anatomy Lesson.* Farrar, Straus & Giroux, 1983.

The above titles have also been published in the following collection: *Zuckerman Bound: Trilogy and Epilogue.* Farrar, Straus & Giroux, 1985.

4. *The Counterlife.* Farrar, Straus & Giroux, 1987.
5. *I Married a Communist.* Houghton Mifflin, 1998.
6. *The Human Stain.* Houghton Mifflin, 2000.

From his days as a young writer to a middle-aged successful writer, Nathan Zuckerman seeks to understand himself, his Jewishness, and life. As a young man, he writes a controversial book and seeks the advice of an older Jewish writer. When he finally writes a blockbuster, he can't cope with his success and by age 40 has writer's block. He flies to Prague to find the unpublished manuscript of a great martyred Yiddish writer, but he fails. At the end, his health is bad but he has mastered himself.

Subjects: Authors; Jews; Success; Middle age; Men—psychology; Psychological novels

Place/Time: United States—1945–1980; Prague (Czechoslovakia)—1945–1980; Czechoslovakia—1945–1980

Rouaud, Jean

1358.
1. *Fields of Glory.* Arcade, 1992.
2. *Of Illustrious Men.* Arcade, 1994.
3. *The World More or Less.* Arcade, 1998.

The aged narrator tells the story of his family—first his maternal grandparents, then his father, and finally himself. As a child living in the Loire Valley of France, the narrator remembers his eccentric grandparents, his hard-to-drive car, and his maiden great aunt. Over time he realizes how World War I changed their lives forever. The narrator then looks at his father Joseph's life. Joseph was a salesman, selling porcelain and glassware, who took his family rock hunting on Sundays. He also shows how World War II shaped Joseph's life and his future. Finally, the narrator looks back on his boarding school days and how he was shaped by events in the 1960s.

Genre: Family Saga
Subjects: Family life; Grandfathers; Fathers; Teenagers
Place/Time: France—1900–1945; France—1945–1980

Roubaud, Jacques

1359.
1. *Our Beautiful Heroine.* Overlook Press, 1987, 1985.
2. *Hortense Is Abducted.* Dalkey Archive Press, 1989, 1987.
3. *Hortense in Exile.* Dalkey Archive Press, 1992, 1987.

The delightful Hortense meets a strong, dark, and handsome stranger who turns out to be a missing prince. She and her Parisian neighbors romp through the city and the principaltariat called Poldevia. There is very little plot in these absurdist novels, which are made up of allusions, mathematical permutations and extrapolations, and burlesques of everything.

Subjects: Aristocracy; Princes; Love; Imaginary kingdoms; Parodies

Routley, B. J.

1360.
1. *Mage Heart.* William Morrow, 1996.
2. *Fire Angels.* Avon Eos, 1998.
3. *Aramaya.* Avon Eos, 1999.

Country girl Dion has the honor of being the only woman enrolled in the Gallian College of Magic when suddenly she is summoned by the palace and plunged into the sophisticated life of the court to protect the

Duke's mistress Kitten Avignon from black magic. Back in her homeland Moria, Dion must confront the demonic Great Destroyer who wishes to seduce her. Then she and Kitten cross an ocean and survive a shipwreck to rescue Dion's niece who has been put under a spell by a group of necromancers.

Genre: Fantasy; Coming of Age
Subjects: Imaginary Kingdoms; Magic; Demonology; Courts and courtiers

Routley, Jane. *See Routley, B. J.*

Royle, Edwin Milton
1361.
1. *The Squaw Man.* (Written with Julie Opp Faversham) Harper, 1906.
2. *The Silent Call.* Scribner, 1910.

To preserve his family's honor, James Wynnegate accepts the blame for a crime committed by his cousin, the earl of Kerhill. He exiles himself to the Wild West of the 19th century where he takes an American Indian wife. The sequel follows the life of his son, who is taken back to England to be raised in the aristocratic way of life of his father's family but eventually seeks his roots and the love of an Indian woman in America.

Genre: Historical Fiction
Subjects: Native Americans; Adventure; Aristocracy; Frontier and pioneer life
Place/Time: Western states—19th century

Rubin, Harold. *See Robbins, Harold*

Ruesch, Hans
1362.
1. *Top of the World.* Harper, 1950.
2. *Back to the Top of the World.* Scribner, 1972.

An Eskimo family lives their traditional life, always dealing with the hardships of their arctic environment, but amazingly able to laugh and enjoy their surroundings. Their daughter Ivaloo is both delighted and confused by the teachings of a Christian missionary. The sequel follows the encroachment of 19th and early 20th-century civilization on the Eskimo way of life and the resistance of the family's son Pupik.

Subjects: Inuit; Family life; Society, primitive; Missionaries; Progress; Acculturation
Place/Time: Arctic regions—19th century; Arctic regions—1900–1945

Russell, Mary Doria
1363.
1. *The Sparrow.* Villard, 1996.
2. *Children of God.* Villard, 1998.

In the 21st century, Jesuit priest Emilio Sandoz experiences a tremendous emotional and spiritual crisis as a result of accompanying a mission to the planet Rakhat in the Alpha Centauri star system. Drawn by songs emanating from the planet, the members of the mission find a gentle race, the Runa, who are exploited by the fierce alien Jana'ata in part because of the mission's well-intentioned interference. Shattered to the core, Sandoz returns to Earth but is forced to go back to the turbulent life that now exists on Rakhat.

Genre: Science Fiction
Subjects: Life on other planets; Extraterrestrial beings; Catholic priests

Russell, Sean
1364. Moontide and Magic Rise
1. *World without End.* DAW Books, 1995.
2. *Sea without a Shore.* DAW Books, 1996.

A young naturalist, whose uncle is thought to have been one of the last mages, is sent on an ocean voyage of discovery by his king. His first quest is for a plant with healing powers; his second to a remote island where the natives have had a mysterious premonition of his arrival. In both ventures he is guided by a white bird, which may be the spirit of his uncle's familiar.

Genre: Fantasy
Subjects: Magic; Voyages and travels; Scientists; Birds

1365. River into Darkness
1. *Beneath the Vaulted Hill.* DAW Books, 1997.
2. *The Compass of the Soul.* DAW Books, 1998.

Magic has existed in this world, but is being eradicated by reason and science. Strangely, the most dedicated opponent of magic is the last mage, Lord Eldrich. A rebel group, the Tellerites, with a talented young woman leading them, descend into the earth to search for the seed of a rare flower that will enable them to vanquish Eldrich.

Genre: Fantasy
Subjects: Magic; Imaginary wars and battles

Rybakov, Anatoli
1366. Arbat Trilogy
1. *Children of the Arbat.* Little, Brown, 1988.
2. *Fear.* Little, Brown, 1992.
3. *Dust and Ashes.* Little, Brown, 1996.

The horrors of Stalin's purges of the 1930s are shown through the persecution of intellectual Sasha Pankratov and the tortured mind of Stalin himself. Sasha is well connected politically, but this does not save him from being sent to Siberia. When Sasha returns to Moscow, he must try to avoid being noticed. He ultimately returns to Siberia, but is called into the army service when the Germans attack Russia during

World War II. As Rybakov tells Sasha's story, he also tries to reproduce Stalin's thought process as his paranoia brings on the Yezhov terror and the Great Purge, which wiped out millions.

Genre: Historical Fiction
Subjects: Communism; Stream of consciousness; Mental illness; Persecution
Place/Time: Soviet Union—1917–1945

Ryman, Rebecca

1367.
1. *Olivia and Jai.* St. Martin's, 1990.
2. *The Veil of Illusion.* St. Martin's, 1995.

In the 1840s, Olivia Raventhorne goes to India to live with her British relatives. There she meets Eurasian Jai and despite colonial society disapproval, Olivia marries him. Jai, however, is angry with the British and wants to revenge his people. Eventually he is arrested and hung as a traitor during the Sepay Rebellion. Years later their children Amos and Maya must also deal with the ostracism of both English and Indian society. Maya tries to lure the wealthy Englishman Christian Pendlebury into marriage while brother Amos refuses to marry until he clears his father's name. The family must undergo numerous trials before they finally find happiness.

Genre: Family Saga; Historical Romance
Subjects: Lovers; Husbands and wives; Brothers and sisters; India—British occupation, 1765–1947; Social classes
Place/Time: India—19th century

Sabatier, Robert

1368.
1. *The Safety Matches.* Dutton, 1972, 1969.
2. *Three Mint Lollipops.* Dutton, 1974, 1971.

Orphaned at age nine, Oliver grows up on the streets of Montparnasse in Paris in the 1930s. As he wanders the streets, he befriends all the residents of the area including Mado, a whore, and her lover Mac. Eventually Oliver is sent to live with his rich uncle and aunt. He runs away to his friends in Montparnasse, but finally learns to live in both worlds.

Genre: Coming of Age
Subjects: Boys; Orphans; Aunts; Uncles; Wealth; Runaways
Place/Time: Paris (France)—1900–1945; France—1900–1945

Sabatini, Rafael

1369.
1. *Captain Blood, His Odyssey.* Houghton, 1922.
2. *Captain Blood Returns.* Houghton, 1931.

3. *The Fortunes of Captain Blood.* Houghton, 1936.

The fictionalized life of Harry Pitman, an Englishman sold into slavery in the 1600s, is told through the character of Peter Blood. Blood, a doctor who helped rebels at the Battle of Monmouth, is sold into slavery in the West Indies. When he escapes, he becomes a pirate and battles the corrupt governor of Port Royal. Errol Flynn became a star playing the swashbuckling Peter Blood.

Genre: Adventure; Historical Fiction; Naval Adventure
Subjects: Adventure; Slavery; Pirates; Physicians; Escapes
Place/Time: Caribbean region—17th century

Saberhagen, Fred

1370. Berserker Series
1. *Berserker.* Ballantine, 1967.
2. *Brother Assassin.* Ballantine, 1969.
3. *Berserker's Planet.* DAW Books, 1975.
4. *Berserker Man.* Ace, 1979.
5. *The Ultimate Enemy.* Ace, 1979.
6. *The Berserker Wars.* Tor, 1981.
7. *Berserker Base.* (Short stories by several authors) T. Doherty, 1985.
8. *The Berserker Throne.* Tor, 1985.
9. *Berserker: Blue Death.* Tor, 1985.
10. *The Berserker Attack.* Waldenbooks, 1987.
11. *Berserker Lies.* Tor, 1991.
12. *Berserker Kill.* Tor, 1993.
13. *Berserker Fury.* Tor, 1997.
14. *Shiva in Steel.* Tor, 1998.

The Berserkers, enormous robotic war machines invented to fight an intergalactic war, destroyed not only their enemies, but their creator as well. This series of short stories and novels narrates their fearsome progress toward Earth and the united efforts of the galaxy to combat them.

Genre: Science Fiction
Subjects: Interplanetary wars; Robots; Technology and civilization

1371. Books of the Gods
1. *The Face of Apollo.* Tor, 1998.
2. *Ariadne's Web.* Tor, 2000.

Jeremy Redthorn undertakes a mission for a beautiful stranger, which requires him to wear a strange mask that confers upon him the powers and enemies of the sun god Apollo. In the second tale about the power of the Greek gods, Theseus, the slayer of the Minotaur in ancient Crete, seeks a mask in the form of a god's face with the help of Princess Ariadne.

Genre: Fantasy
Subjects: Gods and goddesses; Masks; Heroes; Princesses

1372. Dracula Series

1. *The Dracula Tape.* Warner, 1975.
2. *The Holmes-Dracula File.* Ace, 1978.
3. *An Old Friend of the Family.* Ace, 1979.
4. *Thorn.* Ace, 1980.
5. *Dominion.* Tor, 1982.
6. *A Matter of Taste.* Tor, 1990.
7. *A Question of Time.* Tor, 1992.
8. *Seance for a Vampire.* Tor, 1994.
9. *A Sharpness on the Neck.* Tor, 1996

Dracula lives in 20th-century Chicago and acts as a friend and protector to the descendants of Mina Harker. Saberhagen sets the record straight about the world's most famous vampire and, in the process, reveals that Dracula was really Mina's lover and a friend and colleague of Sherlock Holmes. The tales dip back in time into Vlad's lengthy life. Historical figures such as Napoleon, Thomas Paine, and the Marquis de Sade make appearances. Through the 18th, 19th, and 20th centuries Vlad's existence is threatened by his evil vampire brother Radu who is bent on his destruction.

Genre: Horror
Subjects: Vampires; Lovers; Detectives
Place/Time: Chicago (Ill.)—1945–1980; Illinois—1945–1980

1373. Empire of the East

1. *The Broken Lands.* Ace, 1968.
2. *The Black Mountains.* Ace, 1971.
3. *Changeling Earth.* (Alternate Title: *Ardneh's World.*) DAW Books, 1973.

The above titles have also been revised and published in the following collection: *The Empire of the East.* Ace, 1979.

After a nuclear holocaust, spirits usually associated with magic and primitive religion take over Earth. Orcus, the nuclear explosion itself in the form of a demon, opposes Ardneh, the spiritual outgrowth of computer technology. Ultimately the mysterious beings dissolve, and Earth returns to the realm of science again.

Genre: Fantasy; Science Fiction
Subjects: Nuclear warfare; Magic; Demonology; Technology and civilization

1374. Swords

1. *The First Book of Swords.* Tor, 1983.
2. *The Second Book of Swords.* Tor, 1984.
3. *The Third Book of Swords.* Tor, 1984.
4. *The First Book of Lost Swords: Woundhealer's Story.* Tor, 1986.
5. *The Second Book of Lost Swords: Sight-Blinder's Story.* Tor, 1987.
6. *The Third Book of Lost Swords: Stonecutter's Story.* Tor, 1988.
7. *The Fourth Book of Lost Swords: Farslayer's Story.* Tor, 1989.
8. *The Fifth Book of Lost Swords: Coinspinner's Story.* Tor, 1989.
9. *The Sixth Book of Lost Swords: Mindsword's Story.* Tor, 1991.
10. *Wayfinder's Story: The Seventh Book of Lost Swords.* Tor, 1992.
11. *The Last Book of Swords: Shieldbreaker's Story.* Tor, 1994.

In the postholocaust world of Saberhagen's Empire of the East series, a set of 12 swords forged for the gods assume tremendous importance. The swords ultimately prove to be more powerful than the gods who created them and, because of their individual properties, figure in a series of swashbuckling adventures.

Genre: Fantasy
Subjects: Arms and armor; Gods and goddesses

Saint, Dora Jessie. See Read, Miss

Sale, Elizabeth

1375.

1. *Recitation from Memory.* Dodd, 1943.
2. *My Mother Bids Me Bind My Hair.* Dodd, 1944.

Turn-of-the-century Tacoma, Washington, is the background for the coming of age of Fenella Rand, a young woman whose passage from childhood to adolescence is at times made difficult, at other times delightful, by her eccentric family.

Genre: Coming of Age
Subjects: Girls; Family life; Eccentrics and eccentricities
Place/Time: Tacoma (Wash.)—1900–1945; Washington (state)—1900–1945

Salvatore, R. A.

1376.

1. *The Demon Awakens.* Ballantine, 1997.
2. *The Demon Spirit.* Ballantine, 1998.
3. *The Demon Apostle.* Ballantine, 1999.

The demon Bestesbulzibar has an evil spirit that seems impossible to kill. In the land of Corona he awakens, assembles an army of sinister creatures and sets off to conquer the world. Opposing him are young Elbryan, armed with knowledge he has gained from the elves, the wizard Pony, and the young monk Avelyn Desbris, who possesses magical gifts. For a time it appears that their powers have shattered the demon's energy, but as they travel through the land trying to heal the wounds of battle, they discover that he has sought sanctuary in a church.

Genre: Fantasy
Subjects: Demonology; Imaginary wars and battles; Good and evil; Magic

1377. The Crimson Shadow

1. *The Sword of Bedwyr.* Warner Books, 1995.
2. *Luthien's Gamble.* Warner Books, 1996.
3. *The Dragon King.* Warner Books, 1996.

In the land of Eriador, the young nobleman Luthien must live as a fugitive among the peasant population to assemble a resistance movement against the evil wizard King Greensparrow, who has enslaved the land. Luthien frees the crown city of Montfort with the help of the ancient wizard Brind D'Amou, who gives him a magical cape, but Luthien must still face another onslaught of demons.

Genre: Fantasy
Subjects: Imaginary wars and battles; Imaginary kingdoms; Good and evil; Magic; Government, resistance to

1378. Forgotten Realms: Dark Elf Series
1. *Homeland.* TSR, 1990.
2. *Exile.* TSR, 1990.
3. *Sojourn.* TSR, 1990.

The dark elf Drizzt Do'Urden is very different from his family and other members of the society of Underdark where cruel schemes and byzantine plots abound. Drizzt leaves his malevolent culture to wander in the caverns of the Underdark and confront the evil in himself. He finally emerges in the world above as a hero who, with his magic panther, battles evil and prejudice. Drizzt's adventures are also a part of the Icewind Dale Trilogy.

Genre: Fantasy
Subjects: Good and evil; Magic; Adventure

1379. Forgotten Realms: Icewind Dale Trilogy
1. *The Crystal Shard.* TSR, 1988.
2. *Streams of Silver.* TSR, 1989.
3. *The Halfling's Gem.* TSR, 1989.

The dark elf Drizzt must deal with the power of the magical crystal shard that threatens peace in the realm of Ten-Towns. He helps to train the young barbarian Wulfar to unite his tribes while at the same time persuading the community to put aside their differences. Drizzt's adventures continue as with Bruenor the dwarf and Regis the halfling he fights his way to the dwarf stronghold Mithril Hall, but when Regis is kidnapped, the friends must battle pirates and monsters to save him.

Genre: Fantasy
Subjects: Magic; Adventure; Imaginary wars and battles

1380. Forgotten Realms: The Cleric Quintet
1. *Canticle.* TSR, 1991.
2. *In Sylvan Shadows.* TSR, 1992.
3. *Night Masks.* TSR, 1992.
4. *The Fallen Fortress.* TSR, 1993.
5. *The Chaos Curse.* TSR, 1994.

Although he lives in a community of intellects and students in the Snowflake Mountains, the scholar priest Cadderly faces a series of dangerous adventures, beginning when a sorcerer creates a powerful potion that may destroy his peaceful community. He is then pitted against monsters who threaten Shilmista Forest nearby. He is pursued by assassins to the village of Carradoon and then finds himself in the midst of a battle between the inhabitants of the village and the forest. Back in the conservatory where he started, Cadderly confronts the curse that has pursued him.

Genre: Fantasy
Subjects: Clergy; Good and evil; Adventure; Imaginary wars and battles

1381. Spearwielder's Tale
1. *The Woods Out Back.* Ace, 1993.
2. *The Dragon's Dagger.* Ace, 1994.
3. *Dragonslayer's Return.* Ace, 1995.

Gary Leger's adventures begin simply enough when he walks into the woods behind his home. Suddenly a leprechaun appears and transports him into the realm of Faerie where he becomes the reluctant replacement for a vanished warrior and learns to wield a magical spear that has a mind of its own. Despite the fear and hesitancy he felt at the beginning of his first adventure, Gary returns to Faerie to do battle with a rampaging dragon and a wicked witch.

Genre: Fantasy
Subjects: Arms and armor; Imaginary wars and battles; Dragons; Magic

Sams, Ferrol

1382.
1. *Run with the Horseman.* Peachtree, 1982.
2. *The Whisper of the River.* Peachtree, 1984.
3. *When All the World Was Young.* Longstreet, 1991.

These loosely autobiographical novels depict a young boy growing up in rural Georgia during the 1920s and 1930s. Porter Osborne, Jr., loves his rural farm life in Breluton County. He relates stories of the memorable and funny characters he sees. In 1938, he goes off to college and finds he is a naive farm boy amidst bettereducated, upper-crust students. When World War II starts, Porter deliberately flunks out of medical school to join the army as a medical technician. He and his army buddies are involved in numerous humorous high jinks, but facing the horrors of war, Porter finally comes of age.

Genre: Coming of Age; Humor
Subjects: Boys; Autobiographical stories; Farm life; Class distinction; World War II, 1939–1945
Place/Time: Georgia—1900–1945; Europe—1900–1945

Sand, George. *Pseud. of* Amantine-Aurore-Lucile Dupin

1383.
1. *Consuelo.* Ticknor, 1846.
2. *The Countess of Rudolstadt.* Ticknor, 1847.

Sand's masterpiece follows a beautiful singer, Consuelo, in the mid-18th century as she tries to launch her career. The morally pure Consuela is repelled by the immorality in the theater and takes a job as a private music tutor to a wealthy family. She and the son fall in love, but are separated by his parents because of her social class. Only when he is dying are they reunited. Later she is inducted into a secret society and devotes herself to her husband and children as they preach the love of humanity through music.

Subjects: Singers; Class distinction; Love; Bereavement; Music
Place/Time: Europe—19th century

1384. Rustic Series
1. *The Haunted Pool.* Shameless Hussy Press, 1976, 1846.
2. *The Country Waif.* University of Nebraska Press, 1977, 1848.
3. *Fadette: A Domestic Story.* (Today translated as *Little Fadette.*) Putnam, 1951, 1849.

The life of peasants in the central provinces of Berry and Creuse in France is idealized in these novels. Sand uses these stories, which are connected only by setting, to deal with the issues of love, marriage, and social class in the provinces. In each book, a young couple must overcome social differences before realizing they are in love and marrying.

Subjects: Peasants; Country life; Social classes; Love; Marriage
Place/Time: France—19th century

Sanders, Leonard
1385.
1. *Fort Worth.* Delacorte, 1984.
2. *Texas Noon.* Delacorte, 1989.

Travis Spurlock, an orphan of the Civil War, founds the fortunes of his family when he moves to Fort Worth, Texas, and helps make it a commercial center. He becomes a U.S. senator and an aid to President Teddy Roosevelt. His sons, Vern and Clay, get into the burgeoning oil business and make a fortune until Vern is killed in an oil well blow out. Clay's son Brod becomes an oil tycoon, but his untimely death in 1950 leaves his widow Joanne to take command of the company and keep it together despite takeover bids and hidden family secrets that threaten to tear the company apart.

Genre: Family Saga; Historical Fiction
Subjects: Cities and towns; Petroleum industry; Wealth; Business
Place/Time: Texas—multicentury span

Sandison, Janet. *See* Duncan, Jane

Sandlin, Tim
1386. GroVont Trilogy
1. *Skipped Parts.* Holt, 1991.
2. *Sorrow Floats.* Holt, 1992.
3. *Social Blunders.* Holt, 1995.

The town of GroVont, Wyoming, is a beautiful, but wild, place for young people to grow up. In 1963, 13-year-old Sam and his mother Lydia are banished to GroVont by Lydia's father. Lydia drinks too much while Sam is a tough kid who tries to adjust to the eccentric town. Sam meets outcast Maurey Talbot who has a baby at 13. Ten years later, Maurey leaves the town after her husband throws her out. Her adventures on the road are similar to Sam's, who also leaves the town. While Maurey wants adventure, Sam wants to find the father he never knew. Neither Sam nor Maurey find what they are looking for, but they do have fun trying.

Genre: Coming of Age
Subjects: Teenagers; Small town life
Place/Time: Wyoming—1945–1980

Sands, Marella
1387.
1. *Sky Knife.* Forge, 1997.
2. *Serpent and Storm.* Forge, 1999.

Sky Knife is a temple attendant in the Mayan city of Tikal when the god of death, Cizin, appears to him. Since this is an evil omen, Sky Knife must learn why. As Sky Knife searches, he discovers biting butterflies, stinging raindrops, and a rainbow serpent with great insights that gives him magic powers. When he becomes a priest, Sky knife has to confront a priest gone bad. Later the king sends Sky Knife to see the king of Teotihuacan to reopen diplomatic ties, but when he arrives, the king dies, and Sky Knife must protect the young son of the king.

Subjects: Mythology; Native Americans; Mayans
Place/Time: Mexico—to 1st century A. D.

Sandstrom, Flora
1388.
1. *The Midwife of Pont-Clery.* Day, 1957.
2. *The Virtuous Women of Pont-Clery.* Day, 1958.

The early 20th-century Norman town of Pont-Clery is never the same after the arrival of Suzette Quimperny, a lovely young widow who comes to serve as the village's midwife. Because men adore her, women plot against her until her marriage to Monsieur Le Comte d'Hautcourt puts her out of their reach—almost.

Genre: Historical Fiction
Subjects: Midwives; Women; Social classes; Widows
Place/Time: France—1900–1945

Saracino, Mary

1389.
1. *No Matter What.* Spinsters Ink, 1993.
2. *Finding Grace.* Spinsters Ink, 1999.

Ten-year-old Peanut Giovanni discovers that her mother is having an affair with a priest and wants to run away with him. The mother takes her three daughters and leaves, but she doesn't find happiness. The girls want their father, and the ex-priest drinks. When he is drunk, he beats six-year-old Rosa. Finally Peanut and Rosa run away. They find shelter with an old woman who offers them a new life without abuse or violence.

Subjects: Girls; Child abuse; Runaways
Place/Time: United States—1980–

Sargent, Pamela

1390. Venus
1. *Venus of Dreams.* Bantam, 1986.
2. *Venus of Shadows.* Bantam, 1990.

The planet Venus represents a challenge to Iris, a young woman who had been involved in a Midwestern women's commune. She and her children attempt to change the environment of the planet so Venus can be inhabited by Earthlings, although Iris must then work under the domination of Earth's patriarchal Muslim society whose philosophy is in direct opposition to her views.

Genre: Science Fiction
Subjects: Venus (planet); Environment; Feminism; Muslims; Life on other planets

Saroyan, William

1391.
1. *Mama, I Love You.* Little, 1956.
2. *Papa, You're Crazy.* Little, 1957.

Told from the viewpoint of a young sister and brother, the story relates their lives with their divorced parents. Nine-year-old Twinkle lives with their mother. Mama wants to be an actress and gets a bit part in a play, but it is Twinkle who gets the big role, though all she wants is to be a baseball player. Her 10-year-old brother lives with their father in Malibu, where they ride bikes, walk the beaches, and drive along the coast. At Christmas, the brother and sister are finally reunited. The relationship between parents and children and between siblings is engagingly portrayed.

Subjects: Brothers and sisters; Divorce; Family life
Place/Time: California—1945–1980

Sartre, Jean-Paul

1392. The Roads to Freedom Series
1. *The Age of Reason.* Knopf, 1947.
2. *The Reprieve.* Knopf, 1947.
3. *Troubled Sleep.* Knopf, 1951.

Using the events of 1938 and the fall of Paris as background, Sartre demonstrates his ideas of freedom, first through Nathien, who lives his life by the abstract principle of freedom. Then Sartre follows people from all walks of life and their reactions to France's defeat. No books give more insight into the anguished feelings of the French before and after the fall of Paris.

Subjects: Liberty; World War II, 1939–1945; Philosophical novels
Place/Time: France—1900–1945

Saunders, Raymond M.

1393.
1. *Fenwick Travers and the Years of Empire.* Presidio, 1993.
2. *Fenwick Travers and the Forbidden Kingdom.* Presidio, 1994.
3. *Fenwick Travers and the Panama Canal.* Presidio, 1996.

Army officer Fenwick Travers is a coward, liar, womanizer, and thief, but somehow he is quite lovable. In 1897, when he graduates from West Point, he is sent to Cuba during the Spanish-American War, but he is constantly scheming to avoid combat. Whatever he does makes him appear a hero, so he is sent to China to help put down the Boxer Rebellion. When he comes back to America, he is acclaimed a hero and sent to the Philippines to quell a rebellion. He goes after the rebels but is really looking for Spanish gold. Travers is a lovable rogue whose cockeyed adventures somehow come out all right in the end.

Genre: Adventure
Subjects: Army, United States; Picaresque novels; Rogues and vagabonds
Place/Time: United States—19th century; Cuba—19th century; Philippines—19th century

Savage, Felicity

1394. Ever
1. *The War in the Waste.* HarperPrism, 1997.
2. *The Daemon in the Machine.* HarperPrism, 1998.
3. *Trickster in the Ashes.* HarperPrism, 1998.

In this alternate-reality Europe, technology is powered, not by mechanical means, but by daemons. In a war between the Queen's followers and lizard-like creatures, Crispin, a daemon handler who was once with the circus, joins the Queen's Air Force and has a series of adventures before he is falsely implicated in the death of an American businessman. While Crispin is on the run, he is briefly reunited with Rae, a former girlfriend, who is now part of a sinister religious cult.

Genre: Fantasy
Subjects: Imaginary wars and battles; Demonology; Adventure; Technology and civilization

1395. Humility Garden

1. *Humility Garden: An Unfinished Biography.* Roc, 1995.
2. *Delta City.* Penguin Group, 1996.

In the land of Salt where ghosts are very much a part of daily life, Humility Garden ascends to the powerful position of Divinarch, but is deposed by the aggressive Pati. Blinded and powerless, she is still the best hope of the population who turn to her to lead a revolution.

Genre: Fantasy
Subjects: Imaginary wars and battles; Ghost stories; Revolutions and revolutionists

Sawyer, Robert J.

1396.

1. *Far-Seer.* Ace, 1992.
2. *Fossil Hunter.* Ace, 1993.

On the moon revolving around an enormous planet called the Face of God, a race of sentient dinosaurs called Quintaglios have evolved to become the dominant species. The young Quintaglio apprentice astronomer Afsan makes the alarming discovery that the world on which the Quintaglios live will crash into its own planet in 100 years. Since his discoveries challenge Quintaglio religious beliefs, Afsan is punished and his efforts to help his people thwarted. A power struggle ensues, but Afsan's former mate discovers a ruined alien spacecraft whose technical secrets may help the Quintaglios escape their doomed world.

Genre: Science Fiction
Subjects: Astronomers; Life on other planets; Dinosaurs; Religion

Sayers, Valerie

1397.

1. *Due East.* Doubleday, 1987.
2. *How I Got Him Back, or Under the Cold Moon's Shine.* Doubleday, 1989.

Mary Faith Rapple is 15 and pregnant in a small town in South Carolina. Her mother is dead, her father is preoccupied, and the baby's father committed suicide. She fantasizes about her future, but takes responsibility for her baby. Once baby Jesse is born, Mary Faith has to deal with him and Stephen Dugan, who loves her but is married. The situations Mary Faith and her friends get involved in are both comic and touching.

Genre: Coming of Age
Subjects: Small town life; Teenagers; Unmarried mothers; Pregnancy
Place/Time: South Carolina—1980–

Scarborough, Elizabeth Ann. *See also* McCaffrey, Anne

1398.

1. *The Godmother.* Ace, 1994.
2. *The Godmother's Apprentice.* Ace, 1995.
3. *The Godmother's Web.* Ace, 1998.

Godmothers with ancient, mystical origins work their magic in modern day situations. Summoned by the wish of a Seattle social worker, Felicity Fortune takes command of the fate of Sno Quatrill, the runaway daughter of a rock star. Then Sno's apprenticeship with Felicity in Ireland keeps her out of the clutches of her truly evil stepmother, who is soon out of the picture. Then Sno's not terribly fatherly "King of Rock-n-Roll" dad takes up with Cindy Ellis, who herself needs the assistance of a Native American godmother when she escapes West Coast materialism to train horses in the Southwest.

Genre: Fantasy
Subjects: Fathers and daughters; Native Americans; Teenagers; Magic
Place/Time: Seattle (Wash.)—1980–; Ireland—1980–; Western states—1980–

1399.

1. *Nothing Sacred.* Doubleday, 1991.
2. *Last Refuge.* Bantam, 1992.

A valley in Tibet that had been a prison camp during the war-torn 21st century becomes a refuge from the effects of the inevitable nuclear holocaust. Called by mysterious voices seeming to beg for help and salvation, a young woman ventures out from this sanctuary on a mission to rebuild a ravaged, dangerous world.

Genre: Science Fiction
Subjects: Nuclear warfare; Mysticism; Technology and civilization

1400. Songkiller

1. *Phantom Banjo.* Bantam, 1991.
2. *Picking the Ballad's Bones.* Bantam, 1991.
3. *Strum Again?* Bantam, 1992.

Working through such likely channels as lawyers and bureaucrats, a group of devils attempts to wipe out music. Their reason: music is the enemy of evil because it makes the horrors, pain, and disappointment of the human condition easier to bear.

Genre: Fantasy
Subjects: Devil; Music; Good and evil

Schaub, Mary. *See* Nolan, William F. (Witch World series—*Flight of Vengeance* and *The Magestone*)

Schine, Cathleen

1401.

1. *Alice in Bed.* Knopf, 1983.

2. *To the Birdhouse.* Farrar, Straus & Giroux, 1990.

Alice Brody, a sophomore in college in the hospital, has legs that won't move. Her doctor can't find anything wrong, and her mother Brenda spends every day with her and is driving her crazy. As Alice is poked and prodded, she fights to gain control of her life. When she leaves the hospital, she becomes a photographer and marries, but her mother's crazy escapades keep her busy. These novels satirize crazy families and upper-middle-class society in contemporary New York.

Genre: Humor
Subjects: Mothers and daughters; Middle classes; Paralysis; Satire
Place/Time: New York (N. Y.)—1980–

Scholefield, Alan

1402.
1. *View of Vultures.* Doubleday, 1966.
2. *Great Elephant.* Morrow, 1968.

Although bound for imprisonment in a South African penal colony, Jamie Black manages to escape, is adopted by a Dutch family, marries, and raises a family. The sequel follows the adventures of his son Robie into the middle of the 19th century.

Genre: Historical Fiction
Subjects: Escapes; Adventure; Family life
Place/Time: South Africa—19th century

Schonstedt, Walter

1403.
1. *In Praise of Life.* Farrar, 1938.
2. *The Cradle Builder.* Farrar, 1940.

Peter Volkers experiences the dangers and hardships of life in Nazi Germany as a small child. He is rescued from the misery of the postwar period by an American, then marries and settles down in New England.

Genre: Historical Fiction
Subjects: World War II, 1939–1945; Family life
Place/Time: Germany—1945–1980; New England—1945–1980

Scott, Melissa

1404.
1. *Dreamships.* Tor, 1992.
2. *Dreaming Metal.* Tor, 1997.

Persephone is a planet on which the nature of artificial intelligence becomes a political issue. Various factions form around the question of whether AI's are sentient beings with their own rights. Class warfare breaks out when it becomes evident that this sophisticated technology could replace the lowest level of workers on the planet.

Genre: Science Fiction

Subjects: Life on other planets; Technology and civilization

Scott, Michael. *See Llewelyn, Morgan*

Scott, Paul

1405. The Raj Quartet
1. *The Jewel in the Crown.* Morrow, 1966.
2. *The Day of the Scorpion.* Morrow, 1968.
3. *The Towers of Silence.* Morrow, 1972.
4. *A Division of the Spoils.* Morrow, 1975.

The above titles have also been published in the following collection: *The Raj Quartet.* Morrow, 1976.

5. *Staying On.* Morrow, 1977.

The rape of a young Englishwoman in India in 1942 becomes part of the growing tension as India moves toward independence. Sarah and Susan Layton, Lady Manners, Kasim, and the evil Captain Merrick are all caught up in the violence of World War II and the strife of India. The intertwined lives of these characters show the corruption of the colonial system.

Genre: Historical Fiction
Subjects: World War II, 1939–1945; Cultural conflict; Social classes; Race relations; England—colonies; India—British occupation, 1765–1947
Place/Time: India—1900–1945; India—1945–1980

Seals, David

1406.
1. *The Powwow Highway.* Sky Books, 1983.
2. *Sweet Medicine.* Orion Books, 1992.

Three-hundred-pound, slow-witted Philbert Bono and friend Buddy rescue Buddy's sister Bonnie from jail. As the three escape, they make their way across New Mexico and back to their Montana Cheyenne reservation home. They are followed by police and Indian supporters as the trio have a series of crazy and hilarious adventures that satirize both Native Americans and whites.

Genre: Humor
Subjects: Native Americans; Escapes; Satire
Place/Time: Western states—1980–

Segal, Erich

1407.
1. *Love Story.* Harper, 1970.
2. *Oliver's Story.* Harper, 1977.

The ultimate tearjerker tells the story of wealthy Oliver Barrett IV, who goes to Harvard and meets Radcliffe scholarship student Jenny Cavilleri. Against all obstacles, they fall in love and marry. She puts Oliver through law school, but when everything seems to be going right, she dies. He is plagued by grief, but finally comes out of it when he meets Marcie Nash.

Genre: Romance
Subjects: Marriage; Class distinction; Leukemia; Bereavement; Death
Place/Time: New England—1945–1980

Selby, John

1408.
1. *Elegant Journey.* Farrar & Rinehart, 1944.
2. *Island in the Corn.* Farrar & Rinehart, 1941.
3. *Starbuck.* Farrar & Rinehart, 1943.

In 1839, the wealthy Trace family frees their slaves, leaves Maryland, and goes to Wisconsin to found the town of Hasselmans. The family builds the town, but their fortune begins to decline in the 1880s. They move to Missouri, where one of the grandchildren, Brant Starbuck, is a musical prodigy. His piano career is cut short when he injures his hands.

Genre: Historical Fiction
Subjects: Wealth; Cities and towns; Family life; Music
Place/Time: Maryland—19th century; Wisconsin—19th century; Missouri—19th century

Semprun, Jorge

1409.
1. *The Long Voyage.* McClelland & Stewart, 1964.
2. *Literature or Life.* Viking, 1997.

A young Spaniard fighting with the French Resistance during World War II is captured by the Nazis. He and 119 men are put in a cattle truck and sent to Buchenwald concentration camp. For five days he daydreams about his childhood and Resistance days. When the truck arrives at Buchenwald, he is left to face the horrors of the camp. The horrors of the camp, which burden his soul, stay with him even after the concentration camp is liberated. Even 50 years after the war, he feels burdened by his memories and uses literary references to detail his search for meaning.

Subjects: Autobiographical stories; Holocaust, Jewish, 1933–1945; Concentration camps
Place/Time: Germany—1900–1945; Spain—1945–1980

Settle, Mary Lee

1410. Beulah Quintet
1. *Prisons.* Putnam, 1973.
2. *O Beulah Land.* Viking, 1956.
3. *Know Nothing.* Viking, 1960.
4. *The Scapegoat.* Random House, 1980.
5. *The Killing Ground.* Farrar, 1982.

The turbulent history of West Virginia is told through the Lacey family. Jonathan Church leaves Cromwell-

ian England and settles in Virginia. His descendants fight in the American Revolution, then settle in rural West Virginia where they build their plantation. Later family members fight in the Civil War, battle the mine owners, and try to come to terms with life in West Virginia.

Genre: Family Saga; Historical Fiction
Subjects: Plantation life; United States—revolution, 1775–1783; United States—Civil War, 1861–1865; Coal mines and mining
Place/Time: West Virginia—multicentury span

Shaara, Jeff. *See* Shaara, Michael

Shaara, Michael *and* Shaara, Jeff

1411.
1. *Gods and Generals.* Ballantine, 1996.
2. *The Killer Angels.* McKay, 1974.
3. *The Last Full Measure.* Ballantine, 1998.

The Civil War, from its beginnings to the surrender at Appomattox, is seen through the eyes of four soldiers—Confederates Robert E. Lee and Thomas "Stonewall" Jackson and Union leaders Winfield Scott Hancock and Joshua Chamberlain. Lee and Hancock are disillusioned over their early careers, but go into their respective armies and soon make their mark as outstanding leaders. Chamberlain and Jackson are inexperienced but soon become outstanding soldiers. At the Battle of Fredericksburg, all the men see the horror and glory of war. At Chancellorville, Jackson is killed by his own men, and Lee realizes he must attack Washington if the South is to win. At Gettysburg, the three men are again on the same battlefield, and the bloody battle is relived through their eyes. When Lee is repelled, he retreats and tries to outmaneuver Grant's army, but eventually he surrenders at Appomattox. The lives of Civil War soldiers and the horrendous battles are vividly portrayed.

Genre: Historical Fiction; War
Subjects: United States—Civil War, 1861–1865; War; Soldiers—American; Lee, Robert E., 1807–1870; Jackson, Thomas Jonathan (Stonewall), 1824–1863; Hancock, Winfield Scott, 1824–1886; Chamberlain, Joshua, 1828–1914
Place/Time: Southern states—19th century

Shalom Rabinowitz. *See* Sholem Aleichem

Sharp, Margery

1412.
1. *Martha in Paris.* Little, 1962.
2. *Martha, Eric and George.* Little, 1964.

Martha was left on the doorstep of Eric Taylor's apartment in Paris. Eric is a reluctant father, but Mama Taylor takes the ungainly Martha to heart. She also encourages Martha's desire to be an artist. Ten years later, Martha is becoming famous, and she comes back to Paris from London where she is living. Eric brings his son George to see her paintings, and she must come to terms with him.

Genre: Coming of Age; Humor
Subjects: Abandoned children; Girls; Family life; Success; Artists
Place/Time: Paris (France)—1945–1980; France—1945–1980

Sharpe, Tom

1413.
1. *Wilt.* Vintage, 1984, 1976.
2. *The Wilt Alternative.* St. Martin's, 1979.
3. *Wilt on High.* Random House, 1984.

Professor Henry Wilt teaches liberal arts at the Fenland College of Arts and Technology in England. He is beset by stupid students, boorish superiors, and a dumb wife. When he dreams of killing his idiotic wife, he acts it out by disposing of a life-sized doll at a building site. He is arrested for murder when his wife disappears, but she does come back to clear him. Now, however, he is saddled with quadruplets and has to face terrorists and antinuclear protests. Poor Henry can only dream of being a hero, but his misadventures are hilarious.

Genre: Humor
Subjects: College life; Teachers; Dreams
Place/Time: England—1945–1980

Shatner, William

1414. Quest for Tomorrow
1. *Delta Search.* HarperPrism, 1997.
2. *In Alien Hands.* HarperPrism, 1997.
3. *Step into Chaos.* HarperPrism, 1999.
4. *Beyond the Stars.* HarperPrism, 2000.

Jim Endicott's ambition to be a student at the Terran Space Academy is crushed and his life is endangered when the application process reveals his unique DNA configuration, which could provide the key to creating a supercomputer of combined human minds. Jim's biological father, a member of the terran intelligence community, pursues him. He is both hunted and befriended by various superior aliens, loses his first love, and ultimately becomes a mercenary.

Genre: Science Fiction; Coming of Age
Subjects: Genetics; Computers; Extraterrestrial beings; Love; Mercenary soldiers

1415. Tekwar
1. *Tekwar.* Putnam, 1989.
2. *Teklab.* Putnam, 1991.
3. *Teklords.* Putnam, 1991.
4. *Tek Vengeance.* Putnam, 1993.
5. *Tek Secret.* Ace/Putnam, 1993.
6. *Tek Power.* Ace/Putnam, 1994.

7. *Tek Money.* G. P. Putnam, 1995.
8. *Tek Kill.* G. P. Putnam, 1996.
9. *Tek Net.* G. P. Putnam, 1997.

In Los Angeles of the 22nd century, private eye Jack Cardigan and his sidekick Sid Gomez battle crime and corruption surrounded by androids and robots. A recurring menace throughout these futuristic tales is the power of the insidious mind-altering drug Tek.

Genre: Science Fiction; Crime Novel
Subjects: Detectives; Crime and criminals; Technology and civilization; Underworld
Place/Time: Los Angeles (Calif.)—1980–

1416. War
1. *Man O' War.* G. P. Putnam, 1996.
2. *The Law of War.* G. P. Putnam, 1998.

Brilliant, but unconventional, career diplomat Benton Hawkes is assigned to duty on the colonized planet Mars, which in the 22nd century has become a source of minerals and other raw materials for Earth. Initially sent to the planet to subdue a revolutionary movement, Hawkes becomes its leader and attempts peace negotiations with Earth, which put his life in danger.

Genre: Science Fiction
Subjects: Diplomats; Life on other planets; Mines and mining; Mars (planet), exploration of ; Revolutions and revolutionists

Shaw, Bob

1417. Orbitsville
1. *Orbitsville.* Ace, 1975.
2. *Orbitsville Departure.* DAW Books, 1985.
3. *Orbitsville Judgement.* Gollancz, 1990.

Alien beings, the Ultrans, built an enormous sphere, millions of times the size of Earth, which contains its own sun as a trap for sentient beings of the universe. The artificial world attracts the world's population to such an extent that soon Earth is a half-deserted historical curiosity. Scientist Garry Dallen learns of the Ultrans' plans seconds before Orbitsville and its population are whisked millions of light years into outer space.

Genre: Science Fiction
Subjects: Extraterrestrial beings; Space colonies

Shaw, Irwin

1418.
1. *Rich Man, Poor Man.* Delacorte Press, 1970.
2. *Beggarman, Thief.* Delacorte Press, 1977.

This family chronicle tells the story of the children of Axel Jordache, a poor baker in a small town on the Hudson River. Thomas becomes a prizefighter, Rudolph a successful businessman, and Gretchen an actress. From the 1940s to the 1970s, the three siblings fight, love, and win their way from rags to riches. After Tom's murder, his son Wesley tries to uncover his father's past and discovers the tragedies of the whole family.

Genre: Family Saga
Subjects: Brothers and sisters; Wealth
Place/Time: New York (N. Y.)—1945–1980

Shayne, Maggie

1419.
1. *Eternity.* Jove, 1998.
2. *Infinity.* Jove, 1999.

Two witches find that the path to love is both difficult and immortal. When Raven St. James is hung for witchcraft in 17th-century England, only the priest Duncan Wallace tries to help her. Since Raven is immortal, she later shows herself to Duncan, who then follows her to America, but there, the villagers grow suspicious of her. She is again accused of witchcraft, and Duncan is killed trying to save her. Three hundred years later, Duncan is reborn, and he and Raven are finally united. Arianna Sinclair marries her warlock lover Nicodimus Lachlan in 16th-century Scotland, but their happiness is disrupted when Nicodimus's enemy raids their village and kills Arianna. Arianna finds she is immortal, but before she can reappear, Nicodimus is killed. She too must wait hundreds of years for her love to be resurrected. Both woman find that love is immortal.

Genre: Historical Romance; Fantasy
Subjects: Lovers; Witchcraft; Immortality
Place/Time: England—16th century; Scotland—
   16th century; United States—1980–

Sheckley, Robert. *See* Zelazny, Roger

Sheffield, Charles

1420.
1. *Aftermath.* Bantam, 1998.
2. *Starfire.* Bantam, 1999.

In these near-future tales, radiation released from the Alpha Centauri supernova forces scientists and government officials to scramble to control damage to electronic technology and to the Earth's environment. While a protective shield is being put in place in space, a serial killer strikes the space colony of workers. The only way to combat the murderer seems to be to release a despicable criminal who may understand the killer's mind set.

Genre: Science Fiction
Subjects: Technology and civilization; Environment;
   Murder and murderers
Place/Time: United States—1980–

1421. Heritage Universe
1. *Summertide.* Del Rey, 1990.
2. *Divergence.* Del Rey, 1991.
3. *Transcendence.* Del Rey, 1992.

Enormous artifacts scattered throughout the galaxy by a mysterious and possibly extinct race called the Builders represent different things to the central characters in these stories: intellectual challenge to Darya Long, mystery and adventure to Hans Rebka, and wealth to Louis Nenda and Atvar H'sial. As they come closer and closer to the solution, however, it becomes increasingly likely that the Builders were somehow closely related to the dangerous, autocratic Zardalu, who had been defeated but not wiped out by a slave revolt.

Genre: Science Fiction
Subjects: Extraterrestrial beings; Life on other planets

1422. The Jupiter Novels
1. *Higher Education.* (Written with Jerry
   Pournelle) Tor, 1996.
2. *The Billion Dollar Boy.* Tor, 1997.
3. *Putting Up Roots.* Tor, 1997.
4. *The Cyborg from Earth.* Tor, 1998.

In each of these futuristic works, a young man discovers the attractions, challenges, and hazards of life in space. Two of the youths discover their own talents and personal qualities as they brave the hazards of mining in outer space. Abandoned by his family, another young man becomes a part of an interstellar exploration team. The offspring of a terran transportation dynasty, although seemingly unsuited for military life, is sent to a distant outpost of the Space Navy and becomes a pawn in a conspiracy that reaches throughout the solar system.

Genre: Science Fiction; Coming of Age
Subjects: Youth; Adventure; Outer space, exploration of

1423. Proteus
1. *Sight of Proteus.* Ace, 1978.
2. *Proteus Unbound.* Del Rey, 1989.
3. *Proteus in the Underworld.* Simon &
   Schuster, 1995.

In the not-so-distant future, a process called form changing is allowing humans to alter the appearance and functions of their bodies. Behrooz Wolf's job is to track illegal use of form changing and ultimately stop a mad genius who plans to destroy the solar system by tampering with the process.

Genre: Science Fiction
Subjects: Bionics; Earth, destruction of; Insanity

Shelby, Graham

1424.
1. *The Devil Is Loose.* Doubleday, 1974.
2. *The Wolf at the Door.* Doubleday, 1975.

A chronicle of the acquisitive, aggressive war years of 12th-century crusader and English King Richard the Lion Hearted is followed by a narrative of the reign of his brother John I, who possessed none of his sibling's virtues, but most of his faults.

Genre: Historical Fiction
Subjects: Politics—England; Richard I, King of England, 1157–1199; Kings and rulers; Crusades—third, 1189–1192; John, King of England, 1167–1216
Place/Time: England—12th century

1425.
1. *The Knights of Dark Renown.* Weybright & Talley, 1969.
2. *The Kings of Vain Intent.* Weybright & Talley, 1971.

The 12th-century events that precipitated the Third Crusade—Saladin's capture of Jerusalem and the treachery of Reynald of Chatillon—are followed by the saga of the English King Richard the Lion Hearted, who failed in his attempt to capture Jerusalem but negotiated a treaty with Saladin that allowed pilgrims to enter the holy places of Jerusalem.

Genre: Historical Fiction
Subjects: Crusades—third, 1189–1192; Knights and knighthood; Richard I, King of England, 1157–1199; Muslims; Islam; Christianity
Place/Time: Jerusalem (Palestine)—12th century; Palestine—12th century

1426.
1. *The Cannaways.* Doubleday, 1978.
2. *The Cannaway Concern.* Doubleday, 1980.

Georgian England and continental Europe are the background for the story of the Cannaway family, whose patriarch founds a dynasty of wealthy carriage makers. The sequel follows the adventures of his daughter Charlotte through a disastrous elopement and further romantic adventures.

Genre: Family Saga
Subjects: Wealth; Love
Place/Time: England—19th century

Sheldon, Charles Monroe

1427.
1. *In His Steps.* Advance, 1897.
2. *"Jesus is Here."* Doran, 1914.

A shabby young man looking for work appears in the small town of Raymond. Reverend Maxwell gradually realizes that he is a witness to a reappearance of Jesus Christ in the late 1800s. In the sequel, the story of the modern-day appearance of Jesus continues in New York and Washington, D. C.

Genre: Christian Fiction
Subjects: Christianity; Jesus Christ
Place/Time: New York (N. Y.)—19th century; New York (N. Y.)—1900–1945

Sheldon, Sidney

1428.
1. *The Other Side of Midnight.* Morrow, 1974.
2. *Memories of Midnight.* Morrow, 1990.

Two of the great trashy novels tell the story of sexy and successful Chicago businesswoman Catherine Alexander, who marries British playboy Larry Douglas, who loves sexy movie star Noelle Paige, who is mistress to Greek Tycoon Constantin Demiris. When Noelle and Larry get back together, Catherine refuses to divorce him so they plot her murder. Catherine awakens as an amnesiac in a Greek convent, and Demiris engineers numerous plots to get revenge on Catherine, Noelle, and Larry. Melodramatic twists, glamorous locations, and sexy scenes keep the plot moving and exciting.

Subjects: Businesswomen; Actors and actresses; Wealth; Society novels; Amnesia
Place/Time: Chicago (Ill.)—1980–; Greece—1980–; Illinois—1980–

Sherburne, James

1429.
1. *Hacey Miller.* Houghton, 1971.
2. *The Way to Fort Pillow.* Houghton, 1972.

Hacey Miller lives on a small farm in Lexington, Kentucky, in 1845. Because Hacey's family owns slaves, he can't understand the antislavery agitation of Cassius Clay, but attending the trial of a young slave accused of killing Clay's infant son convinces Hacey that he must join the emancipation movement. As Hacey grows up, he teaches at Berea College, fights with the Union in the Civil War, and commands African American troops during the war. Real people from the antislavery movement are portrayed in the books.

Genre: Historical Fiction; War
Subjects: Slavery; Abolitionists; United States—Civil War, 1861–1865; War; African Americans
Place/Time: Kentucky—19th century

Sheridan, Jane. *Pseud. of* Pauline Glen Winslow

1430.
1. *Damaris.* St. Martin's Press, 1978.
2. *My Lady Hoyden.* St. Martin's, 1981.
3. *Love at Sunset.* St. Martin's, 1982.

From the villages of New England to the courts of Europe, three generations of passionate St. Cloud women follow their desires as they find romance and forbidden pleasure. Damaris St. Cloud is the toast of the town in Regency England. She is trapped in a loveless marriage, but follows her lover to America where they find happiness. Her daughter is too lively for Victorian England and is forced to marry a penniless man, but she flees and becomes the darling of Imperial French society. Clarissa, Damaris's granddaughter, also finds she is in love with the wrong man and must fight for the right one.

Genre: Family Saga; Historical Romance
Subjects: Love affairs; Marriage problems
Place/Time: New England—18th century; New England—19th century; England—18th century; England—19th century; France—18th century; France—19th century

Sherman, Jory

1431. Buckskinners Trilogy
1. *The Medicine Horn.* Tor, 1991.
2. *Trapper's Moon.* Forge, 1994.

Lem Hawkes takes his young bride Roberta to Kentucky in 1793 to find better farm land. While Lem is happy farming, Roberta wants wealth, and she eventually leaves him and their young son Morgan. When Morgan is 16, father and son head for the Rocky Mountains to trap beaver. They are looking for mountain man Silas Morgan, but find their way stopped by Josie Montez who blames Silas for his brother's death. Father and son must outwit Josie, live through killer tornados, and fight bad men and Native Americans.

Genre: Western
Subjects: Fathers and sons; Frontier and pioneer life; Mountain life
Place/Time: Western states—19th century

1432. Grass Kingdom
1. *The Barons of Texas.* Forge, 1997.
2. *The Baron Range.* Tor, 1998.
3. *The Baron Brand.* Forge, 2000.
4. *Grass Kingdom.* Tor, 1994.

The saga of the Brand family of Texas begins when Martin Baron and Juanita Salazar land on the coast of Texas in the early 19th century. They set off to find good land but encounter Apaches, Mexicans, and corrupt ranchers. Eventually, Martin starts his ranch and marries Caroline Darnell. Their son Anson grows up to be wild but runs the million acre Box B Ranch when his father Martin runs away after discovering his wife has syphilis. Anson fights Apaches, bandits, and a vengeful Mexican rancher who wants to kill the Brands. Eventually, Martin returns and must decide what to do if Texas secedes from the union as the Civil War opens. In the 1920s, the family head Matt Baron finds his family under attack from a sexual psychopath and must do everything he can to save the family.

Genre: Family Saga
Subjects: Family life; Ranch life; Frontier and pioneer life
Place/Time: Texas—19th century; Texas—1900–1945

Sherwood, Valerie. *Pseud. of* Jeanne Hines

1433.
1. *Bold Breathless Love.* Warner, 1982.
2. *Rash Reckless Love.* Warner, 1981.
3. *Wild Willful Love.* Warner, 1982.
4. *Rich Radiant Love.* Warner, 1983.

Beautiful Imogene falls in love with dashing Caribbean buccaneer Van Ryker, who owns plantations in Carolina and Jamaica, but his conniving brothers and sisters want to become his heirs by getting rid of her. Imogene is reunited with Van Ryker only after surviving shipwrecks, fever, rape, and assaults. Their daughter Georgiana, who was lost at sea and thought dead, also goes through numerous adventures, separations, and sensuous seductions before she is reunited with her parents and her true love Steve.

Genre: Historical Romance
Subjects: Pirates; Love affairs; Sex
Place/Time: Caribbean region—17th century

1434.
1. *Lovesong.* Pocket Books, 1985.
2. *Windsong.* Pocket Books, 1986.
3. *Nightsong.* Pocket Books, 1986.

Platinum-haired Carolina Lightfoot and her lover Kells, king of the Caribbean buccaneers, race from England to Port Royal, to Spain as the lovers overcome obstacles before they can be together. In 16th-century England, Carolina is seduced by a rake and sent home to Virginia. On the way home, her ship is captured by pirate Kells, and it is love at first sight. When they go to England to get Kells a pardon, he discovers that someone is masquerading as him and his Spanish wife is alive. Carolina is captured by the Spanish and must fight for her life and her love.

Genre: Historical Romance
Subjects: Pirates; Love affairs; Sex
Place/Time: England—16th century; Caribbean region—16th century; Spain—16th century

Shinn, Sharon

1435.
1. *Archangel.* Ace, 1996.
2. *Jovah's Angel.* Ace, 1997.
3. *The Alleluia Files.* Ace, 1998.

On the colonized planet Samaria, which is guarded and ruled by genetically engineered angels, there is about to be a change of command. The old angel Raphael is to yield to Gabriel at the next festival of song, but first Gabriel must meet and win the love of Rachel, the bride who has been prophesied for him, but who he finds living as a slave and reluctant to recognize her role in the grand plan. In the next tale, angels and humans use means both mystical and technological to deal with the planet's increasingly violent weather. A hundred years later, an uneasy alliance of renegade angels and humans search for a lost document in their effort to challenge the power of the angel Bael and their ruler Jovah.

Genre: Fantasy; Science Fiction
Subjects: Life on other planets; Angels; Love; Environment

Shirley, John

1436. A Song Called Youth
1. *Eclipse.* Bluejay Books, 1985.
2. *Eclipse Penumbra.* Popular Library, 1988.
3. *Eclipse Corona.* Popular Library, 1990.

Europe following World War III is the scene of this cyberpunk trilogy of the near future. Resistance fighters, many of them rock music enthusiasts, battle fascist forces with advanced technology. Mass media is only one of the villains.

Genre: Science Fiction
Subjects: Imaginary wars and battles; Government, resistance to; Fascism; Technology and civilization

Sholem Aleichem. *Pseud. of* Shalom Rabinowitz

1437.
1. *The Old Country.* Crown, 1946, 1894.
2. *Tevye's Daughters.* Crown, 1949, 1894.

Through a series of interconnected short stories, the tale of Tevye, the dairyman, his family, and his village in the Jewish Pale of Settlements in Russia is told. Tevye is a philosopher, though he has no book learning and is ruled by his heart not his head. Even though he is poor and feels the misery of life, he has a sense of humor and love of life. Through these stories, which formed the basis for the Broadway musical *Fiddler on the Roof*, the vanished world of the Jewish Pale is recaptured.

Subjects: Country life; Family life; Judaism; Jews, persecution of; Jews—Russia
Place/Time: Russia—1900–1917

Sholokhov, Mikhail

1438.
1. *And Quiet Flows the Don.* Knopf, 1934.
2. *The Don Flows Home to the Sea.* Knopf, 1941.
3. *Tales of the Don.* Knopf, 1962.
4. *Seeds of Tomorrow.* Knopf, 1942.
5. *Harvest on the Don.* Knopf, 1960.

Starting before World War I, the Cossack peasants who live by the Don have to use their earthiness, bawdiness, and shrewdness to survive the Russian Revolution. Gregory Melekhov, a young Cossack, fights the Revolution, then fights with the Reds and Whites. As the Communists take control, they force the peasants

into a farm collective system, which ultimately pressures them to revolt.

Genre: Historical Fiction
Subjects: Soviet Union—revolution, 1917–1921; Country life; Communism—Soviet Union; Cossacks; Collective settlements
Place/Time: Soviet Union—1917–1945

Shott, James R.

1439. People of the Promise
1. *Leah.* Herald Press, 1990.
2. *Joseph.* Herald Press, 1992.
3. *Hagar.* Herald Press, 1992.
4. *Esau.* Herald Press, 1993.
5. *Deborah.* Herald Press, 1993.
6. *Othniel.* Herald, 1994.
7. *Abigail.* Herald, 1996.
8. *Bathsheba.* Herald, 1996.

The lives of the people of the Old Testament are recreated to show how faith enables them to triumph over their human weaknesses. Leah must fight to win Jacob's love, while Joseph must overcome being sold into slavery. Hagar is forgotten when Sarah bears a son for Abraham. Esau is denied God's blessing, and Deborah helps lead her people. Othniel must become a judge and leader of his people, while David will become involved with two women, Abigail and Bathsheba, who will change his life.

Genre: Christian Fiction; Gentle Read
Subjects: Religion; Biblical stories; Faith
Place/Time: Palestine—multicentury span

Shuler, Linda Lay

1440.
1. *She Who Remembers.* Arbor House, 1988.
2. *Voice of the Eagle.* Morrow, 1992.
3. *Let the Drum Speak.* Morrow, 1996.

In the 13th century in the region that is now New Mexico, 16-year-old Kwani is driven from her Anasazi clan, because the people think she is a witch. In the wilderness, she meets Kokopelli, a Toltec Indian trader who protects her and takes her to another tribe. There she comes under the wing of spiritual leader She Who Remembers. Later Kwani mates with Tolonqua and goes back to live with Tolonqua's people. There she and her children help build a city on the ridge and live their lives among friends. Kwani's daughter Antelope travels with her mate to what is now Oklahoma to live with the Hasinai people, until her visions force her back to her own people. Faithful to the archaeological and anthropological evidence, these books are filled with authentic details that tell the stories of pre-Columbian Indians.

Genre: Historical Fiction
Subjects: Native Americans; Pueblo Indians
Place/Time: New Mexico—13th century

Shulman, Irving

1441.
1. *The Amboy Dukes.* Doubleday, 1947.
2. *Cry Tough.* Dial, 1949.
3. *The Big Brokers.* Dial, 1951.

Starting with juvenile gangs in the Brownsville section of Brooklyn during World War II, the narrative then moves to the life of Mitchell Wolf, who fluctuates between responsibility and lawlessness and finally becomes involved with a national crime syndicate.

Genre: Crime Novel
Subjects: Gangsters; Crime and criminals; Underworld
Place/Time: New York (N. Y.)—1945–1980

Shulman, Sandra

1442.
1. *The Florentine.* G. K. Hall, 1973.
2. *Francesca: The Madonna of the Shadows.* New English Library, 1973.

Francesca de Narni must disguise herself as a young man when her distinguished family of Renaissance Florence is held responsible for a plot against Lorenzo de Medici. Her life incognito puts her in constant danger, but also allows her to develop her artistic talent, while the magnetic Milanese Ridolfo is always in the background.

Genre: Historical Fiction
Subjects: Medici, Lorenzo De, Il Magnifico, 1449–1492; Impersonations; Renaissance
Place/Time: Florence (Italy)—15th century; Italy—15th century

Sienkiewicz, Henryk

1443. Trilogy Series
1. *With Fire and Sword.* Little, Brown, 1890.
2. *The Deluge.* Little, Brown, 1891.
3. *Fire in the Steppe.* Little, Brown, 1893, 1887. (Original title: *Pan Michael.*)

Better known for *Quo Vadis*, Polish 1905 Nobel laureate Sienkiewicz wrote this thrilling epic of Poland's fight for freedom from 1648 to 1673. Yan Skshetuski goes to gather information about the Cossack rebellion and is captured by the Russians. He escapes to bring help to besieged Poles. Five years after the Cossack attack, the Poles are now threatened by Swedish and Russian troops, and Andrei Kmita fights to save his country and his love from the invaders. Volodyovski, who rode with Skshetuski and Kmita, becomes Poland's greatest hero as he fights the Turks who challenge Poland and the church. Heroic battles, pure love, and superb characters keep the plot racing as it presents a timeless message of hope.

Genre: Adventure; Historical Fiction; War
Subjects: Adventure; War; Cossacks

Place/Time: Poland—17th century

Sillitoe, Alan

1444.
1. *The Death of William Posters.* Knopf, 1965.
2. *A Tree on Fire.* Doubleday, 1968.
3. *The Flame of Life.* W. H. Allen, 1974.

England and Algeria of the 1950s are the backgrounds for the story of Frank Dawley, a young Englishman whose search for freedom and identity propels him toward revolutionary and utopian causes, including the rebellion of Algerian guerrillas against the government of France.

Subjects: Revolutions and revolutionists; Men—psychology
Place/Time: England—1945–1980; Algeria—1945–1980

Silone, Ignazio

1445.
1. *Bread and Wine.* Harper, 1937.
2. *The Seed Beneath the Snow.* Harper, 1942.

Pietro Spina, a young Socialist, secretly returns to Fascist Italy in the 1930s after 15 years in exile. He works for the liberty of his people, but finds the peasants crushed by fear, poverty, ignorance, and superstition. He flees to a mountain village to recuperate, but finds the same poverty. Later he hides in his grandmother's house, eventually turning himself in to the authorities to save a friend.

Subjects: Socialism; Fascism; Poverty; Peasants; Government, resistance to
Place/Time: Italy—1900–1945

Silverberg, Robert

1446. Majipoor
1. *Sorcerers of Majipoor.* HarperPrism, 1996.
2. *Lord Prestimion.* HarperPrism, 1999.
3. *Lord Valentine's Castle.* Harper, 1980.
4. *Majipoor Chronicles.* Arbor House, 1982.
5. *Valentine Pontifex.* Arbor House, 1983.
6. *The Mountains of Majipoor.* Bantam, 1995.

Published more recently, but occupying an earlier place in fictional chronology, the first two works set the stage for the reign of Lord Valentine on the enormous, exotic planet Majipoor by relating the events surrounding a civil war involving the line of succession to the throne. The outcome of the war is that a spell is cast over the population, which produces amnesia and insanity. Lacking any memory of his previous life, Valentine suddenly finds himself on the outskirts of Pidruid, the legendary city of Majipoor. His first quest is simply to discover who he is and what his origins are. With the help of a strange band of performers, Valentine discovers his birthright, assumes the leadership of Majipoor, then deals with internal conflicts and his potential successor, whose nature is very different from his own.

Genre: Science Fiction; Fantasy
Subjects: Amnesia; Imaginary cities; Life on other planets; Inheritance and succession

Simmons, Dan

1447.
1. *Hyperion.* Doubleday, 1989.
2. *The Fall of Hyperion.* Doubleday, 1990.
3. *Endymion.* Bantam, 1995.
4. *The Rise of Endymion.* Bantam, 1997.

In the middle of a 28th-century war that threatens civilization, a group of explorers sets off to the deep space planet, Hyperion. Mysteries and challenges await them in the form of the powerful being called Shrike, who guards the strange tombs that seem about to open to divulge the secrets of the universe. The narrative jumps more than 200 years to a time after the fall of civilization on Hyperion when the Catholic Church and its associated military organization called Pax have become the organizing forces of the universe. Challenging the power of the church is Aenea, who is part human woman, part machine. Aenea is overtly protected and loved by the shepherd Endymion, but also followed and secretly guarded by the mysterious creature Shrike.

Genre: Science Fiction
Subjects: Imaginary wars and battles; Interplanetary voyages; Extraterrestrial beings; Catholic faith

Simpson, Mona

1448.
1. *Anywhere But Here.* Knopf, 1987.
2. *The Lost Father.* Knopf, 1992.

Adele Stevenson takes her daughter Anne and flees their provincial hometown in Wisconsin for California. Adele encourages Anne's success as child star, but for her own selfish motives. Anne, however, longs for the home she left. When she is in medical school, she becomes obsessed with finding her father, who deserted the family when she was a child. Both novels deal with obsession in a dysfunctional family.

Subjects: Girls; Mothers and daughters; Actors and actresses; Desertion and nonsupport
Place/Time: Wisconsin—1980–; California—1980–

Sinclair, Andrew

1449.
1. *Gog.* Macmillan, 1967.
2. *Magog.* Harper, 1972.

The gigantic Gog finds himself on the shore of Scotland just after World War I with no memory of his previous life and with tattoos on his hands reading "Gog"

and "Magog." Gog travels back in time, bringing together some incongruous historical and literary figures before his brother Magog takes the narrative further into the 20th century in a series of guises that include a revolutionary, a movie mogul, and a greedy urban developer.

Genre: Fantasy
Subjects: Amnesia; Time travel

Sinclair, April

1450.
1. *Coffee Will Make You Black.* Hyperion, 1993.
2. *Ain't Gonna Be the Same Fool Twice.* Hyperion, 1995.

Jean "Stevie" Stevenson is an eleven-year-old African American girl living on Chicago's South Side in the late 1960s. She listens to Dr. Martin Luther King and Malcolm X and is caught up in the growth of the black pride movement. Yet as she develops physically, she still looks at dark skin unfavorably and isn't sure breasts are worth the trouble. When she goes to college in the 1970s, she discovers her bisexuality and explores it with female lovers. After college, she keeps her sexuality hidden from her family as she takes a procession of different male and female lovers. When her grandmother becomes ill, she finally finds peace with herself and her life.

Genre: Coming of Age
Subjects: African Americans; Girls; Bisexuality
Place/Time: Chicago (Ill.)—1945–1980; San Francisco (Calif.)—1945–1980

Sinclair, Harold

1451.
1. *The Horse Soldiers.* Harper, 1956.
2. *The Cavalryman.* Harper, 1958.

These fictionalized accounts of real battles show the horrors and devastation of the Civil War. General Jack Marlowe leads a 16-day raid in the South beginning at LaGrange and ending at Baton Rouge. In 1864, Marlowe is ordered to eliminate the Sioux tribes in the Dakotas. Marlowe leads his raw cavalrymen into the Badlands to fight a devastating battle.

Genre: Adventure; War
Subjects: Native Americans; United States—Civil War, 1861–1865; Army, United States; Adventure; Battles
Place/Time: Southern states—19th century; South Dakota—19th century

1452.
1. *American Years.* Doubleday, 1938.
2. *The Years of Growth.* Doubleday, 1940.
3. *Years of Illusion.* Doubleday, 1941.

The history of Everton, Illinois, from 1830 to 1914 is told through its inhabitants. The Ransoms are a prosperous business family, and the McGuires are a poor immigrant family who help settle the town. Both families and the town become involved with the election of Lincoln as president, the Civil War, and the political and social events that change their town.

Genre: Historical Fiction
Subjects: Small town life; Social classes; Family life; United States—Civil War, 1861–1865; Politics—United States
Place/Time: Illinois—19th century

Sinclair, Upton

1453.
1. *Sylvia.* Winston, 1913.
2. *Sylvia's Marriage.* Winston, 1914.

A young Virginia belle marries an upper-class man so that she can have a position in society. However, her life is destroyed when she finds out that her respectable husband has gonorrhea.

Subjects: Social classes; Marriage; Sexually transmitted diseases
Place/Time: Virginia—1900–1945

1454. Lanny Budd Series
1. *World's End.* Viking, 1940.
2. *Between Two Worlds.* Viking, 1941.
3. *Dragon's Teeth.* Viking, 1942.
4. *Wide Is the Gate.* Viking, 1943.
5. *Presidential Agent.* Viking, 1944.
6. *Dragon Harvest.* Viking, 1945.
7. *A World to Win.* Viking, 1946.
8. *Presidential Mission.* Viking, 1947.
9. *One Clear Call.* Viking, 1948.
10. *O Shepherd, Speak!* Viking, 1949.
11. *The Return of Lanny Budd.* Viking, 1953.

In 1913 at the age of 13, Lanny Budd witnesses the important events taking place in Europe. He sees the outbreak of World War I and the peace conference, then the rise of communism and fascism. As he grows up, he sees the forces of freedom fighting the oppression of fascism as America enters World War II. Crucial events and significant historical people are seen through Lanny's eyes as a sweeping world picture of an epoch is drawn.

Genre: Historical Fiction
Subjects: World War I, 1914–1918; World War II, 1939–1945; Politics—Europe; Politics—United States; Good and evil; Fascism; Communism; National Socialism; World politics
Place/Time: United States—1900–1945; Europe—1900–1945

Singer, Isaac Bashevis

1455.
1. *The Manor.* Farrar, Straus & Giroux, 1967.
2. *The Estate.* Farrar, Straus & Giroux, 1969.

During the period from the Polish insurrection of 1863 to the end of the 19th century, Calman Jacoby and his family emerge from the ghetto to seek a new life in a country that is struggling to throw off its feudal past. Jacoby watches as his children draw away from his traditional Jewish ways. He and his children seek a new life as their country changes.

Genre: Historical Fiction
Subjects: Jews; Family life; Parents and children
Place/Time: Poland—19th century

Skelton, C. L. (Clement Lister)

1456. The Regiment Series
1. *The Maclarens.* Dial, 1978.
2. *The Regiment.* Dial, 1979.
3. *Beloved Soldiers.* Crown, 1984.

The tempestuous story of two Scottish families, the Maclarens and the Bruces, is set against the British Empire from the Indian Mutiny through World War II. In 1857, both Andrew Maclaren and Willie Bruce are devoted to their regiment, but they also both love Maud Westburn. Both men's descendants continue to lead the regiment and defend the Empire in World Wars I and II.

Genre: Family Saga; Historical Fiction; War
Subjects: War; Army, British—officers; Adventure; Battles
Place/Time: Scotland—19th century; Scotland—1900–1945

Sladek, John

1457. Roderick
1. *Roderick, or The Education of a Young Machine.* Granada, 1980.
2. *Roderick at Random, or Further Education of a Young Machine.* Carroll & Graf, 1988.

With allusions to the 18th-century author Tobias Smollett and the contemporary author Isaac Asimov, these works satirize modern American life as seen by an impressionable little computer that lacks human experience but is hungry for knowledge.

Genre: Humor; Science Fiction
Subjects: Computers; Education

Slaughter, Frank G.

1458. American Civil War
1. *In a Dark Garden.* Doubleday, 1946.
2. *The Stubborn Heart.* Doubleday, 1950.

A young southern surgeon treats both northern and southern prisoners during the Civil War. His loyalties are stretched still further when the woman he loves turns out to be a northern spy and turns their plantation into a hospital during Reconstruction.

Genre: Historical Fiction

Subjects: United States—Civil War, 1861–1865;
   War; Love; Surgeons; Reconstruction
Place/Time: Southern states—19th century

Sledge, Linda Ching

1459.
1. *Empire of Heaven.* Bantam, 1990.
2. *A Map of Paradise.* Bantam, 1997.

In mid-19th-century China, rural unrest leads to the
Taiping Rebellion. Rulan, a village girl, has the gift of
healing and is sent by the rebels to spy on a wealthy
household. Later, she joins the rebellion, becomes a
woman warrior, and falls in love with rebel general
Pao An. When the rebellion fails, Rulan and Pao An
flee to Hong Kong. They dream of going to Hawaii and
rebuilding their lives. Pao An sells himself as a coolie
laborer to pay for their passage, but Rulan is left in Hawaii while Pao An is sent to California. After seven
years, the two are finally reunited in Hawaii, but their
daughter Molly rejects Chinese customs. Rulan and
Pao An set up a business and flourish, but Molly struggles to find a life that represents a fusing of American
and Chinese traditions.

Genre: Historical Fiction
Subjects: Family life; Peasants; War; Immigrants;
   Chinese—United States
Place/Time: China—19th century; Hawaii—19th
   century; California—19th century

Slonczewski, Joan

1460.
1. *A Door into Ocean.* Arbor House, 1986.
2. *Daughter of Elysium.* AvoNova, 1993.
3. *The Children Star.* Tor, 1998.

The thread connecting these works is the water world
planet of Shora, where the all-female alien population
lives on floating islands of roots. First the idyllic atmosphere of the planet is threatened by an expedition of
human men from Shora's twin planet Valedon, then by
internal strife between the technologically sophisticated Elysians and the rural Windclans, which eventually draws the original inhabitants, the Sharers, into its
complex power play. Two hundred years later a renegade Sharer becomes involved when the stability of
the confederacy of human worlds known as the Fold is
threatened by the plot of greedy Elysian businessmen
to take over Prokaryon, a planet whose ecological system seems to be regulated by mysterious forces.

Genre: Science Fiction
Subjects: Life on other planets; Oceans; Women; Interplanetary wars; Cultural conflict

Small, Bertrice

1461.
1. *Skye O'Malley.* Ballantine, 1982.

2. *All the Sweet Tomorrows.* New American Library, 1984.
3. *A Love for All Time.* Ballantine, 1986.
4. *This Heart of Mine.* Ballantine, 1985.
5. *Lost Love Found.* Ballantine, 1989.

Black-haired, blue-eyed luscious Skye O'Malley
loves and loses four different men as she moves from
the court of Queen Elizabeth I to a harem in Turkey and
back again. This independent female experiences incest, rape, love, sexual bondage, and every other imag-
inable sexual experience during her travels. Her
children, hunky Conn O'Malley and violet-eyed
Valentina, also experience sexual trials as they search
for love.

Genre: Historical Romance
Subjects: Sex; Courts and courtiers; Turks
Place/Time: England—16th century; Turkey—16th
   century

1462. Skye's Legacy Series
1. *Deceived.* Kensington, 1998.
2. *Bedazzled.* Kensington, 1999.
3. *Besieged.* Kensington, 2000.

The 17th-century descendants of Skye O'Malley learn
that love can be sensual when they are kidnapped like
their 14th-century ancestor. Heiress Aurora Kimberly
refuses to marry an English duke she has never seen, so
she runs away. She trades places with her stepsister
and ends up falling in love with the duke she refused to
marry. In 1625, Lady India Lindley tries to elope with
her suitor but is kidnapped by Ottoman pirates. She becomes the wife of the ruler of the Barbary state of El
Sinut, and a sensual body slave. When she is kidnapped again, she finally finds true love. Lady Fortune
Lindley must return to Ireland to marry an Irish
Protestant, William Devers, but it is his disinherited
Catholic brother Kiernan she loves.

Genre: Historical Romance
Subjects: Lovers; Sex; Courts and courtiers
Place/Time: Caribbean region—17th century; Mediterranean region—17th century; Ireland—17th
   century

Smith, C. W.

1463.
1. *Buffalo Nickel.* Poseidon, 1989.
2. *Hunter's Trap.* Texas Christian University,
   1996.

The young Kiowa boy Went on a Journey is sent to
missionary school and renamed David Copperfield.
He knows tribal lore, but no longer fits into the tribe
nor into white man's society. Copperfield, however,
inadvertently becomes an Oklahoma oil millionaire as
he wrestles with who he is. Later, he is killed in a boat
explosion along with the wife of his good friend Will
Hunter. Hunter goes to El Paso, Texas, to avenge the
deaths of Copperfield and his wife. He finds an unscrupulous banker who wanted Copperfield's oil land and
goes after him by kidnaping his daughter Sissy, but

plans go haywire as Hunter sees the greed, bigotry, and betrayal of Texans in the 1920s.

Genre: Historical Fiction
Subjects: Native Americans; Petroleum industry; Revenge
Place/Time: Oklahoma—1900–1945; Texas—1900–1945

Smith, Chard Powers

1464.
1. *Artillery of Time.* Scribner, 1939.
2. *Ladies Day.* Scribner, 1941.

In upstate New York, the Lathrop family experiences the tension and difficulties of the Civil War years, but the real conflict is between brothers Isaac and John, who fall in love with the same woman. The story of Lucy Lathrop's love for a businessman with questionable ethics continues the narrative to 1900.

Genre: Historical Fiction
Subjects: United States—Civil War, 1861–1865; Brothers; Love; Family life
Place/Time: New York (N. Y.)—19th century

Smith, David

1465.
1. *The Leo Conversion.* Dodd Mead, 1980.
2. *Timbuktu.* Dodd Mead, 1983.

Jim Stevens, an American lawyer, and his friend Muntaka, a Nigerian judge, must find a stolen manuscript that was taken from a Nigerian museum. Later they search for missing girls from villages around Timbuktu. As they search, they find clues to the history of the African slave trade.

Genre: Adventure
Subjects: Law and lawyers; Judges; Theft; Missing children; Slave trade
Place/Time: Nigeria—1945–1980; Timbuktu—1945–1980

Smith, E. E. (Edward Elmer) "Doc"

1466. Lensman
1. *Triplanetary.* Fantasy Press, 1948.
2. *First Lensman.* Fantasy Press, 1950.
3. *Galactic Patrol.* Fantasy Press, 1950.
4. *Gray Lensman.* Fantasy Press, 1951.
5. *Second Stage Lensman.* Fantasy Press, 1953.
6. *Children of the Lens.* Fantasy Press, 1954.
7. *The Vortex Blaster.* (Alternate title: *Masters of the Vortex.*) Gnome Press, 1960

Telepathic men and women of the future, aided by magical bracelets called lenses given to them by the alien Arisians, do battle for the forces of good in an expanding conflict that stretches across the universe.

Genre: Science Fiction

Subjects: Telepathy; Interplanetary wars; Extraterrestrial beings; Good and evil

Smith, Helen Zenna. *Pseud. of* Evadne Price

1467. Skinny
1. *Stepdaughters of War.* Dutton, 1930.
2. *One Woman's Freedom.* Longmans, 1932.

A group of upper-class English girls serving as ambulance drivers in France during World War I experience horrors of war that their smug, proud parents at home cannot imagine. The narrative continues with the experiences of one of the girls Nell, who leaves her marriage to a blind war hero, futilely searches for happiness in London nightlife, and finally finds fulfillment in flying a plane.

Genre: War
Subjects: Girls; World War I, 1914–1918; Marriage; Women air pilots
Place/Time: France—1900–1945; England—1900–1945

Smith, Martin Cruz

1468.
1. *Gorky Park.* Random House, 1981.
2. *Polar Star.* Random House, 1989.
3. *Red Square.* Random House, 1992.
4. *Havana Bay.* Random, 1999.

Moscow's chief homicide investigator is complex, world-weary Arkady Renko. Renko is too honest for his Moscow superiors when he investigates three mutilated bodies found in Gorky Park. His search for the murderer puts him on the outs with the KGB, and ultimately forces him to flee to Siberia where he works on a fishing boat. Even there, he cannot avoid investigating murder and running into the KGB. With glasnost, Renko is called back to Moscow to again investigate murder. His last case leads him to his lost love Irina and to helping the masses overthrow the Soviet government. While working as a policeman in the new Russia, Arkady is summoned to Cuba to identify the body of an old friend. When he is attacked by a Russian embassy interpreter, Arkady explores Havana looking for answers, but finding only more questions.

Subjects: Detectives; Police—Moscow (Soviet Union); Murder and murderers; Politics—Soviet Union; Love
Place/Time: Soviet Union—1945–1980; Soviet Union—1980–1991

Smith, Robert Kimmel

1469.
1. *Sadie Shapiro's Knitting Book.* Simon & Schuster, 1973.
2. *Sadie Shapiro in Miami.* Simon & Schuster, 1977.

3. *Sadie Shapiro, Matchmaker.* Simon & Schuster, 1979.

Sadie is 75, a grandmother, a jogger, a knitter, an author, and the supreme "fixit." She and her friends in the Mount Eden Senior Citizens Hotel in Queens get involved in hilarious escapades as they stop scams. When the American Senior Citizens World in Miami may not open because of scandal, Sadie saves the day.

Genre: Gentle Read; Humor
Subjects: Grandmothers; Elderly; Friendship
Place/Time: Queens (N. Y.)—1945–1980; Miami (Fla.)—1945–1980; New York (N. Y.)—1945–1980; Florida—1945–1980

Smith, Sarah

1470.
1. *The Vanished Child.* Ballantine, 1992.
2. *The Knowledge of Water.* Ballantine, 1996.

In 1887, millionaire William Knight is brutally murdered and his grandson Richard, the only witness, disappears. Twenty years later, the family physician Charles Adair recognizes the Baron Alexander von Reisden as the young Richard, even though von Reisden has no memory of his early years. Reisden finally agrees to come to New England and enter the household of his uncle Gilbert Knight. Reisden refuses to say he is Richard, but he does investigate the earlier crime. As he does, he uncovers evidence of child abuse and numerous people with reasons to kill William. He also finds himself falling in love with blind pianist Perdita Halley. When the truth about the murder is finally revealed, Reisden returns to Paris and the mental health institute he runs, and Perdita eventually comes to Paris also to study piano. She is determined to succeed but finds herself having an affair with Reisden, who is trying to find out who is sending threatening letters to him. As the Seine floods Paris, Reisden rushes to save Perdita and untangle the mysteries.

Genre: Crime Novel
Subjects: Murder and murderers; Child abuse; Amnesia
Place/Time: New England—1900–1945; Paris (France)—1900–1945

Smith, Sherwood. *See* Norton, Andre (Time Traders—*Echoes in Time*)

Smith, Thorne

1471.
1. *Topper, an Improbable Adventure.* McBride, 1926.
2. *Topper Takes a Trip.* Doubleday, 1932.

Poor Topper! He's a conservative, middle-aged banker who leads a quiet, uneventful life until the ghosts of wild George and Marion Kerby, who were killed in an car accident, decide to change things.

George and Marion want Topper to have fun, and they materialize at all the wrong times. Even when he retires and goes to the Riviera, Cosmos gets no peace from his ghostly companions.

Genre: Humor
Subjects: Bankers; Middle age; Ghost stories; Husbands and wives; Retirement
Place/Time: United States—1900–1945; France—1900–1945

Smith, Wilbur

1472.
1. *Birds of Prey.* St. Martin's, 1997.
2. *Monsoon.* St. Martin's, 1999.

In this prequel series to "The Courtneys," the adventures of the clan begin with Sir Francis Courtney, a privateer with Sir Francis Drake, as he roams the seas off Africa in 1667. With his son Hal, he attacks the Dutch traders, but is eventually captured and killed. Hal escapes and avenges his father's death. Hal eventually returns to England where he marries and has four sons. To protect his overseas investments, he goes back to sea to fight Arab pirates. Hal takes his three youngest sons who fight among themselves and with pirates. When youngest son Dorian is captured, his brother Tom must do battle with his own brothers and with Arabs to save him.

Genre: Adventure; Family Saga; Historical Fiction
Subjects: Family life; Adventure; Brothers; Voyages and travels; Pirates
Place/Time: England—17th century; Africa—17th century

1473.
1. *River God.* St. Martin's, 1994.
2. *The Seventh Scroll.* St. Martin's, 1995.

Taita is the eunuch slave of Lostris, daughter of Egypt's Grand Vizier Lord Intef in 1750 B.C. He relates Lostris's love for the young army officer Tanus. While Lostris's father plots for her to wed Pharaoh Mamose, Tanus becomes the commander of the army and fights the invading Hyksos. Before the battle, Tanus and Lostris have a brief affair, which leaves her pregnant. Both the Pharaoh and Tanus die in battle, but Lostris's son by Tanus becomes Pharaoh Memnon. In the 20th century, a scroll by Taita helps Sir Nicholas Quenton-Harper and archeologist Royan Al-Sima hunt for the lost tomb of Pharaoh Mamose and his treasures. They must battle rival Gotthold von Schiller and his allies to see who will find the tomb and unravel Taita's secrets and traps in the tomb.

Genre: Historical Fiction; Adventure
Subjects: Adventure; Courts and courtiers; Egypt—Kings and rulers
Place/Time: Egypt—18th century B. C.; Egypt—1980–

1474. The Ballantyne Novels
1. *Flight of the Falcon.* Doubleday, 1982.

2. *Men of Men.* Doubleday, 1983.
3. *The Angels Weep.* Doubleday, 1983.
4. *The Leopard Hunts in Darkness.* Doubleday, 1984.

Searching for their long-lost father, a brother and sister journey to darkest Africa in the 1870s, where the exotic wilderness heightens their obsession. Robyn becomes a missionary-doctor in Rhodesia, while her brother's greed leads him to work with Cecil Rhodes in building a British land and mineral empire. Their children become involved in Rhodes's empire schemes and wars. Their personal lives also are troublesome, as parents, children, and grandchildren fall in love with the wrong people. The turbulent saga continues with the life of great-grandson Craig, a wildlife worker in present-day Zimbabwe who fights poachers and searches for a missing fortune in diamonds.

Genre: Adventure; Family Saga; Historical Fiction
Subjects: Adventure; Physicians; Love affairs; Railroads
Place/Time: Africa—19th century; Africa—1900–1945; Africa—1945–1980

1475. The Courtneys
1. *When the Lion Feeds.* Dell, 1964.
2. *The Roar of Thunder.* Simon & Schuster, 1966.
3. *A Sparrow Falls.* Doubleday, 1977.

The above titles have also been published in the following collection: *The Courtneys.* Little, Brown, 1988.

The saga of the Courtneys begins when Sean Courtney goes to South Africa to farm in the late 1800s. His peaceful farm life is disrupted by the Zulu War. Sean fights Zulus, travels to the wilderness to find gold, and meets the love of his life but loses her. Even in peace time, he can find no peace as disputes and jealousy keep the family torn apart.

Genre: Adventure; Family Saga; Historical Fiction
Subjects: Farm life; Family life; Adventure; Zulus (African people)
Place/Time: South Africa—19th century

1476. The Courtneys of Africa
1. *The Burning Shore.* Doubleday, 1985.
2. *Power of the Sword.* Little, Brown, 1986.
3. *Rage.* Little, Brown, 1987.
4. *A Time to Die.* Random House, 1990.
5. *Golden Fox.* Random House, 1990.

The saga of the Courtney family of South Africa continues in 1917 when Centaine discovers she is pregnant and her lover Michael Courtney is shot down during World War I. She travels to South Africa to be with his family, but her boat is sunk. Taken in by kindly bushmen, she bears a son and then meets Boer Lothar De LaRey with whom she will also have a son. The two half-brothers fight each other over the future of South Africa through the 1930s and 1940s. Their children fight on both sides of the apartheid issue, battle the Cubans in Angola and the civil war in Mozam-

bique, and have numerous love affairs that never go smoothly.

Genre: Adventure; Family Saga; Historical Fiction
Subjects: World War I, 1914–1918; Adventure; Love affairs; Brothers; Apartheid
Place/Time: South Africa—1900–1945; South Africa—1945–1980

Snelling, Lauraine

1477. The Red River of the North
1. *Untamed Land.* Bethany House, 1996.
2. *A New Day Rising.* Bethany House, 1996.
3. *A Land to Call Home.* Bethany House, 1997.
4. *The Reaper's Song.* Bethany House, 1998.
5. *Tender Mercies.* Bethany House, 1999.
6. *Blessing in Disguise.* Bethany House, 1999.

In 1882, Roald and Ingeborg Bjorklund leave their home in Norway and take the perilous voyage across the Atlantic to settle in America. They find the tenements of New York a horror and go by train and wagon to the prairie town of Blessing in Dakota Territory. There, they set out to homestead the land and survive the brutal winter. When Roald dies, his cousin Haakan comes to help Ingeborg with the farm, and she finds that she has strong feelings toward him. More of the Bjorklund family come to the Dakota prairie, and they and the other settlers set out to make a real community with churches, a schoolhouse, and the railroad that brings prosperity. Zeb MacCallister and two orphan girls come to Blessing, and the Bjorklunds help them settle in the community. As the area prospers, Reverend John Solberg falls in love with a young lady, and again the Bjorklunds step in, this time playing matchmakers, helping the Reverend to win the young lady's love. Each of the immigrant families face difficulties and joys as they make a new life.

Genre: Christian Fiction; Historical Fiction
Subjects: Faith; Immigrants; Farm life
Place/Time: South Dakota—19th century

Snow, C. P. (Charles Percy)

1478. Strangers and Brothers Series
1. *Strangers and Brothers.* Scribner, 1960, 1940.
2. *The Light and the Dark.* Macmillan, 1948.
3. *Time of Hope.* Macmillan, 1951.
4. *The Masters.* Macmillan, 1951.
5. *The New Men.* Scribner, 1954.
6. *Homecoming.* Scribner, 1956.
7. *The Conscience of Rich.* Scribner, 1958.
8. *The Affair.* Scribner, 1960.
9. *Corridors of Power.* Scribner, 1964.
10. *The Sleep of Reason.* Scribner, 1968.
11. *Last Things.* Scribner, 1970.

Through his narrator, the lawyer Lewis Eliot, Snow examines the moral climate of England in the years following World War I. Eliot becomes a member of the

Labor Party and lives securely as part of the establishment. He narrates each story and reacts to 50 years of English life. He relates his youth, his Cambridge years, his career as a lawyer, and his marriage. He looks at his friends at the university, in government, and during the war. At the end of his life, he confronts his own personal crises as he resolves the enigma of his life.

Subjects: Law and lawyers; College life; Politics—England; Men—psychology

Place/Time: England—1900–1945; England—1945–1980

Solzhenitsyn, Aleksandr

1479.
1. *August 1914.* Farrar, Straus & Giroux, 1972.
2. *November 1916.* Farrar, Straus & Giroux, 1998.

Solzhenitsyn explores Russia's involvement in World War I and its lead up to the Russian Revolution. When Russia enters the war in 1914, the army is ill-prepared to fight. General Samsonov and Colonel Vorotynsev watch as the army falls apart and then is defeated at the Battle of Tannenberg. As Russia disintegrates, the Tsar struggles to save his crown while revolutionaries plot to overthrow the government. Solzhenitsyn vividly portrays life in Russia as the various groups in society intermingle and clash.

Genre: Historical Fiction
Subjects: World War I, 1914–1918; Army, Russian; Revolutions and revolutionists
Place/Time: Russia—1900–1917; Soviet Union—1917–1945

Somers, Jane. *Pseud. of* Doris Lessing. *See also* Lessing, Doris

1480.
1. *Diary of a Good Neighbor.* Knopf, 1983.
2. *If the Old Could . . . .* Knopf, 1984.

Here is a vivid picture of the forming and maintaining of a friendship between two wildly disparate women—Janna, editor of a successful women's magazine, and Maudie, a woman in her late eighties enmeshed in poverty and furious at her situation. Through their friendship, Janna learns how she made her husband suffer and comes to terms with her lost youth. Janna then takes in her niece Jill, who takes a lover and moves out. Jill's difficult younger sister Kate moves in with Janna just as she finds love with Richard, only to discover that he is married.

Subjects: Friendship; Success; Women editors; Women—relations to other women; Poverty
Place/Time: England—1980–

Somerville, Edith *and* Ross, Martin

1481.
1. *Some Experiences of an Irish R.M.* Longmans, 1899.
2. *Some Further Experiences of an Irish R.M.* Longmans, 1908.
3. *Mr. Knox's Country.* Longmans, 1915.

The above titles have also been published in the following collection: *The Irish R.M. Complete.* Faber & Faber, 1928.

British Major Sinclair Yeates, a resident magistrate who is sent to Skebawn in southwest Ireland, relates his comic episodes with the crazy and disreputable inhabitants of his district. The very straight and proper Major Sinclair is constantly befuddled as he has to deal with the roguish Flurry Knox and his society relatives, his wife Philippa, and the area's preoccupation with horses and horse trading. These comic tales were made into a *Masterpiece Theater* production.

Genre: Humor
Subjects: Local government; Social classes; Rogues and vagabonds; Horse trading
Place/Time: Ireland—19th century

Somtow, S. P. *Pseud. of* Somtow Sucharitkul. *See also* Sucharitkul, Somtow

1482.
1. *Vampire Junction.* Donning, 1984.
2. *Valentine.* Tor, 1992.
3. *Vanitas: Escape from Vampire Junction.* Tor, 1995.

The very wealthy vampire Timmy Valentine can remember the annihilation of Pompeii and the burning of Joan of Arc. In the 20th century, he thrives in the Manhattan rock scene and Hollywood beckons, but an evil psychic, a conniving televangelist, and a group called the Gods of Chaos work against him. Timmy achieves mortality by taking possession of the soul of Angel, a motion picture double, but the invisible spirit of Angel takes revenge and brings about a showdown by manipulating humans into committing crimes for which vampires are blamed.

Genre: Horror
Subjects: Vampires; Wealth; Rock music
Place/Time: New York (N. Y.)—1980–

Sorrentino, Gilbert

1483.
1. *Odd Number.* North Point Press, 1985.
2. *Rose Theatre.* Dalkay Archive, 1987.
3. *Misterioso.* Dalkay Archive, 1989.

These experimental novels explore with Joycean language a parade of characters who are presented to the reader in bits and pieces. The characters appear in all three novels, which contain little plot, a great deal of description, references to great literary works, and comic parodies of popular culture. These densely written novels are for the lover of experimental fiction.

Subjects: Experimental stories; Parodies

Spruill, Steven

1484.
1. *Rulers of Darkness.* St. Martin's, 1995.
2. *Daughter of Darkness.* Doubleday, 1997.

Merrick Chapman, a retired police detective, and his granddaughter, Jenn, a physician, are both hemophaeges, vampiric beings who subsist on human blood without killing. A rash of vampire style killings convince Merrick that his son Zane is on a rampage and must be entombed. Zane escapes and moves inexorably toward a confrontation with his daughter Jenn.

Genre: Horror
Subjects: Detectives; Physicians; Vampires; Murder and murderers
Place/Time: Washington (D. C.)—1980–

1485. Elias Kane
1. *The Psychopath Plague.* Doubleday, 1978.
2. *The Imperator Plot.* Doubleday, 1983.
3. *Paradox Planet.* Doubleday, 1988.

Elias Kane, private eye of the 22nd century, finds the source of a psychic plague, survives the death of his wife, who was the victim of an assassination plot aimed at Earth's Imperator, and deals with rebels on a heavy-gravity world, all with the help of alien Cephantine Pendrake.

Genre: Science Fiction
Subjects: Detectives; Extraterrestrial beings; Interplanetary voyages

Stableford, Brian

1486.
1. *The Werewolves of London.* Carroll & Graf, 1992.
2. *The Angel of Pain.* Carroll & Graf, 1993.
3. *The Carnival of Destruction.* Carroll & Graf, 1994.

A titanic battle between fallen angels, werewolves, and ancient gods takes command of the mind of David Lydyard, a physician in London in 1870, after he is bitten by an asp-like snake in Egypt. He has been infected with the soul of the sphinx, who is slowly awakening. Meanwhile, werewolves of London also try to possess him. He must fight a magician, the queen of the werewolves, and the Egyptian goddess Bast as they use human pawns to gain knowledge of the earthly world that can be used on their astral plane. In the concluding work, an aging Lydyard, is convinced that he is Satan, receives a mysterious message from a young French atheist who has escaped death on the battlefields of

World War I and enters a mystical realm of the imagination.

Genre: Fantasy; Horror
Subjects: Werewolves; Angels; Gods and goddesses; Mysticism

1487.
1. *Inherit the Earth.* Tor, 1998.
2. *Architects of Emortality.* Tor, 1999.

Set in a distant future when a plague has left the sparse population sterile, these tales describe a world in which babies are conceived in artificial wombs and genetically altered flowers are murder weapons. In the first work, a young artist pursues a terrorist group; in the second, a New York investigator tries to solve a murder by deciphering puzzles involving 19th-century literature.

Genre: Science Fiction
Subjects: Diseases; Genetics; Terrorism; Murder and murderers

Stacpoole, H. (Henryk) de Vere

1488.
1. *The Blue Lagoon.* Lippincott, 1908.
2. *The Garden of God.* Dodd, 1923.

Tragedy and romance combine in these tales of a young couple stranded on a South Pacific island, who mature and learn about love in an innocent, primitive manner. Their son, who is found adrift on the sea after his parents' death, is raised by a sailor and falls in love with Kanaka, a young woman who is thought to have been cursed by a sorceress.

Genre: Romance
Subjects: Shipwrecks and castaways; Bereavement; Orphans
Place/Time: Pacific Islands—1900–1945

Stallman, Robert

1489. The Book of the Beast
1. *The Orphan.* Pocket Books, 1980.
2. *The Captive.* Pocket Books, 1981.
3. *The Beast.* Pocket Books, 1982.

The Beast is a mysterious being capable of shifting into human form. In both human and animal form the creature interacts, frequently tragically, with various members of a Midwestern family of the 1930s until he finds peace in a mystical union with a being of his own kind.

Genre: Fantasy
Subjects: Mythical animals; Mysticism

Standiford, Les

1490.
1. *Done Deal.* HarperCollins, 1993.
2. *Raw Deal.* HarperCollins, 1994.

3. *Deal to Die For.* HarperCollins, 1996.
4. *Deal on Ice.* HarperCollins, 1998.
5. *Presidential Deal.* HarperCollins, 1999.

In Miami, John Deal has had several attempts on his life, but he doesn't know why. He's the son of a housing developer, but all he has left is a small bit of land he's developing into a fourplex. As he gets involved with some of his father's old friends who are trying to bring baseball to Miami, his wife is killed. Cuban racketeers are after John and even try to burn his apartment complex. He and former policeman Vernon Driscoll investigate and find that Cuban exiles, big sugar farmers, and even the government are all threatening him. Deal and Driscoll have to race to save themselves in a violent confrontation. Deal's adventures estrange him from his second wife Janice, but they are drawn back together when a friend is killed. Deal must fight rightwingers and their plots to take over the media and then also battle rogue CIA agents and government conspiracies.

Genre: Crime Novel
Subjects: Crime and criminals; Underworld; Businessmen
Place/Time: Miami (Fla.)—1980–

Stasheff, Christopher

1491. Rod Gallowglass
1. *The Warlock in Spite of Himself.* Ace, 1969.
2. *King Kobold.* Ace, 1971. (Revised as *King Kobold Revived.* Ace, 1984.)
3. *The Warlock Unlocked.* Ace, 1982.
4. *Escape Velocity.* Ace, 1983.
5. *The Warlock Enraged.* Ace, 1985.
6. *The Warlock Is Missing.* Ace, 1986.
7. *The Warlock Wandering.* Ace, 1986.
8. *The Warlock Heretical.* Ace, 1987.
9. *The Warlock's Companion.* Ace, 1988.
10. *Warlock Insane.* Ace, 1989.
11. *Warlock Rock.* Ace, 1990.
12. *Warlock and Son.* Ace, 1991.

Fantasy and science fiction combine in these tales of Rodney d'Armond, alias Rod Gallowglass, who attempts to bring democracy to the feudal planet Gramarye, where magic reigns. *Note:* The exploits and adventures of Rod's children continue in The Warlock's Heirs series and Rogue Wizard series.

Genre: Fantasy; Science Fiction
Subjects: Witchcraft; Magic; Life on other planets; Feudalism; Democracy

1492. The Warlock's Heirs
1. *A Wizard in Absentia.* Ace, 1993.
2. *M'Lady Witch.* Ace, 1994.
3. *Quicksilver's Knight.* Ace, 1995.
4. *The Spell-Bound Scholar.* Ace, 1999.

Further adventures of the Gallowglass offspring include Magnus's visit to an asteroid with a robot companion, romance for Cordelia, and Geoffrey's battle with the outlaw Quicksilver. *Note:* This series follows the Rod Gallowglass series and continues in the Rogue Wizard series.

Genre: Science Fiction; Fantasy
Subjects: Brothers and sisters; Life on other planets; Magic; Adventure

1493. Rogue Wizard
1. *A Wizard in Mind.* Tor, 1995.
2. *A Wizard in Bedlam.* Doubleday, 1979.
3. *A Wizard in War.* Tor, 1995.
4. *A Wizard in Peace.* Tor, 1996.
5. *A Wizard in Chaos.* Tor, 1997.
6. *A Wizard in Midgard.* Tor, 1998.
7. *A Wizard and a Warlord.* Tor, 2000.

Rod Gallowglass's son Magnus travels through the galaxy with his sidekick, Dirk, and Herkimer, an intelligent space ship that takes him to colonized planets representing various stages in history. They encounter institutions such as medieval serfdom and Cromwellian Puritanism. Unlike his conscientious father, Magnus frequently makes up his own rules. *Note:* This series follows the Rod Gallowglass series and the Warlock's Heirs series.

Genre: Science Fiction; Fantasy
Subjects: Life on other planets; Magic; Spaceships; History

1494. The Star Stone
1. *The Shaman.* Ballantine, 1995.
2. *The Sage.* Ballantine, 1996.

A race of giants, the Ulin, rules the world as gods, but opposition to their power grows and they are ultimately challenged by the human shaman Ohaern, the half-elf Lucoyo, and one of their own. Centuries later when the defeated Ulin produce another leader, Ohaern returns from his existence in another realm to do battle, but must compensate for his failing strength by training a petty criminal to fill the role of defender and hero.

Genre: Fantasy
Subjects: Imaginary wars and battles; Heroes; Good and evil

1495. Starship Troupers
1. *Company of Stars.* Ballantine, 1991.
2. *We Open on Venus.* Ballantine, 1994.
3. *A Slight Detour.* Ballantine, 1994.

The romance is over, but Ramou Lazarian's ex-girlfriend and her father, who has hired a tenacious detective, are in hot pursuit insisting that he marry her. Ramou takes cover with a company of players. Because this is the 26th century, the itinerary of the Star Company includes Venus where they are to perform *Macbeth*. The actors also need to stay one jump ahead of a terran movement that considers theater immoral.

Genre: Science Fiction
Subjects: Life on other planets; Actors and actresses

1496. A Wizard in Rhyme
1. *Her Majesty's Wizard.* Ballantine, 1986.

2. *The Oathbound Wizard.* Ballantine, 1993.
3. *The Witch Doctor.* Ballantine, 1994.
4. *The Secular Wizard.* Ballantine, 1995.
5. *My Son, the Wizard.* Del Rey, 1997.
6. *The Crusading Wizard.* Ballantine, 2000.
7. *The Haunted Wizard.* Ballantine, 2000.

On a scrap of parchment that he finds in his college library, Matt reads a mysterious spell that transports him to a magical land ruled by beautiful Queen Alisande. Matt becomes the lord wizard of the realm and wins Alisande's love, but cannot share her throne until he defeats the evil ruler of a neighboring kingdom. Back in the mundane world, Matt's friend Saul searches Matt's apartment to find clues to his disappearance, comes in contact with the parchment, and is also transported to Allustria, a realm torn between the magical powers of good and evil. Saul's knowledge of poetry may be crucial to freeing the citizens of the land; but before their adventures can continue, Matt must first return to the ordinary world to rescue his parents from urban decay and danger.

Genre: Fantasy
Subjects: Imaginary kingdoms; Magicians; Imaginary wars and battles; Love

Steen, Marguerite

1497. The Flood Trilogy
1. *The Sun Is My Undoing.* Viking, 1941.
2. *Twilight on the Floods.* Doubleday, 1949.
3. *Jehovah Blues.* Doubleday, 1952.

In the 18th century, Matthew Flood is a slave trader. He marries an English girl, but leaves her when he finds out she is an abolitionist. He reenters the slave trade and takes an African mistress. Only after being captured by pirates does he return home. His great-grandson John goes to Africa in the 1890s to expiate the sins of his forbearers, but after three visits loses his life in the Ashanti wars on the Gold Coast.

Genre: Family Saga; Historical Fiction
Subjects: Slavery; Shipmasters; Slave trade; Abolitionists
Place/Time: England—18th century; England—19th century; Africa—18th century; Africa—19th century

1498. Spanish Trilogy
1. *Matador.* Little, 1934.
2. *One-Eyed Moon.* Little, 1935.
3. *The Tavern.* Bobbs, 1936.

In the Andalusian region of Spain, the people of Granada live out their lives with tragic results. An ex-bullfighter finds he is separated from his sons by their differing political views. A husband is torn between his love for his daughter and his love for his wife, and a tavern keeper who helps his friend have an affair finds it leads to tragedy and death. The stories are only connected by their detailing of the life of people in contemporary Spain.

Subjects: Bullfighters and bullfighting; Politics—Spain; Family life; Love affairs
Place/Time: Andalusia (Spain)—1900–1945; Spain—1900–1945

Steinbeck, John

1499.
1. *Cannery Row.* Viking, 1945.
2. *Sweet Thursday.* Viking, 1954.

This bawdy and sentimental comedy tells the story of the adventures and misadventures of workers in Monterey, California's Cannery Row. Dora runs an efficient brothel, and Doc loves women and music, and runs the Western Biological Laboratories. After World War II, the Row changes until Suzy comes and revives Doc and the other residents.

Genre: Humor
Subjects: Labor and laboring classes; Prostitution
Place/Time: Monterey (Calif.)—1900–1945; Monterey (Calif.)—1945–1980; California—1900–1945; California—1945–1980

Stephens, Michael

1500.
1. *Season at Coole.* Dutton, 1972.
2. *The Brooklyn Book of the Dead.* Dalkey Archive, 1994.

J. Leland Coole is an Irish American customs inspector who lives in Brooklyn with his 16 children. On Christmas day, he plunges into a dark mood so intense that his children recall the experience years later at his funeral when they reflect on the fate of the members of their dysfunctional family. They tell their story in a stream-of-consciousness blend of anecdote and recollection.

Subjects: Family life; Depression, mental; Fathers; Stream of consciousness; Bereavement
Place/Time: Brooklyn (N. Y.)—1945–1980; New York (N. Y.)—1945–1980

Stern, Gladys Bronwyn

1501. The Matriarch Chronicles Series
1. *The Matriarch.* Knopf, 1925.
2. *Shining and Free.* Knopf, 1935.
3. *A Deputy Was King.* Knopf, 1926.
4. *Mosaic.* Knopf, 1930.
5. *The Young Matriarch.* Macmillan, 1942.

From the Napoleonic era to World War II, the Rakonitz family, Viennese Jews, moves from Austria to London and Paris but remains together. At 15, Babette settles in London and sets up her family. When she dies at 89, her granddaughter Toni must lead the family. Toni, however, must also protect her marriage from her cousin Lorraine. The Paris branch of the family has its struggles as Berthe tries to rule her children until her sister Letti helps them escape her oppressive control. The loyal women of the clan keep the family going throughout the turbulent events in history.

Genre: Family Saga; Historical Fiction
Subjects: Jews; Women; Family life
Place/Time: Austria—19th century; Austria—1900–1945; London (England)—19th century; London (England)—1900–1945; Paris (France)—19th century; Paris (France)—1900–1945; England—19th century; England—1900–1945; France—19th century; France—1900–1945

Stevenson, D. E. (Dorothy Emily)

1502.
1. *Celia's House.* Farrar & Rinehart, 1943.
2. *Listening Valley.* Farrar & Rinehart, 1944.

In a small Scottish border town, one house is the key to love for three different women. In 1905, Celia Dunnian owns the house. She passes it to Humphrey and his five children, who love it. His youngest daughter inherits it in 1942 and finds love there. This same house helps another sister find love after her older husband dies.

Genre: Gentle Read; Romance
Subjects: Houses
Place/Time: Scotland—1900–1945

1503.
1. *Miss Buncle's Book.* Farrar & Rinehart, 1937.
2. *Miss Buncle, Married.* Farrar & Rinehart, 1937.
3. *The Two Mrs. Abbotts.* Farrar & Rinehart, 1943.

The above titles have also been published in the following collection: *Miss Buncle.* Holt Rinehart, 1964.

When Barbara Buncle writes a bestseller, her neighbors become angry at her portrayal of them. When she marries her publisher, Mr. Abbott, she moves to the country and settles down to write and raise a family. She becomes friends with her husbands's niece, and together the two muddle through the problems of World War II.

Genre: Gentle Read; Romance
Subjects: Marriage; Husbands and wives; Family life; Authors
Place/Time: England—1900–1945

1504.
1. *Amberwell.* Rinehart, 1955.
2. *Summerhills.* Rinehart, 1956.

Amberwell is the family estate of the Ayrtons in Scotland. There the five Ayrton children grow up, but all but Nell leave the town. She holds the estate together so the family will have a home after World War II. Later Roger Ayrton uses the home as a school for poor boys.

Genre: Gentle Read
Subjects: Family life; Houses; Brothers and sisters
Place/Time: Scotland—1900–1945; Scotland—1945–1980

1505.
1. *Gerald and Elizabeth.* Holt Rinehart, 1969.
2. *The House of the Deer.* Holt Rinehart, 1971.

Dismissed from his job as a mining engineer in South Africa, Gerald returns to London. There he contacts his half-sister Elizabeth Burleigh, who is an actress. She is haunted by her past, and Gerald helps her to love again. On a holiday to Scotland, Gerald falls in love with the daughter of his friend Phil MacAslam and ultimately marries her.

Genre: Gentle Read; Romance
Subjects: Brothers and sisters
Place/Time: London (England)—1945–1980; Scotland—1945–1980; England—1945–1980

1506.
1. *Five Windows.* Rinehart, 1953.
2. *Tall Stranger.* Rinehart, 1957.

From his boyhood to his early twenties, David Kirk grows up, goes to school, and falls in love. When he meets Jan and marries her, a new life starts for them. Their friend Barbie France meets a stranger on her vacation, and when she returns home, meets her attractive stranger again.

Genre: Gentle Read; Romance
Subjects: Husbands and wives
Place/Time: England—1945–1980

1507.
1. *Mrs. Tim Christie.* Holt Rinehart, 1973, 1932.
2. *Mrs. Tim Carries On.* Farrar & Rinehart, 1941.
3. *Mrs. Tim Gets a Job.* Rinehart, 1947.
4. *Mrs. Tim Flies Home.* Rinehart, 1952.

No matter what the situation at home or abroad, Mrs. Tim, the zany wife of a British army officer, can make do. In her diary, she records regimental gossip, the doings of her children, and the trials of her husband being posted all over the world. As a soldier's wife, she records her fears for him as he fights in World War II, then after the war is sent to Kenya and Egypt. No matter what happens, Mrs. Tim finds a way to manage.

Genre: Gentle Read
Subjects: Marriage; Husbands and wives; Army, British; Family life
Place/Time: England—1900–1945; England—1945–1980; Kenya—1900–1945; Kenya—1945–1980; Egypt—1900–1945; Egypt—1945–1980

1508.
1. *Vittoria Cottage.* Rinehart, 1949.
2. *Music in the Hills.* Rinehart, 1950.
3. *Shoulder in the Sky.* Rinehart, 1951.

In the years after World War II, Caroline Daring, a widow with three grown children, falls in love with a stranger who comes to her Scottish village of Ashbridge. Her son James comes home from the war and goes to live with his Aunt and Uncle Johnstone of Mureth to learn to farm and to heal a broken heart. There he meets Rhoda, then falls in love and marries her. These novels reveal the homely business of the farmers and their wives in a rural community and show a simple and happy way of life.

Genre: Gentle Read; Romance
Subjects: Family life; Farm life; Husbands and wives
Place/Time: Scotland—1900–1945; Scotland—1945–1980

Stevenson, Robert Louis

1509.
1. *Kidnapped.* Scribners, 1886.
2. *Catriona.* Scribners, 1893.

In the 18th century, young David Balfour is left to a life of poverty after his father dies. David journeys to his Uncle Ebenezer in Scotland for help, but evil Ebenezer has stolen the Balfour estate from David. He tries to kill David and, when that fails, has him kidnapped. On the ship, David helps save Alan Breck from a sinking ship. Breck is a Jacobite who opposes English rule in Scotland. When the ship is wrecked off the coast of Mull, David and Alan escape. When they witness the murder of Colin Campbell, the king's factor, they are suspected of the crime. Eventually they cross the highlands and confront Ebenezer to recover David's rights. David then works to have James Stewart, who has been falsely accused of Colin Campbell's murder, cleared, but he fails. He does help Alan Breck escape to Europe, and eventually falls in love with Catriona Drummond, the daughter of Scottish renegade James More.

Genre: Historical Fiction
Subjects: Escapes; Adventure; Government, resistance to
Place/Time: Scotland—18th century

Stewart, Fred Mustard

1510.
1. *The Magnificent Savages.* Forge/Tor, 1996.
2. *The Young Savages.* Forge/Tor, 1997.
3. *The Naked Savages.* Tor, 1999.

In the 1850s, young Justin Savage, the illegitimate son of a shipping tycoon, is sent on his first voyage to China as a cabin boy. His evil older half brother Sylvaner has arranged to have Justin murdered, but he survives the attack and begins an adventurous life as a pirate in the South Seas. Through the years he marries the Chinese pirate queen, studies modern warfare in England, and ends up in Italy fighting with Garibaldi. His half-Italian son Johnnie and his half-Chinese daughter Julie continue their father's adventures

around the world. Johnnie fights in Cuba in the Spanish-American War and then returns home to keep his family and business together. Evil intrigue, racy romance, and high spirited adventures keep the family members racing around Europe, America, and Asia.

Genre: Historical Fiction; Family Saga
Subjects: Family Life; Adventure; Sailing vessels; Pirates
Place/Time: United States—19th century; China—19th century; Italy—19th century; United States—1900–1945

Stewart, Mary

1511.
1. *The Crystal Cave.* Morrow, 1970.
2. *The Hollow Hills.* Morrow, 1973.
3. *The Last Enchantment.* Morrow, 1979.
4. *The Wicked Day.* Morrow, 1983.

The Arthurian legend is retold through the life of Merlin as he grows up in the court of King Uther, Arthur's father. The wizard travels the country and monitors the growth of the young Arthur. When Arthur becomes king, Merlin helps him battle the Saxons and build Camelot, but he cannot protect Arthur from his illegitimate son Mordred, who Merlin prophesied would destroy Camelot.

Genre: Fantasy
Subjects: Arthur, King; Merlin (legendary character); Mordred (legendary character)

Stewart, Sean

1512.
1. *Resurrection Man.* Ace, 1995.
2. *The Night Watch.* Ace, 1997.

Demons and angels wield power in a future world where magic and miracles have replaced technology and the laws of physics, following a cataclysmic world war.

Genre: Fantasy; Science Fiction
Subjects: Magic; Angels; Good and evil; War

Stirling, Jessica. *Joint pseud. of* Peggie Coghlan *and* Hugh C. Rae

1513.
1. *The Island Wife.* Thomas Dunne, 1998.
2. *The Wind from the Hills.* St. Martin's, 2000.

On the rugged island of Mull off the coast of Scotland in 1878, the Campbells live on a farm. Father Ronan is usually drunk while mother Vassie runs the farm with her three daughters Bridget, Innis, and Aileen. When Austin and Walter Baverstock buy the estate next to the Campbells, the daughters are attracted to the brothers and to their Roman Catholic shepherd. Bridget ultimately marries Walter, while Innis marries shepherd Michael Tarrant, but the sisters find life isn't smooth.

Bridget's husband dies and Innis resigns herself to a loveless marriage. Innis has her children, and her son Gavin is like his father, aloof and moody. When nephew Donnie Campbell moves to the island and a new school teacher opens a local school, Gavin and brother Michael have trouble adjusting to the changes.

Genre: Historical Fiction; Family Saga
Subjects: Sisters; Family life; Farm life
Place/Time: Scotland—19th century

1514.
1. *Lantern for the Dark.* St. Martin's, 1992.
2. *Shadows on the Shore.* St. Martin's, 1994.

In 1770 in Scotland, Clare Kelso is accused of killing her baby. Her lawyer Cameron Adams is convinced she is innocent and must fight to save her from the gallows. In 1790, Clare comes face-to-face with the man who betrayed her years earlier. She must defend herself and her daughter against his greed and lust.

Genre: Gentle Read; Historical Romance
Subjects: Trials
Place/Time: Scotland—19th century

1515.
1. *The Penny Wedding.* St. Martin's, 1995.
2. *The Marrying Kind.* St. Martin's, 1996.

In Glasgow, the Burnside family are rocked by death and financial devastation during the Great Depression of the 1930s. When Maeve Burnside suddenly dies and husband Alex loses his job, daughter Alison thinks she will have to give up her dream of going to medical school to take care of her father and four brothers. Her teacher, Jim Abbott, helps tutor her and keep her in school even though he has fallen in love with her. Her brothers also pledge to help her stay in school while they find new jobs. When Jim leaves teaching, Alison becomes engaged to him. When Jim becomes ill, the two must reevaluate their love and commitment. The four brothers continue to carve out their careers as the rumbles of the coming World War II intrude on their lives.

Genre: Gentle Read
Subjects: Family life; Brothers and sisters; Love;
    Business depression, 1929
Place/Time: Scotland—1900–1945

1516. Beckman Trilogy
1. *The Drums of Time.* St. Martin's, 1980.
2. *The Blue Evening Gone.* St. Martin's, 1981.
3. *The Gates of Midnight.* St. Martin's, 1983.

In the 1920s, Holly Beckman inherits part of a London antique business. Her hard work in the world of buying and selling fine art helps raise her social and professional status. However, her personal life is in turmoil as her family and her lovers threaten to destroy her. As World War II starts, she must fight the dangers of the blitz and worry about her son David, who is a pilot in the Royal Air Force.

Genre: Family Saga; Historical Romance

Subjects: Business; Women; World War II, 1939–1945
Place/Time: London (England)—1900–1945; England—1900–1945

1517. Glasgow Saga
1. *The Good Provider.* St. Martin's, 1988.
2. *The Asking Price.* St. Martin's, 1989.
3. *The Wise Child.* St. Martin's, 1990.
4. *The Welcome Light.* St. Martin's, 1991.

Kristy Barnes and her sweetheart Craig escape life as servants in rural Scotland in 1900 and flee to Glasgow where they live together, but do not marry. Their hopes for a better future are dashed when Craig falls in with Danny Malone, the leader of a gang. Kristy falls in love with missionary David Lockhart while Craig takes up with another woman. Eventually Kristy and Craig reconcile and have a son, but their marriage is troubled. Kristy uses some money she inherits to set up a shop to help save her marriage, but a series of near-fatal events finally bring them together.

Genre: Historical Romance
Subjects: Marriage problems; Women
Place/Time: Scotland—1900–1945

1518. Patterson Trilogy
1. *Treasures on Earth.* St. Martin's, 1985.
2. *Creature Comforts.* St. Martin's, 1986.
3. *Hearts of Gold.* St. Martin's, 1987.

Elspeth's life begins when she is taken in by Gaddy Patterson after her mother dies in 19th-century Scotland. Gaddy works hard and eventually marries and has another daughter. The two girls compete until Anna steals Elspeth's boyfriend. Elspeth marries James Moodie, but their strange platonic marriage forces her into a love affair with a young man by whom she has a daughter. When she discovers that James is her long-lost father, she runs away. Only after his suicide is Elspeth able to inherit her rightful estate.

Genre: Historical Romance
Subjects: Women; Sisters
Place/Time: Scotland—19th century

1519. Stalker Trilogy
1. *Strathmore.* Delacorte Press, 1975.
2. *Call Home the Heart.* St. Martin's, 1977.
3. *The Dark Pasture.* St. Martin's, 1978.

In 1875, Houston Lamont owns the Scottish mining town Blacklaw. The Stalkers are a mining family who want to escape the poverty of the town. Son Drew is sent to Edinburgh to study law while daughter Mirrin falls in love with mine owner Houston, only to be rejected. She takes to the road and tries life on the stage, but later falls in love with Tom Armstrong. They marry and live happily on a farm, but they and Drew, now a successful lawyer, are pulled back to Blacklaw during a miners' strike.

Genre: Historical Romance
Subjects: Family life; Coal mines and mining; Farm life

Stirling, S. M. (Stephen Michael) *and* Drake, David

1520. The General
1. *The Forge.* Baen, 1991.
2. *The Hammer.* Baen, 1992.
3. *The Anvil.* Baen, 1993.
4. *The Steel.* Baen, 1993.
5. *The Sword.* Baen, 1995.
6. *The Chosen.* Baen, 1996.
7. *The Reformer.* Baen, 1999.

Far in the future, Raj Whitehall is a military officer on the planet Bellevue, which is now isolated and close to barbarism because of an interstellar war that has destroyed humanity's ability to travel among the stars. The war has also regressed technology to the point that remnants and artifacts of the earlier, more sophisticated civilization are viewed as holy. Aided by the only computer still in existence, Raj brings order to his own planet, works to restore space travel, and sets off to deal with cultures on other planets that have become even more violent and primitive than Bellevue.

Genre: Science Fiction
Subjects: Soldiers; Interplanetary wars; Computers; Society, primitive; Technology and civilization; Space flight

Stirling, S. M. (Stephen Michael). *See also* Doohan, James and Weber, David

1521.
1. *Island in the Sea of Time.* Roc, 1998.
2. *Against the Tide of Years.* Roc, 1999.
3. *On the Oceans of Eternity.* Roc, 2000.

Residents of Nantucket are grateful for surviving a terrible storm, but when the weather clears, they discover that a mysterious phenomena, which they call the Event, has carried them back to the Europe of the Bronze Age. Surrounded by people with whom they can barely communicate, the time travelers set up their own Republic of Nantucket complete with a constitution. However, one of their own citizens decides to take advantage of the situation by using his knowledge of modern technology to form alliances with powerful figures of this world and a dangerous confrontation seems inevitable.

Genre: Science Fiction
Subjects: Time travel; Bronze Age; Cultural conflict; Technology and civilization
Place/Time: Europe—prehistoric times

1522. Draka
1. *Marching through Georgia.* Baen, 1988.
2. *Under the Yoke.* Baen, 1988.
3. *The Stone Dogs.* Baen, 1990.
4. *Drakon.* Baen, 1996.

Starting in the past and projecting into the future, this series narrates an alternate timeline in world history. It starts just after the American Revolution when a group of exiled Loyalists set up a nation in Africa in which they are in control despite the defection of a population of serfs and slaves. The Dominion of Draka allies itself with the United States during World War II and continues as a partner in the exploration of space. From far in the future, a genetically altered Draka warrior travels in time to New York City and brings with her the threat of a technologically superior Draka army from centuries away that could conquer Earth.

Genre: Science Fiction
Subjects: Time; American Loyalists; World War II, 1939–1945; Space flight
Place/Time: United States—multicentury span

1523. Fifth Millennium
1. *Snowbrother.* Signet, 1985. Expanded edition. Baen, 1992.
2. *The Sharpest Edge.* Signet, 1986. (Written with Shirley Meier.)
3. *Saber and Shadow.* Baen, 1992. (Written with Shirley Meier.)

Centuries in the future after a great war has all but destroyed civilization, men and women who are warlike and skilled in military arts dominate the population. At the age of 19, the swordswoman Shkai'ra is ordered by the elders of her tribe to subdue the city of a neighboring tribe. Shkai'ra grows in skill and is joined by Megan, a dagger-wielding thief and illusionist. They use their talents in a society of warring factions led by a high priest, a military commander, and a group of mysterious shamans.

Genre: Science Fiction
Subjects: Imaginary wars and battles; Violence; Arms and armor; Women; Society, primitive

Stockton, Frank

1524.
1. *The Casting Away of Mrs. Lecks and Mrs. Aleshine.* Century, 1886.
2. *The Dusantes.* Century, 1888.

In this funny fantasy, two middle-aged Pennsylvania housewives, Mrs. Lecks and Mrs. Aleshine, are shipwrecked on a deserted Pacific island with Mr. Craig in the late 1880s. They are later joined by a missionary, his daughter, and three sailors. When they are finally rescued, they land in the United States and travel east by stagecoach. Their stagecoach is wrecked, and they have numerous adventures, including meeting the Dusantes, who owned the island. Eventually they all get home, and true love triumphs.

Genre: Humor
Subjects: Shipwrecks and castaways; Women; Missionaries; Seamen; Rescues
Place/Time: Pacific Islands—19th century

Stokes, Penelope J.

1525. Faith on the Home Front
1. *Home Fires Burning.* Tyndale House, 1996.
2. *Till We Meet Again.* Tyndale House, 1997.
3. *Remembering You.* Tyndale House, 1997.

As World War II opens, Link Winsom, Owen Slaughter, and Stork Simpson leave their wives and their homes in Mississippi to fight in Europe. They fight for their lives in France, while their wives must face their own problems at home. When Link and Stork are wounded, they are sent home to recover. Stork must deal with his newborn child who is gravely ill, and Link and his wife must try to renew their love. Owen, who was trapped in a Nazi internment camp, finally returns home after the war, but his amnesia makes him forget his true love. For all three couples, faith in God helps them through the horrors of war and separation.

Genre: Christian Fiction
Subjects: Husbands and wives; Marriage problems; World War II, 1939–1945
Place/Time: Mississippi—1900–1945; France—1900–1945

Stong, Phil

1526.
1. *State Fair.* Century, 1932.
2. *Return in August.* Doubleday, 1953.

While their parents concern themselves with a hog and homemade pickles that may or may not win a prize at the fair, Wayne and Margie meet a young woman and a young man who are bit more sophisticated than anyone they have known in their rural Iowa farm town of the early 1900s. Twenty years later, Pat Gilbert, the reporter who met Margie at the fair, returns, finds her a widow, and tries to rekindle their brief romance.

Subjects: Farm life; Fairs; Teenagers; Love
Place/Time: Iowa—1900–1945

Storey, Gail Donohue

1527.
1. *The Lord's Motel.* Persea Books, 1992.
2. *God's Country Clc.* Persea Books, 1996.

Colleen Sweeney is a former Bostonian who is now living in Houston in an old apartment building called the Lord's Motel. She and her eccentric friends try to understand the contemporary scene but get it wrong, especially Colleen who is in love with the wrong man—Web Desiderio. Web is a playboy and a social director on a cruise ship. Eventually he leads her into an arrest for prostitution. After leaving Web, Colleen works as a librarian specializing in service to the homeless. After one of her patrons is rushed to the hospital, Colleen meets Mr. Right—emergency room doctor Gabriel Benedict. They move in together and struggle to make their relationship work. She's from a dysfunctional family while he's from a wealthy Texas family. With a cast of characters around them, the two discover that love can be both funny and elusive.

Genre: Humor; Romance
Subjects: Love affairs; Librarians
Place/Time: Houston (Tex.)—1980–

Stover, Matthew Woodring

1528.
1. *Iron Dawn.* Roc, 1997.
2. *Jericho Moon.* Roc, 1998.

The ancient world is the backdrop for these tales of warrior princess Barra the Pict, who battles pirates and then returns to the Phoenician city of Tyre, which is under Egyptian domination. In Tyre, Barra must fight the power of a sorcerer who is creating distrust among the royal houses. While trying to rescue a kidnapped tribal prince, Barra becomes part of a conflict over the fortress of Jerusalem.

Genre: Fantasy
Subjects: Mercenary soldiers; Witchcraft; Jerusalem—Antiquities; Egypt—Antiquities

Strangeland, Katharina Marie (Bech-Brondum) Michaelis. *See Michaelis, Karin*

Straub, Peter

1529. Blue Rose Trilogy
1. *Koko.* Dutton, 1988.
2. *Mystery.* Dutton, 1990.
3. *The Throat.* Dutton, 1993.

Tim Underhill, thought to be a serial killer by his Vietnam buddies but proved innocent, and Tom Pasmore, a poor little rich boy turned detective, are brought together in their hometown of Millhaven, Illinois, to pursue a serial killer.

Genre: Crime Novel
Subjects: Murder and murderers; Detectives; Serial murders
Place/Time: Illinois—1980–

Street, James Howell

1530.
1. *Oh, Promised Land.* Dial, 1940.
2. *Tap Roots.* Dial, 1942.
3. *Tomorrow We Reap.* Dial, 1949.
4. *Mingo Dabney.* Dial, 1950.

From the opening of southern Georgia in 1794 to the battlefields of Cuba in the Spanish-American War, this panoramic saga follows the Dabney family as they move from Georgia to Mississippi. Sam Dabney and his sister Honoria leave Georgia in 1794 and settle in Lebanon Valley, Mississippi, where they establish a plantation. They become wealthy aristocrats, but being abolitionists they rebel and are left with little but their farm when their revolt is put down. They fight to rebuild their land and see the coming of lumber companies to their secluded area in the 1890s. The youngest, Mingo Dabney, leaves the estate to fight in the Spanish Civil War and find his love Rafaela, a Cuban patriot.

Genre: Family Saga; Historical Fiction
Subjects: Plantation life; Abolitionists; Reconstruction; United States—Spanish-American War
Place/Time: Georgia—19th century; Mississippi—19th century

1531.
1. *The Gauntlet.* Doubleday Doran, 1945.
2. *High Calling.* Doubleday, 1951.

London Wingo comes to a small Missouri town to be the minister of the local Baptist Church. Only after working with the people does he realize he has chosen the right vocation. Years later, he returns to the first church to be its minister again. These books lovingly recreate the everyday life of a man of God and his work with his flock.

Genre: Christian Fiction; Gentle Read
Subjects: Christian life; Clergy; Faith
Place/Time: Missouri—1900–1945

Streeter, Edward

1532.
1. *Dere Mable.* Stokes, 1918.
2. *That's Me All Over.* Stokes, 1919.
3. *Same Ole Bill, Eh Mable!* Stokes, 1919.

The spelling and grammar may not be quite perfect, but these letters from Pvt. Bill Smith to his girlfriend provide a witty narrative of his World War I experiences.

Genre: Humor
Subjects: World War I, 1914–1918; Soldiers; Letters (stories in letter form)
Place/Time: Europe—1900–1945

Stribling, Thomas Sigismund

1533.
1. *The Forge.* Doubleday, 1931.
2. *The Store.* Doubleday, 1932.
3. *The Unfinished Cathedral.* Doubleday, 1934.

The death of the Old South and the rise of the New South is depicted in the life of Colonel Militadas Vaiden of Florence, Alabama. Before the Civil War, Vaiden was a farmer. When the war broke out, he fought for the South at Shiloh. After the war, he led the Ku Klux Klan during Reconstruction while establishing the town bank and helping rebuild the town. Vaiden and his family help the New South, but are deeply involved with the segregation that was part of it.

Genre: Historical Fiction
Subjects: United States—Civil War, 1861–1865; Reconstruction; Prejudices; Ku Klux Klan; Segregation
Place/Time: Alabama—19th century

Strindberg, August

1534.
1. *Son of a Servant.* Putnam, 1913.
2. *Red Room.* Putnam, 1913.
3. *Confession of a Fool.* (Alternate title: *A Madman's Defense.*) Small, 1913.

Strindberg's autobiographical novels set in Sweden of the late 1800s reflect his childhood hatred for his stepmother, his participation in artistic and intellectual circles, and his disastrous first marriage to a woman who was far too independent to adapt to the sort of life he wanted.

Subjects: Autobiographical stories; Boys; Stepmothers; Intellectuals; Marriage problems
Place/Time: Sweden—19th century

Stringer, Arthur

1535. Prairie Trilogy
1. *The Prairie Wife.* Bobbs Merrill, 1915.
2. *The Prairie Mother.* Bobbs Merrill, 1920.
3. *The Prairie Child.* McClelland, 1922.

Chaddie and Duncan McKail are sophisticates from the East who go west in the late 1800s to make their fortunes. They establish a farm on the prairie, but it is not successful. Chaddie comes to love farm life, but Duncan becomes morose and abusive. As their love dies, Chaddie falls in love with another man, Peter. When Duncan finally returns to the East, Chaddie divorces him and returns to her farm and Peter.

Genre: Historical Fiction
Subjects: Farm life; Marriage problems; Love; Husbands and wives; Prairie life
Place/Time: Western states—19th century

Stuart, V. (Vivian) A. *See also* Long, William

1536.
1. *The Valiant Sailors.* Pinnacle, 1972, 1964.
2. *The Brave Captains.* Pinnacle, 1972.
3. *Hazard's Command.* Pinnacle, 1972.
4. *Hazard of Huntress.* Pinnacle, 1972.
5. *Victory at Sebastapol.* Pinnacle, 1972.
6. *Hazard in Circassia.* Pinnacle, 1973.
7. *Hazard to the Rescue.* Pinnacle, 1974.
8. *Guns to the Far East.* Pinnacle, 1975.

Philip Horatio Hazard joins the Royal Navy in the 1850s and rises through the ranks. He sees the navy change from sailing ships to steamships. He is involved with the fleet during the 1850s Indian Mutiny and the Crimean War.

Genre: Naval Adventure; War
Subjects: Naval battles; War; Navy, British—officers; Adventure; Sailing vessels; Steamboats
Place/Time: Atlantic Ocean—19th century; Mediterranean Sea—19th century

1537.
1. *Victors and Lords.* Pinnacle, 1972, 1964.
2. *The Sepoy Mutiny.* Pinnacle, 1973.
3. *Massacre at Cawnpore.* Pinnacle, 1973.
4. *The Cannons of Lucknow.* Pinnacle, 1974.
5. *The Heroic Garrison.* Pinnacle, 1975.
6. *Guns to the Far East.* Pinnacle, 1976.
7. *Escape from Hell.* Pinnacle, 1976.

Alexander Sheridan serves with the British forces in India during the Indian mutiny of 1857. He must survive attempted murder and high adventure as he puts down the revolt.

Genre: Adventure; War
Subjects: Army, British; Adventure; Mutiny; War; India—Sepoy Rebellion, 1857–1858; India—British occupation, 1765–1947
Place/Time: India—19th century

Stubbs, Jean

1538.
1. *By Our Beginnings.* St. Martin's, 1979.
2. *An Imperfect Joy.* St. Martin's, 1981.
3. *The Vivian Inheritance.* St. Martin's, 1982.
4. *The Northern Correspondent.* St. Martin's, 1984.

Farmers and townspeople are worlds apart, but when Ned Howarth and Dorcas Wilde marry, they found a dynasty that survives ostracism and hostility from their friends. Howarth's farm in 1760 Lancashire prospers with the Industrial Revolution. His children and grandchildren seize the new industrial opportunities to start mills, railroads, and newspapers. The family also fights social injustice as they search for love.

Genre: Family Saga; Historical Romance
Subjects: Business; Industrial conditions
Place/Time: England—18th century; England—19th century

Sucharitkul, Somtow. *See also* Somtow, S. P.

1539. Inquestor
1. *Light on the Sound.* Pocket Books, 1982.
2. *The Throne of Madness.* Pocket Books, 1983.
3. *Utopia Hunters.* Pocket Books, 1984.
4. *The Darkling Wind.* Bantam, 1985.

Inquestors are powerful creatures who feel responsible for controlling flawed humanity, but hardly in a kind or paternalistic way. The downfall of the Inquestors be-

gins when from their own ranks arise heretics who are sympathetic to humans and to the Windbringers, whalelike magical beings whom the Inquestors are bent on exploiting.

Genre: Fantasy
Subjects: Totalitarianism; Mythical animals; Imaginary wars and battles; Mythology

Suhl, Yuri

1540.
1. *One Foot in America.* Macmillan, 1950.
2. *Cowboy on a Wooden Horse.* Macmillan, 1953.

A young Galician Jewish boy comes to Brooklyn in 1923 to join his family. As a recent immigrant, he is a greenhorn in American ways and has bewildering adventures as he adjusts to America. As he grows up, he finds an American girlfriend who teaches him the American way of love with the aid of *True Romances* magazine. His friends in the upholsterers' union help him become a man. The world of the Jewish immigrants in the Williamsburg section of Brooklyn is lovingly and humorously shown through Sol, his family, and his friends.

Genre: Coming of Age; Historical Fiction; Humor
Subjects: Jews; Immigrants; Teenagers; Labor unions; Labor and laboring classes
Place/Time: New York (N. Y.)—1900–1945

Sukichi, Saito. *See* Kita, Morio

Surtees, Robert Smith

1541.
1. *Hillingdon Hall.* Payson, 1933.
2. *Jorrocks's Jaunts and Jollies.* Cary & Hart, 1938.
3. *Handley Cross.* Colburn, 1943.

English country life of the early years of Victoria's reign is personified in John Jorrocks, who travels through Europe, finding himself out of place when not pursuing his passion for hunting. His adventures continue as master of foxes at a hunting spa, then as a country squire fascinated with the new applications of scientific agriculture.

Genre: Historical Fiction; Humor
Subjects: Country life; Fox hunting; Farm life
Place/Time: England—19th century

Suthren, Victor

1542.
1. *Royal Yankee.* St. Martin's, 1987.
2. *The Golden Galleon.* St. Martin's, 1989.
3. *Admiral of Fear.* St. Martin's, 1991.
4. *Captain Monsoon.* St. Martin's, 1993.

American colonial Edward Mainwaring is a captain in the British Royal Navy in the 1740s. His service for H.M. George II takes him to the Caribbean, the Mediterranean, and the Indian Ocean as he fights privateers and the French. He falls in love with Anne Brixham, a Caribbean planter's daughter, and has to save her from pirates. Even when faced with impossible odds in attacking French ships and forts, Mainwaring does his service for king and country.

Genre: Historical Fiction; Naval Adventure; War
Subjects: Navy, British; Naval battles; Adventure; War; Pirates
Place/Time: Caribbean region—18th century; Mediterranean Sea—18th century; Indian Ocean—18th century

1543.
1. *A King's Ransom.* St. Martin's, 1981.
2. *The Black Cockade.* St. Martin's, 1982.
3. *The Perilous Seas.* St. Martin's, 1983.

Acadian-born French naval officer Paul Gallant sails the seas in the New World for Louis XV. On his ship *Echo*, Gallant has to protect a golden treasure sent to Louis from the king of Spain. Later he has to guard the French fortress of Louisbourg from the English as the French and Indian War spreads in 1747. Gallant fights the British, saves ladies in harems, defeats pirates, and finally rescues the king's cousin Marianne, who becomes his love. Nonstop naval action keeps Gallant swashbuckling his way across the seas.

Genre: Historical Fiction; Naval Adventure; War
Subjects: Naval battles; Navy, French; Adventure; War; Pirates
Place/Time: Atlantic Ocean—18th century; Caribbean region—18th century

Swann, Lois

1544.
1. *The Mists of Manitoo.* Scribner, 1976.
2. *Tom Covenants.* Scribner, 1981.

In colonial Massachusetts, Elizabeth Dowland, upset over an arranged marriage, walks into the forest and meets Native American Wakwa Manunnappu. He helps her when she becomes ill, and she falls in love with him. They try to build a life together, but Indians in their village are jealous of Elizabeth and betray Wakwa when he tries to unite the tribes. Her family tries to get the British crown to recognize Elizabeth's marriage so her son can inherit their property.

Genre: Historical Fiction
Subjects: Native Americans; Interracial marriage; Love; United States—to 1776;
Place/Time: Massachusetts—17th century

Swann, Thomas Burnett

1545. Minotaur
1. *Cry Silver Bells.* DAW Books, 1977.

2. *The Forest of Forever.* Ace, 1971.
3. *The Day of the Minotaur.* Ace, 1966.

The minotaurs, Silver Bells and his son Eunostos, and their fellow forest creatures interact with the all-too-human Achaens, sometimes helping and saving them. Finally an attack on the forest and its inhabitants leaves Eunostos the last minotaur.

Genre: Fantasy
Subjects: Mythology; Mythical animals; Imaginary wars and battles

1546. Rome
1. *Queens Walk in the Dust.* Heritage Press, 1977.
2. *Lady of the Bees.* Ace, 1976.
3. *Green Phoenix.* DAW Books, 1972.

Set in the realm of classical legend, these tales tell of the eternal dryad Mellonia, whose love for the Trojan warrior Aenas leads to his death. Mellonia's tragic romantic life also involves her in the conflict between Remus, whom she loves, and his twin brother Romulus, the founder of Rome.

Genre: Fantasy
Subjects: Mythology; Love; Twins; Bereavement

Swanson, Neil Harmon

1547.
1. *The Judas Tree.* Putnam, 1933.
2. *The First Rebel.* Farrar, 1937.
3. *The Silent Drum.* Farrar, 1940.
4. *Unconquered.* Doubleday, 1947.

Westward expansion and the first stirring of resentment toward the British crown are the subject of these works of historical fiction, which include the Siege of Fort Pitt, the Pontiac Conspiracy, and two books set in the 1760s that deal with revolutionary movements in Pennsylvania and Maryland.

Genre: Historical Fiction
Subjects: United States—to 1776; War; Native Americans; Frontier and pioneer life
Place/Time: Pennsylvania—18th century; Maryland—18th century

Swinnerton, Frank

1548.
1. *The Woman from Sicily.* Doubleday, 1957.
2. *A Tigress in the Village.* Doubleday, 1959.
3. *The Grace Divorce.* Doubleday, 1960.
4. *Quadrille.* Doubleday, 1965.

From 1920 to 1960, the Grace family struggles to overcome tragedy and find love. Jerome Grace and his wife Mary live in the East Anglian town of Prothero with their children. His mother is a malevolent force who brings about the disintegration of her son. Wife Mary is forced to support the family and raise Jane, Philip, and Raymond. When Jerome finally dies, Mary is free to remarry her devoted friend Tom Tamplin, while her children have their own love problems. Even granddaughter Laura finds love is elusive.

Genre: Family Saga
Subjects: Marriage problems; Family life; Mothers and sons
Place/Time: England—1945–1980

Talbot, Michael

1549.
1. *To the Ends of the Earth.* Knopf, 1986.
2. *A Wilful Woman.* Knopf, 1988.

The settling of Australia is told through four condemned criminals sent to Botany Bay in 1785. Joe Cribb, former soldier, Kitty Brandon, convicted murderer, Ben Thorpe, petty thief, and Abraham Levy, Jewish refugee, must pool their skills to survive the long voyage to Australia. Once they have landed, they must fight hostile natives, soldiers, and each other to set up a colony.

Genre: Historical Fiction
Subjects: Penal colonies; Frontier and pioneer life; England— colonies; Prisoners and prisons
Place/Time: Australia—19th century

Tanner, Edward. *See Dennis, Patrick*

Tanner, Janet

1550. Hillsbridge Trilogy
1. *The Hours of Light.* St. Martin's, 1981.
2. *The Emerald Valley.* St. Martin's, 1985.
3. *The Hills and the Valley.* St. Martin's, 1988.

Charlotte Hall does not want her son Jack to become a miner in Hillsbridge, England. Son Ted and daughter Amy also want to better themselves. When World War I starts, both Jack and Ted go off to fight in France, where one becomes a pilot and the other a soldier in the trenches. After the war, Amy marries a contractor and shocks the town by learning to drive and running her husband's business. Charlotte's grandchildren fight greedy mine owners and must face the horrors of World War II.

Genre: Family Saga; Historical Fiction
Subjects: World War I, 1914–1918; World War II, 1939–1945; Coal mines and mining; Family life
Place/Time: England—1900–1945

Tarr, Judith

1551.
1. *Alamut.* Doubleday, 1989.
2. *The Dagger and the Crown: A Novel of the Crusades.* Doubleday, 1991.

Prince Aidin, with his elfin heritage that grants immortality, travels to the Holy Land between the Second and Third Crusades only to find his nephew murdered by the beautiful Muslim assassin Morgiana, who, like him, is immortal. As unlikely as it may seem, the two fall in love, but both religious and secular forces conspire against them.

Genre: Fantasy
Subjects: Crusades; Assassination; Immortality; Love

1552. Avaryan Rising
1. *The Hall of the Mountain King.* Tor, 1986.
2. *The Lady of Han-Gilen.* Tor, 1987.
3. *A Fall of Princes.* Tor, 1988.
4. *Arrows of the Sun.* Tor, 1993.
5. *Spear of Heaven.* Tor, 1994. (The first three works are collected in Avaryan Rising. Tom Doherty, 1997.)

In the land of Han-lanon, an uncle and his nephew, who are rival princes, vie for the leadership of the realm. As the saga continues, Princess Elian of Han-Gilen rejects an arranged marriage to be with Prince Mirain, the victor of the struggle. Again two princes who share a strange bond compete, but with miraculous results. A century later, Prince Estarion must deal with the loss of his magical powers and a challenge to his authority as he ascends to the throne. The exploits of Estarion's granddaughter and great granddaughter continue the Avaryan saga as the two do battle by using their own magical powers.

Genre: Fantasy
Subjects: Princes; Imaginary wars and battles; Inheritance and succession; Magic; Love

1553. The Hound and the Falcon Trilogy
1. *The Isle of Glass.* Bluejay Books, 1985.
2. *The Golden Horn.* Bluejay Books, 1985.
3. *The Hounds of God.* Bluejay Books, 1986.

Alfred is born of elfin parents in 12th-century England and lives his early adult life as a monk. His psychic ability and healing power bring him into the court of Richard Lionheart and then into the Siege of Constantinople. His plans to return to the quiet life with his beloved Thea are shattered when their twins are spirited away by demons.

Genre: Fantasy
Subjects: Religious life; Extrasensory perception; Richard I, King of England, 1157–1199; Courts and courtiers; Demonology
Place/Time: England—12th century; Turkey—12th century

Tennant, Emma

1554.
1. *Pemberley.* St. Martin's, 1993.
2. *An Unequal Marriage.* St. Martin's, 1994.

In this continuation of Jane Austen's *Pride and Prejudice*, Elizabeth Bennet is now married to Fitzwilliam Darcy and the mistress of Pemberley. As she prepares for the Christmas visit of her mother, three sisters, and Lady Catherine de Bourgh, she is upset over her failure to conceive a child. Her sister Jane will soon give birth, and this further raises her anxiety. She also fears that the young boy in the village is Darcy's illegitimate son by a deceased Frenchwoman. Darcy seems to withdraw, but Elizabeth finally becomes pregnant. Twenty years later, 17-year-old Miranda is a lovely girl and her parents' pride and joy. Brother Edward is a student at Eton and always in trouble. Edward now is gambling, and Darcy tries to control the situation, while Elizabeth sees her marriage coming apart. As she finds herself attracted to another man, Elizabeth flees Pemberley to find herself.

Genre: Historical Fiction
Subjects: Marriage; Lovers; Husbands and wives; Aristocracy
Place/Time: England—19th century

Tepper, Sheri S.

1555.
1. *Grass.* Doubleday, 1989.
2. *Raising the Stones.* Doubleday, 1990.
3. *Sideshow.* Bantam, 1992.

In a future galaxy, humans have spread out to colonize various planets. One group leaves Earth to escape religious domination. Another begins to build a utopian society, but accidentally unleashes beings who seem to be primitive gods attempting to dominate a planet that had enjoyed cultural and social diversity.

Genre: Fantasy; Science Fiction
Subjects: Space colonies; Freedom of religion; Utopias; Gods and goddesses

1556. The Revenants
1. *Marianne, the Magus and the Manticore.* Ace, 1985.
2. *Marianne, the Madame and the Momentary Gods.* Ace, 1988.
3. *Marianne, the Matchbox and the Malachite Mouse.* Berkley, 1989.

Although born to wealthy parents in the tiny country of Alphenlicht, Marianne is a struggling student in the United States, fearful of the brother who has inherited their parents' estate. Suddenly she finds herself in a frightening fantasy world pursued by the vicious manticore and must put into use the magic she learned from an intriguing magus from Alphenlicht.

Genre: Fantasy
Subjects: Students; Brothers and sisters; Inheritance and succession; Mythical animals; Magic

Tevis, Walter

1557.
1. *The Hustler.* Harper, 1959.
2. *The Color of Money.* Warner, 1984.

Fast Eddie Felson hustles his way through the pool halls of Chicago. His big break comes when he gets into a game with Minnesota Fats. Even though he loses, he prepares for the rematch and the right to be the greatest pool player. Twenty years later, Fast Eddie has quit pool until he takes on a young protege and teaches him the game. Ultimately teacher and student must meet for a showdown.

Subjects: Games; Pool (game)
Place/Time: Chicago (Ill.)—1945–1980; Illinois—1945–1980

Thackeray, William Makepeace

1558.
1. *The History of Henry Esmond.* Harper, 1879, 1852.
2. *The Virginians.* Fields, Osgood, 1869, 1857.

In the early 1700s, Henry Esmond is brought up by Francis Esmond on the Castlewood estate. Francis' children believe Henry is the illegitimate son of the late viscount of Castlewood. Only when Francis is dying does he reveal to Henry that he is the real heir. Henry keeps the information secret, and when he is disappointed in love, moves to America. His grandsons fight in the American Revolution, but on different sides.

Genre: Historical Fiction
Subjects: Aristocracy; Illegitimacy; United States—revolution, 1775–1783
Place/Time: England—18th century; United States—18th century

Thane, Elswyth

1559.
1. *Dawn's Early Light.* Duell, Sloan & Pearce, 1943.
2. *Yankee Stranger.* Duell, Sloan & Pearce, 1944.
3. *Ever After.* Duell, Sloan & Pearce, 1945.
4. *The Light Heart.* Duell, Sloan & Pearce, 1947.
5. *Kissing Kin.* Duell, Sloan & Pearce, 1948.
6. *This Was Tomorrow.* Duell, Sloan & Pearce, 1951.
7. *Homing.* Duell, Sloan & Pearce, 1957.

Beginning in 1774, Julian Day arrives in Williamsburg, Virginia, to make his fortune. For the next 200 years, his descendants marry, serve in the Civil War, the Spanish American War, World War I, and World War II. Later generations intermarry with the Sprague family of Williamsburg, the Murray family of New York, and the Campion family of England. The family chronicle comes full circle when Jeff Day, who looks like the original Julian, returns to London in the 1940s as a foreign correspondent and meets his distant cousin, who looks like the first Julian's wife.

Genre: Family Saga; Historical Fiction; War

Subjects: War; Family life
Place/Time: Williamsburg (Va.)—multicentury span; London (England)—multicentury span; Virginia—multicentury span; England—multicentury span

Thibault, Francois-Anatole. *See* France, Anatole

Thirkell, Angela

1560. Barsetshire Novels
1. *High Rising.* Knopf, 1951, 1933.
2. *Wild Strawberries.* Smith & Haas, 1934.
3. *The Demon in the House.* Smith & Haas, 1935.
4. *August Folly.* Knopf, 1937.
5. *Summer Half.* Knopf, 1938.
6. *The Pomfret Towers.* Knopf, 1938.
7. *The Brandons.* Knopf, 1939.
8. *Before Lunch.* Knopf, 1940.
9. *Cheerfulness Breaks In.* Knopf, 1940.
10. *Northbridge Rectory.* Knopf, 1942.
11. *Marling Hall.* Knopf, 1942.
12. *Growing Up.* Knopf, 1944.
13. *The Headmistress.* Knopf, 1945.
14. *Miss Bunting.* Knopf, 1946.
15. *Peace Breaks Out.* Knopf, 1947.
16. *Private Enterprise.* Knopf, 1948.
17. *Love Among the Ruins.* Knopf, 1948.
18. *The Old Bank.* Knopf, 1949.
19. *Country Chronicle.* Knopf, 1950.
20. *The Duke's Daughter.* Knopf, 1951.
21. *Happy Return.* Knopf, 1952.
22. *Jutland Cottage.* Knopf, 1953.
23. *What Did It Mean?* Knopf, 1954.
24. *Enter Sir Robert.* Knopf, 1955.
25. *Never Too Late.* Knopf, 1955.
26. *A Double Affair.* Knopf, 1957.
27. *Close Quarters.* Knopf, 1958.
28. *Love at All Ages.* Knopf, 1959.
29. *Three Score and Ten.* Knopf, 1961.

In the town of Barsetshire in England, the upper middle-class residents who dominate the town live, love, marry, and entertain from the 1930s to 1960. While each novel tells a separate story, characters such as Laura Morland, Lady Leslie, Mrs. Brandon, the Grahams, Sam Adams, and others interact with each other and appear in many of the novels. Children grow up, men and women fall in love, newcomers to the town try to enter society, and the residents live quiet refined lives in their country homes. These delightful comedies of manners reveal a way of life that has disappeared.

Genre: Gentle Read; Romance
Subjects: Small town life; Friendship; Family life; Society novels
Place/Time: England—1900–1945; England—1945–1980

Thoene, Bodie

1561. Saga of the Sierras
1. *The Man from Shadow Ridge.* Bethany House, 1990.
2. *Riders of the Silver Rim.* Bethany House, 1990.
3. *Gold Rush Prodigal.* Bethany House, 1991.
4. *Sequoia Scout.* Bethany House, 1991.
5. *Cannons of the Comstock.* Bethany House, 1992.
6. *The Year of the Grizzly.* Bethany House, 1992.
7. *Shooting Star.* Bethany House, 1993.
8. *Flames on the Barbary Coast.* Bethany House, 1993.

Through his memoirs, Andrew Jackson Sinnickson brings the western frontier to life as he relates his adventures in the Civil War, in the Gold Rush, in cattle drives, and in the settling of San Francisco. The books follow Sinnickson and his descendants in these authentic stories of the West.

Genre: Christian Fiction; Western
Subjects: Frontier and pioneer life; United States—Civil War, 1861–1865; Western states; Christian life; Faith
Place/Time: Western states—19th century

1562. Shiloh Legacy
1. *In My Father's House.* Bethany House, 1992.
2. *A Thousand Shall Fall.* Bethany House, 1992.
3. *Say to This Mountain.* Bethany House, 1993.

Max Meyer, a Jew from New York, Ellis Warne, an Irish doctor's son from Ohio, Birch Tucker, an Arkansas farm boy, and Jefferson Canfield, the son of a black sharecropper, fight together on the battlefields of World War I. When they come home, they each find that they have to fight racial, religious, and cultural intolerance. Their own personal struggles for peace and security on the home front form the core of the series.

Genre: Christian Fiction; Historical Fiction
Subjects: Segregation; World War I, 1914–1918; War; Christian life; Faith; Prejudices; Anti-Semitism; Race relations
Place/Time: Europe—1900–1945; United States—1900–1945

1563. The Zion Chronicles
1. *The Gates of Zion.* Bethany House, 1986.
2. *A Daughter of Zion.* Bethany House, 1987.
3. *The Return to Zion.* Bethany House, 1987.
4. *A Light in Zion.* Bethany House, 1988.
5. *The Key to Zion.* Bethany House, 1988.

A sweeping historical drama of the birth of Israel out of the ashes of the Holocaust reveals the bravery of her people and their struggle against overwhelming odds. Rachel returns to Israel after the Holocaust and is caught up in Israel's war for survival in 1948. This story is told from a Christian perspective.

Genre: Christian Fiction; Historical Fiction
Subjects: Jews; Faith; Holocaust, Jewish,
     1933–1945; Israel; Jewish-Arab relations
Place/Time: Israel—1945–1980

1564. The Zion Covenant
1. *Vienna Prelude.* Bethany House, 1989.
2. *Prague Counterpoint.* Bethany House, 1989.
3. *Munich Signature.* Bethany House, 1990.
4. *Jerusalem Interlude.* Bethany House, 1990.
5. *Danzig Passage.* Bethany House, 1991.
6. *Warsaw Requiem.* Bethany House, 1991.

Elisa Lindheim, Shimon and Leah Feldstein, and others are caught in the terror of Nazi rule. Elisa, a Christian, struggles to resist and save those she can from the horrors of being Jewish in Europe during World War II. She and the Feldstein's focus on saving Jewish children by smuggling them to Palestine.

Genre: Christian Fiction; Historical Fiction
Subjects: World War II, 1939–1945; Christian life;
     Holocaust, Jewish, 1933–1945; Jews; Smuggling;
     Faith; War
Place/Time: Europe—1900–1945

Thoene, Bodie *and* Thoene, Brock

1565. Galway Chronicles
1. *Only the River Runs Free.* Thomas Nelson,
     1997.
2. *Of Men and of Angels.* Thomas Nelson, 1998.
3. *Ashes of Remembrance.* Thomas Nelson,
     1999.
4. *All Rivers to the Sea.* Thomas Nelson, 2000.

In the 1840s, Joseph Connor comes to the small Irish village of Ballynockanor where he meets Tom Donovan and his children. Kate, the oldest daughter, tries to avoid Connor as she is ashamed of the scars on her body; she was burned in a fire that killed her husband. Slowly she is attracted to Connor, and as she learns to love him, she also finds faith in God again. Soon they find themselves caught up in the tenant farmers' revolt against the British government. The farmers elect Connor to lead them, but he realizes that if he takes the position he and Kate may have to leave Ireland. As they grow closer together, they have to deal with a smallpox epidemic and violence. Events try their faith, but they also find it is faith that keeps them together.

Genre: Christian Fiction; Historical Fiction
Subjects: Faith; Rural life; Ireland—country life;
     Government, resistance to; Love
Place/Time: Ireland—19th century

Thoene, Brock. *See* Thoene, Bodie

Thomas, Craig

1566.
1. *Firefox!* Holt, Rinehart & Winston, 1977.
2. *Firefox Down!* Bantam, 1983.

3. *Winter Hawk.* Morrow, 1987.

The Soviets have crafted an unparalleled warplane, the Firefox, which the West wants but is unable to duplicate. Pilot Mitchell Gant is hired by the Allies to steal the plane on its test run. The plan seems to be successful as Gant and the Firefox cross the Russian border, but a fuel leak forces the plane down on a lake in Finland. The Russians and the West race to get the plane from where it has sunk. Gant is then sent back to the Soviet Union to steal a helicopter and a spy with information that could stop the nuclear arms reduction talks between the Soviets and the United States. Gant has to use all his flying abilities to avoid crack Russian pilots.

Genre: Adventure; Technothriller
Subjects: Airplanes; Air pilots; International intrigue
Place/Time: Soviet Union—1945–1980; Soviet Union—1980–1991; United States—1945–1980;
     Finland—1945–1980

Thomas, D. M.

1567. Russian Quartet
1. *Ararat.* Viking Press, 1983.
2. *Swallow.* Viking Press, 1984.
3. *Sphinx.* Viking Press, 1986.
4. *Summit.* Viking Press, 1988.
5. *Lying Together.* Viking Press, 1990.

Sergei Rozonov, a Russian poet, is troubled by the compromises he must make to stay alive. He invents stories about Victor Surkov, who becomes his alter ego. He travels to Finland to be in a storytelling competition, then is put into a Soviet psychiatric hospital for rebellious visionaries. He ultimately meets the real Victor Surkov as Thomas parodies Soviet life.

Subjects: Poets; Intellectual freedom
Place/Time: United States—1945–1980; Finland—1945–1980

Thompson, E. V. (Ernest Victor)

1568.
1. *Chase the Wind.* Coward McCann &
     Geoghegan, 1977.
2. *Ben Retallick.* St. Martin's, 1981.

In the early 1800s, Josh Retallick is a young miner in Cornwall who is bent on reforming the horrible conditions miners face. He falls in love with Miriam Trago, a child of the moors, but a tragic misunderstanding drives them apart. Both marry others but are unhappy. Only after their children are grown up do they finally reunite, then watch their children struggle to find love.

Genre: Historical Romance
Subjects: Coal mines and mining; Family life
Place/Time: England—19th century

Thompson, Flora

1569.

1. *Lark Rise.* Oxford, 1939.
2. *Over to Candleford.* Oxford, 1941.
3. *Candleford Green.* Oxford, 1943.
4. *Still Glides the Stream.* Oxford, 1948.

Using the Oxfordshire towns of Lark Rise and Candleford Green of the 1890s as a setting, Thompson recreates rural life in England without romanticizing. Laura grows up with her father and mother and becomes the apprentice to Miss Lane, the postmistress, but she leaves Lark Rise to be assistant postmistress at Candleford Green. Charity Finch, a middle-aged schoolteacher, returns to the village and recalls her life in the little hamlet.

Genre: Historical Fiction
Subjects: Country life; Small town life
Place/Time: England—19th century

Thornley, Diann

1570.

1. *Ganwold's Child.* Tor, 1995.
2. *Echoes of Issel.* Tor, 1996.
3. *Dominion's Reach.* Tor, 1997.

Tristan, the son of the military leader of the Unified Worlds, escapes the alien Masuki only to be trapped with his mother on the primitive planet Ganwold. A search for his father plunges him into the enemy's hands, where he gleans information that is useful to the Unified Worlds when he is rescued. Finally, he and his mother help his severely injured father discover the treachery in their own government.

Genre: Science Fiction
Subjects: Interplanetary wars; Extraterrestrial beings; Fathers and sons; Mothers and sons

Thornton, Lawrence

1571.

1. *Imaging Argentina.* Doubleday, 1987.
2. *Naming the Spirits.* Doubleday, 1995.
3. *Tales from the Blue Archives.* Doubleday, 1997.

During Argentina's "dirty war" in the 1970s, thousands of people were kidnapped by the military and then they disappeared. Journalist Cecilia Rueda is one of those who disappeared. As her playwright husband, Carlos, searches for her, he discovers he has the gift of being able to see the present situation of someone who has disappeared. A young girl who is the only survivor of a death squad massacre can not remember her own name or the names of the others who were killed. The girl is taken to Carlos Rueda and the stories of the massacre are told. After the Civil War, Dolores Masson searches for her grandsons who were kidnapped and given to a childless couple. As she searches, she tries to understand how this could happen.

Subjects: Argentina—Civil War; Government, resistance to; Death; Kidnapping
Place/Time: Argentina—1945–1980; Argentina—1980–

Tilley, Patrick

1572. Amtrak Wars

1. *Cloud Warrior.* Macmillan, 1984.
2. *First Family.* Baen, 1986.
3. *Iron Master.* Baen, 1988.
4. *Blood River.* Sphere, 1988.
5. *Death-Bringer.* Sphere, 1989.
6. *Earth-Thunder.* Sphere, 1990.

In a post-nuclear-holocaust America of the 30th century, tribal cultures are in conflict and in danger of being controlled by a military federation originating in Texas. For a time, peace seems in sight, but is threatened by a Chinese and Japanese mercantile culture in the Northwest.

Genre: Science Fiction
Subjects: Nuclear warfare; Tribes; Imaginary wars and battles; Militarism; Business

Toer, Pramoedya Ananta

1573. Buru Tetralogy

1. *This Earth of Mankind.* Morrow, 1991.
2. *Child of All Nations.* Morrow, 1993.
3. *Footsteps.* Morrow, 1995.
4. *House of Glass.* Morrow, 1996.

In the late 19th century, Minke, a Javanese native in the Dutch-controlled colony, is the champion of science, technology, and openness in his racially segregated society. He becomes romantically involved with Annelies, the daughter of a concubine and a white settler. His marriage to her brings them in conflict with the legal system, and ultimately they are punished and parted. Minke then works to reclaim his dignity from the Dutch oppression by becoming an activist for Indonesian freedom. He is opposed by Police Commissioner Pangemanann who will try to thwart Minke through legal and illegal means, but these actions only destroy Pangemanann.

Genre: Historical Fiction
Subjects: Cultural conflict; Netherlands—colonies; Race relations; Segregation
Place/Time: Java—19th century

Toland, John

1574.

1. *Gods of War.* Doubleday, 1985.
2. *Occupation.* Doubleday, 1987.

Historian Toland tells the story of the American McGlyn and Japanese Toda families in World War II. Members of the families become friends and intermarry, but they are divided when the Japanese bomb

Pearl Harbor. The men of the families see the horrors of combat and prison camps. When the war ends, the families live through the postwar occupation of Japan.

Genre: Historical Fiction; War
Subjects: World War II, 1939–1945; War; Family life; Interracial marriage; Prisoners of war
Place/Time: United States—1900–1945; Japan—1900–1945

Tolkien, J. R. R. (John Ronald Ruel)

1575. The Chronicles of Middle-Earth
1. *The Hobbit.* Allen & Unwin, 1937.
2. *The Fellowship of the Ring.* Allen & Unwin, 1954.
3. *The Two Towers.* Allen & Unwin, 1954.
4. *The Return of the King.* Allen & Unwin, 1955.

The above three titles make up The Lord of the Rings Trilogy.

5. *The Silmarillion.* Allen & Unwin, 1977.
6. *Unfinished Tales of Numenor and Middle-Earth.* Allen & Unwin, 1980.
7. *The Book of Lost Tales, Part I.* Allen & Unwin, 1983.
8. *The Book of Lost Tales, Part II.* Allen & Unwin, 1984.

It all starts when hobbit Bilbo Baggins, one of the many fantastic inhabitants of Middle Earth, finds a ring, which had belonged to the dreadful Gollum, during an adventure with the wizard Gandalf and a group of dwarves who are trying to retrieve their gold from a dragon. In the next three books, which form The Lord of the Rings Trilogy, Bilbo's kinsman Frodo inherits the ring with its awesome magical powers that become more and more evident to Gandalf. Frodo and his companions undergo many trials and tribulations in their quest to keep the ring from falling into the wrong hands. *The Silmarillion,* unfinished at Tolkien's death and put into final form by his son Christopher, goes back in time to trace the magical history of Middle-Earth. Despite its position in fictional chronology, it is generally considered to be more meaningful if read following the Lord of the Rings Trilogy.

Genre: Fantasy
Subjects: Imaginary kingdoms; Rings; Good and evil; Magic

Townsend, Sue

1576.
1. *The Secret Diary of Adrian Mole, Aged 13 3/4.* Avon, 1984.
2. *The Growing Pains of Adrian Mole.* Avon, 1986.

The above titles have also been published in the following collection: *The Adrian Mole Diaries.* Grove, 1986.

3. *Adrian Mole: The Lost Years.* Soho, 1994.

In his diary, 14-year-old Adrian Mole recounts the difficulties of growing up in a wacky English family. His mother runs away with an insurance salesman, and his father loses his job. Adrian has to pay protection money to the local school bully, and he is in love with the beautiful Pandora, who does not love him. As he grows up, he tries to become a writer, falls in love, and travels to Moscow and Greece. Adrian's daily diary recounts his humorous adventures.

Genre: Coming of Age; Humor
Subjects: Teenagers
Place/Time: England—1980–

Tranter, Nigel

1577.
1. *Robert the Bruce: The Steps to the Empty Throne.* St. Martin's, 1969.
2. *Robert the Bruce: The Path of the Hero King.* St. Martin's, 1972.
3. *Robert the Bruce: The Price of the King's Peace.* St. Martin's, 1972.

In the brutal time of the 13th century, Robert the Bruce fights English King Edward I for the throne of Scotland. His battle goes from 1306 to 1328, as Robert faces defeat, victory, and finally death in his quest. Even when he is deserted by his wife, children, and supporters, Robert continues his fight until he becomes King Robert I.

Genre: Historical Fiction
Subjects: Robert I, King of Scotland, 1274–1329; Edward I, King of England, 1239–1307; Courts and courtiers; Kings and rulers
Place/Time: Scotland—13th century; England—13th century

Traven, B.

1578. The Jungle Novel Series
1. *The Carreta.* Hill & Wang, 1970, 1931.
2. *Government.* Hill & Wang, 1971, 1931.
3. *March to the Monteria.* Hill & Wang, 1971, 1931.
4. *The Rebellion of the Hanged.* Hill & Wang, 1972, 1936.
5. *General from the Jungle.* Hill & Wang, 1972, 1940.

These novels tell of the birth of the Mexican Revolution in the late 1800s. The peasants suffer under the dictator Diaz and eventually rebellion spreads among the laborers and farm workers. When the revolt becomes widespread, it brings bloody results.

Genre: Historical Fiction; War
Subjects: Revolutions and revolutionists; Politics—Mexico; Peasant life; Dictators
Place/Time: Mexico—19th century

Treece, Henry

1579.
1. *Jason.* Random House, 1961.
2. *The Amber Princess.* Random House, 1962.
3. *The Eagle King.* Random House, 1965.

In these retellings of the Greek myths, Treece emphasizes the prehistoric origins of the myths. He fictionalizes the myths of Jason and Oedipus, as he portrays the grim dark forces behind the stories.

Genre: Fantasy
Subjects: Mythology; Jason (Greek mythology)

Trenhaile, John

1580.
1. *A View from the Square.* Congdon & Weed, 1983.
2. *Nocturne for the General.* Congdon & Weed, 1984.

In exchange for aid in defecting to the West, KGB agent Stepan Povin informs on a Soviet plan to steal an American AWAC. Before the Americans can act, the plane is stolen. Povin, now interred in a prison camp by his rival, is interrogated daily in an effort to break a western spy ring within the Soviet Union.

Genre: Adventure; Espionage
Subjects: Informers; Airplanes; Spies; International intrigue
Place/Time: United States—1945–1980; Soviet Union—1945–1980; Soviet Union—1980–1991

Trollope, Anthony

1581. Chronicles of Barsetshire Series
1. *The Warden.* Dick & Fitzgerald, 1862, 1855.
2. *Barchester Towers.* Dick & Fitzgerald, 1860, 1857.
3. *Doctor Thorne.* Harper, 1858.
4. *Framley Parsonage.* Harper, 1861.
5. *The Small House at Allington.* Harper, 1864.
6. *The Last Chronicle of Barset.* Harper, 1867.

Mr. Harding is a gentle Church of England priest in Barchester who is in charge of a home of 12 retired men. When a reformer challenges his charge of the home, a scandal erupts and Mr. Harding ultimately resigns. His son-in-law the archdeacon tries to dominate the old man, but Harding, in his kind way, refuses to do what he is told. He is the man of principle surrounded by those who would use the church for their own purposes. Harding's daughter Eleanor must choose between numerous suitors. The machinations of the aristocrats, the leaders of the church, and the humble men who serve society are faithfully drawn as Trollope explores the role of the church, power, and marriage in Victorian society.

Subjects: Clergy; Aristocracy—England
Place/Time: England—19th century

1582. The Pallisers Series
1. *Can You Forgive Her?* Harper, 1865.
2. *Phineas Finn: The Irish Member.* Harper, 1869.
3. *The Eustace Diamonds.* Chapman & Hall, 1873.
4. *Phineas Redux.* Harper, 1874.
5. *The Prime Minister.* Harper, 1876.
6. *The Duke's Children.* Munro, 1880.

Young Plantagenet Palliser is a dedicated politician and heir to the Duke of Omnium. He and his wife Lady Glencora have marital problems, but their political power grows until Palliser becomes prime minister of England. With his rise to power, Palliser meets many charming and unscrupulous people who are involved with politics. Trollope explores the balance between a politician's conscience and his allegiance to the party and the role financing plays in electing men to Parliament. Although each story is separate, characters introduced in one novel recur in the others playing lesser or more major roles.

Subjects: Politics—England; Marriage problems; Society novels
Place/Time: England—19th century

Trott, Susan

1583.
1. *The Holy Man.* Riverhead, 1995.
2. *The Holy Man's Journey.* Riverhead, 1997.

Atop a mountain, 72-year-old holy man Joe dispenses advice to thousands who come to see him. Joe answers the door and ushers them through the hermitage in a few minutes, but in that time the pilgrims learn that all men are holy. Later Joe leaves the hermitage with his chosen successor, Anna, an Irish healer. They travel to see Joe's teacher, Chen, who has built a lavish retreat. Chen has lost his principles, and Joe must teach him the message of tolerance and self-knowledge.

Subjects: Allegories; Hermits; Philosophical novels
Place/Time: 1980–

Troyat, Henri

1584. The Seed and the Fruit Series
1. *Amelie in Love.* Simon & Schuster, 1956.
2. *Amelie and Pierre.* Simon & Schuster, 1957.
3. *Elizabeth.* Simon & Schuster, 1959.
4. *Tender and Violent Elizabeth.* Simon & Schuster, 1960.
5. *The Encounter.* Simon & Schuster, 1962.

Ordinary middle-class family life in France from 1912 to the occupation of Paris in World War II is depicted through the experiences of Amelia and Pierre. When she is 17, Amelia breaks her engagement and marries Pierre. They take their daughter Elizabeth to Paris when she is 10 to experience the joy of the city. During World War II, Pierre is wounded and nursed by

Amelia. Elizabeth, now grown, falls in love with Boris Danoff, whose family was killed in the war.

Genre: Historical Fiction; War
Subjects: Family life; World War II, 1939–1945;
   Love; Middle classes
Place/Time: France—1900–1945

Trump, Ivana

1585.
   1. *For Love Alone.* Pocket Books, 1992.
   2. *Free to Love.* Pocket Books, 1993.

Ivana Trump fictionalizes her life with Donald into the story of Czech ski champ and model Katrinka Graham who marries wealthy shipping magnate Adam Graham. Together they lead a charmed life in society and business until Katrinka tries to have a baby and cannot and her mother-in-law and friends sabotage her marriage. After divorcing Adam, she marries a new millionaire, has a baby, finds her long-lost first son, and jet sets around the world. Her love life is jeopardized by ex-husband Adam, who tries to destroy her and her lovers. The glitzy world of the super rich comes alive in these novels.

Genre: Romance
Subjects: Autobiographical stories; Millionaires;
   Marriage problems; Divorce; Society novels
Place/Time: United States—1980–

Truscott, Lucian K., IV

1586.
   1. *Dress Gray.* Doubleday, 1979.
   2. *Full Dress Gray.* Morrow, 1998.

West Point cadet Ry Slaight refuses to accept the official verdict on the drowning death of his friend. He believes that officials are stonewalling the investigation and threatens to expose the coverup. Thirty years later, Slaight comes back to West Point as the new superintendent. His daughter Jacey is a company commander there. When one of her female plebs dies from supposed heat stroke, the autopsy reveals otherwise. Also the autopsy shows she had rough sex the night before. Jacey investigates whether she was gang raped and finds herself threatened. Eventually, her father Ry and his enemy General Gibson battle over the presence of women in the military.

Genre: Crime Novel
Subjects: Murder and murderers; Army, United
   States—officers;
Place/Time: New York (state)—1980–

Tryon, Thomas

1587.
   1. *The Wings of the Morning.* Knopf, 1990.
   2. *In the Fire of Spring.* Knopf, 1992.

In the town of Pequot Landing, Connecticut, in the 1820s, the Grimeses and the Talcotts are the town's first families and constant rivals. What ties them together is their love for Georgie Ross, a friend to both families. Independent Georgie is involved in a failed elopement, a shipwreck, and later a school for runaway slaves. The town is divided over the school, which the Talcotts support and the Grimeses oppose. The rival families continue their feud through adventures and loves.

Genre: Historical Romance
Subjects: Cities and towns; Abolitionists; Social
   classes
Place/Time: Connecticut—19th century

Tsukiyama, Gail

1588.
   1. *Women of the Silk.* St. Martin's, 1991.
   2. *The Language of Threads.* St. Martin's,
     1999.

In pre-World War II China, young girls like Pei are sent to work in the silk factories. She stays with Auntie Yee, a woman who runs a boarding house that gives girls food, clothing, and lodging. Pei at first feels alone and abandoned, but she gradually makes friends with the other girls at the factory. They face brutal working conditions and resist forced marriage. When the Japanese invade Pei's village in 1938, Pei flees to Hong Kong with an orphaned 13-year old. There they work to rebuild their lives, but when the Japanese take over Hong Kong, they lose everything again. When the war ends, Pei starts a reweaving business and looks for her long-lost sister. Against this decade of violence, Pei becomes a woman.

Genre: Historical Fiction
Subjects: Girls; Industrial conditions; Silk; World
   War II, 1939–1945
Place/Time: China—1900–1945

Tucci, Niccolo

1589.
   1. *Before My Time.* Simon & Schuster, 1962.
   2. *The Sun and the Moon.* Knopf, 1977.

In Rome at the turn of the century, wealthy widow Sophie von Randen moves heaven and earth to bring about the marriage of her daughter Mary to Leonardo, a poor Italian country doctor. Mary is pale and passionate while Leonardo is ardent and passionate, but both are married to others. Mary and Leonardo are together for nine days of love and guilt while Sophie uses her money to buy off their spouses.

Genre: Historical Romance
Subjects: Love affairs; Marriage problems
Place/Time: Rome (Italy)—1900–1945; Italy—1900–1945

Turtledove, Harry

1590.

1. *The Great War: American Front.* Ballantine, 1998.
2. *The Great War: Walk in Hell.* Ballantine, 1999.

In this version of alternate United States history, the Civil War did not produce a victory by the North. Both sides, still separate entities at the beginning of World War I, form separate alliances: the North with Germany and the South with England and France. Trench warfare takes place on American soil, Canada faces occupation forces, and a communist inspired uprising of blacks occurs in the Confederate states. *Note:* These works, which begin a projected tetralogy, are loosely connected to the author's earlier work *How Few Remain.* Ballantine, 1997.

Genre: Science Fiction
Subjects: World War I, 1914–1918; History
Place/Time: United States—1900–1945

1591.

1. *Into the Darkness.* Tom Doherty Assoc., 1999.
2. *Darkness Descending.* Tor, 2000.

In a setting rather like medieval Europe, a world war is fought with magic as an important weapon. A power vacuum in the country of Bari encourages the ruler of their neighbor country, Algarve, to seek revenge for a military defeat suffered a generation ago. A series of treaties bring other nations into the conflict, and soon dragons are flying overhead raining fire on the towns below, and sea monsters are attacking ships.

Genre: Fantasy
Subjects: Imaginary wars and battles; Magic; Revenge

1592. Worldwar

1. *Worldwar: In the Balance.* Ballantine, 1994.
2. *Worldwar: Tilting the Balance.* Ballantine, 1995.
3. *Worldwar: Upsetting the Balance.* Ballantine, 1996.
4. *Worldwar: Striking the Balance.* Ballantine, 1996.

Historical figures such as Albert Einstein and Joseph Stalin inhabit the pages of these alternate history works that imagine a version of World War II in which lizard-like aliens from space become a common enemy uniting Axis and Allied powers. Finally, an uneasy truce prevails despite fear in the human population about a group of reptilian colonists due to arrive on Earth in the 1960s. *Note:* This series is continued in the Colonization series.

Genre: Science Fiction
Subjects: World War II, 1939–1945; Extraterrestrial beings; Imaginary wars and battles

Place/Time: United States—1900–1945; Europe—1900–1945; United States—1945–1980; Europe—1945–1980

1593. Colonization

1. *Colonization: Second Contact.* Ballantine, 1999.
2. *Colonization: Down to Earth.* Ballantine, 2000.

The alternate history narrative started in the Worldwar series continues in these works. The uneasy balance of power between Lizards and humans is disrupted with the arrival of a colonizing fleet of Lizards, who are under the mistaken impression that the humans have been completely subdued. The Lizards are weakened by the human discovery that they can become addicted to ginger. Further undermining their position on Earth is the necessity for forming an alliance against the Third Reich, which still exists in the 1960s. *Note:* This series follows the Worldwar series.

Genre: Science Fiction
Subjects: Extraterrestrial beings; Imaginary wars and battles; Drug addiction;
Place/Time: United States—1945–1980; Europe—1945–1980

1594. The Tale of Krispos

1. *Krispos Rising.* Ballantine, 1991.
2. *Krispos of Videssos.* Ballantine, 1991.
3. *Krispos the Emperor.* Ballantine, 1994.

A series of misfortunes drive the young adventurer Krispos from his home into the court of the land of Videssos. He survives an assassination attempt, becomes the ruler of the land, and marries the Empress Dara. Although plagued by conspiracies and rebel movements, he prevails, but must deal with his son Phostis's interest in a religious heresy.

Genre: Fantasy
Subjects: Imaginary kingdoms; Kings and rulers; Government, Resistance to; Fathers and sons

Tyler-Whittle, Michael Sidney. *See* Whittle, Tyler

Undset, Sigrid

1595.

1. *The Axe.* Knopf, 1928.
2. *The Snake Pit.* Knopf, 1929.
3. *In the Wilderness.* Knopf, 1929.
4. *The Son Avenger.* Knopf, 1930.

The above titles have also been published in the following collection: *The Master of Hestviken.* Knopf, 1934.

Olaf is the foster son of Steinfinn in 13th-century Norway. He is also betrothed to Steinfinn's daughter Ingunn. Olaf is forced to flee when he kills a kinsman, but comes back to take Ingunn away to Hestviken, his new home. He tries to rekindle their love, but her illness and death leaves him lonely. Their children also experience only tragedy, and Olaf finally finds repentance and death.

Genre: Historical Fiction
Subjects: Marriage problems; Love affairs
Place/Time: Norway—13th century

1596.
1. *Wild Orchid.* Knopf, 1931.
2. *Burning Bush.* Knopf, 1932.

Paul Selmer has experienced neither love nor religious fervor. As he grows up he discovers love. After World War I, he converts to Catholicism, but finds he is growing away from his young wife Bjorg.

Genre: Historical Fiction
Subjects: Love affairs; Religion; Catholic faith; Conversion; Faith
Place/Time: Europe—1900–1945

1597.
1. *Bridal Wreath.* Knopf, 1923.
2. *The Mistress of Husaby.* Knopf, 1925.
3. *The Cross.* Knopf, 1927.

The above titles have also been published in the following collection: *Kristin Lavransdatter.* Knopf, 1938.

In medieval Norway of the 14th century, Kristin grows up to be a beautiful young women. She is betrothed to Simon Andresson, though in love with Erland Nikolausson. She knows Erland is fickle and will bring her anguish, but she marries him and goes to his estate of Husaby. There she raises two sons. When Erland dies, she is stripped of the land and her sons and dies of the plague.

Genre: Historical Fiction; Historical Romance
Subjects: Marriage problems; Love affairs; Middle Ages
Place/Time: Norway—14th century

Updike, John

1598.
1. *Bech.* Knopf, 1970.
2. *Bech Is Back.* Knopf, 1982.
3. *Bech at Bay.* Knopf, 1998.

Interrelated stories narrate the literary and personal life of Henry Bech, a distinguished Jewish American author who is having trouble writing. He becomes involved with a cultural exchange in Russia, with hippies in London, and with Third World countries as a cultural ambassador. He marries an Episcopalian who falls in love with Israel, while he becomes enthralled with Scotland. As he ages, Bech is given the Nobel Prize although many critics protest, and Bech attacks the critics. These sketches are concerned with illusion, reality, fame, and art.

Subjects: Authors; Jews—United States; Creation (literary, artistic, etc.); Marriage

Place/Time: United States—1945–1980; London (England)—1945–1980; Soviet Union—1945–1980; Soviet Union—1980–1991; England—1945–1980

1599.
1. *Rabbit, Run.* Knopf, 1960.
2. *Rabbit Redux.* Knopf, 1971.
3. *Rabbit Is Rich.* Knopf, 1981.
4. *Rabbit at Rest.* Knopf, 1990.

From his first married years to the end of his life, Harry (Rabbit) Angstrom tries to understand himself, his wife, and his life. The frustrations of family life force him to run away. Ten years later as a suburbanite, he is deserted by his wife who wants to find herself. Problems with their son and daughter-in-law plague Harry and his wife through their middle age and beyond.

Subjects: Men—psychology; Family life; Marriage problems
Place/Time: United States—1945–1980

Uris, Leon

1600.
1. *Trinity.* Doubleday, 1976.
2. *Redemption.* HarperCollins, 1995.

From the 1840s through World War I, the Larkins, the Hubbles, and the MacLeods of Ireland interact as the Irish struggle to free themselves from British rule. The Larkins are Catholic farmers who eke out a living on the land and finally become revolutionaries. The Hubbles are British aristocracy who have dominated the country and who do everything they can to oppress the Irish. The MacLeods of Belfast are Scottish Presbyterian industrialists who are caught in the conflict between the Irish and the British. Their struggles culminate in World War I as all three families send sons to the war and then become involved in the Easter uprising.

Genre: Historical Fiction; Family Saga
Subjects: Family life; Irish; Ireland—country life; Catholic faith; World War I, 1914–1918
Place/Time: Ireland—19th century; Ireland—1900–1945

Van de Water, Frederic Franklyn

1601. American Revolution Series
1. *Reluctant Rebel.* Duell, 1948.
2. *Wings of the Morning.* Washburn, 1956.
3. *Day of Battle.* Washburn, 1958.
4. *Catch a Falling Star.* Duell, 1949.

New England of the Revolutionary War period is the scene of these works, which focus on Vermont and New Hampshire at the time of Ethan Allen and the Green Mountain Boys and the Battle of Ticonderoga.

Genre: Historical Fiction; War
Subjects: United States—revolution, 1775–1783; War; Battles; Allen, Ethan, 1738–1789

Place/Time: New England—18th century

Van der Post, Laurens

1602.
1. *A Story Like the Wind.* Morrow, 1972
2. *A Far Off Place.* Morrow, 1974.

The political upheaval of South Africa of the middle of the 20th century shatters the idyllic life of Francois Joubert on his father's isolated farm. After his family is murdered by Maoist guerrillas, Francois sets off through the bush to seek safety, accompanied by a young colonial girl, a bushman couple, and his dog Hintza.

Genre: Historical Fiction
Subjects: Politics—South Africa; Farm life; Revolutions and revolutionists; Escapes
Place/Time: South Africa—1945–1980

Van Dyke, Henry

1603.
1. *Ladies of the Rachmaninoff Eyes.* Farrar, 1965.
2. *Blood of the Strawberries.* Farrar, 1969.

Oliver is a young African American who reads Baudelaire and lives in a crazy household where his aunt Harriet Gibbs works as a companion to Etta Klein. Oliver dodges seduction by the maid Della and breaks up a seance. When Oliver goes to Cornell for college, he marries and acts as a producer for a Gertrude Stein play in which some strange events are happening.

Genre: Coming of Age
Subjects: African Americans; Eccentrics and eccentricities; Students; Theater life
Place/Time: United States—1945–1980

Van Scyoc, Sydney J.

1604. The Darkchild Trilogy
1. *Darkchild.* Berkley, 1982.
2. *Bluesong.* Berkley, 1983.
3. *Starsilk.* Berkley, 1984.

On the forbidding planet Brakrath, sentient beings known as starsilk form symbiotic, mind-enhancing relationships with humans and other inhabitants. The powers of the starsilk eventually stretch across the galaxy.

Genre: Science Fiction
Subjects: Life on other planets; Extraterrestrial beings; Telepathy

Van Vogt, A. E. (Alfred Elton)

1605. Null-A
1. *The World of A.* Simon & Schuster, 1948. (This title was revised as *The World of Null-A.* Berkley, 1970.)
2. *The Pawns of Null-A.* Ace, 1956. (This title was revised as *The Players of Null-A.* Berkley, 1966.)
3. *Null-A Three.* DAW Books, 1985.

Gilbert Gosseyn is unique in the universe. A super being who is the product of an experiment, he has an extra brain and the ability to resurrect himself from death. Gosseyn has many adventures defending the Null-A civilization of Venus from militaristic forces of the galaxy.

Genre: Science Fiction
Subjects: Bionics; Life on other planets; Venus (planet); Interplanetary wars

Vance, Jack

1606. Cadwal Chronicles
1. *Araminta Station.* Tor, 1988.
2. *Ecce and Old Earth.* Tor, 1991.
3. *Throy.* Tor, 1993.

Cadwal was designated a sort of planetary nature preserve a thousand year ago, but the pressure of population and political maneuvering threaten its status at this point in the future. Glawen Clattus, a descendant of one of the families entrusted with conserving the planet, must defend his world against commercial exploitation, but finds that members of his own family are behind the scheming.

Genre: Science Fiction
Subjects: Life on other planets; Nature conservation

1607. The Demon Princes
1. *Star King.* Berkley, 1964.
2. *The Killing Machine.* Berkley, 1964.
3. *The Palace of Love.* Berkley, 1967.
4. *The Face.* DAW Books, 1979.
5. *A Book of Dreams.* DAW Books, 1981.

Keith Gersen swashbuckles through the galaxy seeking revenge for the destruction of his family by the Demon Princes, a network of criminals who wield their power in secret.

Genre: Science Fiction
Subjects: Interplanetary voyages; Crime and criminals; Revenge

1608. Lyonesse Trilogy
1. *Lyonesse Book 1, Suldrun's Garden.* Berkley, 1983.
2. *The Green Pearl.* Underwood Miller, 1985.
3. *Madouc.* Underwood Miller, 1989.

Being the ruler of Lyonesse, a mythical island kingdom off the coast of France, is not enough for Casimir. His plans to be king of all of the Elder Isles threaten the happiness of his daughter Suldrun and everyone around him, including Madouc, who is believed to be Suldrun's daughter, but who is in fact the daughter of the fairy Twisk.

Genre: Fantasy
Subjects: Imaginary kingdoms; Kings and rulers; Ambition

1609. Tschai: Planet of Adventure
1. *City of the Chasch.* Ace, 1968.
2. *Servants of the Wankh.* Ace, 1969.
3. *The Dirdir.* Ace, 1969.
4. *The Pnume.* Ace, 1970.

The planet Tschai is inhabited by six sentient races: the alien Chasch, Dirdir, and Wankh, the aboriginal Pnume and Phing, and human prisoners brought from prehistoric Earth who eventually come to dominate their former rulers.

Genre: Science Fiction
Subjects: Life on other planets; Extraterrestrial beings; Man, prehistoric; Prisoners and prisons

Varley, John
1610. Gaea
1. *Titan.* Berkley, 1979.
2. *Wizard.* Berkley, 1980.
3. *Demon.* Putnam, 1984.

Space adventurer Cirocco Jones is part of a NASA mission to Saturn that is literally swallowed by a newly discovered moon named Gaea, which proves to be a sort of sentient female spaceship. Gaea is at times Cirocco's friend, at others, her foe, but finally Cirocco must deal with definite indications that Gaea is becoming insane.

Genre: Science Fiction
Subjects: Interplanetary voyages; Spaceships; Insanity

Vaughn, Richard
1611.
1. *Moulded in Earth.* Dutton, 1951.
2. *Son of Justin.* Dutton, 1955.

A family feud between the Peeles and the Ellises in a Welsh village of the late 1800s is brought to a close by the death of two young men and marriage between members of the families. The sequel follows the experiences of the next Peele generation.

Genre: Family Saga; Historical Fiction
Subjects: Feuds; Family life
Place/Time: Wales—19th century

Verga, Giovanni
1612. The Vanquished
1. *The House by the Medlar Tree.* Grove 1953.
2. *Maestro-don Gesualdo.* Seltzer, 1923.

Intended to be the first two of a five volume series, these novels show the effect of progress on 18th-century Sicilian families of different social standing. In the first book, a family of fisherman deals with their own internal conflicts and the encroachment of the modern competitive business world. In the second, an ambitious laborer tries to advance socially by allying himself with aristocrats through marriage.

Genre: Historical Fiction
Subjects: Social classes; Peasant life
Place/Time: Sicily (Italy)—19th century; Italy—19th century

Verne, Jules
1613.
1. *Robur the Conqueror.* George Munro, 1887.
2. *The Master of the World.* Lippincott, 1914, 1904.

Robur the Conqueror, in his helicopterlike airship, becomes insane and threatens the Earth with his high-tech inventions. He is stopped by a lightning bolt.

Genre: Science Fiction
Subjects: Helicopters; Insanity; Technology and civilization

1614.
1. *At the North Pole, or The Adventures of Captain Hatteras.* Porter & Coates, 1874, 1866.
2. *The Desert of Ice.* Porter & Coates, 1876, 1866.

Captain Hatteras, the only son of a millionaire, is determined to find the North Pole. An earlier search had resulted in the death of his crew. Now he charters another ship and tries again, but his men desert him. Eventually Hatteras finds the Pole, but he goes mad and is confined to an asylum.

Genre: Science Fiction
Subjects: Explorers; Millionaires; Insanity
Place/Time: Arctic regions—19th century

1615.
1. *Twenty Thousand Leagues Under the Sea.* George M. Smith, 1873, 1869.
2. *The Mysterious Island.* Scribner, 1875.

In 1866, the United States sends out an expedition to discover the cause of mysterious encounters at sea. When the ship is sunk, Professor Aronnax, his assistant Conseil, and whaler Ned Land are held captive by the mysterious Captain Nemo on his submarine. After numerous undersea adventures, the three escape, and Nemo disappears among the Maelstrom Islands, where three American soldiers are wrecked. There they meet Nemo and learn his strange past.

Genre: Science Fiction
Subjects: Ships; Submarines; Shipwrecks and castaways

1616.
1. *From the Earth to the Moon.* Newark Printing, 1869, 1865.
2. *Round the Moon.* George Munro, 1878, 1870.

Michel Arden, a Frenchman, and his American partners Barbican and Captain Nicholl plan a trip to the moon. They build a cannon and finally shoot their rocket to the moon. They complete their trip through the deflection of their rocket by a second earthly moon. They pass the dark side of the moon and finally splash down in the Pacific.

Genre: Science Fiction
Subjects: Space flight to the moon

Veryan, Patricia

1617.
1. *The Riddle of Alabaster Royal.* St. Martin's, 1997.
2. *The Riddle of the Lost Lover.* St. Martin's, 1998.
3. *The Riddle of the Reluctant Rake.* St. Martin's, 1999.

Captain Jack Vespas is injured in a battle against Napoleon, and Lord Wellington sends him home to England to recuperate. He finds his parents' home in London too hectic during the social season, so he goes to his country estate, Alabaster Royal, to rest. At the estate, he find a mysterious young woman, Consuela Jones, who is searching for the murderer of her father. As Jack helps her, he falls in love with her. In searching the estate, Jack finds a cache of weapons and in a fight with his father, Jack discovers he is not his son. Jack must discover his real father if he is to win the hand of his love, Consuela Jones, but various villains try to thwart his search. Later Jack must come to the aid of his friend, Lieutenant Colonel Hastings Adair who is being accused of taking a woman's virtue. As Jack helps Hastings, they begin to uncover the riddle to the poor girl's family.

Genre: Historical Romance
Subjects: Lovers; Soldiers—British; Aristocracy
Place/Time: England—19th century

1618. The Golden Chronicles
1. *Practice to Deceive.* St. Martin's, 1985.
2. *Journey to Enchantment.* St. Martin's, 1986.
3. *The Tyrant.* St. Martin's, 1987.
4. *Love Alters Not.* St. Martin's, 1987.
5. *Cherished Enemy.* St. Martin's, 1987.
6. *The Dedicated Villain.* St. Martin's, 1989.

In Georgian England in 1746, six different couples become involved with the Jacobite rebellion. Each star-crossed couple meets, falls in love, has a spat, and then gets back together, but they do this while trying to carry the cypher that will lead to the source of Bonnie Prince Charlie's treasure. The underground Jacobites want to return the treasure to its rightful owners and keep it out of the hands of King George II. Love and duty triumph in all six novels.

Genre: Historical Romance
Subjects: Charles Edward, Prince, Grandson of James II, King of England, 1720–1788
Place/Time: England—18th century

1619. Sanguinet Saga
1. *Nanette.* Walker, 1981.
2. *Feather Castles.* St. Martin's, 1982.
3. *Married Past Redemption.* St. Martin's, 1983.
4. *The Noblest Frailty.* St. Martin's, 1983.
5. *Sanguinet's Crown.* St. Martin's, 1985.
6. *Give All to Love.* St. Martin's, 1987.

In Regent England, Sir Harry Redmond and his brother Mitchell race to save the Prince Regent when plotters try to kill him. They also become involved with the evil Claude Sanguinet as he weaves plots and tries to foil the love lives of the Redmonds.

Genre: Historical Romance
Subjects: Love; Aristocracy
Place/Time: England—19th century

1620. The Tales of the Jeweled Men
1. *Time's Fool.* St. Martin's, 1991.
2. *Had We Never Learned.* St. Martin's, 1992.
3. *Ask Me No Questions.* St. Martin's, 1993.
4. *A Shadow's Bliss.* St. Martin's, 1994.
5. *Never Doubt I Love.* St. Martin's, 1995.
6. *The Mandarin of Mayfair.* St. Martin's, 1995.

When Captain Gideon Rossiter returns from the European wars of the 1740s, he finds that the family name is disgraced and his fiancee Lady Naomi loathes him. All this is due to a secret cabal known as the Jeweled Men, who discredit the country's best families in a scheme to rid the country of the Hanoverian King. Gideon and Naomi, Horatio Glendenning, Amy Consett, Ruth Allington, Crazy Jack, Peregrine Cranford, Zoe Grainger, James Morris, and August Falcon, all victims of the Jeweled Men, work to uncover the plot while finding romance.

Genre: Historical Romance
Subjects: Aristocracy; Politics—England
Place/Time: England—18th century

Vidal, Gore

1621. American Chronicle Series
1. *Burr.* Random House, 1973.
2. *Lincoln.* Random House, 1984.
3. *1876.* Random House, 1976.
4. *Empire.* Random House, 1987.
5. *Washington, D. C.* Little, Brown, 1967.

Vidal retells American history in an imaginative and intimate way by focusing on one major figure during a critical time. The power elite of Washington, D. C., are shown through the plots of Aaron Burr and the leadership mastery of Lincoln. The power struggles in Washington in the 1870s, then during the McCarthy era come alive as Vidal recounts the scandals, manipulations, and blackmail of the times.

Genre: Historical Fiction
Subjects: Burr, Aaron, 1754–1836; Lincoln, Abraham, 1809–1865; Politics—United States; McCarthy, Joseph, 1908–1957
Place/Time: Washington (D. C.)—19th century; Washington (D. C.)—1945–1980

Viereck, George Sylvester *and* Eldridge, Paul

1622. The Three Immortals
1. *My First Two Thousand Years.* Macauley, 1928.
2. *Salome: The Wandering Jewess.* Liveright, 1930.
3. *The Invincible Adam.* Liveright, 1932.

Immortality is a curse for the first two of these immortals: Cartaphilus, who mocked Christ as he carried the cross, and Salome, who is condemned to an eternal quest for freedom by the words of the severed head of John the Baptist. For the third immortal, Kotikokura, a divine bridge between ape and man, immortality represents youth and sensuality.

Subjects: Immortality; Biblical stories

Vinge, Joan D.

1623. Cat
1. *Psion.* Delacorte, 1982.
2. *Catspaw.* Warner, 1988.
3. *Dreamfall.* Warner, 1996.

Cat's mixed ancestry of human and alien Hydran make him an outcast in both societies. He escapes a life of the streets to become a bodyguard in the home of a wealthy, powerful family where his psychic gifts are both feared and valued. On the planet Refuge, where he was sent to investigate clouds that are the strange manifestations of the thoughts of mysterious cloud whales, Cat becomes inadvertently involved in a kidnapping, which is part of a Hydran terrorist plot.

Genre: Science Fiction; Coming of Age
Subjects: Mixed blood; Extrasensory perception; Discrimination

1624. The Snow Queen
1. *The Snow Queen.* Dial, 1980.
2. *World's End.* Bluejay Books, 1984.
3. *The Summer Queen.* Warner, 1991.

The story of the Summer Queen Moon Dawntreader, cloned daughter of the Snow Queen Arienrhod, takes place on Tiamat, a planet whose primitive society is isolated for its century-and-a-half-long summer season by a star gate. Seal-like creatures called mers, whose blood confers immortality, figure in the plans of forces determined to exploit Tiamat. Involved in the

political intrigue are two men whom Moon loves: Sparks, her childhood sweetheart and husband, and BZ, the police officer who defies authority to protect and support her.

Genre: Science Fiction
Subjects: Queens; Life on other planets; Society, primitive; Animals; Love; Technology and civilization

Vinge, Vernor

1625.
1. *A Deepness in the Sky.* Tor, 1999.
2. *A Fire Upon the Deep.* Tor, 1992.

Set thousands of years in the future, these stories describe a time when humanity has spread among many worlds where societies have developed, flourished, and collapsed. The prequel describes the encounter of humans with spider-like aliens whom one human faction wishes to enslave. Set still further in the future, the previously published work tells the story of a family who escapes from the power of an ancient artifact that is capable of destroying worlds and dominating all intelligent entities.

Genre: Science Fiction
Subjects: Outer space, exploration of; Life on other planets; Extraterrestrial beings; Escapes

Vitola, Denise

1626.
1. *Quantum Moon.* Ace, 1996.
2. *Opalite Moon.* Ace, 1997.
3. *Manjinn Moon.* Ace, 1998.

Dealing with a dangerous urban society is difficult enough for a police detective in this near future world where an oppressive government is riddled with corruption, but Ty Merrick has an additional problem. When the moon is full, she develops symptoms of lycanthropy or werewolfism. Between full moons, Ty investigates a case involving voodoo and designer drugs, tries to find the murderer of members of a secret sect, and chases an assassin who has kidnapped the man she loves.

Genre: Science Fiction; Crime Novel
Subjects: Detectives; Werewolves; Crime and criminals
Place/Time: United States—1980–

Vivian, Daisy

1627.
1. *Rose White, Rose Red.* Walker, 1983.
2. *The Wild Rose: Meg's Tale.* Walker, 1986.

As companion to her aunt, the Countess of Ravenspur, Blanche Montague meets and falls in love with Gareth McQuahae. Gareth, however, is involved with the Jacobite rebellion of the 18th century, and his estate has been confiscated. The two lovers meet at the Countess's house where Gareth and the young cockney servant girl Meg are hiding. As Meg grows up, she is guided by Lady Ravenspur, who must flee because she is caught supporting the Jacobites. Meg is asked to watch Robert Delancy, a pamphleteer, but she falls in love with Jared Almonses, the young son of an earl. Meg is kept busy with the men in her life and the rebellion.

Genre: Historical Romance
Subjects: Jacobites; Aristocracy
Place/Time: London (England)—18th century; England—18th century

Vollmann, William T.

1628. Seven Dreams: A Book of North American Landscapes
1. *The Ice-Shirt.* Viking, 1990.
2. *Fathers and Crows.* Viking, 1992.
3. *The Rifles.* Viking, 1994.

In this imaginative retelling of the history of North America, Vollmann stresses the exploitation of the country and the natives by its explorers and settlers. First came the Scandinavians in A.D. 1000. Erik the Red and his family come to Vinland, where they cheat the native Indians. Six hundred years later, French explorers, trappers, and missionaries come to Canada to discover wealth and save souls. They find both but ultimately exploit and destroy the Huron people. The disastrous Franklin expedition to the North Pole in the 1840s and the Canadian government's forced relocation of the Inuit families in the 1950s are also retold.

Genre: Historical Fiction
Subjects: Explorers; Native Americans; Missionaries; Vikings
Place/Time: United States—multicentury span; Canada—multicentury span

Voynich, E. L. (Ethel Lillian)

1629.
1. *Put Off Thy Shoes.* Macmillan, 1945.
2. *The Gadfly.* H. Holt, 1897.
3. *An Interrupted Friendship.* Macmillan, 1910.

Beginning in Warwickshire and Cornwall of the 1700s, this series narrates the family history of a young woman who participates in the Italian Revolution of 1848.

Genre: Family Saga; Historical Fiction
Subjects: Politics—Italy; Revolutions and revolutionists
Place/Time: England—18th century; Italy—19th century

Walker, David Harry

1630.
1. *Geordie.* Houghton Mifflin, 1950.
2. *Come Back, Geordie.* Houghton Mifflin, 1966.

Geordie MacTaggat is a "wee" Scot, but through bodybuilding he grows to 6'5". At the Boston Olympics, he wins the shot put, then comes home to marry his sweetheart Jean. Parental problems begin when son Charlie reaches his teens and will not practice the bagpipes. Geordie sees life with humor and warmth.

Genre: Humor
Subjects: Athletes; Olympic games; Conflict of generations; Love
Place/Time: Scotland—1945–1980; Boston (Mass.)—1945–1980; Massachusetts—1945–1980

Walker, Jim

1631. Wells Fargo Trail
1. *The Dreamgivers.* Bethany House, 1994.
2. *The Nightriders.* Bethany House, 1994.
3. *The Rail Kings.* Bethany House, 1995.
4. *The Rawhiders.* Bethany House, 1995.
5. *The Desert Hawks.* Bethany House, 1996.
6. *The Oyster Pirates.* Bethany House, 1996.
7. *The Warriors.* Bethany House, 1997.
8. *The Ice Princess.* Bethany House, 1998.

At the end of the Civil War, Zachary Cobb leaves the South with bitter memories and goes West as an undercover agent for Wells Fargo. Zach goes to the Mojave Desert to stop payroll holdups and there meets Jenny Hays with whom he falls in love. He finds adventure in the gold fields of California, the railroad passages of the Rocky Mountains, the Arizona army posts and the ice fields of Alaska. He has to fight bandits, Apaches, Mexican soldiers, cattle rustlers, and even his own brother. Throughout his fights, he must keep his faith in God and his love for Jenny as he tries to build a new life in the West.

Genre: Christian Fiction; Western
Subjects: Faith; Adventure; Western states; Frontier and pioneer life; Detectives
Place/Time: Western states—19th century

Walpole, Hugh Seymour

1632.
1. *Bright Pavilions.* Doubleday, 1940.
2. *Katherine Christian.* Doubleday, 1943.
3. *Rogue Herries.* Doubleday, 1930.
4. *Judith Paris.* Doubleday, 1931.
5. *The Fortress.* Doubleday, 1932.
6. *Vanessa.* Doubleday, 1933.

In Elizabethan England, the Herries brothers set up their estate as they fight their enemy Philip Irvine. Their descendants build the family fortune as Rogue

Herries recounts his life with his two wives. His daughter Judith must fight her father's descendants. Judith will rule the family until she is 100, when her granddaughter Vanessa takes over. She finds she falls in love with a scamp who is just like the old Rogue Herries. All four generations from 1700 to 1932 play out their fights and hates against a panoramic view of England.

Genre: Family Saga; Historical Fiction
Subjects: Women
Place/Time: England—multicentury span

1633.
1. *The Cathedral.* Doran, 1922.
2. *Harmer John.* Doran, 1926.
3. *The Old Ladies.* Doran, 1924.
4. *The Inquisitor.* Doubleday, 1935.

The small English cathedral town of Polchester is the setting for these four stories about different people of the town. Archdeacon Brandon is beset by troubles that include the ambitious Canon Ronder. Harmer John, a Swede, comes to the town to open a gymnasium, but ends up preaching against poverty. Three ladies are drawn together by old age and poverty while a strange ghost walks the streets of the town. These novels paint a portrait of the town and its people.

Subjects: Small town life; Ghost stories
Place/Time: England—1900–1945

1634.
1. *Green Mirror: A Quiet Story.* Doran, 1918.
2. *Young Enchanted.* Doran, 1922.
3. *Dark Forest.* Doran, 1916. (This book is also part of the series listed below that ends with *Secret City.*)

The fortunes of Henry Trenchard are followed from his childhood to when he falls in love, and then into World War I. The Trenchards are distinctively British. Henry's parents try to force ideas onto their children, but Henry and his sister have their own values. When Henry falls in love, his poetic nature makes him ignore the fact that the girl does not respond to his advances. When he goes to war, his poetic nature makes him unsure.

Subjects: Boys; Conflict of generations; Love; World War I, 1914–1918
Place/Time: England—1900–1945

1635.
1. *Dark Forest.* Doran, 1916. (This book is also part of the series listed above that begins with *Green Mirror.*)
2. *Secret City.* Doran, 1919.

During World War I, the sensitive Englishman Trenchard and the businesslike Russian Semyonov try to survive the war while the Russian army advances then retreats. In Petrograd in 1917, the two men are drawn together by chance along with Semyonov's niece, Vera; her husband Markovitch; her sister Nina; two Englishmen, Lawrence and Bohun; and the revolutionary Grogoff. As the Russian Revolution starts, the group is drawn into murder.

Genre: War
Subjects: World War I, 1914–1918; Soviet Union—revolution, 1917–1921; Revolutions and revolutionists; Homicide
Place/Time: Soviet Union—1917–1945

1636.
1. *Jeremy.* Doran, 1919.
2. *Jeremy and Hamlet.* Doran, 1924.
3. *Jeremy at Crale: His Friends, His Ambitions, and His One Great Enemy.* Doran, 1927.

The story of a child's life from eight to 15 is vividly portrayed through the inner and outer life of Jeremy. As a young boy Jeremy torments his governess, does his school work, and plays with his sisters. On his first trip home after he is sent to school, his Christmas is almost ruined by his obtuse father, but kindly Uncle Samuel saves the day. As he gets older, Jeremy has troubles with a friend at school, but Uncle Samuel again comes to the rescue.

Genre: Coming of Age; Gentle Read
Subjects: Boys; Uncles; Nephews; Family life
Place/Time: England—1900–1945

Waltari, Mika

1637.
1. *Adventurer.* Putnam, 1950.
2. *Wanderer.* Putnam, 1951.

Mikail, born in 1502, is raised by his Finnish grandparents until they are killed by Jutes, when he is taken in by the witchwoman Pirijo. He attends school and receives a degree, but he is restless and travels around Europe. During his travels he meets Charles V, Martin Luther, and other notable men. He travels to North Africa and the Ottoman Empire as he searches for adventure.

Genre: Historical Fiction
Subjects: Teenagers; Rogues and vagabonds; Adventure
Place/Time: Finland—16th century; Europe—16th century

Walther, Daniel

1638. Shai
1. *The Book of Shai.* DAW Books, 1984.
2. *Shai's Destiny.* DAW Books, 1985.

In the distant future, Earth's inhabitants have been thrust into barbaric, ritualistic cultures by a combination of natural disasters, warfare, and the perversion of science for political purposes. Meanwhile, a colony that represents a remnant of the earlier advanced culture still exists on a space station. Out of this volatile mixture comes the young man Shai, who is at first seen as a traitor but later as a force for good.

Genre: Science Fiction
Subjects: Society, primitive; Space stations; Treason; Technology and civilization

Walton, Evangeline. *Pseud. of* Evangeline Ensley

1639. Books of the Welsh Mabinogion

1. *Prince of Annwn.* Ballantine, 1974.
2. *The Children of Llyr.* Ballantine, 1971.
3. *The Song of Rhiannon.* Ballantine, 1972.
4. *The Virgin and the Swine.* (Alternate title: *The Island of the Mighty*) Willett Clark, 1936.

In this telling of the Mabinogion, a cycle of Welsh folk tales with pagan roots, gods, goddesses, and royalty intermarry, the enormous Bran the Blessed wades across the ocean to save his sister, and shape shifters melt back and forth between human and animal form.

Genre: Fantasy
Subjects: Legends and folk tales; Gods and goddesses; Brothers and sisters; Supernatural phenomena

Wangerin, Walter, Jr.

1640. The Coop

1. *The Book of the Dun Cow.* Harper, 1978.
2. *The Book of Sorrows.* Harper, 1985.

Chaucerian characters Chauntecleer, the rooster, and Pertellote, the hen, live in an idyllic time when animals could speak. Their happy lives are threatened when the evil Wyrm escapes from the subterranean depths to which he has been consigned.

Genre: Animal Story; Fantasy
Subjects: Chaucer, Geoffrey, d. 1400—characters; Animals; Good and evil

Ward, Christopher

1641.

1. *The Strange Adventures of Jonathan Drew.* Simon & Schuster, 1932.
2. *Yankee Rover.* Simon & Schuster, 1932.

The picaresque adventures of Jonathan Drew tell the story of a young man in 1820 who has to try everything. He starts as an apprentice in a saddle shop, then tries his hand as a highwayman, peddler, manservant, farmer, hunter, fiddler, riverboat captain, and more. He travels to the Ozarks, Charleston, west to Sante Fe, and finally back east.

Genre: Adventure; Historical Fiction
Subjects: Picaresque novels; Adventure; Voyages and travels
Place/Time: United States—19th century

Ward-Thomas, Evelyn Bridget Patricia Stephens. *See* Anthony, Evelyn

Warner, Rex

1642.

1. *The Young Caesar.* Little, 1958.
2. *Imperial Caesar.* Little, 1960.

Told in flashbacks with Julius Caesar as the narrator, this series describes his youth and rise to power in Rome. Caesar tells the story of his consulship prior to his departure for Gaul. As he thinks back, he remembers the conquest of Gaul and Egypt, his love affair with Cleopatra, and his rise to imperial power. He thinks about all of this on the evening before the Ides of March in 44 B.C.

Genre: Historical Fiction
Subjects: Cleopatra, Queen of Egypt, d. 30 B.C.; Caesar, Julius, 100–44 B.C.; Politics—Rome; Rome—kings and rulers; War
Place/Time: Rome (Italy)—1st century B. C.; Italy—1st century B. C.

Warren, Lella

1643. Whetstone Saga

1. *Foundation Stone.* Knopf, 1940.
2. *Whetstone Walls.* Appleton Century Crofts, 1942.

In 1830, Yarborough Whetstone marries Gerda van Ifort, then moves from South Carolina to Alabama, where they start their plantation and build a fortune. They and their children fight in the Civil War, struggle through Reconstruction, and build their fortune again as the New South rises.

Genre: Family Saga; Historical Fiction
Subjects: Plantation life; Reconstruction; Wealth; United States—Civil War, 1861–1865
Place/Time: Alabama—19th century

Warren, Patricia Nell

1644.

1. *Front-runner.* Morrow, 1974.
2. *Harlan's Race.* Wildcat Press, 1994.
3. *Billy's Boy.* Wildcat, 1997.

In the 1970s, ex-marine track coach Harlan Brown is a closeted gay who falls in love with an "out" gay college distance runner, Billy Sive. Sive is training for the Olympics. When Sive is killed at the Olympics, Betsy, a lesbian athlete, is artificially inseminated with Sive's semen. Harlan must come to terms with his lover's death and with his own homosexuality. He tries to remain close with Betsy and her son William, but Betsy takes the child away. She hides her lesbianism from the boy, but William eventually has a sexual affair with the boy next door. Finally William begins to search for information about his father and his own sexual leanings.

Subjects: Homosexuality; Boys; Sports
Place/Time: California—1945–1980; California—1980–

Watson, Ian

1645. Black Current Trilogy

1. *The Book of the River.* DAW Books, 1986.
2. *The Book of the Stars.* Gollancz, 1985.
3. *The Book of Being.* DAW Books, 1986.

In a distant world, male and female societies are divided by a mystical river that drives insane the men who attempt to cross it. Yalen realizes her ambition to become a river woman. She meets a violent death, but her soul, guided by the river spirit, travels to Earth. After doing battle with the destructive Godmind, Yalen's soul returns to her own world where she is reborn as a priestess.

Genre: Fantasy; Science Fiction
Subjects: Men; Women; Rivers; Reincarnation; Life on other planets

Watson, Larry

1646.

1. *Justice.* Milkweed, 1995.
2. *Montana 1948.* Milkweed, 1993.
3. *White Crosses.* Pocket, 1997.

From 1899 to 1960, the people of Bentrock, Montana, are dominated by the Hayden family. Father Julian is the sheriff of the town. His two teenage sons Wesley and Frank get in trouble and even their father can't help them. As the boys grow up, Wesley becomes a softhearted man. He marries but tends to ignore his own son. When Wesley becomes sheriff of the town, he is forced to arrest his brother Frank for raping Native American women. Instead of putting Frank in jail, Wesley locks him in the basement where Frank finally kills himself. Wesley packs up his family and leaves town. Later, Jack Nevelson becomes the sheriff of Bentrock and hides secrets about a fatal accident that could destroy the town.

Subjects: Fathers and sons; Brothers; Sheriffs; Small town life
Place/Time: Montana—1900–1945; Montana—1945–1980

Watt-Evans, Lawrence

1647. The Three Worlds Trilogy

1. *Out of This World.* Random, 1994.
2. *In the Empire of Shadow.* Ballantine, 1995.
3. *The Reign of the Brown Magician.* Ballantine, 1996.

When a magic portal opens in the basement of his suburban home, Pel Brown finds himself transported into not one, but two alternate realities: the fantasy land of Faery and the futuristic Galactic Empire where he is recruited to fight the malevolent Shadow who is tyrannizing both realms. Joining forces with spacemen and warrior wizards, Pel wages war against the evil menace, but in the process, his wife and daughter are killed. Overcome with grief, Pel gradually realizes that the mysterious matrix, which is at the core of the Shadow's power, could give him control over life and death.

Genre: Fantasy; Science Fiction
Subjects: Imaginary kingdoms; Imaginary wars and battles; Good and evil; Magic

Waugh, Evelyn

1648.

1. *Men at Arms.* Little, Brown, 1952.
2. *Officers and Gentlemen.* Little, Brown, 1955.
3. *The End of the Battle.* Little, Brown, 1961.

Guy Crouchback is an Englishman descended from an old Roman Catholic family, but he finds life empty since his non-Catholic wife divorced him. When World War II starts, he joins the army where he sees military blunders, indifference, and confusion. Many of the missions he is sent on end in failure, but in Yugoslavia he helps save 100 Jewish refugees from a concentration camp. He even offers to remarry his ex-wife when she becomes pregnant and is deserted by her lover. Guy's transformation from an unloving loner to a man of compassion illustrates Waugh's belief in the importance of humanitarian actions.

Genre: War
Subjects: Men—psychology; Loneliness; Holocaust, Jewish, 1933–1945
Place/Time: England—1900–1945; Yugoslavia—1900–1945

1649.

1. *Black Mischief.* Farrar & Rinehart, 1932.
2. *Put Out More Flags.* Little, Brown, 1942.
3. *Basil Seal Rides Again.* Little, Brown, 1963.

Englishman Basil Seal goes to Africa to help a young Emperor Seth bring his primitive society up to date. Basil becomes the emperor's chief minister and tries to impose modern theories on the country, but the plan backfires, as does his love affair with the British ambassador's daughter. Back in Britain, Basil becomes involved with the World War II effort as he evacuates children from London. Waugh uses these novels to satirize human vice and folly. The third book is a short story.

Subjects: Society, primitive; Cultural conflict; Love; World War II, 1939–1945
Place/Time: Africa—1900–1945; England—1900–1945

1650.

1. *A Handful of Dust.* Farrar & Rinehart, 1934.

  2. *Mr. Loveday's Little Outing and Other Sad Stories*. Little, Brown, 1936.

Tony and Brenda Last live on a rundown English country estate. They have been married for a few years and Brenda has become bored. She has an affair with an indolent, worthless lover and is encouraged by the well-to-do "smart" set of London. Her husband is shattered by the affair and leaves her. Waugh uses biting irony to show the amorality of modern society.

Subjects: Marriage problems; Love affairs; Country life
Place/Time: England—1900–1945

Weale, Anne

1651.
  1. *All My Worldly Goods*. St. Martin's, 1990.
  2. *The Fountain of Delight*. St. Martin's, 1990.

American heiress Jane Graham marries North, the ninth earl of Carlyon, for his title, and he marries her for her money so he can restore his estate, Longwarden. Jane falls in love with him and is determined to win his love. Her sister-in-law, Lady Allegro Lomax, becomes a talented writer, but her love for an Italian artist keeps her torn between her career and marriage. Her mother-in-law Penelope, whose only interest has been in plants, now finds she is falling in love. Penelope's niece Sarah and Jane's secretary also find love, but for none of these people does the path of love run smoothly. Only after many trials and heartaches do they find happiness.

Genre: Romance
Subjects: Wealth; Aristocracy—England; Love; Marriage
Place/Time: England—1980–

Weber, David

1652.
  1. *Oath of Swords*. Baen, 1995.
  2. *The War God's Own*. Baen, 1998.

Prince Bahzell Bahnakson of the Hradni, a tall fox-like humanoid tribe, must flee the realm after avenging the honor of a ward of the crown who was raped and nearly killed by the evil Crown Prince Harnak. Having survived Harnak's revenge, Bahzell works to overcome prejudice against the Hradni and does battle with the demon god Sharna.

Genre: Fantasy
Subjects: Imaginary kingdoms; Imaginary wars and battles; Good and evil; Princes; Revenge

1653.
  1. *Mutineer's Moon*. Baen, 1991.
  2. *The Armageddon Inheritance*. Baen, 1993.
  3. *Heirs of Empire*. Baen, 1996.

While investigating the moon, spaceship captain Colin MacIntyre is captured by Dahak, an artificial intelligence evolved from a spaceship computer, whose mission is to save humanity from the alien Achuultani. Colin joins forces with Dahak and becomes Earth's emperor, but must deal with a rebel movement and a superbomb while trying to defeat the aliens.

Genre: Science Fiction
Subjects: Extraterrestrial beings; Interplanetary wars; Computers

1654. Honor Harrington
  1. *On Basilisk Station*. Baen, 1993.
  2. *The Honor of the Queen*. Baen, 1993.
  3. *The Short Victorious War*. Baen, 1994.
  4. *Field of Dishonor*. Baen, 1994.
  5. *Flag in Exile*. Baen, 1995.
  6. *Honor among Enemies*. Baen, 1996.
  7. *In Enemy Hands*. Baen, 1997.
  8. *Echoes of Honor*. Baen, 1998.
  9. *More than Honor*. (Written with David Drake and S. M. Stirling) Baen, 1998.
 10. *Ashes of Victory*. Baen, 2000.

Honor Harrington is a genetically engineered officer in the space fleet of the Star Kingdom of Manticore, which is at war with the People's Republic of Haven. Honor survives the death of her lover, a battle with space pirates, and a temporary dismissal from the fleet, all with the support and wisdom of her empathetic treecat Nimitz. Seemingly having been executed by the enemy, she is in fact trapped on the appropriately named planet, Hell, but escapes to be showered with glory and honor and to help Nimitz recover from his war wounds.

Genre: Science Fiction
Subjects: Women; Interplanetary wars; Adventure

Webster, Jan

1655.
  1. *Colliers Row*. Lippincott, 1977.
  2. *Saturday City*. St. Martin's, 1979.
  3. *Beggarman's Country*. St. Martin's, 1979.

Gossip in her small Scottish town forces Kate Kilgour, with her illegitimate son, to leave her job as housekeeper to James Galbraith in 1840. Later she discovers she is related to the wealthy Balfour family. She marries and raises three children, and when they are gone she returns to James Galbraith. Her descendants intermarry with the Balfours and the Flemings. In Glasgow, Sadie Kilgour helps Duncan Fleming fight for coal miners.

Genre: Family Saga; Historical Romance
Subjects: Unmarried mothers; Family life; Housekeepers
Place/Time: Scotland—19th century

Webster, Jean

1656.
  1. *Daddy Long-Legs*. Century, 1912.

2. *Dear Enemy.* Century, 1915.

Jerusha Abbott is the oldest orphan in the John Grier home. When she is sent to college by a mysterious trustee, she writes him letters telling him all the things she does. At graduation, she finally finds out who is her Daddy Long-Legs. Sullee McBride is asked by Judy and Jervis Pendleton to be the superintendent of the John Grier Home. Her letters to the Pendletons tell of her work with the orphans.

Genre: Gentle Read
Subjects: Letters (stories in letter form); Orphans; College life
Place/Time: United States—1900–1945

Weidman, Jerome

1657.
1. *Fourth Street Easy.* Random House, 1970.
2. *Last Respects.* Random House, 1971.
3. *Tiffany Street.* Random House, 1974.

Benny Kramer looks back over 50 years and remembers what it was like to grow up on New York's Lower East Side in the 1920s. At seven, Benny sees his father bring in immigrants and his mother work as a bootlegger to make more money. He helps her because she cannot speak English. At ten, Benny remembers forcing the Mafia to save his junior high. In the 1930s, his family moves to the Bronx where his mother takes in a boarder, Sebastian, who forces Benny to grow up.

Genre: Coming of Age; Historical Fiction
Subjects: Teenagers; Immigrants; Boarding houses
Place/Time: New York (N. Y.)—1900–1945

1658.
1. *I Can Get It for You Wholesale.* Simon & Schuster, 1937.
2. *What's in It for Me.* Simon & Schuster, 1938.

Harry Bogan is ambitious and unscrupulous. He begins as a shipping clerk in a New York garment factory in the 1930s and ruthlessly rises to become a successful dress manufacturer. Along the way, he double-crosses every friend he has, but grows ragged as he ages and finds it harder to keep his fortunes up.

Subjects: Ambition; Self-made men; Fashion industry and trade
Place/Time: New York (N. Y.)—1900–1945

Weis, Margaret

1659. Star of the Guardian
1. *The Lost King.* Bantam, 1990.
2. *King's Test.* Bantam, 1991.
3. *King's Sacrifice.* Bantam, 1991.
4. *Ghost Legion.* Bantam, 1993.

A harsh, corrupt regime has usurped the power of the galactic Starfire dynasty and murdered the galaxy's king; however, a few rebels work against the regime's powerful Warlord to shield the heir to the Starfire throne and eventually bring him back to power.

Genre: Science Fiction
Subjects: Imaginary kingdoms; Inheritance and succession; Government, resistance to

Weis, Margaret *and* Hickman, Tracy

1660.
1. *Forging the Darksword.* Bantam, 1987.
2. *Doom of the Darksword.* Bantam, 1988.
3. *Triumph of the Darksword.* Bantam, 1988.
4. *Legacy of the Darksword.* Bantam, 1997.

Refugees from the Earth's persecution of witches found their own world, Thimhallan. Here, almost everyone can wield the power of magic except beings such as Saryon and Joram, who create the Darksword, a fearsome weapon that annihilates Thimhallan civilization by attracting and destroying magic. Forced to return to Earth, the survivors of the disaster must face the possibility that a second Darksword may save them from the ruthless alien Hch'nyv.

Genre: Fantasy
Subjects: Witchcraft; Refugees; Imaginary kingdoms; Arms and armor; Magic

1661. Deathgate Cycle
1. *Dragon Wing.* Bantam, 1990.
2. *Elven Star.* Bantam, 1990.
3. *Fire Sea.* Bantam, 1991.
4. *Serpent Magic.* Bantam, 1992.
5. *The Hand of Chaos.* Bantam, 1992.
6. *Into the Labyrinth.* Bantam, 1993.
7. *The Seventh Gate.* Bantam, 1994.

This fantasy saga imagines a world divided into four realms—sky, stone, fire, and sea—by ancient magicians who then vanished. As the magic weakens, Haplo, an inhabitant of the mysterious and treacherous Labyrinth comes through the Death Gate to explore the realms. Warfare and chaos ensue. Haplo joins with a sorceress and other creatures to keep the villains from subjugating the different worlds or destroying them completely.

Genre: Fantasy
Subjects: Imaginary kingdoms; Magic; Imaginary wars and battles; Explorers

1662. Starshield
1. *Starshield: Sentinels.* Ballantine, 1996. (This title was also published in a somewhat different form as *The Mantle of Kendis-Dai.* Ballantine, 1997.)
2. *Nightsword.* Ballantine, 1998.

Far in the future, the computer network called Omnet, which is at the heart of a vast interstellar civilization, is threatened by a revolt of its own components. The key to restoring it lies in the search for a mystical ancient artifact, the mantle of Kendis-Dai. Computer expert Merinda Neskat and earthling space explorer, Jeremy

Griffiths join forces to retrieve the mantle and then race across the galaxy, through a series of intrigues to find still another key artifact, the powerful Nightsword.

Genre: Science Fiction
Subjects: Computers; Mysticism; Interplanetary voyages

Weis, Margaret *and* Perrin, Don

1663. Mag Force 7
1. *The Knights of the Black Earth.* Roc, 1995.
2. *Robot Blues.* Roc, 1996.
3. *Hung Out.* Roc, 1998.

Cyborg Xris was once totally human. While leading his Mag Force 7 team of mercenaries in an attempt to foil a plot to overthrow the current government, he also seeks revenge against the traitor who deprived him of his humanity. Xris's next assignment is to steal a seemingly obsolete robot from a crash site for a museum, but the robot proves to be more adversary than antique. While the rest of his force is on a mission, Xris is suddenly framed with false charges and incarcerated on a prison planet. *Note:* This series takes place in the same universe as the Star of the Guardian series.

Genre: Science Fiction
Subjects: Bionics; Mercenary soldiers; Government, resistance to; Revenge; Robots

Weisman, John. *See Marcinko, Richard*

Weiss, David

1664.
1. *Sacred and Profane.* Morrow, 1968.
2. *The Assassination of Mozart.* Morrow, 1971

Mozart's precocity, genius, and flamboyant personality bring him to the heights and depths of experience. In 1823, approximately 30 years after Mozart's mysterious death, a young American couple venture into the political and musical worlds of Salzburg and Vienna to investigate the possibility that the brilliant composer was assassinated.

Genre: Historical Fiction
Subjects: Mozart, Wolfgang Amadeus, 1756–1791; Music; Politics—Austria
Place/Time: Vienna (Austria)—18th century; Vienna (Austria)—19th century; Austria—18th century; Austria—19th century

Weld, William F.

1665.
1. *Mackerel by Moonlight.* Simon & Schuster, 1998.
2. *Big Ugly.* Simon & Schuster, 1999.

After being fired from his job as assistant United States attorney for Brooklyn, Terry Mullally goes to Boston and the safety of a law firm. However, he becomes interested in politics. With the help of a labor organizer and gossip columnist, Mullally runs for district attorney and wins. His charm and luck make him successful and even bring him a lovely wife, but just as he's running for senator, his past catches up with him. After buying off his blackmailers and dealing with the mafia, Mullally wins his senate seat and finds himself in the midst of Washington politics. As he is being courted for his vote, he finds that his past transgressions may come to light. While at Camp David with the Vice President, he sees a senator having an affair with the daughter of a Supreme Court justice. He has to use all of his luck and charm to save himself and keep on the right side of the law.

Subjects: Politics—United States
Place/Time: Boston (Mass.)—1980–; Washington (D. C.)—1980–

Wellman, Manly Wade

1666. Silver John
1. *Who Fears the Devil?* Arkham House, 1963.
2. *Worse Things Waiting.* Carcosa, 1973.
3. *The Old Gods Waken.* Doubleday, 1979.
4. *After Dark.* Doubleday, 1980.
5. *The Lost and the Lurking.* Doubleday, 1981.
6. *The Hanging Stones.* Doubleday, 1982.
7. *The Voice of the Mountain.* Doubleday, 1984.

Beginning as short stories, these tales tell of Silver John, a balladeer who wanders through the Ozarks and Appalachian Mountains frequently confronting the forces of evil featured in American folklore.

Genre: Fantasy
Subjects: Legends and folk tales; Good and evil; Singers; Mountain life

Wellman, Paul I.

1667.
1. *Bowl of Brass.* Lippincott, 1944.
2. *The Walls of Jericho.* Lippincott, 1947.
3. *The Chain.* Doubleday, 1949.
4. *Jericho's Daughters.* Doubleday, 1956.

In the 1880s, two towns in Kansas vie to become the western county seat, using any method to win. Ultimately the wheat town of Jericho succeeds, but the citizens in the town continue their own personal feuds. The Episcopal minister tries to help the poor, but his country club church members force him out. The lives of the people in the early 20th century are vividly portrayed as they fight, love, and scheme.

Genre: Historical Fiction
Subjects: Cities and towns; Small town life; Social classes
Place/Time: Kansas—19th century; Kansas—1900–1945

Wells, Angus

1668. Book of the Kingdoms
1. *The Wrath of Asher.* Bantam, 1990.
2. *The Usurper.* Bantam, 1991.
3. *The Way Beneath.* Bantam, 1991.

The demon messenger Taws threatens the Three Kingdoms, but Prince Kedryn of Tamur seems to be the fulfillment of a prophecy that a hero will save the realms. With his triumph close at hand, Kedryn is blinded by a magic sword. Taws lies in wait for Kedryn to appear from the underworld. While in the underworld, Kedryn encounters the fire god Asher, the source of Taws' evil power.

Genre: Fantasy
Subjects: Imaginary wars and battles; Prophecies; Princes; Good and evil

1669. Exiles Saga
1. *Exile's Children.* Bantam, 1995.
2. *Exile's Challenge.* Bantam, 1996.

Inmates of a prison colony called Salvation are the focus of attention in these tales. In the first story, the tribes of the country Ket-Ta-Witko are feuding and beset by demons. The only possibility of help seems to be the abilities of escaped prisoners from Salvation, who were wrongly convicted of crimes. In the sequel, reluctant hero Major Tomas Var works to quell demonic unrest in the prison colony.

Genre: Fantasy
Subjects: Prisoners and prisons; Demonology; Feuds

1670. Godwars
1. *Forbidden Magic.* Bantam, 1992.
2. *Dark Magic.* Bantam, 1992.
3. *Wild Magic.* Bantam, 1993.

The young nobleman Calandryll and his companions undertake a quest to keep the sorcerer Rythamun from awakening the Mad God by using sorcery from the legendary book the *Arcanum*. Complicating their efforts is Rythamun's ability to inhabit bodies other than his own. Calandryll falls in love with Cennaire, the beautiful woman who must do the bidding of the wizard Anomius. Her love for Calandryll enables her to oppose Anomius and to help her beloved fight Rythamun.

Genre: Fantasy
Subjects: Gods and goddesses; Witchcraft; Good and evil; Love

Wells, Marian

1671. Starlight Trilogy
1. *The Wishing Star.* Bethany House, 1985.
2. *Starlight, Star Bright.* Bethany House, 1986.
3. *Morning Star.* Bethany House, 1986.

Living in New York and the frontier districts of Ohio in the early 1800s, Jenny is a bright and unusually inquisitive young girl. Her search for truth takes her from poverty and abuse by her drunken father to an initially unhappy marriage to a young lawyer, then to fulfillment as she discovers for herself the results of her husband's painful spiritual journey.

Genre: Christian Fiction; Historical Fiction
Subjects: Faith; Christian life; Marriage problems
Place/Time: New York (N. Y.)—19th century; Ohio—19th century

1672. Treasure Quest
1. *The Silver Highway.* Bethany House, 1989.
2. *Colorado Gold.* Bethany House, 1988.
3. *Out of the Crucible.* Bethany House, 1988.
4. *Jewel of Promise.* Bethany House, 1990.

Drawn into the abolitionist cause, Alexander and Thomas help slaves escape by the underground railroad to find freedom in the North. Amy is a single woman in a rough western mining town, which challenges her values. The Civil War brings separation between members of families and tests their love.

Genre: Christian Fiction; Historical Fiction
Subjects: Abolitionists; Slavery; Christian life; Faith; United States—Civil War, 1861–1865
Place/Time: Midwestern states—19th century; Western states—19th century

Wells, Rebecca

1673.
1. *Little Altars Everywhere.* Broken Moon, 1992.
2. *Divine Secrets of the Ya-Ya Sisterhood.* HarperCollins, 1996.

In Thornton, Louisiana, Siddalee Walker's life has always been dominated by her mother, Viviane, and her mother's wacky friends, the "Ya-Ya Sisterhood." Her childhood is marred by abuse and her parents' alcoholism. As an adult, Siddalee achieves fame as a theater director in New York. When an article in *The New York Times* describes her mother as a "tap dancing child abuser," Viviane disowns Siddalee. As mother and daughter try to resolve their differences, Viviane sends her daughter a scrapbook about her Ya-Ya Sisterhood friends that reveals life in Thornton. These crazy friends are smart, funny, and inseparable. Both mother and daughter learn to forgive.

Subjects: Mothers and daughters; Women; Friendship; Small town life
Place/Time: Louisiana—1980–; New York (N. Y.)—1980–

West, Jessamyn

1674.
1. *Except for Me and Thee.* Harcourt Brace, 1969.
2. *The Friendly Persuasion.* Harcourt Brace, 1945.

Quaker Jess Birdwell courts Eliza, and the two move from Ohio to southern Indiana in the 1840s. There they start a farm, have children, and help runaway slaves on the underground railroad. When the Civil War starts, Josh, the oldest son, is torn between loyalty to the Union cause and his religion1235. Mattie is trying to be a young woman, and little Jess is in constant trouble. These novels show a warm, loving, and funny family with very human problems.

Genre: Gentle Read; Historical Fiction
Subjects: Family life; Farm life; United States—Civil War, 1861–1865; Religion; Faith; Abolitionists; Society of Friends
Place/Time: Indiana—19th century

West, Morris L.

1675. Vatican Trilogy
1. *The Shoes of the Fisherman.* Morrow, 1963.
2. *The Clowns of God.* Morrow, 1981.
3. *Lazarus.* St. Martin's, 1990.

These novels follow the Roman Catholic Church and its leaders in the last decades of the 20th century as they deal with religion and power in a rapidly changing political climate. More importantly, the novels deal with the ways in which people communicate. A Ukrainian pope must try to stop World War III. Later Pope Gregory XVIII is forced to abdicate when he preaches the approaching end of the world. Leo XIV, threatened with a serious illness, emerges a changed man. Each pope works to change himself, the church, and the world.

Subjects: Catholic faith; Popes; Faith; World politics
Place/Time: Vatican City (Italy)—1980–; Italy—1980–

West, Paul

1676. Alley Jaggers
1. *Alley Jaggers.* Harper, 1966.
2. *I'm Expecting to Live Quite Soon.* Harper, 1969.
3. *Bela Lugosi's White Christmas.* Harper, 1973.

This inventive trilogy explores the world of insanity through the experiences of a young English plasterer, who is so disgusted and discouraged by his unpleasant domestic circumstances that he escapes into a world of his own with bizarre and horrifying results.

Subjects: Men—psychology; Insanity; Family life
Place/Time: England—1945–1980

West, Rebecca

1677.
1. *The Fountain Overflows.* Viking, 1956.
2. *This Real Night.* Viking, 1985.
3. *Cousin Rosamund.* Viking, 1986.

In Edwardian England, the Aubrey family tries to scrape by even though their father's repeated failures keep them poor. When he deserts the family, their mother works to raise the three girls. Once grown, the three sisters follow their own paths to happiness.

Genre: Historical Fiction
Subjects: Marriage problems; Sisters; Mothers and daughters
Place/Time: England—1900–1945

Westheimer, David

1678.
1. *Von Ryan's Express.* Doubleday, 1964.
2. *Von Ryan's Return.* Coward, McCann & Geoghegan, 1980.

Colonel Joseph "Von" Ryan engineers a spectacular escape from Nazi Germany when he hijacks a prison train. After his escape to neutral Switzerland, he accepts an OSS directive to find and eliminate a dangerous German infiltrator among northern Italy's partisan bands.

Genre: Adventure; War
Subjects: Army, United States—officers; Prisoners of war; Railroads; World War II, 1939–1945; Escapes; International intrigue
Place/Time: Germany—1900–1945; Switzerland—1900–1945; Italy—1900–1945

Wharton, Edith

1679.
1. *Hudson River Bracketed.* Appleton, 1929.
2. *The Gods Arrive.* Appleton, 1932.

Vance Weston, a young literary genius, comes to New York in the late 19th century from a poor and deprived background in the Midwest. He brings his childlike wife Laura Lou with him. In an old house's library, he discovers the rich culture he has lacked. His friend Halo Tarrant encourages his artistic soul. When his wife dies, Vance and Halo decide to travel in Europe until she can get a divorce so they can marry. However, her husband changes his mind, and Halo and Vance struggle until they finally find a way to be together.

Genre: Historical Fiction
Subjects: Society novels; Love affairs; Literary life
Place/Time: New York (N. Y.)—19th century; Europe—19th century

Wheaton, Philip

1680.
1. *Razzmatazz.* Everest House, 1980.
2. *The Best Is Yet to Be.* Dodd, Mead, 1983.

It is 1938, and 12-year-old Willie and 16-year-old Penny are going to New England to live with their Aunt Addie and Uncle Lambot. They have to cope with the deaths of people they love and grow up. When the town is destroyed in a flood, Penny discovers the mystery of her parentage. When World War II comes, Willie goes into the army and Penny becomes a reporter. They survive the war, but find that they have lost in love.

Genre: Coming of Age; Historical Fiction
Subjects: Teenagers; Orphans; Death; World War II, 1939–1945
Place/Time: New England—1900–1945

Wheeler, Richard S.

1681.
1. *Flint's Gift.* Forge, 1997.
2. *Flint's Truth.* Forge, 1998.
3. *Flint's Honor.* Forge, 1999.

Itinerant newspaperman Sam Flint wanders the West setting up his one-man newspaper and uses it to fight corruption. In 1877, he goes to Payday, Arizona, where he sets up shop and attracts settlers to the town. When Payday becomes too prosperous, gunslingers and gamblers invade the town, and Sam and some unlikely allies must fight them. Sam leaves Arizona for a New Mexico gold mining town where the westerners and the Mexicans are struggling. As Sam digs around for stories, he finds a conspiracy that soon makes him unwelcome in the town. He finally leaves and goes to Silver City, Colorado, where he works with a voluptuous prostitute to bring down a corrupt tycoon who controls the town.

Genre: Western
Subjects: Journalists; Adventure
Place/Time: Western states—19th century

White, Antonia

1682.
1. *Frost in May.* Viking, 1934.
2. *The Lost Traveller.* Viking, 1950.
3. *The Sugar Horse.* Eyre & Spotswode, 1953.
4. *Beyond the Glass.* Regnery, 1955.

These autobiographical novels are based on White's life in England in the early 1900s. The young daughter of a Catholic convert is sent to the Convent of the Five Wounds for school. Religion and conformity are the standards impressed on her until at 13 she breaks a rule and pays a high price for her transgression. After graduation, Clara (who is called Nanda in the first book) takes charge of the young son of a titled family until a terrible accident occurs. Clara then marries, but goes insane when she finds her marriage must be annulled. Her stay in the asylum and eventual release are vividly recounted.

Genre: Coming of Age
Subjects: Autobiographical stories; Girls; Catholic faith; Insanity
Place/Time: England—1900–1945

White, Edmund

1683.
1. *A Boy's Own Story.* Dutton, 1982.
2. *The Beautiful Room Is Empty.* Knopf, 1988.
3. *The Farewell Symphony.* Knopf, 1997.

During the 1950s, a young boy tries to come to terms with his homosexuality. He goes to his prep school psychiatrist for help, but the man only discusses his own problems. The boy longs to be popular and to belong, but realizes he is different. As he goes through college, he still denies his emotions and only stands up for himself at the Stonewall uprising of 1969 in New York City, where the patrons of a gay bar will not allow it to be shut down by the police. As he travels through New York, Paris, and Rome, he meets a variety of men both closeted and out who lead him through the heady days of the 1970s to the AIDS-ravaged 1980s.

Genre: Coming of Age
Subjects: Boys; Homosexuality; Conformity; AIDS (disease)
Place/Time: New York (N. Y.)—1980–

White, James

1684. Sector General
1. *Hospital Station.* Ballantine, 1962. (Short stories)
2. *Star Surgeon.* Ballantine, 1963.
3. *Major Operation.* Ballantine, 1971. (Short stories)
4. *Ambulance Ship.* Ballantine, 1979.
5. *Sector General.* Ballantine, 1983. (Short stories)
6. *Star Healer.* Ballantine, 1985.
7. *Code Blue—Emergency.* Ballantine, 1987.
8. *The Genocidal Healer.* Ballantine, 1992.
9. *The Galactic Gourmet.* Tor, 1996.
10. *Final Diagnosis.* Tor, 1997.
11. *Mind Changer.* Tor, 1998.
12. *Double Contact.* Tor, 1999.

Sector 12 General Hospital is a 384-level space station in deep space on the edge of the Galactic Rim, where humans mingle with alien species as both staff members and patients. As new species arrive at the hospital, their unique anatomy and psychology present continuing challenges for the staff. The focus of this mix of novels and short stories ranges from a suicidal doctor, who feels responsible for the death of an entire planet's population, to the quality of the food in the cafeteria.

Genre: Science Fiction
Subjects: Medicine; Physicians; Extraterrestrial beings

White, Jude Gilliam. *See* Deveraux, Jude

White, Stewart Edward

1685.

1. *Skookum Chuck.* Doubleday, 1925.
2. *Secret Harbour.* Doubleday, 1926.

The mysterious X, Anaxagoras, is a healer of souls who is also a two-fisted, red-blooded he-man. He and his sister take on wealthy patient Jerry Marshall as they try to help him. When Marshall is cured of his indifference, he marries X's sister, but finds he needs the mysterious X to help him fight crooks.

Genre: Adventure
Subjects: Adventure; Brothers and sisters
Place/Time: United States—1900–1945

1686. Andy Burnett Saga

1. *Long Rifle.* Doubleday, 1932.
2. *Ranchero.* Doubleday, 1933.
3. *Folded Hills.* Doubleday, 1934.
4. *Stampede.* Doubleday, 1942.

Young Andy Burnett goes west with the long rifle his grandfather got from Daniel Boone. In the 1820s, he seeks adventure with the mountain men and fur trappers. In the mountains, he is captured by the Blackfeet and becomes one of them. In 1832, he crosses the mountains to California, where he marries the daughter of a Spanish settler. Andy and Carmel build their hidalgo, the Folded Hills, then they must protect it from American soldiers during the Mexican War and from squatters during the Gold Rush.

Genre: Adventure; Historical Fiction; Western
Subjects: Frontier and pioneer life; Fur trade; Native Americans; Ranch life
Place/Time: Western states—19th century; California—19th century

1687. California Trilogy

1. *Gold.* Doubleday, 1913.
2. *The Gray Dawn.* Doubleday, 1915.
3. *Rose Dawn.* Doubleday, 1920.

The history of California is told through the men and women who settled and built the state. During the Gold Rush of 1849, four young men go west through Panama to make their fortune, but find it is not as easy as they thought. In the 1850s, vigilantes flourish as they try to control the lawlessness of the Gold Rush and make California a state. Milton Keith and his wife come to San Francisco in 1852 and are plunged into this violent world. In the 1880s, the great ranches are giving way to small fruit farms. Colonel Payton's ranch is threatened, and his friends rally to save it from the land busters.

Genre: Adventure; Historical Fiction; Western
Subjects: Ranch life; Gold mines and mining; California—gold discoveries; Adventure
Place/Time: California—19th century

White, T. H. (Terence Hanbury)

1688.

1. *The Sword in the Stone.* Putnam, 1939.
2. *The Witch in the Wood.* Putnam, 1939.
3. *The Ill-Made Knight.* Putnam, 1940.
4. *The Candle in the Wind.* (This book has not been published separately but only as part of *The Once and Future King.*)

The above titles have also been published in the following collection: *The Once and Future King.* Putnam, 1958.

5. *The Book of Merlin.* University of Texas Press, 1977.

The legend of King Arthur and the Round Table is retold in this magical fantasy. The young Arthur, called Wart, is tutored by Merlyn. As he grows up, he must fight other kings to establish his kingdom, but that heroic age is brought down by the plotting of Mordred and the doomed love of Lancelot and Guenevere. In a conclusion to the famous legend that was published after White's death, Merlyn takes a defeated Arthur into a badger's sett where Arthur learns the futility of war.

Genre: Fantasy
Subjects: Arthur, King; Merlin (legendary character); Guenevere, Queen (legendary character a.k.a. Guinevere); Love; Legends and folk tales

Whittle, Tyler. *Pseud. of* Michael Sidney Tyler-Whittle

1689.

1. *The Young Victoria.* St. Martin's, 1972.
2. *Albert's Victoria.* St. Martin's, 1972.
3. *The Widow of Windsor.* St. Martin's, 1973.

From the time she is seven until her death, Tyler-Whittle retells Queen Victoria's life. As a protected princess, she grows up alone in Kensington Palace. After her marriage to Albert, she has 21 years of happiness and comes to rely on the Prince Consort. After Albert's death, she secludes herself in Windsor and only gradually returns to public life. She favors Disraeli and disapproves of Gladstone, but she shapes the monarchy through her actions.

Genre: Historical Fiction
Subjects: Family life; Victoria, Queen of England, 1819–1901; Queens; Courts and courtiers
Place/Time: England—19th century

Whyte, Jack

1690. The Camulod Chronicles

1. *The Skystone.* Forge, 1996.
2. *The Singing Sword.* Forge, 1996.
3. *The Eagle's Brood.* Forge, 1997.
4. *The Saxon Shore.* Forge, 1998.
5. *The Fort at River's Bend.* Forge, 1999.
6. *The Sorcerer: Metamorphosis.* Forge, 1999.

These realistic, earthy tales of the rise of the Arthurian kingdom Camulod and the decay of the Roman Empire are told in part by the Roman soldier and blacksmith Gaius Publius Varrus, who watches and participates in the consolidation of the power of the Briton population.

Genre: Fantasy; Historical Fiction
Subjects: Arthur, King; Rome
Place/Time: England—5th century

Wideman, John Edgar

1691.
1. *Damballah.* Avon, 1981.
2. *The Hiding Place.* Avon, 1981.
3. *Sent for You Yesterday.* Avon, 1983.

The above titles have also been published in the following collection: *The Homewood Trilogy.* Avon, 1985.

Through a series of interconnected short stories, the lives of African Americans in the Homewood section of Pittsburgh are illustrated. For 100 years, Bess, Tommy, Clement, Albert Wilkes, Brother Tate, and many others tell the story of blacks in urban America as they try to survive.

Subjects: African Americans; Cities and towns
Place/Time: Pittsburgh (Pa.)—1900–1945; Pittsburgh (Pa.)—1945–1980; Pennsylvania—1900–1945; Pennsylvania—1945–1980

Wilder, Cherry. *Pseud. of* Grimm, Cherry Barbara

1692.
1. *Second Nature.* Pocket Books, 1982.
2. *Signs of Life.* Tor, 1996.

Two waves of interstellar castaways, whose spaceships have either crashed or become lost, arrive on the planet Rhomary centuries apart. They encounter strange life forms such as the enormous intelligent marine creatures called Vail and six legged camels called parmels. They long for Earth and weave their home planet's history and legends into their life. Their efforts to build a stable colony are often limited by their prejudices and violent tendencies.

Genre: Science Fiction
Subjects: Space colonies; Life on other planets

Willard, Tom

1693. Black Sabre Chronicles
1. *Bufflalo Soldiers.* Forge, 1996.
2. *Sable Doughboys.* Forge, 1997.
3. *Wings of Honor.* Forge, 1999.
4. *The Stone Ponies.* Forge, 2000.

From the western frontier of the late 19th century to the battlefields of World War II, the men of the Sharp family fight for their country in the segregated African American units of the U.S. Army. Augustus Sharp is saved from death on the Great Plains by the Buffalo soldiers of the Tenth Cavalry. He joins their ranks and protects the settlers from marauding Native Americans. From Kansas to New Mexico, Augustus earns his stripes on the battlefields, marries a good woman, and meets men like George Armstrong Custer and Wild Bill Hickock. After he retires, he watches his two sons, Adrian and David, join the 93rd Division's 372nd Infantry Regiment in World War I. When they find out they will be used behind the lines instead of in battle, they risk court-martial to get a battlefield assignment. At the Argonne offensive, David is killed and Adrian wounded. Adrian's son Samuel enrolls at Tuskeegee Institute so that he can become one of the first African American Army Air Corps officers. Like his father and grandfather, Samuel challenges the segregation he must face in the Army. He and his men in the 99th Pursuit Squadron fly more missions and earn more awards than any other unit in Europe.

Genre: Family Saga; War
Subjects: African Americans; Fathers and sons; War; Soldiers—American; World War I, 1914–1918; World War II, 1939–1945
Place/Time: Western states—19th century; Europe—1900–1945

Willey, Elizabeth

1694.
1. *A Sorcerer and a Gentleman.* Tor, 1995.
2. *The Price of Blood and Honor.* Tor, 1996.
3. *The Well-Favored Man.* Tor, 1993.

Difficult family situations become intense in this fantasy land where members of the nobility are nearly immortal sorcerers and warriors. The prequel narrates a royal family feud between Avril, who has seized the throne from his older brother Prospero, who battles back by creating an army of birds and beasts with human qualities. *The Price of Blood and Honor* continues the story of the conflict between the brothers. Prospero tries to regain power by secretly preserving his magical books and instruments and by attempting to marry his daughter to Avril's son. Written earlier, but describing a later time in the history of the Dominion of Argylle is the story of Prince Gwydion who ascends to the throne when both his father and uncle disappear mysteriously.

Genre: Fantasy
Subjects: Imaginary kingdoms; Imaginary wars and battles; Feuds; Princes; Magic

Williams, Ben Ames

1695.
1. *House Divided.* Houghton Mifflin, 1947.
2. *The Unconquered.* Houghton Mifflin, 1953.

The wealthy Currian family of Virginia and the Carolinas remain loyal to the Confederate cause and feel the full impact of the Civil War on their plantations. General James Longstreet is their friend and tries to help them. After the war, the New Orleans branch of the family fights to rebuild their wealth during the Reconstruction period.

Genre: Historical Fiction; War
Subjects: Plantation life; United States—Civil War, 1861–1865; Reconstruction; Confederate States of America
Place/Time: Virginia—19th century; New Orleans (La.)—19th century; Louisiana—19th century

Williams, Jeanne

1696.
1. *The Island Harp.* St. Martin's, 1991.
2. *Daughter of the Storm.* St. Martin's, 1994.

Mairi MacLeod becomes the head of her clan upon the death of her grandfather. In 19th-century Scotland, this position puts her up against greedy landlords who wish to use the land she and her family have farmed for centuries for their own purposes. Because of the hardships of the struggle, Mairi's pregnancy ends in a miscarriage. She takes in Christy, a talented girl whose parents were killed in the conflict over land.

Genre: Historical Fiction
Subjects: Landlord and tenant; Clans; Farm life; Orphans; Family life
Place/Time: Scotland—19th century

Williams, Paul O.

1697. The Pelbar Cycle
1. *The Breaking of Northwall.* Ballantine, 1981.
2. *The Ends of the Circle.* Ballantine, 1981.
3. *The Dome in the Forest.* Ballantine, 1981.
4. *The Fall of the Shell.* Ballantine, 1982.
5. *An Ambush of Shadows.* Ballantine, 1983.
6. *The Song of the Axe.* Ballantine, 1984.

A thousand years in the future, the descendants of survivors of a nuclear holocaust have formed insular tribal societies. A group called the Pelbar have developed cities in the American heartland along the Mississippi River, but these communities, each with its own strong character, are now becoming less isolated as their members migrate and reach out for other experiences.

Genre: Science Fiction
Subjects: Nuclear warfare; Tribes; Mississippi River; Social isolation

Williams, Tad

1698. Memory, Sorrow, and Thorn Series
1. *The Dragonbone Chair.* NAL, 1988.
2. *Stone of Farewell.* DAW Books, 1990.

3. *To Green Angel Tower.* NAL, 1993.

In the kingdom of Osten Ard, the arch foe of kitchen-boy-turned-knight Simon appears to be the evil Prince Elias, who has imprisoned Simon's brother Joshua. Simon and Joshua join forces only to encounter an even more powerful enemy, The Storm King. The showdown for good and evil, which involves elves, swamp creatures, and other mystical forces, takes place at the Green Angel Tower.

Genre: Fantasy
Subjects: Imaginary kingdoms; Imaginary wars and battles; Brothers; Good and evil

1699. Otherland
1. *Otherland: City of Golden Shadow.* DAW Books, 1996.
2. *Otherland: River of Blue Fire.* DAW Books, 1998.
3. *Otherland: Mountain of Black Glass.* DAW Books, 1999.

In search of the secret of eternal life, a mysterious near-future cabal of the wealthy and corrupt, who call themselves the Grail Brotherhood, have created a virtual reality called Otherland, where they have ensnared the minds of hundreds of children. A small unlikely band of rescuers and explorers breaks into Otherland and encounters such strange phenomena as giant insects and advertisements that come to life. They must also deal with treachery in the form of a Grail Brother in their midst.

Genre: Science Fiction; Fantasy
Subjects: Immortality; Computers; Good and evil; Technology and civilization

Williams, Walter Jon

1700.
1. *Hardwired.* Tom Doherty Associates, 1986.
2. *Voice of the Whirlwind.* Tom Doherty Associates, 1987.

These futuristic works take place 200 years apart in a world where corporate blocs increasingly control both legal and illegal activities. In this crumbling, corrupt society, two cyborgs start a rebellion against the tyranny of powerful businesses. In the second story, a cloned mercenary tries to recover 15 years for which he has no memory.

Genre: Science Fiction
Subjects: Business; Bionics; Mercenary soldiers

1701.
1. *Metropolitan.* HarperPrism, 1995.
2. *City on Fire.* HarperPrism, 1997.

Aiah was a humble worker in the Plasm Authority, an agency that regulates the supply of plasm, a mysterious and powerful substance that has appeared as part of the urban sprawl of the future. But, her life changes when she discovers an enormous well of the shimmering material. Aiah sells the plasm to Constantine, a deposed urban social leader. Aiah rises to a position of authority when Constantine seizes power and, although she is irresistibly drawn to him, she questions his tyrannical methods.

Genre: Science Fiction
Subjects: Technology and civilization; Urbanization; Power (social sciences)

1702. Crown Jewels
1. *The Crown Jewels.* Tor, 1987.
2. *House of Shards.* Tor, 1988.
3. *Rock of Ages.* Tor, 1995.

In this future universe where style is all-important, Drake Maijstral commits robberies with such grace and panache that he has become an Allowed Burglar of the Human Constellation and has reached the pinnacle of celebrity status. However, fame has its price. Friends are suspicious. Unwanted marriage proposals and challenges to duel are frequent. Worst of all, Drake is robbed!

Genre: Science Fiction; Humor
Subjects: Theft; Rogues and vagabonds; Crime and criminals; Success

Williams, William Carlos

1703. The Stecher Trilogy
1. *White Mule.* New Directions, 1937.
2. *In the Money.* New Directions, 1940.
3. *The Build-Up.* Random House, 1952.

Joe and Gurlie Stecher establish themselves in New York State in the years before World War I. Joe is persuaded by Gurlie to abandon his craftsman's interest in printing and become a businessman. He is successful, but there is a hollowness at the core of his accomplishment that the death of their son only intensifies.

Subjects: Marriage; Business; Success; Bereavement; Parents and children
Place/Time: New York (state)—1900–1945

Williamson, Jack. *See also* Pohl, Frederik

1704.
1. *Lifeburst.* Ballantine, 1984.
2. *Mazeway.* Ballantine, 1990.

Seekers, giant cyborg war machines unleashed on the universe by aliens who were their first victims, have ravaged Earth and plunged humanity into violence and barbarism. However, an idealistic young man, Ben Dain, is willing to try to survive an alien testing ground to get help from the advanced Eldren civilization.

Genre: Science Fiction
Subjects: Bionics; Technology and civilization; Interplanetary wars; Extraterrestrial beings

Willis, Ted

1705.
1. *Spring at the Winged Horse.* Morrow, 1983.
2. *The Green Leaves of Summer: The Second Season of Rosie Carr.* St. Martin's, 1989.
3. *The Bells of Autumn.* St. Martin's, 1991.

In Edwardian England, street waif Rosie Carr is taken in by her Aunt May, who works herself to death in a pub. Rosie's humor and vitality help lift her out of poverty. When she loses her job in a laundry for helping another worker, street trader Jack Cameron helps her. She marries, sets up a catering business, and runs for Parliament. In the 1930s, she sees the rise of the Fascists and tries to help German Jews escape from Hitler. Lovable Rosie has a life full of adventure, humor, and love.

Genre: Historical Fiction; Humor
Subjects: National Socialism; Businesswomen; Labor and laboring classes
Place/Time: England—1900–1945

Willson, David A.

1706.
1. *R E M F Diary: A Novel of the Vietnam War Zone.* Black Heron, 1988.
2. *The R E M F Returns.* Black Heron, 1992.

A 24-year-old nameless soldier in Vietnam is a clerk in the rear areas of Saigon in 1966. Through his diary, he comments on the paperwork war, the food in the mess hall, the boredom, and the horror of the war. He uses comic irony to comment on a war that makes no sense, and his only goal is to survive and enjoy himself.

Genre: War
Subjects: Diaries (stories in diary form); Vietnamese War, 1961–1975; Soldiers
Place/Time: Vietnam—1945–1980

Wilson, A. N.

1707. Lampitt Papers
1. *Incline Our Hearts.* Viking, 1989.
2. *Bottle in the Smoke.* Viking, 1990.
3. *Daughters of Albion.* Viking, 1992.
4. *Hearing Voices.* Norton, 1995.
5. *A Watch in the Night.* Norton, 1996.

Young Julian Ramsay is brought up by his aunt and uncle in a small East Anglian village. His crazy uncle is obsessed with the aristocratic Lampitt family who live in the town. Throughout his life, Julian also finds his life entangled with the Lampitts. When Sargent Lampitt's brother James, a famous writer, dies, Raphael Hunter writes a biography of him. Later Hunter helps Julian get his first novel published. Julian also marries Anne Lampitt. In his forties, when he thinks he is free of the Lampitts, Julian manages to get involved with them again through a protege of James Lampitt. Only at the end of his life does Julian discover the answer to the mystery around James Lampitt's death. Wilson uses the high jinks of Julian to satirize the nature of literature and to wickedly dissect the English character.

Subjects: Small town life; Authors; Class distinction
Place/Time: England—1945–1980

Wilson, Doug. *See* McGehee, Peter

Wilson, F. Paul

1708.
1. *The Keep.* Morrow, 1981.
2. *The Tomb.* Berkley, 1984.
3. *Reborn.* Dark Harvest, 1990.
4. *Reprisal.* Dark Harvest, 1991.
5. *Nightworld.* Dark Harvest, 1992.

Rasalom, the ancient evil spirit that is released by the Nazis in World War II, reappears as a soulless clone, then as a genius baby, and finally gathers all the forces of evil from each earlier book as he fights to take over the world. Glacken, his ancient enemy who fights for good, must summon all his strength to defeat Rasalom. Each of the first four volumes can be read as a separate novel, but the final volume brings all the heroes and evil creatures from the first four together as they line up to fight the ultimate battle of good versus evil.

Genre: Horror
Subjects: Good and evil; Imaginary wars and battles; National Socialism

Wilson, John Anthony Burgess. *See* Burgess, Anthony

Wilson, Sloan

1709.
1. *The Man in the Gray Flannel Suit.* Simon & Schuster, 1955.
2. *The Man in the Gray Flannel Suit II.* Arbor, 1984.

Tom Rath is the organization man. He is a middle-class businessman who works his way up the corporate ladder in 1953 by being the perfect conformist. He plays by the rules, but muses about his past. Ten years later he has a midlife crisis when he finds his suburban dream and the rest of the world are going crazy after John F. Kennedy is killed. Rath has an affair with a much younger woman, but he finally seems to find himself and pull out of the affair before it destroys his marriage.

Subjects: Business; Ambition; Conformity; Marriage problems; Love affairs
Place/Time: United States—1945–1980

Windle, Janice Woods

1710.
1. *True Women.* Putnam, 1993.
2. *Hill Country.* Longstreet, 1998.

In Sequin, Texas, in the 19th century, the women of the Woods, King, and Lawshe families must survive Indian raids and the Civil War. Their ancestor Laura Hoge Woods fights for women's suffrage and gets elected to office at age 87. As a young girl, Laura loves a Native American but later falls in love with rancher Peter Woods. They raise horses that are ridden by people like Teddy Roosevelt and Lyndon Johnson. A strong woman, Laura fights for women's rights and her own dreams.

Genre: Family Saga
Subjects: Women; Autobiographical stories; Frontier and pioneer life; Ranch life; Family life
Place/Time: Texas—19th century; Texas—1900–1945; Texas—1945–

Wingrove, David

1711. Chung Kuo
1. *The Middle Kingdom.* Delacorte, 1990.
2. *The Broken Wheel.* Delacorte, 1991.
3. *The White Mountain.* Delacorte, 1992.
4. *The Stone Within.* Dell, 1993.
5. *Beneath the Tree of Heaven.* Dell, 1994.
6. *White Moon, Red Dragon.* Dell, 1996.
7. *Days of Bitter Strength.* Dell, 1997.

This series portrays an alternate future in which the world is controlled by Chinese overlords called T'ang. A group of western industrialists are willing to use any means to overthrow this government, which prohibits technological innovation and change. After a time, the T'ang's power begins to crumble beset by treachery from within, civil unrest on Earth, a revolutionary movement on Mars, and the activities of rebel Mama Em.

Genre: Science Fiction
Subjects: Cultural conflict; Totalitarianism; Business; Technology and civilization

Winslow, Pauline Glen. *See* Sheridan, Jane

Wodehouse, P. G. (Pelham Grenville)

1712.
1. *Mike: A Public School Story.* (Alternate title: *Enter Psmith.*) Macmillan, 1910.
2. *Psmith in the City.* Macmillan, 1910.
3. *Psmith, Journalist.* Macmillan, 1915.
4. *Leave It to Psmith.* Doran, 1924. (This title appears in two of Wodehouse's series.)

During and after his days as a student at Cambridge, Psmith is the typical English schoolboy. He travels to New York where he helps renovate a slum tenement, then comes back to England where he helps a young man who needs money. These lighthearted tales poke fun at the English school system.

Genre: Humor
Subjects: College life; Teenagers
Place/Time: England—1900–1945

1713.
1. *Young Men in Spats.* Doubleday, 1936.
2. *Eggs, Beans, and Crumpets.* Doubleday, 1940.
3. *A Few Quick Ones.* Simon & Schuster, 1959.

The Drones Club is a group of young English gentlemen who in the true Wodehouse manner all lack something and will resort to any means to get it. They do so, of course, in a series of humorous stories.

Genre: Humor
Subjects: Social classes; Society novels; Clubs
Place/Time: England—1900–1945

1714.
1. *My Man Jeeves.* Newnes, 1919. (This title has been published only in England.)
2. *The Inimitable Jeeves.* Doran, 1923.
3. *Carry On, Jeeves!* Doran, 1925.
4. *Very Good, Jeeves.* Doubleday, 1930.
5. *Thank You, Jeeves.* Little, Brown, 1934.
6. *Brinkley Manor.* Little, Brown, 1934.
7. *The Code of the Woosters.* Doubleday, 1938.
8. *Joy in the Morning.* Doubleday, 1946.
9. *The Mating Season.* Didier, 1949.
10. *The Return of Jeeves.* Simon & Schuster, 1954.
11. *Bertie Wooster Sees It Through.* Simon & Schuster, 1955.
12. *How Right You Are, Jeeves.* Simon & Schuster, 1960.
13. *Stiff Upper Lip, Jeeves.* Simon & Schuster, 1963.
14. *Jeeves and the Tie That Binds.* Simon & Schuster, 1971.
15. *The Cat-Nappers.* Simon & Schuster, 1974.

Jeeves is a gentleman's gentleman to Bertie Wooster, a none-too-bright young English gentleman who is constantly in trouble with his friends, women, and his family. It is the ever-upright Jeeves who uses his infinite resources to save Bertie from his aunts, husband-hunting females, and assorted menaces. Jeeves recognizes that Bertie has little intelligence, but knows he is kind, modest, and honorable. Their hilarious adventures are always a treat. The first Jeeves book has only been published in England, and there have been many omnibus volumes with a variety of stories from the 15 books.

Genre: Humor
Subjects: Valets; Aristocracy

Place/Time: England—1900–1945; England—1945–1980

1715.
1. *Something New.* Appleton, 1915.
2. *Leave It to Psmith.* Doran, 1924. (This title appears in two of Wodehouse's series.)
3. *Blandings Castle.* Doubleday, 1935.
4. *Fish Preferred.* Doubleday, 1929.
5. *Heavy Weather.* Little, 1933.
6. *Full Moon.* Doubleday, 1947.
7. *Pigs Have Wings.* Doubleday, 1952.
8. *Service with a Smile.* Simon & Schuster, 1962.
9. *The Brinkmanship of Galahad.* Simon & Schuster, 1965.
10. *No Nudes Is Good Nudes.* Simon & Schuster, 1970.
11. *Sunset at Blandings.* Simon & Schuster, 1978.

At Blandings Castle, the daffy aristocracy are constantly involved in hilarious complications. Clarence, ninth earl of Emsworth, worries about the Empress of Blandings, his prize pig who has won the title at the Shropshire agriculture show. Lady Constance, Clarence's sister, worries about the love lives of her niece Millicent and nephew Ronnie. Pongo the butler and Uncle Fred, fifth earl of Ickenhan, make up the rest of the crazy cast who cannot keep out of trouble.

Genre: Humor
Subjects: Aristocracy; Society novels
Place/Time: England—1900–1945

1716.
1. *Meet Mr. Mulliner.* Doubleday, 1928.
2. *Mr. Mulliner Speaking.* Doubleday, 1930.
3. *Mulliner Nights.* Doubleday, 1933.

In a series of interconnected stories, Mr. Mulliner regales his cronies at the Angler's Rest pub in England with stories about his family. Mulliners far and wide have one thing in common—they are always involved in hilarious adventures that Mulliner relates to his pals.

Genre: Humor
Subjects: Hotels, taverns, etc.
Place/Time: England—1900–1945

1717.
1. *The Luck of the Bodkins.* Little, 1935.
2. *The Plot That Thickened.* Simon & Schuster, 1973.

Model steward Albert Peasemarch is on his way to Hollywood with Monty Bodkin, who is in love with Gertrude. When they get to the film capital, they become involved with film magnate Ivor Llewellyn, film star Lotus Blossom, Ambrose Tennyson, and other zany characters.

Genre: Humor
Subjects: Motion pictures
Place/Time: Hollywood (Calif.)—1900–1945; California—1900–1945

Woiwode, Larry

1718.

1. *What I'm Going to Do, I Think.* Farrar, Straus & Giroux, 1969.
2. *Indian Affairs.* Atheneum, 1992.

Chris is a bright but troubled young man who is unsure of himself and his future. At college, he meets Ellen who is beautiful but troubled. They fall in love and have an on-again, off-again romance until Ellen gets pregnant. They marry but find marriage is not as blissful as they thought. Ellen miscarries, then cannot get pregnant again. Seven years later in a cabin in the Michigan north woods, they struggle to find themselves and come to terms with their past and their future.

Subjects: College life; Love affairs; Marriage problems
Place/Time: Michigan—1945–1980

1719.

1. *Beyond the Bedroom Wall: A Family Album.* Farrar, Straus & Giroux, 1975.
2. *Born Brothers.* Farrar, Straus & Giroux, 1988.
3. *The Neumiller Stories.* Farrar, Straus & Giroux, 1989.

The Neumiller family live in North Dakota and Illinois in the 1930s. Martin and his wife Alpha and their five children, Jerome, Charles, Tim, Marie, and Susan, see the changing landscape. They bury their grandfather, and the children grow up and marry. When the children are older, they remember their childhood and the fights they had with each other. The third volume in the series contains the original short stories that were reworked as the first novel in the series. The book also contains three original stories that continue the Neumiller story.

Genre: Family Saga; Historical Fiction
Subjects: Family life; Brothers and sisters
Place/Time: North Dakota—1900–1945; Illinois—1900–1945

Wolf, Joan

1720.

1. *Daughter of the Red Deer.* Dutton, 1991.
2. *The Horsemasters.* Dutton, 1993.
3. *The Reindeer Hunters.* Dutton, 1994.

In the prehistoric world of Cro-Magnon man in the Pyrenees of Southern France, Alin is to be inducted into the mysteries of the Sacred Marriage, a rite where the women of the Tribe of the Red Deer choose their mates. Before the ceremony begins, she and other women are kidnapped by the men of the Tribe of the Horse. She becomes the mate of Mar and discovers the difference between her matriarchal society and Mar's patriarchal tribe. The two eventually build a new society. Their son Ronan is exiled from his tribe. He forms a new tribe, the Kindred, with the misfits and outcasts of all tribes and welds them into a group capable of fighting the invaders from the North who have mastered the horse. However, the Kindred are forced to move further south as the climate changes. Kindred warrior Rorig weds Alane of the Worakamo tribe as the two tribes try to live together.

Genre: Historical Fiction
Subjects: Women; Tribes; Clans; Stone Age; Man, prehistoric
Place/Time: France—prehistoric times

1721. Dark Age England Trilogy

1. *The Road to Avalon.* NAL, 1988.
2. *Born of the Sun.* NAL, 1989.
3. *Edge of Light.* NAL, 1990.

Beginning with the legendary reign of King Arthur, this series continues with the events surrounding the end of Arthur's peace between the Celts and Saxons in the sixth century A.D. The last work narrates the ninth-century reign of Alfred the Great, King of West Saxony, and the beginning of English unification.

Genre: Historical Fiction
Subjects: Arthur, King; Anglo-Saxons; Kings and rulers; Alfred the Great, King of England, 849–899
Place/Time: England—multicentury span

Wolfe, Gene

1722. The Book of the Long Sun

1. *Nightside the Long Sun.* Tor, 1993.
2. *Lake of the Long Sun.* Tor, 1994.
3. *Caldé of the Long Sun.* Tor, 1994.
4. *Exodus from the Long Sun.* Tor, 1996.

This projected tetralogy takes place on Whorl, an enormous starship that sets out from Urth to colonize a new world. As time goes by, the colony develops its own institutions and forgets its purpose. In the second book, a religious leader becomes involved with criminals and discovers some of Whorl's secrets. In the concluding volumes, the hero, Patera Silk, saves the Holy City Viron and continues to work against the forces that threaten peace on Whorl. *Note:* This series is set in the same universe as the New Sun series.

Genre: Fantasy; Science Fiction
Subjects: Space colonies; Interplanetary voyages; Spaceships

1723. The Book of the New Sun

1. *The Shadow of the Torturer.* Simon & Schuster, 1980.
2. *The Claw of the Conciliator.* Simon & Schuster, 1981.
3. *The Sword of the Lictor.* Simon & Schuster, 1982.
4. *The Citadel of the Autarch.* Simon & Schuster, 1983.
5. *The Urth of the New Sun.* Tor, 1987.

One million years in the future, young Severian is thrust into membership in a guild of torturers, then exiled and threatened with death because he falls in love with one of his victims. During a series of adventures, the appearance of a magical sword and a powerful jewel prophesy Severian's fate as the new autarch of Urth.

Genre: Fantasy; Science Fiction
Subjects: Exiles; Love; Prophecies

1724. Book of the Short Sun
  1. *On Blue's Waters.* Tor, 1999.

This projected trilogy, which continues the narrative of the Book of the Long Sun, tells of the adventures of the leader of colonists who have left the spaceship Whorl and settled on the planet Blue. Horn sets off on a quest, first to find a vehicle capable of returning to Whorl and then to find the legendary leader Patera Silk, who may be able to rejuvenate the decaying civilization on Blue. *Note:* This projected series follows the Book of the Long Sun series.

Genre: Science Fiction
Subjects: Space colonies; Life on other planets

1725. Latro
  1. *Soldier of the Mist.* Tor, 1986.
  2. *Soldier of Arete.* Tor, 1989.

In Greece of the fifth century B.C., gods and other supernatural beings walk the earth unseen by most mortals. The Greek mercenary Latro receives a head wound in battle that distorts his memory and time sense, but allows him to see and communicate with these other-worldly creatures. As a result of his heightened powers, he must escape a murder plot and seek counsel from the Delphic Oracle.

Genre: Fantasy
Subjects: Mercenary soldiers; Gods and goddesses; Extrasensory perception
Place/Time: Greece—5th century B. C.

Wolfe, Thomas

1726.
  1. *The Web and the Rock.* Harper, 1939.
  2. *You Can't Go Home Again.* Harper, 1940.

Wolfe relates his own life through the fictional character of George Webber. George grows up in the South, goes to college, teaches, and goes to Europe. He has an affair with Esther Jack, which ends unhappily. He resumes the affair and finally becomes an author. He discovers that you cannot go home when he returns to his childhood home and finds it does not live up to his expectations. Throughout his travels, he searches himself and life for understanding.

Genre: Coming of Age
Subjects: Teenagers; Love affairs; College life; Authors
Place/Time: Southern states—1900–1945; Europe—1900–1945

1727.
  1. *Look Homeward Angel: A Story of the Buried Life.* Scribner, 1929.
  2. *Of Time and the River: A Legend of Man's Hunger in His Youth.* Scribner, 1935.

In the town of Altamont (a fictionalized Asheville, North Carolina), Eugene Gant grows up among the eccentric townspeople and his even stranger relatives. When he goes to college, he discovers ideas, culture, and books that feed his burning soul. He has love affairs and finally leaves home to find himself. He studies at Harvard, teaches in New York, and travels to Europe. When he finally returns home, he is emotionally and physically drained. There he must face the death of his father.

Genre: Coming of Age
Subjects: Teenagers; College life; Fathers and sons
Place/Time: North Carolina—1900–1945; Massachusetts—1900–1945; New York (N. Y.)—1900–1945

Wolitzer, Hilma

1728.
  1. *Hearts.* Ivy Books, 1990.
  2. *Tunnel of Love.* HarperCollins, 1994.

Lots of things happen in a short period of time to 26-year-old social dance instructor Linda Reismann. Her six-week-old marriage ends with her husband's death, she acquires Robin, a 13-year-old far-from-perfect stepdaughter, with whom she sets off on a cross-country trip to find a resting place for her husband's ashes, and she discovers that she is pregnant. Linda's trail of boyfriends begins with an intriguing hitchhiker she meets on the road and continues in Los Angeles. Always hovering on the criminal fringe, Robin has to deal with finding out the truth about her real mother and assorted difficulties that bring her to a closer relationship with Linda.

Subjects: Widows; Teenagers; Stepmothers; Stepdaughters; Travel
Place/Time: Newark (N. J.)—1980–; Los Angeles (Calif.)—1980–; New Jersey—1980–; California—1980–

Womack, Jack

1729.
  1. *Random Acts of Senseless Violence.* Grove, 1994.
  2. *Ambient.* Weidenfeld & Nicholson, 1987.
  3. *Terraplane.* Weidenfeld & Nicholson, 1988.
  4. *Heathern.* Tor, 1990.

New York of the 21st century is violent and decaying. Lola, a young girl, describes the city's decay in her diary. The city is dominated by the Ambients, who have their own culture and language and can time travel. The city is run by ruthless CEO Thatcher Drydon. He uses people such as his bodyguard O'Malley and his girlfriend. When the people become desperate, Drydon tries to manipulate them by creating a messiah. His bodyguard O'Malley is sent back in time to New York of 1939 to stop a plague that is infecting time travelers.

Genre: Science Fiction
Subjects: Time travel; Social problems; Dictators
Place/Time: New York (N. Y.)—1980–

Wood, Jane Roberts

1730.
1. *The Train to Estelline.* Ellen Temple, 1987.
2. *A Place Called Sweet Shrub.* Delacorte, 1990.
3. *Dance a Little Longer.* Delacorte, 1993.

At 17, Lucinda Richards leaves home to teach in the small west Texas town of Estelline in 1911. She discovers prejudice, ignorance, and violence as she teaches in her one-room schoolhouse, but she also gains wisdom and strength from her experience. When she returns home, she weds Josh Roberts and moves to Sweet Shrub, Arkansas, where Josh will be principal. They find a racial powder keg in the town where whites treat African Americans as if they are indentured servants. In 1931, they move again to Deere County in west Texas to teach, but are met with hostility. Their love and devotion to each other help them surmount the trials and tragedies they face.

Genre: Gentle Read; Historical Fiction; Historical Romance
Subjects: Teachers; Prejudices; Small town life; Race relations
Place/Time: Texas—1900–1945; Arkansas—1900–1945

Woodman, Richard

1731.
1. *Nathaniel Drinkwater: Midshipman.* Pinnacle, 1983.
2. *Nathaniel Drinkwater: An Eye of the Fleet.* Pinnacle, 1983.
3. *A King's Cutter.* Pinnacle, 1984.
4. *A Brig of War.* Pinnacle, 1985.
5. *Arctic Treachery.* Walker, 1987.
6. *The Bomb Vessel.* Walker, 1986.
7. *Decision at Trafalgar.* Walker, 1987.
8. *Baltic Mission.* Walker, 1988.
9. *In Distant Waters.* St. Martin's, 1989.
10. *A Private Revenge.* St. Martin's, 1989.

In 1800, midshipman Nathaniel Drinkwater enters the Royal Navy. During the Napoleonic Wars, he rises through the ranks to become commander of a ship. The decisive and risk-taking young man becomes involved with secret agents, undercover plots, and numerous battles. His service to the crown takes him into French waters, the Baltic, Cape Horn, and the China seas. Besides adventures, he finds love while serving the king.

The series very accurately portrays the 18th-century navy.

Genre: Historical Fiction; Naval Adventure; War
Subjects: Naval battles; Adventure; Navy, British—officers; Sailing vessels; Napoleonic Wars, 1800–1814
Place/Time: Atlantic Ocean—19th century; Pacific Ocean—19th century

Woolley, Persia

1732.
1. *Child of the Northern Spring.* Poseidon Press, 1987.
2. *Queen of the Summer Stars.* Poseidon Press, 1990.
3. *Guinevere: The Legend in Autumn.* Poseidon Press, 1991.

This retelling of the Arthurian legend seen through Guinevere's eyes begins with Guinevere as a young high-spirited girl who grows up to be a passionate woman. Although she does not want to marry Arthur, she obeys her family. As Queen, she sees the revolt of the pagans and Druids against the Christians. She tells of her love for Lancelot, Arthur's development of the law code, her trial for adultery, and the final battle between Arthur and his son Mordred. In her convent, Guinevere reflects on all that has happened.

Genre: Fantasy
Subjects: Guenevere, Queen (legendary character a.k.a. Guinevere); Arthur, King; Love; Lancelot (legendary character); Mordred (legendary character)

Wouk, Herman

1733.
1. *The Hope.* Little, Brown, 1993.
2. *The Glory.* Little, Brown, 1994.

The epic story of the state of Israel is told through two families who participate in every major war and political crisis in Israel's history. Zev Barak is an aide to Israel's first general, American Mickey Marcus. Don Kishote is a soldier who fights in Israel's wars and eventually becomes chief of staff. These men, their families, and their friends fight for independence, the Suez crisis, the Six Day War, and the Yom Kippur War. They work with David Ben-Gurion, Moshe Dayan, Golda Meir, Anwar Sadat, and others as they build the country and finally see peace.

Genre: Historical Fiction; War
Subjects: Jews; Israel-Arab War, 1967; War
Place/Time: Israel—1945–1980; Israel—1980–

1734.
1. *The Winds of War.* Little, Brown, 1971.
2. *War and Remembrance.* Little, Brown, 1978.

A rich narrative follows the career of Captain Victor (Pug) Henry before and during World War II. Henry and his family become intertwined with the life of President Roosevelt as Henry performs special missions for the President in Washington, Berlin, Rome, London, and Moscow. He encounters Hitler and Goering on his missions. When he becomes captain of his own ship, he is involved in the major battles of the war, but tragedy strikes his family. One son is killed, and the other son loses his Jewish wife and son to the Nazis.

Genre: Historical Fiction; War
Subjects: World War II, 1939–1945; World politics; Navy, United States; Roosevelt, Franklin D., 1882–1945; Naval battles; Holocaust, Jewish, 1933–1945
Place/Time: United States—1900–1945; Europe—1900–1945

Wrede, Patricia C.

1735.
1. *Mairelon the Magician.* Tor, 1991.
2. *The Magician's Ward.* Tor, 1997.

Disguised as a boy living on the streets of London of the Regency era, Kim is offered money to steal a silver bowl from traveling magician Mairelon. She is rescued from her life on the streets by Mairelon and his aunt and gradually begins to realize that his magical powers are more than an illusion. Kim acquires social graces and learns magic from Mairelon with whom she falls in love, but must use skills and talents from her street life when their home is burglarized.

Genre: Fantasy
Subjects: Homelessness; Magic; Theft; Rescues; Love
Place/Time: London (England)—19th century

Wren, P. C. (Percival Christopher)

1736.
1. *Soldiers of Misfortune: The Story of Otto Belleme.* Stokes, 1929.
2. *Valiant Dust.* Stokes, 1932.

Otto is a remarkable boxer who fights his way to the top of the boxing world. In his love of adventure, he joins the Foreign Legion and continues his daring ways. Otto is quixotic, sentimental, romantic, and a fighter.

Genre: Adventure
Subjects: Adventure; Army, French; Foreign Legion, French; Boxing
Place/Time: England—1900–1945; North Africa—1900–1945

1737.
1. *Action and Passion.* Stokes, 1933.
2. *Sinbad the Soldier.* Houghton, 1935.
3. *Fort in the Jungle.* Houghton, 1936.

Sinclair Dyart rises from a naval apprentice in the English Royal Navy to become captain of the Valkyrie. He has to battle hurricanes, mutinies, and Arabs. When he is captured by Arabs, he is sold into slavery to the white sultan Chandos. He fights in the jungles for the sultan as he swashbuckles from adventure to adventure.

Genre: Naval Adventure
Subjects: Navy, British; Adventure; Arabs
Place/Time: Africa—19th century; Atlantic Ocean—19th century

1738.
1. *Beau Geste.* Stokes, 1925.
2. *Beau Sabreur.* Stokes, 1926.
3. *Beau Ideal.* Stokes, 1928.
4. *Good Gestes: Stories of Beau Geste, His Brothers, and Certain of Their Comrades in the French Foreign Legion.* Stokes, 1929.
5. *The Desert Heritage.* Houghton Mifflin, 1935.

When Blue Water, a priceless gem, is stolen from Lady Branden as she shows it to her guests, her nephew Beau takes the blame and joins the French Foreign Legion. His two brothers follow him as they try to preserve their family honor and fulfill their boyhood military fantasies. In the Legion, they find adventure and death. Only the youngest brother John survives to go back to England where he finds more adventure.

Genre: Adventure; War
Subjects: Army, French; Foreign Legion, French; Adventure; Brothers; War
Place/Time: England—1900–1945; North Africa—1900–1945

Wright, Harold Bell

1739. Dan Matthews Series
1. *The Shepherd of the Hills.* Book Supply Co., 1907.
2. *The Calling of Dan Matthews.* Book Supply Co., 1907.
3. *God and the Groceryman.* Appleton, 1927.

The Ozark Mountain region at the turn of the century is the scene of these romances built around the central character of a minister and the theme of technological encroachment on the pure life of the hills.

Genre: Gentle Read; Christian Fiction
Subjects: Clergy; Mountain life; Technology and civilization
Place/Time: Ozark Mountains—1900–1945

Wright, Sydney Fowler

1740. Marguerite Cranleigh
1. *Dream, or The Simian Maid.* Harrup, 1931.
2. *Spider's War.* Abelard-Schuman, 1954.

Ape girls, hostile river rats, and giant spiders figure in the dreams of Marguerite, who is transported into fantasy realms with the help of a psychologist, who also happens to be a magician.

Genre: Fantasy
Subjects: Dreams; Psychologists; Magicians

Wubbels, Lance

1741. The Gentle Hills Series
1. *Far from the Dream.* Bethany House, 1994.
2. *Whispers in the Valley.* Bethany House, 1995.
3. *Keeper of the Harvest.* Bethany House, 1995.
4. *Some Things Last Forever.* Bethany House, 1996.

When the Japanese bomb Pearl Harbor, Jerry Macmillan leaves the family farm in Minnesota to join the navy. He marries Marjie Livingstone before he leaves. Marjie finds she is pregnant and prepares to have their child while Jerry faces the horrors of war. When his aircraft carrier sinks, he returns home to find his father ill and a new daughter. When Jerry is given a special hardship discharge, he takes over running the farm. They soon hear that Marjie's brother is missing in action in Sicily. Then an American missionary who escapes the Japanese in Borneo shows all of them what true faith is. When their friends decide to become missionaries, Marjie and Jerry support their decision to work among the defeated Japanese. They must also take care of Marjie's brother who was wounded in Italy, and they face adopting two children who have become orphans. Their faith helps them weather all of life's challenges.

Genre: Christian Fiction
Subjects: Faith; Marriage; Farm life; Family life; World War II, 1939–1945
Place/Time: Minnesota—1900–1945; Minnesota—1945–1980

Wurts, Janny

1742. Wars of Light and Shadow
1. *Curse of the Mistwraith.* Penguin, 1993.
2. *Ships of Merior.* HarperCollins, 1995.
3. *Warhost of Vastmark.* HarperCollins, 1996.
4. *Fugitive Prince.* HarperPrism, 1998.
5. *Grand Conspiracy.* HarperPrism, 2000.

Plagued by the evil spirit of the Mistwraith, the planet Athera is afflicted with war and chaos, forcing the royal family to flee into another dimension. However, there is a prophecy that a prince descended from the absent family will oppose the malevolent Mistwraith that has gripped the land. Two princes who are half-brothers appear to be the fulfillment of that prophecy, but the power to heal the planet's wounds is divided between them. Lysaer, lord of light, and Arithon, master of shadow, must deal with their world's problems and their own conflicts and differing natures before the Mistwraith's power is dispelled.

Genre: Fantasy
Subjects: Prophecies; Good and evil; Princes; Imaginary kingdoms; Magic

Wurts, Janny. *See* Feist, Raymond E.

Wylie, Philip. *See* Balmer, Edwin

Yarbro, Chelsea Quinn

1743.
1. *The Law in Charity.* Doubleday, 1989.
2. *Charity, Colorado.* Evans, 1994.

When the town of Charity, Colorado, needs a sheriff, they hire an eccentric Englishman, Jason Russell. Jason's idea is to use his wits, not guns, to keep order. He does fine until he has to fight Coffin Mayhew, a real bad guy. He also must settle a Spanish land grant dispute and find a serial killer while stopping the criminal growing pains of the town.

Genre: Adventure; Western
Subjects: Sheriffs; Adventure; Outlaws
Place/Time: Colorado—19th century

1744. Saint-Germain
1. *Hotel Transylvania: A Novel of Forbidden Love.* St. Martin's, 1978.
2. *The Palace.* St. Martin's, 1979.
3. *Blood Games.* St. Martin's, 1980.
4. *Path of the Eclipse.* St. Martin's, 1981.
5. *Tempting Fate.* St. Martin's, 1982.
6. *The Saint-Germain Chronicles.* Pocket Books, 1983.
7. *Out of the House of Life.* Tor, 1990.
8. *Spider Glass.* Tor, 1991.
9. *Darker Jewels.* Tor, 1993.
10. *Better in the Dark.* Tor, 1993.
11. *Mansions of Darkness.* Tor, 1996.
12. *Writ in Blood.* Tor, 1997.
13. *Blood Roses.* Tor, 1998.
14. *Communion Blood.* Tor, 1999.

The vampire Saint-Germain is a cultured, considerate, charming gentleman. He was made an immortal by a dark prehistoric god and subsequently appears in Nero's Rome, Saxony of the Dark Ages, Renaissance Florence, the China of powerful warlords, and the vanquished Incan culture of 17th-century Peru. His Russian experiences include the reign of Ivan the Terrible, the court of Czar Nicholas II, and the violence of the Bolshevik Revolution. In decadent, prerevolutionary Paris, he rescues the beautiful young aristocrat Madeleine de Montalia from a satanic cult and brings her into immortal existence. Their love relationship continues by long distance as she excavates Egyptian ruins guided by Saint-Germain's firsthand knowledge. *Note:*This series spins off to the Atta Olivia Clemens series.

Genre: Horror
Subjects: Vampires; Aristocracy; Love
Place/Time: Rome (Italy)—multicentury span; China—multicentury span; Paris (France)—multicentury span; Egypt—multicentury span; Russia—multicentury

span; Italy—multicentury span;
France—multicentury span; Peru—multicentury
span

1745. Atta Olivia Clemens
1. *A Flame in Byzantium.* Tor, 1987.
2. *Crusader's Torch.* Tor, 1988.
3. *A Candle for D'Artagnan.* Tor, 1989.

Introduced in *Blood Games* in ancient Rome, where
the vampire Saint-Germain rescues her, falls in love
with her, and makes her an immortal, Atta Olivia
Clemens assumes a very long life of her own. At the
age of 500, she is involved in complex political intrigues in Constantinople. The 12th century finds her
making her way through the violence of the Crusades
from the ancient city of Tyre back to her beloved
Rome. From Rome, she travels to 17th-century France
and the milieu of Dumas's *The Three Musketeers.*
Note: This series is a spin-off of the Saint-Germain series.

Genre: Horror
Subjects: Vampires; Love; Rescues; Crusades—third, 1189–1192
Place/Time: Rome (Italy)—multicentury span; Istanbul (Turkey)—multicentury span;
  France—multicentury span; Italy—multicentury
  span; Turkey—multicentury span

Yasar, Kemal

1746.
1. *Memed, My Hawk.* Pantheon, 1961.
2. *They Burn the Thistles.* Morrow, 1973.

Memed is a young boy growing up in a small village in
the mountains of Turkey. The town is ruled by the
cruel Agha who wants Memed's sweetheart to marry
another. The two flee, and Memed is forced to kill the
Agha's nephew. He is imprisoned, flees, and joins
bandits. Eventually he rescues his sweetheart and kills
the Agha. He becomes the scourge of the corrupt beys
and aghas, as he comes out of the mountains to fight for
the peasants in the feudal world of modern Turkey.

Subjects: Country life; Peasant life; Turks; Brigands
  and robbers
Place/Time: Turkey—1900–1945

1747.
1. *Iron Earth, Copper Sky.* Morrow, 1979,
    1963.
2. *The Undying Grass.* Morrow, 1978, 1968.

The villagers of Yalak, Turkey, are poor people who
depend on the cotton crop for their livelihood.
Memidik, a young hunter, cannot pick cotton and
wants to kill the tyrannous headman Muhtar Sefer.
When Sefer humiliates him, Memidik tries to kill him,
but cannot. Memidik then accidentally kills another
man and has to flee. The old woman Meryemdje clings
to life and will not give up. Life in this rural village is
portrayed through the different characters.

Genre: Historical Fiction
Subjects: Country life; Peasant life; Turks
Place/Time: Turkey—1900–1945

Yerby, Frank

1748.
1. *The Dahomean.* Dial, 1971.
2. *A Darkness at Ingraham's Crest: A Tale of
    the Slaveholding South.* Dial, 1979.

In the West African kingdom of Dahomey, Nyasnu is a
powerful chief with many wives. Eventually he is betrayed and shipped to America as a slave. In America,
Wes, as he is called, feels he is superior to his white
master. The powerful Wes can heal the sick—both
people and animals. On Ingraham Plantation, he comes under the sway of Pamela who must conceal her
love for him. The slave relationship brutalizes the
whites and dehumanizes the blacks. Wes fights his
way to freedom with his two wives, one who kills herself after being raped by a white man. These powerful
stories show the brutality of slavery and its impact on
all.

Genre: Historical Fiction
Subjects: Plantation life; Slavery; Race relations;
  Prejudices; African Americans
Place/Time: Africa—18th century; Southern
  states—18th century

Yglesias, Jose

1749.
1. *Home Again.* Arbor House, 1987.
2. *Tristan and the Hispanics.* Simon &
    Schuster, 1989.

Pinpin is a retired Hispanic author who has lost touch
with his roots and his work. He goes back to Tampa,
Florida, where he is immediately caught up with the hilarious and bizarre quest of his Latin cousins to find
niece Dulcie who has run away. He remembers growing up in Tampa and his adult life in New York in the
1940s and 1950s. After Pinpin's death, his grandson
Tristan is sent to Tampa to settle Pinpin's estate. The
WASP-like Tristan is bewildered by his cousin's passion and schemes. Eventually he comes to understand
himself, his grandfather, and his heritage.

Genre: Humor
Subjects: Authors; Family life
Place/Time: Florida—1945–1980; New York (N.
  Y.)—1945–1980

Yolen, Jane

1750.
1. *Sister Light, Sister Dark.* St. Martin's, 1988.
2. *White Jenna.* St. Martin's, 1989.

In this feminist fantasy, Jenna, an orphaned girl, is
brought up in a mountain sisterhood. As she grows to

adulthood, Jenna must fulfill the prophecy to become the warrior queen who leads her people out of oppression. She calls upon her dark sisters, souls who can only appear in the flesh under moonlight, and on her two friends Petra and Catrona to lead a band to overthrow Lord Kales.

Genre: Fantasy
Subjects: Orphans; Women; Prophecies; Imaginary wars and battles

Young, E. H. (Emily Hilda)

1751.
1. *Jenny Wren.* Harcourt Brace, 1933.
2. *The Curate's Wife.* Harcourt Brace, 1934.

Jenny and Dahlia Rendall have the airs and graces of their father's refined background, but must live in the scruffy boarding house atmosphere to which their mother brings them after his death. Dreamy Jenny and outgoing Dahlia must deal with their unique station in life as they navigate the social and romantic shoals of England in the 1920s, each searching for love in her own way.

Genre: Romance
Subjects: Sisters; Boarding houses; Class distinction; Love
Place/Time: England—1900–1945

Young, Francis Brett

1752.
1. *They Seek a Country.* Reynal, 1937.
2. *City of Gold.* Reynal, 1939.

Having been convicted of poaching in England, John Oakley escapes while being shipped to South Africa. He learns to farm and marries the daughter of the Boer family, who gives him shelter. The sequel follows the fates of their children as they are involved in the founding of Johannesburg, the first Boer War, and the quest for gold in South Africa during the middle of the 19th century.

Genre: Family Saga; Historical Fiction
Subjects: Farm life; Gold; Afrikaners
Place/Time: South Africa—19th century

Zahn, Timothy

1753. Blackcollar
1. *The Blackcollar.* DAW Books, 1983.
2. *The Backlash Mission.* DAW Books, 1986.

Earth has been conquered by alien forces despite the efforts of Blackcollar units consisting of warriors with technologically enhanced bodies. A resurgence against the aliens seems likely to succeed, but only with the help of a drug that is in the hands of the enemy.

Genre: Science Fiction

Subjects: Extraterrestrial beings; Imaginary wars and battles; Bionics

1754. Cobra
1. *Cobra.* Baen, 1985.
2. *Cobra Strike.* Baen, 1986.
3. *Cobra Bargain.* Baen, 1988.

Cobras are warriors of the future whose bodies have been altered to make them effective fighting machines, but frightening to those who must deal with them on a day-to-day basis in peace time. These fears are put aside, however, when an alien invasion appears imminent.

Genre: Science Fiction
Subjects: Soldiers; Bionics; Extraterrestrial beings; Imaginary wars and battles

Zelazny, Roger

1755. Amber Series
1. *Nine Princes in Amber.* Doubleday, 1970.
2. *The Guns of Avalon.* Doubleday, 1972.
3. *Sign of the Unicorn.* Doubleday, 1975.
4. *The Hand of Oberon.* Doubleday, 1976.
5. *The Courts of Chaos.* Doubleday, 1978.
6. *Trumps of Doom.* Arbor House, 1985.
7. *Blood of Amber.* Arbor House, 1986.
8. *Sign of Chaos.* Arbor House, 1987.
9. *Knight of Shadows.* Morrow, 1989.
10. *Prince of Chaos.* Morrow, 1991.

Corwin wakes up in a hospital room with no memory of his past or the accident that put him there. He gradually discovers that he is a prince from the planet Amber, the real world of which Earth is only a shadow. After many adventures, Corwin disappears. While his son Merlin lives a precarious existence on Earth searching for him, Corwin's brother rules Amber.

Genre: Fantasy; Science Fiction
Subjects: Interplanetary visitors; Amnesia; Princes; Life on other planets

1756. The Changeling Saga
1. *Changeling.* Ace, 1980.
2. *Madwand.* Phantasia Press, 1981.

Pol, the changeling offspring of the Dragon Lord, is exiled from his realm of magic and must live on Earth where he battles evil technological forces that threaten both the world on which he lives and the one on which he was born.

Genre: Fantasy
Subjects: Exiles; Imaginary kingdoms; Technology and civilization; Good and evil

Zelazny, Roger *and* Sheckley, Robert

1757. Millennial Contest
1. *Bring Me the Head of Prince Charming.* Bantam, 1991.

2.   *If at Faust You Don't Succeed.* Bantam,
     1993.
3.   *A Farce to Be Reckoned With.* Bantam, 1995.

Angels, demons, fairy tale characters, and historical figures battle it out in this light-hearted approach to the good versus evil confrontation, which tends to become intense around the turn of the century. Demon Azzie Elbub attempts to change the outcome of the story of Sleeping Beauty and later tries to write and produce an immorality play. Mephistopheles presents Johann Faust with the chance to rewrite history, but finds that he has been fooled by an imposter.

Genre: Fantasy; Humor
Subjects: Demonology; Devil; Angels; Good and
    evil

Zenowich, Christopher

1758.

1.   *Economies of the Heart.* Harper, 1990.
2.   *The Cost of Living.* Harper & Row, 1989.

Bob Bodewicz grows up in the small town of Litchfield, Connecticut. He is given numerous tasks so he can raise money. Through his chores, he learns that one job is like another. This is further brought home when he graduates from college and trains for a sales job with a retail chain. He is the first in his family to go to college, and his family thinks he has done well.

Genre: Coming of Age
Subjects: Small town life; Business; Ambition;
    Teenagers
Place/Time: Connecticut—1980–

Zilahy, Lajos

1759.

1.   *Century of Scarlet.* McGraw-Hill, 1965.
2.   *The Dukays.* Prentice Hall, 1949.
3.   *The Angry Angel.* Prentice Hall, 1953.

As the Congress of Vienna opens in 1814, the Dukay twins, Count Antal and Count Adalbert, are members of an aristocratic Hungarian family caught up in the turbulence of Europe. Antal is loyal to the Habsburgs, but Adalbert is a revolutionary. They pursue their fortunes across a changing Europe. Their descendants continue to fight for Hungary. Count Istran Dukay's daughter Kristina is in love with the last Habsburg monarch, while Zia gives her lands to peasants. Their children fight both the Nazis and the communists.

Genre: Family Saga; Historical Fiction
Subjects: Twins; Aristocracy; Congress of Vienna,
    1814–1815; Habsburg, house of; Revolutions and
    revolutionists
Place/Time: Austria—19th century; Eu-
    rope—1900–1945

Zola, Emile

1760. Four Gospels Series

1.   *Fruitfulness.* Chatto & Windus, 1900.
2.   *Travail.* Chatto & Windus, 1901.
3.   *Truth.* Chatto & Windus, 1903.

The above titles have been published only in England.

The four sons of Pierre Froment—Matthieu, Marc, Luc, and Jean— are the heroes of these novels that explore what life will be like in the future. Zola pictures a world where socialism triumphs over capitalism and scientific truth over darkness. Work is deified, and a utopian society is created.

Subjects: Utopias; Socialism; Philosophical novels

1761. Rougon-Macquart Family

1.   *The Rougon-Macquart Family.* T. B. Peter-
     son, 1879, 1871.
2.   *In the Whirlpool.* T. B. Peterson, 1879, 1871.
3.   *The Markets of Paris.* T. B. Peterson, 1879,
     1873.
4.   *The Conquest of Plassons: A Tale of Provin-
     cial Life.* T. B. Peterson, 1879, 1874.
5.   *The Abbe's Temptation.* T. B. Peterson, 1879,
     1875.
6.   *Clorinda, or the Rise and Reign of His Excel-
     lency Eugene Rougon, the Man of Progress,
     Three Times Minister.* T. B. Peterson, 1880,
     1876.
7.   *Gevaise: The Natural and Social Life of a
     Family Under the Second Empire.* G. W.
     Carleton, 1879, 1877.
8.   *Helene, a Love Episode.* T. B. Peterson,
     1880.
9.   *Nana.* T. B. Peterson, 1880.
10. *Pot-Bouille.* T. B. Peterson, 1882.
11. *The Ladies' Paradise.* T. B. Peterson, 1883.
12. *Joys of Life.* T. B. Peterson, 1884.
13. *Germinal.* Belford, 1885.
14. *His Masterpiece? or Claude Lantier's Strug-
     gle for Fame.* Vizetelly, 1888.
15. *The Soil.* Vizetelly, 1888.
16. *The Dream.* T. B. Peterson, 1888.
17. *Human Brutes.* Laird & Lee, 1890.
18. *Money.* Laird & Lee, 1891.
19. *The Downfall: A Story of the Horrors of War.*
     Chatto & Windus, 1892.
20. *Doctor Pascal or Life and Heredity.* Chatto
     & Windus, 1893.

In this monumental series, Zola depicts the social, cultural, and historical atmosphere of the Second Empire (1852–1870) of France. He evokes its energy, impatience, democratic fevers, social mobility, unbridled ambitions, nervous tensions, dazzling rewards, and murderous competition through every stratum of society. The scenes follow one extended family—the Rougons and Macquarts—through mines, slums, middle-class houses, churches, factories, banks, and brothels in Paris and the provinces. The series begins with the origins of the family in Plassans, continues showing how they overcome the effects of war, the industrial revolution, poverty, and immorality, then follows them through their decline with the fall of the Second Empire.

Genre: Family Saga
Subjects: Politics—France; Social classes; Industrial conditions
Place/Time: France—19th century

1762. Three Cities Trilogy

1. *Lourdes.* Chatto & Windus, 1894.
2. *Rome.* Chatto & Windus, 1896.
3. *Paris.* Chatto & Windus, 1900.

The above title have been published only in England.

In the late 19th century, Pierre Froment is a spiritually troubled priest. He travels to Lourdes in the hopes that he will be cured of his doubts. He then goes to Rome to try to get the pope to approve his book calling for a new Christian socialist social order, but he fails. He returns to Paris and leaves the church. He then devotes himself to charity work and embraces the new religion of science. Zola portrays a world where traditional religion is declining and people are searching for faith.

Subjects: Catholic faith; Catholic priests; Faith; Ex-priests
Place/Time: France—19th century

TITLE INDEX

The numbers listed below refer to entries in the main entry section, not to page numbers. Book titles are italicized in this index. Series titles are in regular type.

A

Abbe Coignard Series (France, Anatole), 528

The Abbe's Temptation (Zola, Emile), 1761

The Abiding Gospel of Claude Dee Moran Jr. (Farris, Jack), 481

Abigail (Shott, James R.), 1439

About Harry Towns (Friedman, Bruce Jay), 541

Absolute Truths (Howatch, Susan), 760

The Acceptance World (Powell, Anthony), 1264

The Accidental Bride (Feather, Jane), 487

The Accursed King Series (Druon, Maurice), 405

Acorna: The Unicorn Girl (McCaffrey, Anne and Ball, Margaret), 1033

Acorna's People (McCaffrey, Anne and Ball, Margaret), 1033

Acorna's Quest (McCaffrey, Anne and Ball, Margaret), 1033

Across the Sea of Suns (Benford, Gregory), 95

Action and Passion (Wren, P. C. [Percival Christopher]), 1737

Adam and the Serpent (Fisher, Vardis), 506

The Adept (Kurtz, Katherine and Harris, Deborah Turner), 874

The Adept Series (Kurtz, Katherine and Harris, Deborah Turner), 874

Admiral Hornblower in the West Indies (Forester, C. S. [Cecil Scott]), 515

Admiral of Fear (Suthren, Victor), 1542

The Adrian Mole Diaries (Townsend, Sue), 1576

Adrian Mole: The Lost Years (Townsend, Sue), 1576

Adulthood Rites (Butler, Octavia E.), 192

The Adultress (Carr, Philippa), 210

Adventurer (Waltari, Mika), 1637

The Adventurers (Long, William), 956

The Adventures of David Simple: In Search of a Faithful Friend (Fielding, Sarah), 499

Adventures of David Simple: Volume the Last (Fielding, Sarah), 499

The Adventures of Flinx of the Commonwealth Series (Foster, Alan Dean), 521

The Adventures of Hajji Baba of Ispahan (Morier, James), 1108

The Adventures of Tapiola Series (Nathan, Robert), 1141

Adventures of the Scarlet Pimpernel (Orczy, Emmuska, Baroness), 1194

The Adventures of the Stainless Steel Rat (Harrison, Harry), 685

The Adventuress (Chesney, Marion), 247

The Adversaries (Cavanaugh, Jack), 217

The Adversary (May, Julian), 1023

Advise and Consent (Drury, Allen), 406

The Affair (Snow, C. P. [Charles Percy]), 1478

Affairs at Thrush Green (Read, Miss), 1293

After All (Landis, Jill Marie), 897

After Dark (Wellman, Manly Wade), 1666

After the Rainbow (Kalman, Yvonne), 820

After the Reunion (Jaffe, Rona), 782

After Worlds Collide (Balmer, Edwin and Wylie, Philip), 64

Aftermath (Habe, Hans), 647

Aftermath (Romains, Jules), 1342

Aftermath (Sheffield, Charles), 1420

Aftermath: Part Second of "A Kentucky Cardinal." (Allen, James Lane), 13

Against the Fall of Night (Clarke, Arthur C.), 257

Against the Tide of Years (Stirling, S. M. [Stephen Michael]), 1521

Agatha (Colegate, Isabel), 275

The Age of Miracles (Gilchrist, Ellen), 586

The Age of Reason (Sartre, Jean-Paul), 1392

The Age of Unreason Series (Keyes, Greg), 846

Aggressor Six (McCarthy, Wil), 1038

Ain't Gonna Be the Same Fool Twice (Sinclair, April), 1450

Air Force Eagles (Boyne, Walter J.), 151

Aisling (Cooper, Louise), 301

Alamut (Tarr, Judith), 1551

Albany Cycle Series (Kennedy, William), 837

Albatross (Anthony, Evelyn), 32

Albert's Victoria (Whittle, Tyler), 1689

The Albino Knife (Perry, Steve), 1227

Albion's Story (Grenville, Kate), 631

Alexa (Melville, Anne), 1063

The Alexandria Quartet (Durrell, Lawrence), 427

The Alexandria Quartet Series (Durrell, Lawrence), 427

The Alexandrian Ring (Forstchen, William R.), 517

Alice in Bed (Schine, Cathleen), 1401

Alice's Adventures in Wonderland (Carroll, Lewis), 212

An Alien Heat (Moorcock, Michael), 1100

The Alien Series (Ore, Rebecca), 1196

The Alien Within (Bova, Ben), 142

The Alienist (Carr, Caleb), 209

Alinor (Gellis, Roberta), 569

The Alkahest (Balzac, Honore de), 65

All About Lucia (Benson, E. F. [Edward Frederic]), 98

All Manner of Riches (Elmblad, Mary), 457

All My Friends Are Going to Be Strangers (McMurtry, Larry), 1059

All My Worldly Goods (Weale, Anne), 1651

All or Nothing (Longstreet, Stephen), 959

All Quiet on the Western Front (Remarque, Erich Maria), 1302

Mosaic (Stern, Gladys Bronwyn), 1501

Moscow (Plievier, Theodor), 1255

Moses (Asch, Sholem), 51

Mostly Canallers (Edmonds, Walter Dumaux), 442

Mostly Harmless (Adams, Douglas), 2

The Mote in God's Eye (Niven, Larry and Pournelle, Jerry), 1159

Mother Earth, Father Sky (Harrison, Sue), 690

Mother of Winter (Hambly, Barbara), 661

Motherlines (Charnas, Suzy McKee), 233

Motown (Estleman, Loren D.), 462

Moulded in Earth (Vaughn, Richard), 1611

The Mountains of Majipoor (Silverberg, Robert), 1446

Mountolive (Durrell, Lawrence), 427

Mouvar's Magic (Anthony, Piers), 34

Moving Pictures (Pratchett, Terry), 1268

Mr. Bridge (Connell, Evan S.), 284

Mr. Knox's Country (Somerville, Edith and Ross, Martin), 1481

Mr. Loveday's Little Outing and Other Sad Stories (Waugh, Evelyn), 1650

Mr. Midshipman Hornblower (Forester, C. S. [Cecil Scott]), 515

Mr. Mulliner Speaking (Wodehouse, P. G. [Pelham Grenville]), 1716

Mr. Seidman and the Geisha (Moll, Elick), 1091

Mrs. Appleyard's Year (Kent, Louise Andrews), 840

Mrs. 'Arris Goes to Moscow (Gallico, Paul), 557

Mrs. 'Arris Goes to New York (Gallico, Paul), 557

Mrs. 'Arris Goes to Paris (Gallico, Paul), 557

Mrs. 'Arris Goes to Parliament (Gallico, Paul), 557

Mrs. Bridge (Connell, Evan S.), 284

Mrs. Budley Falls from Grace (Chesney, Marion), 248

Mrs. Pringle (Read, Miss), 1292

Mrs. Tim Carries On (Stevenson, D. E. [Dorothy Emily]), 1507

Mrs. Tim Christie (Stevenson, D. E. [Dorothy Emily]), 1507

Mrs. Tim Flies Home (Stevenson, D. E. [Dorothy Emily]), 1507

Mrs. Tim Gets a Job (Stevenson, D. E. [Dorothy Emily]), 1507

Mrs. Washington and Horowitz Too (Denker, Henry), 368

Much in Evidence (Boyd, Martin), 147

The Mullah from Kashmir (MacNeil, Duncan), 993

Mulliner Nights (Wodehouse, P. G. [Pelham Grenville]), 1716

A Multitude of Monsters (Gardner, Craig Shaw), 562

Munich Signature (Thoene, Bodie), 1564

The Murder in the Tower (Plaidy, Jean), 1251

Murder Most Royal (Plaidy, Jean), 1252

A Murder of Quality (Le Carre, John), 909

The Murderers (Griffin, W. E. B.), 633

Murphy (Paulsen, Gary), 1207

Murphy's Ambush (Paulsen, Gary), 1207

Murphy's Gold (Paulsen, Gary), 1207

Murphy's Herd (Paulsen, Gary), 1207

Murphy's Stand (Paulsen, Gary), 1207

Murphy's Trail (Paulsen, Gary), 1207

Murphy's War (Paulsen, Gary), 1207

Muse of Art (Anthony, Piers), 39

Music from Behind the Moon (Cabell, James Branch), 197

Music in the Hills (Stevenson, D. E. [Dorothy Emily]), 1508

The Music of Time Series (Powell, Anthony), 1264

Mustang Man (L'Amour, Louis), 876

The Mutant Legacy (Haber, Karen), 648

The Mutant Prime (Haber, Karen), 648

The Mutant Season (Haber, Karen), 648

The Mutant Star (Haber, Karen), 648

The Muted Swan (Arnold, Bruce), 48

Mutineer's Moon (Weber, David), 1653

Mutiny on the Bounty (Nordhoff, Charles and Hall, James Norman), 1164

My Blue-Checker Corker and Me (Radley, Paul), 1283

My Brilliant Career (Franklin, Miles), 535

My Brother Jack (Johnston, George Henry), 798

My Days of Anger (Farrell, James T.), 476

My Father's World (Phillips, Michael R.), 1235

My First Two Thousand Years (Viereck, George Sylvester and Eldridge, Paul), 1622

My Friend Annie (Duncan, Jane), 422

My Friend Emmie (Duncan, Jane), 422

My Friend Flora (Duncan, Jane), 422

My Friend Madame Zora (Duncan, Jane), 422

My Friend Martha's Aunt (Duncan, Jane), 422

My Friend Monica (Duncan, Jane), 422

My Friend Muriel (Duncan, Jane), 422

My Friend My Father (Duncan, Jane), 422

My Friend Rose (Duncan, Jane), 422

My Friend Sandy (Duncan, Jane), 422

My Friend Sashie (Duncan, Jane), 422

My Friend the Swallow (Duncan, Jane), 422

My Friend's Book (France, Anatole), 530

My Friends from Cairnton (Duncan, Jane), 422

My Friends George and Tom (Duncan, Jane), 422

My Friends the Hungry Generation (Duncan, Jane), 422

My Friends the Macleans (Duncan, Jane), 422

My Friends the Miss Boyds (Duncan, Jane), 422

My Friends the Misses Kindness (Duncan, Jane), 422

My Friends the Mrs. Millers (Duncan, Jane), 422

My Heart's Desire (Bacher, June Masters), 58

My Holy Satan: A Novel on Christian Twilight (Fisher, Vardis), 506

My Lady Hoyden (Sheridan, Jane), 1430

My Man Jeeves (Wodehouse, P. G. [Pelham Grenville]), 1714

My Mother Bids Me Bind My Hair (Sale, Elizabeth), 1375

"My Novel" by Pisistratus Caxton, or "Varieties in English Life" (Lytton, Edward Bulwer, Baron), 975

My Self, My Enemy (Plaidy, Jean), 1250

My Sister the Moon (Harrison, Sue), 690

My Son, the Wizard (Stasheff, Christopher), 1496

The Mysterious Island (Verne, Jules), 1615

Mystery (Straub, Peter), 1529

Mystical Paths (Howatch, Susan), 760

Mythago Wood (Holdstock, Robert), 742

N

Nail Down the Stars (Morressy, John), 1110

Naked Lunch (Burroughs, William S.), 189

GENRE INDEX

The numbers listed below refer to entries in the main entry section, not to page numbers.

Coming of Age

Crime Novel

Espionage

Family Saga

Fantasy

Gentle Read

Historical Fiction

Historical Romance

Horror

Humor

Naval Adventure

Romance

Science Fiction

Sports

Technothriller

War

Western

SUBJECTS AND LITERARY FORMS INDEX

The numbers listed below refer to entries in the main entry section, not to page numbers.

Stuart, V. (Vivian) A., 1536, 1537
Suthren, Victor, 1542, 1543
Walker, Jim, 1631
Waltari, Mika, 1637
Ward, Christopher, 1641
Weber, David, 1654
Wheeler, Richard S., 1681
White, Stewart Edward, 1685, 1687
Woodman, Richard, 1731
Wren, P. C. (Percival Christopher), 1736, 1737, 1738
Yarbro, Chelsea Quinn, 1743

Advertising
Faust, Joe Clifford, 486
Pohl, Frederik, 1257

Aeronautics, military
Herman, Richard, Jr., 722, 723
Rosenbaum, Ray, 1345

Aesthetics
Fuller, Henry Blake, 547

Africa—native peoples
Harris, Wilson, 683
Monsarrat, Nicholas, 1094
Palmer, Catherine, 1198

Africa—race relations
Monsarrat, Nicholas, 1094

African Americans
Andrews, Raymond, 23
Chase-Riboud, Barbara, 235
Denker, Henry, 368
Habe, Hans, 647
Harris, E. Lynn, 678
Kress, Nancy, 865
Lauber, Lynn, 901
Sherburne, James, 1429
Sinclair, April, 1450
Van Dyke, Henry, 1603
Wideman, John Edgar, 1691
Willard, Tom, 1693
Yerby, Frank, 1748

Afrikaners
Cloete, Stuart, 264
Young, Francis Brett, 1752

Aging
See also Elderly; Middle age
McMurtry, Larry, 1057
Moll, Elick, 1091

AIDS (disease)
McGehee, Peter, 1049
White, Edmund, 1683

Air Force, British
Gavin, Catherine, 567
Hennessy, Max, 716

Air Force, United States
Boyne, Walter J., 151
Herman, Richard, Jr., 722, 723
Rosenbaum, Ray, 1345

Air pilots
Berent, Mark, 101
Boyne, Walter J., 151
Coonts, Stephen, 298
Herman, Richard, Jr., 723
Jack, Donald, 777
Morris, Janet and Morris, Chris, 1123
Rosenbaum, Ray, 1345
Thomas, Craig, 1566

Air warfare
See Aeronautics, military; World War II, 1939–1945—aerial operations

Airplanes
Boyne, Walter J., 151
Herman, Richard, Jr., 722
Thomas, Craig, 1566
Trenhaile, John, 1580

Akhenaton, King of Egypt, 1388–1348 B.C.
Drury, Allen, 408

Alaska—gold discoveries
Morris, Gilbert, 1116

Alcoholism
Exley, Frederick, 465
Farrell, James T., 478
Gold, Ivan, 602
McGahan, Andrew, 1048

Alexander the Great, 356–323 B.C.
Forstchen, William R., 517
Renault, Mary, 1303

Alfred the Great, King of England, 849–899
Duggan, Alfred Leo, 412
Wolf, Joan, 1721

Algeria—revolution, 1954–1962
Larteguy, Jean, 899

Aliens from Outer Space
See Extraterrestrial beings

Allegories
Adams, Richard, 3
Evans, Max, 463
Gilman, Charlotte Perkins, 591
Hardy, Robin, 676
Kristof, Agota, 866
LaHaye, Tim and Jenkins, Jerry B., 893
Leroux, Etienne, 928
Lewis, C. S. (Clive Staples), 937

Mishima, Yukio, 1081
Monsarrat, Nicholas, 1095
Murakami, Haruki, 1133
Okri, Ben, 1191
Trott, Susan, 1583

Allen, Ethan, 1738–1789
Van de Water, Frederic Franklyn, 1601

Amateur theater
Davies, Robertson, 348

Amazons
Charnas, Suzy McKee, 233

Ambassadors
See Diplomats

Ambition
See also Self-made men; Self-made women; Success
Braine, John, 161
Conrad, Joseph, 286
Downing, John Hyatt, 398
Dreiser, Theodore, 403
Farrell, James T., 478
Giles, Janice Holt, 588
Hill, Deborah, 728
Howatch, Susan, 759
Loos, Anita, 960
Vance, Jack, 1608
Weidman, Jerome, 1658
Wilson, Sloan, 1709
Zenowich, Christopher, 1758

American Loyalists
Stirling, S. M. (Stephen Michael), 1522

American Revolution
See United States—revolution, 1775–1783

Americanization
Gold, Herbert, 601
Rosten, Leo Calvin, 1355

Amish
Bender, Carrie, 92, 93
Borntrager, Mary Christner, 135
Lewis, Beverly, 935, 936

Amnesia
Ludlum, Robert, 964
Sheldon, Sidney, 1428
Silverberg, Robert, 1446
Sinclair, Andrew, 1449
Smith, Sarah, 1470
Zelazny, Roger, 1755

Angels
Edwards, Gene, 443
MacAvoy, R. A. (Roberta Ann), 978
Shinn, Sharon, 1435
Stableford, Brian, 1486
Stewart, Sean, 1512

Family chronicles
See **Family life; Genre Index—Family Saga**

Family life
See also **Marriage; Marriage problems; Genre Index— Family Saga**

Horror stories
See Genre Index—Horror

Horse breeding
De Blasis, Celeste, 352

Horse racing
McCord, John S., 1039

Horse trading
Cotton, Ralph W., 312
Somerville, Edith and Ross,
Martin, 1481

Horses
Cherryh, C. J., 237
Dexter, Susan, 375
Durgin, Doranna, 426

Hostages
Gaskell, Jane, 566

Hotels, taverns, etc.
Chesney, Marion, 248
Hamilton, Patrick, 666
Harvey, Kathryn, 697
Peterson, Tracie, 1230
Richardson, Bill, 1312
Robinson, Spider, 1334
Wodehouse, P. G. (Pelham
Grenville), 1716

Housekeepers
Webster, Jan, 1655

Houses
Cadell, Elizabeth, 198
Chesney, Marion, 247
Cradock, Fanny, 324
De la Roche, Mazo, 356
Delderfield, R. F. (Ronald
Frederick), 364
Graham, Winston, 618
Gregory, Philippa, 629
Heaven, Constance, 706
Kettle, Jocelyn, 844
Lofts, Norah, 952
O'Grady, Leslie, 1179
Stevenson, D. E. (Dorothy
Emily), 1502, 1504

Hughes, Howard, 1905–1976
Lupoff, Richard A., 971

Humans, origin of
Hogan, James P., 741

Humans, prehistoric
Bruchac, Joseph, 176
Gear, W. Michael and Gear,
Kathleen O'Neal, 568
Harrison, Sue, 691
Mackcy, Mary, 989

Humor
See Genre Index—Humor

Hunters
Haggard, H. Rider, 652

Husbands and wives
See also Marriage
Allen, James Lane, 13
Anand, Valerie, 18
Barstow, Stan, 74
Barthelme, Frederick, 75
Bennett, Arnold, 96
Borchardt, Alice, 134
Bova, Ben, 139
Condon, Richard, 281
Connell, Evan S., 284
Coulter, Catherine, 317
Deighton, Len, 360, 361, 362
Dew, Robb Forman, 374
Donati, Sara, 387
Evans, Richard Paul, 464
Funderburk, Robert, 549
Galsworthy, John, 558
Golon, Sergeanne, 606
Hambly, Barbara, 659, 660
Hodge, Jane Aiken, 735
Hoff, B. J. (Brenda Jane), 737
Johnstone, William W., 803
Kennelly, Ardyth, 838
Michaels, Fern, 1073
Nielsen, Elizabeth, 1156
Oke, Janette, 1184
Phillips, Michael, 1234
Phillips, Michael R., 1236
Plaidy, Jean, 1252
Riefe, Barbara, 1316
Ryman, Rebecca, 1367
Smith, Thorne, 1471
Stevenson, D. E. (Dorothy
Emily), 1503, 1506, 1507,
1508
Stokes, Penelope J., 1525
Stringer, Arthur, 1535
Tennant, Emma, 1554

Hypocrisy
Metalious, Grace, 1066

Ice
Forstchen, William R., 519
Foster, Alan Dean, 523
Rohan, Michael Scott, 1340

Idealism
Franken, Rose, 534

Illegitimacy
Coulter, Catherine, 315
D'Annunzio, Gabriele, 334
Hobb, Robin, 733
Parry, Richard, 1206
Robin, Maxwell, 1331
Thackeray, William Makepeace,
1558

Imaginary cities
Bishop, Michael, 115
Blish, James, 125
Clarke, Arthur C., 257
Lee, Tanith, 918
Nathan, Robert, 1142
Silverberg, Robert, 1446

Imaginary kingdoms
Anthony, Mark, 33
Anthony, Piers, 34
Beagle, Peter S., 81
Bradley, Marion Zimmer, 154
Bradley, Marion Zimmer and
Lisle, Holly, 157
Brooks, Terry, 170, 171, 172
Brust, Steven, 178
Cabell, James Branch, 197
Carroll, Lewis, 212
Chalker, Jack, 228
Cherryh, C. J., 240, 243
Claremont, Chris and Lucas,
George, 255
Cole, Allan, 273
Cole, Allan and Bunch, Chris,
274
Cook, Hugh, 291
Daley, Brian, 337
De Haven, Tom, 355
de Lint, Charles, 357
Dexter, Susan, 375
Dickson, Gordon R., 377
Douglas, Carole Nelson, 392, 393
Drake, David, 402
Duane, Diane, 410
Duncan, Dave, 417, 418, 419
Eddings, David, 432, 433, 434
Edgerton, Teresa, 440, 441
Farland, David, 470
Farmer, Philip Jose, 472
Feist, Raymond E., 490, 491, 492
Feist, Raymond E. and Wurts,
Janny, 493
Gentle, Mary, 572
Gunn, Neil, 644
Hancock, Niel, 672
Harris, Deborah Turner, 677
Hazel, Paul, 704
Hobb, Robin, 733
Jones, J. V. (Julie Victoria), 813
Kay, Guy Gavriel, 825
Kerr, Katharine, 841
Keyes, Greg, 847
Kurtz, Katherine, 870, 871, 872,
873
Lackey, Mercedes, 882, 883, 884,
885
Lackey, Mercedes and Dixon,
Larry, 880
Lancour, Gene, 896
Laumer, Keith, 902
Lawhead, Steve, 904, 906
Lee, Adam, 913
Leiber, Fritz, 922
Lynn, Elizabeth A., 974
MacAvoy, R. A. (Roberta Ann),
977

Science fiction
See **Genre Index—Science Fiction**

Scientific experiments
See **Experiments, scientific**

Scientists
Bova, Ben, 138
Djerassi, Carl, 380
Farmer, Philip Jose, 472
Haldeman, Joe, 655
Keyes, Greg, 846
Laumer, Keith, 902
Russell, Sean, 1364

Scipio Africanus, ca. 236–183 B.C.
Leckie, Ross, 912

Scouts and scouting
Cooper, James Fenimore, 299

Sculptors
Alexander, Sidney, 10
James, Henry, 787

Sea stories
See **Adventure; Voyages and travels; Genre Index—Naval Adventure**

Seamen
Dos Passos, John, 390
Forester, C. S. (Cecil Scott), 515
Gallacher, Tom, 556
Golding, William, 604
Haislip, Harvey, 654
Hartog, Jan de, 695
Hobb, Robin, 734
Hough, Richard Alexander, 754
Kent, Alexander, 839
Kraus, Jim, 863
Lambdin, Dewey, 895
Maynard, Kenneth, 1025
McCutchan, Philip, 1041
Morris, Gilbert and Funderburk, Bobby, 1119
Nordhoff, Charles and Hall, James Norman, 1164
O'Brian, Patrick, 1175
Parkinson, C. (Cyril) Northcote, 1205
Stockton, Frank, 1524

Seasons
Aldiss, Brian W., 7

Secret service
Anthony, Evelyn, 32
Armstrong, Campbell, 47
Egleton, Clive, 445
Elgin, Suzette Haden, 450
Forbes, Bryan, 511
Forrest, Anthony, 516
Gardner, John E., 563
Hagberg, David, 650

Hunter, Jack D., 766
Le Carre, John, 909

Sects
Ing, Dean, 772
Lagerlof, Selma, 891

Segregation
Stribling, Thomas Sigismund, 1533
Thoene, Bodie, 1562
Toer, Pramoedya Ananta, 1573

Self-confidence
Donaldson, Stephen R., 386

Self-made men
See also **Ambition; Success**
Archer, Jeffrey, 43
Weidman, Jerome, 1658

Self-made women
See also **Ambition; Success**
Bradford, Barbara Taylor, 152

Self-realization
Frank, Waldo David, 532

Selfishness
Beckett, Samuel, 85

Serial murders
Carr, Caleb, 209
Diehl, William, 378
Harris, Thomas, 682
Straub, Peter, 1529

Servants
Chesney, Marion, 247
Dodd, Christina, 382
Duncan, Jane, 421
Peake, Mervyn Laurence, 1211

Sex
Calder, Richard, 200
Chamberlin, Ann, 232
Dixon, Stephen, 379
Harvey, Kathryn, 697
Lawrence, D. H. (David Herbert), 907
Lenz, Frederick, 926
Maillard, Keith, 996
McGahan, Andrew, 1048
Miller, Henry, 1075, 1076
Powell, Padgett, 1265
Robinson, Spider, 1334
Rogers, Rosemary, 1338
Sherwood, Valerie, 1433, 1434
Small, Bertrice, 1461, 1462

Sex discrimination
Charnas, Suzy McKee, 233
Elgin, Suzette Haden, 452

Sex roles
Metalious, Grace, 1066

Sexually transmitted diseases
Sinclair, Upton, 1453

Shakespeare, William, 1564–1616
Fisher, Edward, 504

Shakespeare, William, 1564–1616—characters
Anderson, Poul, 21

Sheep and sheep farming
Doig, Ivan, 383

Sheriffs
Davis, W. E., 351
Jones, Douglas C., 809
Paulsen, Gary, 1207
Watson, Larry, 1646
Yarbro, Chelsea Quinn, 1743

Shipmasters
Argo, Ellen, 45
Golding, William, 604
Hartog, Jan de, 695
Steen, Marguerite, 1497

Shipping
Aldridge, James, 9
Fast, Howard, 482
Gallacher, Tom, 556

Ships
See also **Sailing vessels**
Hobb, Robin, 734
O'Brian, Patrick, 1174
Verne, Jules, 1615

Shipwrecks and castaways
Stacpoole, H. (Henryk) de Vere, 1488
Stockton, Frank, 1524
Verne, Jules, 1615

Short stories
Fuller, Anna, 546

Show business
McMurtry, Larry, 1056

Silk
Tsukiyama, Gail, 1588

Singers
Blackwell, Lawana, 120
McCaffrey, Anne, 1030
Meredith, George, 1064
Modesitt, L. E., Jr., 1089
Moore, George, 1105
Sand, George, 1383
Wellman, Manly Wade, 1666

Sisters
See also **Brothers and sisters**
Alcott, Louisa May, 6
Alvarez, Julia, 17
Boissard, Janine, 129
Bradley, Marion Zimmer, 154

TIME AND PLACE INDEX

The numbers listed below refer to entries in the main entry section, not to page numbers.

MERLE LYNN JACOB is director of library collection development for the Chicago Public Library and a mysteries advisor for NoveList. She has been a chair of the Adult Reading Roundtable, the oldest readers' advisory group in the country, and she founded the Readers Advisory Committee of the American Library Association. A frequent workshop presenter on collection development topics, she also does independent consulting. In addition to *To Be Continued: An Annotated Guide to Sequels*, *Second Edition*, she is the author of several magazine articles.

HOPE APPLE is a researcher and writer. She is the former head of reference services for the Skokie (Illinois) Public Library and has nearly 20 years of experience as a reference librarian.